HUMAN RESOURCE MANAGEMENT
STRATEGY, DESIGN, AND IMPLEMENTATION

DOUGLAS T. HALL
Boston University

JAMES G. GOODALE
Philbrook, Goodale Associates,
Consultants in Organizational Management

SCOTT, FORESMAN AND COMPANY
Glenview, Illinois
London, England

TO THE MEMORY OF ANNE T. HALL

Scott, Foresman Series in Organizational Behavior and Human Resources

Lyman W. Porter, Editor

Library of Congress Cataloging-in-Publication Data

Hall, Douglas T.
  Human resource management.

  (Scott, Foresman series in organizational behavior and human resources)
  Includes bibliographies and index.
  1. Personnel management.   I. Goodale, James G.
II. Title.   III. Series.
HF5549.M267   1986   658.3   85-22216
ISBN 0-673-16552-3

Public recognition of the importance of human resource management has grown dramatically in the last two decades. Turbulent economic conditions, increased foreign competition, and changing employee attitudes challenge employers to find and retain more productive employees. *Human Resource Management: Strategy, Design and Implementation* shows how human resource professionals and line managers can meet this challenge by planning, designing, and implementing policies and practices to recruit, select, train, develop, evaluate, and compensate effective employees.

A number of features make this text unique:

- *Dual Responsibility of Line Managers and Human Resource Professionals.* This text is directed not only to students interested in becoming human resource managers, but also to general management students, who will need to understand human resource policies and practices in any supervisory or managerial position. The role of the line manager as a consumer and sometime implementer of human resource programs is discussed, while the human resource manager is presented as an internal consultant who diagnoses the needs of the organization and its employees and then designs and implements policies and practices to meet those needs.
- *Strategic Focus.* The strategic implications of designing and implementing human resource functions are discussed throughout, and the importance of linking human resource activities with strategic business planning for the whole organization is emphasized. Chapters Two, Seven, Eleven, and Eighteen are devoted to the strategic implications of human resource planning, staffing, employee development, and compensation.
- *Applied Approach.* Drawing on the latest research, this book describes specific HRM skills and techniques. Major functions are presented in chronological order as they relate to the employee—beginning with recruitment and ending with termination and retirement (Parts Three and Four).
- *Interesting Examples from Practice.* Complex and abstract concepts are made more concrete and interesting through the use of chapter-opening vignettes that illustrate major topics in the chapter, boxed examples of how companies have applied concepts and approaches under discussion, frequent references to the human resource policies and practices of specific organizations, and interviews with human resource practitioners.
- *Management of the Human Resource Function.* The concluding part explains why human resource professionals need increased power and influence in their organizations, and describes tactics they can use to en-

hance their credibility. The book concludes on the vital topic of evaluation by stressing ways to document the costs and benefits of human resource management in financial terms.

Our approach throughout this book has been primarily *descriptive;* we have presented many examples of how human resource management is actually practiced. But we have also been *prescriptive;* we have made specific recommendations for the effective practice of human resource management, and we have cited examples of organizations whose practices conform with those recommendations.

ACKNOWLEDGMENTS

We are grateful to many people who have added to the quality of *Human Resource Management.* The following colleagues reviewed preliminary drafts and made valuable comments and suggestions:

Stephen C. Burshardt, The University of Southern Mississippi
Paul S. Greenlaw, The Pennsylvania State University
Frederick S. Hills, Virginia Polytechnic Institute and State University
Marilyn D. Jacobson, The University of Illinois-Chicago
Benson Rosen, The University of North Carolina at Chapel Hill
Jo Ann Verdin, The University of Illinois-Chicago

We are especially grateful to the following human resource practitioners who generously discussed their activities with us and contributed many anecdotes and illustrations that enhance the realism of this book:

Edward F. Adams, AT&T
Charles S. Arnold, Monsanto Company
Gene Banks, United Gas Pipe Line Company
Frank Chadwick, Exxon, USA
Eugene Croisant, Continental Bank
David Montross, The Norton Company
Curtis Paulson, Mark Producing
Robert Ripston, Ingersoll-Rand

We also thank Lyman W. Porter, Consulting Editor to Scott, Foresman, whose excellent suggestions helped us improve initial drafts. John Nolan, Diane Culhane, Jeanne Schwaba and Jacqueline Kolb of Scott, Foresman contributed immeasurably to its quality and clarity. We are particularly grateful to Jim Sitlington, Editorial Vice-President, for his enthusiasm and energy at a critical point in this book's development. We offer special thanks to Steve Locke, who first encouraged us to write this book.

We also wish to acknowledge the continuing support of Dr. Tom Philbrook of Philbrook, Goodale Associates and Dean Henry Morgan of the Graduate School of Management at Boston University. The Human Resources

Policy Institute at Boston University and its director, Fred Foulkes, were important sources of ideas. A team of world-class word processor operators, Emily Phillips and Vincent Mahler, typed the entire book in at least two drafts, and for their patience and skill we are eternally grateful. Neil Gladstone did an excellent job conducting interviews of human resource practitioners. Two secretaries in the Organizational Behavior Department at Boston University, Sara Tarbox and Leslie Lomasson, shepherded the manuscript from the "early concept" stage to the final details of reference checks and permission requests. We also thank Robin Goodale for her help in editing and proofreading the final draft of the manuscript.

Finally, our deepest appreciation goes to our families, whose understanding and encouragement made *Human Resource Management* possible. In particular we dedicate this book to the memory of Anne T. Hall, the first author's mother, who played a major role in shaping his ideas about working with people.

Douglas T. Hall
James G. Goodale

CONTENTS

CHAPTER NINETEEN

EMPLOYEE HEALTH AND SAFETY 540

CHAPTER TWENTY

EMPLOYEE COMMUNICATIONS 572

INTERVIEW

PART SIX

IMPLEMENTING HUMAN RESOURCE STRATEGY 598

CHAPTER TWENTY-ONE

STRUCTURING THE HUMAN RESOURCE FUNCTION 600

PART ONE

STRATEGIC HUMAN RESOURCE MANAGEMENT

Human resource management is the process of bringing people and organizations together so that the goals of each are met. In Part One, we elaborate on this process and explain how it requires a joint effort between human resource professionals and line managers of an organization. We also discuss how human resource management has evolved during the twentieth century, how rapidly it has undergone change in the past two decades, and how it has increased in importance in today's organizations.

Part One introduces four key themes that are stressed throughout this book. First, dramatic changes in organizations and the business environment in the past two decades have increased pressure on employers to deal effectively with employees. The importance of human resource management has grown accordingly. Amidst turbulent economic conditions, government regulations, and social values, employers must make special efforts to find and retain productive employees.

Second, human resource professionals increasingly function as internal consultants in a partnership with line managers and supervisors. They advise and assist supervisory personnel who implement many human resource programs for selection, training, performance appraisal, and career development. Chapter One concentrates on these first two themes.

The third theme, which is discussed in depth in Chapter Two, concerns the growing need to link strategic planning for the organization with human resource planning. For example, as an organization makes plans to develop a new product line or enter a new market, it must also consider how it will secure the right people to staff the venture. Senior human resource professionals participate in business planning with the top management group of many of today's organizations.

The fourth theme, also addressed in Chapter Two, is that human resource management is best practiced in an integrated way in concert with major line functions. As line managers make key strategic and operational decisions (e.g., changing the flow of work in a department or replacing old equipment with new technology), they must also consider how these decisions will affect their employees and how management can make adjustments, for example, through training or career development, to maintain productivity.

CHAPTER ONE

AN INTEGRATED APPROACH

Peter Brown, the Vice-President of Financial Controls in a major division of Confederated, Inc., has a serious problem in his department of 100 accountants and accounting clerks.[1] Employee morale is low, and job performance is barely acceptable. The managers and supervisors of the department appear to be overworked, and recently hired employees are not reaching expected levels of performance quickly enough. Nearly half of the department's new accountants and accounting clerks are quitting within their first twelve months of employment, and turnover is 25 percent among accountants with three to four years with the company. The department is meeting routine accounting deadlines only through extensive overtime work. Special projects and requests from top management, while interesting and challenging, are increasingly viewed by the staff as intrusions and crises.

The problem began eighteen months ago just after a major reorganization of Confederated. At that time, the decision was made to split the company into two divisions to accommodate rapid growth and product diversification. The reorganization was routine for many operating departments that produced various groups of products, but it was far more dramatic for staff departments. In particular, the accounting department, which had served the entire organization, was split into two new departments. Jobs and functional units were allocated to one division or the other, and people who used to work side by side found themselves in separate buildings. The original accounting department's controller and assistant controller became vice-presidents of the two new departments.

Peter Brown realized that such a disruption would affect staff morale and performance for some time, but now that eighteen months have passed, he is convinced that his problems have other causes. A number of questions go through his mind.

- *Were the wrong kinds of employees hired in the past eighteen months?*
- *Are new employees receiving inadequate training on the job?*
- *Are supervisors and managers delegating too little work?*
- *Are the performance standards in the department unclear?*

Are the organization's salaries and benefits competitive?
Are there too few opportunities for promotion and career development in the department?

How can Peter learn what is interfering with the job performance of seemingly talented people?

The most important resource of any organization is often said to be its people. Such claims appear in organizations' annual reports and mission statements. Of course, an organization is simply a collection of people whose activities have been planned and coordinated to meet organizational goals. An organization that exists to produce goods or services has a good chance to survive and prosper if it consists of the right people. This is true for all organizations, whether they are privately or publicly owned, or created by the government to serve the public.

Similarly, people need organizations. The vast majority of people must work to support themselves and their families. But people work for many reasons other than economic security. For example, many also work to keep busy and feel useful, to create and achieve, to gain recognition and status, or to test and stretch their abilities.

To meet their respective needs, people and organizations join forces. Unfortunately, this union seldom approaches perfection. All organizations, from the small business of a few employees to the giant corporation of over 100,000 employees, encounter obstacles in meeting their goals. And similarly, almost all employees report some problems in their attempts to be productive and efficient in their jobs and to feel satisfied in their work lives. The challenge of human resource management is to minimize these obstacles and problems.

EXHIBIT 1.1 **FOUR COMPONENTS OF HUMAN RESOURCE MANAGEMENT**

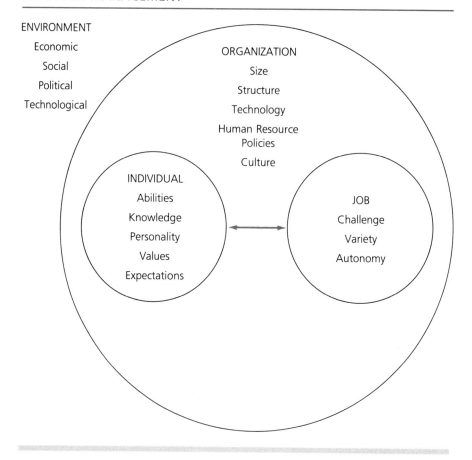

HUMAN RESOURCE MANAGEMENT DEFINED

Human resource management is the process of bringing people and organizations together so that the goals of each are met. It can be viewed as the process of combining four components, shown in Exhibit 1.1, in a harmonious and productive fashion. Its goal is an optimal degree of fit among these four components—the environment, organization, job, and individual.

The Environment

Every organization exists in an environment and survives by interacting effectively with it. The environment can be divided into four parts—economic, social, political, and technological. The *economic* environment consists of such influences as the number and strength of competing organizations, interest and inflation rates, and level of unemployment. One has only to watch the fluctuation in the number of want ads during economic recessions and recoveries to note the impact of the economic environment on human resource management.

The *social* environment is shaped by the society in which the organization functions. Potential customers and employees of the organization, with their attitudes and values concerning work, products, and business, their educational and skill levels, and their expectations, are integral parts of the social environment. To prosper, the organization must achieve a fine balance between meeting the needs of its employees and customers and meeting its own organizational goals.

The *political* environment consists of the laws and regulations governing an organization's operation. A myriad of federal, state, and local legislation affects the basic nature of private, public, and government organizations in addition to their policies and practices concerning employees. For example, laws regulate the way employers hire, promote, and pay employees, the way they negotiate with unions, and their efforts to ensure employee health and safety.

The *technological* environment consists of the raw materials the organization uses and the market demand for its products and services. **Technology** is *the process through which the organization turns raw material into finished products or services*. In some kinds of business, the technological environment is relatively stable, and organizations can prosper by continuing to operate as in the past, drawing on the same types of employees to produce the same products and services. In other fields, such as computers, telecommunications, and genetic engineering, raw materials and market demands change very rapidly, and the organization must respond by changing technology, jobs, and the skills and knowledge of its employees.

technology

The Organization

The second component is the organization and its many characteristics that contribute to employee satisfaction and performance. Some key organizational characteristics are listed in Exhibit 1.1. One obvious characteristic is *size;* some people have strong preferences about the size of the organization they want to join. Organizations also differ in their *structure*. Some are tall and hierarchical, with a boss for every small group of employees, while others are flat, with a large number of employees to each supervisor. Some are organized into functional departments (e.g., marketing, production, and sales), while others rely on project teams consisting of members from several different functional areas. Another key characteristic of organizations is *technology*, which governs how work is done and the types of employees who must be hired and trained. The organization's *human resource policies* show its orientation toward people and play a major part in attracting and retaining productive and satisfied employees. Finally, the **culture** of the organization is *the shared values and beliefs that form informal ground rules about how employ-*

culture

ees are expected to behave. A mismatch between the personality of an employee and the culture of an organization can frustrate both personal and organizational goals.

The Job

job

The **job** is *the collection of tasks and activities in which an employee is engaged.* Since the U.S. Department of Labor's *Dictionary of Occupational Titles* includes over 40,000 different jobs, this component of the individual-job-organization-environment fit can vary in an almost endless number of ways. Among the key characteristics of jobs that directly affect employee performance and satisfaction are the degrees of *challenge, variety,* and *autonomy* they offer to employees. Challenge is the level of difficulty of a job's tasks and activities. Variety refers to the number of different tasks and activities included in the job, and autonomy is the extent to which an employee works independently on a job.

The Individual

Finally, each individual brings a unique combination of attributes to an employer. Some personal characteristics that cause people to succeed or fail on a job are their *abilities, knowledge, personality, values,* and *expectations.* Abilities and knowledge determine an employee's potential to perform specific jobs successfully. Personality, values, and expectations are related to an individual's preference for different kinds of jobs and organizations and therefore determine the choice of a specific job or employer.

Given that the goal of human resource management is an optimal degree of fit among these four components, we can now expand the definition: **human resource management** is the *process through which an optimal fit is achieved among the employee, job, organization, and environment so that employees reach their desired level of satisfaction and performance and the organization meets its goals.*

human resource management

Defined in this way, human resource management encompasses a wide range of activities. Once an organization has been established and jobs have been created, people are recruited and selected to fill the jobs. Once hired, they are oriented to their new department and organization, and trained in their job functions. Employee performance is monitored and reviewed, and salaries and benefits are distributed. Steps can be taken to help employees progress in their careers. Various health and safety programs are established in accordance with government regulations and company policies. Someone in the organization engages in contract negotiation with unions representing employee groups. Employee problems such as low morale, poor motivation, or dependence on alcohol or drugs can be addressed effectively for the benefit of both the employee and the organization.

EXHIBIT 1.2

JOINT LINE MANAGER—HUMAN RESOURCE PROFESSIONAL APPROACH TO SELECTION

	Strategy	Design	Implementation
Individuals Responsible	Top management and Senior Human Resource Professional	Human Resource Professional	Human Resource Professional and Line Manager
Key Activities	Project 40% increase in gross revenues, requiring a 20% increase in staff, and identify employees needed in 1 to 3 years Identify sources of needed employees Establish guidelines for salaries and benefits required to attract needed employees	Prepare recruiting materials such as brochures and ads Design and administer selection tools such as application forms, tests, assessment centers, etc.	Participate in recruiting activities on college campuses, open houses, etc. Interview all applicants recommended by human resource professionals Review all information on each applicant and make employment decisions

DUAL RESPONSIBILITY FOR HUMAN RESOURCE MANAGEMENT

In most organizations of more than 100 employees, a staff specialist, a *human resource professional*, coordinates the activities mentioned above. But line managers also engage in these activities when seeking the optimal degree of fit among employees, jobs, the organization, and environment. Throughout this book we will show how line managers and human resource professionals work as a *team* to plan, design, and implement human resource policies and activities that further organizational goals.

Strategy

The top management group of virtually all organizations meets annually to make long-term plans for change. Plans may be made to increase gross revenues or market share, to cut costs, or to expand into a new line of business. Since these plans usually require an adjustment in the organization's labor force, the organization's senior human resource professional meets with top management to make plans to train employees, hire new ones, or lay off workers no longer needed (see Chapter Two). In Exhibit 1.2, for example, plans to increase gross revenues by 40 percent require a 20 percent increase in employees. The senior human resource professional and top management would discuss the kinds of employees needed and the costs to train and recruit the necessary employees. The result would be a strategy to make the right kinds of employees available at the right time.

Design

Once the strategy has been set, human resource professionals work relatively independently to design appropriate human resource programs that will meet the organization's needs for employees. In the example in Exhibit 1.2, they prepare recruiting materials such as brochures and advertisements and design selection tools such as application forms, tests, and assessment centers. Next, they distribute the recruiting materials, administer the selection tools, and conduct preliminary interviews with all applicants.

Implementation

After the appropriate human resource programs have been designed, they must be implemented. This requires a team effort between human resource professionals and line managers who directly supervise employees. For example, managers and supervisors in the accounting, engineering, and marketing departments will visit college campuses and recruit graduating seniors in their respective disciplines. Middle managers will interview experienced applicants who have passed the tests and interviews administered by human resource professionals. Finally, hiring managers and human resource professionals will review all information on each applicant and decide who is to be hired.

Personnel Management or Human Resource Management?

In many organizations titles like personnel department, personnel director, and personnel manager are common. Traditional books about personnel management concentrate on how programs for selection, training, compensation, and career planning are designed by members of the personnel department, and their audience is students who plan to specialize in personnel management. We have chosen to use the term *human resource management* for two major reasons. First, we view it as a process much broader than designing personnel programs; it also involves strategic planning and implementation. Second, the expanded definition of human resource management includes responsibilities that can only be assumed by line managers. Therefore, our audience is not only students who wish to become human resource professionals, but also business students who plan to become line managers.

THE EVOLUTION OF HUMAN RESOURCE MANAGEMENT

The large organization with its highly specialized departments is a relatively recent development. Until the time of the Industrial Revolution in the nineteenth century, organizations were small, and there was a complete absence of human resource professionals and departments.[2] But new employees still had to be selected and trained, performance had to be evaluated, and wages had to be paid. Of course, these human resource functions were performed in organizations before the Industrial Revolution, but not by human resource professionals. They were handled by the owner of the business or by supervisors who directed the work of employees. This remains true of small organizations. It is rare to find a human resource professional in a business employing fewer than one hundred people. Many human resource functions are performed by supervisors, and the record keeping for hours worked, salaries paid, and payroll deductions made is delegated to a clerk.

In the twentieth century, three major trends increased the emphasis and formality placed on human resource functions in organizations. The first trend was simply the *growth in the size of organizations*. As more and more organizations grew in size to several thousand employees, the need arose for various small teams of human resource professionals to recruit and screen new employees, to design and conduct training programs, to conduct salary surveys and to adjust annual salaries to keep the firm competitive. This trend gave rise to human resource management as a staff function, with human resource professionals to help set employment policies for the organization and provide service and advice on employee-related matters to line managers and supervisors.

The second major trend was the *growth of government regulations on organizations*. The 16th Amendment to the U.S. Constitution, which gave Congress the right to tax incomes, and the law that established the Social Security system have led to standardized payroll deductions which all employers in the nation must incorporate into their procedures for paying employees. The Fair Labor Standards Act of 1938 created more policies and record keeping for employers by imposing limits on the number of hours certain employees can work in a week without being paid for overtime. The National Labor Relations Act (Wagner Act) of 1935 gave employees the legal right to organize into labor unions and also led to the need for human resource professionals to represent management in the collective bargaining process. And more recently, the Civil Rights Act of 1964 and subsequent laws and executive orders required organizations to keep records of the number of female job applicants or members of specified minorities to ensure equal employment opportunities for all applicants. These laws and many others have added responsibilities and positions to human resource departments throughout the United States.

The third major trend was *changes in the social environment*—the employees and customers of organizations. The changes in Western society since 1900 are staggering in scope. Research on the social needs of employees ushered in the human relations movement, and employers turned to human resource professionals to design and implement more employee-oriented policies. The result was the evolution of policies regarding working conditions and employee benefits beyond the most ambitious dreams of the union organizers of the 1920s. Recent increases in employees' educational level and expectations for a high quality work life have prompted organizations to become even more sophisticated in their interaction with employees. These trends

EXHIBIT 1.3   **RECENT ENVIRONMENTAL CHANGES**

Economic	Social	Political	Technological
Fluctuating energy supplies	Lost trust in business and government	Equal employment and affirmative action legislation	Word processors and personal computers
Foreign competition	Challenges to corporate profits	Pension plan reform	Industrial robots
Variations in interest rates and levels of unemployment	Changing work ethic	Health and safety standards	Rapid technological obsolescence

have firmly established human resource management as an important responsibility to be carried out in all organizations.

RECENT CHANGES IN THE ORGANIZATION'S ENVIRONMENT

The years since 1970 have seen even greater expansion of human resource management in many U.S. organizations, due primarily to pronounced changes in the environment in which organizations must compete and survive (see Exhibit 1.3). Organizations have called upon the expertise of human resource professionals to help them deal effectively with major environmental changes that affect the way they do business and their relationships with employees. These changes marked the beginning of a new era in which human resource professionals were thrust into the role of "new corporate heroes"[3] who provide guidance and assistance to organizations (see Box 1.1). In this new role, they increasingly collaborated with senior managers to develop human resource strategies.

Economic Changes

Organizations in the United States have experienced high levels of uncertainty and stress due to major economic changes since 1970. Fluctuating energy supplies have driven up manufacturing costs and revolutionized consumer demand for automobiles, traditionally one of the most competitive U.S. products. Foreign competition in the automotive, steel, and home entertainment industries has forced greater attention to labor costs and worker productivity. Periods of high unemployment and interest rates have discouraged business expansion and pressured organizations to make the best possible use of limited financial and human resources.

In an effort to improve productivity, human resource professionals provide assistance through selection and training procedures to achieve a good

THE BEGINNING OF A NEW ERA OF HUMAN RESOURCE MANAGEMENT

BOX 1.1

The personnel department has been represented on many a corporate organization chart as an orphaned box—one that came from nowhere and didn't seem to fit anywhere. To many businessmen, including many chief executives, the people who worked in "personnel" were considered harmless chaps who spent their careers worshiping files, arranging company picnics, and generally accomplishing nothing whatsoever of any fundamental importance.

In some cases, this depressing image was accurate. Companies *have* been known to use their personnel departments as a sort of dumping ground for executive misfits, or for burned-out vice-presidents who needed just a little while longer on the payroll to be eligible for their pensions. But there have always been some personnel directors who found the job a springboard to higher corporate office, and in some companies the executive in charge of personnel management has traditionally been regarded not as an outcast but as an heir apparent.

The current chairman and chief executive of Delta Airlines, W.T. Beebe, was once Delta's senior vice-president for personnel. Both Richard D. Wood, the chairman of Eli Lilly & Co., and one of his predecessors as chief executive served as corporate personnel directors on their way to the top.

In the last few years, many companies have joined Delta and Lilly in putting their personnel departments in the hands of powerful senior executives. Absolutely no one at First National City Bank viewed it as a setback for Lawrence M. Small when he was transferred from the commercial-banking division to head the personnel division in August 1974. Indeed, it was universally regarded as one very impressive step up the ladder: the job carries the title of senior vice-president, and Small was only thirty-two years old at the time.

At Dow Chemical Co., the man in charge of personnel, Herbert Lyon, reports directly to President Ben Branch, the chief executive. Lyon is a member of Dow's board of directors, and is responsible for, among other things, global product planning and corporate administration.

The executives who are being put in charge of personnel departments today are hard-driving business managers who speak what they call "bottom-line language": they are as interested in profits as any other executives. George A. Rieder, senior vice-president for personnel at Indiana National Bank in Indianapolis, provides an almost textbook example of how today's personnel executives perceive their role. "I'm not a personnel manager," Rieder says, in a tone of voice conveying scorn for that traditional title. "I'm a business manager with responsibilities for personnel."

Rieder quickly adds that this difference is much more than merely semantic. "It's a difference of style, scope, and approach. I view myself as a businessman first, whose job has as much of an impact on the bottom line around here as anybody else's. To be effective I have got to understand every aspect of my company's business, and I have got to participate actively in major management decisions before they're made." Rieder reports to the bank's president, and participates actively in day-to-day management of the business.

match between employees and jobs. Career development also receives attention as organizations strive to make the best possible use of available employees.

Social Changes

During the Vietnam War and the Watergate scandal, many Americans lost trust in government and big business. Windfall profits of U.S. oil companies, the result of OPEC price increases, negatively affected the public's view of the profit motive; and environmental concerns cast serious doubts on the morality of organizations' waste disposal practices. In sum, businesses have found themselves on the defensive in trying to attract customers and employees.[4] A gradual change in the work ethic and the degree of commitment employees are willing to make to an organization also appears to have taken place. Working people are placing a greater emphasis on quality of life and expect satisfaction at work, as well as in their leisure activities. As a result, changing jobs has become more common and is perceived as an acceptable method of developing one's career. Similarly, dedication to one's work life and employer at the expense of family and friends is being questioned. Employees are more likely today to refuse transfers and even promotions if they involve relocation or more time away from the family.

Organizations have turned to human resource professionals for help in recruiting and orienting this "new breed" of employee. Human resource policies and practices have also been developed to meet the needs of today's employees. Assistance programs for employees with alcohol- or drug-related problems and fitness programs for all employees reflect recent health and fitness trends in our society. Flexible working hours and a choice of fringe benefits are other examples of human resource policies that evolved recently in response to employee needs.

Political Changes

Recent federal and state legislation has revolutionized the practice of human resource management. Major laws and court decisions now require all U.S. organizations to review and alter many policies and practices that previously had been widely accepted. Equal employment and affirmative action regulations have forced organizations to change the way they make decisions to hire, promote, transfer, train, and compensate employees. Company pension plans have been significantly revised to conform to a new federal law. The health and safety standards and practices of virtually all U.S. organizations have been placed under the jurisdiction of federal law.

Human resource professionals are perhaps most essential to the organization as it responds to these changes in the political environment. They have guided organizations through the legislative regulations of the 1970s and have been instrumental in designing and implementing new policies and practices to conform with regulations and avoid costly lawsuits.

Technological Changes

One need only walk into any office today to see how changes in technology have affected human resource management. Word processors and personal computers with letter-quality printers are replacing the typewriter. Industrial robots are used in manufacturing companies, and smaller, more efficient "user-friendly" computers have become common in all types of organizations. This rapid technological change has created new jobs, while significantly altering some existing jobs and eliminating others. Many organizations must find employees to fill these new jobs.

Human resource professionals have helped organizations and employees deal with advances in technology. They have provided guidance not only in redesigning jobs, but also in selecting and training people to perform those jobs. They have also assisted their organizations in dealing with experienced employees whose jobs become obsolete because of rapid technological changes. In the steel and auto industries, for example, the jobs of some employees with twenty years' experience have simply disappeared. Human resource professionals have designed career planning and development programs to prepare for and address this problem.

THE LINK BETWEEN HUMAN RESOURCE MANAGEMENT AND STRATEGIC PLANNING

Environmental pressures such as those discussed above have increased the involvement of human resource professionals in policy making, planning, and control activities in their organizations.[5] It has become increasingly necessary for strategic planning by the top management of an organization to be coordinated with planning activities of human resource professionals. For example, the strategic planning that precedes an organization's decision to diversify and produce a new product requires not only market research, financial analysis, research and development, and production tests, but also human resource planning to determine how the new venture will be staffed. Answers to the following questions must be found:

- What new jobs will be created?
- What skills and knowledge are necessary to perform them?
- Where can good people be found to fill them?
- What level of compensation is appropriate?
- How long will it take to recruit or train people?

The increasing expertise and influence of human resource professionals is illustrated in Box 1.1. As the box makes clear, the human resource function is being viewed with growing respect by senior managers throughout the organization, and seasoned business managers are bringing broad management skills into human resource departments.

Further evidence of the strengthened relationship between human resource professionals and senior management is found in a major survey of over 700 companies conducted by the Conference Board.[6] One key finding indicates that the movement toward a relationship between human resource professionals and top management has been initiated by both parties. Senior executives have become actively involved in what used to be solely human resource functions, and human resource professionals have become involved in business planning and policy making—formerly the responsibility of the organization's senior managers. The survey noted the following six major changes:

1. A greater involvement by top management in the planning and control of the personnel function;
2. An increased orientation of the corporate personnel staff to company-wide planning and control activities;
3. An increased emphasis on activities of an external relations nature, especially those connected with government regulation;
4. The involvement of a number of other corporate staff units—especially the legal and public affairs staffs—in support of the personnel planning, control, and representative roles;
5. A more technically competent personnel staff reporting to local managers, to provide better quality advice and services to local units;
6. Expanded general management accountability for personnel management performance, and increased emphasis on personnel management information systems to provide communication and control.[7]

The survey also described four major human resource topics and investigated how much corporate executives participated in each. The results, summarized in Exhibit 1.4, show a high level of senior executive involvement in policy formulation of these topics.

The close relationship between senior corporate executives and human resource professionals is further emphasized by the responsibilities assigned to the human resource professionals in major companies. They are in direct communication with top management and give advice and guidance on matters affecting the organization's employees. This increased responsibility is illustrated in the goals of the human resource department at Honeywell (Exhibit 1.5).

ROLE OF THE HUMAN RESOURCE PROFESSIONAL

As we explained earlier, human resource functions were originally performed by owners or managers of small organizations. As organizations grew in size, specialists were hired to provide a *service* to the organization by securing the number and type of employees needed to meet organizational goals. Just as with any other staff function (marketing, advertising, financial management),

WHO PARTICIPATES IN HUMAN RESOURCE MANAGEMENT?   *EXHIBIT 1.4*

	President		Senior Level Executives		Senior Human Resource Professional		Operating Level Managers	
	Companies	%	Companies	%	Companies	%	Companies	%
Participates significantly in policy formulation regarding:								
EEO*	363	56	150	38	596	92	37	24
Manpower training	125	19	15	4	497	77	29	19
OSHA**	122	19	77	20	463	72	52	34
Benefits	360	56	113	29	582	90	32	21
Participates significantly in program design regarding:								
EEO	108	17	66	17	596	92	51	33
Manpower training	52	8	5	1	485	75	43	28
OSHA	39	6	38	10	436	67	60	39
Benefits	180	28	79	20	584	90	35	23
Participates significantly in monitoring company performance regarding:								
EEO	145	23	51	13	603	93	52	34
Manpower training	53	8	8	2	468	72	32	21
OSHA	60	9	38	10	437	68	67	43
Benefits	130	20	42	11	574	89	39	25
Prepares company's position for legislative hearings on personnel matters:								
Before Congress	87	14	171	44	205	32	9	6
Before state legislatures and local governments	96	15	191	49	237	37	14	9
Principal spokesperson on personnel matters:								
Before Congress	78	12	63	16	144	22	6	4
Before state legislatures and local governments	91	14	89	23	180	28	12	8

*Equal Employment Opportunity
**Occupational Safety & Health Administration

SOURCE: Adapted from "Who Participates in Human Resource Management?" *The Personnel Function: Changing Objectives and Organization,* by A.R. Janger. Reprinted by permission.

EXHIBIT 1.5

CHARTER OF CORPORATE HUMAN RESOURCES, HONEYWELL, INC.

1. To provide leadership in the employee relations function throughout the corporation.
2. To support the attainment of operating objectives of the company—earnings, growth, and continuity.
3. To maintain a staff of competently trained and experienced professionals who can provide consultative, developmental, and implemental services.
4. To advise operating executives and employee relations departments on important employee relations policy matters.
5. To perceive long and short range company and employee needs, and to develop strategies to deal with these needs.
6. To furnish certain professional services which cannot be performed cost effectively at other organizational levels.
7. To provide functional approval prior to the appointment of a group, division, or location personnel manager or the personnel manager of a large subsidiary.

The importance a corporation places on human resource management is often reflected in the goals of the human resource department. The Charter of the Employee Relations (Human Resource) Department above establishes a direct link between human resource activities and company operating objectives and also requires the department to provide advice to operating executives.

SOURCE: The authors are grateful to Arnold F. Kanarick, Ph.D., Vice-President, Human Resource Planning & Development, Honeywell, Inc., for providing this document.

experts in human resource management were expected to assist managers and supervisors in the line organization. But what assistance do line managers want? A recent study divided human resource management into four categories:

1. *Policy initiation and formulation:* proposal and drafting of new policies or policy revisions to cover recurring problems or to prevent anticipated problems. Ordinarily it is on the authority of the president that the policy is actually issued.
2. *Advice:* the counseling and advising of line managers. Human resource professionals are expected to be fully familiar with human resource policy, labor agreements, past practices, and the needs and welfare of both the organization and the employees in order to develop sound solutions.
3. *Service:* the recruiting, testing, and planning of training programs by human resource professionals.
4. *Control:* the monitoring of performance of line departments and other staff departments to ensure that they conform to established human resource policy, procedures, and practices.[8]

Each senior human resource professional in the study asked the executive to whom he or she reported, and two line managers in the same organization, to participate. The executives and managers were asked how well human resource activities were currently carried out and how the activities should be conducted. The results indicated a strong endorsement of the importance of human resource management. Over 58 percent of the sixty-nine executives and 145 managers who responded indicated they wanted human resource professionals to provide *service* in such areas as labor market surveys and recruiting, Affirmative Action/Equal Employment Opportunity, wage surveys, personal counseling, and human resource research. Ranked second in importance was *advice*, with particular emphasis on discipline, performance appraisal, discharges, employee selection, and job design. These highly sensitive topics require a high degree of skill from line managers, and the survey suggests they want help in these matters from experts in human resource management.

The rank of third given to *policy making* reflects the growing need for organizational policies and practices that incorporate governmental regulations on human resource management. Executives and managers emphasized the need for policy making in Affirmative Action/Equal Employment Opportunity, performance appraisal, discharges, pay structure design, wage/salary administration, and human resource planning. Finally, *control* was ranked a distant fourth.

While *control* was the least popular category, in the past thirty years human resource professionals have assumed a control function in the organizations they serve. With the increasing size of organizations has come a greater need for policies and practices that standardize human resource functions. For example, in many organizations salary policy requires that all employees in a job category be paid the same base salary. Performance appraisals are to be conducted on the anniversary date of the individual's date of employment. Salary increases are not to exceed a given percentage of base salary. All applicants for a given position must achieve a specified score on a designated selection test. All supervisors must follow the union contract when responding to an employee grievance. These are limitations that human resource management has placed on the way line managers and supervisors deal with their employees. They represent control.

Local, state, and federal governments also exercise control over organizations. Major legislation that regulates the way in which organizations deal with employees is presented in Chapter Five. Safe working conditions must be maintained for employees, minimum wages and hours of work must be enforced, equal opportunity for employment must be ensured, employee health and benefit packages must be offered, etc. Human resource professionals often establish organizational policies and procedures to meet government regulations and ensure that they are not violated. Just as the organization's accountants and auditors establish and maintain essential cash management and reporting policies, human resource professionals establish and maintain necessary policies and procedures concerning the organization's dealings with its employees.

This increasing emphasis on control has led to a perplexing dilemma in today's organizations. The human resource function originally evolved from the need of managers and supervisors for assistance. Human resource professionals responded to that need by initiating and formulating policy, giving advice, and providing service. More recently, however, human resource professionals are often perceived as telling managers and supervisors what they can and cannot do. Consider the following examples.

- Betsy Hawkins has just created a new position in her department and wants to promote her key assistant. She contacts the human resource department for assistance in making the promotion official and is told the job must be posted for two weeks and applicants must be sought throughout the organization. Betsy claims that she already has the applicant she wants and complains about the two-week delay.
- Val Orantes, a foreman in the production department, wants to provide special training to a bright new employee on the assembly line, but the plant's human resource professional blocks the plan because it will violate the union agreement.

These and similar situations underscore the human resource control function. Of course, the vast majority of government rules and organization policies are in the best interest of both the employees and the organization. Many human resource policies that are perceived by managers as restrictive actually provide a service. In the examples above, the job posting procedure may indeed turn up another applicant, unknown to Betsy Hawkins, who is far more qualified than the department employee under consideration for the job, and the union may already have five employees with more seniority who also want the training. To overlook them would lead to a major grievance.

STEPS IN THE CONSULTANT-CLIENT RELATIONSHIP

Although standardization and control are essential features of the process of human resource management in today's organizations, the primary goal of the process is service. Research has shown that executives and managers of the line organization want advice and service from human research managers whom they perceive as the organization's experts in achieving the best fit between people, jobs, the organization, and the environment. As a result, human resource professionals find themselves increasingly in the role of internal consultant to their organizations, providing advice and guidance to executives and managers.

Experienced human resource professionals report that it takes a number of years to establish the level of expertise and credibility in their organizations needed to assume the role of internal consultant. They do so by identifying and solving problems for line managers. In essence, they become the consultant and the line managers take the role of client.

EXHIBIT 1.6

STEPS IN THE CONSULTANT-CLIENT RELATIONSHIP

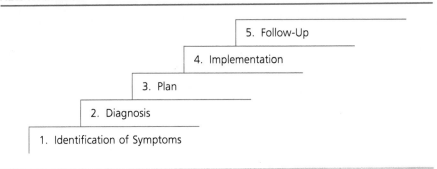

Human resource professionals and line managers establish a consultant-client relationship through a series of steps, outlined in Exhibit 1.6 (Chapter Twenty-Two deals with this topic in detail). It begins with the *identification of symptoms*. An employee-related problem must first be identified. Frequently line managers, because of their close contact with employees, first become aware of a problem and bring it to the attention of a human resource professional. The next step is *diagnosis*. The human resource professional collects information about the employees, jobs, the organization, and the environment to identify potential causes of the problem. A *plan* is then made to alleviate the problem. This may involve establishing or revising human resource policies and practices to address the problem. Next, *implementation* of the plan occurs, often through the joint efforts of human resource professionals and line managers. The last step is *follow-up*. The initial symptoms of the problem are examined again to detect improvements.

To show this process in action, let's return to the financial controls department described at the beginning of the chapter. Peter Brown, the Vice-President of Financial Controls, told Julie Martin, Director of Human Resources of Confederated, Inc., about the recent problem in his department.

Identification of Symptoms

Peter Brown's appraisal noted the following symptoms:

- Department turnover is high, morale is low, and performance has dropped since the reorganization.
- Complaints are up substantially from operating departments about missed deadlines and incomplete budgets.

Additional data from the human resource department's records indicate:

- Turnover among new accountants and accounting clerks was 20 percent per year before reorganization and 52 percent since.

▬ Turnover among accountants with three or four years of experience with the company has doubled since reorganization.

▬ Authorized overtime is up 20 percent since the reorganization.

Diagnosis

Julie Martin analyzed the environment, organization, jobs, and employees to try to identify potential causes of these problems. She gathered information on the local employment market, competitors' salaries, and industry turnover rates, and conducted confidential interviews with all members of the financial controls department. The interviews were designed to focus on specific areas of concern.

▬ The perceived mission and goals of the department,

▬ Clarity of job definitions and work procedures,

▬ Orientation and training of new employees,

▬ Quality of supervision,

▬ Frequency of performance appraisals with new and experienced employees,

▬ Interest in and satisfaction with the work,

▬ Qualifications of new employees.

All of this information was analyzed by Julie Martin and presented to Peter Brown and his immediate staff. The results were grouped into the four potential causes.

Environment ▬ Since the reorganization, employment opportunities in accounting had improved only slightly and industry turnover figures were unchanged. Further, the salary survey indicated that the department's starting salaries and raises were competitive in the local market. Therefore, environmental factors were ruled out as a significant cause.

Organization ▬ The interviews revealed major internal changes that could be traced back to the reorganization. When the original department was split, some functions were retained in both new departments, while others were assigned to either of the two. The result, the interviews showed, was widespread confusion about the mission and goals of each new department. Even seasoned employees were unsure of their current job duties. There were no job descriptions or work procedures for entry-level accounting positions. The interviews showed that formal orientation and training for new accountants had been discontinued since the reorganization. Therefore, new accountants had to train themselves by asking questions of more experienced accountants or their supervisors. However, supervisors often did the accounting work themselves under time pressure, rather than teaching new employees how to do it. Furthermore, there was no formal performance appraisal system in the new department. New employees complained of not knowing "where they stood." Supervisors seldom provided informal feedback.

Jobs ▰▰▰ Most of the entry-level jobs were initially challenging but became routine in a few months. New employees complained of limited opportunities for job rotation or promotion and felt they were not using all of their accounting knowledge and skills. They were particularly concerned about the lack of job definition.

Employees ▰▰▰ Since reorganization, the department continued the practice of hiring well-qualified applicants for all entry-level jobs. Some supervisors were viewed by their employees and Peter Brown as excellent accountants but poor supervisors. Therefore, a potentially troublesome combination of highly qualified new employees and mediocre supervisors existed in the department.

In summary, a number of issues were identified as potential causes.

▰▰▰ Unclear departmental goals,
▰▰▰ Unclear definition of jobs and work procedures,
▰▰▰ Inadequate orientation and training of entry-level employees,
▰▰▰ Lack of systematic feedback to entry-level employees about their performance,
▰▰▰ Limited opportunities for job rotation and promotion.

Plan

Peter Brown and his staff met with Julie Martin to work out a plan to remedy the situation of high turnover, low morale, and poor performance in the department. They proposed a series of steps to cover a two-year period:

▰▰▰ New job descriptions and work procedures would be written for each entry-level job, and departmental goals would be established.
▰▰▰ Orientation and training programs for new employees would be designed. Employee performance would be regularly reviewed.
▰▰▰ New employees would be rotated and promoted when possible.

Implementation

The plans were then implemented by Julie Martin and key members of the financial controls department. The following five changes were made:

1. Accounting managers and supervisors met with members of the human resource department to write new job descriptions and work procedures for each entry-level job. They also prepared statements of goals for the five sections in the department.
2. The job descriptions were used to identify the knowledge and skills that graduate accountants needed to acquire *after* being hired. This material (e.g., sources of accounting data within the company, work and information flows within the department, company accounting and control procedures) was incorporated into orientation and training programs for new accountants and accounting clerks.

3.   A new performance appraisal system was developed for all employees in the department. After it was developed, a departmental meeting was held to introduce the system to all new employees. Managers and supervisors were trained in the use of the appraisal system and in performance appraisal interviewing. The new appraisal system was then implemented.

4.   A job rotation system was developed for new accountants and accounting clerks based on the new job descriptions and required knowledge and skill for each job. Time spent in each job varied according to the job's complexity and the need for staff in the department.

5.   Supervisory manuals were revised to ensure that the new practices remain in operation, and to incorporate the following policies:

   a. Periodic review and updating of job descriptions and desk procedures.

   b. Regular orientation and training courses for entry-level employees when they enter the department or upon their transfer to another section within the department.

   c. Quarterly performance appraisals for new hires and annual performance appraisals for experienced employees. Appraisal interviews include discussions of employee development and career planning, with special attention to job rotation.

   d. Annual review of all salaries within the financial controls department to maintain competitiveness with other firms.

Follow-up

After two years, turnover has dropped markedly and morale is up in the department. Overtime has also been reduced substantially, and overall performance has improved. Employees have expressed satisfaction with the feedback and developmental elements of the performance appraisal system and the job rotation program. Orientation and training courses are routinely held.

It should be noted that this two-year project was a joint effort of the senior management of the financial controls department and the company's human resource department. Expert guidance was given by a senior human resource professional, but the managers and supervisors of the client department were actively involved in the planning and the implementation of new policies to achieve a better fit between employees and jobs within the department.

THE PARTNERSHIP BETWEEN LINE MANAGERS AND HUMAN RESOURCE PROFESSIONALS

The story above illustrates a trend that we expect to continue. Rapid environmental changes have prompted more interaction between human resource professionals and line managers and have enabled them to work as a team to plan, design, and implement human resource policies and practices. Human resource management is likely to be most effective if it is based on a *partner-ship* between human resource professionals and line managers. As we noted earlier, human resource professionals consult with senior management to plan human resource policies for the organization. They then design human resource policies and programs which are ultimately implemented by line managers and supervisors throughout the organization.

Human resource professionals communicate policies to the relevant supervisory personnel, instruct them in their application, and provide advice in carrying out the policies. But the bottom line in human resource management is implementation, and individual supervisors and managers of any organization play a major role in performing most of the human resource activities described in this book. They recruit, select, orient, and train their own employees. They also appraise employee performance and recommend salary increases, transfers, and promotions. In addition, they are directly involved in such programs as career development and employee health and safety.

Consequently, our audience is two groups, human resource professionals as well as line managers and supervisors. Our intention is to educate students and practitioners of human resource management in the underlying principles and effective practice of their discipline, but also to reach the other half of the partnership that is so essential to effective human resource management—students of general management and practicing supervisors, managers, and executives. We want to acquaint those of you in this category with the field of human resource management so you can make informed choices among various human resource policies and programs and implement them effectively.

THE PLAN OF THIS BOOK

This book is divided into six major parts. Part One defines human resource management and emphasizes the growing relationship between human resource management and strategic planning in today's organizations. Chapter One presents human resource management as a process of combining the environment, organization, job, and individual. Chapter Two demonstrates how the process can be integrated with strategic planning for the entire organization. Part Two, The Organization and the Environment, deals with two of the four components that human resource management seeks to combine. Chapter Three portrays the work force from which employers draw employees, and Chapter Four traces recent changes in the work place. Other environmental influences on organizations are included in Chapter Five, which summarizes legislation that regulates the practice of human resource management, and in Chapter Six, which focuses on laws and procedures that govern the relationship between employers and unions.

Parts Three and Four focus on two fundamental ways to attain the best fit between employees and jobs. The first is staffing, presented in Part Three as the specific steps required to secure people who will successfully perform the organization's jobs. Chapter Seven describes approaches to defining the staffing needs of the organization, and Chapters Eight through Ten outline the techniques for recruiting, selecting, and orienting new employees.

Part Four, Employee Development and Performance, describes ways to improve employee performance by increasing employee knowledge and skill or by altering the work environment. Chapter Eleven introduces the strategic issues involved in human resource development, and Chapters Twelve through Fourteen present the principles of training and career development. Procedures for measuring and improving employee performance are included in Chapter Fifteen, and Chapter Sixteen deals with the growing trend in today's organizations to assist employees as they leave their current employer to seek other employment or to retire.

Part Five, Human Resource Systems, presents a number of programs used by organizations to maintain employee performance and satisfaction. These programs are initiated by the organization itself or prompted by environmental influences. Chapter Seventeen includes a thorough discussion of the strategic considerations necessary to design an organization's compensation system, and Chapter Eighteen presents the procedures needed to design and implement various compensation systems. Chapter Nineteen reflects the impact of government health and safety legislation as well as an emerging concern among progressive employers for employee fitness and health. Organizations' attempts to keep employees informed and to measure employee work attitudes are examined in Chapter Twenty.

Part Six, Implementing Human Resource Strategy, ends the book on the vital and practical note of implementation. Human resource management cannot be effective if it is not conceived and implemented properly. Chapter Twenty-One emphasizes the need to structure the human resource function so that it is compatible with the needs and structure of the organization. Chapter Twenty-Two deals with the ways in which the human resource process can be managed and underscores the role of the human resource professional as an internal consultant. Finally, Chapter Twenty-Three focuses on the bottom line of human resource management—its impact on the organization—and presents an approach to evaluating that impact.

KEY POINTS

■ Human resource management is the process of achieving the best fit between individuals, jobs, organizations, and the environment. As the rate of change in these four components has accelerated in the past two decades, human resource management has grown in complexity and importance.

■ There is growing interaction between top management and senior human resource professionals in today's organizations. Top management contributes to human resource policy making, and human resource professionals are actively involved in strategic planning for the organization.

▬ Managers and supervisors want service and advice from human resource professionals to help them deal more effectively with their employees, but they dislike the restrictions that standardized human resource policies sometimes place on them.

▬ To assist managers and supervisors in solving employee-related problems, human resource professionals act as internal consultants to diagnose the causes of the problems and recommend changes in human resource policies and practices.

ISSUES FOR DISCUSSION

1. Compare economic conditions and employee values and expectations today with those of fifteen years ago. How have the differences affected human resource management?

2. Choose a number of human resource policies that you have encountered in organizations where you have worked. From your perspective, did their primary purpose appear to be to *control* you or to *assist* you? Why?

3. Consider the case of Peter Brown and the Financial Controls Department. Which problems could have been anticipated and avoided if the Vice-President of Human Resources had been involved in the strategic planning that led to the reorganization of the division?

4. Imagine that you are a manager with serious employee-related problems in your department. What are the risks of sharing these problems with a human resource professional and asking for help? What kind of human resource professional would you prefer to approach for assistance?

5. What are the advantages of transferring line managers to head human resource departments in today's organizations, as illustrated in Box 1.1? What are the disadvantages to such a staffing strategy?

6. Even today, many small organizations do not employ human resource professionals and have no standardized human resource policies and procedures. What risks are these organizations taking?

NOTES

1. Based on a real organization with a disguised name.

2. C. Ling, *The Management of Personnel Relations: History and Origins* (Homewood, Ill.: Irwin, 1965), p. 19.

3. H.E. Meyer, "Personnel Directors Are the New Corporate Heroes," *Fortune,* February 1976, pp. 84–88 and 140.

4. D. Kelley "Critical Issues for Issue Ads," *Harvard Business Review,* July–August 1982, pp. 87–89.

5. A.R. Janger, *The Personnel Function: Changing Objectives and Organization,* Report No. 712 (The Conference Board, Inc., 1977).

6. Ibid.

7.   Ibid., pp. 1 and 2.

8.   H.C. White, and M.N. Wolfe,"Industrial Management Views Personnel Admin-
     istration," *Industrial Management, 23*, 1981, pp. 10–14, and G.W. Bohlander,
     H.C. White, and M.N. Wolfe, "The Three Faces of Personnel—or, PAIR De-
     partment Activities as Seen by Executives, Line Managers, and Personnel Di-
     rectors," *Personnel*, July–August 1983, *60*, pp. 12–22.

ANNOTATED BIBLIOGRAPHY

A list of books, journals, and professional associations relevant to the topic under
discussion appears at the end of each chapter throughout this book. Interested
readers will find them to be excellent sources for additional information on the
topic. In this first bibliography we present a number of academic and applied
sources about human resource management and general management.

Human Resource Management— Applied

Personnel Journal. Published monthly by A.C. Croft, Inc.

A solid source of current practices and thinking in human resource management
with many articles on survey research data. A regular feature is "Resource Marketplace," a description of products, services, and books on human resource
management. The "Conference Calendar" and extensive advertising in each issue are useful to human resource practitioners.

Additional useful sources are: *Personnel; Human Resource Planning; Labor Letter* appearing weekly in the *Wall Street Journal;* Yoder, D., and Heneman, H.G., Jr. (Editors) *ASPA Handbook of Personnel and Industrial Relations.* Washington, D.C.: Bureau of National Affairs, 1979.

Human Resource Management— Academic

Human Resource Management. Published quarterly by John Wiley & Sons for the
Graduate School of Business Administration of the University of Michigan.

An excellent source of data-based and review articles on current practices and
trends in human resource management. Also includes book reviews and lists
current books on human resource management and general management.

Additional useful sources are: *Personnel Psychology; Journal of Applied Psychology;*
Dunnette, M.D. (Editor) *Handbook of Industrial and Organizational Psychology.*
Chicago: Rand McNally, 1976.

General Management—Applied

California Management Review. Published quarterly by the University of California
Graduate School of Business Administration, Berkeley, and Graduate School of Management, Los Angeles.

Includes a wide range of articles on management, well grounded in research or theory, but with an applied orientation. Also publishes book reviews.

Additional useful sources are: *Organizational Dynamics; Harvard Business Review;* Grove, A.J. *High Output Management.* New York: Random House, 1983.

General Management—Academic

Academy of Management Journal. Published quarterly by the Academy of Management.

An excellent source of empirical research on a wide range of management topics, such as business policy and planning, international management, organizational behavior, and health care administration.

Additional useful sources are: *Journal of Management, Administrative Science Quarterly;* Fombrun, C., Tichy, N., and Devanna, M.A. (Editors) *Strategic Human Resource Management.* Reading, Mass.: Addison-Wesley, 1984.

CHAPTER TWO

STRATEGIC HUMAN RESOURCE PLANNING

Even the most astute observer would never recognize the nondescript single-story building in Boca Raton, FL, as a product development laboratory of International Business Machines Corporation, the world's premier computer maker. The converted warehouse has a leaky roof, few windows, and a malfunctioning air conditioner. Yet a small team of IBM engineers began working here in 1980 and managed to design the computer that has ended up significantly changing the entire personal computer business—and IBM as well. . . .*

In 1980 the home computer market was highly fragmented. There were no industry-wide standards. When IBM entered the competition it dominated the market.

The design team was not expecting such grandiose results that first summer. They were not developing a computer to fit IBM's traditional product lines but creating instead a product that would enable the computer giant to enter the already exploding personal computer market. . . .

To create what became the industry-dominating Personal Computer (PC), an autonomous task force was created. It was separate from IBM's normal bureaucratic procedures and rules. This new form of human organization was central to the PC's success.

"We were allowed to develop like a startup company," says Philip D. "Don" Estridge, the project leader, whose personal star in IBM has risen just as fast as the Personal Computer. "IBM acted as a venture capitalist," he explains. "It gave us management guidance, money, and allowed us to operate on our own."

Their triumph is dramatically changing the entire corporation. "The PC has reinvigorated the company," declares Stephen T. McClellan, who has long followed IBM for Salomon Brothers. . . .

*Reprinted from the October 3, 1983 issue of *Business Week* by special permission. Copyright © 1983 by McGraw-Hill, Inc.

The rocketing triumph of the Personal Computer also provides the most visible confirmation yet of the aggressive strategy that IBM put in place in 1979 and 1980. During the 1970s, the computer giant was unable to establish a strong position in such high-growth markets as distributed data processing and office automation. As a result, its overall market share slipped from 60 percent to about 32 percent of the broadly defined information processing market. To ensure that IBM did not continue to miss market opportunities, then-Chairman Frank T. Cary radically changed the company's operations. . . .

In the late 1970s the growth area in the computer industry was in home computers. Management was encouraged to examine this market. They were also encouraged to consider different channels of distribution, for example, independent retailers such as Computerland. This was a radical departure for a firm with a marketing organization as strong as IBM's.

And in a broad effort to lower production costs, IBM invested many millions of dollars in automated production facilities. "The success of the PC justifies the grand strategy that IBM put in place in 1979," says William D. Easterbrook, computer industry analyst for Kidder Peabody and Company.

IBM certainly developed the PC in an uncharacteristic manner for a large, structured company. Unlike most of its product design teams, which must account for their every move, the Boca Raton group was on its own, except for quarterly corporate reviews. . . .

But this was a new ball game for IBM, competing with the numerous entrepreneurs in the personal computer business. Work conditions were Spartan. Eighty and 100 hour weeks were not uncommon.

"If you're going to compete with five men in a garage, you have to do something different" than what IBM usually does, says David J. Bradley, one of the designers of the PC.

This autonomy was largely responsible for the Personal Computer's quick penetration of the market. . . .[1]

*I*n Chapter One, we discussed the role of the human resource manager as a consultant and partner to line managers. We also stressed the importance of managing human resources (people) as a critical element in the line manager's responsibilities. In this chapter we will get more specific and see how human resources are integrated into the functioning of the organization's line management.

A key to the stunning success of IBM's PC project was the *strategic use of human resources*. IBM combined a select group of employees and jobs to form a business unit in a dynamic technological and economic environment. Let us consider the components of the human resource strategy in this case.

First, a *new organization design* (the autonomous design team) was created. It operated much like the free-standing entrepreneurial ventures of their competitors, the proverbial "five men in a garage." This autonomous organizational unit in turn dictated new types of *jobs* for the project team members: more autonomy, the chance to see a complete project through from beginning to end, the chance to work on a project which was extremely significant to the future of IBM, and great task variety, since a small group had to do the whole range of tasks associated with designing and developing the new machine. *Staffing* had to be done strategically to select and recruit just the right kind of employee to fit into an entrepreneurial subunit. We are not told about *compensation*, but perhaps there were special incentives or bonuses linked to the attainment of the team's objective. Thus, to achieve the strategic business objective of successfully developing the PC, a particular strategy for managing people also had to be developed.

In contrast to this IBM example, many organizations are notorious for making poor use of available human resources because they do not systematically analyze the environment, organization, and jobs and anticipate how, when, and where the people will be needed. Stories are told of the U.S. Army training graduate engineers to be cooks, and then six months later training qualified chefs to do drafting work. Similar tales abound about managers who telephone the human resource department and request that ten new, highly qualified employees be hired by the end of the week (usually in an area in which good applicants are very scarce). Similarly, organizations may wait until employees have struggled in newly created jobs for six months and turnover has increased dramatically before developing a training program. What can be done to reduce such poor planning?

The solution, of course, is to know ahead of time when the organization will need a certan kind of employee in a certain type of job and plan to meet that need in the most efficient way possible. *Human resource planning* is the process through which the organization strives to have the right people available for the right jobs at the right time. It occurs through the strategic use of all the basic human resource functions (e.g., selection, training, career development, and compensation). This chapter describes how the management of human resources can be conducted in a strategic manner. (We will define *strategic* human resource planning and discuss it in detail in a later section in this chapter.)

Remember that human resource management is primarily a staff function that provides service and guidance to the line organization. It is the line organization (and the line manager) that is ultimately accountable for the management of people. One common style of operation of a human resource department is the reactive one. The **reactive style** is a *response to the needs of line managers and supervisors as they bring those needs to the department's attention.* In the extreme, this method of operation is very inefficient because it represents human resource management by crisis. Every time a crisis erupts, the human resource department reacts to address it; there is no systematic diagnosis of the environment, organization, jobs, and employees to identify potential problems and plan to avoid the crisis.

reactive style

Of course, not all problems can be anticipated, and human resource professionals will inevitably have to react to poor matches between available people and jobs within the organization. For example, a new government regulation may require a major change in human resource policies and practices. Changes in the economy or market conditions may require phasing out certain departments and retraining current employees. Reacting to unanticipated problems is part of the human resource professional's role of internal consultant, discussed in Chapter One.

But there is a second possible method of operation of the human resource function, exemplified by the IBM example, which should be used as much as possible. The **proactive style** *actively anticipates and influences the future.* With a proactive approach, managers and human resource professionals systematically analyze the fit between available employees and needed jobs in the organization and take appropriate action to meet strategic organizational objectives. This proactive approach is facilitated when line managers see the management of human resources as *their* responsibility, in partnership with the human resource department. This partnership makes possible the process of strategic human resource planning, which, in turn, leads to enhanced organizational performance.

proactive style

WHAT IS STRATEGIC PLANNING?

Before we can discuss strategic human resource planning, we need first to discuss what we mean by the general process of strategic planning. **Strategic planning** is *"the process of setting organizational objectives and deciding on comprehensive programs of action which will achieve these objectives."*[2] This requires three core elements:

strategic planning

1. *A mission and strategy.* The **mission** is a *statement of the organization's reason for existing;* **strategy** is *the process whereby the resources available are used most effectively to achieve the objectives related to an organization's mission.* Using strategy entails developing a plan to maximize the impact of the organization's resources. In the IBM PC example, the basic strategy was to pursue high-growth markets (such as personal computers), to use new distribution channels (independent

mission
strategy

EXHIBIT 2.1 ENVIRONMENTAL PRESSURES ON
STRATEGIC MANAGEMENT

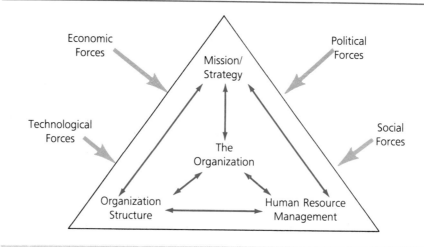

retailers, such as Computerland), and to lower production cost through automation.

structure

2. *A structure.* The **structure** is *the way work is organized into logical groupings, such as functional departments, products, markets, or geographic regions, as well as the way authority is distributed and top management control is exercised.* These groupings of activity and authority essentially represent the division of labor in the organization, the way people are organized to execute the mission of the organization. In terms of our IBM example, again, the basic structure to implement the PC strategy was the small, autonomous design team.

3. *A human resource process.* The mission, strategy, and structure represent the skeleton of the organization. The final element is people to fill the positions in the structure. Effective human performance requires a *staffing* process to get people in the appropriate positions, *training and employee development* so they are capable of good performance, *management of performance, compensation,* and other human resource systems for effective performance, and an ability to create *organizational change* to facilitate the first four processes. All of these activities relate to recruiting and managing people who can operate effectively in the structure of the organization. These five critical steps in the human resource process need to be managed strategically, in relation to the mission and strategy of the organization.[3]

DEVELOPMENT OF ORGANIZATIONAL
STRATEGIES

EXHIBIT 2.2

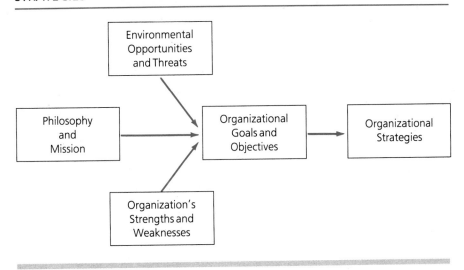

In the IBM example, the PC team was staffed with entrepreneurial, talented people, starting with the leader, fast-tracker Don Estridge. Performance was stimulated through clear goals given to small special business units. "The idea was to have a small group of people with a single result orientation," explained Estridge.[4]

The interrelationships among the elements of the management process are shown in Exhibit 2.1. Forces in the economy, in the political system, in the society, and in technology all impinge upon organizational effectiveness.

Basic Steps in Strategic Planning

Although the steps that follow may appear quite simple and straightforward, in practice they entail a great deal of data collection, analysis, and successive reviews by different levels of management. The major steps (see Exhibit 2.2) in this process, with implications for human resource planning, are as follows:[5]

1.   *Define the corporate philosophy and mission.* This is perhaps the most difficult part of the process. Critical questions include: What is the basic purpose for which this organization exists? Why are we in business? What are our underlying values? For example, Dayton-Hudson (a retailing organization) defines its mission as follows:

    Dayton-Hudson Corporation is a diversified retailing company whose business is to serve the American consumer through the retailing of fashion-oriented quality merchandise.

Serving the consumer over time requires skilled and motivated employees, healthy communities in which to operate, and maximum long-range profit. We are committed to meaningful and comprehensive employee development, to serving the business, social, and cultural needs of our communities, and to achieving levels of profitability equivalent to the leading firms in industry.[6]

2.   *Scan the environmental conditions.* In terms of the model in Exhibit 2.1, it is next necessary to analyze systematically the technological, economic, political, and social forces affecting the organization's ability to pursue its mission. What are current and future trends in the labor market? What changes in government regulations are forecast? Which way are the national and international economies moving?

3.   *Evaluate the organization's strengths and weaknesses.* The environmental scan in step 2 identified facilitating and restraining forces in the external environment, and step 3 does the same thing in relation to the organization's internal resources. What are the organization's distinctive strengths or advantages? What critical limitations does it have? For example, one organization stopped at this point in their strategic planning to develop a new foreign subsidiary, because they realized they lacked the managerial talent to run the operation in that particular country.

4.   *Develop objectives and goals.* After the organization's capabilities are assessed, it can realistically determine specific goals and objectives which would fulfill its mission. Specific important questions are, What are our objectives for sales, profit, and return on investment? How can we measure performance in more qualitative areas, such as customer service or employee development?

5.   *Develop strategies.* It is only after the first four steps are completed that the issue of strategy can be addressed. The main questions are, What would be the most effective approach or course of action to achieve our goals and objectives? What specific changes of direction are needed? What new programs, organization structure, technology developments, financial activities, human resource policies, etc., are needed? Here the organization begins to start to plan strategically for human resources—acquiring, assigning, developing, and rewarding people for the attainment of objectives. This is the point at which human resource planning ties in most directly to strategic planning.

Three Levels of Planning

There are three levels of activity and planning within the organization, each with distinct responsibilities and concerns (Exhibit 2.3). The *strategic level* generally consists of the board of directors, the president, and the executives reporting to the president. Here the concern is for the institution as a whole, and a major responsibility at this level is to manage the interface between the organization and its external environment. In the area of human resource strategy, the vice-president for human resources would play a lead role in decisions made by this top-level team.

EXHIBIT 2.3

THREE LEVELS OF ORGANIZATIONAL PLANNING

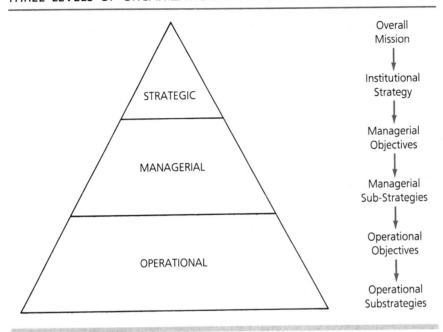

The next part of the organization, moving down, is the *managerial level.* This is the portion of the organization between the president and vice-presidents on the one hand, and first-line supervisors on the other. In general, a *manager* is defined as any person who directly supervises other supervisory personnel. A first-line supervisor, in contrast, is responsible for nonsupervisory personnel, such as hourly workers. At the managerial level, the concern is planning, organizing, motivating, and controlling the major resources available to the organization: capital, information, and people. Whereas at the institutional level there is great concern for communication beyond the organization and for negotiating with a complex variety of constituencies, at the managerial level there is more focus on internal systems, policies, and practices.

The lowest level in the organization is the *operational level.* This is the part of the organization that produces and delivers its actual goods or services. In the words of one vice-president, "This is where the rubber meets the road." The operational level consists of the people who produce the goods and/or services of the organization and their immediate supervisors.

Strategic Human Resource Planning

Strategic human resource planning is *the process of linking the management of human resources to the organization's overall strategies for achieving its goals and objectives.* This planning process entails relating the basic human resource activities (staffing, performance management, employee develop-

strategic human resource planning

ment, compensation and other human resource systems, and environmental and organizational change) to business strategy at each level of the organization. At the strategic level the work in these areas is *long-term,* such as succession planning for future generations of managers and developing policies for rewards (e.g., should there be incentive compensation for executives tied to long-term organizational performance?). Human resource plans are connected to strategic business plans at this level. Indeed, in many organizations the senior people at this level do both strategic business planning and strategic human resource planning.

At the managerial level, long-term plans and policies are translated into specific human resource systems, such as the development of a recruiting plan or a compensation program. If long-term plans and policies are not clearly communicated from the institutional level, there can be no corporate framework and guidance for the creation of specific human resource programs and systems at the operational level.

For example, one large bank had a clear business strategy that it would move aggressively into new, nontraditional markets: financial services, leasing, and consulting. At the strategic level, it decided on a human resource policy of a differentiated compensation structure (i.e., different pay systems for different groups of employees), so it could meet the market compensation rates for consultants, marketing-oriented financial experts, and leasing specialists. It was the responsibility of people at the managerial level (in this case, the line department heads and the corporate compensation director) to develop these differentiated compensation systems.

At the operational level, these human resource systems are put into operation: training programs are administered, pay and benefits are distributed, and performance appraisals are conducted. In the bank example above, operational activities consisted of developng new software for the computerized salary system and communicating with department personnel about the new plan, etc.

It is the strategic level which is most likely to fail to perform its appropriate activities. Here, senior executives are supposed to deal with long-term conceptual issues related to the basic aims and objectives of the enterprise.

On staffing, the top level should decide what type of people will be needed in the next five or ten years, and how they are to be recruited, developed, promoted, and moved laterally. On performance management, executives at the strategic level must decide what kind of evaluation system will be most effective with these future employees, so that positive results are achieved and dysfunctional side-effects are avoided. They need to decide on effective compensation plans for the future, and the kinds of rewards to be linked to the attainment of long-term business objectives. They must determine the general developmental policies that will produce the future managers and work force that will be needed. And they should agree on the philosophy and general policies for change that are consistent with the culture of the organization. Examples of how Honeywell's and Polaroid's senior managements formulate human resource strategy are shown in Box 2.1.

FORMULATING HUMAN RESOURCE POLICY

BOX 2.1

Edwin H. Land, chief executive officer of the Polaroid Corporation, describes the strategies of his company:

"We have two basic aims. One is to make products that are genuinely new and useful to the public, products of the highest quality and at reasonable cost. In this way we assure the financial success of the company and each of us has the satisfaction of helping to make a creative contribution to the society.

The other is to give everyone working for the company a personal opportunity within the company for full exercise of his talents—to express his opinions, to share in the progress of the company as far as his capacities permit, and to earn enough money so that the need for earning more will not always be the first thing on his mind. The opportunity, in short, to make his work here a fully rewarding and important part of his life."

All personnel strategies at Polaroid flow from the second basic aim. The personnel policy committee consists of top corporate officers and is chaired by a senior vice-president, with members of the personnel department serving as staff to the committee. In addition, all levels of the organization, through a "yellow draft" system, extensively review proposed policy changes before their formal adoption. . . .

In another case, Honeywell recently formed an executive employee relations committee composed of five operating group vice-presidents and five staff vice-presidents. This committee serves as a senior policy board in respect to employee relations. Commenting on this, Charles Brown, Honeywell's vice-president for employee relations, said: "We go to the committee with one or more proposals for changing something at every meeting, and we have had practically 100% acceptance. Once an idea is endorsed by the committee, its implementation becomes relatively easy." The executive employee relations committee at Honeywell is also responsible for evaluating the top 200 management positions in the company.

At Honeywell, proposals approved during 1976 included a significantly upgraded employee communications program, improvements in the company's merit pay plan, and increased emphasis on recruiting talented minorities and women.

Does any set of personnel policies universally fit all situations? We think not. If they did, management could simply find and adopt them. The best personnel policies are like the best organizational strategies—they are contingent upon the particular situation and they depend on the strategy of the company.

Policy ▬ One term which has been conspicuously absent to this point in the chapter is "policy." Its use here is downplayed because of differing ways it is used. On the one hand, it is commonly used to describe simple administrative procedures, such as the length of coffee breaks. At the other extreme, human resource policy can cover broad issues such as attitudes toward unions and whether or not to "grow" managers via promotion from within. Our definition will take the latter approach. **Human resource policy** is *strategy related specifically to the human resource function.*

human resource policy

In the words of two noted human resource researchers, Fred Foulkes and Henry Morgan, "In general the formulation of [human resource] policy is simply too important to be left to the [human resource] departments alone. . . . We believe that top management should formulate the critical policy decisions relating to [human resources]. Such decisions should not be allowed to develop in response to crises, and they should be integrated with basic corporate strategies."

Strategy vs. Fire Fighting ▬ Unfortunately, in many organizations senior people (vice-presidents and above) do not think in a long-term fashion about these human resource policy issues. Ironically, they frequently do long-term planning for financial and business matters, but they may never plan for people in the same systematic way. In these organizations, the human resource vice-president may act as a personal counselor or consultant to the chief executive officer or key line officers, only after a crisis has arisen, rather than as the leader of an executive team involved in strategic-level human resource planning that would have prevented the crisis. For example, if the top management team that decided to divide Confederated, Inc., into two divisions (opening case in Chapter One) had also considered the effect of the reorganization on jobs and employees, many of the problems in the new Financial Controls Department could have been avoided.

Please note that we are not saying that the counselor/consultant role of the senior human resource executive is not appropriate or important—in fact, we will discuss this role in detail in Chapter Twenty-Two. Our point is that the more proactive role senior human resource people play in human resource planning, the less need there may be for providing assistance in crises.

The senior human resource officer is often drawn away from strategic planning because of human resource and labor relations crises "fire fighting." A difficult contract negotiation, strike, employee discrimination law suit, or unexpected resignation of a key executive with no back-up candidate can "burn up" months of a human resource vice-president's time. The irony is that if the vice-president had spent more time doing strategic planning and less time doing the work of managerial-level or operational-level people, these crises might never have arisen in the first place.

In some organizations, in fact, responding to crises is seen as a valued part of the culture. Examples of ways some organizations avoid these problems and do, in fact, make human resources part of their strategic functioning are shown in Box 2.2.

BOX 2.2

HUMAN RESOURCES AS PART OF THE TOP MANAGEMENT TEAM

Until three years ago, the personnel department at Standard Brands Inc. was virtually indistinguishable from those that have existed since the dawn of the corporate era. Composed of a director of labor relations and a director of benefits—each with a salary in the $30,000 range—and a staff of about 20, the department routinely administered hiring and firing procedures, handled labor negotiations, maintained employee records, administered benefits, and saw to it that paychecks went out on time. Its decisions could vitally affect individual employees, but they had little impact on the direction of the corporation. . . .

Things have changed at Standard Brands. The personnel department has been incorporated into the new human resources department. The new department has grown in size and status and is directed by a corporate vice-president, Madelyn P. Jennings.

Part of that growth is the result of a flood of new government regulations that have increased the importance and the complexity of traditional personnel administration tasks. Since joining the company in 1976, Jennings had instituted a national compensation program, overhauled benefits, and developed an employee appraisal system.

But much of the stunning growth of Jennings' department is the result of a brand-new role that has been assigned to personnel administration at Standard Brands: the development and implementation of the company's first manpower planning system, one that is directly tied to carrying out corporate strategies. . . .

Changes taking place at Standard Brands are occurring in other large corporations as well. Personnel administrators are using the human resources title and are becoming increasingly powerful members of the corporate structure.

Already, experts estimate, such human resources executives—whether they carry the title or not—now hold key manpower planning responsibilities in almost all of the nation's 500 largest industrial companies, compared with only a handful of companies five years ago.

While their staffs still handle such mundane chores as allocating spaces in the company parking lot, they are also expected to work closely with senior operating managers to create staffing plans that are designed to meet corporate goals and to satisfy the growing demands by employees for clear career paths they can follow. . . .

The advantages of having the right people in the right place at the right time have become abundantly clear to today's management. Company assets are not limited to financial resources, and staffing has high priority.

Chief executive officers are increasingly taking an active role in such searches, a clear indication that the human resources position is gaining importance. Standard Brands' Jennings recalls one prehiring interview with F. Ross Johnson, the company's chairman, that lasted seven hours. . . .

Reprinted from the February 26, 1979 issue of *Business Week* by special permission. Copyright © 1979 by McGraw-Hill, Inc.

EXHIBIT 2.4   FOUR STRATEGIC APPROACHES TO HUMAN
RESOURCE MANAGEMENT

	Individual	
	Assumed Stable	Assumed Flexible

Assumed Stable	I
	Staffing
	  Recruiting
	  Selection and Placement
	  Entry
		II
		Performance Management
		and Employee Development
		  Training
		  Career development
		  Motivation
		  Performance appraisal
		  Exit

Assumed Flexible	III
	Human Resource Systems
	  Compensation
	  Employee health and safety
	  Communication
		IV
		Environmental and
		Organizational Change
		  Organization development
		  Quality of work life
		    programs
		  Organization redesign
		  Labor relations

(Row label, left of the table: **Job Situation**)

AN INTEGRATED PLAN FOR HUMAN RESOURCE MANAGEMENT

Now let's return to the fundamental objective of human resource management—to achieve the optimal fit among the individual, job, organization, and environment. We will present four alternative approaches for achieving this fit through the use of the five functions of human resource management described earlier (staffing, performance management, employee development, compensation and other related human resource systems, and organizational change). These five functions can be combined into *four basic strategic approaches* (Exhibit 2.4).

The choice of an appropriate human resource strategy depends upon the assumed state of two components: the individual and the job situation. The job situation is composed of the individual's job, the parts of the organization that affect him or her directly (e.g., supervisor's style, co-workers, department in which the job is found, other departments he or she interacts with), and the environment in which the organization exists (e.g., stable or unstable business climate, dynamic or static technology). Each component, the job situation and the individual, can be assumed to be in one of two states: relatively stable or relatively flexible. The result is four different combinations: stable person and stable job situation, stable person and flexible job situation, flexible person and stable job situation, and flexible person and flexible job situation. Under each of these four conditions, a different strategy for managing human resources is most appropriate. Let us consider each condition in turn. (In practice, of course, these strategies are often used together, but we will consider them separately.)

I. *Stable person, stable job situation: Match the individual to the job.* The first approach to the optimal individual-job situation fit is based on the assumption that both the individual and the job situation are relatively stable, and the challenge is to put the two together. The basic human resource strategy under these conditions, then, is *staffing* (i.e., matching the right people with the right jobs). There are a number of human resource functions that can be used to implement a staffing strategy. Examples are recruitment and selection of applicants and placement of new or current employees into the jobs for which they are best suited. These topics are addressed in Chapters Eight and Nine.

The staffing strategy begins with a thorough analysis of the job situation to determine the duties that must be performed, the working conditions, skills and knowledge needed, etc. Next, a search is begun to identify and attract applicants who fit the job situation. Finally, these applicants are assessed in terms of potential and willingness to perform the job, and a final choice is made.

II. *Flexible person, stable job: Change the employee to fit the job.* The second fundamental strategy to obtain a person-job fit is based on the assumption that the job situation is relatively stable but the individual is malleable. Here, then, the task is to influence the way the person changes through *employee development and performance management*. Specific human resource functions such as training and career development illustrate this approach, as do entry, performance appraisal and feedback, internal communication, and employee counseling or coaching. Most typically, this approach is used for current employees who must learn new attitudes, skills, or knowledge. This approach also requires a thorough understanding of the job in terms of the duties and responsibilities the employee must perform. In addition, if the objective is to change employees so that they can perform the job better, one must know the specific skills and knowledge the job requires, because these are the characteristics the employee will need to acquire.

A thorough assessment of the employees is also necessary. Emphasis is placed on their current level of skill and knowledge and their potential to gain proficiency in these areas. Finally, one must determine if the employees are interested in changing as the job requires, and whether they are motivated to work hard enough to make the necessary changes.

III. *Stable person, flexible job: Change the job to fit the employee.* The situation in which the employee is relatively stable but the job situation is open to change suggests the third approach. In its pure form, this approach accepts the employee as a given and involves attempts to design *human resource systems* which create a job situation that enables the employee to achieve optimal levels of performance and satisfaction. This approach is followed in activities like job design, collective bargaining with unions, compensation programs, various supervisory motivational techniques, and employee health and safety programs.

Extensive analysis of the job and organization is required, with special emphasis on the effect these two components have on individual employees. Pertinent questions are: Does the job provide the challenge, variety, and responsibility the employee needs? What demands of the union can be met economically? What techniques of supervision and motivation are appropriate for individual employees? What level of salary and benefits meets employee needs most effectively? How safe and healthful is the work environment of employees?

Employees must be assessed primarily in terms of the value they place on work and the needs they hope to satisfy on the job.

IV. *Flexible person, flexible job: Change both.* The fourth approach is based on the assumption that both the employee and the job situation are subject to change. This is a *system-wide organizational change* approach because the components—individual, job, organization, and environment—are viewed as distinct but closely connected parts of a whole, parts which may need to be changed simultaneously. A change in any one part inevitably influences the other parts. For example, training not only changes an employee's current level of knowledge and skill, but also alters his or her perception of the challenge the job offers and may require adjustments in job responsibilities and supervisory style. Similarly, major breakthroughs in technology may dramatically alter the mission of a department and the nature of the jobs in that department. These changes may increase job stress among employees and lead to demands for greater job security.

An example of this approach would be the state of the U.S. automobile industry in the 1970s. With massive changes in markets, energy supplies, automated technologies, government regulation, and employee work values, system-wide changes were necessary. Cost reduction, quality of work life, layoffs, retraining, supervisory training, and other changes were used to create massive organizational change. A system-wide approach to human resource management is suited to organization development and supervisory changes. In each, changes are made in both individuals and the work environment to reach that elusive optimal fit. In a system-wide approach it is necessary to understand as much as possible about the individual, job, organization, and environment and how these four interact. Chapter Four will give more detail on ways organizations (such as General Motors) have changed the work place to adapt to major changes in employees and in job situations.

Obtaining Information About the Job and the Individual

Job Analysis ▬▬ To analyze the nature of the person-job relationships reflected in Exhibit 2.4, it is critical to have a thorough understanding of the job. In fact, job analysis is probably one of the most crucial activities in the entire process of human resource management. Understanding the job situation is important not only to the choice of a strategy for managing human resources, but also for any specific operational human resource activity (e.g., selection and compensation).

Traditionally, **job analysis** is the *process "in which jobs are studied to determine what tasks and responsibilities they include, their relationships to other jobs, the conditions under which work is performed, and the personal capabilities required for satisfactory performance."*[8] A **job description** is the *written statement of these tasks, responsibilities, work conditions, and needed skills.*

job analysis

job description

Information About the Individual ▬ In the quest for an optimal fit between people and job situations, the individual is certainly the most interesting and diverse of the components to be analyzed. Analyzing individuals provides the basis for predicting and altering their work performance—an objective which is the subject of several chapters in this text.

Much of the text deals with the way in which this analytical information can be used in the process of human resource management. All of this information can be grouped into three categories:

▬ Past performance—what the individual *has done*,
▬ Potential to perform—what the individual *can do*,
▬ Intention to perform—what the individual *will do*.

The best predictor of future performance is past performance. A major goal of human resource management is to predict future performance; therefore, assessing how an individual has performed in the past is important. In the selection process, the past performance of applicants can be assessed in interviews and through reference checks or letters of recommendation from previous employers. Similarly, past performance of current employees is assessed through various methods of performance appraisal. This information provides the basis for such human resource decisions as salary increases and promotions.

Potential to perform includes basic personal characteristics that determine what individuals are capable of doing, such as intelligence, knowledge, skills, and personality traits. Analysis of these characteristics helps us understand what is required for successful performance. This kind of information is particularly useful in selecting from a group of applicants those who have the best chance to perform a given job well. In addition, an understanding of the personal characteristics that lead to successful job performance is an essential first step in training. If one wishes to alter people to fit the job, one must first know what level of those characteristics the people possess and to what extent these qualities can be changed.

Other information determines how people *choose* to perform, and why. One of the great mysteries in human resource management is why people perform as they do. Why does an employee with ten years' experience in computer programming and all the required knowledge and skill abruptly quit and begin a new career? Why does an employee with minimal intelligence and skills excel over more capable co-workers? Partial answers to these questions involve an understanding of what people like and need to do at work. Individuals' needs, values, and interests strongly influence their choice of a job and how well they perform that job. The myriad factors that influence *work motivation* and *job satisfaction* are important to the process of human resource management. Analysis of employees' intention to perform is a part of virtually every human resource function covered in this text.

Choosing Which Strategy to Use

The four strategic options in Exhibit 2.4 represent alternative approaches to the same objective—the optimal individual-job-organization-environment fit. Various combinations of these approaches are in common practice. For example, applicants may be chosen through extensive recruitment and selection procedures (I), and immediately upon entry into the organization be enrolled in a one year training course (II) or encounter supervisors' attempts to motivate and challenge them (III).

The fact that these four approaches are alternative means to the same objective leads to an important point that is stressed throughout this text. That is, careful analysis is necessary before choices among these approaches are made. When is training the best choice? When is selection most appropriate? When is a combination of approaches called for? Furthermore, once the approaches are chosen, they must be properly coordinated. Everyone in the organization who is responsible for planning, designing, or implementing human resource policies and practices must understand the interactions among these approaches in order to evaluate alternatives and make appropriate choices. Otherwise, chaos will ensue. Training programs may be offered that nobody needs. Recruiters may interview applicants without having a good understanding of the jobs they are trying to fill. Departmental policies may call for job enrichment but an individual supervisor may be taking responsibility away from subordinates. These inconsistencies can be reduced through a well-coordinated program of human resource management and the commitment of members of the organization to that program.

Human Resource Activities at Different Organizational Levels

How, specifically, should human resource activities be incorporated into strategic management? Exhibit 2.5 shows how human resource activities can be related to business strategy at each level.[9] The five major human resource activities mentioned earlier are considered: staffing, performance management, development, compensation, and environmental and organizational change. At the strategic level the work in these areas tends to be *long-term*, such as succession planning for future generations of managers and developing policies for compensation and career development. This is also the level where human resource plans are connected to strategic business plans. Indeed, in many organizations, the senior people at the strategic level do both

EXHIBIT 2.5   LEVELS OF HUMAN RESOURCE ACTIVITIES

	Staffing	Performance Management	Employee Development	Compensation and other Human Resource Systems	Environmental and Organizational Change
Strategic Level Policies and plans	Specify the policies for the characteristics of people needed to run business in long term Alter internal and external systems to reflect future Succession planning	Policy question: in long term what should be valued? Develop means to appraise future dimensions Early identification of potential	Plan developmental experiences for people running business of the future Systems with flexibility to adjust to change	In world as it might be in long term, how will work force be rewarded? Link to the long-term business strategy Develop long-term career paths	Environmental scanning and issue tracking Analysis and possible redirection of corporate culture
Managerial Level Programs and systems	Longitudinal validation of selection criteria Development of recruitment marketing plan New markets	Validated systems relating current and future potential Assessment centers for development	General management development Organization development Fostering self development	Five-year compensation plans for individuals Cafeteria fringe package	Organizational survey programs Creation of interdepartmental task forces for planning change Development of new methods of change
Operational Level Implementation	Staffing activities Recruitment plans Day-to-day monitoring systems	Annual or semiannual performance appraisal system Day-to-day control systems	Specific job skill training On-the-job training Career planning seminar	Wage and salary administration Benefits package	Job redesign Quality circles Productivity and quality of work life experiments Employee involvement teams

SOURCE: Adapted from "Strategic Human Resource Management" by Noel Tichy, Charles J. Fombrun, and Mary Ann Devanna, *Sloan Management Review*, Winter 1982, by permission of the publisher. Copyright © 1982 by the Sloan Management Review Association. All rights reserved.

strategic business planning and human resource planning, as does Joe Henson, the CEO at Prime Computer (see Chapter Twenty-One).

At the managerial level, long-term plans and policies are translated into specific human resource systems, such as recruiting plans or compensation programs. If long-term plans and policies are not clearly communicated from the institutional level, there would be no corporate framework and guidance for the creation of specific human resource programs and systems at the operational level.

At the operational level, these systems are implemented: training programs are given, pay and benefits are given, performance appraisal is conducted, and so forth. Again, obviously the next higher level has to have done its job (developing programs and systems) before the operational level can do its planning for how best to deliver these activities.

INTEGRATING HUMAN RESOURCES INTO THE BUSINESS PLAN

Issues to Consider

Eugene Croisant, an experienced human resource executive, has described how an organization motivates both line officers and human resource professionals to integrate human resource planning and business planning.[10]

The first issue to be considered is *why* line executives should care about bringing human resource considerations into strategic business planning. What is in it for a division general manager who, for example, has countless pressing business crises to consider? Isn't human resource planning one of those "motherhood and apple pie" things that receive "lip service" but is time-consuming and not really essential?

Croisant cites three reasons why even the most "hard-nosed" line executives are motivated to incorporate human resource plans into their business plans:

1. Increasing productivity and quality are priorities in most businesses today, and productivity and quality require people to deliver them. In service industries, such as banking, health care, and transportation, the impact of the employee's contribution is especially critical. This point is reinforced by the fact that service is the fastest growing component of the American economy.

2. The human resource department can be a true support group to assist line management to achieve its objectives. In some organizations, it acts more as a "police" arm of corporate policy and government regulation (such as safety and equal employment opportunity), but if members of the department are included in the mainstream business planning process, they will better understand line management's objectives and be better able to assist.

3.   Perhaps most important, a big part of the success of any business plan is having the right people in the right places to implement the plan. Thus, when human resource considerations are incorporated into the business plan from the very beginning of the planning process, the quality of the business plan is greatly enhanced. "In fact," says Croisant, "a [business] plan which ignores such [human resource] issues may well be impossible to follow."

There are several requirements for the successful integration of human resource planning and corporate strategic planning. First, there must be *close cooperation between human resource planners and corporate planners*. This means starting with both groups working together to plan the planning process. If the groups have an equal say in determining how the process will work, they can help ensure that both human resource and business considerations will receive sufficient weight.

The human resource planners must also provide basic statistical information, such as projections of employee turnover, future recruiting needs, internal personnel flows, salary growth, etc. Each group should perform critical analysis of proposed plans based upon their own unique perspective. So, for example, if Bank X were planning to start up a new operation in Country Y, it would need a detailed analysis of the market opportunities, government regulations, tax considerations, foreign exchange effects, competition, and other factors related to profitability. However, suppose the bank found, as it began to start up the new subsidiary, that it had no managers with the right background and experience to create a top executive team for the organization? It would then be faced with the unpleasant choice of either hiring from the outside for these critical top positions or abandoning the new venture.

A second requirement is an *understanding of the human resource needs of the line units*, which is obtained from analysis of the business plans and from discussions with line managers. Particular emphasis is placed on areas with specialized needs for talent and on events which will strongly affect human resource requirements, such as a new business venture, geographic expansion, introduction of new products or services, discontinuance of old products or services, increased automation, and mergers and acquisitions. Detailed discussions with managers are necessary to help think through the full human resource ramifications of these plans and to identify areas of uncertainty that must be taken into account. These discussions should also include the anticipated labor market and the feasibility of finding suitable employees in that market.

Third, *external events must be considered* as factors affecting the management of human resources. Some of these factors are: economic developments (world, national, and local), demographic changes, changes in values and attitudes in the work force, new government regulations, changes in the firm's industry, actions of pressure groups, new public issues, corporate expansion or change, and changes in the human resource department. Each of the existing business goals and objectives should be considered in the light of these developments. The goals may need to be modified or supplemented.

Fourth, *plans for the human resource unit should be developed* in such a way as to address the needs of other units in the organization in the face of likely developments. This entails four steps:

1.   Setting goals consistent with corporate goals and with good human resource management.
2.   Defining strategies for meeting human resource needs.
3.   Defining strategies for adapting human resource policies and procedures to meet changing trends or likely events. (This is the key place for building flexibility into the planning process.)
4.   Identifying significant issues which must be addressed in pursuing these strategies. This is a form of contingency planning: anticipating events which might interfere with successful implementation and deciding *in advance* how to deal with them.

The fifth and final critical requirement is to build in *regular reviews* of progress in the plan. Croisant's experience shows quarterly reviews to be effective. This means that line managers should periodically review the human resource plan as it relates to the implementation of the business plan, and human resource managers should review business plans to be sure that they are consistent with planned human resource activities. The line manager's review of the human resource plan should cover important elements such as staff growth, turnover, salary expense, affirmative action progress, and staffing new activities. The requirement to review human resources each quarter along with business leads naturally to the realization that the two are, in fact, inseparable. Changes in the human resource environment should be considered continually. As Croisant indicates, much of this linking of human resource planning to business planning is simply a process of "educating" top management to the critical role of people in achieving business objectives. These five requirements are summarized in Exhibit 2.6.

Important Design Features

We have been discussing a fundamentally different conception of the human resource function from that found in many organizations today: a conception of human resources as a "mainstream" activity, integrally linked to the value-producing line activities of the organization. How do we move from a traditional "nuts and bolts" human resource department, with a focus on operational human resource tasks, to a strategic human resource orientation? Tichy, Fombrun, and Devanna have identified seven critical steps.[11] The first four deal with the internal organization of the human resource function, and the last three involve making the link between the human resource function and the line organization.

Organizing the Human Resource Function ▬▬▬ The first step in developing a strategic human resource function is to identify the various human resource tasks to be performed at the strategic, managerial, and operational level for each of the five basic human resource activities: staffing, performance

Requirement	Components	Responsibility
1. Develop close cooperation between human resource planners and corporate planners	Both groups plan the planning process together Equal power for both groups	Human resource planners provide basic human resource statistical information Corporate planners provide data on business outlook and plans
2. Identify human resource needs of line units	Special focus on areas with unique talent needs Special focus on events which will impact on human resources (e.g., major shutdown, geographic expansion, new product line)	Detailed discussions of human resource implications of business plans, between both planning groups Human resource planners lead the discussion
3. Examine external events for human resource implications	Economic developments Demographic changes New government regulations New public issues	Human resource planners give input on social changes. Business planners give input on economic, competitive changes
4. Develop plans for human resource unit, based on information from points 1–3 above	Set goals consistent with corporate goals and goals of human resource management Define strategies for meeting human resource needs Define strategies for meeting human resource policies	Human resource planners draft human resource plans Business planners review human resource plans Both groups discuss plans and reach agreement

5. Plan for regular reviews of progress	Quarterly reviews
	Cover elements such as:
	   staff growth
	   turnover
	   affirmative action
	   progress
		Human resource planners periodically review business plans for consistency with human resource plans
		
		Business planners periodically review human resource plans for consistency with business plans

management, development, compensation, and managing environmental and organizational change. The second step is to reorganize the human resource function based upon the three levels. The operational level is probably best handled in a traditional personnel department with separate divisions to execute the traditional activities of recruiting, training, compensation, etc. At the managerial level, linking designs would be needed to integrate these various divisions. For example, human resource teams might be assigned to line business units consisting of specialists in compensation, training, and recruiting and selection. Their job would be to assist the manager of the business unit in meeting the human resource needs of the unit. One large bank in Boston has assigned human resource teams to each branch location, with dual reporting relationships to both the branch manager and the corporate human resources director. Each team looks like a "mini human resource department'" and is charged with designing and delivering tailor-made services to its particular branch office.

Other types of linking designs might be project or task force teams made up of personnel specialists who help the organization deal with new issues and events affecting human resources. For example, many companies employ *issue-tracking teams* to diagnose emerging issues and to provide analysis for management. (See Chapter Twenty for more detail on issue tracking to aid communication with the external environment.) Another approach could be the use of a matrix design, in which members of the human resource department serve on the corporate personnel staff in their specialized area (e.g., training), but are also assigned to a particular operating unit and do most of their work for that unit. (See Chapter Twenty-One).

At the institutional level an influential senior human resource management team or individual should participate in key line management committees such as the executive compensation committee, the succession planning group, or the top management team (often called the "management policy committee"). One good way to build in credibility for this team is to put "fast track"executives in some of these positions or in the human resource vice-president's role. These may or may not be career human resource specialists; if not, it would be important to maintain a good mix of human resource professionals and general managers.

The third step in developing a strategic human resource function is to select and train the human resource staff for the strategic orientation. At the operational level, start with professional human resource specialists or recent graduates who received training in state-of-the-art methods. At the managerial level, select people with a general management orientation from the people at the operational level, or bring in good managers from other functions. Training here is aimed at organizational and management skills.

At the strategic level, look for people with broad conceptual and political skills, a good business background, and a solid human resource background. Ideally, these would be people who have had successful work experience in the "mainstream" areas of the organization. For example, in a high-technology company like Honeywell, a senior staff person with educational training or career experience as an engineer, will have far higher credibility than someone whose background is limited to the present area of staff specialization.

The fourth step is to revise the reward and control systems in light of the strategic orientation. Most rewards in human resource departments currently are geared toward how well they deliver at the operational level, which is one important part of human resource effectiveness.

However, people at the managerial level need to be rewarded on the basis of their ability to integrate human resource functions and to make them responsive to the needs of line business units. Too many human resource units are so concerned about being "professional" (e.g., having the most sophisticated compensation system possible) that they totally lose sight of what line managers need. For example, a simple ranking of the worth of jobs may be far more useful to a division manager than a more complex system of job evaluation that assigns points to each job and computes base salaries with detailed equations. (See Chapter Eighteen).

At the institutional level, the top team or person should be rewarded in relation to the performance of the total organization, since that person or group is part of the senior corporate executive team. Specifically, this would mean that the human resource vice-president should participate in the same executive bonus plan as the other officers of the organization.

Linking the Human Resource Department to the Line Organization ▬ Once the human resource function is strategically organized, new kinds of links are necessary between the human resource department and the line organization. Since most links exist at the operational level, more must be added at the managerial and institutional levels. An example of how a new position and person (David Montross) were added to the managerial level at Norton Company is shown in Box 2.3. (Note that Montross spends 40 percent of his time at the strategic level, relating staffing needs to business plans, 30 percent at the managerial level, designing new programs and systems, and 15 percent at the operational level, on program delivery.)

The fifth step, then, in developing a strategic human resource function is to provide the business units with good human resource data, including information on external labor markets, as well as economic and social issues that affect the work force. A human resource record system is often useful to provide quick information to managers on the internal labor market.

For example, Monsanto, facing declining business in certain operating companies, needed information to help assess the extent to which reduced career advancement opportunities were a problem for its employees. With a human resource information system (described in this chapter), it was possible to identify immediately what proportion of employees in these companies were in a career plateau (as determined by how long they had been with the company and in their current positions). When the computer immediately produced a massive list of plateaued employees, the dimensions of the problem were clear. There was no need to conduct a long study to determine *if* there was a problem with plateauing. Instead, the human resource planners could move directly to a study of employee reactions to plateauing and to ways to deal with the problem. Without easily accessible, accurate human resource information, at least a year would have been wasted.

Sixth, the role of senior management regarding human resources must be revised. Top management must be willing to give large amounts of quality time to human resource issues, such as a day each month on succession planning, or several days each year on compensation awards. This really requires the commitment of the top person in the organization; if the chief executive officer says human resource issues are important and spends time on them, these issues will also receive attention from other members of the management team.

A HUMAN RESOURCE PLANNING MANAGER

BOX 2.3

David Montross, co-editor of the book *Career Development in the 1980s,* made the switch from education to industry several years ago. Formerly at Holy Cross College, he is now manager of Human Resource Planning and Career Development at the Norton Company in central Massachusetts. Norton, $1.5 billion company employing some 21,000 people, manufactures a wide range of engineering materials, petroleum and drilling supplies, and industrial abrasives. Recently he discussed his work with the company.

He broke down his schedule in the following way:

- 40% of his time is spent with the human resource implications of the Norton business plans, and what the staffing needs are. Included in this time is work in the areas of recruiting, benefits, and training and development.

- 30% of his schedule involves setting up career development programs and internal information resources, including the new discover III computer system.

- 15% is used for arranging in-house educational programs for employees, taught by staff as well as local educators.

- 5% is reserved for professional affiliations and associations.

- 10% remaining involves reading, keeping current with other human resource professionals.

He has a number of suggestions for those considering a similar move. First, take a two-year perspective, during which time it would be beneficial to enroll in some business-related courses and gain some knowledge of how the business world is changing. Information interviewing is also important, as some companies have a strong interest in people from education, but others do not. Some companies will hire career counselors on a part-time basis, and establishing some identity and credibility in a business setting is a plus.

And finally, Montross recommends a book titled *How to Enter the Field of Human Resources and Organizational Development: A Guide to Entry-Level People, Recent College Graduates, and Mid-Career Changers.* It's written by Stephen Rosenthal and published by the O.D. Network, 1011 Park Avenue, Plainfield, NJ 07060. Cost: $5.

Adapted from "From Education to Industry," by Michael Durall, *Career Planning and Adult Development Newsletter,* Vol. 5, No. 12, December 1983. Reprinted by permission of Career Planning and Adult Development Newsletter, 4965 Sierra Rd., San Jose, California 95132.

The seventh step in developing a strategic human resource management process requires the line organization to revise its reward and control system for managing the human resource function. The organization must have ways to measure outputs at the operational, managerial, and strategic levels of human resource activities. Too often, because human resources is seen as a staff activity, it is not expected to produce accurate results, and it is not held accountable for results. Effective evaluation involves ongoing audits and inputs from line managers as the clients of human resource services. Such a client-driven evaluation system can certainly "get the attention" of human resource professionals and encourage them to develop more of a business orientation.

Human Resource Planning and the Corporate Life Cycle

In recent years it has become very clear that organizations have life cycles, just like people. An organization has to be *born*, or created. It has to get *established*, a period when it is getting "settled down." After becoming established, it enters a period of *growth*, during which it acquires more employees, a larger market, more products, and, hopefully, more profit. Then, as its products and markets enter *maturity*, it may reach a sort of plateau period. Later, if it does not develop new markets and products, it may enter a period of *decline*, where sales, profits, and later the size of the organization's work force drop off.

These phases in the organizational life cycle are very much like the stages in the individual's career cycle, as we will discuss in Chapter Thirteen. The person begins the career with exploration and trial jobs. These mark the entry into the work force (or the birth of the career, if you will). Next, after a good-fitting niche has been found, there is a period of settling down and becoming established. Once set in a field, the person goes through a period of growth through advancement and/or the development of expertise. Then the promotions begin to level off and the person reaches a point in mid life where the job and career are under control. This is a period of maturity or maintenance. Near the end of the career, the person begins to withdraw from the world of work and move into retirement.

The kind of human resource planning needed by the organization varies with its stage in the corporate life cycle. In the *birth stage*, the main need is staffing—the organization needs to recruit and select entrepreneurial types of people who can envision a new organization and who have a unique product or service to produce and sell. The whole notion of *planning* for human resources may seem foreign to the founders of an organization at the early stage, because there are such pressing day-to-day concerns for getting the product out, making contacts, paying the bills, etc. However, without some thought for the future of the people in the organization, unwise commitments may be made.

One example of a critical issue is compensation. Often a fledgling organization has no cash for paying people. Some employees may work on faith or for low pay. However, one common arrangement is to compensate people with equity, or stock in the company, at this early cash-poor stage. One of the best-known examples here was the equity compensation to the secretary of Ray Kroc, founder of McDonald's, during the company's early years. She is now a millionaire because she accepted McDonald's stock instead of cash years ago.

In the growth stage, a more dependable selection and retention process is needed. Recruiting is again critical, but this time the recruiting of competent producers in specific functional areas is needed. For example, in the peak growth period of the high-tech industry in areas like Massachusetts and California, the number one human resource problem was how to hire and retain enough engineers. Groups like the Massachusetts High Technology Council made recruiting a major priority and became involved in state politics to influence property taxes, education, and other aspects of the environment that would make the state attractive to engineers. (Of course, the changes also made the state attractive to new high-tech companies, as well.)

Training becomes important at this stage for several reasons. First, since the company's products and services are distinctive, the company is growing fast, and new employees must be oriented and trained in these special activities. Second, because the labor market may be tight, if less than perfectly qualified people are being hired, training may be needed to upgrade the skills of the entering people (or to develop people through internal transfers). And finally, training itself can be an inducement to accept a job with a particular company.

Compensation during the growth stage might take the form of a bonus or other incentive for the person to share in the growth of the business. With growth assured, top management may be reluctant to give out additional equity to employees, and may have to sell equity externally to raise funds to finance this growth.

The need for good appraisal methods may not be immediately evident here, but again in the well-run organization, top management will want to establish a clear tradition of paying for performance. It is easy at this point to pay for loyalty or length of service, since the staffing needs are so great. However, this can result in the retention of the wrong people, which could be disastrous in the maturity stage. Many contemporary organizations are plagued by "deadwood" employees who were needed in the "early days" and were promoted far beyond their capabilities to meet pressing needs. The more the growing organization can plan for future management and professional needs and can reward and place people in terms of actual performance, the stronger the future organization will be.

In the maturity stage, activities become more structured and routine. There may be more specialized departments (e.g., human resources and purchasing) and more standard operating procedures. Recruitment and selection may not be the life-and-death matters they were before, but rewards and development may assume higher priority as a means to maintain motivation and performance.

Compensation in the maturity phase may take the form of straight salary. Development becomes critical, for both people and products, as innovation must be fostered to prevent the organization's decline. The more organizations plan for continuing renewal of people, the longer the maturity period will last, and the more likely a new growth surge might be. In this way both the organization and the employee benefit.

In the decline stage, the type of rewards provided becomes a key issue. Since people can see "the handwriting on the wall," there may be little intrinsic reward from the work itself. If a manager is put into a declining business to close it down smoothly, it is obviously unwise and unfair to base his or her pay on the performance of the business. It is important to establish clear performance objectives that the manager is expected to accomplish in terms of a certain time schedule and then pay a bonus based upon successful completion of these tasks. Some organizations have found to their chagrin that when managers are put into declining businesses (or businesses that the firm wanted to phase out) and paid bonuses based on the business's profits, the managers successfully developed new products and got the business growing again. Contradictory though it may seem, if the corporation has made a strategic decision to phase out the business, renewed growth can create great problems.

On the other hand, if a business unit is declining and the corporation wants it to survive, a performance bonus to the unit's management might be a very appropriate form of compensation. A selection strategy to hire new types of people ("new blood") might also help turn it around. If people are to be let go, accurate appraisal becomes critical so that only the most competent people are retained.

If the survival strategy is to get into new markets, development is critical, as people must be retrained for new products and services. For example, Lawrence Livermore Laboratories in Livermore, California, had been extremely successful as a government contractor on nuclear weapons research and development. It had numerous scientists and engineers who were specialists in the nuclear field. However, in the late 1960s, after the nuclear test ban treaty was signed and as government research and development money was cut back as the Vietnam War wound down, Livermore was left with a diminished market and a declining organization. The strategy Livermore management adopted was to retrain many of its professionals in energy research, as the energy crisis was becoming serious in the early 1970s. So weapons experts became experts in solar and geothermal energy. Thus, development of human resources became a key element in the strategy for corporate survival. Livermore has since become not only a very successful organization but also a recognized leader in the field of career and human resource development.

HUMAN RESOURCE INFORMATION SYSTEMS (HRIS)

*human resource
information system*

An important resource which greatly facilitates the collection and analysis of the various types of information just described is the human resource information system. A **human resource information system** (**HRIS**) is a *computerized data base containing information on employees to be used for both routine human resource administration (e.g., compensation) and management decision-making.* The basic purpose of the HRIS is to provide information to management in a more efficient manner than was possible with manual employee records. Typical employee information found in such an HRIS might include demographics, job histories, performance ratings, review dates, salary histories, assessments of potential for advancement, employee career interests, job position openings, manpower forecasting and planning data, union membership, and grievance data. A survey of nineteen organizations (including business, health care, and educational organizations) revealed widespread use of HRISs for a variety of functions, as shown in Exhibit 2.7. Basic employee records and compensation data seem to be the most common applications, however.[12]

There is a growing trend, however, to use HRISs for human resource planning activities, such as forecasting, succession planning, and career planning. (At IBM, for example, succession planning is a high priority activity, according to Donald Laidlaw, Director of Succession Planning.[13]) A related move with HRISs is toward using them to assist employees in searching out new career path opportunities and job openings.

Although packaged software (computer programming) for HRISs is available, most organizations develop their own programs, to meet their own unique needs. The majority of systems have on-line interactive capability, meaning users can call up data and receive it almost immediately through a video terminal in the human resource department.

Generally the idea for developing an HRIS is initiated by a senior human resource manager. In a growing number of cases, human resource departments are adding to their own staff's professionals with systems and programming skills.

The major benefit of an HRIS is the accurate and timely access to diverse data which it provides to management. In conducting human resource planning, it is extremely useful (and simple) to examine numerous "what if" scenarios (simulations) to test out different strategic alternatives. This is especially important in large, decentralized organizations, where manual data collection would be almost impossible. This increased speed and responsiveness can also permit smaller human resource departments.

Any powerful technology produces concerns as well as benefits. The quality of the input data is obviously key to the quality of the system's operation. Updating the information must be done frequently, and the support of line managers is needed if managers are to provide timely and accurate data to the system.

HUMAN RESOURCE INFORMATION SYSTEMS SERVICES

EXHIBIT 2.7

Employee Record Keeping	% of Organizations	Employment Functions	% of Organizations
New hire report	100	Application-job matching	21
Separations report	100	Applicant tracking	26
Anniversary listing	89	Job requisition tracking	16
Demographic information	95	Position openings	32
Job history report	79	Recruitment information system	21
Wage history report	74	Personnel tracking	58
Performance ratings	68	College recruiting tie-in	5
Absence tracking	58		
Earnings and benefits	74	**Skill Inventory/Manpower Planning**	
EEO/Affirmative Action	74		
Scheduled review dates	84	Employee-job matching	21
		Manpower forecasting	21
Wage and Salary Data		Systematic employee searches	10
		Training and Development tracking	47
Pay rates by employee	79	Future replacement candidates	16
Pay rate by job class	89		
Pay rate analysis	68	**Other**	
Past salary increases	37		
Internal compensation trends and planning	42	Organizational charts	42
		Human resource accounting	32
External compensation trends and planning	26	Budget planning	26
		Behavioral information system	11
Benefits statements	26	Employee grievances	5
Pension system	5	Union contract	5
		Union membership list	5
Performance Appraisal			
Merit rating reports	47		
Performance analysis over time	32		

SOURCE: Survey of nineteen organizations reported in Arlene Vernon-Oehmke, *Compensation and Benefit Trends and the Computerization of Personnel*, Unpublished report, Boston University, August 1983.

The type of information contained in this system can be a source of conflict in the organization. For example, should performance ratings and assessments of potential be included? This raises the related issue of security: who has access to the system, how is the system's integrity safeguarded, and how are employees protected from invasion of privacy?

The quality of reports and their usefulness to managers can vary widely. This is less likely to be a problem in an on-line system, where a manager has the option to vary the content and the format of data provided.

SUCCESSFUL HUMAN RESOURCE PLANNING

As we have said, systematic analysis of people, jobs, the organization, and the environment is the first step in human resource planning. Information resulting from this analysis must then be shared with decision makers (line executives) in the organization, who, in consultation with human resource professionals, must make choices among various human resource functions. These plans then lead to implementation and evaluation.

Such human resource planning procedures are difficult to implement successfully in many organizations. There are two major reasons for this: first, traditional human resource planning has not been fully integrated into the entire process of human resource management. Frequently it has been perceived as a long-term planning process that should lead to human resource programs but actually has had little influence on the day-to-day running of the human resource department. For example, some training may be derived through human resource planning, while other training courses are mounted to meet very localized unit needs. This disjointed approach tends to isolate traditional human resource planning from human resource functions such as selection, training, and performance appraisal.

A second major reason for this failure is the low level of involvement in human resource planning by supervisory and managerial personnel of the line organization. Too much human resource activity is conducted primarily at the operational level (often reactive "fire fighting") and fails to involve the institutional and managerial levels. Bennett argues for an initial "corporate push"[14] to a human resource planning program by top-level institutional executives in the organization and the formation of teams of human resource people and line managers (management level) to collect information needed for planning human resource programs.

The approach to human resource planning presented in this chapter minimizes the impact of those two major reasons for failure. First, planning is an integral part of the process of human resource management. Second, collaboration is necessary between human resource professionals and members of the line organization. A partnership between human resource specialists and senior executives of the organization links corporate planning and human resource planning. A similar partnership links human resource specialists and the supervisors, managers, and employees who implement human resource policies and practices throughout the organization. Through these partnerships it is possible to plan and implement human resource functions that truly serve the needs of the organization.

KEY POINTS

▪ Traditionally, human resource management has been a low-power staff function, performing routine personnel administration activities. It has tended to be passive and reactive, responding to initiatives of line management.

▬ Well-managed contemporary organizations are moving more toward a strategic operation of the human resource function, meaning the function is being more closely integrated with the long-term mission and objectives of the institution. This is resulting in a more proactive, business-oriented human resource organization.

▬ The human resource function must carry out different types of activities at different levels of the organization. At the *strategic* level, human resources must help the organization position itself effectively in relation to its environment and its long-run objectives. At the *managerial* level, the concern is with availability and allocation of resources to carry out the strategic plan. And at the *operational* level, day-to-day human resource programs and activities must be carried out.

▬ The choice of an appropriate human resource strategy depends upon whether the person and the job situation are relatively stable or flexible. If both are stable, a stress on *staffing* is appropriate. If the person is stable and the job situation is flexible, a stress on *human resource systems* may be more effective. If the person is changeable and the job environment is relatively stable, a *performance development* strategy may be the best fit. And if both person and job are flexible, then a strategy of *planned organizational change* is appropriate.

▬ The process of integrating human resources into the business plan consists of 1) developing close cooperation between human resource planners and corporate planners, 2) identifying human resource needs of line units, 3) examining external events for human implications, 4) developing plans for the human resource department, based upon information from steps 1–3 above, and 5) planning for regular reviews of progress.

▬ Human resource information systems (HRISs) are an important tool to aid strategic human resource planning. An HRIS is a computerized data base containing information on employees to be used for both routine human administration (e.g., compensation) and management decision-making.

ISSUES FOR DISCUSSION

1. What is strategic business planning? What are the elements in the process of strategic business planning? What makes it "strategic"? Why is "strategic" important?

2. How can human resource planning be linked to strategic business planning? Why should this link be made? What examples have you seen of the positive effects of making this link? What would be some results of not making this link?

3. Pick a human resource function (e.g., selection, compensation). How would you approach this function at a strategic level? At the operational level? What problems could arise at the managerial or operational levels if the necessary work at the strategic level were not done?

4. Pick a specific organization with which everyone in the class is familiar (such as a university or a big local company, hospital, or government agency). Using the

framework for analyzing the environment, organization, job, and person, conduct a diagnosis and develop a strategic human resource plan for this organization.

5.   How would you describe the operation of a human resource information system (HRIS)? Give some examples of human resource management problems which could be solved more effectively with an HRIS. How does an HRIS facilitate strategic human resource planning?

NOTES

1.   "How the PC Project Changed the Way IBM Thinks," *Business Week*, October 3, 1983, pp. 86, 90.

2.   J.W. Walker, *Human Resource Planning* (New York: McGraw-Hill, 1980) p. 78.

3.   N. Tichy, M.A. Devanna, and C. Fombrun, "Strategic Human Resource Management," *Sloan Management Review*, Winter 1982, 28, p. 47.

4.   P.D. Estridge, quoted in *Business Week*, October 3, 1983, p. 9.

5.   J.W. Walker, op. cit., p. 79.

6.   W. Ouchi, *Theory Z: How American Industry Can Meet the Japanese Challenge* (Reading, Mass.: Addison-Wesley, 1981), p. 200.

7.   F.K. Foulkes and H.M. Morgan, "Organizing and Staffing the Personnel Function," *Harvard Business Review*, May–June 1977, 55, No. 3, p. 144.

8.   D. Yoder, *Personnel Management and Industrial Relations* (Englewood Cliffs, NJ: Prentice-Hall, Sixth Edition, 1970), p. 85.

9.   N. Tichy, C. Fombrun, and M.A. Devanna, "Strategic Human Resources Management," *Sloan Management Review*, Winter 1982, 28, pp. 47–61.

10.   E. Croisant, "Strategic Planning for Human Resources," presentation at meeting of the Human Resources Policy Institute, School of Management, Boston University, December 1981.

11.   Tichy et al., op. cit.

12.   The following information on HRISs is from Arlene Vernon-Oehmke, *Compensation and Benefit Trends and the Computerization of Personnel*, Unpublished report, Boston University, August 1983.

13.   D. Laidlaw, "Succession Planning at IBM," presentation at Annual Meeting of American Society for Personnel Administration, Chicago, June 27, 1984.

14.   J.E. Bennett, "What Went Wrong with Manpower Planning?" *The Business Quarterly*, Summer 1972, 37, pp. 54–61.

ANNOTATED BILBIOGRAPHY

ANDREWS, K. *The Concept of Corporate Strategy*. Homewood, Ill.: Dow-Jones Irwin, 1971.

> This is a classic work in the area of strategic business planning. While it does not deal specifically with human resource management, it is the most authoritative work available on business strategy. To successfully implement strategic

human resource management, you must first have a sound understanding of how business strategy operates.

FOMBRUN, C., TICHY, N., and DEVANNA, M.A. (eds.). *Strategic Human Resource Management.* New York: Wiley, 1984.

This is a major work related to the topic of this chapter. It uses the model of strategic management presented in this chapter and contains invited chapters describing how each of five major human resource functions can be done strategically: structure, selection, appraisal, rewards, and development. Also, for each function there is a case illustration, a chapter describing how a major corporation developed a strategic approach in that area.

FREDRICKSON, J.W. "Strategic Process Research: Questions and Recommendations." *Academy of Management Review*, 1983, 8, pp. 565–75; ASTLEY, W.G. and FOMBRUN, C.J. "Collective Strategy: Social Ecology or Organizational Environments." *Academy of Management Review*, 1983, 8, pp. 576–87.

Many questions and points of debate have arisen with regard to the concept of corporate strategy. These two papers identify and discuss several of these issues and suggest approaches for research on strategy.

TICHY, N. *Managing Strategic Change.* New York: Wiley-Interscience, 1983.

This volume examines strategic issues as a framework for managing organizational change more effectively than traditional models of organization development might allow. The author introduces "TPC theory," which poses three major foci involved in change: 1) the technical aspects of work, 2) power, and 3) values. These correspond to other strands—technical (T), political (P), and cultural (C)—of the "strategic rope." The book shows how explicit work on each strand is necessary and possible for effective strategic change.

WALKER, J.W., *Human Resource Planning.* New York: McGraw-Hill, 1980.

This is another major text, by now a classic, in the area covered by this chapter. The author makes clear distinctions between *strategic planning* (long-range perspectives), *operational planning* (middle-range perspectives), and *budgeting* (annual perspectives). The book is full of practical ideas and case examples on how to do human resource planning most effectively.

INTERVIEW

F. C. CHADWICK,* MANAGER OF PLANNING, EMPLOYEE RELATIONS DEPARTMENT, EXXON, USA

▬▬ *First, could you tell us something about your role at Exxon, and how your department fits in the overall organization?*

Exxon Corporation is headquartered in New York City. The corporation manages its business throughout the free world through a decentralized organization using broad policy guidance, financial controls, and a high level of coordination among affiliates. In general, Exxon tends to operate as a matrix organization. It is decentralized into organizations called "regions" on either a geographical or functional basis. On a geographical basis, the energy business is assigned to Exxon USA in the United States, Esso Europe in Europe, Esso Interamerica in Central and South America, and Esson Eastern in the Far East and Australia. An example of a functionally based region is Exxon Production Research. It does research on the exploration for and production of natural resources and applies that research to affiliate operations worldwide.

Each of the regional organizations includes staff departments that function similarly and each has similar operating departments. My position is manager of planning in the headquarters Employee Relations Department of Exxon Company, U.S.A. There are people with equivalent responsibilities in each of the regions. There is also a human resource planning department in the corporate Employee Relations Department in New York. Each region is responsible for human resource planning within the region, and for coordinating plans with other regions and the corporate human resource planning department. This coordination helps to identify areas in which actions in one region might impact upon another and helps develop compatible approaches to solving problems.

Human resource planning considerations are very broad. They include factors both internal and external to the company. Examples would be company business plans, legislative and regulatory environment, economic environment, recruiting environment, internal and external work force skills and demographics, and work force attitudes and values.

▬▬ *Could you give us a general overview of how the human resource planning process operates at Exxon?*

Human resource planning is an integral part of business planning and is conducted in two phases. One is long-range plan development which begins in April and concludes in October. The other is short-range plan development which starts in October and ends in January. The short-range plan is a detailed operating program for the first year or two of the long-range plan.

The long-range plan changes from year to year. It could cover from four to twenty years depending on the environment. These long-term plans are used to develop a framework of possible environments against which to test short-term actions. The most frequently used time frames are five to ten years.

The complete company plan includes all aspects of the business. Forecasts are made for operating programs, capital expenditures, cash flow, new technologies, human resources, public affairs, governmental factors, etc. These are all put together in a plan outlining the company's goals and objectives, operating strategies, and action steps. Each operating function (i.e., department or similar unit) has a planning manager, whose principal task is to coordinate the long-range plan development within the function. Each staff function develops plans to support the operating functions. It is a cooperative effort to make sure the pieces are fully integrated.

The planning cycle usually starts in the first quarter of each year. Staff groups in the corporation and their counterparts in the regions discuss the environment and operating challenges. Frequently, top management participates in this dialogue, which may be in the form of meetings, phone conversations, data exchanges, and correspondence. The planning officially begins when the Contact executives on the Corporate Management Committee forward letters to the CEO of each region. These letters document the broad planning bases, and include operating strategies, areas of the business to be emphasized, and a schedule for each region to complete its plan. Usually the letters are issued in late April and the plan is to be completed in September for review by the corporation in October and November.

Within Exxon USA, the Corporate Planning Department (CPD) coordinates development of the plan. CPD takes the lead in developing strategy, forecasting price structures and market conditions, defining the economic outlook, and documenting the regulatory environment. The Controller's Department takes the lead in coordinating operating forecasts, developing capital budgets and expense forecasts, and forecasting cash flows and profits. Employee Relations takes the lead in developing the human resources environment, coordinating manpower forecasts, and defining critical skill requirements.

The planning manager in headquarters Employee Relations writes to functional staffs sometime in the spring to request human resources planning information, and to emphasize the need for human resource plans based on specific business plans. Through a series of tables and narratives each function submits detailed forecasts of total people requirements, numbers and kinds of critical skills required, attrition, transfers, hires by skills, problems and challenges, and actions planned to ensure human resources do not limit business plan implementation. Operating managers are responsible for forecasting and meeting human resource needs. Each of the operating departments has field and headquarters employee relations staffs to assist the operating managers in the development and implementation of their human resource plan.

Human resource forecasts are received in headquarters Employee Relations planning in August. The environment and forecasts are summarized and analyzed for inconsistencies, and the problems and challenges are outlined along with the strategies and actions proposed to handle them. These summaries are forwarded to corporate planning for inclusion in the company plan. The assembled plan is reviewed by the Exxon USA Management Committee. It is then forwarded to the corporation, which assembles the worldwide plan. Paralleling this process, Exxon USA Employee Relations sends the human resource portion of the plan to Employee Relations in the corporation, which in turn develops a worldwide human resource plan for the corporation. There are numerous reviews throughout the process to ensure the pieces of the plan are integrated, limitations defined, and solutions available.

Toward the end of the long-range planning cycle, in the fall, corporate Employee Relations schedules a meeting of human resource planning managers from all the regions. The two-day meeting is used to define issues that have global implications. Company-wide issues are sifted out and put on an agenda for worldwide strategy consideration. This work is wrapped up in December with specific recommendations.

In January the corporate Employee Relations manager calls a meeting of the top Employee Relations people. They review the planning manager's recommendations and adjustments. Lead responsibility is assigned to one region to coordinate studies and achieve consensus on actions to be taken.

■■■■ *Could you explain how short-range planning works?*
By late September the long-range plan has been completed and work has begun on the detailed short-range plan.

Requests are made for specific operating programs. Short-range planning involves getting down to nuts and bolts—exact numbers and skills of people needed, which wells to drill, how much oil to refine, and what products to market. Requests for short-range plan information are sent to the same staffs that develop the long-range human resource plan. In addition, an Employee Relations managers' meeting is held within Exxon USA in mid-November. During this meeting a series of presentations, workshops, and general discussions are scheduled in order to: discuss current issues and activities such as next year's recruiting, training program development, cross functional skill transfer, compensation policy, benefit changes, and attrition.

How has the planning process helped Exxon respond to unplanned events in the environment?

The planning process provides a good basis for making adjustments to meet the new environment. Unexpected events are more easily handled and changes are more readily measured against the detailed program of the plan. The environment predicted in the long-range plan is compared with the changes, and then the total business and human resource plans are adjusted. The planning process helps to define what revisions need to be made.

To summarize, there is commitment to planning at Exxon. Planning is treated as a necessary part of managing the business.

*Mr. Chadwick held this position at the time this material was written. He has since moved to a new assignment.

PART TWO

THE ORGANIZATION AND THE ENVIRONMENT

In Part One, the process of human resource management was introduced and shown to be an integral component of the operation of the organization. An enterprise will simply not function without people.

A key element which will be stressed in this book is strategy in managing human resources. Chapter Two described how strategic human resource planning is a process linking the organization's human resource activities to its strategic business mission and objectives. This planning process is an important mechanism the organization can use to adapt to the demands and opportunities presented by the external environment. The **external environment** is the combination of social, economic, technological, and political forces which influence the organization. Examples of various components of the environment are competitors, government regulatory agencies, culture change and social movements, product and process innovations, customers and clients, labor unions, suppliers, and distributors.

Organizations can be thought of as open systems which are constantly interacting with their environments—buying materials from suppliers, hiring new employees from schools and competitors, negotiating with unions and regulatory commissions, selling products to customers, dealing with *foreign governments, and so forth. The organization receives inputs from the environment (e.g., raw materials, new employees, new capital, new ideas), it transforms them (e.g., manufactures products, delivers services, trains employees), and then sends outputs back to the environment (e.g., sells products, disseminates ideas, pays dividends and taxes). As it functions, it receives feedback on the quality of its outputs and makes revisions in its operations if the outputs are not at desired levels. If any of these links are weak or missing, the effectiveness of the organization will be impaired.*

In Part Two we will discuss four critical elements of the environment which influence the human resource functioning of any organization. First, in Chapter Three we will examine the changing work force, the new types of employees entering work roles and the ways they affect organizations. Chapter Four looks at the ways the work environment has changed, largely because of new workers, but also because of new technologies and new forms of work design. Chapter Five examines government, a critical factor in the external environment, whose role has changed greatly since the 1970s. And finally, Chapter Six discusses the history and procedures of labor relations, a subject which almost always seems to be in the day's headlines.

CHAPTER THREE

THE CHANGING WORK FORCE

More than fifty years ago, when Sigmund Freud was asked the prescription for a healthy life he came up with two simple ingredients: work and love. But what the doctor had in mind was an integrated personality, not an integrated work force.[1]

The corporate executives of today may also believe wholeheartedly in love and work, but they appear to be wary of love AT work. Since Mary Cunningham and Bill Agee became a case study in how not to mix business and pleasure, a torrid interest has grown around the subject of love between executives.

Now the Harvard Business Review, *which caters to the classiest of corporate leaders, has come out with some advice on dealing with dalliance at the top. In this month's issue, senior director Eliza Collins concludes after studying the business dynamics of four affairs, that "Love between managers is dangerous because it challenges—and can break down—the organizational structure."*

The new coalition, the love coalition, makes everybody anxious, she says. It threatens to exclude others, makes subordinates worry about the judgment and the fairness of bosses who are blinded by love.

Having analyzed this, Collins makes some fairly bold recommendations. The senior executive should intervene in the executive love affair because "of the high degree of stress in the corporation."

"If the company sees rats in the basement they've got to get them out," said Collins in an interview. "It does have a responsibility to run an environment in which people can work."

Short of hiring a pied piper then, the best interest of business is apparently to separate love, or at least one lover, from work. Collins suggests that the senior executive persuade "the person least essential to the company" to leave. She advises this reluctantly because the less important person is still "in almost all cases a woman."

Much of Collins' description of how a love affair can disrupt the office environment is astute. But her generalizations and recommendations are somewhere between offensive and dangerous.

For openers, a piece like this in the prestigious Review *feeds into the wave of literature on how women are confronting the corporate world with all "their" messy little problems. The* Wall Street Journal, *for example, has been running an apparently endless series on the woes of young executive mothers. Apparently there are no young executive fathers.*

Now the women are mucking up the structure, by bringing love relationships into the board room, instead of keeping them where they belong, say, in the steno pool. The notion is that executives are so freaked out by their love that they cease functioning rationally at work. Love comes in and business school training goes out.

But there are others, like Ann Jardim, a dean of the Simmons Graduate School of Management, who remain unconvinced of Collins' basic premise. For every bungled relationship, Jardim can count another "in which the people involved handled it with discretion, became scrupulously fair and survived."

Rosabeth Kanter, professor of sociology and management at Yale University, suggests that senior executives handle love affairs the way they handle alcohol. Do nothing until there is an issue in job performance. Perhaps, she suggests, there should be a checklist for problem lovers that asks: How is this showing up at work?

The reality is that there are all sorts of special relationships between executives, all sorts of political and personal alliances in the corporate power structure that are untinged by sex. Kanter is not convinced that sexual love between executives is either widespread or disruptive enough for the sort of radical advice Collins has offered.

"People can behave in absolutely adolescent ways," says Kanter of executive lovers, "but it doesn't last that long in that stage. If we can indulge people when they are going through divorce or alcoholism, then we can indulge them with love."

What is most unsettling about the new advice on executives in love is that, once again, the business world is being fed the illusion that they can, and, indeed, should manage emotions by removing them from the work place. The prime candidate for emotional excision is, as always, love: first family love and, now, sexual love.

In this case, the solution Collins recommends would effectively remove even the "carrier" of love in this society: women. We go back again to the *notion that a healthy business personality is different from a healthy human personality. The message? If you want to get ahead in business, keep love off the books.**

*H*ow do executives deal with love affairs among their subordinates? How do executives deal with their own feelings of attraction toward colleagues? Historically, there has not been much mention of these issues in books on management.

Love entering the executive suite is not the only change we have had to contend with in the work force. The future isn't what it used to be. Less than ten years ago, experts painted the years ahead as a rosy scene with rising education, limitless affluence, an end to poverty and scarcity, boundless choices, and mass fulfillment. In the meantime, however, as Warren Bennis once commented, "A funny thing happened on the way to the future."[2] Energy became scarce and therefore expensive. Inflation and interest rates skyrocketed. Unemployment at first refused to go down, stubbornly ignoring the "laws" of economics which forbid unemployment and inflation to be high at the same time. Millions of "undocumented aliens" were added to the work force, along with large numbers of "baby boomers" and women. Eventually, the economy recovered to absorb these new members.

Two-income couples began to appear on the scene, attempting to combine loving and working. But, said the labor economists, because they are a "new breed," they will not have so many children. And, in fact, fertility rates were dropping, so the complicated issues of combining dual careers and families did not seem too problematic. But then employed couples surprised everyone by starting to have babies in their thirties, after their careers had been securely launched. And they continued their careers. So, in fact, it has been necessary for couples and corporations to learn how to cope with the pressures of parenting and employment.

Chapter Two discussed the types of information about the environment and about people (among other entities) one would need to collect in order to do good strategic human resource planning. In this chapter we will examine the dramatic changes which have been occurring in one part of the environment, the labor force. We will describe how management's assumptions about workers have changed and we will report on changes in employee work values which support these new assumptions. We will then describe the changing demographics of the work force—more women, more two-career couples, more older workers, and more heterogeneity. Chapter Four will go on to show the concomitant changes which have been made in the work place.

MANAGERIAL ASSUMPTIONS
ABOUT WORKERS

In 1960, Professor Douglas McGregor of the Sloan School of Management at the Massachusetts Institute of Technology discussed "**Theory X,**" *the traditional view of managerial control* at that time. He argued that every managerial decision or action was based on assumptions about human nature and human behavior. McGregor felt that some of these assumptions were pervasive and implicit in much managerial thinking, organization, and in much current managerial policy and practice:

theory X

> The average human being has an inherent dislike of work and will avoid it if he can . . .
>
> Because of this human characteristic of dislike of work, most people must be coerced, controlled, directed, threatened with punishment to get them to put forth adequate effort towards the achievement of organizational objectives . . .
>
> The average human being prefers to be directed, wishes to avoid responsibility, has relatively little ambition, wants security above all.[3]

Most managers behave on the basis of their own "theory" of management, their own assumptions about what motivates people and how to treat people most effectively in relation to these motivators, and, in 1960, Theory X was a good summary of the assumptions about employee motivation that most managers carried around in their heads.

Next McGregor reviewed research which provided a modest beginning for "**Theory Y,**" *a new set of assumptions about intrinsic human motivation in the management of human resources:*[4]

theory Y

> The expenditure of physical and mental effort in work is as natural as play or rest . . .
>
> External control and the threat of punishment are not the only means for bringing about effort toward organizational objectives. Man will exercise self-direction and self-control in the service of objectives to which he is committed . . .
>
> Commitment to objectives is a function of the rewards associated with their achievement . . .
>
> The average human being learns, under proper conditions, not only to accept but to seek responsibility . . .
>
> The capacity to exercise a relatively high degree of imagination, ingenuity, and creativity in the solution of organizational problems is widely, not narrowly, distributed in the population . . .
>
> Under the conditions of modern industrial life, the intellectual potentialities of the average human being are only partially utilized.[5]

Bear in mind that in 1960, Theory Y was seen by many managers as a pretty fuzzy-headed, idealistic view of human motivation at work. It was called a *normative* view of employee motivation, a view of *what could be*, but certainly not a description of what actually existed.

One of the "funny things" about the future is that Theory Y has quietly come true. Employee values are now remarkably congruent with the assumptions of Theory Y. And, in Chapter Four, we will see that the move to more participative management in the work place shows managerial acceptance of Theory Y assumptions. The status of Theory Y has changed from a normative view to a descriptive one. Let us review the research on work values which is consistent with Theory Y.

CHANGING VALUES IN THE WORK FORCE

In the 1970s, a "new breed" of employees was making the transition from the campus into the world of work. Vietnam-era students and young employees had new beliefs:[6] There was now more concern about basic values, not just different values, but values *per se*. Action was more important. Merely talking about one's values was suspect. The operative slogan was "do it!" Personal integrity, honesty, and openness were more important. Many of the "youth" values were humanistic, oriented toward personal fulfillment. This reflected a shift away from extrinsic symbols of success and security. There was increased concern for the ultimate meaning and social value of one's work, the consequences of that work and not just its content. Authority based on age or position was less highly regarded and the authority of one's expertise, personal style, convictions, or competence carried much more weight with youth. Shared authority was more valued and expected.

Survey results indicate that these humanistic, self-fulfillment values (i.e., Theory Y-type values) of the students of the 1970s now have become firmly implanted in the new work force.[7] A study by Renwick and Lawler[8] asked people how important various job features were to them, as well as how satisfied people were with each feature. Respondents assigned importance to various job features by ranking them from 1 (most important) to 18 (least important). The results are presented in Exhibit 3.1.

Obviously, self-fulfillment, self-control, learning, and worthwhile activity were strongly valued. Among the lowest-rated aspects were fringe benefits, promotion prospects, the physical environment at work, and friendliness of people at work.

How did self-actualization compare in importance with money? Renwick and Lawler asked if people would accept a higher-paying job if it meant less interesting work. Almost two-thirds of the people responding said they would not. However, 46 percent said they would not take a more interesting job that paid less than their present job (41 percent would.) The researchers concluded:

> The data suggest that people have in mind a level of compensation that they consider adequate for them. If their pay falls below this level, then money becomes more important than interesting work. If wages or sal-

IMPORTANCE OF VARIOUS JOB EXPERIENCES

EXHIBIT 3.1

Rank Order of Importance

1. Chances to do something that makes you feel good about yourself
2. Chances to accomplish something worthwhile
3. Chances to learn new things
4. Opportunity to develop your skills and abilities
5. The amount of freedom you have on your job
6. Chances you have to do things you do best
7. The resources you have to do your job
8. The respect you receive from people you work with
9. Amount of information you get about your job performance
10. Your chances for taking part in making decisions
11. The amount of job security you have
12. Amount of pay you get
13. The way you are treated by the people you work with
14. The friendliness of people you work with
15. Amount of praise you get for job well done
16. The amount of fringe benefits you get
17. Chances for getting a promotion
18. Physical surroundings of your job

SOURCE: "What You Really Want from Your Job," by Patricia Renwick and Edward Lawler, *Psychology Today*, May 1978. Copyright © 1978 American Psychological Association. Reprinted by permission.

ary are above this level, then whether they consider their job interesting assumes more importance.[9]

Renwick and Lawler asked why people work. The most frequent response was "I enjoy what I do on my job" (29 percent of respondents, male and female). The next most common reply was "I derive a major part of my identity from my job" (26 percent of the men, 28 percent of the women). Third was "Work keeps me from being bored" (17 percent of men, 18 percent of women), followed by "My work is important and valuable to others" (14 percent of men and 11 percent of women).

The common element in these responses was that work provided a major source of *meaning* and *personal identity* to people. Work helped people structure their lives with valued and rewarding activity. As one person described the meaning of her work to one of the authors, "If I weren't a nurse, I just wouldn't be the same person."

There were other noteworthy results in this survey, as well. Forty-three percent of the respondents felt they had been discriminated against at work in the past five years, yet 82 percent opposed affirmative action programs to

EXHIBIT 3.2

HIGH SCHOOL STUDENTS RATE THE
IMPORTANCE OF JOB-RELATED FACETS

Job Facet	Rated "Very Important"
A job that is interesting to do	89.2%
A job that uses your skills and abilities—lets you do things you can do best	71.4%
A job where you can see the results of what you do	60.6%
A job that provides you with a chance to earn a good deal of money	50.3%
A job that gives you an opportunity to be directly helpful to others	49.5%
A job that leaves a lot of time for other things in life	41.0%
A job that has high status and prestige	24.4%

SOURCE: L.D. Johnston, J.G. Bachman, and P.M. O'Malley, "Monitoring the Future: Questionnaire Responses From the Nation's High School Seniors, 1979" (Ann Arbor, MI: Institute for Social Research, University of Michigan, 1979).

make up for past discrimination against underrepresented groups. Seventy-five percent would like more control over their starting and quitting times (through plans such as "flextime"). Forty-four percent felt "locked in" to their jobs, yet most would continue working, even if money were no object. When the job became stressful, the most popular method of reducing stress was physical exercise, not drugs or alcohol. And, finally, despite everything being said about gender equality, in two-career families, the men's careers came first, and women did most of the housework.

The Renwick and Lawler study was based on a poll of the readers of *Psychology Today,* and the respondents tended to be younger, better educated, more highly paid, and more progressive than the national average. Therefore, it would be useful to examine other, more representative surveys, as well. In a national sample of workers, Seashore and Barnowe found a comparable set of values. And when they compared blue-collar, white-collar, and pink-collar (i.e., clerical) workers, there were no differences between occupational groups.[10]

One good predictor of what future employees will value is the values of high school students. A national high school survey by Johnston, Bachman, and O'Malley asked students to rate the importance to them of various job facets. Most of these students entered the work force in the early 1980s. Their responses are shown in Exhibit 3.2.[11]

The Johnston *et al.* study shows that high school students have rather high aspirations for their work careers. Like the Renwick and Lawler study, Johnston and colleagues also found that students expected work to be a central part of their lives (75 percent), and that they would continue to work even if they had enough money to live comfortably without working (80 percent). Thus, this study suggests that "the work ethic is hardly dead." Instead, they suggest a "new work ethic" which includes the desire for interesting work, the chance to use one's skills and abilities, to see the results of one's efforts, to earn money, to help others, and to have time to develop personal interests off the job. Thus, whereas the "old" work ethic said simply that work provides meaning to one's life and hard work is its own reward, the "new" work ethic is more specific: *meaningful* work provides meaning in one's life.

Perhaps the most influential writer on work-related values is Daniel Yankelovich. Yankelovich uses the terms "old values" and "new values."[12] Old values were reflected in the following features of the work force of the 1950s and 1960s, based upon surveys conducted at that time:[13]

- If women could afford it, they would prefer to stay at home.
- As long as a job provided a man with economic security, he would tolerate all kinds of job dissatisfaction so he could be a good provider to his family.
- The incentive system—mainly money and status rewards—was effective as a motivator.
- People were tied to their jobs in large part by loyalty to their employing organizations.
- Most people defined their identity through their work role, and work took priority over personal interests.

In contrast, there are three important ways in which "New Breed" values are becoming important, according to Yankelovich.

The increasing importance of leisure. While work, family, and leisure time always have been highly important for most workers, in recent years work and family have become less important and leisure has become more important. In Yankelovich's surveys, when work and leisure were compared as causes of satisfaction, only 21 percent (one out of five) of the people responding stated that work meant more to them than leisure. Sixty percent of the respondents said that work was not their major source of satisfaction, even though they enjoyed it. Yankelovich also reports similar increases in the importance of leisure in other countries, such as Sweden.

The symbolic significance of a paid job. This is the issue that seems to affect women more than men, at least in terms of direct effects. In recent years, the status of homemaking has dropped sharply. A paid job is seen as a means of achieving independence and self-esteem. In fact, many women are the only source of support for themselves and their dependent children as a result of divorce, widowhood, or the husband's disability. Even if the woman has a husband who is the major breadwinner, she is likely to prefer a paid job to home activities or volunteer work, feeling that she will be respected more if she receives money for her work.

The insistence that jobs become less depersonalized. The critical factor here is the New Breed's concern for self-fulfillment. When Yankelovich asked people what aspects of their jobs were becoming more important to them, they stressed "being recognized as an individual person." Thus, not only do people want their job to provide challenge, purpose, and significance, they want the job to provide self-expression, so that the person is significant, as well. Yankelovich estimates that nearly 80 percent of the U.S. population is now motivated by a desire for self-fulfillment, in one way or another.

Yankelovich goes on to argue that these new values call for an entirely new set of motivators in work organizations. Under the old values, the employee would work hard to hold a job, because simply *having* a job was the main objective. Now the objective is to have a satisfying job, and if the job is unfulfilling, the person will either become alienated or quit. The burden for motivation now falls more heavily on the employer:

> As long as the traditional carrot-and-stick worked well, those at the top could afford to pay less attention to the human side of the organization. Perhaps the chief lesson we should draw from the changes shaped by the new values is that concern for the human side of the enterprise can no longer be relegated to low-level personnel departments. In the 1980s, knowledge of how the changed American value system affects incentives and motivations to work hard may well become a key requirement for entering the ranks of top management in both the private and public sector. If this occurs, we shall see a New Breed of managers to correspond to the New Breed of employees.[14]

The material in Box 3.1 describes the conclusions one corporation, Honeywell, reached regarding this new success ethic. As the box shows, some long-held managerial beliefs about employee motivation are being called into question.

CHANGING DEMOGRAPHICS AT WORK

Not only are we finding different values among the people in our work organizations, but we are also finding different types of people. These new types, like the New Breed, will also exert strong influences on the process of managing human resources. Let us consider who the new workers are.

More Women and Two-Career Couples

We have already described the increasing symbolic importance of paid jobs for women, and in fact there are more women in paid jobs than ever before. By the late 1970s, the majority of American women, for the first time in history, were working outside the home. Whereas a generation ago, the "typical" worker was a man working for a wife and children at home, today fewer than one out of five employees fits this description. And we are also seeing greater proportions of women in previously male-dominated professional and managerial job categories. It is not uncommon for MBA programs to be 25 to 50 percent female.

CRACKING CULTURES—AND CRACKING MYTHS AT HONEYWELL

BOX 3.1

As part of a Honeywell program to keep managers up to date, Thomas L. Brown spent five years researching, interviewing, and teaching about the increasingly important field of human resource management.

This brief report of the results of that study is organized around five widely-held beliefs about human motivation—which Brown found to be myths.

MYTH #1: The values of workers in the work place are heavily influenced by age, the young having "young" values, those older sharing more "traditional" values.

It is sometimes assumed that those holding "new" values (self-fulfillment, challenge, etc.) are chronologically young. However, research shows that shifting work values affect all ages.

MYTH #2: Pay and promotion remain the dominant motivators in human attitudes toward work.

The consensus of the overwhelming majority of managers and workers alike held that money and rank were simply not enough to provide total incentive and reward for work today. By far, the prime motivator holding many of those interviewed to their job was a sense of personal commitment.

MYTH #3: Turnover is the prime measure of worker unrest and dissatisfaction.

It often appears that the prime indicator of employee *and* manager self-esteem, job satisfaction, and work involvement is turnover. The reality, however, is that employees who are dissatisfied are not as likely to turn a job over as they are to turn the job off.

MYTH #4: There is such a thing as a "model manager," who can be identified and exemplified through an organization.

In trying to identify those managers who simultaneously seemed most keen about their jobs, most respected by their subordinates, and most valued by their superiors, Brown quickly became perplexed. He found some departments enslaved by *easy-going, mod* Theory-X managers, and others headed by managers with participative values yet a demeanor cold and stony.

Greater credibility is found in the "management system" employed rather than the style of the person at the top—systems in which workers and managers are able to contribute to their destinies and their work styles and where workers are able to share in the determination of rewards (for some, more pay; for others, increased time off or more education).

MYTH #5: Quality of Work Life (QWL) issues are organizationally defined and begin and end on the job.

The vitality of a number of QWL programs seems to vary in direct proportion to worker involvement in creating the programs. Where workers help to define QWL issues, the ensuing program is more self-sustaining.

We have come to recognize that the employee has a life beyond the job, a personal life which impacts on-the-job performance. QWL issues come as much from the relationship between work life and private life as they do from the job alone.

The authors wish to thank Dr. Thomas L. Brown, now president of Situation Management Systems, Inc., Plymouth, Mass., for his help in preparing this material.

Related to the increased number of women in the work force, there are approximately thirty million married two-career couples in the U.S. work force.[15] There are no statistics available yet on unmarried couples (or as the census calls them, P.O.S.S.L.Q.s, for Persons of Opposite Sex Sharing Living Quarters), but the ranks of unmarried two-career couples would undoubtedly add several more million to that estimate. (It is estimated that by 1990, 90 percent of U.S. family units will have two earners.)[16] By 1980, more than two of every five women with children aged six or under worked for pay. And in families earning over $25,000, the majority depend on both a husband's and a wife's income.[17]

This increase in the number of working couples means that over half of employees will be concerned about two jobs—their own and their partner's. It will also mean that pressures from home and family will affect the employee's attitudes and behavior at work. It may be that "sick" days come to be seen as personal entitlements, redefined as "personal days," to be used for taking sick children to the doctor, covering for a baby sitter who doesn't show up, and other family emergencies. A survey of companies reported the ten major ways the organization is affected by two-career couples.[18]

Recruiting difficulty. It is very hard to attract a person to a new location if the employed spouse does not find the move attractive for his or her career. Companies are beginning to provide job placement assistance to spouses to make a relocation more appealing to an employee.

Work scheduling. There is need for greater flexibility to allow for family needs, such as children who don't leave for school until 8:00 or who arrive home at 2:30. This need fits well with other forces leading toward "flextime" and more part-time work opportunities.

Transfers and relocation. This is now the number one problem for employers. Like recruiting, moving an employee whose spouse is well settled in a job is extremely difficult. Employers are becoming more flexible about letting employees turn down moves without jeopardizing their careers, and employers are also using more consultation in career management to reduce these strains.

Promotions. There is the possibility working couples may be less upwardly mobile than single-career couples. They may be more likely to trade off promotions for marital happiness, because promotions often require relocation.

Travel. Travel can make demands on family life and may be hard to arrange if the spouse's job also requires being away from home. There is also the issue of traveling with opposite-sex colleagues and spouse jealousy. Child care is also more difficult with a heavy travel schedule.

Benefits. There is greater need for maternity/paternity leave, leave without pay, and personal days. There is a problem of overlapping benefits and there is a strong interest in employer assistance with child care.

Conflicts of interest. Organizations are beginning to develop policies to deal with situations where the employee's spouse works for a competitor, a client, or a regulatory agency. However, in many cases the situation is left to the professional discretion of the employee.

Career development programs. There is a greater need to design new career paths, with less geographical movement. For example, is an assignment "in the field" really necessary? Job moves are being planned more carefully. Often temporary assignments can achieve the same objective as a longer-term move, with lower cost.

Potential deadwood. If a member of a two-career couple is comfortable in the present job, does not want to relocate, and has a fairly high family income, there may be insufficient incentive to continue learning and growing. This can increase the likelihood of frustration and conflict later in the career.

Career bargaining. Members of two-career couples are bargaining for career assistance for the spouse as part of the necessary "package" of benefits before accepting a job or a transfer. The spouse's career is now seen as an extension of the employee's, a career for which the employer feels increased responsibility.

In the past, a person's work life often put strong demands on personal and family life. But rarely did the family make demands on the work organization. If the person had to work overtime with no extra pay, so be it. That was part of the job. Out-of-town travel? Transfers to distant cities? They all "came with the territory."

With the "new" work force, however, these work demands on personal time are more likely to be seen as intrusions, and not as legitimate. In contrast, it is now legitimate for family and personal needs to make demands on the employing organization. If an employed parent needs to rush a sick child to the doctor, it's reasonable to be late for work. Chances are, the employee will take the responsibility to make up the time, either by working late, by working at home, or by working harder. If an employee with an employed spouse is offered a transfer from Tulsa to Houston and the spouse is not willing or able to relocate, declining the transfer is no longer seen as an end to the person's career advancement. Spouse and family needs are now seen as a legitimate part of the employment relationship. While this is true for most employees, it is especially important for two-career couples.

One fairly simple activity employed by some organizations is seminars on topics such as "Balancing Work and Family Life." For example, a number of organizations in the Boston area have used a series of 10 lunch-hour seminars on this topic developed by Professor Fran Litman of Wheelock College. Karen Atkinson, vice president for personnel at New England Merchants National Bank, says that employees who worry about their families probably perform less effectively, "but if we help them get over hurdles, they'll produce better. It's an intangible gain."[19] These seminars, first given at New England Mutual Life Insurance Company, were subsequently offered by many other firms around the country. The topics covered are selected by participants, but usually include issues such as how to rear children, how to handle household chores, and how to cope with time pressure and conflicting demands of job and home.

Participation is voluntary, and participants include large numbers of men, as well as women. An alternative to the lunch-hour format, which uses only the employee's personal time, is to meet at the end of the day, half of the time before quitting time and half afterward. Thus, the firm and the employee share the time. This method has been used successfully at Continental Bank in Chicago. An added benefit of this late-afternoon format is that the employee's partner or spouse is more likely to participate.

Research by the Catalyst organization on corporate response to two-career couples shows a general awareness of the issue but a reluctance to take specific actions. The most common response is the *absence of restrictions against hiring husband and wife* (reported by approximately 80 percent of the companies responding in two separate studies).[20] *Flexible work hours* are widely used (in about half of the reporting firms), as well as *employment assistance for spouses* (30 percent) and *relocation counseling* (about 20 percent). Clearly, the burden of combining work and family rests with the employee.

A Graying Work Force, with Age Gaps

The American work force is aging.[21] In 1970 the median age in the U.S. population was twenty-eight. By 1980 it was thirty, and by the year 2000 it should hit thirty-five. This change is complicated by the fact that there are important gaps in the size of certain age groups (or "cohorts," as demographers call them), as they move through the life cycle. There were low birth rates (fertility rates around 2.1 children per family) during the Depression years, followed by the post-World-War II "baby boom," which continued into the early 1960s (fertility rates hit 3.8 in the mid-1950s), and then the "baby bust" of the 1970s, with more women in the work force planning smaller families or no families at all. The fertility rate fell to 1.76 in 1976. There appears to be a "baby boomlet" today, with couples in their thirties deciding to have their deferred families before the "biological time clock" too greatly increases the perceived health risk of later motherhood. A report in *Business Week* examined the implications for business organizations of these demographic peaks and valleys, and is shown in Exhibit 3.3. The combined effects of a low birthrate before and after the baby boom have created great instability in the work force. Demographers compare the baby boom age cohort to a melon being digested by a boa constrictor. As this group ages and passes through society, it creates a series of fairly predictable strains. In the 1960s, schools had to expand rapidly, and the culture of educational institutions was changed profoundly by baby boomers' social activist, anti-establishment concerns. With the baby bust, communities were left with empty classrooms and unpaid school bonds. As the cohort moves into middle age, many unneeded schools are serving baby boomers a second time, through conversion to condominiums, to meet housing shortages.

Perhaps the greatest impact, however, was in the early 1970s, as the baby boomers entered the labor market. With a greatly increased supply of labor and a slow-growing economy (accentuated by a rising number of women entering the work force), unemployment rose sharply. By the mid-1980s, the cohort had been absorbed, and unemployment decreased.

EXHIBIT 3.3

SOURCE: "How Drastic Shifts in Demographics Affect the Economy" reprinted from the February 20, 1978 issue of *Business Week* by special permission, © 1978 by McGraw-Hill, Inc. Illustration by Francois Colos.

Let us now consider more specific changes within particular age groups. The changing age composition of people in the work force is shown in Exhibit 3.4. Let us consider a few of the major issues raised by the demographic curves in Exhibit 3.4.

In the 1980s the size of the 18-to-24-year-old group is declining steadily and will decline for about fifteen years. This change has already shown up as declining enrollments in colleges and universities, and this small cohort earlier caused significant retrenchment in the public school system. The 18-24-year age group, of course, is the major age of entry into the labor market, so that the supply of potential new employees is declining steadily. This is why we have the paradoxical situation of high unemployment for the economy as a whole, because of the world business situation, yet severe labor shortages in certain growth industries, such as information processing, biosciences, and financial services.

EXHIBIT 3.4   *AGE COMPOSITION OF THE LABOR FORCE*

| Age Group | Percent of Labor Force | | |
	1970	1980	1995
16–24	22	23	17
25–44	40	45	53
45–64	34	29	28
65+	4	3	2

The most rapidly increasing group until the 1990s will be the 25-44-year group. This is the age range where career and salary growth are traditionally found to be the greatest, as are individuals' career aspirations. Yet, with slow growth and organizational retrenchment, these aspirations may not be met, and we may see a greater incidence of plateauing in mid-career. This raises severe problems regarding potential stagnation, alienation, career switching, and the need for new methods of career development. We will need alternatives to upward mobility to provide continuing career growth.

The 45-54-year group will shrink slightly until the late 1980s, when it will grow sharply. This age range is the source of senior management talent, meaning there will continue to be a shortage of senior talent for a few more years, with a resulting stress on "early identification" programs to spot high-potential younger candidates. Another irony here, then, is that while the bulk of the 25-44-year group will experience slower-than-normal advancement, a select few from this age group will be tapped for "fast-track" development to fill gaps in senior management. By the 1990s there will be rapid growth in the 45-54-year group.

Around 2010 there will be an enormous increase in the over-64 group, as the baby boom cohort hits retirement age. As the ratio of employed people to retired people (collecting pensions and Social Security) decreases, great strain will be placed on the economy's ability to support its senior citizens. The future of the Social Security system has been a source of great concern for the last several years, as employed people become more resistant to increased Social Security taxes.

A Segmented Work Force, with Diverse Needs

A reflection of the larger society in which it is embedded—the work force is becoming more segmented or differentiated into special interest groups. As already discussed, growing numbers of female employees, entering and advancing in traditionally male positions, are making their special concerns felt. As the baby boomers age, the special problems of the mature employee (stagnation, plateauing, burnout, drop out, and career change) will receive increasing attention. Handicapped workers have emerged as a strong influence on the business environment, and this group will certainly grow as the work force ages and develops various physical problems. Physical access to the work place and the physical design of work equipment will become more important as elements of equal employment opportunity.

A mosaic of minority groups exists, with Hispanics becoming the largest minority group in the 1990s. Language skills, especially Spanish, will become increasingly important for managers in the future. (More international business activity will also create this need.) The ability to be sensitive to and deal with cultural differences will become an increasingly important management skill. Previous waves of immigration saw new groups seek to become integrated into the work place, whereas now new groups tend to maintain their languages and cultural identity.

Highly educated employees will bring new skills and make new demands on the organization. As people with college and graduate degrees are either displaced from professional positions or unable to find jobs for which they are educationally qualified, they will move toward white-collar or blue-collar jobs. Some will do so by choice, to support themselves while they pursue their true vocation (e.g., writing, teaching, service) in their "leisure" time.

With reduced promotion opportunities, more employees will define their careers as technical specialists of various kinds (e.g., engineers, financial analysts, information systems specialists) and will not aspire to management positions. This change will coincide with the desire for leisure time and the reluctance to let work pressures (such as from managerial responsibilities) spill over into personal time.

With a larger work force and a sluggish economy producing continued high levels of unemployment, and more-educated people displacing less-educated people from clerical and blue-collar jobs, the specter of social conflict between educated and uneducated groups looms large. We may become increasingly a two-class society, the haves and the have-nots. As government-funded social programs are cut back in a period of fiscal conservatism, this possibility is further enhanced.

This more heterogeneous and better-educated employee population is also characterized by a strong sense of the unique special interests of each subgroup. Thus, older employees are becoming more aware of their rights under the Age Discrimination in Employment Act, women and minority group members are sensitive to their equal opportunity rights, the handicapped are conscious of physical access rights, and so forth. As the general society has become more litigious, individual employees or groups of employees have become more likely to take (or, more often, threaten to take) legal action against their employers if they perceive that important rights violations have taken place.

There has also been a trend toward external support for employee "whistle-blowers," people who draw public attention to their employer's violations of legal or ethical procedures. Ralph Nader has been a leading advocate of employee rights in this area of public interest. David Ewing in *Freedom Inside the Organization* proposed an "Employee Bill of Rights" (Exhibit 3.5), which captures the spirit of this concern for due process at work.

IMPLICATIONS FOR HUMAN RESOURCE MANAGEMENT

What do these changes in the work force mean for the management of people? This chapter has discussed many of these implications, but let us focus on some of the more important issues facing managers and human resource professionals. We said earlier the goal of human resource management is a good fit between the person, the job, and the organization. If the employee has changed in the ways described in this chapter, the job and organization must change accordingly. Following are some of the ways that management has had to adapt to the contemporary norm.

Increased Demands on Managers' Human Resource Skills

The rapidly changing nature of the work force makes the job of managing people far more complex than it was years ago. Within line managers' departments or units, there is far greater *diversity* than before. Whereas in the past managers might have advanced through the ranks and ended up supervising people similar to themselves, now those subordinates may be quite different from their managers. Managers must be able to individualize their treatment of employees as well as motivate and lead each one on the basis of the employee's needs and interests. And employees are more aware that they represent different groups and are more sensitive to how they are treated. A white male manager who makes unintended sexist, racist, ethnic, ageist, or other remarks will not have the luxury of employees shrugging the remarks off forgivingly with the attitude that "that's the way he is." Managers now have to be more *sensitive* to differences among employees and more *flexible* in their treatment of different employees.

Improved Human Relations Training for Managers

One implication of these greater people-management demands on managers is the need for better training for managers in this area. This training includes skills in motivating employees (diagnosing individual needs and administering rewards), assessing performance, giving performance feedback, counseling and coaching employees, negotiating with employees, peers, and superiors, recruiting and selecting employees (especially those who are "different"), disciplining subordinates, firing people, etc. In short, all of the human resource

THE LEGALISTIC CLIMATE OF THE WORK FORCE

EXHIBIT 3.5

A Proposed "Employee Bill of Rights"

1. No organization or manager shall discharge, demote, or in other ways discriminate against an employee who criticizes, in speech or press, the ethics, legality, or social responsibility of management actions.

2. No employee shall be penalized for engaging in outside activities of his or her choice after working hours, whether political, economic, civic, or cultural, nor for buying products and services of his or her choice for personal use, nor for expressing or encouraging political, economic, and social ideas.

3. No organization or manager shall penalize an employee for refusing to carry out a directive that violates common norms of morality.

4. No organization shall allow audio or visual recordings of an employee's conversations or actions to be made without his or her prior knowledge and consent. Nor may an organization require an employee or applicant to take a personality test, polygraph examinations, or other tests that constitute, in the person's opinion, an invasion of privacy.

5. No employee's desk, files, or locker may be examined in the employee's absence by anyone but a senior manager who has sound reason to believe that the files contain information needed for a management decision that must be made in the employee's absence.

6. No employer may collect or keep on file information on an employee that is not relevant and necessary for efficient management. Every employee shall have the right to inspect his or her personnel file and challenge the accuracy, relevance, or necessity of data in it, except for personal evaluations and comments by other employees which could not reasonably be obtained if confidentiality were not promised. Access to an employee's file by outside individuals and organizations shall be limited to inquiries about the essential facts of employment.

7. No manager may communicate to prospective employers of an employee who is about to be or has been discharged gratuitous opinions that might hamper the individual in obtaining a new position.

8. An employee who is discharged, demoted, or transferred to a less desirable job is entitled to a written statement from management of its reasons for the penalty.

9. Every employee who feels that he or she has been penalized for asserting any right described in this bill shall be entitled to a fair hearing before an impartial official, board, or arbitrator. The findings and conclusions of the hearing shall be delivered in writing to the employee and management.

SOURCE: Excerpts adapted from *Freedom Inside the Organization,* copyright © 1977 by David W. Ewing. Reprinted by permission of the publisher, E.P. Dutton, a division of New American Library.

activities to be covered in later chapters represent critical skills to be mastered by the effective manager. These activities cannot be delegated to the human resource department.

Strategic Level Planning: Include Employee Diversity

At the strategic level, more work will be needed to factor in the employee of the future to the organization's human resource plans. Although information about employees is an important part of the human resource planning process, as we saw in Chapter Two, many senior executives do an inadequate job of gathering this information. As a senior human resource executive at AT&T admitted when asked how the Baby Boom cohort has affected or will affect his organization, "We haven't seen much effect. But then, we haven't really been looking for it or thinking about it much. Perhaps we should be." Similar sentiments were expressed to a *Business Week* reporter when asked about the future impact of changing demographics: "We've simply not given much thought to the subject. . . ."[22] Thus, it appears that senior executives tend not to anticipate changes in the work force. They are more likely to react to such changes after they have occurred. Ironically, demographics is the area of human behavior which is quite predictable (e.g., we *know* that in 10 years a given cohort group will be ten years older), and there is no reason for not doing better strategic work force planning.

Continued Stress on Legal Issues

With the work force divided into various special interest groups, and with the "due process" climate described earlier, the need for legal expertise in managing people will continue to grow. Three parts of the organization will be affected here. First, the line manager will need to be aware of legal constraints on his or her behavior, due to possible employee discrimination suits over actions such as hiring or promotion decisions, supervisory treatment, pay raises, etc. Second, the human resource department will need staff with specialized legal training. And third, the organization's legal department will also need more staff with expertise in human resource and labor law.

There will be a growing need for information on legal issues in labor relations and human resource management. Organizations such as the Bureau of National Affairs (BNA) and the Research Institute of America provide newsletters, management advisories, and other reports which summarize recent regulations, court decisions, and research studies to meet this need for current legal information in the human resource area.

Uneven Staffing

Great fluctuations from surplus to shortage in the various organizational levels will be a continuing problem for human resource planning. Senior management talent will be relatively scarce in the late 1980s. As Arch Patton of McKinsey & Co. said:

> In the years 1985 to 1990, managers in the 45-65-year age group, a group that has traditionally held 60 percent to 70 percent of senior management jobs, will number only between 11 percent and 18 percent of

the total population segment in management. . . . Management's ranks will contain 88 percent more 20-34-year-olds than 45-59-year-olds, an inexperienced to experienced ratio of almost two to one.[23]

And then as the Baby Boom cohort hits the 1990s, this 45-to-59-year group will expand sharply, and the supply of management slots will become very tight.

Labor Relations

At the worker level, the Baby Boom has already had its impact, as this group now dominates the labor force. However, neither labor leadership nor management has fully adjusted to the new social values which this generation of employees brings to the work place. These changes are present both in the blue-collar ranks, where rank-and-file members are becoming increasingly difficult for their (older) leaders to manage, and among white-collar and service employees, who are one of the fastest-growing sources of new union membership (see Chapter Six). The demands of these "new value" workers for more leisure time and more participation in decision-making, in addition to the traditional high wages, benefits, and job security, are sources of conflict in labor-management relations.

The big problem in labor will be the surplus of workers from today's huge 25-44 age group as it moves through the life cycle. Competition for high-paying jobs will be intense, and the newly-created hourly jobs in the service and high-technology industries will not be highly paid.

Strains between the "haves" and the "have nots" will be great. People who are already employed will try to strengthen seniority clauses, in an attempt to protect their jobs. Strain between seniority and affirmative action issues will remain a problem. The most highly-educated cohort in our society will, by and large, be in jobs for which they are seriously overqualified.

Unions may react with demands to reduce the 40-hour workweek in an attempt to spread the work over more people. They may be willing to trade off money for this increased leisure time, especially if inflation is low. However, as the "Baby Bust" group comes along after the Baby Boomers, there suddenly may be a shortage of labor, and a shorter workweek could present real difficulties.

As the Baby Boomers move toward retirement, the prospects for intergenerational conflict will increase: the Baby Boomers may be concerned about increasing their pension benefits, while their younger colleagues will probably want more take-home pay. There will be more concern for cost-of-living escalator clauses in pension plans and more concern about health care benefits for retirees. We already can see harbingers of this generational conflict in the growing unwillingness of current workers to pay in more to Social Security to cover benefits for today's retirees.

In the next decade, the Baby Boomers will become leaders of the labor movement. Their values for individuality, freedom, flexible work arrangements, and a voice in decision making will produce significant changes in the process of labor relations.

Compensation

Pay has been and will continue to be a major facet of human resource management to be affected by the changing work force. The diversity of employees has led to more flexible pay systems. Part-time employees in some organizations receive pro-rated benefits, based on the number of days or hours worked. For instance, the American Institute for Research, in Palo Alto, California, which employs many part-time professionals, gives one day of vacation time for each twenty days worked. "Cafeteria" benefit plans permit an employee to choose among various options: health insurance, life insurance, disability, etc. To attract senior executives, the differential in pay and "perks" between junior and senior management has been increased in many organizations. For example, one manufacturing firm recently raised the level at which bonuses were paid from plant manager to vice-president. And with more baby boom employees facing plateaued careers, compensation systems which uncouple pay from position (through technical ladders or cash performance awards) are becoming more widespread.

Also, the impact of pay as a reward may be changing. With the diversity of employees comes a diversity of needs. This means that a wider range of factors may serve as rewards—e.g., the opportunity to have more flexible work schedules, individualized benefits, parental leaves of absence, opportunities to do career planning and to have more control over one's future. All of these facets of the work environment are important to today's workers, and people often would trade off a certain amount of money for them.

Career Development

With more employees concerned about their special needs, there are more concerns about future rewards and, in particular, about their careers. As organizations continue to experience slow growth, and as we see uneven flows of people in different age groups, a great premium will be put on individual career planning and organizational career management. The individual employee can no longer count on organizational growth to provide career opportunities. And the organization will have to find more creative ways for people to have broadening and stretching experiences. The line manager will feel increasing pressure from employees to provide career counseling and coaching. The human resource department will be called upon to provide training for managers in career coaching skills and to facilitate interdepartmental career moves.

Leadership

All of these human resource implications add up to far greater demands for strong leadership from line management and from the human resource department. With greater employee *diversity* will come a need for *integration* of these members into a committed, motivated, and productive work force. Management will be forced to provide excellent direction and excitement in pursuit of the organization's mission. Those organizations will need to have an IBM- or Procter & Gamble-type climate where everyone feels like a "winner" by being part of a superior organization. A key task of human resource management will be to create a strong sense of shared meaning and purpose among this diversified work force.

These changes in the composition of human resources in the work organization are no less dramatic than recent changes in the nature of financial and technological resources. The "internal environment" (i.e., people) of the organization is just as complex and turbulent as the external environment. All of the human resources tasks performed by the manager, from recruitment and selection, through training and development, to outplacement and retirement, are affected by the new flows of people in the work force.

In Chapter Four, we will move from the employee to the setting in which that employee works: the work place. We will see that the changes in the work environment have been just as dramatic as those in the worker. The theme of *management flexibility* which has been running through this chapter will be shown in more detail as it appears in contemporary work settings.

KEY POINTS

- Contemporary employee work values, while still recognizing the importance of pay and security, show a strong concern for intrinsic work rewards, such as self-fulfillment, meaningful work, and job satisfaction.

- Demographic trends indicate growing numbers of women, two-career couples, older workers, Hispanics, handicapped, and other diverse groups in the work force. The result will be an increasingly heterogeneous employee population.

- Changes in age composition are occurring unevenly. Thus, there are growing numbers of middle-aged workers, declining numbers of young workers, and growing numbers of retired people. The importance of careful human resource planning and management development for different age cohorts is clear.

- These changes in the work force are placing great demands upon the human resource capabilities of the organization (e.g., greater people-management skills for managers, ability to incorporate employee diversity into strategic planning, uneven staffing patterns, and new forms of compensation).

ISSUES FOR DISCUSSION

1. In your own work experiences, what do you see as important work values in today's work force?
2. If you were a line manager, how would you try to motivate people with these values?

3. How well suited are today's organizations for managing this new work force?

4. With such a diverse work force, how would you, as a manager, deal with the issue of *equality?* Is it possible to treat all employees the same? If it were possible, would it be effective?

5. What *managerial skills* are required to manage a heterogeneous work force?

6. What implications does this employee diversity have for designing human resource systems (e.g., compensation, benefits, training, labor relations, recruiting)?

NOTES

1. *Boston Globe*, September 27, 1983, p. 19.

2. W. G. Bennis, *Beyond Bureaucracy* (New York: McGraw-Hill, 1973), p. 3.

3. D. McGregor, *The Human Side of Enterprise* (New York: Harper, 1960), pp. 33–34.

4. Ibid., p. 47.

5. Ibid., pp. 47–48.

6. D. T. Hall, "Potential for Career Growth," *Personal Administration, 34*, pp. 18–30.

7. P. Pascarella, *The New Achievers* (New York: Free Press, 1984), and J. Naisbitt, *Megatrends: Ten New Directions Transforming Our Lives* (New York: Warner Books, 1982).

8. P. Renwick and E. E. Lawler III, "What You Really Want from Your Job," *Psychology Today*, May 1978, pp. 53–58, 60, 62, 65, 118.

9. Ibid., p. 57.

10. S. E. Seashore and J. T. Barnowe, "Collar Color Doesn't Count," *Psychology Today*, August 1972, pp. 53–54, 80–82.

11. L. D. Johnston, J. G. Bachman, and P. M. O'Malley, "Monitoring the Future: Questionnaire Responses from the Nation's High School Seniors, 1979" (Ann Arbor, MI: Institute for Social Research, University of Michigan, 1979), p. 26A.

12. D. Yankelovich, *New Rules* (New York: Random House, 1981).

13. D. Yankelovich and J. Immerwahr, "Putting the New Work Ethic to Work" (New York: The Public Agenda Foundation, September 1983); and D. Yankelovich, "Work, Values, and the New Breed." In C. Kerr and J. M. Rosow (Eds.), *Work in America: The Decade Ahead* (New York: Van Nostrand, 1979), pp. 3–26.

14. Ibid., p. 21.

15. F. S. Hall and D. T. Hall, *The Two-Career Couple* (Reading, MA: Addison-Wesley, 1979), p. 10.

16. C. Fukami, State University of New York at Buffalo, verbal communication with D. T. Hall, May 1981.

17. Ibid.

18. Hall and Hall, op. cit.

19. "Employees Get Help on Delicate Balance Between Work and Family," *Wall Street Journal*, April 3, 1980, p. 16.

20. Catalyst, *Corporations and Two-Career Families: Directions for the Future* (New York: Catalyst, 1981); and R.E. Kopelman, L. Rosenzweig, and L.H. Lally, "Dual Career Couples: The Organizational Response." *Personnel Administrator*, September 1982, 27, no. 9, pp. 73–78.

21. L. B. Russell, *The Baby Boom Generation and the Economy* (Washington, DC: The Brookings Institution, 1982); Richard A. Easterlin, *Birth and Fortune: The Impact of Numbers on Human Welfare* (New York: Basic Books, 1980); and "Americans Change," *Business Week*, February 20, 1978, pp. 65–66.

22. *Business Week*, op., cit. p. 60.

23. Ibid.

ANNOTATED BIBLIOGRAPHY

EVANS, P. A. L., and BARTOLEMÉ, F. *Must Success Cost So Much?* New York: Basic Books, 1981.

> This is a study of the relationship between professional lives and private lives of male middle managers. The samples consisted of 532 managers (95 percent of whom were European), twenty-two British executives and their wives, and twenty-two French executives and their wives. The study examined lifestyles, satisfactions, life and career stages, and ways managers attempt to create balance between work and personal life. The study makes a strong argument for considering the employee's family and personal needs in the management of human resources.

HALL, F. S. and HALL, D. T. *The Two-Career Couple.* Reading, MA: Addison-Wesley, 1979.

> This book examines a rapidly-growing segment of the contemporary work force: the dual-income couple. Like the Evans and Bartolemé book, it examines the interaction of work lives and family lives, but the focus is on the couple, rather than the individual employee. Based in part on the Halls' own research with more than 60 two-career couples, the book describes conflicts, stresses, and sources of satisfaction for two-career couples. It also discusses methods of coping with two-career conflicts, time management, career planning, family planning, and child care.

McGREGOR, D. *The Human Side of Enterprise.* New York: Harper, 1960.

> This is one of the earliest and perhaps most influential of the new, humanistic approaches to management which appeared in the 1960s. Very readable and insightful, it is based on McGregor's own work as an administrator (he was president of Antioch College), consultant, and scholar. It covers issues such as human motivation (based upon the theories of Abraham Maslow), management styles, control systems, and one of the earliest discussions of management by objectives. The ideas are every bit as current today as they were in 1960.

NAISBITT, J. *Megatrends: Ten New Directions Transforming Our Lives.* New York: Warner Books, 1982.

> This important book is one of those rare combinations of influential scholarly work and popular reading (it was at the top of the best-seller list for months). Based on years of trend analysis, Naisbitt identified ten overarching "mega-

trends" which he feels are changing our lives. The trends which relate to this chapter are:

A move from industry to information (and brainpower).

A tendency for the new high technologies to be complemented by a human response ("high-tech-high-touch," as he calls them). Example: individualized-compensation plans.

A switch from dependence on large institutions to self-help. Examples would be wellness and fitness activities, home-study, entrepreneurialism, and self-employment.

An increasing demand by people for a say in decisions that affect their lives. Workers' rights movements, employee participation programs, and consumerism are all examples of this desire for more personal control.

Moving from "either/or" to multiple choice in employment, arts, marriage, religion, entertainment, and even language.

PASCARELLA, P. *The New Achievers.* New York: Free Press, 1984.

This book is a survey of the values found in the contemporary work force, written by the editor of *Industry Week.* It examines the work ethic in the past, present, and future, and the effects of these changes in the work place. There is extensive discussion of the implications of these changes for management practices, with many examples of organizations that are creating more flexible, autonomous, and fulfilling work environments.

YANKELOVICH, D. *New Rules: Searching for Self-Fulfillment in a World Turned Upside Down.* New York: Random House, 1981.

Daniel Yankelovich is the leading chronicler of changes in American values. The theme of this book is that the more Americans have been turning inward in the 1970s and early 1980s (the so-called "Me Generation") in search of self-fulfillment, the less likely they have been to find it. This is because fulfillment is most likely to be found through a sense of meaning, which entails commitment and relating to others. Yankelovich predicts that the next social trend will be toward more connectedness and commitment.

THE CHANGING WORK PLACE

Secretaries tittered when Kim Chappell, his short hair already damp, his white uniform soaked with sweat, barged into the tweedy executive offices of the Westin Hotel.* He looked like an escapee from somewhere, and he was—from the laundry room. He strode into the serene rosewood-paneled office of the managing director as if it were his own.[1]

It was—but not for today.

"Look at this!" he exploded. "He's drinking my Cokes! And he didn't get through my 'in' box. I finished his work!"

Greg Alston, a large, dignified man in a black three-piece suit, looked Chappell over. "How was your day?" he asked, smiling benignly.

"I'm sweaty. I stink . . ." answered Chappell. And then they both laughed.

Chappell, 40, who runs the Westin, and Alston, 26, a Westin laundry worker, had traded jobs Monday, which was National Boss/Employee Exchange Day. Chappell, a boss who likes to keep in touch with his 1,150 employees by regularly eating in the employees' cafeteria and frequently touring all the hotel departments, approved a contest to pick one hourly employee to replace him.

Alston's winning essay, one of 125, said in part, "I will become more aware of the problems in management and Mr. Chappell will learn about the problems we face in the laundry. Maybe we can help solve each other's problems."

The main problem in the laundry Monday morning was that the Westin's 1,400 rooms had all been booked over the weekend, leaving an elephantine heap of towels, sheets, pillowcases, and bath mats for the hapless Chappell and thirty-one other launderers to sort, wash, dry, press, and fold.

Hollow-eyed with fatigue by 3 P.M., Chappell said he hadn't done so much physical work since he started with the Westin chain eighteen years ago as a stock clerk.

On the phone with Jack Skinner, Westin resident manager, Chappell sat

---

*Adaptation of "Job swap at the Westin Hotel was more than trading spaces" by Lona O'Connor, Detroit Free Press, September 15, 1983. Reprinted by permission.

still for a little ribbing from his majordomo, then reported, lest there be any question about which job he prefers, "I'm telling you now, I'm coming back up. I ain't staying down here. I've had two breaks and a half-hour lunch. And I really looked forward to those breaks . . ."

"I certainly have a lot more respect for the laundry workers," he concluded, staring at his laundry-reddened palms. "And I intend to get down there more often. There's a need for someone to say they appreciate it. When I come down and slap people on the back and feel the perspiration on their backs, I'll know what it means.

*I*n the previous chapter, we noted that the work force is changing. And, as we said in Chapter Two, if the employee changes, the job must change as well to provide a good person-job fit. We now see another change—a change in the work place. Twenty years ago, the idea of a "National Boss/Employee Exchange Day" would have seemed ludicrous. Since that time, the nature of work has been redesigned as programs aimed at "quality of work life" (QWL), job enrichment, employee participation, team management, organization redesign, and product quality improvement have advanced from the status of "industrial experiments" to the level of effective human resource management. In this chapter we will examine the new work place and the skills in human resource management it demands.

EVOLVING THEORIES OF WORK DESIGN

Let us start by tracing changes in the way managerial thinking has related to the work environment. We will see that management philosophy has moved from a bureaucratic, organization-centered approach to a more participative, employee-centered style of design for the work environment.

Bureaucratic Theory

Traditionally, work organizations have been administered as *bureaucracies.* While this term is often used in a negative way (i.e., to mean "red tape"), in its technical sense **bureaucracy** is *a form of highly structured administration based upon rational-legal principles* (as expressed in the writings of sociologist Max Weber). Some of the characteristics of a bureaucratic administration include:

bureaucracy

- Fixed and official areas of jurisdiction governed by rules, laws, or administrative regulations.
- Prescribed duties for officeholders.
- A system of authority in which officeholders give commands to carry out these duties, and rules govern the use of rewards or sanctions.

- A hierarchy of authority in which there is supervision of lower offices by higher ones.
- Management of an office based upon written documents ("the files"), which are preserved.
- Management of an office based upon general rules, which are stable and exhaustive and which can be learned.
- Thorough and expert training for office managers.
- Full-time employment of all officials.[2]

These characteristics of the bureaucratic form of managing an organization hold certain implications for the people who occupy positions in the organization. For people in a "pure form" of bureaucracy, holding an office is thought of as a *"vocation involving long-term training and service."* The official is held in higher *esteem* than people at lower levels. The bureaucratic official is *appointed* by a higher authority. Normally, there is *tenure for life*. *Salary and a pension* are the forms of compensation. And, finally, employment in the organization represents a *career*, with advancement from lower to higher positions.[3]

Obviously, this ideal form of bureaucracy is not found in many organizations today, nor was it ever widespread in practice when Weber was writing. However, many organizations demonstrated certain characteristics of the bureaucratic form, such as the hierarchy of offices, bureaucratic authority, and a system of rules governing employee behavior. According to Weber, the two organizations closest to the bureaucratic form were the German military and the Roman Catholic Church.

The most important feature of the bureaucratic form of administration was the *rationality and efficiency* it introduced into the management of an organization. Whereas under a system such as feudalism, decisions might be based on the whims of the local baron, who exercised a high degree of autonomy, a bureaucratic structure forced a rational coordination of goals and activities and a fairer system of rewards and punishments.

The bureaucratic form represented progress for the employee, in that it provided more separation of the work role from the employee's personal life. Under bureaucracy, the person's work duties were formally defined and not subject to the capricious demands of a ruler. Employees' rights, as well as their responsibilities, were more formally recognized, and the limits of authority were identified. The copy of a Wisconsin teacher's contract for 1922 (at a salary of $75 a month), shown in Exhibit 4.1, indicates that employees were not totally free of employer influence over their private lives when Weber's work was published in 1921. However, the concept of rationality vs. personal whim in the exercise of authority was firmly established.

Scientific Management

Whereas Weber's ideas related to the overall administrative structure and processes of the organization, the ideas in "scientific management" during the early 1900s strongly affected the design of jobs. The person most closely as-

EXHIBIT 4.1   *GOOD OLD DAYS WERE TERRIBLE*

Miss _____ agrees:

1. Not to get married. This contract becomes null and void immediately if the teacher marries.
2. Not to have company with men.
3. To be home between the hours of 8 P.M. and 6 A.M. unless in attendance at a school function.
4. Not to loiter downtown in ice cream stores.
5. Not to leave town at any time without the permission of the chairman of the Trustees.
6. Not to smoke cigarettes. This contract becomes null and void immediately if the teacher is found smoking.
7. Not to drink beer, wine, or whisky. This contract becomes null and void immediately if the teacher is found drinking beer, wine, or whisky.
8. Not to ride in a carriage or automobile with any man except her brother or father.
9. Not to dress in bright colors.
10. Not to dye her hair.
11. To wear at least two petticoats.
12. Not to wear dresses more than two inches above the ankles.
13. To keep the classroom clean:
    a. To sweep the classroom floor at least once daily.
    b. To scrub the classroom floor at least once weekly with soap and hot water.
    c. To clean the blackboard at least once daily.
    d. To start the fire at 7 A.M. so that the room will be warm at 8 A.M. when the children arrive.
14. Not to wear face powder, mascara or to paint the lips.

SOURCE: From "Good old days were terrible" from "City schools face loss of $100 million" by Casey Banas and James Coates, *Chicago Tribune,* September 28, 1975. Reprinted by courtesy of the Chicago Tribune.

sociated with scientific management was an industrial engineer, Frederick Winslow Taylor (1856–1917). Taylor advanced from laborer to chief engineer at the Midvale Steel Works, later worked for Bethlehem Steel Works, and then became a business consultant. Others who contributed to the early work of industrial engineering were H. L. Gantt and Frank and Lillian Gilbreth.

Four main principles formed the basis of scientific management:

1. *There is "one best way"* to do a job. Like Weber's approach, this was a highly *rational* way of viewing work, making the important assumption that there was *one and only one* "best way." Through scientifically determined procedures, the job was analyzed, and the most efficient method was determined. (For this reason, industrial engineers were sometimes called methods engineers. "Efficiency expert" was also used, but with pejorative overtones.) The proper method was prescribed to the employee, and expected (standard) rates of output were established.

In addition, pay incentives were provided for work above the standard.

2. *There is a "right person" to do a job.* Along with the idea of the "best way" was the notion of the "right person," the one best qualified to fit the job. Scientific hiring criteria were established as a basis for selection. Training activities were carefully geared to specific job requirements.

3. *There should be a matching of method, selection, and training.* With the right method, the right people, and the right training, Taylor felt that management and labor alike would benefit. The company would cut costs and increase output levels and quality, while the workers exerted less effort and made more (incentive) money.

4. *There should be cooperation between labor and management.* This teamwork involved a division of labor, with management doing the planning and thinking, and workers doing the physical labor. Again, cooperation was expected, since it was in the rational best interests of all parties.

The following example illustrates how the principles of scientific management were applied. In observing bricklayers at work, Frank Gilbreth was puzzled by the variety of ways in which experienced bricklayers carried out their work. Gilbreth had assumed that since bricklaying was one of the oldest crafts in the world (dating back to pre-biblical times), some sort of trial-and-error learning over the centuries would have established the "one best way." But this learning had not taken place.

As an experiment, Gilbreth developed his own system, using standard materials and processes. He designed a scaffolding system which put the bricklayer at one level, the bricks at an easily accessible second level, and the mortar at a third level. He specialized the tasks by having a laborer carry the bricks to the mason and sort them so that the best edge was up (previously, the mason had carried and sorted the bricks himself). Also, Gilbreth worked out a standard formula for mixing mortar so that the consistency was always the same.

Using these standard methods and materials, Gilbreth was able to reduce the movements of the mason from eighteen to five. He also increased his output of bricks laid from 120 to 250 per hour. Using scientific management, Gilbreth was able to achieve what bricklayers had not been able to accomplish in thousands of years of experience.[4]

Gilbreth's method of analyzing the job was to break it up into small discrete components, and he called a small piece of a task activity a "therblig" (which is close to "Gilbreth" spelled backwards). This approach to task design was called *job simplification.* Two major elements of this approach were:

- Simplified tasks were largely repetitive,
- The tasks did not require complex thinking or problem-solving by the operator.

The aim of this approach was to make the job literally "fool-proof," so that no fool could possibly do the job incorrectly.

Problems with Bureaucratic and Scientific Management Theories

The difficulty with these classical theories lies more in what they leave out than what they say.

First, they are based upon incomplete models of human motivation. They assume people are motivated primarily by money. Now we realize that a whole set of motivators are found in the work force, including social, ego, achievement, and self-fulfillment needs.

Second, these theories assume that humans rationally decide how to behave at work. Later work on decision-making by Herbert Simon and others found that people will not always search for the optimal solution to a problem, because there are *costs* associated with search (e.g., it takes time and effort). Also, decisions are often influenced by *feelings* rather than facts, and people may have personal biases which might lead them to choose to behave in ways that are personally satisfying (e.g., socializing with co-workers) but not necessarily efficient.

Third, the assumption of "one best way" can be questioned. Organizations are complex entities and there are often multiple methods of achieving a particular outcome. As we saw in Chapter Two, there are different strategies available in managing people. Also, we know that a particular method or practice may have multiple consequences, some positive and some negative. Thus, choosing a particular administrative practice may be more a matter of making trade-offs among various objectives than finding *the* perfect method.

Fourth, these classical theories assume the individual employee has little ability and motivation to make intelligent decisions about how work should be performed. This implies that managers should think, and employees should work. We know now, however, that the employee is often the real expert about the job and is the major source of creative ideas for ways to improve productivity.

The Human Relations Era

What started as an attempt to extend "scientific management" type knowledge about job characteristics eventually ushered in a new era of management theory. **The human relations approach** is *the use of interpersonal relations, communication, and group concepts to manage people.* A team of researchers from Harvard University, headed by Elton Mayo, conducted a series of studies at the Hawthorne Plant of Western Electric in Chicago between 1927 and 1932. Their original attempt was to assess the impact of the physical environment on productivity. They focused on factors such as lighting and fatigue.

human relations approach

Illumination Studies ▬ The first research attempted to determine the effect of lighting on the efficiency of the workers. As the ilumination level was increased, the researchers found, as expected, that output increased. This appeared to be a very promising discovery indeed. To get more work out, simply turn up the lights.

Then, to confirm this relationship between lighting and output, the researchers turned down the lights. They figured that, if their illumination principle was valid, lowering the lights should lower output. So the lights were dimmed. And . . . output increased again. And so on. Not until the lighting reached the level of moonlight did output begin to drop off.

What happened? Because employees were being treated in a special way, they wanted to show how well they could work. This *tendency for people to perform well simply because they are singled out for special treatment* has been labeled the *Hawthorne Effect*.

Bank Wiring Room Experiment ▬▬ In another study, the bank wiring room experiment, the effects of a group piecework pay incentive plan were examined. The hypothesis was that the existence of the pay incentive scheme would motivate the group to work harder to make more money.

What researchers found, instead, was that the group established its own *norms* about the appropriate level of output for its members. If one member produced too much, he was termed a "rate buster," because his high output might lead management to "tighten" the rate to keep pay down. If a member produced too little, he was called a "chiseler" or "goldbricker." This study led to the conclusion that group norms and members' needs for social acceptance were more important motivators than was the financial incentive.

The Hawthorne studies led to decades of research and to management practices which focused on work as a social activity. Interpersonal relations, communication, and group behavior were seen as important facets of the function of the social organization. Human relations training became "big business" for supervisors and managers, and led to the fields of organizational behavior and human resource management.

Unfortunately, human relations theory was also incomplete. Its central assumption was "a satisfied worker is a productive worker." We know now that the link between satisfaction and performance is more likely to work in the opposite direction: good performance leads to increased satisfaction (through pride in work and intrinsic rewards). However, the identification of emotional and social influences on work behavior helped "round out" what had been learned earlier about task and structure by scientific management and the administrative theorists.

Self-Actualization Approaches

In the late 1950s and early 1960s, a more refined view of the individual's role in organizational effectiveness began to emerge. This view acknowledged that the human relations approach was incomplete and also a bit naive. Led by thinkers like Chris Argyris (*Personality and Organization*, 1957), Douglas McGregor (*The Human Side of Enterprise*, 1960), and Rensis Likert (*New Patterns of Management*, 1961), this school of thought argued that the key was not satisfaction alone, but the *kinds of needs* being satisfied that were critical to effective performance.

The central assumption in this approach was that employees could be motivated by a range of needs, from security, money, and social belonging, to achievement, autonomy, self-esteem, and self-actualization. The classical approach, these writers argued, was missing out on a great deal of motivation potential by focusing only on the lower-level needs like money and affiliation. The self-actualization approach argued that, with the right kind of supervision, the right job design, and the right organizational climate, it should be possible to tap people's higher order needs so that by performing effectively in a valued job, they would at once satisfy their own important needs and work toward the goals of the organization.

The most compelling expression of this self-actualization theory was found in Douglas McGregor's "Theory Y," which we examined in Chapter Three. Theory Y claimed that employees *could* be self-directed and inner-motivated *if* conditions such as job challenge and employee participation in setting work goals were present. At that time, most organizations fit Theory X better than Theory Y, and Theory Y was seen as nice but hopelessly naive by many managers.

Chris Argyris explained why Theory X seemed to work better than Theory Y: formal management control systems created a self-fulfilling prophecy which confirmed management's Theory X assumptions. Argyris describes a "vicious cycle" which traps managers in their pessimistic assumptions about human potential in the work force. If top management behaved as if employees were lazy and needed strict external control, management would, in fact, create tight systems to control employee behavior. Employees, in turn, would react to these controls and try to establish more self-control by "beating the system." As employees were successful in outsmarting the system, management would react by tightening controls even more, thus increasing employee frustration and alienation. Then employees would fight the revised system in ever more counter-productive ways, and the cycle would continue. Management had created a self-fulfilling prophecy.[5]

Human Resource Management Implications ▬▬ What did these self-actualization approaches imply for managing people? First, they implied that *the key to high or low productivity lay with management, not employees*. If people were not motivated, it was not because they were lazy or inept, but probably because their job, their bosses, and the organizational climate did not arouse their achievement and self-actualization needs.

Second, they called for *more collaborative decision-making* between managers and employees. In contrast to the scientific management approach, where managers did the thinking and employees did the work, the self-actualization approach indicated that employees could be extremely creative and helpful in solving job problems and helping decide on better methods. This approach called for a whole employee; people were no longer expected to check their brains at the factory gate.

Third, they called for *new management behaviors*. Robert Blake and Jane Mouton, in their famous *Managerial Grid* (1964), argued that concern for both production *and* relationships was critical to produce a sense of motivated team spirit at work. The concern for relationships was not meant to imply a social, "country club" atmosphere, but rather a concern for open communication on issues related to effective performance. Argyris called this "reality centered leadership," where the basis of a manager's actions and authority was the demands of the task at hand rather than the formal power of the managerial position.

Fourth, they established the *need for job redesign*. If people were apathetic or alienated because jobs were intrinsically alienating, then jobs could be redesigned to make them intrinsically rewarding, providing the employee with a sense of pride in a worthwhile accomplishment. The thinking was, "If you want employees to take pride in their work, give them a job they can be proud of."

Fifth, they called for *mutual goal setting* to provide a way to introduce several of the elements listed above: collaborative decision making, new management styles, and more challenging jobs. McGregor (1960), in a chapter on joint target setting, described a process by which a manager and employee could discuss the employee's performance for the coming year in terms of goals to be achieved. The employee might make the initial list of planned goals; it could then be modified and jointly agreed upon in the discussion between the employee and the boss. This process was later elaborated on and popularized as *management by objectives*.

Resulting Activities ▬ Two specific kinds of human resource activities grew out of this self-actualizing approach to management. *Sensitivity training groups* (also called T-groups and encounter groups) applied the concepts and skills of group dynamics and used a professional human relations trainer to improve the competence of groups in organizational settings.

Richard Beckhard defined a related spin-off activity, **organization development** (O.D.), as " . . . *an effort (1) planned, (2) organization-wide, and (3) managed from the top, to (4) increase organization effectiveness and health through (5) planned interventions in the organization's 'process,' using behavioral-science knowledge*."[6] Organization development encompasses a wide range of behavioral science techniques, including T-groups, or an outgrowth called team building (the group being trained is a natural work group), job redesign, organization (structure) redesign, career planning, goal setting, work role clarification, and intergroup conflict resolution, to name a few. During the 1970s organization development activities became widespread, first as a specialized function (e.g., through organization development departments). Later, through a process of diffusion, organization development concepts and skills became integrated into the regular activities of the human resource or personnel function. The skills included problem diagnosis, consultation, and participative decision-making. Organization development diffused throughout the entire organization through the inclusion of its components into management training programs, so that over time managers acquired organization development skills to help them more effectively work with people.

organization development

THE INDIVIDUALIZED ORGANIZATION

As we said in Chapter Three, the assumptions of Theory Y are becoming increasingly valid, as workers' values move toward self-fulfillment and as the work place becomes more participative. Organizations today have become more flexible than ever, as they increase their ability to adapt quickly to changes in financial, competitive, and human resource conditions. Pressures for cost containment and for productivity *demand* that employee potential be tapped more creatively. On the human resource side, much of the flexibility of today's organizations is due to the great variety in employees today, as we saw in Chapter Three, with wide ranges in education (but a high average level), and growing numbers of women, minorities, two-career couples, technical/professional employees, unskilled employees (especially in service industries), and "new value" employees. Because of the contributions of organization development, today's organizations have developed many activities to improve productivity and competitiveness.

Source of the Individualized Organization

What we are seeing in the more innovative organizations today is a range of new forms of management. Perhaps the most common elements in many of these forms are *employee participation in decision-making* and *opportunities for individual choice* by employees. These activities are often developed through processes like job enrichment, team management, productivity improvement, and organization development, but they are often not labeled as such. These processes have simply been adopted and internalized by many line managers and human resource specialists and are often not seen as "new" or "innovative." They are seen simply as "good management."

For example, Motorola introduced job enrichment and switched from an assembly line to individual assembly of its "Pageboy II" paging radios in its Fort Lauderdale, Florida, plant in the mid-1970s. This change was made because the individual assembly method produced higher-quality radios, since the assembler was highly involved and felt personally responsible for the performance of each radio. However, this change in work design was done *not* for the purpose of enriching the operators' jobs (although this was a fortunate side effect). The change was initiated by the industrial engineers and the plant manager for the purpose of assuring product quality. In other words, job redesign was simply "good management" in this case.

In addition to job enrichment, numerous innovations are often found in individualized organizations (such as General Foods, PPG Industries, Procter & Gamble, Sherwin-Williams, TRW, H. J. Heinz, Dana Corporation, Rockwell, General Motors, Ford, McMead Corporation, and Cummins Engine).

Greater employee self-selection. Rather than seeing selection solely as the organization's task (through interviews, tests, etc.), there is also a desire to give the applicant realistic information to help make a valid decision about accepting the job. Group interviews with managers and employees who could be the applicant's future co-workers are often used to make a mutual decision. More details on these decisions, "realistic job previews" for prospective employees, will be found in Chapter Ten, "Organizational Entry."

Participative plant design. If a new plant is going to be constructed, there is often an attempt to utilize employees' ideas about the layout of machinery, equipment, and the personal and recreational areas of the plant. The atmosphere tends to be egalitarian, and separate areas for managers and non-management employees (e.g., cafeterias, parking areas, restrooms) are discouraged.

Skill-based pay systems. Instead of using job evaluation (which we will describe in Chapter Eighteen) to set pay levels for various kinds of positions, the new pay system is often based upon the number of skills the employee possesses. As experience is acquired, the employee also learns new skills. The more skills the person has, the higher the pay.

Flatter organization structure. The hierarchy of the individualized organization is far flatter than a traditional system. Because employees usually work in self-managed teams in enriched jobs, there is less need for levels of supervision, such as general foremen and superintendents.

Greater stress on training. Because today's employees have more autonomy, responsibility and challenge, and because pay is based often on skill levels, there is a greater need for effective training. A rich set of in-plant training programs, career development workshops, and support for off-the-job training is found in the new work place.

Participative management style. To further stimulate and support these qualities of the new work place, a new form of leadership is required. Rather than top-down, authority-based leadership, the most effective management style in this setting involves a more democratic, participative form, using greater channels for employee involvement in decision-making and problem solving.[7]

Thus, the current individualized work place represents the application of the 1960s era self-actualization management writings of Douglas McGregor, Chris Argyris, and Blake and Mouton. Of course, we still see elements of bureaucratic administration (rules, hierarchies, career progressions, etc.), scientific management (we still have industrial engineers, but they are more people-oriented, as the Motorola example shows), administrative efficiency (updated by computer information technology), and human relations (participative team management uses the group as a central unit for performance improvement).

Each generation of theory has added some new insight to our understanding of management; no one theory is right or wrong—each is incomplete in some way. As the time line for the various approaches shows (Exhibit 4.2), each set of new insights was superimposed on our previous knowledge from

EXHIBIT 4.2   TIME LINE: THEORIES OF MANAGEMENT

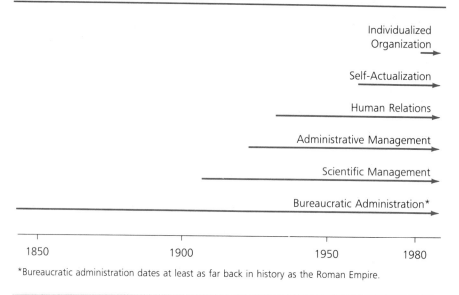

*Bureaucratic administration dates at least as far back in history as the Roman Empire.

earlier theories. Thus, our understanding of how to manage people in the work place has become more complete over the years.

Referring back to the model of external influences on the management process shown in Exhibit 2.1, we can categorize the forces we have just described which led us to the individualized organization (shown in Exhibit 4.3). The key changes in the *social* environment were the new employee intrinsic work values and the new (Theory Y) managerial assumptions about employee motivation. In the *economic* environment, we had serious external competition (especially foreign competition and the emergence of what is truly a world economy), economic constraints from a long recession and slow economic growth, and a resulting need for labor-management cooperation. In the *political* environment we had deregulation (and reduced government protection for certain industries, such as utilities and transportation), pressure for social responsibility and public accountability, greater concern for employee rights, and constraints of formal authority (through government legislation, as we will see in Chapter Six). In the *technological* environment, there was rapid change in products, in processes, in knowledge, and in information-processing capability (i.e., computer technology). All of these influences supported the use of human resource management technologies, such as job redesign, team building, etc. And the use of these human resource activities led naturally to new forms of management, which we will discuss now.

DEVELOPMENT OF NEW FORMS OF INDIVIDUALIZED MANAGEMENT

EXHIBIT 4.3

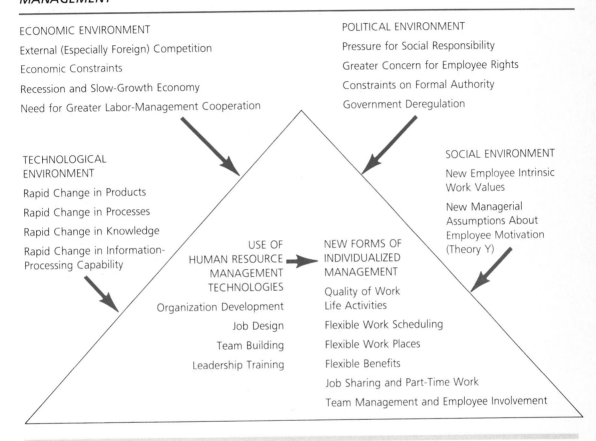

ECONOMIC ENVIRONMENT

External (Especially Foreign) Competition

Economic Constraints

Recession and Slow-Growth Economy

Need for Greater Labor-Management Cooperation

POLITICAL ENVIRONMENT

Pressure for Social Responsibility

Greater Concern for Employee Rights

Constraints on Formal Authority

Government Deregulation

TECHNOLOGICAL ENVIRONMENT

Rapid Change in Products

Rapid Change in Processes

Rapid Change in Knowledge

Rapid Change in Information-Processing Capability

SOCIAL ENVIRONMENT

New Employee Intrinsic Work Values

New Managerial Assumptions About Employee Motivation (Theory Y)

USE OF HUMAN RESOURCE MANAGEMENT TECHNOLOGIES

Organization Development

Job Design

Team Building

Leadership Training

NEW FORMS OF INDIVIDUALIZED MANAGEMENT

Quality of Work Life Activities

Flexible Work Scheduling

Flexible Work Places

Flexible Benefits

Job Sharing and Part-Time Work

Team Management and Employee Involvement

Quality of Work Life

The phrase "quality of work life" is a generic one encompassing an employee's feelings about all dimensions of work, including economic rewards and benefits, security, working conditions, organizational and interpersonal relationships (especially with the supervisor), job tasks, unions, work rules, decision-making discretion, and the intrinsic meaning of that work in the person's life.[8] The important feature here is that quality of work life is what exists in the *perception of the employee;* it is how the employee evaluates the work elements in the above definition.

    Quality of work life is a *process by which an organization attempts to unlock the creative potential of its people by involving them in decisions af-*

quality of work life

fecting their work lives. In practice, the abbreviation *QWL* is the term more generally used. Its goals are both extrinsic, focusing on productivity and efficiency, and intrinsic, focusing on what the employee sees as self-fulfilling and self-enhancing ends in themselves.[9] Literally thousands of articles and books have been written on the subject, many national and international centers focus on the subject, and countless QWL programs are in existence. The Tarrytown, N.Y., program of General Motors is described in Box 4.1.

The following conclusions about QWL programs grew out of the Tarrytown experience.[10] First, management must be competent if a QWL program is to succeed. QWL is not a substitute for managerial competence. Workers will not become involved in decision-making if they feel management lacks the skills to utilize their ideas.

QWL requires a strong union (if a union is present). The venture must be a cooperative labor-management effort, and workers must trust their union leaders' competence, openness, and influence. Management often has to be the one to initiate the ideas of a joint venture, however.

QWL should exist outside of the labor-management contract and should never circumvent the contract (i.e., wage issues, grievance-handling, and contract negotiations are all handled in the traditional manner). Top management and the union leadership must make a strong personal commitment to the QWL program. (And the QWL program will probably *not* work if management's real motivation is to speed up production or to reduce the work force; workers will see through such motivation as a new form of exploitation.)

The QWL effort should be *voluntary* for all participants. The program should start small, be flexible, and grow organically. There can never be a fully developed, detailed "master plan" for QWL. Problems must be worked out as they arise, while they are small (otherwise they could grow to explosive proportions later). Thus, QWL is not a finite "program" with a specific beginning and ending. It is ongoing and dynamic and continues, regardless of which people are involved at any particular time.

The *risk* to management and the union is that once employees become involved in work decisions, they will have gained a unique power over their own work lives, and they will want to continue the process. Even though management may have the *formal* power to stop the QWL activity and the union may have the *political* means to do so, it would cause great employee dissatisfaction and hostility if either tried to reverse the QWL process.

Quality Circles

quality circles

Quality circles (QCs) are *natural work groups of employees who meet on a regular basis to share ideas to improve product quality, process efficiency, and quality of work life.* The concerns of QCs, then, tend to be more task-centered than QWL groups, although QWL issues might be covered by QCs. There is usually a formal leader and agenda, a recorder, and a stress on specific follow-up actions to be taken. The original interest in QCs came primarily from their successful application in Japanese organizations.

QWL AT GENERAL MOTORS' TARRYTOWN PLANT

BOX 4.1

This is the story of the General Motors car assembly plant at Tarrytown, New York. In 1970, the plant was known as having one of the poorest labor relations and production records in GM. In seven years, the plant turned around to become one of the company's better run sites.

In April 1971, Tarrytown faced a serious threat. The plant manager saw the need for change, and also an opportunity. He approached some of the key union officers who, though traditionally suspicious of management overtures, listened to him.

The company decided to stop assembling trucks at Tarrytown and to shuffle the entire layout around. Two departments, Hard Trim and Soft Trim, were to be moved to a renovated area of the former truck line.

Two of the production supervisors in Hard Trim, sensing that top plant management was looking for new approaches, asked a question that was to have a profound effect on events to follow: "Why not ask the workers themselves to get involved in the move? They are experts in their own right. They know as much about trim operations as anyone else."

The consensus of the Hard Trim management group was that they would involve the workers. The Soft Trim Department followed suit. The union was brought in on the planning and told that management wanted to ask the workers' advice.

Moving the two departments was carried out successfully with remarkably few grievances. The plant easily made its production schedule deadlines.

In 1973, the UAW and GM negotiated a national agreement. In the contract was a brief "letter of agreement" signed by Irving Bluestone and George Morris, head of industrial relations for GM. Both parties committed themselves to establishing formal mechanisms, at least at top levels, for exploring new ways of dealing with the quality of work life. *This was the first time QWL was explicitly addressed in any major U.S. labor-management contract.*

Early in the year, 1977, Tarrytown made the "big commitment." The QWL effort was to be launched on a plant-wide scale involving approximately 3,800 workers and supervisors.

On September 13, 1977 the program was launched. Each week, 25 different workers (or 50 in all from both shifts) reported to the training rooms on Tuesdays, Wednesdays, and Thursdays, for nine hours a day. Those taking the sessions had to be replaced at their work stations by substitutes. Given an average hourly wage rate of more than $7 per attendee and per replacement (for over 3,000 persons), one can begin to get an idea of the magnitude of the costs.

What are the measurable results of quality of work life at Tarrytown?

Although not confirmed by management, the union claims that Tarrytown went from one of the poorest plants in its quality performance (inspection counts or dealer complaints) to one of the best among the 18 plants in the division.

The major characteristics of QCs have been summarized by Robert Cole.

- Training for foremen in participative management techniques and statistical methods applied to practical shop problems.
- Instruction by foremen of small groups in their work setting.
- Spontaneous participation of workers and their participation in self-improvement activities.
- QC as a spontaneous study group operating on a continuous basis.
- QC as a group effort with all members of the group participating.
- Extensive staff and managerial assistance to QCs provided by company.
- Recognition of circle members through public demonstrations, company awards, and national and regional QC conventions. Financial incentives are downplayed.[11]

A pioneer in the application of QCs has been Honeywell, Inc. Much of the impetus for QCs and other forms of participative management at Honeywell came from James Ranier, who was then president of the Control Systems Division (and is now corporate vice-chairman). Ranier holds a strong Theory Y view that people *want* to be productive and that sometimes management frustrates that desire:

> People are working harder today than I did, and the constraints on them are far worse. Because of high housing costs, for example, a person might live thirty miles from work. She may have to stop on her way to work to leave the children at a day-care center. She may get up at 4:30 A.M. for a 7 A.M. shift. And then a foreman who hasn't thought out his week very well asks her to work overtime—when she is worried about getting back to the day-care center.
>
> We miss the point about the work ethic by not knowing the individual's objectives. Unfortunately, we (in management) ask, "What's the bottom line," rather than, "How far do you drive to work?"[12]

Intense competition, both domestic and foreign, is heightening Honeywell's concern for participative management, as is the need to avoid losing good workers to that competition. This is especially true in high-turnover areas like Silicon Valley in California, where the culture virtually demands a participative approach.

In 1981 nearly 300 QCs were in operation in Honeywell's U.S. plants, with another 300 in their plants in Japan. The workers were interested in QCs because of better working conditions, greater involvement in work decisions, and better community spirit. Management's interest was due to both the improved work climate and improved productivity. These productivity payoffs covered many areas.

- Ten teams at one facility improved assembly productivity by 46 percent over two years. Also, there were improvements in communication, cooperation, and attitudes, as well.

▬ Twenty-eight teams in another plant reduced assembly hours in one
year, for a savings of $625,724.

▬ At a third facility, in nine months, eleven teams implemented solutions
to 109 production problems. This resulted in savings of $86,430, a 36
percent assembly cost reduction, and a marked improvement in attitude
and working climate.[13]

Two questions which are still unresolved at this point are: 1) What can
be done to sustain a QC that has been effective for several years, and 2)
Should the financial gains that result from greater productivity be shared?
Honeywell was investigating financial incentives as of this writing. Also, the
company has found that training for supervisors and managers is necessary to
support QC activities. Now nearly 1,000 middle managers per year go
through Honeywell's Management Development Center in Minneapolis. The
corporate human resource staff has been increased to forty (from thirty in
1979).

One implication of the use of participative management techniques is
that these activities have come to be used in corporate advertising. Motorola,
which has been a leader in this area, has used advertisements which describe
their participative management program in some detail (e.g., *Newsweek*, October 26, 1981, pp. 92, 93). The ads end with the words, "Motorola, world
leader in electronics. Quality and productivity through employee participation
in management."

Japanese Management and "Theory Z" Organization   *important.*

Interest in specific techniques such as quality circles was part of a broader
American fascination, starting in the late 1970s and early 1980s, with Japanese
management practices. As Japanese industries, such as electronics, automobiles, and steel, began to dominate their American counterparts, American
executives wanted to learn more about Japanese practices through field trips
to Japan, books on Japan, consultants in Japanese management, and the like.
Books such as Ezra Vogel's *Japan as Number One*, William Ouchi's *Theory
Z: How American Business Can Meet the Japanese Challenge*, and Anthony
Athos and Richard Pascale's *The Art of Japanese Management* became best
sellers—not just management best sellers, but general best sellers, at the top
of the weekly non-fiction lists. Television specials such as NBC's "If Japan
Can Do It, Why Can't We?"[14] were widely viewed and immediately influen-
tial.

William Ouchi has summarized the major differences between Japanese
and American management (shown in Exhibit 4.4). Perhaps the most widely
publicized contrast is the system of lifetime employment in Japan. However,
this system is practiced only by the larger firms in Japan and covers only
about 35 percent of their work force. Briefly, the person is hired right out of
school, promotion is entirely from within, and a person with experience in

EXHIBIT 4.4

**THE CONTRAST BETWEEN JAPANESE
AND AMERICAN ORGANIZATIONS**

Japanese Organizations	vs.	American Organizations
Lifetime employment		Short-term employment
Slow evaluation and promotion		Rapid evaluation and promotion
Non-specialized career paths		Specialized career paths
Implicit control mechanisms		Explicit control mechanisms
Collective decision making		Individual decision making
Collective responsibility		Individual responsibility
Holistic concern for people		Segmented concern for people

SOURCE: William Ouchi, *Theory Z*, © 1981, Addison-Wesley, Reading, Massachusetts, p. 58 (chart). Reprinted with permission.

one company will not be hired by another with lifetime employment. Once employed, the employee is retained until the mandatory retirement age of 55. Only a major criminal offense is a basis for termination. At 55, the person receives no pension but does get a lump-sum separation payment equivalent to five or six years' salary. As an alternative to a pension, the large firm will place the retiree in a smaller firm with which it does business (a "satellite company"), and the person continues to work, perhaps on a part-time basis. This income, plus savings, will carry the employee comfortably into retirement.

Performance evaluation and career advancement are much more gradual processes in Japan than in the U.S. It may take as long as ten years for members of a group hired together to receive differential promotions. This long-term process discourages corporate "game-playing" and builds strong commitment. Career paths take Japanese managers through a range of different departments and functions. This develops generalized skills, but at the expense of strong expertise in any one area.

Control mechanisms in Japan are subtle, operating through the corporate culture (symbols, ceremonies, and myths), as opposed to rules and "standard operating procedures" (SOPs) in the U.S. Over time in the organization, the person comes to understand and internalize the norms of acceptable behavior. Decision making and responsibility for executive decisions are collective (or shared) processes in Japan. The disadvantage of this approach, very frustrating to American executives, is that it takes a *long* time to make a decision in Japan. However, once the decision is made, the people with responsibility for implementing the decision are already "on board," so that the necessary action is taken quickly, with no resistance. Americans, on the other hand, make decisions quickly, with little involvement of the implementors; then the process of implementing the decision is lengthy. Thus, in Japan, the total time spent deciding and implementing may be shorter than in the U.S.

And finally, in the Japanese firm there is more concern for the total person, not just the person as a worker. Companies often provide employees with housing, child care, recreation, and social activities. This is a system which a U.S. observer might term "paternalistic." It develops a strong sense of community and intimacy in the work force.

As Ouchi continued his research, he found that these qualities of organizations were *not necessarily unique to Japan*. He was able to identify several U.S. companies which possessed many of these qualities: IBM, Procter & Gamble, Hewlett-Packard, Kodak, Eli Lilly, the U.S. military, and others. (The one feature of Japanese firms which was *least* likely to be found in U.S. businesses was slow promotion.) Ouchi referred to **Theory Z** as those *firms which have developed naturally in the United States but have many characteristics similar to firms in Japan.* (Ouchi chose the term Theory Z to build on the work of Douglas McGregor with Theory X and Theory Y.)[15]

theory Z

American Influence

It is ironic that the "discovery" by American managers of Japanese management methods (such as quality circles) led many people to conclude that these methods were new and unique to Japan. The opposite is true. As we have seen, experiments in work redesign, team management, and other forms of employee-management cooperation have been going on in the United States since the 1960s.

Robert Cole, in a chapter entitled "Borrowing: The Case of Work Redesign in Japan," gave several reasons why American management practices were adopted by Japanese management. First, the Japanese paid great attention to the latest developments in Western theory and practice. Extensive survey research in Japan showed a high level of worker discontent, especially for young workers. An increasingly tight labor market in the late 1960s, difficulty in recruitment and retention, rising education levels, and mature industries made job redesign an attractive way to maintain high worker commitment. Japanese managers, unlike their Western counterparts, take the social sciences extremely seriously, particularly American social science. Much of the published management literature in Japan consists of translations of Western scholars (9 percent, in one estimate). As Cole put it:

> The research and proposals of American organizational specialists such as Rensis Likert, Chris Argyris, and Douglas McGregor are widely diffused, and the use of their techniques is commonplace in large Japanese firms. This may be seen as part of a larger "management boom," as it was called in Japan, during which American management formulas and techniques were introduced into all spheres of business administration from the late 1950s on; personnel administration was no exception.[16]

Thus, we have the ironic situation in which postwar Japan borrowed new management practices and theory from United States businesses, which in turn re-borrowed them following the success of Japanese business in the 1970s and 1980s.

Factory and Office Automation

One of the major types of technological change indicated in Exhibit 4.2 is automation. A general term, **automation** is a *self-controlled electronic and/or mechanical process*. Typical examples of automation in the work place could be electronic office equipment (such as personal computers, word processors, and electronic mail systems), computer-aided manufacturing (CAM) systems (such as robot-assisted assembly lines), computer-aided design (CAD) systems (such as computer software to test alternative versions of automobile or air-craft designs), and computer-integrated manufacturing (CIM) systems (to tie together separate production operations).

The field of computer and information technology has traditionally been a critical area of superiority for United States industry. Major developments in computer hardware and software and in production of industrial robots were almost exclusively the domain of U.S. companies (such as IBM, Control Data Corporation, Digital Equipment Corporation, Cincinnati Milicron, and Computervision). Yet as we have just seen in the area of management theory, Japanese companies were faster to *apply* this new technology to manufacturing processes (through robotics), and U.S. companies have been struggling to catch up. (Although Japanese companies have been ahead in CAM, U.S. firms have been stronger in CAD.) Even so, in 1984 the population of robots in the U.S. was growing at 30 percent a year, compared to a human population growth rate of 2 percent, according to the World Future Society. This group also predicted the U.S. robot population will be 35,000 by 1990.[17]

The consequences of automated manufacturing are considerable. Reliability, accuracy, and predictability are far greater than with conventional processes.

The factory of the future is characterized by high flexibility, information richness at low cost, improved control and optimization of factory operations, increased integration of separate operations, as well as greater integration of the production function with other business operations (especially product design and marketing).[18]

Human Resource Management Implications of Automation

What effect will these developments in automated processes have on the work place? Because developments in this area have been so dramatic and rapid, there is considerable uncertainty about just what all of the organizational implications might be. However, there are a number of effects that are likely to occur.

Job elimination. While experts do not see a massive displacement of workers as automation proceeds, certain tasks will be transferred from people to machines.

Upgraded jobs. As the new equipment takes over more physical tasks, people will still be needed to monitor and operate it. Large numbers of enginéers, programmers, systems analysts, and hardware specialists will be needed. Alex C. Nair, vice-president for technical staffs of General Motors Corporation, predicts that by the year 2000 the percentage of skilled tradespeople in GM plants may be 50 percent, up from 16 percent in 1981.[19]

New training and retraining. As the newly created jobs become more complex, more effort is directed toward training people to acquire the necessary skills. These people may be either new employees or displaced employees who are being retrained for the new jobs. For example, one chemical manufacturing firm developed a mid-career retraining program for surplus chemical engineers. They went to school full-time for one year, at company expense, and earned masters degrees in process control engineering. This helped the company deal with a shortage of process control specialists *and* the oversupply of chemical engineers.

Less mobility. As organizations move information more, there will be less need to move people. Within a work station, computerized information processes, such as electronic mail and teleconferencing, can bring people in contact without being physically together.

Health hazards. Long hours at a video display terminal can cause eye, neck, and back strain. Possible radiation hazards may be a problem as well. Standards are currently evolving for length of exposure to terminals, proper distance, lighting, and furniture.

Intrusion of work on home life. As new technologies give the person more flexibility about where work is performed (a topic we will examine in the following section), it will become easier and more convenient to perform work at home, through communication and computer technology. While this flexibility may be attractive in some ways, it could blur the boundaries between work and home and lead to disruptions of family and personal life.

Security problems. As more sensitive information becomes controlled by computer networks, this information becomes increasingly accessible to skillful unauthorized people. Computer crime is already a major problem for banks, brokerage firms, and other financial institutions.

Labor relations. Because of the variety of ways this new technology can affect jobs, some labor relations experts are predicting that automation will be *the* central bargaining issue in the new decade.

Flexible Work Scheduling

Flexible scheduling of work hours has gained widespread popularity since the early 1970s. Current estimates indicate that over a million employees in the United States are benefiting from flextime, as are about five million in Europe.[20]

The basic idea of **flextime** is that, *employees can choose when they will report to work and when they will leave outside of a "core" of hours* (for example, between 10 a.m. and 3 p.m.). Of course, the total number of hours worked per week must equal thirty-five, thirty-seven, forty, or whatever

flextime

number the company requires. The following types of programs are most common:

1. *Daily flextime, fixed lunch, and core time.* Under this approach, the person works a full number of hours (usually eight) each day.
2. *Daily flextime, flexible lunch.* This is the same as number 1. above, except that the person has more choice about the lunch period.
3. *Weekly flextime.* Employees have to work the core hours each day, but do not work a fixed number of hours per day. They do, however, have to work a fixed number of hours per week.
4. *Monthly flextime.* This is like number 3., except the requirement is for a certain number of hours per month, rather than a weekly quota.[21]

Research on flextime has shown that employees (especially working parents) are usually more satisfied with flextime than with standard work hours. The group most likely to report dissatisfaction is supervisors, who may feel they have to work additional hours to be able to supervise both the early-arriving and late-leaving employees.

Flexible Work Places

flexplace

Along with flextime, some organizations have been introducing the concept of flexplace. **Flexplace** *allows employees the freedom to do some or most of their work at home.* Of course, working at home has always been found in some craft industries, and in creative fields such as writing and poetry. Some unions are concerned about at-home work, since such labor may represent lower-cost competition to the work of their members.

With the increase in information processing technology (for example, computers and word processors) we are finding increased evidence of the emerging *electronic cottage.* Computer programmers and information systems specialists are able to have a terminal at home which is connected by telephone to the company's computer. In this way, they can do many components of their job at home. CDC, for example, has endorsed at-home work for many of its computer specialists, taking the following approach:

> Analysts, computer programmers, educational-courseware writers and clerical workers, because they are task and project-oriented employees, can most easily participate in the program.
>
> In our experimental programs, nearly all participants have both an alternate work site and a central office station. Their central offices are used for group meetings and the distribution of supplemental work materials.
>
> Our satellite office—located near a cluster of employee residences—permits employees to share lawyer services, word-processing equipment, copy duplicators, and libraries.[22]

One possible problem with a work-at-home system is that employees may feel socially isolated, cut off from their peers in the office. Ironically, by working at home, people may feel less "at home" at work (i.e., in the main office). Therefore, some companies attempt to provide employees with regular opportunities to attend meetings and get together with other employees periodically. A special attempt is also made to make employees feel welcome when visiting the main office facility by providing special meeting rooms, mailboxes, lockers, and special stations for picking up work assignments.

Also, since the employee works alone, without supervision, it is important to have clear expectations and feedback about performance.

Flexible Benefits

With a more differentiated work force, organizations are finding that employees have differing needs in the area of benefits. Young people may not care much about health insurance or family medical plans, but they may want more vacation time than the two weeks newer employees typically receive. A person with an employed spouse may find that the spouse's family medical coverage is superior to his or her own and would like to trade off the company's medical contribution against some other benefit, say, child care credits.

Many companies are now using *cafeteria benefit programs*, in which employees are able to make these choices. There may be a core of benefits which everyone receives, and then beyond that, people can select different combinations. The whole idea is that company contributions to a person's benefits are part of that person's total compensation package, and if part of the package is not accepted, the employee still should be able to get that value through some other benefit.

A variant of this approach is to let people have the value of unwanted benefits in *time*, rather than as cash applied to other benefits. Continental Bank, for example, has found that computing the cash value of benefits is too complex to be feasible, so it uses time as the "currency" instead of money. Thus, people who opt not to receive certain benefits can have them counted toward more vacation days and personal days each year.

Job Sharing and Part-Time Work

There are now more ways to be employed than in the past. As we have seen, one manifestation of this development is the increase in home work. A second is exercised options for part-time work. It used to be that part-time jobs were only lower-level, unrewarding, low-paying positions with no upward career path. Now, however, companies are becoming more open to part-time work in higher-level technical and professional positions. This is especially common with new parents who do not want a long maternity/paternity leave but also do not want to start back on a full-time schedule initially. Given the choice between losing an established employee and relaxing human resource policies to permit more part-time work, many organizations have chosen the latter course. The organization benefits in two ways: 1) it attracts or retains competent people who would not be there if full-time work were the only option,

job sharing

and 2) even though the employees are *paid* part-time, they may be *involved* full-time, especially in a professional job. Thus, the organization may receive far more time and effort than it pays for.

Job sharing is *a process by which two people, sharing jointly, assume responsibility for a full-time position.* Job sharing is thus a way to work part-time when there is no actual part-time job. This means the incumbents have to be able to communicate well with each other about what they did when it was their turn to work. Performance evaluation, pay, and benefits are somewhat more complicated, but once the organization develops policies about job-sharing, these should not be major problems. Our impression, despite an occasional well-publicized example, is that job sharing is not used as frequently as the other types of flexible work arrangements described earlier.

Temporary Employment

Another way in which flexibility is being added to the modern work force is temporary employment. For years, organizations have leased physical resources (equipment such as cars, trucks, furniture, computers, copiers, etc.). Now more and more firms are "leasing" people through agencies which provide workers in specific job categories. For example, the Pinkerton Agency was leasing security personnel during the Wild West heyday of Jesse James and Butch Cassidy. And clerical help has long been available from firms such as Kelly Services (formerly Kelly Girls). But now all varieties of employees can be hired through broker firms: scientists, accountants, computer specialists, etc.

There are three sources of temporary employees. The most familiar is the *temporary help agency* (e.g., Kelly Services), which is usually used for short-term needs (unexpected resignations, peak work periods). *Leasing companies* will provide all types of employees (managers through hourly production personnel) for indefinite time periods.

The third option is *job shops*, which provide various types of professional personnel (e.g., systems analysts, marketing specialists), generally on a per-project basis. Given the fluctuations in the business levels of research and consulting firms, leasing from job shops allows the organization to operate at full capacity in peak periods without a long-term commitment to those employees. Richard Botwinick, manager of administration and planning for the Air Pollution Control Division of Research-Cottrell, Inc., in Somerville, N.J., recalled a time when the firm had hired many regular employees for a big project, which was then canceled at the last minute. "We had to have some layoffs." Now when the company lands a big contract, "we hire about two dozen job shoppers for the life of the project and drop them when it's done."[23] These three sources of temporary help make up "one of the fastest-growing industries ' today's economy," according to Samuel R. Sacco, executive vice-president of the National Association of Temporary Services, a trade association located in Alexandria, Va.[24] A description of one organization's experience with employee leasing is found in Box 4.2

FOR RENT: AN ENTIRE WORK FORCE

BOX 4.2

On a Friday afternoon last year, Walter Klein, president of Klein Meat Company, passed out pink slips to each of his fifteen employees. He saved the last one for himself.

The following Monday the staff of the Forth Worth, Tex., meat company returned to work as usual. But over the weekend they had become employees of Omnistaff Inc., a Dallas leasing firm, and Klein Meat Company was leasing their services from Omnistaff.

Mr. Klein, whose business had been in his family for forty-four years, opted to lease his employees because he could no longer afford a decent benefits package. There was no retirement plan, and even medical coverage was getting out of reach. "As costs went up it became more difficult to negotiate a good health plan," he said.

Now Mr. Klein and his workers are covered by Omnistaff's medical insurance, and have been given immediate vesting in a pension plan. "I was beginning to see my own retirement on the horizon, so I found the pension plan an attractive feature," said Mr. Klein, who is 61 years old. "I also think the pension plan will help our long-term retention."

None of the benefits are free to Klein Meat. The company's payroll had totaled $7,000 a week. Now Mr. Klein pays Omnistaff that amount plus a premium between 20 and 30 percent.

Omnistaff, in turn, negotiates all of the benefits for the workers. Because it has an employee roster of more than 7,000 people, it gets a far better rate from insurance companies than would any small business negotiating on its own.

"What our clients can buy in the market for $100, we can buy for $80," claimed James Borgelt, Omnistaff's general manager. "I compared the costs of leasing every way I could," said Mr. Klein. "There was no doubt it was cost effective."

Employee leasing firms also shoulder their clients' paperwork burdens. They prepare the payroll, file payroll deductions, keep tabs on vacation days, file quarterly and annual payroll taxes, prepare federal and state unemployment filings, handle workers compensation audits, take care of income tax paperwork, and administer the pension plans.

A study by the Heller/Roper Small Business barometer found that almost three-quarters of small businessmen consider federal tax forms and laws one of their biggest problems. Only finding competent help caused more worry.

Leasing firms apparently are filling a real vacuum. According to Mr. Borgelt, Omnistaff alone services about 100 companies and bills more than $100 million annually. The largest of these companies has a staff of 200, but the average client only employs seven workers. Mr. Borgelt estimates that there are about two dozen employee leasing firms across the country, and that together they employ about 50,000 people. That is up from 3,000 people just five years ago.

"There is a groundswell of demand," Mr. Borgelt said.

Adaptation of, "For Rent: An Entire Workforce," by Beth Ellyn Rosenthal, *The New York Times*, December 16, 1984. Copyright © 1984 by The New York Times Company. Reprinted by permission.

NEEDED HUMAN RESOURCE SKILLS FOR THE MANAGER

What do these changes mean for the manager? How does the effective manager have to behave to supervise people in the work place? Let us examine a few implications.

Restricted Formal Authority; More Personal Authority

As one manager put it, "The boss is dead; long live the leader!" The formal authority of the manager has been decreasing over the years. From the employee's perspective, acceptance of authority has also been decreasing since the 1960s.[25] Thus, the manager will not be able to obtain results simply because "I told you so." Also, increasing legal restraints, employee rights, and union agreements will force managers to be much more careful to avoid arbitrary attempts to use "position power." Personal competence, trustworthiness, and powers of persuasion will be required.

Increased Sensitivity and Diagnostic Skills

It will be far more important for the manager to understand the motivation of individual employees, to know "where they are coming from." The manager will have to know what motivator is most appropriate for each employee. It may be pay for one person, recognition for another, and an occasional kick in the pants for a third.

Behavioral Flexibility

The manager must also be able to *act effectively* to motivate each employee. This means the manager must have a wide range of *behavioral skills* to be effective in influencing employees. This is where leadership comes in, the ability to move people in directions they might not otherwise choose to move. Communication skills are an important element here, as well.

Coaching and Helping

The new manager is more of a coach and helper than a traditional "authority" figure. Since contemporary employees value autonomy and achievement, the effective manager will be one who can help employees work effectively while working independently. This means being able to provide "supportive autonomy."[26] Also, since contemporary employees are likely to have special needs, such as a physical handicap, the inability to speak English, a young family, or a mid-career plateau, it will be important for managers to be able to counsel people about problems as well as about task behavior.

Dealing with the Employee's Personal Life

In the past, the employee's personal and family life were seen as unrelated to the work organization. Now it has become clear that personal and family situations can affect the employee at work, and vice versa. Managers should consider aspects of the employee's personal life as part of the organization's concern. This may involve such actions as counseling the employee and the spouse about a proposed job transfer, consulting with the family about an employee with an alcohol or drug problem, or helping a spouse search for employment.

Negotiation Skills

Since the manager's formal authority has decreased and employees are making more demands on organizations, the manager may find it necessary to develop skill in the role of the company negotiator. The manager may have to bargain with employees about work hours, deadlines, future assignments, travel, and acceptance of undesirable projects. The astute manager will, when asked for special favors by employees, grant them in return for outstanding performance in some behavior the manager desires.

Focus on Performance

With resources of all types (financial, human, capital) becoming scarcer all the time in today's "lean and mean" organization, performance is more important than ever. One of the most viable means of motivation will be the ability to focus the employee's attention on outstanding performance. Managers need to: focus on realistic, challenging goals, establish standards of excellence, shape employee effort, evaluate performance objectively, and give clear, descriptive feedback on performance.

This requires what Chris Argyris in 1957 called "reality-centered leadership."[27] The more a manager can focus on job performance and not on the employee as a person, the less defensive and more motivated the employee will be.

CONCLUSION

As we can see, there has been a great deal of change from the bureaucratic form of administration to the more flexible, individualized organization of today. This does not mean that *all* modern organizations have the individualized structures described here; bureaucracy is still alive in many places today. However, well-managed organizations tend to be more flexible and employee-centered than are less effective organizations. And effective managers are likely to use more participative leadership styles than their less effective colleagues. Even though the reader may eventually work in a bureaucratic organization, it will still be possible to practice some degree of participative management within his or her area of discretion. With today's better-educated, more discriminating work force, taking individual differences between employees into account in managing even a part of the business will produce a better employee-job fit—and thus more effective management of human resources.

KEY POINTS

- There has been an evolution of management theory, starting with bureaucratic theory, then scientific management, administrative management, human relations, and self-actualization theory. Each of these theories added elements which had been missing from earlier theories.

- The current theory of management might be termed "individualized management," in which flexibility exists to tailor the work place largely to the needs of each individual employee.

- Many of the recent innovations in the U.S. work place have been inspired by Japanese management practices, which in turn were largely borrowed from U.S. business and theory after World War II.

- The individualized work place often includes elements such as quality of work life (QWL) programs, quality circles, and flexible work schedules, locations, and benefits.

- To be effective in today's work place, a supervisor must possess: the ability to share authority, sensitivity, flexibility, coaching skills, ability to help employees with personal problems, negotiation skills, and a strong performance orientation.

ISSUES FOR DISCUSSION

1. If you were working in a "modern" bureaucratic organization (say, a government department) in 1880, in what ways would employment here be *better* than working for a less-formal, small (say, six-person) firm? (Consider Bob Cratchit in *A Christmas Carol.*) In what ways would the bureaucracy be worse?

2. Which theory of management seemed to prevail in the organization where you were most recently employed? Describe one or two specific incidents which illustrate this approach to management. How did supervisors behave?

3. What elements do you think are most critical to the success of a QWL program? What elements do you think would be most difficult to implement? Can a QWL program be sustained over a long period of time (say, ten years or more)?

4. What are the advantages to an employing organization of the individualized work place? Disadvantages? What are the costs of *not* individualizing the work place to some extent?

5. What implications does the individualized organization have for the basic human resource functions (compensation, recruiting, training, labor relations, etc.)?

NOTES

1. From the *Detroit Free Press*, September 15, 1983, p. 1B.

2. M. Weber, *From Max Weber: Essays in Sociology*, H. H. Gerth, translator, (New York: Oxford University Press, 1946).

3. Weber, op. cit.

4. A. Filley, and R. House, *Managerial Process and Organizational Behavior* (Glenview, Ill: Scott, Foresman and Company, 1969).

5. C. Argyris, *Personality and Organization* (New York: Harper, 1957).

6. R. Beckhard, *Organization Development: Strategies and Models* (Reading, Mass: Addison-Wesley, 1969), p. 9.

7. E. E. Lawler, III, "The New Plant Revolution," *Organizational Dynamics*, Winter 1978, pp. 3–12.

8. Adapted from W. Skinner, "The Impact of Changing Technology on the Working Environment." In C. Kerr and J. M. Rosow (eds.), *Work in America: the Decade Ahead* (New York: D. Van Nostrand, 1979), pp. 204–30; and R. H. Guest, "Quality of Work Life—Learning from Tarrytown," *Harvard Business Review*, July–August 1979, pp. 76–87.

9. Guest, op. cit.

10. Guest, op. cit.

11. R. E. Cole, *Work, Mobility, and Participation: A Comparative Study of American and Japanese Industry* (Berkeley, Calif: University of California Press, 1979), p. 141.

12. James Ranier, quoted in "Humanagement at Honeywell," *Industry Week*, July 27, 1981, p. 34.

13. "Humanagement at Honeywell," op. cit., p. 35.

14. This documentary is now available as a film through NBC Film Enterprises, Inc.

15. W. G. Ouchi, *Theory Z: How American Business Can Meet the Japanese Challenge* (Reading, Mass: Addison-Wesley, 1981).

16. Cole, op. cit., p. 130. This quotation includes references to K. Nodal, "Big Business Organization." In E. Vogel (ed.), *Modern Japanese Organization and Decision-Making* (Berkeley, Calif: University of California Press, 1975); and S. Takezawa, "The Quality of Working Life: Trends in Japan," *Labour and Society*, 1976, *1*, pp. 29–48.

17. "Futurists See Growth in Robot Population," *New York Times*, December 27, 1984, p. A16.

18. M. Jelinek, and J. D. Goldhar, "The Strategic Implications of the Factory of the Future," *Sloan Management Review*, Summer 1984, 25, pp. 29–37. (Both the Swedish example and the consequences of the factory of the future are described in this article.)

19. "The Speedup in Automation," *Business Week*, Aug. 31, 1981, pp. 56–67.

20. A. Cohen, and H. A. Gadon, *Alternate Work Schedules* (Reading, Mass: Addison-Wesley, 1978).

21. D. Fleuter, *The Workweek Revolution* (Reading, Mass: Addison-Wesley, 1975).

22. R. A. Manning, "Alternative Work Sites," speech presented to the U.S. Department of Transportation (Minneapolis, Minn.: Control Data Corporation, 1981). For a discussion about how Continental Bank is trying similar homework

activities, see H. Louis Mertos, "Doing You Over—Electronically," *Harvard Business Review*, April 1981.

23.   B. E. Rosenthal, "What's New in Temporary Employment," *New York Times*, December 16, 1984, p. F15.

24.   Ibid.

25.   D. A. Ondrack, "Emerging Occupational Values: A Review and Some Findings," *Academy of Management Journal* 1973, *16*, pp. 423–32.

26.   D. T. Hall, and B. Schneider, *Organizational Climates and Careers* (New York: Academic Press, 1973).

27.   Argyris, op. cit.

ANNOTATED BIBLIOGRAPHY

COHEN, A. and GADON, H. *Alternate Work Schedules.* Reading, Mass: Addison-Wesley, 1978.

> This is an excellent review of corporate practices in creating flexible work hours. It surveys the relevant literature on the advantages and disadvantages of flextime, considers conditions under which it is most appropriate, and describes ways to implement it most effectively.

COLE, R. E. *Work, Mobility, and Participation: A Comparative Study of American and Japanese Industry.* Berkeley, Calif: University of California Press, 1979.

> This is an in-depth comparison of U.S. and Japanese business practices, particularly as they relate to the automobile industry. Cole uses a unique data set of male respondents in Detroit and Yokohama in 1970–71 to examine issues of inter- and intra-firm job changing. He also analyzes Japanese borrowing of U.S. management concepts, work design at Toyota, the work design movement in Japan (vs. U.S., Yugoslavian, and Chinese practices), and the Japanese work ethic. This is one of the most authoritative sources available on Japanese management.

KERR, C. and ROSOW, J. M. *Work in America: The Decade Ahead.* New York: D. Van Nostrand, 1979.

> The second part of this book, which was in the Chapter Three bibliography as well, focuses on the emerging work environment. It considers quality of work life issues for the 1980s, productivity trends, changing technology, new forms of collective bargaining, public policy and QWL, and the labor market of the 1980s. This is an excellent single source for original writings of major thinkers in the literature on work: Jerome Rosow, Irving Bluestone, A. H. Raskin, and Wickham Skinner, among others.

CHAPTER FIVE

THE IMPACT OF GOVERNMENT REGULATION

Uncle Sam will pose the biggest problems for personnel chiefs in the '80s.*

So say 316 executives interviewed by Opinion Research Corporation for Human Resources Service, Inc., N.Y. Of the personnel specialists among those interviewed, 45 percent listed government regulation as having the biggest potential impact: 35 percent of the other top executives put government regulation first.

Fully 65 percent of the non-personnel executives expect personnel executives to become more heavily involved in developing corporate strategies and policies in the years ahead. And 69 percent of the personnel executives said they already serve on operating, planning, and other policy committees.[1]

General Motors Corporation settled 10-year-old government job-bias charges by agreeing to spend at least $42.5 million to hire, train, and promote more women and minorities.

The five-year agreement, resolving an Equal Employment Opportunity Commission administrative complaint brought in 1973, is the biggest such settlement ever, the agency said. Commission officials said that by closing the GM probe, they will have the time and resources to pursue a greater number of cases involving companywide patterns of employment discrimination.

The Commission also seems to be easing its reliance on back pay as a primary remedy.

A main feature of the agreement is a $15 million education package of endowments and scholarships for more than 100,000 employed and laid-off women and minorities at the auto maker. The workers' families also will be eligible. A GM spokesman said twenty-eight colleges and universities will receive endowments of $250,000 each over the five years.

"Back pay (was) an issue," agrees Edmond Dilworth, a GM assistant general counsel. "In this case we felt the money would be better spent on education and training."[2]

Government regulations pertaining to the relationship between employees and employers have grown dramatically in the past two decades, and their impact on human resource management has remained strong in spite of the politics of the White House and Congress. In short, nearly every human resource activity covered in this text is regulated by some form of federal or state legislation. For example, human resource managers must ensure that the organization's policies for selection, performance appraisal, compensation, promotion, employee health and safety, and labor relations comply with regulations of federal and state governments. Failure to comply can lead to costly settlements such as the one involving General Motors Corporation. Furthermore, all members of the organization who are involved in any of these functions—especially the managers and supervisors who implement human resource policies—are required by law to comply with government regulations. This explains the concern that top executives have expressed regarding government regulation. It also explains the increasing role that human resource executives are playing in strategic and operational planning. Top management needs to know the legal implications of organizational policies that affect employees, and this need has strengthened the partnership between human resource professionals and line managers discussed in Chapter One.

The purpose of this chapter is twofold. First, we present an overview of the legal environment in which organizations manage human resources. The government regulations presented here apply directly to the many functions of human resource management covered in this text. As each function is addressed in more detail in later chapters, the impact of the government regulations will be discussed more extensively.

Second, we stress how line managers and human resource professionals work together to ensure that all the organization's employees comply with government regulations. Efforts must be made to keep abreast of relevant regulations, and human resource policies must be established to comply. Supervisory personnel must then be informed of the policies to ensure that they do not violate any regulations in day-to-day interactions with their employees and job applicants. Finally, line managers and human resource professionals must attempt to anticipate political, social, and economic trends and strive to influence future regulations.

THE NEED FOR REGULATION

The social commentary since the Industrial Revolution in the middle 1800s has clearly shown that the relationship between employers and employees has often been viewed as less than congenial. Although Bob Cratchit in Charles Dickens's *A Christmas Carol* and the beleaguered assembly line workers in Charlie Chaplin's classic film *Modern Times* may be extreme examples, many employees have felt unappreciated, or even exploited, by their employers. The relationship between employer and employee has always had some adversarial elements as each party seeks to negotiate a fair exchange with the other. Employers attempt to purchase the services of employees at the lowest possible cost, and employees try to sell their services at the highest possible rate of exchange.

Following the Industrial Revolution, and stretching into the second quarter of the twentieth century, the employer had the upper hand, as evidenced by poor ventilation, heating, and lighting, as well as long work weeks and low wages. Let's consider the lot of persons employed in the United States in the 1920s. The average worker could be hired, promoted, laid off, or fired for whatever reason the employer chose. He (most were men) could be refused employment because of his age, color, religious beliefs, or ethnic background or for any other reason. The work place was dangerous, and measures to protect employees were taken solely at the discretion of the employer. Employees who suffered work-related injuries or illnesses had no recourse except to bring a costly and time-consuming common-law suit against their employers. Wages were less than $.25 per hour and a six-day week of ten-or-twelve-hour days was common. Company benefits such as health insurance, life insurance, and pensions were unheard of. Finally, workers could be fired for trying to organize labor unions, employers could legally block certain union activities, such as strikes, and employers could require newly hired workers not to join a union.

Major social and economic changes during the twentieth century brought about three significant waves of government regulations affecting the relationship between employers and employees. The first wave was initiated primarily by the states, which passed child labor laws and workers' compensation laws in the first two decades of the 1900s. The conservative federal government of this era, however, refrained from imposing federal regulations on business.

The Great Depression of the 1930s spawned the second wave of government regulation, as evidenced by the New Deal and extensive state and federal legislation that dealt with the rights of unions and management, wages and hours of work, and compensation for work-related injuries and illnesses.

The third wave began with the civil rights movement of the 1960s, which exposed the nation to the discrimination faced by blacks and other minorities and provided the impetus for legislation that required employers to provide equal opportunities for employment to women and minorities. In the 1970s major federal legislation followed to protect employee health and safety and to guarantee employee pensions. It was this third wave of government regulations during the 1960s and 1970s that had the most broad and dramatic effect on the relationship between employers and employees. These regulations revolutionized the practice of human resource management.

Many people view the government regulations that emerged from these three waves of legislation as a quagmire of laws, court decisions, agencies, constraints, and paperwork that exist only to confuse them and complicate their lives. This view is especially common in the field of human resource

EXHIBIT 5.1   REGULATORY MODEL

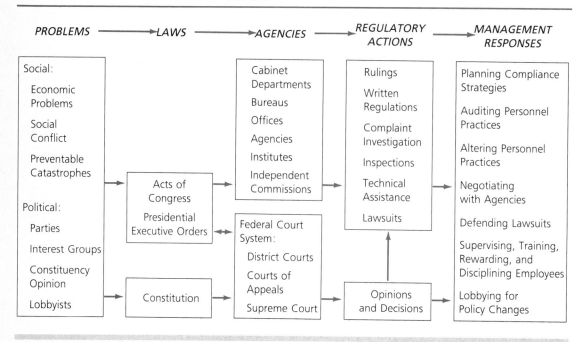

SOURCE: James Ledvinka, *Federal Regulation of Personnel and Human Resource Management* (Boston: Kent Publishing Company, 1982), p. 10. Copyright © 1982 by Wadsworth, Inc. Reprinted by permission of Kent Publishing Company, a division of Wadsworth, Inc.

management because government regulations, many of which have been produced in the past twenty years, have significantly altered policies and practices that had gone unchecked for decades.

The rationale behind government regulations is more easily understood when the components of the regulatory process are put together in a model, such as the one in Exhibit 5.1. In explaining this model, James Ledvinka states that 1) regulation begins with social and political problems, which cause lawmakers to pass laws; 2) those laws empower agencies to take the regulatory actions that trigger management responses; and 3) the courts oversee this process by settling disputes between the parties to it. Management is most naturally concerned with appropriate responses. Unfortunately, management often neglects the "problems" side (as shown in the left hand column of Exhibit 5.1); it is easy for management, in its quest for the "legal" practices, to overlook the cause-and-effect relationships of the process. Until the organization understands what leads to the regulatory action, it cannot hope to forecast directions of the agency or to speculate on what the agency might do when presented with a new situation.[3]

Ledvinka adds that employers will become aware of two fundamental principles of government regulations when they examine both the causes of the laws and their effects. First, to understand the purpose and authority of the agencies which enforce a law, one must examine the law itself. For example, a human resource professional may feel that Occupational Safety and Health Administration officials are unreasonable when they make a surprise inspection of a work site and issue a citation for employer violations but take no action against employees who are acting unsafely. But close examination of the Occupational Safety and Health Act, described later in this chapter and in Chapter Nineteen, makes it clear that the responsibility to ensure not only safe working conditions but also safe employee behavior rests primarily with the employer. Therefore, the officials' actions are consistent with the purpose of the law.

Second and more importantly, one must understand that laws are passed for specific purposes; namely, to solve social and political problems. Therefore, any ambiguity about the interpretation of a law will be resolved in favor of its original purpose. For example, the Civil Rights Act of 1964 prohibits discrimination with respect to the terms, conditions, and privileges of employment on the basis of race, color, religion, sex, or national origin. Suppose that 100 women charge that they were refused employment unfairly, and the employer claims that its recruiters did not *intentionally* turn down qualified female applicants. How might a court rule on the interpretation of an employer's intention to discriminate? Since the primary purpose of the law is to eliminate discrimination, the courts have ruled that it is the *effect* of the hiring practices, regardless of intent, that is relevant. Whether intentional or not, the employer's selection practices would therefore be judged discriminatory (see Chapter Nine).

These two principles—to understand the law itself and to understand the social and political problems the law was passed to solve—are essential if an employer is to deal effectively with government regulations. Employers must also realize that regulations are established through a political process. While regulations are passed by Congress or the President primarily to address social and economic problems, there are many special interest groups and lobbyists who have vested interests in specific regulations and strive to influence the regulatory process. Such political pressure sometimes leads to regulations with unintended effects and costs.

MAJOR GOVERNMENT REGULATIONS

Our purpose in this section is to describe major federal and state legislation under which human resource management is currently practiced in the United States. The specific regulations are listed in Exhibit 5.2, along with their major provisions and the employers they cover. The regulations fall into the following five categories:

1. Equal employment opportunity
2. Employee health and safety

EXHIBIT 5.2   MAJOR GOVERNMENT REGULATIONS

Equal Employment Opportunity

Law	Major Provisions	Employers Covered
Title VII of the Civil Rights Act of 1964, as amended in 1972	Prohibits discrimination in terms, conditions, and privileges of employment on the basis of race, color, religion, sex, or national origin.	Private employers with 15 or more employees, governments, unions, and employment agencies.
Age Discrimination in Employment Act of 1967, as amended in 1978.	Prohibits discrimination in employment for persons between the ages of 40 and 70.	Private employers with 20 or more employees, unions with 25 or more members, and employment agencies.
Pregnancy Discrimination Act of 1978	Prohibits discrimination in employment on the basis of pregnancy, childbirth, and related conditions.	Private employers with 15 or more employees, governments, unions, and employment agencies.
Executive Order Number 11246 (1965)	Prohibits discrimination in employment based on race, color, religion, sex, or national origin and requires affirmative action.	Federal contractors and subcontractors.
Vocational Rehabilitation Act of 1973; Executive Order Number 11914	Prohibits discrimination in employment based on physical or mental handicap and requires affirmative action.	Federal contractors and subcontractors and the federal government.
Vietnam Era Veterans' Readjustment Act of 1974; Executive Order Number 11701 (1973)	Prohibits discrimination against disabled veterans and Vietnam era veterans and requires affirmative action.	Federal contractors and subcontractors and the federal government.

Employee Health and Safety

Law	Major Provisions	Employers Covered
State Workers' Compensation Laws	To employees who suffer work-related injury, illness, or death, replaces lost income, pays medical expenses, and provides some rehabilitation, lump-sum disability payments, and death benefits to survivors.	All private employers in most states and public employers in some states.
Occupational Safety and Health Act of 1970	Establishes safety standards, conducts inspections of work places, allows variances from standards, and issues citations for violations.	All private and public employers.

Compensation and Benefits

Law	Major Provisions	Employers Covered
Fair Labor Standards Act of 1938, as amended	Establishes minimum hourly wage and requires payment of time and a half for work on many jobs in excess of 40 hours per week.	Employers engaged in interstate commerce and many government employees (comparable state legislation covers other private employers).
Equal Pay Act of 1963	Prohibits discrimination in pay for substantially equal work on the basis of sex.	All employers and labor organizations.
Title VII of the Civil Rights Act of 1964	Prohibits discrimination in pay for jobs of comparable worth on the basis of sex.	Private employers with 15 or more employees, governments, unions, and employment agencies.
Employment Retirement Income Security Act of 1974	Establishes standards for employee funding, participation, and vesting in pension plans to ensure that employees receive payment of benefits.	All employers with private pension programs.

Labor Relations

Law	Major Provisions	Employers Covered
National Labor Relations Act of 1935 (Wagner Act)	Establishes the National Labor Relations Board to assist workers in choosing a labor union. Prohibits management from interfering with workers' choice of a labor union.	Private employers and unions.
Taft-Hartley Act of 1947 (Labor-Management Relations Act)	Amends the Wagner Act to place government in a more neutral position of neither encouraging nor discouraging union organization.	Private employers and unions.

Employee Privacy

Law	Major Provisions	Employers Covered
Privacy Act of 1974	Gives employees the right to inspect, review, and amend their employee records and to prevent their misuse.	All federal agencies.

3. Compensation and benefits
4. Labor relations
5. Employee Privacy

Each of these five categories of regulations is discussed in the context of the regulatory model (Exhibit 5.1). The social problems that prompted the regulations are noted, along with the major provisions of the regulations and significant court decisions. Finally, the impact of the regulations is assessed.

Equal Employment Opportunity

Laws that ensure equal opportunity of employment for all persons with the right to work in the United States (U.S. citizens and resident aliens but not illegal aliens) are probably the best-known government regulations. These laws were triggered in the 1960s by major social problems, such as school segregation that resulted in poorer job skills for blacks, systematic discrimination in employment practices against minorities and women, and significant discrepancies between employment and income levels for blacks and whites. Prior to 1964, hiring practices were commonly discriminatory; it was not unusual to see age or sex specified in advertisements for employment. The civil rights movement brought these problems to the attention of all Americans, and many laws were enacted to address them.

Title VII of the Civil Rights Act of 1964 (as amended by the Equal Employment Opportunity Act of 1972) is probably the most far reaching federal law. It prohibits discrimination with respect to the terms, conditions, and privileges of employment on the basis of *race, color, religion, sex,* or *national origin.* This is the broadest of the equal employment opportunity (EEO) laws and covers such human resource functions as selection, job assignment, training, promotion, discipline, compensation, layoffs, and all other conditions of employment. Title VII applies to all employers having fifteen or more employees and essentially requires that all human resource functions be made *without* consideration of the five personal characteristics mentioned above.

Later laws added to the list of personal characteristics that cannot affect employees' terms, conditions, and privileges of employment. The *Age Discrimination in Employment Act of 1967* (amended in 1978) prohibits discrimination against applicants and employees aged forty through seventy in terms of hiring, compensation, discharge, and other major aspects of employment. Similarly, the *Pregnancy Discrimination Act of 1978* (an amendment to Title VII) prohibits discrimination in employment on the basis of pregnancy, childbirth, and related conditions.

Additional laws and executive orders require employers to take *affirmative action* in the employment and treatment of women and minorities. This involves such activities as increasing the employer's efforts to recruit black applicants, providing special training to female employees to increase their opportunities for promotion, and restructuring the work setting to accommodate a physically handicapped employee. The objective of affirmative action is to provide women and minorities with additional opportunities to achieve equal employment.

NONDISCRIMINATION UNDER FEDERAL CONTRACTS

EXHIBIT 5.3

Excerpts from Executive Order 11246 Amended by Executive Order 12086, 1978.
Subpart B—Contractors' Agreements

Sec. 202. Except in contracts exempted in accordance with Section 204 of this Order, all Government contracting agencies shall include in every Government contract hereafter entered into the following provisions:

During the performance of the contract the contractor agrees as follows:

(1) The contractor will not discriminate against any employee or applicant for employment because of race, color, religion, sex, or national origin. The contractor will take affirmative action to ensure that applicants are employed, and that employees are treated during employment, without regard to their race, color, religion, sex, or national origin. Such action shall include, but not be limited to the following: employment, upgrading, demotion, or transfer; recruitment or recruitment advertising; layoff or termination; rates of pay or other forms of compensation; and selection for training, including apprenticeship. The contractor agrees to post in conspicuous places, available to employees and applicants for employment, notices to be provided by the contracting officer setting forth the provisions of this nondiscrimination clause.

(2) The contractor will, in all solicitations or advertisements for employees placed by or on behalf of the contractor, state that all qualified applicants will receive consideration for employment without regard to race, color, religion, sex, or national origin.

Subpart D—Sanctions and Penalties

Sec. 209. (a) In accordance with such rules, regulations, or orders as the Secretary of Labor may issue or adopt, the Secretary may:

(1) Publish, or cause to be published, the names of contractors or unions which it has concluded have complied or have failed to comply with the provisions of this Order or of the rules, regulations, and orders of the Secretary of Labor.

(2) Recommend to the Department of Justice that, in cases in which there is substantial or material violation or the threat of substantial or material violation of the contractual provisions set forth in Section 202 of this Order, appropriate proceedings be brought to enforce those provisions, including the enjoining, within the limitations of applicable law, of organizations, individuals, or groups who prevent directly or indirectly, or seek to prevent directly or indirectly, compliance with the provisions of this Order.

(5) After consulting with the contracting agency, direct the contracting agency to cancel, terminate, suspend, or cause to be cancelled, terminated, or suspended, any contract, or any portion or portions thereof, for failure of the contractor or subcontractor to comply with the equal employment opportunity provisions of the contract. Contracts may be cancelled, terminated, or suspended absolutely or continuance of contracts may be conditioned upon a program for future compliance approved by the Secretary of Labor.

Executive order number 11246 (1965) applies to all employers with government contracts or subcontracts of $10,000 or more. It not only prohibits discrimination in employment practices on the basis of race, color, religion, sex, and national origin but also requires employers to take affirmative action in employment for groups that have traditionally been discriminated against. As Section 209 in Exhibit 5.3 shows, the penalties for noncompliance are severe and include cancellation, termination, or suspension of the contract.

The Vocational Rehabilitation Act of 1973 prohibits the same employers from discriminating against physically and mentally handicapped persons and requires employers to take affirmative action in their behalf. The *Vietnam Era Veterans' Readjustment Assistance Act of 1974* prohibits government contractors and subcontractors from discriminating against veterans of the Vietnam era and all disabled veterans and requires affirmative action.

Various federal laws and executive orders (see Exhibit 5.2) prohibit discrimination and require affirmative action with regard to public sector employment practices for all the groups mentioned above and add *political affiliation* and *marital status* as conditions on the basis of which discrimination is prohibited.

There is little doubt that this legislation was needed. Many organizations, and a much greater number of line managers and supervisors, had a history of systematic discrimination against women and minorities. Because many discriminatory practices were subtle or even unintentional, they were continued in spite of new government regulations. This led to many charges of discrimination that were settled in federal court.

As is common with new laws, their scope and impact are not clearly established until lawsuits force their interpretation in court. Two major court cases have set precedents which have significantly influenced employers' attempts to conform with EEO legislation. The first case was *Griggs v. Duke Power Company.*[4] Duke Power Company, an electric utility, required that applicants have a high school diploma and pass two aptitude tests to be hired for higher paying jobs. Black applicants who could not meet these requirements filed charges of racial discrimination. The Supreme Court ruled against Duke Power Company on the grounds that the employment requirements favored white applicants, who were more likely than blacks to have a high school diploma and enough education to pass the employment tests. The Court maintained that employment requirements on which whites perform better than blacks are not necessarily illegal, but *they must be shown to be related to job performance.* The need to demonstrate the relationship between an employment requirement and job performance is critical in the selection process and is addressed in Chapter Nine of this text.

Another court case clearly established the principle that *employers need to avoid basing human resource decisions on highly subjective grounds.* In the case of *Rowe v. General Motors Corporation,* the Court of Appeals for the Fifth District ruled that blacks had been unfairly denied promotions and transfers because the performance appraisal system on which the promotions and transfers were based was subjective and vague.[5] Performance appraisals were made primarily in terms of personal characteristics (see the section on trait-rating scales in Chapter Fifteen) rather than job performance.

Such court cases have made employers acutely aware of human resource policies and practices that discriminate against women and minorities and have sent a clear message that major changes were necessary to ensure compliance with EEO regulations. As a result, employers have substantially revamped their human resource policies and practices. Selection procedures have been revised to minimize the impact of applicants' personal characteristics on the employment decision. For example, application forms no longer include questions about sex, marital status, age, etc. In addition, sophisticated validation procedures (see Chapter Nine) are followed in many organizations to ensure that employment tests predict job performance and do not discriminate against women and minorities.

There are also many examples of affirmative action, such as special attempts to attract minorities and women to vocations traditionally dominated by white males (see Chapter Eight for examples of progressive recruiting practices). As a result, the number of women and minorities in disciplines like business and engineering has grown. Increased recruiting efforts at black high schools and colleges as well as special company training programs for minorities and women can also be found.

It is important to recognize that these changes in human resource policies and practices to comply with EEO and affirmative action legislation are entirely consistent with sound human resource management. If human resource management is viewed as the process of seeking an optimal degree of fit between people, jobs, organizations, and the environment, then it is in the best interests of every employer to consider *all* available people in its quest for the optimal fit and to base human resource decisions on each person's *potential to perform the job*. Personal characteristics covered by EEO legislation are unrelated to an individual's potential to perform the vast majority of jobs. There are some jobs for which personal characteristics such as sex, religion, and physical health are allowed by EEO legislation as bona fide occupational qualifications. For example, sex and religion are relevant and legal qualifications for the job of Catholic priest, and a deaf person cannot perform effectively as a music teacher. But for almost all jobs, personal characteristics covered by EEO legislation are irrelevant to any human resource decisions.

Although many organizations have changed human resource policies and practices to comply with EEO and affirmative action regulations, a crucial question remains. Is there evidence of less discrimination in employment against women and minorities? Isolated instances of change can be noticed through casual observation. For example, the job of airline stewardess, almost always occupied by women in the 1950s and 1960s, has given way to the job of flight attendant, occupied today by both men and women. Women and minorities can be found today in many other jobs that were traditionally reserved for white males. But a comprehensive examination of changes in the economic and employment conditions since EEO legislation was initiated reveals a discouraging picture.[6] In terms of unemployment, occupational mobility, earnings, and prospects for economic advancement, the differences between men and women and between non-minorities and minorities have actually *increased*. Of course, the difference might have been even greater without government regulations, but the fact remains that EEO legislation has not yet produced equality in employment and economic status.

It must be noted that equal opportunity does not automatically produce equal *results*. Change of this magnitude takes a great deal of time. Although discrimination in employment very likely still exists, changes in human re-source policies and practices have made equal opportunity for employment standard operating procedure in most organizations. In addition, large orga-nizations have added specialists in EEO and affirmative action to ensure that federal and local laws are followed throughout the organization. These spe-cialists have done much to educate and guide managers and supervisors who must avoid discriminatory practices as they carry out human resource policies. The specialists also handle employee complaints and serve as the employee's advocate to resolve charges of discrimination within the organization. In short, the changes that are necessary for equal opportunity in employment have been made in many organizations. With time, these changes can be expected to narrow the gaps in employment and economic status between men and women, and between non-minorities and minorities.

Employee Health and Safety

Employees have always been under some degree of risk in the work setting, and the complex machinery and large factories of the Industrial Revolution greatly increased that risk. It was not until 1948, however, that employees in every state had any significant recourse if they suffered a work-related illness or injury.[7] Prior to the enactment of two major groups of government regu-lation, the ill or injured employee's only course was to sue the employer under common law, which strongly favored the employer.

Furthermore, federal legislation that required employers to regulate the work setting to *prevent* work-related illness and injury did not exist until 1970. Until then, employers could voluntarily minimize hazards in the work setting and protect employees from illness and injury and although some em-ployers did so, there was no legal means to compel such action. As a result, many employees had little choice except to work in hazardous conditions.

To eliminate the inefficiency and inequity of common law suits, all states have passed *Workers' Compensation Laws*, which establish a no-fault insur-ance program to compensate employees who sustain job-related illnesses or injuries. These laws vary from state to state, but they all grant basic remedies to the ill or injured employees, whether the employee or the employer was at fault. Employers' contributions to the insurance program are based on their claim rate, so there is some incentive to maintain safe working conditions. But the primary purpose of these laws is not to regulate the working condi-tions of employers. It is to provide compensation to employees in the form of replacement for lost income, payment for medical expenses, and rehabilita-tion, as well as payment for disability or even death.

Through the *Occupational Safety and Health Act of 1970*, the federal government attempted to place a much greater emphasis on *preventing* work-related illnesses and injuries. This highly controversial law dramatically and abruptly changed the employee health and safety practices of all employers in the United States. The Occupational Safety and Health Administration (OSHA), created as an agency of the U.S. Department of Labor, imposed new regulations on all employers. It established numerous safety standards to be met by employers, and in some cases allowed temporary variances from the standards to allow time for compliance. OSHA officials conduct inspections of work places to ensure compliance and issue citations for violations.

The impact of this legislation has been mixed. Workers' compensation laws exist in all states and certainly provide far better compensation to the ill or injured worker than was available through common law settlements. But state workers' compensation laws vary widely, and the benefits range from satisfactory to inadequate. The Occupational Safety and Health Act was exceedingly controversial in 1970 and is no less so today (see Chapter Nineteen). Employers claim that many OSHA standards are arbitrary, unattainable, or too expensive. Nevertheless, employers have altered human resource policies and practices to comply, and many required safety standards and practices presented in Chapter Nineteen have become commonplace. There is still major disagreement, however, on whether this legislation has actually been instrumental in *preventing* work-related illness and injury. Its impact on accident rates is inconclusive, and some studies question whether small reductions in worker injuries are worth the millions of dollars spent to comply with OSHA standards.[8]

Compensation and Benefits

As we mentioned earlier, employees were generally at the mercy of their employers early in the twentieth century. This was particularly true with regard to wages and benefits before workers won the right to organize labor unions and bargain collectively with employers. Before the 1930s, employers could demand long work days and pay low wages, and a worker's only option was to quit and find a more generous employer. The Great Depression, which underscored the economic vulnerability of working people, led to the first major federal legislation regulating compensation and benefits.

The *Fair Labor Standards Act* was originally passed in 1938 and has been amended several times. This federal law established the *minimum wage* (which has grown from $.25 per hour in 1938 to $3.35 today) that employers are required to pay all employees covered by the act. It also required payment of 1.5 times the regular wage for work in excess of forty hours per week. Most employees are currently covered by this law or by comparable state laws. As Section 13 in Exhibit 5.4 shows, exceptions are granted for *exempt* employees, generally salaried employees involved in predominantly "executive, administrative, or professional" work. Employers' compensation policies must differentiate between employees who are exempt or non-exempt from the provisions of The Fair Labor Standards Act. For example, employers are not required to pay exempt employees for overtime.

As we have already noted, the civil rights movement led to extensive legislation to provide equal opportunity for employment to women and minorities. This period also produced comparable regulations regarding wages. The *Equal Pay Act of 1963*, an amendment to the Fair Labor Standards Act,

EXHIBIT 5.4

EXCERPTS FROM FAIR LABOR STANDARDS ACT OF 1938, AS AMENDED

Minimum Wages

Sec. 6. (a) Every employer shall pay to each of his employees who in any workweek is engaged in commerce or in the production of goods for commerce, *or is employed in an enterprise engaged in commerce or in the production of goods for commerce, wages at the following rates:*

(1) not less than $2.65 an hour during the year beginning January 1, 1978, not less than $2.90 an hour during the year beginning January 1, 1979, not less than $3.10 an hour during the year beginning January 1, 1980, and not less than $3.35 an hour after December 31, 1980, except as otherwise provided in this section; . . .

Investigations, Inspections, Records, and Home-Work Regulations

Sec. 11. (a) The Secretary of Labor or his designated representatives may investigate and gather data regarding the wages, hours, and other conditions and practices of employment in any industry subject to this Act, and may enter and inspect such places and such records (and make such transcriptions thereof), question such employees, and investigate such facts, conditions, practices, or matters as he may deem necessary or appropriate to determine whether any person has violated any provision of this Act, or which may aid in the enforcement of the provisions of this Act. Except as provided in section 12 and in subsection (b) of this section, the Secretary shall utilize the bureaus and divisions of the Department of Labor for all the investigations and inspections necessary under this section. Except as provided in section 12, the Secretary shall bring all actions under section 17 to restrain violations of this act. . . .

Exemptions

Sec. 13. (a) The provisions of section 6 (except section 6(d) in the case of paragraph (1) of this subsection) and 7 shall not apply with respect to—

(1) any employee employed in a bona fide executive, administrative, or professional capacity (including any employee employed in the capacity of academic administrative personnel or teacher in elementary or secondary schools), or in the capacity of outside salesman (as such terms are defined and delimited from time to time by regulations of the Secretary, subject to the provisions of the Administrative Procedure Act, except that an employee of a retail or service establishment shall not be excluded from the definition of employee employed in a bona fide executive or administrative capacity because of the number of hours in his workweek which he devotes to activities not directly or closely related to the performance of executive or administrative activities, if less than 40 per centum of his hours worked in the workweek are devoted to such activities). . . .

prohibits sex discrimination in the wages paid to employees doing equal work, defined in Exhibit 5.5 as requiring "equal skill, effort, and responsibility, and . . . performed under similar working conditions . . . ." This legislation was intended to eliminate the traditional practice of paying men more than women in the same job because the man was the family "bread-winner." Practices such as establishing different pay scales for men and women or giving different titles to the same job held by men and women were also the target of these regulations. The act allows pay differences based on seniority, merit,

EXHIBIT 5.5

EXCERPTS FROM THE EQUAL PAY ACT OF 1963

Sec. 3. (d) (1) No employer having employees subject to any provisions of this section shall discriminate within any establishment in which such employees are employed, between employees on the basis of sex by paying wages to employees in such establishment at a rate less than the rate at which he pays wages to employees of the opposite sex in such establishment for equal work on jobs the performance of which requires equal skill, effort, and responsibility, and which are performed under similar working conditions, except where such payment is made pursuant to (i) a seniority system; (ii) a merit system; (iii) a system which measures earnings by quantity or quality of production; or (iv) a differential based on any other factor other than sex: *Provided,* That an employer who is paying a wage rate differential in violation of this subsection shall not, in order to comply with the provisions of this subsection, reduce the wage rate of any employee.

(2) No labor organization, or its agents, representing employees of an employer having employees subject to any provision of this section shall cause or attempt to cause such an employer to discriminate against an employee in violation of paragraph (1) of this subsection.

(3) For purposes of administration and enforcement, any amounts owing to any employee which have been withheld in violation of this subsection shall be deemed to be unpaid minimum wages or unpaid overtime compensation under this Act.

(4) As used in this subsection, the term "labor organization" means any organization of any kind, or any agency or employee representation committee or plan, in which employees participate and which exists for the purpose, in whole or in part, of dealing with employers concerning grievances, labor disputes, wages, rates of pay, hours of employment, or conditions of work.

---

or quality and quantity of production. It also permits differences in pay for jobs that require different levels of skill, effort, and responsibility. But it prohibits pay differences between men and women that cannot be attributed to these specific factors.

Sex discrimination in compensation is relatively difficult to prove under the Equal Pay Act of 1963 because it applies only in the case of male and female employees doing *equal work* in the same organization. *Title VII of the Civil Rights Act of 1964* is far less restrictive, however. It can be interpreted as prohibiting sex discrimination in pay for jobs of *comparable worth.* This highly controversial concept (see Chapter Eighteen) stems from the argument that employees in traditionally female-dominated jobs should receive the same pay as employees in traditionally male-dominated jobs that involve similar degrees of skill, effort, and responsibility. In short, Title VII prohibits differences in pay for men and women doing different jobs that are of comparable worth to an employer. For example, if two jobs in the same organization—clerk typist, held primarily by women, and engineering clerk, held primarily by men—are judged to be of comparable value, they must be assigned the same salary. In 1983 a federal judge found intentional discrimination in Washington State's pay practices because employees in female-dominated jobs were paid less than employees in comparable male-dominated jobs and awarded $140 million to 15,000 state employees (see Chapter Eighteen). As Box 5.1 illustrates, the issue of comparable worth is very complex and highly controversial and may pit the law of supply and demand in the labor market against the federal courts.

The *Employee Retirement Income Security Act* (ERISA) of 1974 is one of the most influential pieces of federal legislation ever passed in the area of compensation and benefits. It regulates retirement or pension plans established by an employer that provide income to employees upon retirement. This legislation was prompted by many problems in the private pension funds that resulted in the loss of benefits to employees.[9] Prior to this legislation, for example, employees could lose their pensions because they moved from one employer to another, or because they violated complicated vesting rules that determine the eligibility of employees to receive pension benefits. ERISA established standards for the funding and financial management of private pensions to ensure their financial security. It also established standards for employee eligibility and participation in pension plans and required that employers clearly and regularly inform employees about the pension program and their status in the program.

Many provisions of these regulations have become standard human resource policy in today's organizations. Certainly most readers who have worked part-time or full-time are familiar with the minimum wage and "time-and-a-half" for overtime, and exempt employees are well aware that they usually receive the same salary, regardless of how many hours they work. Similarly, the requirements of ERISA are routinely met by employers who offer pension plans to employees.

The impact of the Equal Pay Act and the Civil Rights Act has not been so clear, however, As is discussed in Chapter Eighteen, it is very difficult to demonstrate that two jobs are of comparable or equal value. In addition, many jobs continue to be filled by mostly men or mostly women, and most women today are still in traditionally low-paying jobs. In spite of hundreds of equal pay suits, many of which have resulted in increased pay for women, Bureau of Labor Statistics figures show that the average American woman working full-time earned about two-thirds of the pay of the average working man in 1983.

Labor Relations

When the trade union movement was in an embryonic stage in the United States in the early 1900s, the federal government assumed a neutral position. The spirit of free enterprise was strong during this period, and the government adopted a stance of noninterference with the rights of employers. This was definitely a time when the employer had the upper hand in the employer-employee relationship, and various management tactics to discourage unionism, such as firing union organizers and legally blocking union activities, were commonplace.

THE CONTROVERSY OVER COMPARABLE WORTH

BOX 5.1

Every so often, an idea pops up with superficial appeal that ultimately collapses of its own weight. I think this fate awaits "comparable worth," the notion that different jobs can be rated equal and paid equally; in practice, it's intended to raise women's wages and offset alleged sex discrimination. The Civil Rights Commission voted 5–2 against comparable worth last week. I think the vote's correct because, if widely adopted, comparable worth would raise prices, hurt low-skilled workers, and ultimately harm the economy.

Comparable worth assumes that, within the same firm, objective evaluations could rate quite different jobs equivalent for purposes of pay. While such a world of assured objectivity sounds nice, I think most of us also sense that it's unattainable and probably undesirable.

In a complex economy, "fairness" is a fictional ideal. Your pay reflects luck, skill, the supply and demand for different jobs, whether or not you work for a profitable firm or in a profitable industry, or whether you belong to a union. Fairness has little to do with it.

Our existing pay system is decentralized and diverse. Most companies pay what they must. Many large companies use job evaluation systems, but most use them differently and adjust—up or down—internal job and pay rankings to take into account what similar jobs pay elsewhere. This patchwork pay system may not be fair, but it produces jobs because it is flexible and can adjust to changing circumstances. Comparable worth threatens this flexibility and diversity; wage-setting would become more rigid and prone to lawsuits.

I am not saying that comparisons between male- and female-dominated jobs are illegitimate. Women working full-time in 1983 earned only 64 percent of what men did. But employers will have to deal with this difference through normal human resource policies or labor negotiations, not through comparable worth. Half or more of the gap can be explained statistically. Women have less work experience, less seniority, a lower rate of unionization, etc. . . .

It's hard to argue discrimination when women have made huge gains in occupations once dominated by men. Between 1972 and 1981 woman accountants rose from 22 to 38 percent of the total; women economists from 12 to 25 percent; and women bartenders from 28 to 48 percent.

Our job markets meet people's full needs, not just their work needs. In some jobs, the clustering of women may depress wages, which is unfair. Other women interrupt their careers to care for children. Life is full of choices, not all of them fair. I don't deny discrimination and sex stereotyping exist, but I doubt they have a huge effect on wages. As sociologist Brigitte Berger of Wellesley College writes: "Both career pattern differences as well as income differences can be explained—and to my mind convincingly—in terms of women's . . . overall life plans."

Raising women's wages will not raise the economy's output. It will simply push up prices and make the cost of labor higher for employers. . . .

This laissez-faire stance on the part of government proved rather ineffective for all concerned, however. Tension and mistrust grew between union and management, and strikes and violence interfered significantly with free enterprise. Hence, the federal government took steps to regulate the interaction between management and organized labor via the *National Labor Relations Act* of 1935. This major piece of legislation explicitly encouraged the growth of trade unions and the process of collective bargaining. It established the National Labor Relations Board to assist groups of workers who wished to form a labor union by setting up election procedures. In addition, the board investigated complaints of unfair labor practices by management. This law also prohibited management from engaging in a number of activities that would interfere with the formation of unions. These regulations were clearly pro-labor, and union membership increased dramatically during the next decade.[10]

The *Taft-Hartley Act* was passed in 1947 as an amendment to the National Labor Relations Act to eliminate this strong pro-labor bias. This legislation placed the federal government in the role of impartial referee of labor-management relations. It neither encouraged nor discouraged union organization, but stated that employees have the right either to organize into labor unions or to refrain from doing so. The role of the National Labor Relations Board became one of ensuring that the collective bargaining process proceeded fairly, and the board continues to function that way today.

Although decisions and interpretations by the National Labor Relations Board have varied over the years, no labor legislation in the past three decades has had significant impact on the process of human resource management. The collective bargaining procedures that resulted from the Taft-Hartley Act are still commonly practiced in today's organizations.

Employee Privacy

As the practice of human resource management has become more sophisticated, employers have collected more information about job applicants and employees as a basis for specific human resource decisions. For example, in a routine selection process, applicants supply data about their education and previous employers, take tests measuring intelligence and personality characteristics, and may be subjected to credit checks or lie detector tests. New employees provide detailed medical information as they complete routine paperwork relating to employee benefits. After they have been on the job for several months, their supervisors' assessments of their level of job performance and comments about their strengths and weaknesses also become part of the employee records. Since some of this information can be quite personal, applicants and employees, as well as human resource professionals, have raised concerns about how the information is to be used, who will have access to it, and how long it will be stored. Will such information be made available to an employee's co-workers, boss, human resource professionals in the employee's organization, or even other potential employers? Such questions are answered by the organization's policies and procedures governing the storage and management of employee records.

Unlike the other major topics included in this chapter, concern for employee privacy has resulted in relatively little regulation by the federal government. The only federal law that relates directly to employee privacy is the *Privacy Act of 1974,* which gives federal employees the right to inspect, review, and amend their employee records and ensure that they are not misused. Some states have passed legislation to regulate the use of employee records by private-sector employers. In general, state laws give employees access to their human resource records to ensure that the information is correct and is not misused.

Much of the initiative to manage employee records, however, has been taken voluntarily by individual employers. For example, IBM's guidelines to prevent the collection of unnecessary personal information and to protect the privacy of human resource records have gone far beyond legal requirements.[11] Recent surveys have indicated growing concern by employers about employee privacy, and as a result, policies to ensure the privacy of employee records are becoming common in today's organizations.[12] Exhibit 5.6 shows a typical example of a policy on employee privacy. But employees don't seem very interested in seeing their own private files. According to American Motors Corporation, fewer than fifty of 26,000 employees ask to see their files annually, and other companies also report little interest.[13]

State and federal privacy legislation, along with voluntary initiatives in the private sector, has opened up an employee's human resource and medical records to that employee, while closing them to others. This trend toward the more stringent management of employee records is particularly important today in view of the increasing use of computerized human resource information systems to store employee records. Since computerized records are potentially more accessible than bulky files locked in cabinets, the need to control access has increased.

EMPLOYER RESPONSES TO A REGULATED ENVIRONMENT

The vast majority of regulations, while sometimes confusing and burdensome, are beneficial to both employees and employers. It is therefore the responsibility of human resource professionals and line managers to ensure that their organization complies with all relevant legislation. Both line and staff must work together to ensure compliance. Human resource professionals design policies and procedures that conform to regulations, but it is the line manager who implements the policies and procedures. To the government agency, the line manager *is* the organization, and if he or she violates a regulation, the organization is liable.

EXHIBIT 5.6 **COMPANY POLICY ON PERSONNEL AND MEDICAL FILES**

Purpose

Inasmuch as the personnel files contain private and confidential information, the company restricts access to these files and to other confidential information about employees. The following procedure specifies who has access to personnel and medical files. It also indicates how Human Resources handles inquiries for information regarding present or past employment, department transfers, and from employees requesting information from their files.

Scope

This policy is applicable to all employees.

Procedure

Personnel files:

1. Access to personnel files is restricted to authorized employees of Human Resources; a respective employee's supervisor, manager, division director; and officers of the company.

2. All inquiries received by personnel from other departments, including requests for references regarding past employment, should be directed to the employee relations managers.

    a. Telephone inquiries

    Human Resources *will* verify the following information:
    date of hire or date of termination;
    Social Security numbers;
    job title.

    Human Resources *will not* verify the following information:
    telephone numbers;
    addresses;
    rates of pay;
    job performance;
    reason for termination.

    b. Written inquiries

    If the employee has signed a release of information, Human Resources will verify the following information:
    date of hire or date of termination;
    Social Security number;
    telephone number;
    address;
    rate of pay;
    job title.

    A written request without the employee's authorization to release information will be handled like a telephone inquiry.

Medical files:

1. Access to the medical files is restricted to the medical services coordinator, human resource managers, and officers of the company.

2. Medical information can be released only upon written authorization of the employee, by the medical services coordinator, to persons or agencies who have legitimate claims to the information.

3. In the event of an emergency situation, any information to be released will be handled with discretion by the medical services coordinator or by the human resource manager.

Employee's accessibility to files:
1. With reasonable notice, an employee may review his/her own personnel file in Human Resources, with a human resource manager present.

Proactive Response

As the regulatory model of Exhibit 5.1 shows, laws governing the relationship between employees and employers are enacted to address specific problems. Each major category of government regulation arose in response to social and economic problems and conditions. It is therefore possible for organizations to continually scan the social, political, and economic environment and anticipate likely regulatory changes.

This *proactive* response to a regulated environment has many advantages. First, it gives organizations longer lead time to implement human resource policies and practices before they are forced to do so by law. Indeed, if enough organizations identify a social or economic problem and design human resource policies to alleviate it, they may eliminate the need for a new regulation. Second, voluntary innovations made by individual organizations or industries can be tailored to specific needs and therefore are more likely to be effective than broad government policies designed to apply to all employers. Third, organizations that voluntarily adopt advanced human resource policies and practices are likely to be viewed as progressive by their employees and potential employees and may enjoy greater success in attracting and retaining high-quality employees. Fourth, internally developed human resource policies are more likely to be accepted and implemented by line managers than are government-imposed policies.

Environmental Scanning ▬ Both the human resource professionals and line managers can systematically monitor the *external* environment to keep abreast of changes in the labor market from which their organization draws employees and adjust human resource policies accordingly (see Tenneco, Inc.'s approach in Chapter Seven). For example, if they detect an increase of two-income couples in the labor market, they may add child care facilities as an employee benefit. Similarly, *internal* scanning of the organization's current employees is also useful in identifying potential problems. Data can be drawn from human resource information systems (see Chapter Two) to analyze trends in the organization's work force. For example, if systematic observation by line managers or the human resource department's analysis of employee records indicates that minorities and women are being promoted from entry-level jobs more slowly than white males, special training and career counseling programs may be initiated to correct the discrepancy. In short, environmental scanning enables the organization to identify potential problems and solve them internally.

Lobbying ▬▬ Another common proactive response to regulations is for members of an organization or various industry and professional groups to encourage legislators to endorse or oppose specific government regulations. Lobbying may also be done by senior managers or members of the organization's corporate affairs or human resource departments (see Chapter Twenty). In 1983, for example, the federal law that made employer-provided education assistance a non-taxable employee benefit was allowed to expire in Congress, and employers were required to deduct social security and income taxes from tuition reimbursements of employees who attended school to upgrade their skills and knowledge to move up the job ladder. A massive lobbying effort by labor, management, professional, and educational groups contributed to Congressional action in 1984 to restore the tax exclusion.

Consent Decree ▬▬ Finally, if an employer is under investigation by a government agency for alleged violation of a regulation, it can agree to take appropriate action to address the violation through a consent decree. A **consent decree** is *an agreement by the defendant to cease the activities asserted as illegal by the government; in return, the government's action against the defendant is dropped.* By entering into the consent decree, the organization avoids the legal fees, time, and administrative costs of going to court. Consent decree is an effective response if senior management feels that solving the alleged problem is in the best interests of the organization and its employees. In 1973, for example, AT&T was being investigated for alleged discrimination against women because only 22.4 percent of its managers were female. Under a consent decree with the Department of Labor and the Equal Employment Opportunity Commission, AT&T initiated extensive programs of management development and career development and by 1979, when the consent decree had expired, 28.5 percent of management jobs were held by women.[14]

Many organizations respond proactively to today's regulatory environment by identifying the needs of their employees and society and designing

consent decree

EMPLOYER RESPONSES TO GOVERNMENT REGULATIONS

EXHIBIT 5.7

or revising human resource policies and practices accordingly. Throughout this book, human resource policies are cited that were initiated voluntarily by organizations, rather than mandated by government regulations.

Reactive Response

And yet, even the most progressive organizations will not detect all of their own regulatory violations or anticipate the need for all new government regulations. It then becomes the responsibility of line managers and human resource professionals to develop and implement policies and practices that conform to relevant legislation to protect the legal position and reputation of their organization. The result is a two-pronged reaction to the regulatory environment. Senior executives can take a strong, visible position in favor of compliance with regulations and motivate line managers throughout the organization to view regulations positively and follow them closely. Human resource professionals can monitor all relevant regulations, review existing policies and practices, and encourage line managers to comply. The way senior management and human resource professionals seek to ensure compliance with government regulations is crucial. They must strive to ensure compliance without being seen as policing agents for the government and alienating members of the organization. As we noted in Chapter One, it is possible for human resource professionals to gain a reputation for interfering with the work of line managers when they seek to ensure their organization's compliance with government regulations.

Staying Informed of Regulations ▬▬ There are five major steps that can be taken by organizations as they respond to government regulation (see Exhibit 5.7). The first is to become informed of the specific legislation that applies to a given organization. The responsibility to keep abreast of new regulations or changes in existing regulations that affect human resource management can be assumed by company employees directly involved in the human resource functions of the organization. Line managers can keep informed by reading business and government publications on regulations and discussing their impact with colleagues in other organizations. But the responsibility for monitoring regulatory changes rests primarily with human resource professionals. For example, in large organizations the specialists in the various human resource functions, such as labor relations, safety, and EEO, would maintain up-to-date information on government regulations. In smaller organizations, the director of human resources or perhaps the organization's legal counsel would assume this responsibility.

Human resource managers must also remain informed of major strategic changes in their organizations so they can advise top management on the legal implications for human resource practices. For example, a company that plans to enter a new area of manufacturing would need advice on OSHA regulations for a new factory. Similarly, a company planning to pursue contract work with the federal government should be informed that legislation requiring affirmative action would apply to its human resource policies as soon as the first contract was landed.

Reviewing Current Human Resource Policies and Practices

The next step involves a thorough review of the organization's current human resource policies and practices to determine the impact of new or amended regulations on them. All written documents—policy statements, procedures, and forms—will require scrutiny to assess their relevance to the government regulations. This review is usually spearheaded by human resource professionals. The passage of some laws, such as the Employee Retirement Income Security Act of 1974, rendered all existing policies unacceptable. In other cases, such as the passage of EEO legislation, application forms required revision to delete requests for information that could no longer be collected as part of the selection process.

In addition, actual human resource practices that presumably follow written policies and procedures need review. It is entirely possible for some managers to continue favoring male applicants even after "sex" has been removed from an organization's application form. It is also possible for employees to ignore clearly written and posted safety procedures. Line managers must take a major role in monitoring and reviewing their practices and those of their employees to ensure that no government regulations are violated. In particular, senior managers can make it clear that the organization views government regulations positively and can encourage their employees to do the same. In addition, human resource professionals can—through observation and record keeping—also review how human resource policies and procedures affected by legislation are actually implemented. For example, if records show that no female applicants have been hired in a specific department for an entire year, they could investigate for possible discriminatory selection practices.

Changing Policies and Practices to Comply ▬ The third step is for the organization to make the necessary changes to comply with government regulations or to go to court to challenge the interpretation or application of the regulations. Written policies and procedures may be revised or completely replaced. For example, compliance with amendments to the Fair Labor Standards Act to increase the minimum wage involves a simple raise in pay to the appropriate employees of an organization. Other regulations, however, require far more major changes for compliance. OSHA called for major revisions in health and safety standards that cost some companies years of effort and millions of dollars to comply and forced others out of business. Usually, human resource professionals in consultation with senior management assume the responsibility of initiating changes in policies and procedures to ensure compliance with regulations.

Educating and Training Employees ▬ Ultimately, federal and state regulations govern *behavior* and the *results* of that behavior. It is therefore essential for line managers and human resource professionals to educate employees about how the regulations affect their job performance and train them to alter their performance accordingly. Issuing a new policy that promotion is to be based only on job performance will not ensure that veteran supervisors will end their practice of denying promotions to blacks and women. Attempts to coerce compliance with regulations are likely to be ineffective. A more effective approach is for line managers to explain the regulation and help employees change through one-on-one coaching, or for human resource professionals to launch orientation and training programs and help employees to comply. For example, training is helpful in teaching managers how to conduct selection interviews that do not discriminate against minorities or women or in teaching employees how to follow safety procedures (Chapter Nineteen).

Documenting Compliance ▬ The final step is to document compliance with government regulations through data collection and testing. Virtually all of the regulations covered in this chapter require that routine reports be submitted to the appropriate agency to demonstrate compliance, and human resource professionals must collect or generate appropriate data. For example, evidence of compliance with EEO legislation is based on records of the race, color, religion, sex, and national origin of applicants and the percentages of protected groups that were hired. More elaborate validation procedures, described in Chapter Nine, are also used to demonstrate that selection procedures do not discriminate against protected groups. While this record keeping and documentation can be burdensome, they are essential to demonstrate compliance and avoid penalties.

In summary, human resource professionals and line managers work together to ensure that their organizations comply with government regulations. First, they need to keep abreast of new or amended regulations that apply to their organization as well as strategic changes that make their organization liable under existing regulations. Second, they must review existing human resource policies and practices and make appropriate changes as directed by the legislation. Finally, they must monitor the changes to ensure compliance. Although these responsibilities may not be among their favorite duties, they are an essential part of the process of human resource management in today's organization.

The Future of Government Regulation

As we explained earlier, major legislation of the 1960s and 1970s has revolutionized the process of human resource management. But what does the future hold? Is another revolution just around the corner? We think not. Nearly all of the regulations of the past two decades have become standard operating procedure in today's organizations, and federal and state agencies and courts continue to monitor human resource practices. The regulations have moved our society much closer to the goals of equal employment opportunity, safe working conditions, secure pensions, and fair labor-management relations.

Remember that regulations emerge through a political process, and there is little evidence in the social and political environment of another wave of major government regulations in the next five to ten years. Instead, a trend toward voluntary innovations tailored to the needs of specific organizations and their employees seems to be emerging. Examples of such innovations are programs for employees with alcohol- or drug-related problems, flexible working hours and benefit packages, fitness centers, and progressive approaches to career development. If human resource professionals and line managers continue to ensure that their organizations comply with existing government regulations and also play a central role in the development of voluntary innovations, we expect less impetus for new government regulations.

KEY POINTS

- Throughout the twentieth century, federal and state laws have been enacted to solve social and political problems by regulating the relationship between employers and employees.

- The dramatic growth of government regulations during the 1960s and 1970s has revolutionized the process of human resource management and has strengthened the role of human resource managers in today's organizations.

- Organizations need to continually scan the social and political environment to anticipate future likely regulatory changes, thus permitting longer lead-time and more careful planning to respond effectively.

▬ Line managers and human resource professionals can promote compliance with government regulations by reviewing and revising organizational policies and providing orientation and training to employees who implement and follow human resource policies.

▬ No major wave of new regulations is expected in the next decade, but a trend toward voluntary innovations tailored to the needs of specific organizations appears to be emerging.

ISSUES FOR DISCUSSION

1. List some of the major social and political problems that produced the major government regulations described in this chapter. Do you think these problems could have been addressed effectively in any other way? If yes, how?

2. Your company has secured its first major contract with the federal government and is therefore required to take affirmative action in its employment practices. As the human resource professional, how would you implement a policy of affirmative action throughout the company?

3. Compare the proactive and reactive responses to a regulatory environment. How can organizations become more proactive and strive to decrease the need for government regulations?

4. Consider some of today's major social problems and speculate on the kind of government regulations that might be proposed to address them. What voluntary actions might be taken by organizations to address the same problems?

5. What are the two fundamental principles of government regulations mentioned by Ledvinka? How can human resource professionals use these two principles to encourage line managers to comply with government regulations?

6. What are the five major steps in responding to government regulations? How can human resource professionals approach these steps to minimize employee resistance to regulations?

NOTES

1. Robert W. Merry, "Labor Letter," *Wall Street Journal*, February 12, 1980, p. 1.

2. J. S. Lublin, "GM to Spend $42.5 Million to Hire, Train Women and Minorities, Settling Bias Case," *Wall Street Journal*, October 19, 1983, p. 8.

3. J. Ledvinka, *Federal Regulation of Personnel and Human Resource Management* (Belmont, CA: Wadsworth, 1982), p. 11.

4. *Griggs v. Duke Power Company*, 401 U.S. 424, 1971.

5. G. L. Lubben, D. E. Thompson, and C. R. Klasson, "Performance Appraisal: The Legal Implications of Title VII," *Personnel*, 1980, 57, pp. 11–21.

6. U.S. Commission on Civil Rights, *Social Indicators of Equality for Minorities and Women*, August 1978.

7. Ledvinka, op. cit., p. 143.

8.   Ledvinka, op. cit., Chapter 9.
9.   Ledvinka, op. cit., pp. 213–215.
10. I. Bernstein, "The Growth of American Unions," *American Economic Review*, 1954, *44*, pp. 308–17.
11. *Wall Street Journal*, December 1, 1981, p. 1.
12. F. T. Cary, "IBM's Guidelines to Employee Privacy," *Harvard Business Review*, September-October 1976, pp. 82–90.
13. *Wall Street Journal*, June 12, 1984, p. 1.
14. H. J. McLane, *Selecting, Developing and Retaining Women Executives* (New York: Van Nostrand Reinhold, 1980), p. 2.

ANNOTATED BIBLIOGRAPHY

LEDVINKA, J., *Federal Regulation of Personnel and Human Resource Management.* Belmont, CA: Wadsworth, 1982.

> Describes the major legislation concerning equal employment opportunity, employee safety and health, employee pension and benefit plans, unemployment compensation, wages and hours, and employee privacy. The book's real strength is in its comprehensive coverage of each area of legislation. The social, economic, and political problems leading to the regulations are discussed, the legislation is explained, and its impact on organizations and society is assessed. An excellent and comprehensive source.

Several private and professional organizations publish newsletters and more extensive handbooks that contain recent developments in government regulations, court decisions, and their impact on human resource management. Some key sources are:

The Bureau of National Affairs, Inc. (BNA), Washington, D.C.

> A leading private publisher of labor and employee relations information, BNA publishes a myriad of newsletters like the *Daily Labor Report* and the *Labor Relations Reporter*, as well as more extensive handbooks (e.g., the *Affirmative Action Compliance Manual*) which provide information and advice for human resource professionals and line managers who deal with government regulations.

The American Society for Training and Development (ASTD), Washington, D.C.

> ASTD, a non-profit association of over 23,000 professionals involved in human resource development, publishes the biweekly *National Report*, containing the latest government actions, and recommends responses that organizations can take.

The Bureau of Law & Business, Inc. (BLB), Madison, CT.

> Another private publisher, the BLB produces the *Human Resources Reporter* and the *Personnel Manager's Legal Reporter* with the latest developments in employment law. It also publishes more extensive handbooks to guide human resource policy and practices.

CHAPTER SIX

LABOR-MANAGEMENT RELATIONS

C. Richard Rough, the general manager of Bethlehem Steel Corp.'s Burns Harbor plant near Chicago, has never met David Wilborn, the president of the United Steelworkers of America local at the facility. It isn't for lack of trying, Mr. Rough says. Two meetings were scheduled, but the union leader didn't show up.*

"I'm just giving him the same snub he gave me," counters Mr. Wilborn, who says he asked for a meeting with Mr. Rough shortly after being elected president of Local 6787 in April 1979. Instead of coming himself, Mr. Rough sent an assistant, says Mr. Wilborn, who agrees with Mr. Rough that "we have a terrible labor-management situation here."

Meanwhile, at Nippon Kokan's Ohgishima plant near Tokyo, Gyoichi Suzuki, the general manager, was recently invited to attend an evening meeting of current and retired blast-furnace workers at the facility. The meeting's purpose? "Drinking," Mr. Suzuki says with a grin.

The relationships that Mr. Rough and Mr. Suzuki have with the workers at their respective plants go a long way toward explaining how, in the past thirty years, Japanese steelmakers have become the world's premier steel industry while the American companies have slumped to a poor second.[1]

As the steel industry experience has shown dramatically, unions and labor-management relations play a critical role in the economy and world of work in America. The impact of unions is far greater than their membership would indicate. While only 20 percent of America's over 100 million workers belong to one of the nation's 175 unions, unions touch the lives of everyone, including union members, nonunion employees of unionized organizations, employees of nonunion organizations, and consumers of goods and services produced (in whole or part) by union members. The degree of antagonism

*Adaptation of "Steel Blues: Poor Labor Relations at U.S. Steelmakers Cut Ability to Compete" by Douglas R. Sease and Urban Lehner, *The Wall Street Journal*, April 7, 1981. Copyright © 1981 Dow Jones & Company, Inc. All Rights Reserved. Reprinted by permission.

(often found in the U.S.) or cooperation (often found in Japan) in union-management relations can affect the productivity and survival of entire industries, such as steel and automotive. And the union's influence extends far beyond its immediate membership. Unionized labor usually leads the way in areas such as wages, benefits, and conditions of employment. The political influence of unions can be considerable. And in nonunion organizations, simply the prospect of a union organizing attempt often results in sensitive, responsive, and employee-centered personnel and grievance policies. Thus, the direct and indirect effects of unions can be considerable.

LABOR RELATIONS AND HUMAN RESOURCE STRATEGY

The relationship between labor and management is a critical element in the design and implementation of the organization's human resource management strategy. On the one hand, a labor contract can be viewed as a strong *constraint* on the freedom of management to deploy and motivate the work force. Also, labor costs are often the greatest single component of an organization's total operating expenses. On the other hand, the union may be viewed as a potential *resource* in the organization's attempts to increase productivity and competitiveness. The role of the labor-management relationship depends greatly upon the attitude of management toward the union. The *company's policy toward unions* is the first strategic issue top management must address. Will the policy be to maintain (or restore) nonunion status? Will the policy be to accept the existence of unions but assume that the basic interests of the union and management conflict? If the latter, it will be necessary to develop an effective adversarial or competitive relationship with the union. Or will the policy be to cooperate, to assume that there are large areas of common interest between the employees, as represented by the union, and the company? Such a policy implies participation of labor in certain areas of problem-solving and decision-making and a tendency to resolve conflict through problem-solving discussions rather than confrontation (e.g., job actions and strikes).

The basic policy toward unions affects all aspects of employee relations and human resource management. It affects how compensation is determined, how staffing, training, and career development are done, how performance is appraised, and how organizational exit is managed. A number of factors, including the past history of labor relationships, the stance of the union toward management, and competitive pressures in the industry, affect union policy.

In general, however, management in contemporary organizations tends to adopt a more cooperative stance *vis-a-vis* unions. One reason for this is that rigid, inefficient work rules, which grow out of adversarial labor-management relationships, lead to low production, high costs, and low-quality products, which hurt profitability. Also, in an adversarial relationship, wages become inflated because management may be less open to bargaining on other issues and more willing to trade off high pay to maintain "management prerogatives" in other areas of the business. Another consequence of an adversarial labor relations climate is the low commitment and involvement of workers (or worse, hostility and sabotage), which hurts quality and productivity. All of these costs have tended to motivate management to explore more cooperative relationships with unions.

At the opposite extreme, many companies with unions have attempted to win decertification elections and remove the union. The recession of 1982–83 produced a wave of union decertifications. These decertifications were often influenced by management's communications with employees and employee-centered human resource activities which demonstrated management's concerns and raised questions about the union's role in the company's productivity problems. In such organizations, much stress was placed on training line managers in various human resource management skills (e.g., effective feedback, recognition, communication, and positive leadership). More competent behavior by managers created a more positive employee relations climate, which in turn reduced the employees' perceived need for a union.[2]

Thus, the behavior of line managers is critical in affecting the employees' stance toward a union. In turn, top management's policy toward unions is critical in influencing lower-level line managers' behavior. And the nature of the everyday labor relations climate has a strong impact on how well various human resource management activities will work. In the following section, we will provide more detail on why employees do or do not want unions, and we will see more clearly the role line management plays in determining employee needs for formal representation.

WHY EMPLOYEES JOIN UNIONS

Why do employees want unions? Union supporters will often cite the following as important on-the-job benefits of unionization:

- Higher wages and more influence in the wage-setting process;
- Increased job security;
- Improved benefits (insurance, pensions, personal and sick leave time, vacations, work breaks, etc.);
- Improved working conditions (physical conditions, work pace, etc.);
- Clearer, fairer rules and processes for handling job transfers, discipline, promotion, and grievances;
- Greater self-control in the work place.

In addition to job-related factors, the political impact of unions is also cited. Examples of political effects would be organized lobbying at state and federal government levels and formal union support of political candidates.

Management often perceives unions in a less favorable way. Managers often feel betrayed by employees who want to vote in a union; union activity is often associated with a lack of loyalty to and confidence in management. In some organizations, however, management views the union as a positive, constructive influence, as a respected representative of the work force and a useful agent for problem-solving and communications with employees. It may recognize that its goals and those of the union are legitimately different in some areas (e.g., management may be more concerned with financial return to stockholders, while the union is more interested in compensation and benefits for its members), although there are probably goals upon which they can agree (e.g., the survival and growth of the company).

Thus, there may be wide differences between and within management and unions about the value of unions. How about the employees themselves? What affects employee attitudes toward a union? Thomas Kochan has summarized factors that influence employees' decisions to join unions:[3]

1. *Perceptions of the work environment.* This includes job satisfaction or dissatisfaction, attitudes toward supervisors, and feelings about pay, benefits, working conditions, etc.
2. *Perceptions of influence.* If employees want to influence the job and other conditions in the organization and feel they have no way to do so without a union, they will tend to want to join a union. If their desire to influence is low or they feel they can influence management without a union, the propensity to join a union will be lower.
3. *Beliefs about unions.* If employees tend to see unions as effective in improving workers' satisfaction, they will be more likely to want to join. If they see unions as "Big Labor" and "just another big bureaucracy," they will be less inclined to join.

Earlier we mentioned that employees' attitudes toward a union are affected by the ways managers treat people. Evidence for this point is found in a study of thirty-one union representation elections by Getman, Goldberg, and Herman (whose results also strongly supported the findings of Kochan). Employees (1,239 of them) were randomly selected and interviewed twice, immediately after the election date was set and again just after the election. In the first interview they were asked about their attitudes toward working conditions and unions, whether they had signed an authorization card, and whether they intended to vote. In the second they were asked about the content of the campaign and how they had actually voted.[4]

The results of this study are shown in Exhibit 6.1. Exhibit 6.1 shows that job dissatisfaction was a good predictor of voting for the union, especially for dissatisfaction with job security and pay. These measures of work dissatisfaction enabled the researchers to predict an employee's vote with 75 percent accuracy. Exhibit 6.1 also shows the strong role of general attitudes toward unions in the employees' representation vote. These favorable attitudes toward unions led to accurate predictions about the employee's vote 79 percent of the time. As one author put it, "In sum, our study results indicate that employees' interest in unionization is triggered by real frustration in the work place and strong beliefs that the way to remove that frustration is through collective action.[5]

EMPLOYEES AND UNION REPRESENTATION

EXHIBIT 6.1

Job Satisfaction Dimensions	Correlations with Vote for Union*
1. Wages	−.40
2. Perceptions that supervisors treat all employees alike	−.34
3. Type of work you are doing	−.14
4. Appreciation shown by supervisors for a good job	−.30
5. Fringe benefits	−.31
6. Chance for promotion	−.30
7. Job security	−.42
8. Overall satisfaction	−.36

Attitudes toward Unions and Voting for Union Representation

Employees who voted for union representation tended to *agree* that:

1. Unions make sure that supervisors treat employees fairly.
2. Unions help working men and women to get better wages and hours.
3. Unions call strikes for good reasons.
4. Their overall attitude toward unions is favorable.

Employees who voted for union representation tended to *disagree* that:

1. Unions are becoming too strong.
2. Unions interfere with good relations between companies and workers.
3. Union dues are too high.
4. Unions are a major cause of high prices.

*All correlation coefficients are statistically significant at the .99 level of confidence. Sample size was 1,000. Negative correlations mean that employees who were satisfied tended to vote against union representation.

SOURCE: Adapted by permission of the publisher, from ''Why Employees Want Unions,'' by Jeanne M. Brett, *Organizational Dynamics*, Spring 1980, p. 57. Copyright © 1980 AMACOM, a division of American Management Associations, New York. All rights reserved.

A related study by W. Clay Hamner and Frank Smith was conducted in 250 units of the Sears, Roebuck organization.[6] Sears routinely surveys employee perceptions of the work environment, so good attitude survey data were available from these 250 units. There were also records on the extent of union organizing activity and union success. By correlating prior work attitudes with later organizing activity, the researchers were able to measure the impact of work attitudes on employee unionization attempts. The results showed a positive relationship between employee dissatisfaction within a unit and the level of union organizing which later took place in that unit. Hamner and Smith determined that dissatisfaction with *leadership* and *supervision* was especially important in affecting union activity. Thus, it seems clear from all of those studies that satisfied employees support the company in a union representation election. And the factor that seems most strongly related to employee satisfaction is the *competence with which managers deal with human resource management issues such as pay, supervision, job design, recognition, motivation, and career development.*

Jeanne Brett has identified five principles of union organizing.

1. The factors stimulating employee interest in union representation existed long before the union-organizing campaign was begun.
2. Employers wishing to remain non-union should be concerned with employee satisfaction. . . . Satisfied workers are seldom interested in unionization; they don't need it.
3. Employee attitude surveys can provide accurate information about the degree to which employees may be willing to vote for a union if given a chance.
4. Unions should focus their organizing efforts on units in which employees are dissatisfied.
5. Union organizers should concentrate on getting employees to attend union meetings. . . . Attending a union meeting and familiarizing oneself with the union campaign were related to switching from a pro-company to a pro-union vote.[7]

A major study, conducted by Fred Foulkes, of labor relations in non-union companies yielded results consistent with what Brett and others have learned about the impact of human resource management practices on employees' decisions to join unions.[8] Foulkes found that firms which have remained nonunion are characterized by progressive and equitable human resource practices and highly attractive work environments. These include firms such as Black and Decker, Eli Lilly, Gillette, Gruman, IBM, and Polaroid. Foulkes concluded that the accomplishments of these firms could not easily be copied or duplicated and that a key element in their success was a "strong top management concern for employees [that] becomes institutionalized through implementation of various policies."[9] The innovative personnel practices of these firms yield high productivity, high employee involvement and loyalty, and low turnover, low absenteeism and low resistance to technological change. In the opinion of the company people Foulkes interviewed, these benefits resulted from the firm's freedom to experiment with new human resource programs, their ability to deal directly with workers, and the atmosphere of trust and cooperation in management-employee relations.

Foulkes found a set of characteristic policies and practices in these large nonunion companies:

- *A sense of caring:* managing the business with strongly egalitarian views about the treatment of employees.
- *Carefully considered surroundings:* choosing plant locations in areas with good public schools, often in rural areas, with access to a university, and without aggressive and militant unions.

- *High profits, fast growth, and family ties:* a strong financial position and strong control by the founding family which supports the implementation of the ideas of the founders.
- *Employment security:* maximizing workers' job security by pursuing various techniques to ensure full employment.
- *Promotion from within:* keeping advancement opportunities open for present employees, rather than outsiders, supported by training, education, career development, and job posting.
- *Influential human resource department:* maintaining a high-powered, well-staffed human resource function, with the human resource vice-president often reporting directly to the president and sometimes even serving on the board of directors.
- *Competitive pay and benefits:* maintaining total compensation well above industry and community standards.
- *Managements that listen:* communicating constantly with employees through attitude surveys, regular meetings, speak-out programs, and effective grievance procedures.
- *Careful preparation of managers:* using carefully considered professional procedures for selecting, training, and rewarding managers throughout their careers.

Taken together, these characteristics of effective nonunion companies suggest a *personal involvement of top management in human resource management.* Put another way, in these firms, human resource management is not a specialized function but simply part of management.

THE HISTORY OF THE LABOR MOVEMENT

As we have just seen, unions have been employees' response to unsatisfactory wages, working conditions, and management practices. Whereas before the advent of unions, employees did not have much power as individuals, particularly when there was an ample supply of labor, they realized that if they were organized into a cohesive group with a common goal, they could exert power as an organized union.

The earliest such labor organizations were guilds. **Guilds** were *associations in which merchants and skilled craftsmen (journeymen) met to discuss issues such as common prices, quality standards, and terms of apprenticeships* (for entry into the craft or skilled trade). In time, as the Industrial Revolution progressed in eighteenth century Europe and as trade increased and business became more complex, journeymen in each craft (e.g., shoemakers) organized to regulate work and trade for their craft; this was the beginning of *trade unions.*

guilds

In the United States, the early trade unions developed to resist the growing power of merchant capitalists who bought the tradesman's goods for later sale to the ultimate customer. (Earlier, each tradesman had sold his own products directly to the customer.) As markets and technology grew in size and complexity, so did the role of the merchant-middleman.

Increased competition between merchants led to more competition among craftsmen. Journeymen began using cheaper apprentice labor, and the work of the apprentices became more specialized to make it more efficient (e.g., each apprentice carpenter would make only certain parts of a chair, such as the arms). This tended to weaken the craft, as the work became more fragmented and there was less need for the highly skilled craftsman who could build the complete product. This change also tended to keep wages down. In turn, this development led to the creation of unions to insure a minimum price for the product of the craft.

In 1827, a group of trade unions merged in Philadelphia to fight for the ten hour day. This group was called the Mechanics Union of Trade Associations, and the date, 1827, has been marked by labor historians as the founding of the American labor movement.

In 1886, the American Federation of Labor (AFL) was formed as a federation of national craft unions. The nationals had been formed during the Civil War period by combining local unions for the same craft. The national organizations were responsible for collecting and allocating strike funds, which provided control over the actions of locals. The national unions also assumed authority for organizing new workers and providing insurance and benefits. Thus the financial resources which came to be controlled by the national unions were considerable.

The vicissitudes of the labor movement in the twentieth century have been great. In the early 1900s, there was much labor unrest. Management practices were often inhumane. Workers were fired for little or no cause. Even the suspicion of union activity could lead to dismissal. Companies kept "black lists" of known union sympathizers, which discouraged union activity. "Yellow dog" contracts were used, which prohibited employees from belonging to unions. Many companies set up company towns which provided housing, stores, banking, recreation, and other services, in addition to employment. Thus, both the employee's private life and work life were controlled by the company.

During World War I, organized labor's strength increased, as labor was in short supply as a result of military manpower needs. The National War Labor Board was formed to handle labor disputes, and this gave the labor movement a new legitimacy. AFL membership in 1920 reached its peak, with over four million members.

In the post-war years, unions again faced difficult times. "Scientific management," which entailed an objective approach to supervision, was on the rise. Time and motion studies were conducted to determine the most efficient method of doing a certain job, quantitative measures were taken of employee performance, and piece-rate incentive plans were devised. Even after the importance of "human relations" was discovered, employee participation at work and communication with management was always on management's terms. Managers occasionally became more sensitive to employee needs and ideas, but only if managers chose to do so. Management was clearly in control.

The CIO

With industry becoming more specialized through mass production technology, the notion of a *craft* (or skilled trade), upon which the AFL was based, was clearly weakening. The transition from the AFL crafts to the factory or industrial unions (of the CIO) was under way.

The 1920s were a period of decline for the AFL, with membership by 1933 only half of its level in 1920. The depression was a contributing factor, as were employer opposition and union organizing practices.

John L. Lewis, the head of the AFL's United Mine Workers, was one of the first to organize along industry lines. He created an unofficial "Committee for Industrial Organization" in 1935, which attempted to organize all of the workers in a factory into a single union. Because this activity was in direct opposition to the AFL's policy of separate unions for each trade or craft, Lewis was expelled from the AFL. The CIO (Congress of Industrial Organization) was created in 1938.

The long depression had created a great interest in unionization on the part of industrial workers. With the regulation of election procedures provided by the Wagner Act in 1935, union membership rose dramatically, from three million in 1933 to nine million in 1939, one third of the labor force. However, labor growth was not easily achieved, for employers strongly resisted union organizing attempts.

Labor Legislation

Before the 1930s, there was no specific legal framework for dealing with labor-management relations. Under common law, private property rights were liberally interpreted, and employers had great freedom to run their businesses and treat their employees as they saw fit.

The Sherman Anti-Trust Act of 1890, which prohibited actions in restraint of trade, was interpreted to cover union activities as well as those of businesses. Thus, the act effectively meant that boycott and strike activities, whose purpose was to prevent the interstate movement of goods, were declared illegal. This severe limitation of their ultimate primary tactic severely weakened the unions.

However, political activity by the unions began to win them important gains in the 1920s and 1930s. In 1926, the Railway Labor Act was passed through the efforts of the powerful railroad unions. This act guaranteed organization rights to railroad workers. In 1932, the Norris-LaGuardia Act outlawed "yellow dog" contracts and limited the ability of federal courts to issue injunctions to stop union picketing activities.

A major piece of legislation, the National Labor Relations Act (NLRA) of 1935, also called the Wagner Act for the senator from New York who introduced it, provided a legal framework for labor-management relations with clear rules and an appeals process. The U.S. government was now on record as encouraging collective, good-faith bargaining by management and labor. This act defined the rights of workers, listed a set of unfair (i.e., illegal) labor practices, and created a National Labor Relations Board (NLRB) to oversee union representation elections and to judge complaints about unfair labor practices.

The NLRA gave workers the right to "self-organization, to form, join, or assist labor organizations, and to bargain collectively through representatives of their own choosing—all without employer influence, coercion, or restraint."[10] Other unfair labor practices were defined as employer domination in creation of unions and discrimination against workers who participate in union activity.

The act created a union certification process, in which the NLRB conducted elections among groups of employees of organizations to determine which unions, if any, would represent those groups. Once a union was certified, it obtained exclusive jurisdiction over the group of workers who voted; no other union could represent them. After certification, the employer was required to bargain in good faith with the union over wages and benefits, work rules, and certain areas of plant operations. The act did not require *agreement* on these matters; it only specified a *process*, bargaining in good faith by the employer.

During and after World War II, there was another jump in union membership (from nine million in 1940 to fifteen million in 1950). After unions took a no-strike pledge during the war, there were almost 5,000 strikes in 1945–46, as workers attempted to reestablish their strike power and gain economic ground in the face of post-war inflation.

In response to the view that the NLRA and post-war events had given too much power to unions, the Taft-Hartley Act was passed in 1947 to serve as a check on union influence. Taft-Hartley was, in a sense, "management's NLRA." It specified that unions could also commit unfair labor practices, and it allowed for elections to decertify a union. In addition, it created procedures whereby strikes which created a "national emergency" could be halted for a period of time, and permitted states to outlaw contracts requiring union membership as a condition of employment (i.e., it permitted the "open shop").

Union growth began to slow in the 1950s. The AFL and the CIO, formerly rivals, merged in 1955 to form the AFL-CIO. Concern about illegal activities of union leaders, particularly in the Teamsters, led to the passage in 1959 of the Landrum-Griffin Act. It provided a bill of rights for union members regarding union leadership and required public disclosure of union financial activities.

The Labor Movement Today

Since the 1930s, the percent of the U.S. labor force which was organized has decreased from almost one third of the work force to less than 20 percent now. Most of the drop has been in the private sector (see Exhibit 6.2); in the public sector (i.e., government) there has been great growth in union membership since the 1960s (13 percent in 1960 to 20 percent in 1976 and 36 percent in 1984).

EXHIBIT 6.2

*DECLINE IN UNION MEMBERSHIP
IN THE PRIVATE SECTOR*

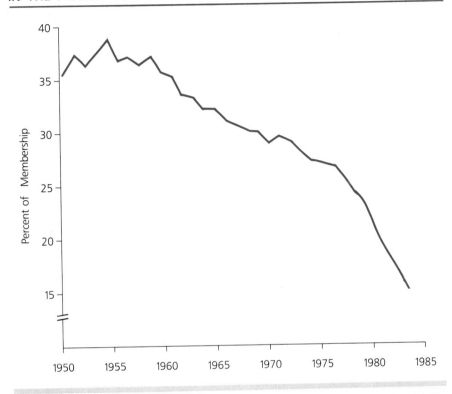

SOURCE: U.S. Bureau of Labor Statistics, *Handbook of Labor Statistics* Bulletin 2070 (1980), tables 72, 162, and 165; Bulletin 2000 (1978), table 42; and "Changing Employment Patterns of Organized Workers," by Larry T. Adams, *Monthly Labor Review*, February 1985, p. 26.

At the federal level, the Postal Service and the Departments of Defense, Education, and Health and Human Services have the highest rates of participation. At the state and local levels, most cities with populations over one million have municipal unions for police officers, fire fighters, sanitation workers, teachers, etc. Teachers represent the largest single group of unionized public employees in many municipalities.

As the economy moves from manufacturing and goods producing toward the production of *knowledge* and *services*, white-collar workers represent the "growth market" for union organizing efforts. Thus, union membership also is increasing among hospital workers, nurses, technicians, and other health-care providers. Day-care workers are another growing group, as the percentage of working parents increases. Organizations for secretarial and clerical workers are growing in size and importance.

UNIONS MOVE INTO OFFICE

BOX 6.1

Except in the case of public employees and actors, U.S. unions have often shunned white-collar workers as a poor organizing risk. But the decline of heavily organized industries is forcing unions to seek more members among the office workers who now constitute 57 percent of non-agricultural employees. . . .

Many unions are increasing efforts to organize white-collar workers. District 65 of the United Auto Workers has 10,000 clerical workers (out of a total membership of 38,000). A new division in District 65 will consist solely of office workers.

The 600,000-member Communications Workers of America (CWA) last July set up a department for public employees, primarily white-collar workers. A group of ten California unions called the Council of Engineers and Scientists Organizations hopes next fall to found a new union to bargain for the 50,000 professionals it represents and to organize new members.

Each year sees additional millions of dollars spent to aid the effort to unionize clerical and technical workers. Frequently, organizing into some type of unit precedes union organization.

But the pressures on business to avoid unions also are strong. Robert Lewis, whose New York law firm of Jackson, Lewis, Schnitzler and Krupman is branded an antiunion consultant by labor, contends that employers would lose much of their flexibility to manage white-collar workers. He adds that unionization would mean higher wage costs for many office jobs, including clerical work and jobs in banking.

In banks, union organizing attempts have often been unsuccessful. Data from the NLRB indicate unions lose over half of their white-collar organizing campaigns. However, such campaigns continue in great numbers.

But the unions that are most successful at organizing white-collar workers have also developed some new tactics. One is more education of potential members in how flexible collective activity can be. "Professionals often think that once you join a union, there'll be rules over who gets to do which work," says the Office & Professional Employee International Union's Mark Reader.

More careful selection of union organizers is another part of the unions' human resource strategy. Organizers are better educated than in the past and the 625,000-member Service Employees International Union now has 35 percent female organizers (vs. 20 percent ten years ago).

Larry Nathan, an attorney and the executive director of the 2,000-member New York State Federation of Physicians and Dentists, recruits doctors individually by phone, promising anonymity. He avoids the word union, which infers a lower status than doctors like to claim, and instead of "dues," he speaks of providing services for a fee. . . .

Lewis, the management lawyer, thinks enlightened management, among other factors, will prevent unions from adding to their share of the white-collar work force. But unions do not agree and he admits "if unions are to survive, white-collar organizing is what they have to do."

Business Week, January 25, 1982, pp. 90, 92.

Engineering and high technology are two other occupational areas of increased union activity in recent years. Engineers, as professional employees, have always been considered closer to management than to hourly and clerical workers. However, like other professional groups (e.g., teachers, nurses, professors), engineers in some organizations have felt the need to organize for various reasons (e.g., employment security, greater pay and benefits, working conditions). Box 6.1 provides more information about the growth of clerical and professional unions.

Union Organization

Exhibit 6.3 shows the structure of the AFL-CIO. The basic unit of a union is the *local*. A local is made up of the members from a particular department or employing organization (or group of organizations, in the case of amalgamated locals). The AFL-CIO has 71,000 locals in its 177 national and international unions. The national provides leadership in organizing and negotiating, in financial administration, and in maintaining internal discipline.

A constitution sets out the duties and obligations of national officials, locals, and members. Annual or biannual conventions govern the national union. An elected executive board, including the president, handles the administration of the union. National leaders possess great visibility and authority within the union structure, and generally have long tenure in office (perhaps ten–twenty years).

The local exists by virtue of a charter from the national and is the unit closest to the work place. A local may have as few as five members or as many as 40,000. It has a president and a secretary-treasurer, and in the case of craft unions, a business agent who works directly with an employer and makes immediate decisions on the legality of a grievance or a work procedure.

A critical position in the local, the **shop steward** is the *union representative in each plant, department, or other local work area.* The steward is usually elected, and when there are several departments and different work shifts, there is a steward for each. The steward works directly with the department supervisor and is thus the main link between union members and management. When grievances arise, the supervisor and shop steward take the first step toward resolution and their relationship directly affects the labor relations climate in that work unit.

shop steward

Generally, stewards (who may alternatively be called plant representatives or grievance committee members) are elected by union members for one-year terms. Re-election may often hinge on the steward's effectiveness in resolving grievances.

It is usually in the best interests of management and the workers for a union to have strong leadership. A strong union leader is one who can negotiate with management and has confidence that the membership will support the agreements reached. Bargaining is much more difficult if one party (the union, in this case) always has to check for constituent agreement on every detail.

EXHIBIT 6.3   **STRUCTURE OF THE AFL–CIO**

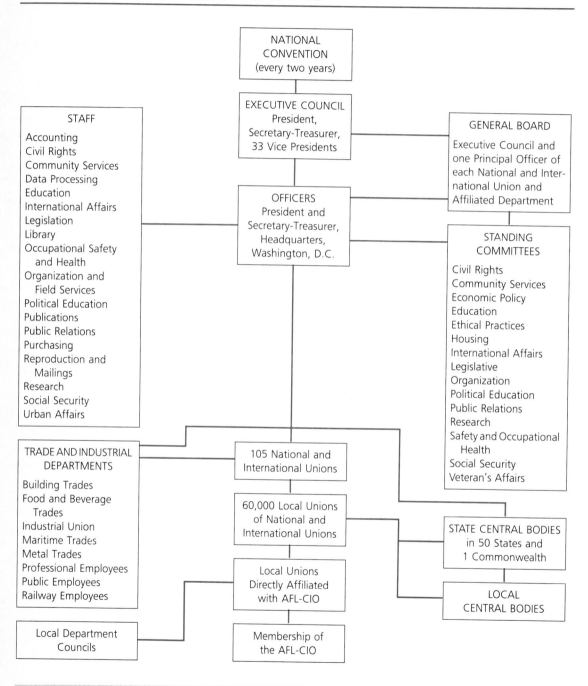

SOURCE: Directory of National Unions and Employee Associations, 1975, U.S. Department of Labor BLS Bulletin (1977), p. 2.

THE COLLECTIVE BARGAINING PROCESS

Collective bargaining is *the process by which unions and employees relate to each other.* The collective bargaining process takes place in several stages (shown in Exhibit 6.4). In the first stage, the *union organizing campaign*, the union attempts to win recognition as the legal bargaining unit for a group of employees. If the campaign is successful, the second stage is *negotiation of a collective bargaining agreement*—i.e., working out a contract. If the negotiation is unsuccessful, the third stage could be a *strike*. On the other hand, if the contract is signed, the next stage would be the day-to-day *administration of the contract*. We will discuss these stages in turn.

collective bargaining

The Union Organizing Campaign

Usually a campaign to organize a union is initiated not by a union but by a group of employees. These employees communicate with the union in which they are interested and obtain cards to distribute to other employees authorizing the union to represent the card signer in negotiating with the employer about pay, hours, benefits, and working conditions.

At least 30 percent of the organization's employees must support the union's election petition before the National Labor Relations Board will agree to conduct an election. If the board agrees to hold the election, union and management must agree on an election date and on the group of employees who will participate in the vote. If the union and management cannot reach agreement on these issues, the board will decide. The time period between these decisions and the actual election is usually two weeks to a month.

During the campaign, employees receive many communications from the union and management. The whole process resembles a political election campaign. Union staff members function as professional organizers, and the company may appoint one of its senior management staff, usually a human resource professional, as a campaign manager. This person has access to top management and usually works full-time at the target location. Union handbills and management newsletters, as well as media communications, may be employed to win over the voters. Propaganda usually abounds on both sides.

The NLRB regulates the conduct of the union and the company during the campaign. Both sides are prevented from using various forms of coercion (e.g., economic threats, promises, physical threats, acts of reprisal) to interfere with the employees' free choice. The board also prohibits factual misrepresentations, racially based appeals, and campaigning at voting locations. If a winning party violates board rules, a second election is held. If the board concludes that employer violations are so severe that a fair election cannot be held, it may certify the union anyway.

Not all union organizing campaigns reach the election stage. In a study of organizing campaigns in 125 units of the Sears, Roebuck organization, Hamner and Smith rank-ordered the activities that indicate the degree of success of the organizing campaign:

EXHIBIT 6.4 **STAGES IN THE COLLECTIVE BARGAINING PROCESS**

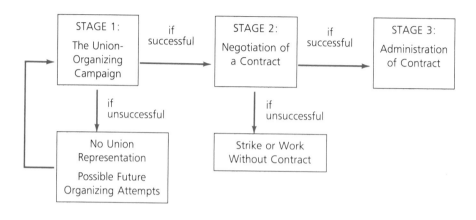

Level 0 = no union activity;

Level 1 = distribution of union handbills at the unit, which may not include any employer activity;

Level 2 = authorization card signing; employees take affirmative action on behalf of union by signing authorization cards;

Level 3 = union meetings (enough employees had signed authorization cards or expressed sympathy for the union to make it worthwhile for the union to hold meetings to plan and initiate a serious organization attempt);

Level 4 = representation petition filed by union (at least 30 percent of the employees in the requested bargaining unit had signed authorization cards);

Level 5 = union election held and won by company;

Level 6 = union election held and won by union.[11]

Hamner and Smith found that if a given level of activity occurred, all the lower levels of activity had probably taken place.

Collective Bargaining

Once a representation election has been held and the union certified, union representatives are authorized to bargain with management and negotiate an employment contract for union members.

Preparation ▬ Preparing to negotiate is a critical part of the process, taking from three to nine months, with more time needed for a larger firm. The first step is to identify key bargaining issues. If either party wants to change an existing contract, 60 days' written notice before the expiration of the old contract is required. During this phase, management and union must establish their own goals and priorities, and have a clear sense of the relative importance of each.[12]

Next, research is conducted. Each side collects statistical data to support and illustrate its demands, along with visual aids which persuasively communicate the information. It is also necessary to compute the cost or value of each demand. Financial data are essential in evaluating one's position on various issues.

The third step is to prepare a detailed analysis of the key parties on the other side. The personalities of the union and management negotiators, as well as the nature of the union membership, are critical factors in the process.

Fourth, if this is to be industry-wide bargaining (for example, the railroad industry), communication and preparation between companies must take place.

Finally, initial meetings between management and union representatives to define and narrow the scope of the bargain and to get a sense of the other party's priorities must occur.

Negotiation ▬ **Negotiation** is *the process of meeting, communicating, and compromising for the purpose of reaching an acceptable agreement.* Negotiating has been described as "an exercise in graceful retreat—retreating without seeming to retreat."[13] Kreps et al. have described the process as follows:

> Since priorities and minimum demands are disguised, the bargaining parties must fend off questions and demands aimed at exposing primary and secondary demands. Both parties have a good idea of the ultimate *settlement range*—those wage and fringe benefit packages that are more rational to accept than go to war over. As the ritual proceeds, demands are repackaged: perhaps the union backs off a demand for longer rest periods in exchange for a five cent an hour wage increase. The negotiating language often concedes true differences: the union's 'no contract, no work' statements may be countered by management's 'this is our final offer.' Despite the apocalyptic language, most negotiations result in agreement *before* the existing contract expires. After an informal agreement is reached, lawyers reduce the agreement to its legal, written form.[14]

negotiation

Most negotiations cover issues such as union security and management rights, wages, work hours and overtime, leave time (paid and unpaid), benefits, seniority arrangements, job security, and dispute resolution procedures.

Contract duration can also be an important issue, since employers prefer longer contracts to reduce uncertainty in labor relations. A longer contract, however, reduces the relevance of the union's ultimate weapon, the strike.

The process of bargaining can take place in basically two ways:

1. *Distributive* (or win-lose) *bargaining.* Here the assumption is that there is a "fixed pie"—what I gain has to come out of your share, so that for me to win, you have to lose. This is a *competitive* process.
2. *Integrative* (or win-win) *bargaining.* This approach assumes shared objectives and a problem-solving approach. Both parties *cooperate* to try to find ways that each can win without hurting the other.[15]

To understand these approaches, assume two pharmaceutical firms both need to obtain the small world-wide supply of the rare Ugli orange in order to make important vaccines—one to protect pregnant women and the other to protect newborn babies. Agents of the two firms meet to bargain over the oranges. If they assume a distributive bargaining stance, they will communicate little and simply propose compromises (e.g., "I'll take half and you take half"). However, if they take the integrative bargaining approach and ask questions such as "What do you need," they can quickly produce important new information: one company needs the pulp to make its vaccine, and the other needs the rind. Thus, through problem-solving, an easy win-win solution can sometimes be worked out.

Generally, contract negotiations are conducted via distributive bargaining, since each side is trying to maximize the other's concessions and to minimize its own. However, even here there can be integrative possibilities. Some issues, such as flexible work hours or a different mix of benefits, might have little or no cost to the company, yet be highly important to employees. In economically troubled industries such as steel, farm equipment, and automobiles, joint problem-solving and cooperative quality-of-work-life agreements might be included in the negotiations in order to save the industry or company. Such cooperation has been critical in the survival attempts of organizations like Chrysler and New York City.

More commonly, however, integrative bargaining occurs after the contract has been negotiated and during the *contract administration.* This approach is a way of building a positive labor-management climate and of preventing small problems and issues from growing into formal grievances. Furthermore, this kind of cooperative problem-solving often results in creative, high-quality solutions that not only solve problems but actually improve performance and satisfaction.

The traffic commissioner of a major U.S. city recently used the integrative approach to solve two problems that arose simultaneously. First, new rules on maximum truck size were about to go into effect, permitting tandem trailers on city streets. The commissioner was concerned about the safety and road-wear effects of these rules. He wanted to ban the tandems from certain areas of the city, but he knew the truckers would oppose such a ban. The second problem was a nationwide strike by the independent truckers' union over increased highway use fees and a higher gasoline tax. The truckers were threatening to block traffic entering the city from several key arteries. When the commissioner was asked by one of the authors how he could possibly deal with these two potential crises, he replied:

> I think we can help each other. They don't really need to use the city streets I'm most worried about, but I'd like the security of a formal ban. And I kind of agree with them on their concern about the higher fees and tax. Their gripe there is with the federal government, not with the city. So I'm going to offer to support them in Washington on their issues if they will help me keep the tandems off the narrowest streets.

And, in fact, this is exactly the agreement that was achieved.

Mediation

When difficulties are encountered in the bargaining process, the participants may seek a **mediator**, *a professional neutral third party who intervenes to facilitate communication and help the two negotiating parties reach an agreement.* Mediators are often provided by government agencies. At the federal level, mediation is provided by the Federal Mediation and Conciliation Service (FMCS). A state mediation agency would typically be housed in the state's department of labor.

Deborah Kolb, who acted as a participant-observer studying state and federal mediators in action, observed three mediating strategies:

mediator

1. *Structuring the session.* Mediators convene and conduct meetings— some with each party alone, some together. State mediators tend to play a more active role than their federal counterparts and tend to have more separate meetings with each party. Federal mediators are more likely to meet with both parties together.
2. *Reducing the issues.* One reason that some negotiations reach an impasse is that the parties often come to the table with a long list of "unweeded" demands—the "shopping list." Before constructive mediation can start, the list must be reduced to a more manageable size. Various tactics are used to get the parties to reduce their lists. Federal mediators tend to push the parties to reduce the lists themselves, while state mediators are likely to push for the elimination of specific items.
3. *Helping the pro.* When one of the two chief negotiators is an outsider (e.g., a hired labor lawyer or a national union leader) known by the mediator as a "pro" (a highly experienced, expert, well-regarded negotiator), the mediator will often focus on this person to facilitate the process. The federal mediators tend to try to further enhance the role and image of the pro with his or her own bargaining committee so the pro can be even more effective. State mediators are more likely to attempt

to isolate the pro from his or her committee, which would make the pro more likely to want to accept the mediator's suggestions so that a solution would be reached. Then the credibility of the pro could be re-established by this "responsive and fair" settlement.[16]

In general, federal mediators appear more likely to play indirect, catalyst roles. They tend to see themselves as "orchestrators." One explained:

> My role is to help the parties reach a settlement. I am just a third party, another forum to talk about your differences. I want to develop a dialogue on these open issues and hopefully reach an agreement, but the burden of reaching that agreement rests with the union and management.[17]

State mediators, on the other hand, are more likely to play an active, direct role. They often describe themselves as "dealmakers." A state mediator said:

> I am here to make a deal. Negotiations are over as far as I am concerned. I refuse to play a passive role and just let the parties talk. I will not be a messenger either. First they have to convince me and then we will see what I can do with it.[18]

One explanation offered for these differences in style was that the federal system is more established and accepted. State mediators usually lack the resources and status of the federal mediators. Thus, being "number two," they have to try harder. Another state mediator noted:

> They [federal mediators] have a reputation. We are newer. We have to be more active; we have to show people we can provide a service.[19]

Strikes and Lockouts

When an agreement cannot be reached by the expiration date of a contract, a strike or lockout becomes possible. A **strike** is *the employees' refusal to work.* A **lockout** is *management's refusal to allow the employees to work.*

strike
lockout

Although strikes are dramatic, they are quite infrequent. Fewer than 4 percent of contract negotiations result in strikes.[20] The strike represents the ultimate weapon which the union can threaten to use, and it is risky to do so. First, unions do not want to strike unless they feel they will win. Second, a strike can hurt the employees (through lost income) more than management in many cases. Third, once the ultimate weapon has been used, one's bargaining chits become severely limited. For the company, the lost income and tarnished image from a strike also are costly. Usually, as the saying goes, there are no winners in a strike.

Before a strike is called, the union must hold a *strike vote* among the members. If the vote is positive, the union is authorized to call a strike at a time it deems appropriate. Thus, the strike vote strengthens the hand of the union in the bargaining process.

The most common strikes are contract and grievance strikes. Ninety percent of all strikes are *contract strikes*—strikes that take place when there is failure to agree on a new contract. A *grievance strike* is the result of an unresolved dispute over the administration of the contract.

One alternative to a total strike is a *work-to-rule* job action or a *slow-down*. In this procedure, all of the rules and regulations governing job behavior are followed to the letter by employees. Many of these procedures are unnecessarily complex and are usually bypassed during normal operations, so when employees work to rule, paralysis occurs. Slowdowns by the air traffic control operators in the U.S. illustrate the delays that such a procedure can cause.

Another non-strike job action is the *sick-out,* in which employees call in "sick" en masse. This is often used by public employees for whom strikes are illegal, such as fire fighters and police officers. (Among police, such large-scale organized absences are called "the blue flu.")

During the strike, the company may or may not continue to operate without the striking employees. If it stays open, employees who continue to work are called "scabs" by the strikers and may be subject to verbal or physical abuse when entering or leaving the place of work. Nails on the road, sugar in gas tanks, rocks through a windshield, or cars overturned are not uncommon during a bitter strike. The company may also attempt to hire new, nonunion ("scab") workers. White-collar and management employees are sometimes pressed into service to take the place of striking workers. Some advantages for the company of continued operation are "teaching the union a lesson," maintaining revenue, providing service, and possibly strengthening the company's bargaining position. The disadvantages are the possible violence and negative public relations.

Arbitration

In contrast to mediation, in which the third party acts to assist the bargaining parties to come to an agreement, **arbitration** is a *process by which a neutral third party makes a decision to which the two parties must agree.* In other words, the arbitrator decides the issue.

arbitration

Arbitration is often seen as a failure in the bargaining process, since the parties are unable to reach a decision themselves. However, like most last resorts, it can be effective under certain circumstances.

There are several types of arbitration:

1. *Voluntary arbitration*—arbitration to which both parties agree.
2. *Compulsory arbitration*—arbitration which is required by law.
3. *Conventional arbitration*—process in which the arbitrator provides a settlement that seems reasonable and fair to him or her.
4. *Final-offer arbitration*—procedure in which the arbitrator accepts one of the two parties' final offers. No compromises or combination of elements from the two competing offers can be generated.

5.   *Single arbitration*—process in which one arbitrator makes the decision.
6.   *Arbitration panel*—procedure in which a group of arbitrators decide the issue. The panel can be either *all neutral* parties or *tripartite*, made up of union, management, and neutral members.

Final-offer arbitration may be superior to conventional arbitration because it motivates the parties to reach agreement, since there is more risk of a major loss to each of them from the arbitrator's decision. With conventional arbitration, there is often a perception that the arbitrator will forge a compromise roughly half-way between the two positions. Thus, the parties might prefer to let the arbitrator make the final decision so that neither party has to accept responsibility for it. This might also reduce their commitment to implementing the solution.

Having heard all the evidence, the arbitrator makes a decision in writing, usually within thirty days of the hearing. The decision is legally binding on both parties.

Arbitration can be used to settle disputes over either contract negotiations or grievances. In the case of grievances, the burden of proof is usually on the party who initiated the action. In writing decisions in grievance cases, the arbitrator will generally attempt to clarify the problem to prevent it from arising again.

Contract Administration

Once a contract is signed and in operation, the final step in the bargaining process is the *administration* of the contract, the day-to-day execution of the terms of the agreement. When disputes arise about conditions of work under the terms of the contract, the employee may file a **grievance**—a *claim that the contract has been violated*. Most grievances arise in relation to discipline, seniority rights, management rights, work assignments, performance of bargaining unit work by people outside the bargaining unit, pay, benefits, promotions, transfers, and layoffs.

grievance

There are several steps in the grievance procedure, designed to encourage settling disputes at the lowest level possible. Although the steps in the process may vary with the structure of the organization, they tend to follow this pattern:

1.   *Informal meeting* with the employee, supervisor, and union steward.
2.   *Formal grievance to supervisor.* If the problem is not resolved at step 1, then a formal, written grievance may be submitted within a specified number of days. The employee, supervisor, and union steward or grievance committee person meet to discuss the issue and a specific remedy is requested.
3.   *Appeal to higher management.* If the grievance is not settled by the supervisor, it is taken to higher levels, such as the director of human

resources or the plant manager. It could ultimately go to top corporate management and the national union for review.

4. *Arbitration*. If the dispute is not settled by top management, it will go to the final step, arbitration.

Most grievances (over 75 percent) are handled at step 1 and an additional 20 percent at step 2. Only about 1 percent reach arbitration.[21] The ability to avoid grievances and to deal effectively with them when they do arise is often an important element in top management's evaluation of a supervisor's effectiveness. In fact, considerable interpersonal and leadership skill is required for effective employee-supervisor problem-solving. An effective day-to-day relationship between supervisor and steward is a critical element here as well.

LABOR RELATIONS AND MANAGEMENT OF HUMAN RESOURCES

Emerging Forms of Labor-Management Cooperation

Contemporary labor relations have had a major impact on the ways line managers work with their employees, and this section will examine how the work of managers has been affected by the various new forms of labor-management activity.

The changing work place described in Chapter Four, and the move away from the adversarial climate described in this chapter's vignette about Bethlehem Steel, demonstrate how labor-management relations in many organizations have expanded beyond the basic administration of the collective bargaining agreement to include the cooperative exploration of new ways to design the work environment. This change entails new roles for employees, line managers, and human resource specialists.

Cooperative efforts are often part of a quality-of-work-life (QWL) program. The steel companies and the United Steelworkers Union are working together to reduce labor costs. Other examples are the joint UAW-Ford Employee Involvement Program and Honeywell's ongoing problem-solving Arrowwood Conferences for Honeywell Avionics and Defense managers and members of Minneapolis Teamsters Local 1145. A union leader who helped initiate the Honeywell activity, Jim Holte, President of Local 1145, described the motivation behind the joint meetings at Arrowwood (in which over 10,000 people have now participated):

> Arrowwood, in its original state, addressed quality—and of course you read in all kinds of periodicals and newspapers about the influx of foreign competition on United States industry. And in looking at the ap-

proach Japan takes toward the making of their products, you'll find that quality is highly rated in their working atmosphere. And a lot of people feel that that's why they are so successful. In the United States, however, quality has not been of the utmost concern. We've tended to think, "How fast can I do it?" But really, when you look at quality and not making mistakes, that's a relatively "free" thing. If you can eliminate those costs of making those mistakes, that puts you in a more competitive state where you hopefully gain bigger shares in the marketplace. From a union standpoint, it helps us on wages, working conditions, and benefits. It's a thing that benefits all of us, I believe, if it can work. It'll improve our competitive edge, number one, and hopefully gain a bigger share of the marketplace and provide job security for all of us in Minneapolis.[22]

In the automobile industry, foreign competition was a major factor leading to cooperative efforts. At Ford, Peter J. Pestillo, Ford's vice-president for labor relations, and Don Ephlin, the UAW's vice-president of the Ford Division, have been strong supporters of employee involvement. This top-level support is critical to the success of such efforts. However, the real activity (and payoff) in employee involvement occurs at the level of the work group, when natural work units (departments, assembly teams, etc.) get together once or twice a week to brainstorm new and better ways to do their job. An example of how the cooperative process works at General Motors is shown in Box 6.2.

Another troubled industry which has been forced to develop more cooperative labor-management problem-solving activities is steel. In 1982, Jones and Laughlin Steel Corp. saved $75 million, mainly through "people programs," in cooperation with the United Steelworkers. This involved worker suggestions and work-force reductions, according to Thomas C. Graham, former president of J and L. The company has cut the man-hours required to make a ton of steel from six in 1978 to three and a half in 1983.[23]

For managers, such cooperative labor relations require skills in participative management, which include group problem solving and decision making, active listening, conflict management, interpersonal sensitivity, and positive reinforcement. As one manager described the change in his approach to managing people, "It's amazing how much you can accomplish if you don't worry about who gets credit for the results."

More Flexible Work Rules

work rules

Many of the changes that come out of these cooperative approaches result in more flexible work rules that boost productivity. **Work rules** are *the regulations in the labor contract which govern the conditions and the conduct of work.* When the economy was growing rapidly and the economic survival of an industry was never in doubt, both labor and management were preoccupied with contractual "rights," such as who performed what tasks and what

A PLANT WHERE TEAMWORK IS MORE THAN JUST TALK

BOX 6.2

Life inside a Cadillac engine plant in Livonia, Mich., is worlds apart from the atmosphere of a typical auto factory. Hourly workers and supervisors dress much the same and cooperate closely on "business teams" that organize the work and make other decisions normally left to management. "It makes you feel like a part of what's going on," says Gary L. Andrews, an hourly worker and assistant team coordinator (ATC). A 14-year Cadillac veteran, Andrews says he would return to a traditional auto plant "only if it was a choice between that and hitting the streets."

Livonia uses the "pay-for-knowledge" concept where a worker's pay rises as more job skills are mastered, and the worker is rotated among all the jobs in one section. The worker earns more and management has more flexibility in job assignments.

The system was introduced in July 1981, when GM's Cadillac Motor Car Division closed its engine works in Detroit and moved to the western suburb of Livonia. About 95 percent of the Detroit workers transferred with Cadillac. Local 22 of the United Auto Workers was involved in planning the change from the start and even had a voice in choosing salaried employees who would function as the team coordinators. (ATCs such as Andrews, 32, are elected from the ranks.)

The basic plant unit is the business team, consisting of ten to twenty workers each. The assembly line is still used, but the employees do a variety of jobs and participate in solving problems and making decisions about the production process. Managers dress in similar ways (often jeans), and share the same cafeteria and parking lot (no reserved spaces).

The teams meet weekly on company time to discuss issues such as safety and housekeeping. They decide when to award raises and rotate jobs, and they may even suggest redesigning the work flow. In the fall of 1981, Andrews took it on himself to analyze every job on two teams that attach components to already-assembled engines. "I sat with pencil and paper and figured out how to make it easier," he recalls. His teammates accepted his idea of spreading the work more evenly along the lines.

A traditional plant would have forty-five different job titles, each with its own pay rate. At Livonia, there are four pay rates. Learning a new range of job skills means moving up to a higher wage rate. The top rate is $10.08 for a "job setter," who sets up tooling.

In a traditional plant, you might have 90 to 100 job setters," says Peter J. Ulbrich, until recently Livonia's personnel administrator. "Here, you have the opportunity for 1,200 to 1,300 people to get there." This system can produce an expensive work force. "It is a neat way to get short-term productivity results," says one teamwork expert, "but you wonder what they will do when everybody reaches the top rate."

Business Week, May 16, 1983, p. 108.

groups were entitled to incentive pay. However, as technology changed rapidly and the competitive environment required higher quality and lower costs, rigid work rules became an impossible burden for both parties.

These rules changes affected many industries, especially the ones in the traditional manufacturing, processing, and transportation industries. Airlines persuaded pilots to fly more hours for the same pay. (Greyhound Bus Lines suffered a strike when it attempted to make similar changes without involving its union.) Trucking companies won the right to pay drivers for hours worked rather than the outmoded miles driven. Auto, rubber, and steel companies combined certain skilled trades.

Not all of these changes have been accepted easily by the unions. Companies often present the same ultimatum that led to wage concessions: "Change the work rules or see the plant close."[24] In some cases, the unions obtained concessions in return. Kaiser and J and L give early retirement and $400 monthly pension supplements to workers 50 and older whose jobs have been eliminated. In its New Castle, Indiana, machining and forge plant, Chrysler gave the UAW a written promise that the plant would remain open through 1985 in return for changes made in early 1982.

These changes have been basically of two types—those that do not change the design of work but make it more efficient, and those that change the work system itself, such as through autonomous work teams. Most changes so far have been of the first type, with the most important being the combining of tasks and the elimination of unneeded jobs.[25] A summary of the major work rule changes is shown in Exhibit 6.5.

New Programs for Job Security

As a result of managerial attempts to reduce the size of the work force to increase productivity and cut costs, unions have become increasingly concerned with job security for their members. And in many cases, through cooperative problem-solving, union and management representatives have found creative ways to achieve both sets of objectives.

One area of joint activity is *worker retraining*. For example, at two automobile companies which have lost hundreds of thousands of employees since 1979 (Ford and General Motors), the contract with the United Auto Workers calls for a special retraining fund. The fund was created by a contribution by the companies of $.05 for each hour worked by a UAW member. This fund has raised millions of dollars to help laid-off workers learn new skills through activities such as college courses, job search assistance, and career planning and change activities. In Dearborn, Michigan, a school which had been closed was bought and converted by Ford to be used as a retraining center. Although many retrained employees have found jobs paying $6.00 or $7.00 an hour, one adjustment they have had to make is that they will probably never again earn the $16 to $20 per hour they once earned in the auto industry.

Another form of security in the Ford and GM contracts is the *Guaranteed Income Stream*, or GIS. Under this system, high seniority workers can

A SUMMARY OF MAJOR WORK RULE CHANGES

EXHIBIT 6.5

Unions Are Granting These Major Changes in Work Rules. . . .	*. . . In These Industries*
Job assignments Cutting size of crews; enlarging jobs by adding duties; eliminating unneeded jobs	Steel, autos, railroads, meatpacking, airlines
Skilled maintenance and construction Combining craft jobs such as millwright, welder, rigger, and boilermaker; allowing journeymen to perform helpers' duties; permitting equipment operators to run more than one machine	Autos, rubber, steel, petroleum, construction
Hours of work Giving up relief and wash-up periods; allowing management more flexibility in scheduling daily and weekly hours; working more hours for the same pay	Autos, rubber, steel, meatpacking, trucking, airlines (pilots), textile
Seniority Restricting use of seniority in filling job vacancies, "bumping" during layoffs, and picking shifts	Autos, rubber, meatpacking, steel
Wages Restricting pay to hours worked rather than miles traveled	Railroads, trucking
Incentive pay Reducing incentives to reflect changing conditions	Rubber, steel
Team work Allowing team members to rotate jobs; permitting pay for knowledge instead of function; allowing management to change crew structure to cope with new technology	Autos, auto suppliers, steel, rubber

SOURCE: "Unions are Granting These Major Changes in Work Rules . . . In These Industries" from the May 16, 1983 issue of *Business Week* by special permission, © 1983 by McGraw-Hill, Inc.

receive a certain percentage of their wages until they reach retirement age, if they are laid off. However, if the employee receives another bona fide job offer and turns it down, he or she then forfeits rights to the GIS. The basic idea of the GIS is that its high cost to the company makes it unattractive to lay people off.

Employee redeployment is the movement of laid-off employees to other plants. Usually the company pays the moving expenses in such a transfer, but not all companies provide this benefit. In the Ford and GM contracts, these expenses are paid by the company.

Guaranteed employment has become another popular form of security, especially in the wake of all of the interest in Japanese management. Firms such as IBM, Procter & Gamble, and Johnson Wax are known for their commitment to no-layoff policies. (In many cases, these are unwritten, but widely publicized and consistently practiced over the years.) In an industry as cyclical as the automobile business, such a policy is difficult to implement. However, at Ford and GM, certain plants have been set up as experimental locations, at which 80 percent of the work force would be protected from layoffs. This program remains to be tested, however, because an improving economy resulted in the recall of large numbers of employees at these plants.

A new tactic of unions faced with a local plant closing is efforts toward *plant conversion.* In this process the union attempts instead to identify other economically viable products which the plant could make.

The biggest task a union faces, however, is not identifying the alternative products which would utilize the workers' skills, but convincing management that plant conversion would be in the company's best interests. Often management had gone through a similar search for alternative uses of the plant before making the difficult decision to close it.[26]

Effects on Traditional Human Resource Activities

When all of these new forms of labor-management relationships are considered together, they have strong implications for the ways in which traditional human resource management activities are conducted. For example, as we have just seen how *training* has become a central element in the organization's human resource strategy in relation to employment security and retraining. By using training to develop new skills in present or laid-off employees (the internal labor market), there will be less need to go to the external labor market for these skills. Thus, *staffing* is also affected, in that the search becomes more internal than external.

Compensation has been affected, as high-paying, less flexible jobs are traded off for low-paying, more flexible jobs. Pay is based more on the number of skills the employee possesses than on a specific job title. And new forms of compensation, such as guaranteed income streams for laid-off high-seniority employees and subsidies for retraining, are being created through cooperative union-management efforts.

Job design has been strongly affected. This had been one of the most jealously guarded "management prerogatives," involving "efficiency experts" (industrial engineers) whose goal was to reduce cost alone, rather than to attain the new twin goals of cost-cutting and quality of work life through cooperation.

Supervisory practices also have been strongly affected by contemporary labor-management relations. Top management now tends to see the first-line supervisor as the company's main implementor of labor relations policy and expects participative leadership styles, communication skills, and collaborative problem-solving from the supervisor.

Human resource planning, usually done at the highest level of the organization, also has become "fair game" for cooperative discussions with the unions. As we see in discussions of plant conversions and other forms of employment security, any consideration of redeployment of human and physical resources has an impact on plans for staffing and thus increases the complexity of strategic planning for human resources.

CONCLUSION

The meaning and the role of unions are changing. While there will always be a need for the union to engage in certain confrontational activities vis-à-vis management (especially in the area of rewards, such as pay and benefits), there are new areas of cooperation to be developed (especially in the areas of productivity and quality of work life). Unions fill an important need for employees, especially where workers are dissatisfied with their work, where they feel powerless, and where their attitudes toward unions are positive. It is important for managers (and future managers) to recognize the legitimate role of unions and to develop skills to bring about win-win relationships with union leaders, both in formal bargaining and in the day-to-day administration of the contract.

KEY POINTS

▬ Unions play a major role in the quality of work life and in the economic viability of organizations and industries.

▬ Employees generally are motivated to join unions because of 1) perception of (or attitudes toward) the work environment, 2) perceptions of employee influence, and 3) beliefs about unions.

▬ The history of the labor movement was one of stormy, uneven progress, affected by economic conditions, employer resistance, and union leadership. Starting with the early craft unions, union activity moved toward industry-based organizing during the depression. The current growth areas in union membership are the public sector, service workers, and information workers.

▬ The stages in the collective bargaining process include the union organizing campaign, negotiation of the contract, administration of the contract (if there is agreement), or a strike (if there is no agreement).

▬ Bargaining can be either distributive (win-lose) or integrative (win-win). The latter results in greater cooperation and trust, although the former may be more common in practice.

▬ Mediation and arbitration are two forms of external, third-party intervention designed to facilitate the bargaining process. In mediation, the third party helps the two parties reach their own solution, while in arbitration the third party makes the decisions.

▬ In recent years, labor-management relations have expanded in many industries to include cooperative problem-solving efforts to improve productivity, cut costs, and enhance quality of work life.

ISSUES FOR DISCUSSION

1. What do you think are the most important reasons why employees want unions? What can management do to respond to these concerns in advance of union organizing activity?

2. What are some of the major differences between a union of secretarial and clerical workers and a union of manufacturing workers? What managerial skills would be most useful for dealing with organized office workers?

3. How involved should top management be in labor relations? What specific activities should top management perform in this area? Why?

4. It is often said that there is no winner in a strike. What is your reaction to this statement? Are there conditions under which a strike does have a positive pay-off, either to the union or to management? Discuss, citing concrete examples.

5. What actions at the strategic or management level could increase the probability that an employee's grievance would be handled satisfactorily at step 1? What supportive human resource policies are useful?

6. Briefly summarize the "new look" in labor-management relations. How would you defend this new approach to a hard-nosed, "Theory X" style supervisor?

NOTES

1. *Wall Street Journal*, April 7, 1981, p. 1.

2. D. Quinn Mills, and Janice McCormick, *Industrial Relations in Transition* (New York: Wiley 1985), p. 647. For more detail on new forms of cooperation *and* efforts to decertify unions, see David Wessel "Fighting off Unions, Ingersoll-Rand Uses Wide Range of Tactics," *Wall Street Journal*, June 13, 1985, pp. 1, 22.

3. T. Kochan, *Collective Bargaining and Industrial Relations* (Homewood, IL: Irwin), 1980.

4. Julius G. Getman, Stephen B. Goldberg, and Jeanne B. Herman, *Union Representation Elections: Law and Reality* (New York: Sage Foundations, 1976).

5. J. M. Brett, "Why Employees Want Unions," *Organizational Dynamics*, Spring 1980, 8, No. 4, p. 53.

6. W. Clay Hamner, and Frank J. Smith, "Work Attitudes as Predictors of Unionization Activity," *Journal of Applied Psychology*, 1978, 63, pp. 415–21.

7. Brett, op. cit., pp. 57–59.

8. Fred K. Foulkes, "How Top Nonunion Companies Manage Employees," *Harvard Business Review*, September-October 1981.

9. Ibid., p. 90.

10. Juanita M. Kreps, Philip L. Martin, Richard Pearlman, and Gerald Somers, *Contemporary Labor Economics and Labor Relations* (Belmont, CA: Wadsworth, Second Edition, 1980), p. 149.

11. Hamner and Smith, op. cit.

12. Steps in preparation for negotiation are based on Meyer Ryder et al. *Management Preparation for Collective Bargaining* (Homewood, IL: Irwin), 1966.

13. Clark Kerr, "Bargaining Processes," in E. Bakke, C. Kerr, and C. Anrod (eds.), *Unions, Management and the Public* (New York: Harcourt, Brace, 1967), p. 307.

14. Kreps, et al., op. cit., p. 180.

15. Richard Walton, and Robert McKersie, *A Behavioral Theory of Labor Negotiations* (New York: McGraw-Hill, 1965).

16. Deborah M. Kolb, "Roles Mediators Play: State and Federal Practice," *Industrial Relations*, 1981, 20, pp. 1–17.

17. Ibid., p. 4.

18. Ibid., p. 4.

19. Ibid., p. 16.

20. *Yearbook of Labour Statistics* (Geneva: International Labour Office, 1975).

21. John Price, et al., "Three Studies of Grievances," *Personnel Journal*, January 1976, pp. 33–37.

22. "Newstape," Honeywell Aerospace and Defense Management Development Center, February 1983.

23. *Business Week*, May 16, 1983, p. 110.

24. Ibid., p. 103.

25. Ibid.

26. Worker retraining, the Guaranteed Income Stream, and guaranteed employment are described in detail in "New Blueprints in the Drive for Job Security," *Business Week*, January 9, 1984, pp. 91, 92; and "A Bold Tactic to Hold on to Jobs," *Business Week*, October 29, 1984, pp. 70, 72.

ANNOTATED BIBLIOGRAPHY

BAZERMAN, M. and LEWICKI, R. J. (eds.) *Negotiation in Organizations*. New York: Russell Sage Foundation, 1983.

> This is a book of invited papers by leading scholars (e.g., Thomas Kochan, Jeanne Brett) in the area of bargaining and negotiation. The focus is on new approaches to bargaining and new arenas in which bargaining is occurring, such as between different divisions within the same organization.

BRETT, J. "Why Employees Want Unions." *Organizational Dynamics*, Spring 1980, 8, No. 4, pp. 47–59.

> This is a detailed and well-written overview on employees' motivation to join unions. Much of the material is based on the author's own research on union organizing campaigns. The theme of the article seems to be that effective human resource management practices, applied consistently over time (not just when there is a threat of union organization), are the strongest factor in employees' decisions not to vote for a union.

FISHER, R. and URY, W. *Getting to Yes: Negotiating Without Giving In*. Boston: Houghton Mifflin, 1981.

> This short volume, also available in a Penguin paperback version published in 1983, is a summary of the studies and conferences conducted by the Harvard Negotiation Project, a group that deals continually with all levels of conflict resolution from domestic to business to international disputes. It describes a step-by-step strategy for coming to mutually acceptable (integrative) solutions in various situations—boss-employee, tenant-landlord, parent-child, etc. The steps describe how to: 1) separate the people from the problem, 2) focus on interests, not positions, 3) establish precise goals at the outset of negotiations, 4) work together to find creative, win-win options, 5) negotiate successfully with opponents who are more powerful, refuse to play by the rules, or use "dirty tricks."

"A Work Revolution in U.S. Industry: More Flexible Rules on the Job Are Boosting Productivity." *Business Week*, May 16, 1983, pp. 102–110.

> This is an excellent examination of the ways in which labor-management agreements are being modified to permit productivity improvements to meet external competition. Many of those changes are based upon cooperative problem-solving processes, such as employee involvement and participative management practices. The changes described point to movement toward more integrative forms of bargaining processes.

PART THREE

STAFFING THE ORGANIZATION

Staffing is the process through which jobs are defined and people are found to fill those jobs. Part Three deals with the methods organizations use to match people and jobs to ensure personal satisfaction and productivity and organizational effectiveness. Each chapter presents a crucial step in the staffing process, starting with the identification of the need for employees, continuing with the recruitment and selection of applicants, and ending with the entrance of the employee into the organization. Part Three also shows how human resource professionals and line managers work together in each step of the staffing process.

The staffing process begins with planning, discussed in Chapter Seven. This chapter emphasizes the need for human resource professionals to collaborate with top management to estimate the number of employees required to meet organizational goals and to identify potential sources of such employees. Methods for forecasting the need for employees and the supply of potential applicants are also discussed.

Chapter Eight concentrates on recruitment, the organization's efforts to attract and screen job applicants. Several recruitment methods in use today are presented, with advertising, campus recruiting, and employment agencies discussed in detail.

The next step in the staffing process is selection, the topic of Chapter Nine. This chapter describes many common selection techniques, such as interviews, tests, and work samples, and provides standards for evaluating their effectiveness. Also discussed is the impact of Equal Employment Opportunity legislation on selection procedures. Chapters Eight and Nine stress how both line managers and human resource professionals are involved in recruitment and selection. For example, human resource professionals may take the lead in preparing recruiting materials and establishing selection procedures, but both parties interview and screen job applicants, and line managers usually make final selection decisions.

Chapter Ten focuses on how the new employee moves from the status of "outsider" to that of "insider" and stresses the need for organizations to consciously manage this entry process. The chapter examines how individuals deal with unrealistically high expectations about their new job and employer and how organizations socialize new members. Techniques for early career planning are also discussed.

CHAPTER SEVEN

STRATEGIC STAFFING

Krack Exploration, Inc., was formed in 1980 by six veterans of the Gulf Coast oil and gas industry.[1] *By the end of 1980 the company employed twenty-five people and became the wholly owned subsidiary of a major European corporation with little experience in oil and gas exploration but with considerable cash to invest in such a venture. Krack executives prepared a five-year strategic plan to chart the growth of the company. Their primary goals were to recoup the parent company's investment by discovering and developing productive oil and gas fields and to become profitable by 1985.*

As they prepared their plans in 1980, Krack executives considered environmental opportunities and threats in their highly competitive and unpredictable business. Both consumer demand and the price of oil and gas had been high and were expected to increase. Many small exploration companies, which were formed to capitalize on the demand for domestic oil and gas, represented a potential threat to Krack, but since most did not have Krack's considerable financial backing they were not viewed as major, long-term threats. Furthermore, Krack executives felt the expertise of their employees gave the company a distinct advantage over small competitors. Their ability to act quickly was also viewed as an advantage over major oil companies.

As Krack executives prepared specific goals for capital investments, number of leases and number of producing wells, they also began a process of strategic planning for staffing their company as it grew. First, they estimated their need for key employees such as geologists, geophysicists, and various types of engineers. Next, they identified two major sources of these professional employees so essential to their success—university campuses and other oil and gas companies. Unlike major oil companies, Krack was not able to hire recent graduates and allow them several years to develop expertise through on-the-job training and experience. Krack needed seasoned professionals who could assume major responsibilities immediately after being hired. In addition, when the company discovered a major well or field, Krack had to be able to hire many experienced employees very quickly. Krack therefore developed a strategy to match people and jobs through recruitment of experienced professionals.

In assessing the strengths and weaknesses of current employees, Krack executives concluded that their managers of technical disciplines were outstanding, but the company needed employees in technical disciplines with five to ten years of Gulf Coast experience. On the basis of exploration and production projections, Krack's vice-president of human resources consulted extensively with technical managers to estimate the numbers of new employees required over the next five years. He then developed a strategy of enticing such employees away from major oil companies through aggressive recruiting and attractive salaries and benefits. Krack set salary levels above the industry average and also implemented a bonus plan for all employees involved in a major discovery of oil or gas. The company also retained search firms to recruit prospective employees from competitors. These firms stressed Krack's small size and ability to act quickly, as well as the autonomy and substantial financial rewards available to employees.

By 1985 Krack had grown to 288 employees, somewhat short of the 350 that had been projected in 1980 for 1985. The oil glut and recession of 1981–82 had forced a revision of growth projections, but the company had found many productive wells. Krack's recruiting efforts had been consistently responsive to company needs for new employees, and Krack's professional staff was considered one of the strongest in the industry.

*T*here is little doubt that in today's dynamic and often hostile business environment few organizations can survive and prosper without continually anticipating and responding to environmental changes. Progressive organizations deal with the uncertainty of the future through strategic planning, the process of setting organizational objectives and deciding on comprehensive programs of action that will achieve these objectives.[2]

Most organizations engage in formal or informal planning to establish objectives and ways of meeting those objectives in the future. Seldom are the plans accurate, but they provide direction and a basis for making adjustments as the future arrives.

Krack Exploration, Inc., followed the strategic planning steps outlined in Exhibit 7.1. The company's mission was to discover and develop productive oil and gas fields that would recoup the parent company's investment in Krack. Company executives analyzed environmental threats and opportuni-

EXHIBIT 7.1   **PLANNING SEQUENCE LEADING**
TO STRATEGIC STAFFING

Strategic Planning	Strategic Human Resource Planning	Strategic Staffing
What philosophy and mission does the organization wish to establish?	What degree of fit between employees and jobs does the organization desire?	What kinds of employees does the organization need?
What environmental opportunities and threats does it face?	What is the current degree of fit and resultant level of employee productivity and satisfaction?	What supply of employees is anticipated inside and outside the organization?
What strengths and weaknesses does the organization have?	What changes in human resource policies and practices are necessary to attain the desired fit between employees and jobs?	What steps are necessary to meet the anticipated need for employees?
What goals and objectives does it wish to achieve?		
How will its goals and objectives be met?		

ties, assessed the organization's strengths and weaknesses, and set specific goals for the investment of capital, number of leases, and number of producing wells. They then prepared plans on how to meet these goals.

The availability and quality of employees are important considerations in the strategic planning process. It is obvious that without the right people in the right jobs at the right time an organization cannot meet its goals. Plans to recruit and select new employees were especially important to Krack because its projections for rapid growth required that the company nearly double its work force every year until 1985. Therefore, as Krack executives engaged in strategic planning, they also considered the fit between jobs and employees and determined that seasoned professionals would be required to perform the complex work involved in finding and producing oil and gas. Finally, they estimated their need for various kinds of employees and the availability of these employees in the labor market. In collaboration with the vice-president of human resources they then made plans to attract and retain the required employees at the appropriate time.

PLANNING STRATEGIES

Strategic planning leads directly to two additional planning activities, strategic human resource planning and strategic staffing (Exhibit 7.1). *Strategic human resource planning* focuses on the organization's need for an optimal degree of fit between employees and jobs and the human resource policies and procedures to satisfy that need. As noted in Chapter Two, strategic human resource planning involves the analysis of people, jobs, the organization, and the environment to set plans for how the optimal degree of fit between employees and jobs can be achieved. This analysis is used to choose among four basic approaches to combining employees and jobs—staffing (matching the person and the job), employee development (changing the person to fit the job), human resource systems (changing the job to fit the person), and organizational change (changing both the person and the job).

Strategic staffing is *the process of forecasting an organization's demand for employees and deciding on a plan of action to secure those employees through recruitment, selection, promotion, and transfers.* Both line managers and human resource professionals are involved in this process. After top management has set organizational goals, departmental managers throughout the organization estimate the number of additional employees they will need to achieve those goals (or, conversely, the size of the *reduction* of their staff). Human resource professionals confer with line managers to estimate the organization's need for specific kinds of employees and the supply of those employees inside and outside the organization. They then plan to obtain the needed employees. When an organization's need for a specific kind of employee is great and the supply of those employees in the labor market is also great, staffing is the most appropriate way to achieve an optimal degree of fit between jobs and people.[3] This is especially true when highly skilled employees are needed in a short period of time. For example, Krack Exploration could not afford the time to hire recent engineering graduates and train them for three or four years to fill the need for intermediate-level engineers. A strategy to recruit experienced technical employees and to compensate them well was more appropriate for Krack.

strategic staffing

In practice, strategic planning, human resource planning, and strategic staffing are seldom as well integrated as they were in Krack Exploration, Inc. Rather than occurring simultaneously, they often take place in sequence with little or no interaction between line managers and human resource managers. This lack of integration contributes to the *reactive* style of human resource management discussed in Chapter Two. For example, corporate executives might make long-term plans to double production of a sophisticated product that requires highly skilled and experienced technical employees, but fail to inform human resource professionals of the increased need for such employees until a few months before the expansion is scheduled to occur. As a result, human resource professionals might have difficulty recruiting and hiring the required employees on such short notice. Human resource practitioners object strongly to a lack of involvement in corporate strategic planning because it often forces them to react to crises that could have been avoided. This lack of integration between strategic planning and human resource planning (discussed in Chapters One and Two) has been widely lamented by academic writers as well as practitioners,[4] and in recent years important steps have been taken to include senior human resource professionals in long-range strategic planning (see Box 2.1 in Chapter Two).

Coordination of long-range business and human resource planning is still relatively rare in practice today but is likely to increase as the work force and work place continue to change dramatically (see Chapters Three and Four) and as a highly competitive and rapidly changing marketplace forces organizations to change more rapidly in order to survive. Successful companies must not only anticipate market trends but also anticipate trends in the labor market. In considering the kinds of products and services it will provide in the future, an organization must also consider the kinds of employees it will need to produce those products and services. It is important for human resource professionals to gather information about developments in the economic, political, social, and technological environments to anticipate the nature of the work force available to the organization five to ten years into the future. Such projections can have a crucial impact on the business planning of an organization. The potential impact of environmental trends on business planning and the way in which an organization can be staffed are illustrated in Box 7.1. In particular, the projections made by human resource planners at Tenneco, Inc., about educational and skill levels, age, and life style have broad implications for the kinds of employees available to Tenneco and the kinds of jobs they will be able and willing to accept.

STAFFING STRATEGIES

Line managers, in consultation with human resource professionals, can choose from a number of strategies to staff their organizations with productive, satisfied employees. Some organizations, such as Krack Exploration, Inc., prefer to hire applicants with considerable related work experience, while others favor inexperienced high school or college graduates, who immediately enter extensive training programs before assuming all the responsibilities of their new jobs. Similarly, some organizations seek applicants with very specialized educational credentials and work experience (e.g., only business school graduates with twenty-seven hours of accounting courses and five years of industrial accounting experience are considered for the job of auditor), while others prefer applicants with a broader range of education and work experience (e.g., applicants with a social science major and two years of any kind of work experience are considered for a sales position).

Eight major strategies are defined by combining three key *dimensions*, each of which is divided into two levels (see Exhibit 7.2). The first dimension concerns the *amount of related work experience* of applicants. They may have the appropriate educational background for the job to be filled but very little related work experience. At the other extreme on this dimension is the applicant with a high level of related work experience. The second dimension represents the *breadth of the applicant's educational and occupational background*.

At one end of the continuum is the specialized applicant whose education and work experience have focused in a particular discipline (e.g., ac-

BOX 7.1

ENVIRONMENTAL SCANNING AT TENNECO, INC.

Richard E. Clinton, Director of Human Resource Planning at Tenneco, Inc., participates actively in the strategic planning by the senior management team of this energy firm consisting of twelve highly autonomous divisions and over 90,000 employees. One of his responsibilities is to gather information that can be used in long-range human resource planning, in concert with the business planning of the firm. Clinton refers to this activity as environmental scanning, or "reading the tea leaves" and defines it as an information gathering process that alerts human resource managers to trends that may present future opportunities and threats to the goals of the organization. Information is gathered about the economic, political, social, technological, and demographic environments and organized and presented monthly to senior human resource managers throughout the company.

For example, when Clinton reads that by 1990 slow population growth will decrease the number of workers entering the labor force, he encourages each operating unit to evaluate this trend's effect on their ability to acquire people with specific skills needed to accomplish projected organizational goals. Environmental scanning offers line managers a tool to reduce risks in business planning, and enables them to make plans that will help the organization avoid unexpected obstacles to achieve long-term goals. Environmental scanning might ask:

Is technology being developed that will change work force composition?

Will people be available with the types of skills required to accomplish your plans?

Will job tasks and career paths need to be adapted to accommodate the increasingly large numbers of women in the work force?

The monthly reports highlight developments of special interest to Tenneco business managers. Among the topics included are human resource planning, recruiting, training and development, attitudes and values, changing technology, productivity, compliance programs, and the potential influence of a variety of activist organizations. Recent developments include:

Significant changes will occur in the work force over the next 15–20 years. Persons aged 18–34, who now comprise 48 percent of the work force, will by the year 2000 represent only 37 percent of the work force. Those aged 35–54 will increase from 35 percent to 49 percent of all workers. The pressure of a large number of middle-aged candidates for a potentially limited number of middle management positions will be considerable.

The growing percentage of single-parent, dual-career, and single-person households will have a direct impact on scheduling, compensation, and counseling needs of workers.

Personal computers are making the use of "home office" employees more feasible. Some of the problems are liability at home, performance measurement, and the absence of staff members from the office environment.

The authors wish to thank Richard E. Clinton for his cooperation in preparing this material.

EXHIBIT 7.2   **MATRIX: STAFFING STRATEGIES**

APPLICANT'S BACKGROUND

		Specialist		Generalist	
		BREADTH OF CAREER PATH		BREADTH OF CAREER PATH	
		Within Function	Between Functions	Within Function	Between Functions
RELATED WORK EXPERIENCE	High	1	2	3	4
	Low	5	6	7	8

counting or geology). The generalist has a much broader background and may have held jobs in several functional areas (e.g., research and development, production, and sales). The third dimension consists of the *breadth of the career paths* available in the organization to new employees. At one extreme is a very narrow career path in which employees can be promoted only within the same functional area of an organization (e.g., from reservoir engineer to intermediate reservoir engineer to senior reservoir engineer to staff reservoir engineer), and at the other is a broad range of career paths which allow employees to be promoted or transferred between departments.

Depending on the job and labor market, an organization defines its staffing strategy by choosing among the eight combinations of these three dimensions. One strategy, represented by cell 1, is to hire experienced specialists and provide them with a narrow career path. Cell 6 represents the strategy of hiring inexperienced, adequately educated specialists to whom a wide range of career paths will be available through transfers between functional areas.

Organizations may choose different staffing strategies to fill different types of positions, but the strategy chosen is determined by the nature of the business environment and the organization itself, as shown in Exhibit 7.3.

Environmental Determinants

A number of environmental characteristics influence the choice of a staffing strategy. Two key characteristics of the business environment are its degree of *complexity* and *rate of change*.[5] Complexity refers to the number of factors that must be considered before decisions are made in the organization. For

DETERMINANTS OF STAFFING STRATEGIES

EXHIBIT 7.3

Business Environment	Organization
Degree of complexity	Organization structure
Rate of change	Size
Degree of business competition	Rate of growth
Availability of applicants	Degree of emphasis on long-term employment

example, computer companies exist in a highly complex environment because of the large number of competitors, suppliers, and customers they must take into account as they make decisions about research and development, manufacturing, and sales. In contrast, the environment of soft drink companies is considered less complex because of the smaller number of competitors, suppliers, and distinctly different customers they must deal with. Rate of change refers to how stable or dynamic these factors remain over time. Rapid changes in technology, competition and customer base have made the environment of telecommunications companies very dynamic in recent years. Organizations in stable, simple environments are likely to pursue a strategy of placing inexperienced specialists in jobs and developing them in narrow career paths (cell 5). This strategy produces highly experienced employees with specialized skills often found in the automobile and steel industry. Organizations in more dynamic, complex environments often prefer to hire generalists with a high degree of work experience who can move from one department to another or work on multi-disciplinary project teams (cell 4).

Degree of business competition in the industry and the *availability of applicants* in the labor market also influence the choice of staffing strategies. In an industry with very little competition, such as the hydroelectric and nuclear power industries, an employer may prefer to hire applicants with several years of related work experience, but find that the source of such applicants is a small number of comparable power plants across the country. Faced with the expense of enticing experienced personnel away from a competitor, the employer may be forced into a strategy of hiring inexperienced applicants and developing them over several years through training and job rotation (see Chapter Eleven). If this strategy is to be successful, the employer must anticipate the need several years before the employees will actually be required. Similarly, the availability of applicants in the labor market limits the choice of staffing strategies that an organization can pursue. An employer may need experienced generalists but find only experienced specialists in the labor market. An employer may plan to hire specialists with narrow career interests, but find that 80 percent of the available applicants want to broaden their careers through training and job assignments outside their area of specialization. Consequently, line managers and human resource professionals of these organizations will have to alter their staffing strategies to accommodate the labor market from which they draw applicants.

In extreme cases, a number of environmental variables change significantly, causing the organization to make rapid, large-scale adjustments in its staffing strategy. Such a case occurred in the telecommunications industry when major competitors like MCI and Sprint began to offer long distance telephone service at reduced rates and AT&T was reorganized through agreements between the Department of Justice and AT&T. Virtually all four factors in the business environment changed markedly. The market became far more complex and dynamic because of technological changes and increased competition, which affected the availability of applicants. Furthermore, the size of AT&T and the nature of key jobs changed significantly. As Box 7.2 shows, staffing strategies were carefully altered to help AT&T find the right kind of employees and remain competitive.

Organizational Determinants

Several characteristics of organizations also influence the choice of a staffing strategy. *Organization structure*, perhaps the most significant determinant of staffing strategy, reflects the way the essential work activities of an organization are grouped into jobs and departments. Three basic organization structures are *functional, decentralized*, and *matrix*.[6] In the functional organization similar work activities are grouped into large, specialized departments such as production, sales, engineering, research and development, and accounting; the managers of these departments report to the president of the organization. A strategy of hiring inexperienced specialists and developing them along a narrow career path (cell 5) is common in functional organizations.

A decentralized organization is divided into divisions that concentrate on a particular product or market. For example, an automotive company might have several divisions (e.g., trucks, luxury cars, intermediate cars, compact cars), each of which operates relatively autonomously and has its own production, sales, engineering, and accounting departments. Decentralized organizations require employees who are specialists in a particular function (e.g., accounting, production, sales), but they offer a broader career path since specialists can move from one product division to another. They also require that division managers be generalists. Consequently, an appropriate staffing strategy is to hire inexperienced specialists who are seeking broad career paths (cell 6).

The matrix organization structure combines elements of both functional and decentralized organizations. It contains the specialized departments of a functional organization and also has the product or market orientation that characterizes a decentralized organization. But in a matrix organization *project teams* that work on a specific product or market are made up of employees drawn from a number of functional specialties. For example, a team of twenty employees to design a new application of a company's established line of computers might consist of employees from the marketing, R and D, software, production, and sales departments. The team is headed by a project manager whose primary responsibility is to coordinate the activities of this diverse

BOX 7.2

FROM ENGINEERING TO MARKETING AT AT&T

The transition of AT&T from a completely regulated telecommunications company to a competitive marketing organization provides a rich example of adapting staffing strategies and procedures to the business environment. Until recently AT&T was simply known as "the Phone Company" and was recognized for providing the highest quality telephone service in the world and acknowledged as a leading engineering company. The company was structured along functional lines to facilitate technological advancements and the integration of the twenty-three Bell system operating companies into a national communications network. Problems were addressed through operations, methods and procedures, product development, and manufacturing.

The January 1, 1984, divestiture changed much of this. AT&T is now an information management company with telecommunications being one of several market segments. It has slimmed down from over one million to 350,000 employees and is structured by product lines.

In 1960 the sales department was staffed with salaried communication consultants who spent 60 percent of their time on service activities. Sales were primarily from customer requests and demand selling. To fill these positions AT&T adopted a strategy of selecting inexperienced college graduates with an interest in selling (cells 7 and 8 in Exhibit 7.2).

But during the 1960s the job of communication consultant began to change. Competition was slowly requiring salespeople to actually sell to clients and customers. To select applicants AT&T developed assessment centers (see Chapter Nine) which evaluated sales-and-service skills, interpersonal skills, and personal qualities.

The mid-1970s brought more radical changes in the business environment. Specialized telecommunications companies were setting up routes competing with AT&T, and this competition necessitated marketing and pricing skills, quicker response times, and the revolution of integrated circuits.

AT&T therefore changed its staffing strategy and began recruiting salespeople with extensive marketing experience (cells 1 and 2 in Exhibit 7.2). The sales team now consists of an account executive (central customer contact), a market administrator (implementation and service coordinator), and a communication systems representative (technical design and telecommunications consultant). The market administrators and account executives require precise product knowledge to deal with very sophisticated customers, and the communication systems representatives must know communications design and applications.

To fill these positions, AT&T has developed new selection procedures. All applicants are required to have demonstrated selling expertise or university training in marketing and/or technical areas and experience in their positions. Special assessment procedures are used to evaluate applicants on consultative selling, team management, and communication skills. Once hired, employees also receive expert training.

The authors wish to thank Richard J. Campbell and Edward F. Adams of AT&T for their help in preparing this material.

group of individuals. Each member of the project team has two supervisors, the project manager, and the manager of the functional department from which he or she is drawn. In practice, it is not uncommon for functional specialists to be assigned to more than one project team. To be effective, matrix organizations require a high degree of communication and coordination of the work activities of employees who must divide their time among several potentially competing assignments. Therefore, matrix organizations often staff their project teams with highly experienced specialists who seek broad career paths and can understand the perspective of team members from other functional specialties (cell 2). Further, project managers are likely to be generalists with many years of work experience in matrix organizations (cell 4).

Another major organizational determinant of staffing strategy is the *size* of the organization. Relatively small organizations, such as Krack Exploration, Inc., require experienced employees who can serve as specialists in functional departments and since they offer limited opportunity for employees to receive promotions or even transfers between functional departments, they seek applicants who are interested in narrow career paths. For example, a 35-year-old engineer who wants to move into production or sales positions currently occupied by 40-year-old employees in a small organization will find it necessary to change employers. Therefore, small organizations often adopt a strategy of hiring experienced specialists with interest in narrow career paths (cell 1). Large organizations of several thousand employees are more likely to hire inexperienced specialists and offer them a wide range of career opportunities (cell 6). In huge corporations like Exxon and General Motors, for example, a vast array of training programs, coupled with frequent opportunities for promotions and transfers, makes it possible for individuals with talent and interest to pursue almost any conceivable career path.

Staffing strategy is also strongly influenced by the *rate of growth* of an organization. Slow growth obviously limits career opportunities, especially in small organizations, while rapid expansion makes broader career paths more readily available. Consistent growth also encourages organizations to hire inexperienced specialists with broad career interests (cell 6). For example, Krack Exploration, which hired only veteran specialists (cell 1) in its first year of operation, began to hire less experienced engineers and geologists as its technical departments grew in size. Krack was able to hire inexperienced applicants *only* after it had established a base of experienced employees in each department. To successfully adopt the strategy of hiring inexperienced employees, the organization must also have the resources available to train and develop these employees (see Chapter Eleven). Relatively stable organizations, however, are less likely to hire inexperienced applicants and develop them for more senior positions because opportunities for promotion are rare.

A final determinant of staffing strategy is an organization's *degree of emphasis on long-term employment*. The human resource policies and practices of some organizations strongly encourage employees to remain with the same employer for their entire work lives. Major corporations like IBM, Exxon, and Hewlett-Packard have developed a reputation for hiring excellent employees and nurturing them within the organization through a wealth of challenging work assignments and training and development activities. Such an emphasis on long-term employment opens up a wide range of staffing strategies, depending on the job and the labor market. For entry-level jobs, these organizations often hire inexperienced specialists and offer them a wide range of career paths (cell 6). For more senior jobs, they seek experienced generalists and move them from one department to another to keep them challenged and growing (cell 4). The objectives or philosophy of an organization often reflect such an emphasis on career development. For example, one of the seven corporate objectives of Hewlett-Packard reads as follows:

Our People
OBJECTIVE: To help HP people share in the company's success, which they make possible; to provide job security based on their performance; to recognize their individual achievements; and to ensure the personal satisfaction that comes from a sense of accomplishment in their work.[7]

Other organizations place less emphasis on long-term employment either by choice or by necessity. Organizations in cyclical markets must have the flexibility to abruptly increase or decrease their number of employees. For example, engineering and construction firms and automobile companies have a history of laying off hundreds or even thousands of employees during economic slowdowns and hiring them back during recoveries. The prospects of long-term employment for any employee are therefore remote until the individual has amassed enough seniority to escape periodic layoffs. These organizations therefore avoid hiring inexperienced specialists and training them on the job because of the possibility of unanticipated layoffs. They are more likely to hire experienced specialists or generalists (cells 1–4).

The environmental and organizational factors discussed above represent constraints on and opportunities in the process of designing and implementing staffing strategies. Line managers and human resource professionals must consider the staffing options available to the organization and the consequences of each and then choose a strategy that serves the best interests of the organization and its employees. The choice of a staffing strategy must be coordinated with the strategic planning of the entire organization and reviewed annually so that it can be adjusted to accommodate changes in the environment and the organization. There are no right or wrong staffing strategies, merely choices and consequences. The decision to hire bright, well-educated, inexperienced applicants into a small, functional organization with a slow rate of growth will very likely lead to low morale and high turnover two or three years after the applicants are hired. On the other hand, a large, rapidly expanding decentralized or matrix organization in a complex, unstable environment would profit from a strategy of hiring inexperienced specialists and experienced generalists with broad career interests. Similarly, a strategy of hiring inexperienced or experienced specialists with narrow career aspirations would be appropriate for a large, stable functional organization in a simple, stable environment.

PROCESS OF STRATEGIC STAFFING

By analyzing the environmental and organizational factors discussed above, line managers and human resource professionals can determine which staffing strategies appear most appropriate for filling specific types of jobs in the organization. But they need far more detailed information before they can begin recruiting, selecting, promoting, or transferring employees to fill those jobs. They must estimate the number of employees needed to meet specific organizational objectives (e.g., to increase next year's gross revenues by 20 percent or to boost market share by opening six new sales and service offices on the West Coast) and determine where and how they can secure the required employees. They can make these judgments through the process of strategic staffing, outlined in Exhibit 7.4.

Let's begin with a brief overview of the process, and then discuss the steps and techniques in more detail. As we have already stressed, strategic staffing should be linked with strategic planning, presented in the left-hand column of the exhibit. In strategic planning, executives set specific objectives for growth, diversification, acquisition, new markets and products, etc. They also set operating budgets to provide the funds to meet those objectives. Since the organization will need the right kind of employees at the right time to achieve its objectives, the executives also confer with line managers and human resource professionals to estimate how many employees will be needed one, two, or even five years from now (Forecasting Demand in the exhibit) and where these employees can be found (Forecasting Supply). Notice that both current employees and prospective employees in the labor market are included in the forecast of supply. These three estimates—the operating budget, demand for employees, and supply of employees—are then compared, and adjustments are made to reconcile the figures. (For example, the operating budget may be increased because the short supply of essential new employees in the labor market will increase recruiting and salary costs.) Finally, plans are made to secure the needed employees through various staffing procedures (recruitment, selection, transfer, or promotion) or through training and development (see Chapter Eleven).

Forecasting Demand

Forecasts are almost invariably derived from an understanding of current or historical conditions. Knowledge of the number of employees required this year to produce 2,000 computers per week, for instance, provides an excellent basis for predicting the number required next year to produce 5,000 computers per week. Therefore, when forecasting demand in order to estimate an organization's future need for employees, an analysis begins with current need, represented by the organization structure with its departments and the number and types of specific jobs. Additional assessments of the work load of current employees also indicate whether the organization is lean or over-staffed.

Line managers and human resource professionals then compare the current demand for employees with short- and long-term organizational objec-

PROCESS OF STRATEGIC STAFFING

EXHIBIT 7.4

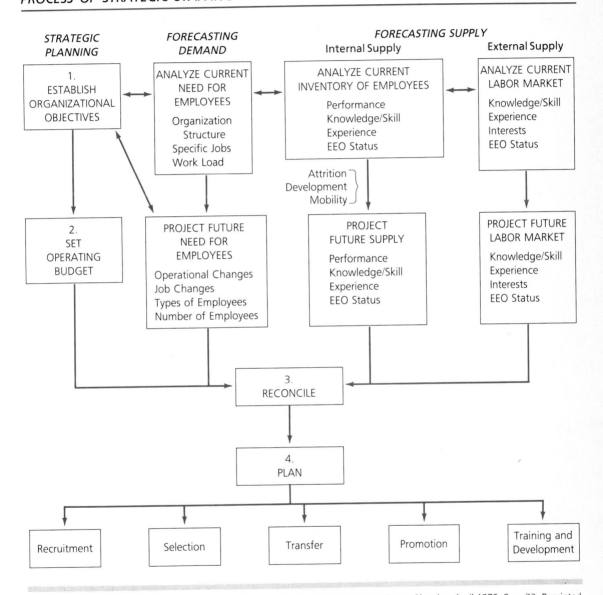

SOURCE: Adapted from "Manpower in Corporate Planning," by D. J. Bell from *Long Range Planning*, April 1976, *9*, p. 33. Reprinted by permission of Pergamon Press Inc., and from *Human Resource Planning* by James Walker, p. 102. McGraw-Hill Book Company, 1980. Reprinted by permission.

tives and estimate the future need for employees. Organizational objectives to develop new products, divest an old division and acquire a new one, or expand a market can then be translated into changes in the work activities and operations of the organization (e.g., marketing and advertising must be emphasized more, and production will need better coordination). From these projections, changes in jobs and the types and number of employees required in the future can be estimated. When an organization is undergoing major change, it is particularly important that corresponding changes in work activities are carefully analyzed and job descriptions are revised before estimates are made of the types and number of employees who will be needed to perform the work. Demand forecasts are typically classified as short-range (less than two years into the future), intermediate-range (two-five years), and long-range (beyond five years). Many organizations make forecasts for all three ranges and revise them annually.

Judgmental Methods

Judgmental Methods ▬▬ There are a variety of methods for forecasting demand, but the most common are subjective.[8] Judgmental methods are based on the assumption that well-informed people can estimate the staff required to complete specified amounts of work and achieve organizational objectives. One procedure often used for short-range forecasts produces *supervisor estimates*, which are the informed guesses by managers and supervisors of how many employees will be needed to achieve the objectives of their group or department in the next one, two, or three years. Specific estimates are often made of new jobs needed, jobs to be dropped or left unfilled, changes in existing jobs, double occupancies, overtime and slack time expected, fluctuations in work load during the forecast period, any changes in overhead, contracted labor and supervision, and the budgetary impact of the changes.[9] Supervisor estimates are usually done from the "bottom up." Initial estimates, made by first-line supervisors for their individual units, are then reviewed and revised by departmental managers, whose estimates are in turn reviewed and revised by divisional managers, etc., up through the organization. Human resource professionals may also compare the estimates for one unit, department, or division with those for others and prepare aggregate estimates for presentation to senior management.

Another method favored by small firms is the *rule-of-thumb*, which governs the number of employees authorized under specified conditions. Directives for, say, one secretary per two department heads or one accounting clerk for every four accountants can be derived from previous experience with workloads to provide clear staffing guidelines. Such guidelines, however, should be periodically reviewed and adjusted to reflect changes in jobs and work procedures.

The *Delphi Technique* is a more complex judgmental method, which capitalizes on the input of a number of managers and supervisors. Through questionnaires or structured interviews, a number of knowledgeable supervisors and managers estimate staffing needs. These estimates are then summarized and submitted to the same group of judges, who review and reevaluate the estimates until agreement is reached. Although this procedure provides accurate forecasts, it is rarely used.[10]

Regression Methods ▬ In larger organizations statistical methods are used to determine relationships between output variables (quantity of product, dollar volume of sales, and number of projects completed) and the number of employees needed. For example, an output variable that is crucial to the organization's success, such as sales volume, might be compared with the number of employees required to generate the sale in previous years. If a ratio of $1,000,000 in sales volume is computed per salesperson, then a projected increase of $30,000,000 in volume will require an additional thirty salespeople. Regression analysis can also be used to derive a more complex way of predicting the number of employees required. Several key output variables can be selected and correlated with one another. Then a regression model can be derived that places a weight on each output variable according to its importance in predicting the number of needed employees. The result is as follows:

$$\text{Number of employees} = .0021 \times (\$ \text{ volume}) + .05 \times (\text{number of sales calls}) + .15 (\text{number of service calls})$$

Regression models are based on the assumption that relationships in the past are valid in the future and may therefore be inaccurate during periods of rapid change in the organization and the environment. They are most commonly used in large organizations for long-range forecasting.

Forecasting Internal Supply

Once line managers and human resource professionals have estimated the organization's future need for employees, they turn their attention to the internal and external supply of employees. They begin by looking inside the organization for employees who can be transferred or promoted into jobs that must be filled in the future. As the exhibit shows, forecasting the internal supply of employees begins with an analysis of the current supply of employees.

Human Resource Inventories ▬ One of the most fundamental methods of forecasting the internal supply of employees is simply to analyze all the organization's current employees and record their performance, knowledge, skills, experience, interests, and personal characteristics relevant to Equal Employment Opportunity legislation (see Chapter Five). Human resource inventories, also called *skills inventories*, are especially useful for short-range forecasts of employees who will be readily available to the organization. Many organizations, in spite of well-publicized policies to "promote from within," are not fully aware of the wealth of talent they currently employ and consequently resort to filling jobs unnecessarily from outside. A complete, regularly updated human resource inventory can provide line managers and human resource professionals with easily accessible information about the availability of current employees who will be qualified for specific jobs within the next year or two.

Recent growth in access to the computer through software and terminals has led to increasing use of computerized human resource information systems (Chapter Two). These new systems are replacing manual files and provide great potential for storage, analysis, updating, and rapid retrieval of data essential for human resource planning.[11] Computerized human resource inventories are especially useful in organizations that strive to fill job openings through promotions or transfers. Once the qualifications (educational background, work experience, knowledge, and skills) have been established for a job opening, a quick scan of the human resource inventory will identify qualified candidates from within the organization.

Replacement and Succession Planning
Two widely used methods for estimating the future supply of employees in an organization are replacement planning and succession planning. These techniques are most often used to identify members of the organization who have high potential to move into middle and upper management positions. Human resource professionals, in collaboration with top management, forecast the short- and intermediate-range need for management positions and prepare an organization chart. Information about anticipated retirements, promotions, and transfers of current job incumbents is also collected to estimate when each position will become vacant. In addition, individual managers conduct annual reviews of their employees' performance, potential, strengths, and weaknesses and identify candidates for rapid development and promotion in the organization.

Then a committee of top managers and human resource professionals meets annually to discuss each candidate and make plans for which positions the employee is considered qualified to assume, when, and what developmental activities (work assignments, training) might ensure that the individual's potential will be reached. In many organizations, organization charts (see Exhibit 7.5) are prepared with summary information on each high-potential employee to aid the committee in comparing candidates and picturing the organization of the future. Information is included about each candidate's age, performance, readiness to replace a current incumbent, and potential for long-term growth in the management ranks. Some large organizations place the charts on a wall so the committee members can move employees around and actually construct the organization chart they anticipate in the next one, two, or three years.

While both methods use the same information, there are differences between replacement planning and succession planning.[12] Replacement planning focuses on the best candidates available in the organization to replace key managers within the next twelve months. Succession planning is oriented more toward the long-term growth and development of high-potential employees (see Chapter Eleven). Their potential to move laterally or vertically in the organization in the next two to five years is considered, and more emphasis is placed on how far they can progress (not whom they can replace)

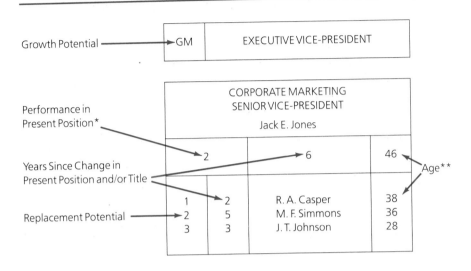

EXHIBIT 7.5

GUIDE TO SUCCESSION PLANNING
ORGANIZATION CHART

Growth Potential ———→ GM EXECUTIVE VICE-PRESIDENT

CORPORATE MARKETING
SENIOR VICE-PRESIDENT

Jack E. Jones

Performance in Present Position*

2   6   46   Age**

Years Since Change in Present Position and/or Title

1	2	R. A. Casper	38
2	5	M. F. Simmons	36
3	3	J. T. Johnson	28

Replacement Potential ———→

GROWTH POTENTIAL CODES	PERFORMANCE CODES	REPLACEMENT POTENTIAL CODES
GM General Management	1 Performance leaves little to be desired	1 Ready now
FM Functional Management	2 Assigned objectives met or exceeded in all areas	2 One–two years
L Limited	3 Adequate for position involved: most objectives achieved	3 Three–five years
	4 Below normal requirements	
	NR Performance not rated in present position	

*Postings represent nearest full years of experience since last position responsibility and/or title change, to be completed through year end. Full year counted if effective date was in first quarter.

**Age attained in review year.

and what specific developmental activities will enable them to reach their potential.

Replacement and succession planning are especially crucial today because of demographic trends that have had a strong influence on the current supply of employees (see Chapter Three). A large number of people who began ther careers just after World War II are now in their sixties and are ready to retire from important management positions. But many organizations have relatively few employees in their fifties because of the low birth rate during the Great Depression. Consequently, they are faced with the challenge of filling senior management positions from the ranks of employees in their forties. The importance of this challenge and the way various organizations are meeting it are discussed in Box 7.3.

Transition Models ━━ Another method of forecasting the internal supply of employees takes into account the historical movement of employees through the organization (shown in Exhibit 7.4 as attrition, development, and mobility). Transition models are developed for a number of employees grouped by some common characteristic such as job level, salary range, or region of the country. For example, if a specific job is chosen, then the percentage of employees who left that job each year through termination, transfer, or promotion can be calculated for the past five years. These percentages are then averaged to estimate the probability that movement will occur next year through termination, transfer, or promotion.

When a number of jobs are considered simultaneously, complex Markov or network flow models can be constructed to account for the fact that the loss of employees from one job through transfer or promotion represents a gain of employees for other jobs.[13] Transition probabilities for each job can then be estimated, and the number of employees in each job can be forecast for any number of years into the future.

Transition models are most often used for long-range forecasts in large organizations.[14] They are based on the assumption that future transition rates will be identical to historical rates, although adjustments in probability estimates can be made by human resource professionals to take into account organizational and environmental changes (e.g., rapid growth in the organization or a high unemployment rate). Estimates of the number of employees available within the organization are useful in planning to add staff through recruitment and selection.

Forecasting External Supply

Human resource professionals and line managers also keep track of the kinds of employees available outside the organization, as shown in Exhibit 7.4. Analysis of the labor market from which an organization hires is generally done on an informal basis. Human resource professionals who specialize in recruitment and selection develop a sense of the supply of people with specific knowledge, skills, experience, and interests through the number of unsolicited applications they receive and the response to their ads for job openings. Line managers also keep track of the supply of prospective employees in their discipline through contacts with their counterparts in other organizations and with professional groups and universities. Human resource planners are especially interested in trends that might affect the organization's ability to attract and retain needed employees in the future and engage in environmental scanning, as illustrated in Box 7.1.

In particular, demographic and economic trends significantly affect the labor market and need to be noted by human resource professionals and line managers. Changes in university enrollment in specific curricula such as busi-

THE IMPORTANCE OF SUCCESSION PLANNING

BOX 7.3

Ruminating over the broad challenges confronting his company, George M. Keller, chairman and CEO of Standard Oil Co. of California (Socal), ticks off two items you'd expect from an oil company CEO: the increasing difficulty of finding oil, and the rigors of staying competitive in a changing marketplace.

Then he pauses, reflects a bit, and brings up a problem you might *not* expect. "We have a large crop of management people who started their careers just after World War II. And now they're about to retire," he says. "We face a fundamental management turnover during the next five years."

To a greater or lesser degree, other CEOs find their firms in similar circumstances. "I don't know of any company that doesn't face the problem," observes David Smith, managing director of Korn/Ferry International, a New York executive-search firm. "Consider the arithmetic of the thing: a surge of young people came out of the war all at once, went to college under the GI bill, entered the work force, and rose to management positions. Now they're in their sixties and it's time for them to step aside. The problem will be worse five years from now than it is today." . . .

Even in companies that have a well-oiled succession-planning process, replacing the World War II crop of managers might not be easy. One reason for the difficulty, believes Korn/Ferry's Mr. Smith, is the low birth rate during the Great Depression of the 1930s. "The 'back-up' people who are moving into the jobs vacated by the retiring World War II veterans are generally in the 43–53 age bracket," he notes. "Because of the lower birth rate when they were born, there simply are fewer of them than in other age brackets."

As a result, he adds, talented men and women of this age group are in high demand. And many are unwilling to wait for the next rung on their firms' management ladder to open up, so they are prone to snap up lucrative offers from the outside.

But many companies—those *with* succession-planning programs—are taking pains to see to it that they don't lose a step when their World War II-vintage leadership departs.

At Socal, for example, the Management Planning & Development Department has been working for years to avert any problems. In fact, says James R. Sylla, vice-president for industrial relations and environmental affairs, Socal already is looking beyond the "crunch of retirements" among the World War II group to what he calls "another peak" of retirements in the next century. This second peak will result, he explains, from the company's sharp increase in hiring of 30-to-35-year-old managers during the go-go 1970s. "We'll have to be ready to replace them," he says.

Socal's succession-planning system, which has been in effect for more than twenty-five years, is based on demographic studies. The firm assigns "probabilities of departure"—for whatever reason—within each age group among its top 3,000 managers at corporate headquarters in San Francisco. "This gives us a statistical idea of how many job openings we'll need to fill," explains Mr. Sylla. "When openings occur, we match them against our inventory of promotable candidates." A similar system tracks some 8,000 managers at other Socal locations. . . .

Adaptation from "Who'll Replace the Vanishing Vets?" by William H. Miller, *Industry Week*, April 16, 1984. Reprinted by permission.

ness administration, computer science, and engineering can also be used to predict increases or decreases in the supply of applicants for specific kinds of jobs. If fluctuations in the external labor market can be accurately forecast, organizations can respond with increased recruiting efforts or with training programs that will produce the required employees over a number of years. Box 7.3 illustrates how demographic trends have produced a severe shortage in the labor market and how progressive companies have attempted to reduce the shortage. Similar long-range planning is also necessary for organizations to meet affirmative action goals of hiring female and minority members of protected groups under EEO legislation. Information about the number of women and minorities in various jobs within the organization and their availability in the labor market can be used to strengthen affirmative action through more ambitious recruiting and selection programs (see Chapters Eight and Nine).

Reconciling and Planning Steps

The last two steps in the process of strategic staffing are to reconcile any differences between operating budgets and forecasts of employee demand and supply, and to make appropriate plans to increase or decrease the number of employees in the organization. Efforts to reconcile these differences requires close consultation and cooperation between human resource professionals and line managers throughout the organization. Supervisors and managers may have to revise estimates of their need for employees because of financial constraints or mandates by top management. Disagreements may arise over the promotability of specific employees because their current managers are reluctant to lose them, or over the recruiting department's assurance that it can find enough new technical and professional employees in the next six months to staff a new operation.

Attempts to reconcile differences in data and opinions can take place over several months and are concluded in many organizations in an annual planning meeting attended by top management and a senior human resource professional. This group reviews strategic plans and financial projections for the entire firm and compares the forecast of the organization's need for employees with the projected internal and external supply of employees and decides what actions are appropriate. If a net increase in employees is needed, then promotions and transfers are planned within the organization, and programs to recruit and select external applicants are conceived. If a net decrease is required, plans are made to reduce the organization's work force. Small reductions can often be achieved through employee turnover and retirements. During the 1981–82 recession, for example, many firms simply imposed a freeze on hiring and waited for normal attrition to reduce their complement of employees. Other firms offered early retirement, which included attractive pensions for employees nearing retirement age. In more extreme cases, organizations were forced to lay off employees.

An integral part of this process is *affirmative action planning*. As Exhibit 7.4 shows, projections of the internal and external supply of employees include information about their status under Equal Employment Opportunity legislation. The Equal Employment Opportunity Commission requires organizations to keep records of the percentage of women and minorities in their work force, compared with the percentage of these groups in the labor market (see Chapter Nine). If these percentages differ, top priority should be given to increased efforts to hire and promote employees from these groups. Similarly, if the percentages differ within a given job category (e.g., a far greater proportion of men than women in middle-management positions) specific plans should be made to hire, develop, and promote women into these positions (see AT&T's example in Chapter Five). Chapters Eight and Nine also provide examples of how employers have taken affirmative action in recruitment and selection.

A FINAL CAUTION

As we have implied throughout this chapter, strategic staffing is more of an art than a science. Virtually all methods for forecasting supply and demand are destined to produce inaccurate estimates because they are either highly subjective or based on the untenable assumption that the future is simply an extrapolation of the present or past. Therefore, plans to staff the organization will also go awry and require regular review and revision. An inaccurate forecast, however, is better than no forecast, and a flawed plan is preferable to no plan. Many human resource professionals have exclaimed, "Throw out the plan, not the planner." They argue convincingly to top management that even a poor plan enables an organization to prepare for the future and make adjustments as the future arrives. Such planning allows human resource professionals and line managers to join forces and become more *proactive*, anticipating problems and challenges, rather than reacting to crises.

In short, strategic staffing is a continuous process that requires periodic review and revision. How often the forecasts and plans need review depends on the nature of the organization and its business environment. The same environmental and organizational variables (see Exhibit 7.3) that lead to staffing strategies also influence the accuracy of forecasts and plans. In a large, functional organization with a slow rate of growth that operates in a simple, stable business environment with few competitors and an ample labor supply, for example, staffing plans may require only minor annual adjustments. But in organizations dealing with dynamic, complex business environments and many competitors, a time horizon of three to six months is far more appropriate. Since technology and entire product lines may have to be changed in a matter of months, forecasts and plans require frequent adjustments. Many organizations make short-, intermediate-, and long-range forecasts and staffing plans at least once a year and review them annually. Through a regular review process, they are able to adjust their staffing plans to changing business conditions and organizational priorities.

KEY POINTS

- When making plans to meet long-range organizational objectives, line managers must also consider how they will staff the organization with the right employees at the right time.

- The staffing strategies available to an organization are determined by such environmental variables as degree of complexity, rate of change, degree of business competition, and availability of applicants, and by such organizational variables as organization structure, size, rate of growth, and degree of emphasis on long-term employment.

- In the process of strategic staffing, the following four forecasts are made and reconciled: the organization's operating budget, its future need for employees, and the internal and external supplies of employees available to the organization. Plans are then made to secure the necessary employees through recruitment, selection, transfer, and promotion.

- The organization's future demand for employees is most often forecast with judgmental methods such as supervisor estimates or rules-of-thumb. In large organizations more sophisticated regression methods are also used.

- Human resource inventories and replacement or succession planning are common methods for forecasting an organization's internal supply of employees.

- Since all forecasting methods are subjective and inaccurate, forecasts are periodically reviewed and revised, and staffing plans are adjusted accordingly.

ISSUES FOR DISCUSSION

1. Analyze the staffing strategy under which you were hired by your current or a past employer. What key environmental and organizational factors appear to have determined the choice of that strategy? Did the strategy produce a good fit between you and your employer?

2. What arguments can you offer for linking strategic staffing and strategic planning for an organization? Why do you think the link is not more common in today's organizations?

3. What information would you include in a human resource inventory of a large, growing organization to ensure effective strategic staffing?

4. Considering the poor accuracy of forecasting methods, why should organizations use them to predict demand for employees?

5. How can EEO status of current employees and external applicants be incorporated into an organizational staffing strategy?

6. Define replacement and succession planning. How do these techniques differ?

NOTES

1. This story is based on a real organization, but with a disguised name. Another good case of strategic staffing is found in C. C. Bowicki and A. F. Lafley, "Strategic Staffing at Chase Manhattan Bank," in C. J. Fombrun, N. M. Tichy, and M. A. Devanna, *Strategic Human Resource Management* (New York: John Wiley and Sons, 1984), pp. 69–86.

2. J. W. Walker, *Human Resource Planning* (New York: McGraw-Hill, 1980), p. 78.

3. H. Weihrich, "A Comprehensive Systems Model for Human Resource Planning," *Human Resource Planning*, 1980, 3, pp. 27–31.

4. L. Baird, I. Meshoulam, and G. DeGive, "Meshing Human Resources Planning with Strategic Business Planning: A Model Approach," *Personnel*, Sept.–Oct. 1983, 60, pp. 14–25; E. J. Kelleher and K. L. Cotter, "An Integrative Model for Human Resource Planning and Strategic Planning," *Human Resource Planning*, 1982, 5, pp. 15–27; J. W. Walker, "Linking Human Resource Planning and Strategic Planning," *Human Resource Planning*, 1978, 1, pp. 1–18.

5. R. B. Duncan, "What Is the Right Organization Structure? Decision Tree Analysis Provides the Answer," *Organizational Dynamics*, Winter 1979, pp. 59–79.

6. Ibid.

7. W. Ouchi, *Theory Z: How American Business Can Meet the Japanese Challenge* (Reading, Mass.: Addison-Wesley, 1981), p. 230.

8. C. R. Greer, and D. Armstrong, "Human Resource Forecasting and Planning: A State-of-the-Art Investigation," *Human Resource Planning*, 1980, 3, pp. 67–78.

9. J. W. Walker, *Human Resource Planning* (New York: McGraw-Hill, 1980), p. 124.

10. C. R. Greer and D. Armstrong, "Human Resource Forecasting and Planning: A State-of-the-Art Investigation," *Human Resource Planning*, 1980, 3, p. 73.

11. R. G. Murdick, and F. Schuster, "Computerized Information Support for the Human Resource Function," *Human Resource Planning*, 1983, 6, pp. 25–33. V. R. Ceriello, "Computerizing the Personnel Department: Make or Buy?" *Personnel Journal*, Sept. 1984, 63, pp. 44–48.

12. J. W. Walker, *Human Resource Planning*, p. 285.

13. Ibid, pp. 133–37.

14. C. R. Greer, and D. Armstrong, "Human Resource Forecasting and Planning: A State-of-the-Art Investigation," *Human Resource Planning*, 1980, 3, p. 72.

ANNOTATED BIBLIOGRAPHY

Human Resource Planning

This journal, published four times annually since 1978 by the Human Resource Planning Society, is an excellent source of articles written by academics and practitioners. It covers a wide range of topics, including surveys of current practices in various aspects of human resource planning, theoretical and conceptual models of strategic planning and human resource planning, and technical applications of forecasting techniques.

Human Resource Planning Society

Founded in 1977, this professional association now has 1,200 individual and 100 corporate members. Among its individual members are human resource planning professionals, staffing analysts, recruiters, and business planners. The Society provides a forum for individuals to exchange experiences and pool knowledge in this relatively new field and holds an annual convention.

MILLER, E. L. "Strategic Staffing." In FOMBRUN, C. J., TICHY, N., and DEVANNA, M. A. (Editors). *Strategic Human Resource Management.* New York: John Wiley and Sons, 1984, pp. 57–68.

This chapter presents a comprehensive discussion of the importance of strategic issues in staffing. Miller emphasizes the need for the involvement of human resource professionals in operational, managerial, and strategic levels of decision making in the organization. He examines the relationship between the staffing process and the organization's purpose, its approach to strategic management, and organizational design and structure. Finally, he discusses staffing strategies such as succession planning, management development, and job assignments.

WALKER, J. W. *Human Resource Planning.* New York: McGraw-Hill, 1980.

This highly regarded book provides a wealth of well-researched, practical information. It stresses the importance of linking human resource planning with strategic planning and provides many illustrations of how this link can be established. Of particular relevance to strategic staffing are the chapters on forecasting human resource needs (Chapter 5), forecasting models and applications (Chapter 6), and management succession and development planning (Chapter 12).

CHAPTER EIGHT

RECRUITMENT

A lot went into Apple Computer Inc.'s coup in luring John Sculley away from PepsiCo Inc. After all, the 44-year-old Mr. Sculley was firmly ensconced as a president at Pepsi-Cola Co., PepsiCo's U.S. soft drink unit, and would have a shot at the chairmanship of the parent company when 62-year-old Donald Kendall retired in three years. Mr. Sculley routinely turned down chances to go elsewhere, as when, five years ago, Norton Simon Inc. tried to hire him for its Canada Dry unit.*

So Apple had to reckon with the usual considerations in any high-level executive search—money, prestige, family, and life-style—as well as Mr. Sculley's securely fast-track status. Such campaigns are arduous . . . .

Often, the most sought-after executives are the most difficult to snare, because the jobs they have promise a bright future. "There's got to be some reason to veer from the fast track," says David Joys, executive vice-president at Russell Reynolds Associates. "More often than not, it tends to be a career opportunity."

And intangibles carry as much weight in a high-level search as cash compensation or an executive's ability. Such considerations counted heavily in Apple's search for a new president, which was led by Gerald Roche, chairman of Heidrick & Struggles, a large executive search firm in New York. When Mr. Roche began working for Apple last fall, its chairman, Steven Jobs, and the current president, A. C. "Mike" Markkula, told him they wanted someone with broad domestic and international management and marketing experience who could adapt to Apple's loosely structured environment.

When Mr. Roche's call came last December, Mr. Sculley wasn't interested in the job. "But I did have a lot of interest in meeting Jobs and Markkula, a couple of guys who took a company that six years ago didn't exist and built it to $1 billion," says Mr. Sculley. After that first meeting, Mr. Roche arranged another for after Christmas, although, says Mr. Sculley, "I reiterated that I still wasn't interested in the job."

*Adaption of "Apple Lured President from Pepsi with Patient Persuasion and Cash" by Janet Guyon, *The Wall Street Journal*, April 15, 1983. Copyright © 1983 Dow Jones & Company Inc. All Rights Reserved. Reprinted by permission.

"I spent an immense amount of time with Sculley getting him from curious to healthily interested," says Mr. Roche. At one point he told the executive he should consider California's Silicon Valley as similar to Florence during the Renaissance—the place where the brightest people of an age congregate. *"To show you how naive I am, I believed that,"* Mr. Sculley said.

The trips to California did bring back for Mr. Sculley an early interest in electronics. In his youth he had built, among other things, his own ham radio. But he still wasn't considering leaving Pepsi. Throughout January, February, and March, Mr. Roche, Mr. Jobs, and Mr. Markkula persisted by staying in constant contact, aware that initial reluctance is almost a given in high-level searches. But the personal relationship between company officials and an executive also helps make a match. After his first meeting with Mr. Jobs and Mr. Markkula, Mr. Sculley saw in Apple *"something that just awakened me and got me excited."*

In late March Mr. Jobs made an offer, and Mr. Sculley turned him down flat. Money was one roadblock. But, says Mr. Roche, *"it wasn't only money; it was a comfort level with Apple."* Additional conversations between Mr. Jobs and Mr. Sculley were necessary to work out an acceptable financial package.

"I told Apple from the start that if my family didn't want to move, that was a deal breaker," Mr. Sculley said. Another deal breaker, says Mr. Roche, was the potential wrath of Mr. Kendall, who had considered Mr. Sculley as a possible successor. Mr. Sculley's family and boss eventually endorsed the opportunity to join Apple, and he called Mr. Roche and told him that he was accepting.

"That's when I bow out," says Mr. Roche, though he tries *"to stay close and make sure things work out."* He adds that *"Sculley turned into a very close friend on this, and I'm not about to take my fee—$333,000—and run."*[1]

recruitment

Recruitment is *the process through which the organization's job openings are clearly defined, and prospective employees are found to fill those openings.* It provides employees, the lifeblood of any organization. The process consists of two major phases. The first is to monitor environmental and organizational changes that create a need for new employees and to define precisely the jobs to be filled and the types of applicants required to fill them. The second is to make a broad range of potential applicants aware of specific job openings, attract them to the employment opportunities, and screen out applicants who lack the necessary qualifications. The second phase may be time-consuming and expensive, as in Apple's search for a new president, or it may involve simply placing an ad in the local newspaper and conducting brief interviews with applicants who respond. Once applicants have been found and screened, they enter the *selection* process described in the next chapter.

Since human resource management is the process through which an optimal fit is sought between the individual, job, organization, and environment, recruitment is a very important first step in that process. Recruitment represents a key contact point between the organization and the environment in which it strives to survive and prosper. As Exhibit 8.1 shows, the organization, with its need for high-quality employees, exists in an environment that

EXHIBIT 8.1

RECRUITMENT: MATCHING THE NEEDS
OF APPLICANTS AND ORGANIZATIONS

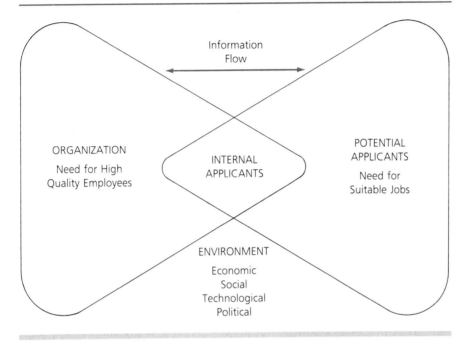

contains a supply of individuals who need suitable jobs. Bringing the organization and appropriate potential applicants together is the goal of recruitment. As part of the recruitment process, information is sent in both directions between applicants and the organization. Not all potential applicants exist outside the organization. The overlap in Exhibit 8.1 represents so-called *internal applicants*, current employees who apply for other jobs in the organization.

DUAL RESPONSIBILITY
FOR RECRUITING

Both line managers and human resource professionals are actively involved in planning, designing, and implementing the recruitment process in their organization. As we discussed in Chapter Seven, senior managers and human resource professionals confer to identify organizational objectives and the numbers and types of employees required to meet those objectives and to set *plans* to secure the needed employees. Next, human resource professionals assume the primary responsibility for *designing* the recruiting program by identifying sources of applicants and preparing necessary materials, such as brochures describing the organization and its benefits, specific job descriptions, and ads to attract prospective applicants. Finally, they are joined by line managers to *implement* the recruitment program. Both human resource professionals and line managers recruit and meet with prospective employees on college campuses, at job fairs, and in their own offices.

ENVIRONMENTAL INFLUENCES ON RECRUITMENT

Since recruitment represents a vital link between the organization and its environment, it is highly susceptible to environmental influences. All four of the environments first discussed in Chapter One—economic, social, technological, and political—have traditionally had a major impact on recruitment. Furthermore, in the past two decades major changes in these environments have increased their influence, and no organization is likely to recruit successfully without paying close attention to those changes.

The Economic Environment

Shifts in the national economy have an obvious influence on the recruitment process in all organizations. Periods of economic recession and recovery significantly affect the organization's need for employees and force the curtailment or expansion of recruiting efforts. Economic conditions also affect the level of unemployment and consequently the internal and external supply (Chapter Seven) from which organizations can draw. Economic recessions, for example, increase not only the supply of external applicants but also the supply of internal applicants, as a result of reduced rates of employee turnover.

These variations in the supply and demand for applicants cause organizations to vary not only the level of recruitment, but also their recruitment techniques. For example, during the 1981–82 recession, when demand for applicants was low and supply was high, organizations dramatically reduced their recruitment costs by decreasing the use of search firms and campus recruiting and concentrating on less expensive media advertising.

The Social Environment

Major social changes in the past two decades have caused organizations to place increased emphasis on recruitment. These social changes have altered basic attitudes toward work (Chapter Three) and today's organizations must contend with these attitudes. People are looking for satisfying careers, rather than "just a job," and commonly do so by leaving one employer and seeking a better position with another. To attract and retain employees, organizations have responded with recruitment efforts that emphasize opportunities for training and development, and progression through a series of jobs within the same organization. They also present more realistic views of the job and career opportunities to avoid disappointing new employees.[2]

Lack of awareness of, or sensitivity to, prevailing social values and norms can be disastrous to an organization's recruitment efforts. Consider the impact of Watergate on the federal government's efforts to recruit bright young applicants. Many became very skeptical of the morality of public officials and sought jobs in the private sector. Major employers that manufactured munitions and supplies for the Vietnam War encountered strong resistance during that period, especially from college students. When U.S. oil companies reaped windfall profits in 1979 and 1980, they prepared their recruiters to deal with hostile questions from college students during campus interviews, and thus avoided bad publicity that might have jeopardized future recruiting trips.

The Technological Environment

Changes in technology have long had an effect on recruitment because as new technology is developed, many existing jobs change substantially and new jobs are created. Consequently, applicants with unusual combinations of skills and knowledge must be found. One major technological trend has been the evolution of the U.S. economy from a manufacturing base to an information-processing base.[3] Old jobs are disappearing and new jobs are difficult to fill because of insufficient numbers of employees with the appropriate skills and knowledge. As technology creates new jobs or changes old ones, organizations step up their recruitment efforts to compete successfully for a small number of suitable applicants. For example, even during the last recession recruiting was brisk for applicants in the data-processing field. We expect competition for limited skills (e.g., electronics and robotics) to grow even fiercer in the next several years.

The Political Environment

A fourth major influence on recruitment is the political environment, especially federal and state laws that regulate the employment process organizations use to find and select applicants (Chapter Five). The most far-reaching impact on recruitment over the past two decades can be traced to *equal employment opportunity* laws and executive orders, which make it unlawful to discriminate against women and minorities in employment practices, and *affirmative action* directives, which require many organizations to make special efforts to recruit and hire women and minorities.

Since 1964, such legislation has directly affected the way virtually all U.S. organizations recruit applicants. This legislation applies to both phases of recruitment: defining the job to be filled and the types of applicants required, and seeking and screening applicants. The organization's need for employees can no longer be arbitrarily defined to exclude certain groups of applicants. For example, the job of flight attendant can no longer be filled only by single women, and the jobs of truck driver, mail carrier, and roustabout

EXHIBIT 8.2   **THE RECRUITMENT PROCESS**

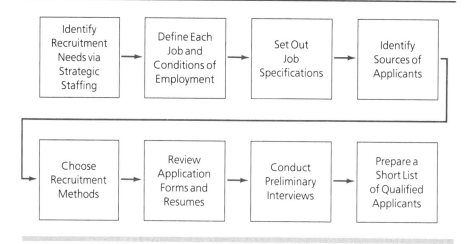

can no longer be considered the exclusive domain of men. In short, employment needs must be defined in terms of ability to perform the job, not in terms of race, color, religion, sex, or national origin. Furthermore, all recruitment policies and procedures, including advertisements for jobs, application forms, and screening interviews, have been affected. Phrases such as "only men need apply" and "age 30–40 preferred" may no longer appear in advertisements for job openings. In addition, application forms cannot request such information as age, race, and sex, and interviewers cannot reject applicants on these grounds.

Affirmative action requirements have caused organizations to recruit far more widely than ever before and have therefore increased the pool of qualified applicants from which organizations can draw. Organizations have taken a number of approaches to find and attract women and minority applicants. One is to place advertisements for job openings in publications directed primarily to women and minorities. Another is to send recruiters to colleges and universities whose enrollments are predominantly minority or female, and to hold "career days" in high schools to encourage female and minority students to pursue careers traditionally open primarily to white men.

THE RECRUITMENT PROCESS

Eight major steps occur in the recruitment process (Exhibit 8.2). Each step is vital to a successful recruiting effort, although some may receive more emphasis than others, depending on the job opening and the organization. For example, a brief "help wanted" ad in the local newspaper is often the primary recruitment method used for semi-skilled factory jobs, while nationwide multi-media ads and trips to university campuses may be used to recruit entry-level engineers and computer programmers.

There is some overlap between the recruitment process and the selection process discussed in the next chapter (Exhibit 9.1). The overlap occurs in the initial steps of each process since both must begin with clear descriptions of the job to be filled and the types of applicants required. The main difference between recruitment and selection, reflected in the latter steps of each process, is in their orientation toward applicants. Recruitment focuses primarily on selling the organization's opportunities for employment and attracting large numbers of applicants who appear qualified, whereas selection is concerned largely with evaluating applicants and rejecting all but the one with the best potential to perform successfully. Recruitment supplies the selection process with relatively well qualified applicants.

Identify Recruitment Needs
Via Strategic Staffing

As we stressed in Chapter Seven, any effort to add employees to an organization must begin with planning. Top management sets organizational goals through strategic planning, and then human resource professionals confer with line managers to estimate the number and types of employees required to meet the goals through strategic staffing. Periodic forecasts of an organization's need for additional employees are especially important to effective recruiting because plans to find and screen suitable applicants must sometimes be made as long as one year before the new employees will be hired.

Box 8.1 describes the recruiting process at Fluor Engineers, Inc. Since Fluor operates in a very dynamic economic environment, recruiting needs are derived directly from sales forecasts prepared by top management and are adjusted frequently as the firm's business prospects change.

Define Each Job and Conditions
of Employment

Recruitment, like other major human resource functions, begins with a thorough understanding of the job. Once estimates have been made of the number of new employees required to achieve organizational goals, the jobs they will fill must be clearly described. Therefore, job descriptions, which list the major duties and responsibilities of a job and its relationship with other jobs, are prepared for new jobs and revised for existing ones that may have changed. Conditions of employment, such as salary, benefits, overtime, travel, and possibility of relocation, are also identified for each job. Human resource professionals often consult with line managers to prepare accurate job descriptions and to specify clearly the conditions of employment in a particular operating department. They use this information to prepare printed

RECRUITMENT AT FLUOR ENGINEERS, INC.

BOX 8.1

Tom Perryman, currently Administrator of Employee Relations of the Houston Division of Fluor Engineers, Inc., was involved in recruiting for Fluor from 1980 to 1982.

Fluor provides engineer, procurement, construction, and project management services to the energy industry and ranks in the top five engineering firms in the United States. The Houston Division specializes in the design and construction of hydrocarbon processing plants and employs many engineers, designers, and support staff. The early 1980s were a particularly turbulent period for Fluor as the Houston economy peaked in 1981 and then dropped into a deep recession.

According to Perryman, recruiting needs of the Houston Division are derived from the sales forecast prepared annually by top management and updated monthly. As new projects are initiated and old ones are completed, the firm's need for employees changes. Recruiting needs are estimated for current projects as well as prospects that Fluor is bidding on and has a good chance of getting. In addition, market trends are monitored by top management to estimate the type of projects that the firm will have the opportunity to bid on in the near future. Key technical experts are sometimes recruited while a project is being bid on to strengthen the firm's chances of winning the project.

Fluor recruiters use various means to identify and attract qualified applicants. They place ads in local newspapers and confer with local search firms to generate as many applicants as possible. They also run newspaper ads in other major cities and if a sizeable number of qualified people respond, recruiters travel to the city for a day or two to interview all interested applicants. Another excellent source of applicants is former employees who have left Fluor voluntarily or have been laid off because of reduced business volume. College recruiting is also used to fill entry-level professional jobs.

"The recruitment process consists of a number of steps to identify and employ those applicants most qualified for Fluor's work," explains Perryman. Recruiters review resumes for the appropriate academic credentials and work experience and conduct reference checks to verify information on the employment application. Then recruiters conduct preliminary interviews to examine applicants' general technical expertise and communication skills. They also sell the job and Fluor realistically and enthusiastically to attractive applicants. Fully qualified applicants are then referred to department managers for additional interviews. Here the applicant is also given an in-depth look at the type of work he or she can expect. Recruiters must be able to quickly generate a flow of applicants so that new positions may be filled within a short time frame. The entire process should not take more than one month from beginning of search to hiring.

Perryman found the dynamic nature of Fluor's business and recruiting needs especially challenging and exciting. Just after he joined Fluor, the firm landed several huge projects and more than doubled its staff during the next two years. "The recruiting staff increased from eight to thirty-five," he recalls, "and we were recruiting continually."

The authors wish to thank Mr. Thomas B. Perryman for his help in preparing this material.

materials such as advertisements and brochures that describe the job and organization to prospective applicants. A complete job description is also very helpful to the organization's recruiters, who describe the job and conditions of employment to applicants in preliminary interviews.

Set Out Job Specifications

At this point in the recruitment process, the first basis for screening applicants is established. **Job specifications,** which are the *qualifications required for successful job performance,* typically include the level of education, field of concentration (e.g., computer science, accounting, electrical engineering), and years of related work experience. Exhibit 8.3 shows an employment requisition for a systems analyst at Fluor. Notice that the requisition is quite specific about the knowledge and competencies, related work experience, and educational background of desired applicants. Detailed and realistic job specifications are important because they help prospective applicants evaluate their own qualifications for a job, and line managers and human resource professionals often prepare them together. An ad with unclear job specifications may attract far too many unqualified applicants, and an ad with inappropriately high job specifications may turn away qualified applicants.

job specifications

Identify Sources of Applicants

As noted in Chapter Seven, a key element in strategic staffing is to analyze the supply of prospective applicants both inside and outside the hiring organization. Human resource inventories, which are records of the educational and occupational background, knowledge, skills, EEO status, and interests of all current employees of the organization, are an excellent starting point for any recruiting effort. By hiring from within, employers avoid recruiting costs and also strengthen employee morale by transferring or promoting qualified employees.

If no qualified applicants are available inside the organization, recruiters analyze the labor market to identify additional sources of applicants. Human resource professionals can monitor the labor market formally through environmental scanning (Chapter Seven) and informally by noting the number of unsolicited applications received in the employment office. Line managers also keep abreast of the market through professional associations and contacts with colleagues in other organizations, and can provide excellent suggestions about where to find qualified applicants. As they identify sources of internal and external applicants, employers must also take into account the applicants' status under EEO legislation and their own affirmative action goals (Chapter Five). If analysis of the organization's current and potential employees suggests discrimination against women or minorities (e.g., only 5 percent of the organization's middle managers are black, whereas 10 percent of qualified applicants in the labor market are black), special efforts must be launched to recruit applicants from these groups.

EXHIBIT 8.3   **EMPLOYMENT REQUISITION**

✦ FLUOR

EMPLOYMENT REQUISITION

EMPLOYMENT DEPT. USE ONLY
REQ. # 2172
DATE FILLED 3-7-83
EMPLOYMENT REP. JBT
AAP CODE

To: EMPLOYMENT OFFICE   Date: December 20, 1982

From: Organization Code   754

               No.   Name

PLEASE REVIEW THE FOLLOWING:

	YES	NO
• Is this position or replacement essential?	☒	☐
• Can the position be eliminated by reassignment of work functions?	☐	☒
• Can the position be filled from the current department staff?	☐	☒
• Can the position be filled from within the division with the assistance of the employment department?	☐	☒
• If this is a new position, have future routes for advancement been determined?	☒	☐
• Are the qualifications for this position defined in reference to the position description?	☒	☐

CHECK ONE: ☒ Replacement   ☐ New Position

NUMBER NEEDED	JOB CODE	JOB CLASSIFICATION	STARTING RATE	DATE NEEDED
1	BO7E	Systems Analyst	per month	12/21/82

COMPETENCIES/QUALIFICATIONS/KNOWLEDGE NEEDED TO PERFORM JOB DUTIES SATISFACTORILY (TECHNICAL AND/OR SUPERVISORY) COBOL programming experience, must have CICS or

data base (IDMS) experience and large IBM mainframe experience, PL/I and

CULPRIT desired.

TYPES OF RELATED EXPERIENCE WHICH MAY INDICATE THAT AN APPLICANT POSSESSES THE COMPETENCIES NEEDED

Commercial Systems, application systems in Project & Financial (such as

cost reporting, payroll, progress reporting and administration).

LENGTH OF PREVIOUS RELATED EXPERIENCE REQUIRED

5 - 10 years

EDUCATIONAL BACKGROUND REQUIRED

College grad. or experience equivalent

RESUMES/APPLICATIONS SHOULD BE SENT TO:

REQUESTED BY: *Charles E. Mitchell*   Name   Office   APPROVED BY: _____

                                                           (Department Manager)

NOTE: It is unlawful employment practice and contrary to company policy to discriminate against any applicant on the basis of race, color, religion, sex, national origin, age, military or handicap status. All criteria used in selecting candidates for positions must be job related.

SOURCE: Mr. Thomas B. Perryman, Fluor Engineers, Inc.

Choose Recruitment Methods

The job to be filled, the selection ratio (percentage of applicants hired), and the supply of prospective applicants determine the choice of recruitment methods. The chosen method must make the appropriate people aware of the employment opportunity and attract enough of them to meet the hiring organization's needs. A telephone call to former employees or an inexpensive ad in a local newspaper can be sufficient if qualified applicants are plentiful and the selection ratio is high. Jobs for which a very small percentage of applicants are hired (e.g., astronaut) require recruiting methods that attract vast numbers of applicants. Similarly, when the need for employees is great and the supply is low, more aggressive and expensive methods are necessary. For example, Fluor chose to recruit on college campuses to fill entry-level engineering jobs at a cost of over $1,000 per new employee, and Apple paid a search firm $333,000 to consider senior executives throughout the United States as prospects for company president.

Review Application Forms and Resumes

The first major screening takes place as recruiters review application forms or resumes of internal or external applicants. The primary objective of this step is to eliminate those who do not meet job specifications. It is a relatively routine task usually handled by human resource professionals, rather than line managers. In periods of high unemployment, organizations can receive hundreds of applications for a single job, and a cursory review of educational background and work experience is often used simply to reduce the number of applicants to a manageable size.

Conduct Preliminary Interviews

Next, interviews are conducted with applicants who have met all of the qualifications for the job. The preliminary interview (also called a recruiting or screening interview) is the most personal step in the recruitment process and enables the recruiter to present the job and conditions of employment to each applicant and to further assess the applicant's ability to perform the job successfully. The quality of these interviews is critical to the success of a recruitment program, and organizations differ in their choice of recruiters. Some favor human resource professionals, who are skillful interviewers and knowledgeable about the company's benefits but may not be very familiar with the specific job and hiring department. Other employers choose line managers or other employees from the hiring department to screen applicants, because of their knowledge of the department and job.

Regardless of which recruiters the organization prefers, they should be well trained in interviewing and also be knowledgeable about the job, department, and organization. In presenting the job and organization in the interview, the recruiter should be enthusiastic but realistic to avoid the problem of unrealistic expectations by new employees. In assessing the applicant's ability to perform, the recruiter should probe education and work experience for specific coursework, projects, and work responsibilities that are directly applicable to the job to be filled. Recruiters quickly learn that the information on resumes and application forms can be relatively general or even inaccurate, and careful probing is necessary to gain a better assessment of applicants. Chapter Nine includes specific guidelines on how to conduct this type of interview.

Prepare a Short List of Qualified Applicants

Finally, recruiters prepare a list of the most qualified applicants, who are then examined more closely through various selection techniques described in Chapter Nine. The number of applicants on the short list varies according to the hiring manager's wishes, but many are satisfied with five to ten carefully screened applicants.

RECRUITMENT METHODS

After an organization's need for additional employees has been estimated and job descriptions and job specifications have been prepared, the search for suitable applicants begins. There are many sources of applicants and many recruitment methods available to an organization.

Recruitment of Current Employees

Almost all organizations endorse the policy of promoting from within, and many pursue it actively by designating their present work force as the first source of applicants to meet recruitment needs. As we noted in Chapter Seven, human resource inventories and replacement and succession planning can be used to estimate the availability of employees to assume various jobs within the organization. Transferring or promoting employees to fill vacant positions has several advantages. Because of their knowledge of the organization, employees can learn new jobs more quickly than outside applicants. In addition, managers know more about internal applicants and can therefore base selection decisions on a broader foundation of job-related information. Finally, recruitment of current employees is less costly and frequently quicker than a search for external applicants. Of course, recruitment of current employees creates as many vacancies as it fills, but the new vacancies are often at a more junior level and are presumably less difficult to fill.

   In many organizations, the human resource department serves as a control point to ensure that current employees are given first consideration for any job openings. A common procedure is to require the line manager to submit a *job requisition* to the human resource department as soon as an opening occurs. All employees are then notified of the opening through a *job-posting system,* in which lists of available jobs and job specifications are posted in all company facilities, and employees are invited to apply. Human resource professionals or line managers then review the applications of all interested employees and conduct preliminary interviews with those who meet the job specifications. A "short list" of the best internal applicants is sent to the manager or supervisor with the job opening. If the job has been posted and a review of internal applicants fails to produce one who is suitable, the recruiting effort is extended outside the organization.

Unsolicited Applicants

Applicants who simply walk into the employment office or send in resumes constitute a fruitful source of new employees at virtually no cost to the employer. Unsolicited applications are most common, of course, during periods of high unemployment, but organizations with good reputations receive them on a regular basis. The "walk-in" is particularly welcome in organizations with many entry-level operational and clerical jobs that often become vacant through turnover or internal promotion.

A common practice is to have the walk-in complete an application form, which is then filed and pulled when a need for new recruits arises. Most organizations take applications even when no jobs are open to maintain a file of interested applicants, although many refuse to do so when unemployment is high. Some organizations interview all walk-ins as a public relations gesture, even when no jobs are open. However, this practice can be very time-consuming and may be discontinued during periods of high unemployment.

Unsolicited resumes are also a useful source of applicants at no cost and can be filed for future reference when a job opening occurs. People who send resumes to organizations are typically seeking technical, professional, or managerial positions, and many organizations make the public relations gesture of sending a brief letter of thanks to people who send resumes. Recruiters can quickly review the resumes to determine whether those who send them meet job specifications. Follow-up screening interviews are often done by telephone with qualified applicants. Desirable applicants are then called in for a personal interview as they enter the organization's selection process (Chapter Nine).

Employee Referrals

Human resource policies that encourage current employees to refer applicants to their organization can be very effective, especially in times of low unemployment and high demand for good applicants. Some organizations offer a lump sum to an employee who refers an applicant who is subsequently hired and stays on the payroll for over six months. Others use a sliding scale that increases with the job level of the opening.

Organizations that encourage employee referrals assume that the employee and the applicant will exchange more information than is exchanged between recruiter and applicant during the usual recruitment process. As a result, applicants will be more familiar with the job and organization and less likely to accept a job and join an organization that does not fit them. This recruiting technique also assumes that current employees, in the interest of maintaining their reputations in the organization, will assess acquaintances carefully and refer only those who appear to have good potential for successful job performance. In addition, the requirement that the new employee remain with the organization for at least six months before the referral fee is awarded would tend to discourage careless referrals. Finally, compared to placement agencies and search firms, employee referrals are very cost effective.

Media Advertising

Advertising job openings in printed material (e.g., newspapers, magazines, trade journals, and directories) or other forms of media, such as radio and television, is a widespread and versatile method of recruitment. Depending on the needs of the hiring organization, media advertisements can convey specific company and job-related information to almost any potential applicant in a selected labor market or geographical location. For example, an ad for pipefitters placed in a local newspaper will attract only people who are interested in that specific job and who reside in or near the city where the newspaper is published. An ad for human resource specialists placed in *Personnel Journal* will reach human resource professionals throughout North America.

Although there is a wide range of media available for recruiting advertising, the vast majority of ads appear in newspapers. There are three main types of newspaper ads: classified, classified display, and nonclassified display[4] (Exhibit 8.4). *Classified ads* are listed alphabetically by job category in the "help wanted" section of the newspaper and are generally used to recruit for blue-collar, clerical, and technical jobs. *Classified display ads* are generally used to recruit for professional and managerial positions. They are more elaborate than classified ads, often include variations in typography and artwork, and usually appear in the newspaper's classified section but are not listed alphabetically. *Nonclassified display ads* are even more elaborate and may appear anywhere in the newspaper. They are generally larger and more expensive than the other two types of ads and are used by organizations seeking a large number of applicants for professional or managerial positions.

Selecting the type of medium and the content of a recruitment ad is a sophisticated process undertaken by human resource professionals, sometimes in collaboration with an advertising agency. Bernard Hodes emphasizes the need to present a realistic picture of the job to attract only those people who will find it appealing. Five key areas to include are job content, working conditions or atmosphere, location of company, company reputation, and compensation.[5]

Classified

MACHINIST

With industrial repair machine shop experience is required. The successful candidate will be adept at using lathe, drill press, grinder, shapers and milling machines. The candidate must also possess a minimum of 6 yrs journeyman's experience and be prepared to work in a challenging fast-paced environment. All interested should send a resume, wage history and wage expectations to:

Box 000 000 Tribune 60611
equal opportunity employer m/f

Classified Display

Insurance

LIFE INSURANCE MANAGER
EMPLOYERS MUTUAL COMPANIES

This position, located in the western suburbs, offers an outstanding opportunity for a career life insurance professional who can assume responsibilities for life production through independent property and casualty agents in Illinois. Degreed individual should have a minimum of 2 years production management. Some travel required,

We offer a base salary, car, extra incentive compensation bonus and liberal benefits. Please write in confidence, include resume and salary history to:

Robert E. Smith

Employers Mutual Companies

MLD 114   TRIBUNE 60611
An Equal Opportunity Employer M/F

Nonclassified Display

ACCOUNTING PROFESSIONALS
The Excitement is Still Growing.

Five years ago, Taco Bell was only half the size we are today. As the fastest growing division of Fortune 50 PepsiCo, Inc., our record setting rate of expansion leads the entire fast service restaurant industry. In order to keep pace with this growth, we are seeking accounting professionals to be involved in the ongoing enhancement of our automated accounting systems.

The following position offers the opportunity to interface with Operations Development and Accounting staffs at our corporate headquarters. If you are an ambitious, success-driven individual you can share both the excitement and the rewards.

MANAGER-PROPERTY ACCOUNTING

- Will define future needs in establishment and installation of automated systems for tracking maintenance and reporting of fixed assets.
- Supervisory experience is essential in order to lead our group of 7 professionals.
- Experience with capital expenditures, fixed assets, and FASB-13 is helpful.
- BS degree in accounting, 3-5 years experience required; MBA/CPA preferred.

Taco Bell offers a highly competitive salary and a wide range of company paid benefits including a tuition reimbursement plan. Please forward your resume with salary history to: Taco Bell, Dept. DK-721, 16808 Armstrong Ave., Irvine, CA 92714. Equal Opportunity Employer.

SOURCE: *Taco Bell* advertisement. Reprinted by permission of Taco Bell. *Employers Mutual Companies* recruitment advertisement from *Chicago Tribune*, June 30, 1985. Reprinted by permission.

Hodes also raises four issues the preparer of advertising copy should consider:

1. Position and conditions of employment—Job title, primary tasks and responsibilities, number of openings, compensation range, fringe benefits, hours, location, and starting date.
2. Target audiences—Work experience and education of desired applicants, their needs, motivations, and availability in specific geographic locations.
3. Advertising message—Selling points, company image, and the manner in which applicants can respond.
4. Presentation and placement of the message—General type of medium (e.g., newspaper, magazine, directory) to be used and the specific medium vehicle (e.g., local newspaper or the *Wall Street Journal*).[6]

This information provides guidance for choosing among major types of media. For example, newspaper ads are best for quickly reaching applicants concentrated in a specific geographic area but are easy to ignore, and are quickly discarded. Magazine ads have a longer life and can be directed to specific occupational groups, but they require longer lead times. Radio and television ads are difficult to ignore and can be limited to specific geographic locations, but they are brief and expensive. The advantages and disadvantages of ads in major media are shown in Exhibit 8.5.

Campus Recruiting

Colleges and universities are excellent sources of applicants for entry-level technical, professional, and management-trainee positions in companies of all sizes. Consequently, large and medium-size organizations throughout the United States send recruiters to selected colleges once or twice a year to inform graduating seniors about their organizations' career opportunities and to conduct screening interviews with students.

Campus recruiting has become a regular event at the vast majority of U.S. colleges and universities and has evolved into a very elaborate and effective method of recruitment. The entire process is governed by the College Placement Council, Inc., which represents seven regional placement associations throughout the United States. These associations draw their members from two major groups that are intimately involved in campus recruiting— directors of career planning and placement employed by the college or university to provide career counseling to students and to coordinate campus recruitment activities, and human resource professionals who plan and coordinate their organizations' campus recruiting efforts.

There are two peak recruiting periods on campus each year: September-November for winter graduates, and February and March for spring graduates. Because placement directors schedule recruiting visits as far as one year in advance, careful planning and coordination by human resource professionals is essential for successful campus recruiting. Careful planning is also necessary to coordinate the efforts of campus placement directors, human re-

ADVANTAGES AND DISADVANTAGES OF THE MAJOR TYPES OF MEDIA

EXHIBIT 8.5

Type of Medium	Advantages	Disadvantages	When to Use
Newspapers	Short deadlines Ad size flexibility Circulation concentrated in specific geographic areas Classified sections well organized for easy access by active job seekers	Easy for prospects to ignore Considerable competitive clutter Circulation not specialized—you must pay for great amount of unwanted readers Poor printing quality	When you want to limit recruiting to a specific area When sufficient numbers of prospects are clustered in a specific area When enough prospects are reading help-wanted ads to fill hiring needs
Magazines	Specialized magazines reach pinpointed occupation categories Ad size flexibility High quality printing Prestigious environment Long life—prospects keep and reread magazines.	Wide geographic circulation—usually cannot be used to limit recruiting to specific area Long lead time for ad placement	When job is specialized When time and geographic limitations are not of utmost importance When involved in ongoing recruiting programs
Directories	Specialized audiences Long life	Not timely Often have competitive clutter	Only appropriate for ongoing recruiting programs
Direct mail	Most personal form of advertising Unlimited number of formats and amount of space By selecting names by zip code, mailing can be pinpointed to precise geographic area	Difficult to find mailing list of prospects by occupation at home addresses Cost for reaching each prospect is high	If the right mailing list can be found, this is potentially the most effective medium—no other medium gives the prospect as much a feeling of being specially selected Particularly valuable in competitive situations
Radio and Television	Difficult to ignore. Can reach prospects who are not actively looking for a job better than newspapers and magazines Can be limited to specific geographic areas Creatively flexible. Can dramatize employment story more effectively than printed ads Little competitive recruitment clutter	Only brief, uncomplicated messages are possible Lack of permanence; prospect cannot refer back to it. (Repeated airings necessary to make impression.) Creation and production of commercials—particularly TV—can be time-consuming and costly Lack of special interest selectivity; paying for waste circulation	In competitive situations when not enough prospects are reading your printed ads When there are multiple job openings and there are enough prospects in specific geographic area When a large impact is needed quickly. A "blitz" campaign can saturate an area in two weeks or less Useful to call attention to printed ads

SOURCE: "Planning for Recruitment Advertising: Part II," by Bernard S. Hodes, copyright June 1983. Reprinted with the permission of *Personnel Journal*, Costa Mesa, California; all rights reserved.

EXHIBIT 8.6   THE CAMPUS RECRUITING PROCESS

Step	Campus Placement Office	Human Resource Professionals	Line Managers or Employees
1. Identify recruitment needs.		Consolidate human resource forecasts and identify numbers and types of additional employees needed.	Estimate needs for additional employees.
2. Select colleges and universities.		Identify colleges and universities to be visited.	Advise human resource professionals regarding good schools for their discipline.
3. Schedule recruiting visits.	Book recruiting dates for the employers.	Contact placement offices of selected schools and request recruiting dates.	
4. Send brochures and post interview schedules.	Post interview schedules and job descriptions; students sign up for interviews.	Send updated recruiting brochures and job descriptions to placement offices. Confer with faculty regarding top students.	
5. Arrange trips and prepare recruiters.		Make all travel arrangements and prepare recruiters for trips.	Select line managers and employees to serve as recruiters and arrange for training.
6. Conduct interviews and evaluate students.	Route students to interview rooms; keep recruiters on schedule.	Conduct interviews on campus and evaluate students.	Conduct interviews on campus and evaluate students.
7. Select students for location visits.		Confer with line managers and employees to select students to visit the organization.	Confer with human resource professionals to select students to be invited to visit the organization.

source professionals, and managers and employees in the department with job openings. The entire campus recruiting process, from identifying the need for applicants to choosing a small number of students to enter the selection process, is outlined in Exhibit 8.6. The process consists of seven steps.

1. Identify Recruitment Needs

Systematic planning is essential in any organization participating in campus recruiting because the size of the recruiting effort depends on estimates of the number of job openings at a given time. The forecasting techniques discussed in Chapter Seven are typically used to identify an organization's recruitment needs.

2. Select Colleges and Universities ▬▬ An obviously crucial step is to identify the best available sources of students. The breadth of the campus recruiting program is determined by the size of the organization, its geographical location, the jobs it must fill, and the funds it is able to invest in this method of recruitment. Representatives of large organizations with offices throughout the country may visit over 200 campuses, medium-size regional organizations may select twenty to thirty colleges and universities in their part of the country, and small organizations may visit one or two campuses within driving distance. Human resource professionals who coordinate the recruiting effort typically confer with line managers and employees about schools that excel in their particular discipline. With this information they can focus the recruiting effort by selecting a limited number of specific schools where they will recruit students for specific job openings. In selecting schools, organizations can give special attention to the quality, majors, interests, and values of students, the area of specialization and national standing of faculty members, and the course content and quality of the curriculum.

3. Schedule Recruiting Visits ▬▬ Next, the organization's human resource professional contacts the appropriate placement offices and schedules the number of days that recruiters will be on campus. Large universities often have a main career planning and placement office as well as placement offices in large departments such as the business school and the engineering school.

4. Send Brochures and Post Interview Schedules ▬▬ Several weeks before the recruiting visit, recruiting brochures and job descriptions are sent to the campus to attract students. Student awareness of a potential employer is obviously crucial to successful recruiting, and experienced recruiters strive to strengthen their organization's image by visiting the campus throughout the year and talking with students about career opportunities.

5. Arrange Trips and Prepare Recruiters ▬▬ The impression students form of the campus recruiter significantly influences their views of the organization as a prospective employer. Consequently, organizations take care in selecting and training their campus recruiters for the interview. Whether human resource professionals or line managers and other employees from the department with job openings conduct these interviews is a matter of organizational policy and personal preference. Since students want to face recruiters who can answer their questions about the nature of the job and department, managers or other employees from highly specialized or technical departments (e.g., engineering, accounting, data processing) often serve as campus recruiters. Human resource professionals more commonly recruit students for less specialized jobs such as management trainees or sales representatives. To be effective, recruiters should be knowledgeable about the employer, department, and specific jobs to be filled and should also know how to conduct interviews properly.[7]

6. Conduct Interviews and Evaluate Students ▬ A typical day of campus recruiting includes as many as sixteen thirty-minute interviews. Recruiters usually arrive the night before and begin seeing students at the career planning and placement office at 8:00 A.M. A quick lunch break, often spent with professors or deans to learn more about the quality of students and the curriculum, is followed by another four hours of interviewing. It is essential for recruiters to write a brief evaluation of the student immediately after each interview. After dinner they rank order the students they saw that day, complete their paperwork, and then repeat the process the next day or catch a plane to the next university. Experienced recruiters sometimes joke that their work is "cruel and unusual punishment," and there is little doubt that such a schedule requires motivation and stamina. Placement office personnel provide valuable assistance by handling the logistics of scheduling, directing students and recruiters to the correct rooms, and keeping the whole process on schedule.

7. Select Students for Location Visits ▬ Next, recruiters confer with members of the hiring department to discuss evaluations of all students, and the most highly regarded ones are invited to visit the organization. The location visit is time-consuming for both parties and costly to the organization, and is therefore offered only to the most promising applicants. The students then enter the selection process of the organization and may undergo additional interviewing, testing, and other techniques described in Chapter Nine.

As the competition for college graduates has grown more intense in recent years, especially for scarce talent, many organizations have become very aggressive in their recruitment practices and go beyond the steps outlined above. Many major corporations have full-time college relations specialists who not only coordinate campus recruiting activities but also engage in college relations throughout the year. To heighten student awareness of their employer, they organize and coordinate many ongoing activities. They invite students in key disciplines to tour their facilities so students can directly observe applictions of the principles they are studying and can talk with recently hired employees. Many major corporations also hire students during summers and make job offers to the best performers after they graduate. In addition, college relations specialists arrange for key managers and professionals from the organization to give guest lectures in their discipline or to host "career days" during which they meet with students and discuss career opportunities in their field.

The effectiveness of campus recruiting can be measured in several ways.[8] The number of students who sign up for interviews with an organization reflects the quality of that organization's printed recruiting material, its reputation, and the number of competing employers visiting the campus. This measure varies according to economic conditions and tends to be very high during recessions. The percentage of invitations for location visits accepted by students is an indicator of the quality of the recruiter representing the organization in campus interviews. After the location visit, job offers are made, and the ratio of job offers to visits reflects how well campus recruiters have evaluated students during the campus interviews. A fourth measure is the percentage of job offers that are accepted by students, which reflects the success of the location visit, as well as the level of competition for good students. During recessions, employers with excellent reputations may have almost all their offers accepted. Finally, all direct and indirect costs (e.g., travel, accommodations, employee time, brochures) can be totaled to determine the average cost per student hired by the organization. Costs in the $1,500–$6,000 range are not uncommon.[9]

Employment Agencies

Many organizations find it necessary to augment their recruiting efforts with the services of employment agencies. Employment agencies are private or public organizations that provide job applicants to employers. They range from publicly funded state employment services that screen and refer applicants to employers at no cost to private agencies that bill employers for their services. Employment agencies provide two basic functions: they expand the pool of applicants available to the hiring organization, and they do preliminary screening of applicants. When they perform both functions well, they serve their clients by producing lists of well-screened job applicants.

Although heavy reliance on employment agencies can be expensive and inefficient, they can be very useful to an organization when the following conditions apply:

1. The employer has found it difficult to generate a pool of qualified applicants.
2. The employer's need for only a few people or an irregular demand for new employees makes it inefficient to maintain an elaborate recruiting capacity.
3. A particular job opening must be filled quickly.
4. More minority or female applicants need to be attracted.
5. The recruitment effort is aimed at reaching individuals who are currently employed (for example, executives, professionals).[10]

The term "employment agency" applies to a wide range of recruitment organizations which can generate comments varying from contempt to praise from the human resource professionals and line managers who interact with them. Employment agencies can be categorized according to the kind of service they provide. They concentrate on either the *placement* of job applicants or the *search* for job applicants.

Placement Agencies ▬▬ The job applicant is the primary client of the placement agency, which concentrates on assessing the client's work qualifications and placing him or her in a job. Consequently, the agency contacts

potential employers to determine whether they have job openings for which its clients might qualify. Private placement agencies charge a fee, usually paid by the employer, for placing an applicant in a job. Public agencies charge no fees.

Placement agencies clearly expand the pool of applicants available to an employer and are particularly good sources of blue-collar and clerical applicants. Some private placement agencies concentrate in a particular discipline (e.g., accounting or computer science) and supply applicants for a wide range of job levels. Employers often contact agencies they respect and request applicants for specific job openings.

Placement agencies earn bad reputations when they fail to screen their applicants thoroughly. A major complaint from human resource professionals and line managers is that agencies not only fail to screen applicants, but make applicants appear more highly qualified than they actually are by embellishing their resumes and coaching them for employment interviews. In the extreme, this practice can increase the work of human resource professionals by flooding the organization's employment office with unqualified applicants. The key to a placement agency's success is thorough screening of applicants and referral of only those that meet the organization's needs.

Search Firms ━━━ The client of a search firm is an employer, rather than an applicant. Organizations call upon search firms when they need help finding highly qualified applicants in a tight labor market. Consequently, search firms deal primarily with executive, managerial, and professional applicants. The recruiting process begins with a "job order" based on a detailed job description and job specifications. Search consultants often visit the organization and interview current employees of the department with the job opening to gain more insight into the type of applicant being sought. Next, they search for applicants in their files or through newspaper ads and carefully screen all who seem qualified. They then choose a small number of applicants to be examined by the employer. Apple Computer's search for a new president illustrates the way a search firm operates.

The fees of search firms are very high, running from 30 percent to 50 percent of the annual salaries of the employees they place. Such high fees can be jusitifed, however, if an agency can fill a crucial job with an outstanding employee. Effective search firms not only expand the pool of applicants but thoroughly screen applicants. But they also have their failings. Human resource professionals and line managers complain about frequent calls from search consultants seeking job orders. The most serious complaint about search firms, however, is the tactics they use in finding applicants. Many engage in the questionable practice of "raiding" by contacting employees of one organization and trying to convince them to apply for a job with their client organization. Some search consultants even raid former clients by tempting employees they had placed a year or two ago to join a current client.

Search firms provide a useful service to employers, but they walk a fine line between conducting legitimate searches for applicants and practices that employers consider unethical.

How can an employer evaluate and select a good search firm? Reputation is probably the most important criterion. When considering a particular search firm, experienced line managers and human resource professionals often confer with their colleagues in other organizations to assess the quality of the firm's services. Another important consideration is the firm's fee structure. As we have already mentioned, many search firms base their fee on the annual salary of the employee they place. This practice places a premium on filling a vacancy quickly and could encourage some firms to try to sell available, somewhat undesirable applicants to a client, rather than taking more time to find a better applicant. To eliminate this incentive, some firms charge a fee for a search (e.g., for a three-month period) regardless of whether they find an acceptable applicant for the client. Employers should also be cautious when dealing with search firms that also provide **outplacement services,** which is *a process by which an organization provides financial and professional support to help a terminated employee find a satisfactory position in another organization* (Chapter Sixteen). A firm engaging in both search and outplacement has an incentive to place the terminated employees of its outplacement clients with its search clients and thereby collect two fees for one transaction. In spite of the short-term incentives for unethical practices, reputable search firms recognize that the key to their success is repeat business with the same clients. Consequently, they avoid shortcuts and unethical practices and spend the time necessary to meet their clients' needs for high-quality employees.

outplacement services

Choosing Recruitment Methods

The recruitment methods discussed in this chapter are ways organizations find needed employees in a timely fashion. Human resource professionals, working in collaboration with line managers and supervisors, must anticipate the organization's job openings and choose appropriate recruitment methods. The use of a wide variety of recruitment methods is discussed in Box 8.2. The choice of a specific method in the organizations surveyed was based on two major factors. The key factor is the availability of applicants; organizations use very aggressive and costly methods, such as search firms and display ads in specialized publications, to attract scarce applicants. A second factor is the applicants' status under equal employment opportunity legislation. Employers showed great ingenuity in their efforts to recruit women and minorities. In choosing recruitment methods for their organizations, human resource professionals and line managers must consider these two factors, as well as the strengths and weaknesses of each method.

USE OF RECRUITMENT METHODS

BOX 8.2

With the economy improving, many organizations are reactivating their recruitment and selection programs. The primary aim of such programs is to attract and choose productive employees who will not only fit the organization's needs, but remain and grow with the organization. Thus, 28 of the 41 respondents to a survey report that their organizations have formal recruitment programs.

Recruitment programs are most frequently directed at groups who are in great demand—such as engineers, nurses, and other professionals. It is not surprising, therefore, to find that the most popular target of respondents' recruitment efforts are professional and technical employees—24 of the 28 formal programs are directed at this group. Following these in order of popularity as targets are salaried employees (21), middle managers (19), hourly employees (16), executives (14), and sales personnel (12).

Because different techniques are considered to be effective in reaching people with different interests and capabilities, a variety of techniques are used by organizations, including some without formal recruitment programs. These range from the most widely used technique, classified advertising in newspapers (used by 35 respondents), to television spot advertisements (used by one). The list below shows the range of recruitment techniques and the number of respondents who used each.

Spurred by various federal and state equal employment opportunity (EEO) requirements, many employers take a variety of steps to ensure that women and minorities are adequately represented in the work force. The most frequently used method for reaching those

Type of Recruitment Techniques Used* (total = 41)

Classified advertisements in newspapers	35
In-house recruitment	34
Walk-in applicants	33
Private agencies	29
State agencies	29
College visits	24
Classified advertisements in specialized periodicals	24
Display advertisements in newspapers	22
Recruiting literature	18
Display advertisements in specialized periodicals	17
Job fairs	14
Recruiting team visits	11
Bonuses to current employees	11
Open houses	8
Radio spots	7
College placement offices	2
Television spots	1
Current employee referral	1
Referrals by others	1

*Total is more than 41 because most organizations use more than one technique.

covered by EEO laws is through agencies or groups that service or represent them. For example, David G. Nelson, corporate manager of selection and placement for Honeywell, Inc., reports that his company contacts the Society of Women Engineers, the National Society of Black Engineers, and similar organizations for eligible candidates.

KEY POINTS

▬▬ Recruitment begins with an estimate of an organization's need for new employees. Then various methods such as media advertising, campus recruiting, and employment agencies are used to attract and screen potential job applicants.

▬▬ Organizations must systematically adapt their recruitment efforts to changes in the economic, social, technological, and political environments. In particular, equal employment opportunity legislation has strongly influenced the recruitment process since the middle 1960s.

▬▬ Media advertising is a common recruiting method that enables employers to send a wide range of information to specific groups of applicants.

▬▬ Campus recruiting, which can cost as much as $6,000 per new employee, requires careful coordination between the college placement office, human resource professionals of the hiring organization, and managers and employees of the department with the job opening.

▬▬ The term "employment agency" refers to placement agencies, whose primary objective is to find jobs for applicants, and search firms, who find and screen applicants for employers.

ISSUES FOR DISCUSSION

1. Consider the impact of the economic, social, technological, and political environment on your current career interests. How would your career interests affect the type of job and employer you would seek in the recruitment process?

2. Review the eight major steps in the recruitment process. Which are the most important? Why?

3. If you have been involved in campus recruiting as a student, discuss what caused you to like or dislike a prospective employer.

4. What is the basic difference between a placement agency and a search firm? Under what circumstances would an organization need the services of each?

5. What are the major types of media advertising? Under what conditions should an organization use each type?

NOTES

1. Adapted from J. Guyon, "Apple Lured President from Pepsi with Patient Persuasion and Cash," *Wall Street Journal*, April 14, 1983, p. 33.

2. J. P. Wanous, *Organizational Entry: Recruitment, Selection, and Socialization of Newcomers* (Reading, MA: Addison-Wesley), 1980, Chapter 3.

3. J. Naisbitt, *Megatrends: Ten New Directions Transforming Our Lives* (New York: Warner Books), 1982, Chapter 1.

4. P. F. Wernimont, "Recruitment Policies and Practices," in *ASPA Handbook of Personnel and Industrial Relations*, Ed. D. Yoder and H. G. Heneman (Washington, DC: Bureau of National Affairs), 1979, p. 4-101.

5.   B. S. Hodes, "Planning for Recruitment Advertising: Part II," *Personnel Journal*, June 1983, *62* (6), pp. 492–501.

6.   Ibid., pp. 496, 498.

7.   The principles of selection interviewing in Chapter Nine also apply to recruiting interviews.

8.   See B. Nunke, "The Components of Successful College Recruitment," *Personnel Journal*, November 1981, *60* (11), pp. 859–62.

9.   T. Bergmann, and M. S. Taylor, "College Recruitment: What Attracts Students to Organizations?" *Personnel*, May–June 1984, *61*, pp. 34–46.

10. S. Rubenfeld, and M. Crino, "Are Employment Agencies Jeopardizing Your Selection Process?" *Personnel*, September–October 1981, *58*, p. 71.

ANNOTATED BIBLIOGRAPHY

College Placement Council, Inc.

  This highly regarded professional association, composed of seven regional placement associations throughout the United States, provides many services to its members. It has established and published *Principles and Practices of College Career Planning, Placement and Recruitment*, which provides ethical standards for college placement personnel, organizational recruiters, and students. It also publishes information and trends in recruitment and placement in the quarterly *Journal of College Placement*. Another major publication is the *College Placement Annual*, in which organizations' job openings and interview dates are listed.

HODES, B. S. *The Principles and Practice of Recruitment Advertising: A Guide for Personnel Professionals*. New York: Frederick Fell, 1982.

  This book, written by the founder of an international company specializing in recruitment advertising, is a practical guide on how advertising principles can be applied to recruitment. The author discusses the similarities between consumer and recruitment advertising and illustrates common advertising formats. The book includes clear guidelines on how to manage a recruitment advertising program and outlines such steps as setting advertising objectives, defining the target audience, and determining the message content. Hodes also offers suggestions on how to select an ad agency and determine its role in an organization's recruitment program. Finally, guidance is given on the production and effectiveness of various types of media.

WANOUS, J. P. *Organizational Entry: Recruitment, Selection, and Socialization of Newcomers*. Reading, MA: Addison-Wesley, 1980.

  Chapters 2 and 3 of this book focus on the conclusions the author has drawn from ten years of research on how new members join organizations. He discusses the problems inherent in the traditional recruitment process, in which applicants and organizations fail to exchange accurate information, and stresses the consequences of unrealistic expectations developed by applicants during recruitment. He then proposes that organizations recruit more realistically by presenting applicants with all relevant information without distortion and explains how realistic recruitment can be implemented. Finally, he presents several examples of organizations that recruit realistically and summarizes many studies which have demonstrated the positive impact of realistic recruitment.

WHITE, C., and THORNER, A. W. *Managing the Recruitment Process.* New York: Harcourt Brace Jovanovich, 1982.

While its focus is on the recruitment of lawyers, this book includes a wealth of detailed, practical information on how to design, administer, and manage a recruitment program for professionals. The authors divide the recruitment process into major steps such as preparing information to be presented by the employer, handling contacts with applicants, interviewing, evaluating, and extending the offer. In addition, they discuss the administration of a recruitment program and list a number of specific tasks to be done by the hiring manager, the recruiting coordinator, and a secretary. This book would be very helpful to human resource professionals who must initiate a campus recruiting program.

CHAPTER NINE

SELECTION

The latest method for invading the privacy of someone's personality goes one step beyond body language.* This is a way of interpreting a person's integrated body movements to come up with an action profile or body "signature". . . .

The theory is being promulgated by Warren Lamb, director of a British consulting firm that specializes in decoding these subtle body movements primarily for firms interested in recruiting and organizing management teams.

The basic premise is that everyone has a distinctive pattern of movements that lasts a lifetime. "Whatever is consistently emphasized in movement holds the key to character," Lamb maintains.

By interpreting these movements, Lamb and his experts can determine whether a person tends to approach or withdraw from others, has an upward or downward sweep or appears outgoing or self-enclosing . . . .

From these actions, determinations are made regarding a person's decision-making abilities, adaptability to change and to other people, as well as basic personality traits . . . .[1]

It sometimes seems that there is no limit to the methods that employers can use to select successful employees. Some organizations rely on tests of job-related skills and abilities, others use interviews and questionnaires to discern personality traits, and still others resort to lie detector tests or even body signature analysis. The goal of all these methods is the same—to select people with the greatest potential to perform the job successfully.

But how often is that goal met? Selection is a very difficult task because it involves collecting information about human beings to predict their performance. How can employers determine what information needs to be collected? Do they have the right to collect the information? And will that information actually help employers select good performers? These are some of the questions about the selection process that are addressed in this chapter.

selection

Selection is *the process through which representatives of an organization define a job to be filled, assess the people applying for that job, and*

---

*"Body 'Signature' called Key to One's Character" KNT News Wire Story. Reprinted by permission: Tribune Media Services.

choose the applicant with the greatest potential to perform the job success-fully. Anyone who has held a job or been admitted to college has gone through a selection process. A selection process may be rather simple, requiring applicants to complete an application form, go through a brief interview, and pass a physical examination. Or it may be quite complex, consisting of reviews of the applicant's resume and letters of recommendation, extensive psychological testing, several interviews, and even credit checks. Each step in the selection process is an attempt by the organization to assess the applicant's potential to perform the job.

Selection is one of the most universal human resource functions included in this text and is simply another way for the organization to attain an optimal degree of fit between the individual, the job, the organization, and the environment, as discussed in Chapter Two. In selection, both the individual and the job are viewed as relatively stable, and the objective is to match people and jobs to the satisfaction of both the employees and the organization.

A key step in the selection process is the assessment of applicants. In this step information is collected to answer two fundamental questions: can the applicant do the job, and will the applicant do the job? While somewhat related, these questions draw upon different information for their answers. The first question examines the education, work experience, knowledge, skills and intelligence that people need to perform job functions successfully. The second question is concerned primarily with applicants' likes and dislikes for various types of work, their interests, and their career goals. Both questions must be answered positively for an applicant to be acceptable. The remainder of this chapter focuses on how organizations can determine which applicants can and will perform specific jobs successfully.

RESPONSIBILITY FOR EMPLOYEE SELECTION

The responsibility for employee selection is shared by line and staff, much as it is for recruitment. Line managers and human resource professionals begin the process by collaborating to define the jobs to be filled. Then human resource professionals design the selection procedures and administer selection tools (e.g., application forms, skill tests, and personality inventories) to applicants from inside or outside the organization. Finally, line managers and supervisors to whom new employees will report become involved again by assessing applicants, usually through interviews. They normally make the final choice of applicants to be hired.

Human resource professionals provide two essential services to the organization in its quest for new qualified employees. First, they *establish and maintain a standardized selection process* to ensure that each applicant is passed through procedures that have been required by the hiring organization or by various state and federal government agencies. For example, many organizations maintain a policy of promoting from within and attempt to fill every vacancy with a current employee before initiating an external search for qualified applicants. This policy not only reduces the cost of selection but also contributes to employees' career development and improves employee morale. Similar standardization is found in efforts to ensure that all applicants have an equal opportunity for employment without consideration of such personal characteristics as race, sex, ethnic background, or national origin. This policy was originally mandated by the Civil Rights Act of 1964.

The second service of human resource professionals is to *secure well-qualified applicants for line managers to consider*. Sometimes this involves very active recruiting to find qualified applicants, as discussed in Chapter Eight. More often, it involves preliminary screening of applicants to save line managers' time by eliminating unqualified applicants. For example, if fifty applicants respond to an ad for a job with an organization, human resource professionals might review application forms, conduct preliminary interviews, and administer tests to all fifty applicants and then eliminate all but the five best applicants from further consideration. This "short list" of five applicants would then be interviewed by the line manager, who would then decide which applicant to hire.

THE SELECTION PROCESS

Exhibit 9.1 outlines the major steps in the selection process of a typical organization. The time and emphasis placed on each step will of course vary from one organization to another and, indeed, from job to job within the same organization. For example, some organizations may place great emphasis on testing, while others may focus on interviews and reference checks. Similarly, a single, brief selection interview might be sufficient for applicants for lower-level jobs, while applicants for professional or managerial jobs might be interviewed by a number of people.

Preliminary Phase

The selection process begins with a job opening. The opening may result from the promotion, transfer, or termination of an employee, or it may result from a new position being added to a department. The line manager with the job

SELECTION PROCESS

EXHIBIT 9.1

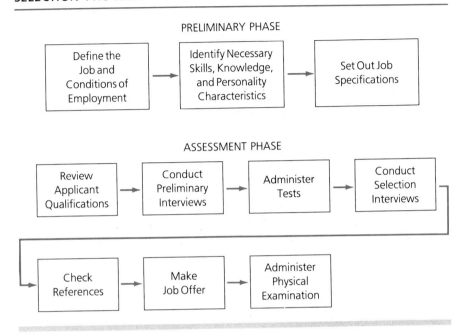

opening then contacts a human resource professional and submits a request for a new employee. At this point, the preliminary phase of the selection process begins. Note that this preliminary phase is very similar to steps 2 and 3 in the recruitment process outlined in Chapter Eight. This overlap is essential since both recruitment and selection must begin with a clear definition of the job and applicant qualifications. The preliminary phase has of three steps.

Define the Job and Conditions of Employment ▬ A crucial but sometimes overlooked starting point in the selection process is to clearly describe the job to be filled. This is essential not only when new jobs are created, but also when existing jobs are vacated, since many jobs change over time and job descriptions may be out of date. The job description should list job responsibilities as well as describe the job's relationship to other jobs. In addition, any unusual conditions of employment, such as extensive travel, overtime, or work hazards, should be noted. Human resource professionals often confer with line managers or current employees to prepare accurate, up-to-date job descriptions. An example of a job description for a current vacancy is shown in Exhibit 9.2.

Identify Necessary Skills, Knowledge, and Personality Characteristics ▬ Once the job has been clearly described, the second step is to identify what the applicant must bring to the job to perform successfully. What level of intelligence is required? What specific skills and abil-

EXHIBIT 9.2   ## JOB DESCRIPTION

STATEMENT OF POSITION RESPONSIBILITIES

Position Title: Clerk/Sr   *Company:*
Reports To: Dir/Empl & Organization Dev   *Functional Area:* Personnel
Directly   *Department:* Emp & Org
Supervises: None   *Section:* Development

BASIC FUNCTION

Performs administrative duties for training programs and the educational refund plan to facilitate effective program implementation, and provides clerical support for department personnel.

PRIMARY DUTIES AND RESPONSIBILITIES

1. Participates in training program administration:
   a. Monitors participant nominations, schedules participants, and confirms attendance, by telephone,
   b. Schedules training room and makes luncheon, hotel, and travel arrangements,
   c. Prepares, edits, and mails correspondence to participants, supervisors, and speakers,
   d. Organizes, formats and produces training manuals and materials,
   e. Updates educational records through batch and on-line computer system,
   f. Operates company vehicle to pick up films and other training materials, and, as required, transports training participants to field locations.
2. Implements Educational Refund Plan:
   a. Processes applications and requests for refunds,
   b. Advises employees of educational refund procedures,
   c. Assists Program Administrator in maintaining and updating educational refund records through batch and on-line computer system.
3. Performs clerical support for departmental personnel:
   a. Operates IBM 8100 System word processor to prepare, proofread, and edit correspondence, reports, forms, schedules, and proposals,
   b. Prepares documents for approval, including account distributions, materials ordered, invoices, expense accounts, time sheets, carpool and busing subsidy forms and reports, automobile mileage reports, sickness and injury reports, monthly departmental budget analysis.
   c. Receives, screens, refers, and/or distributes telephone calls and correspondence,
   d. Organizes and maintains filing systems,
   e. Monitors and maintains office supplies, materials and forms.
4. Participates in collecting and disseminating information regarding outside training programs
5. Ensures the security of classified and confidential employee information.

APPROVED: DATE:

ities are necessary? What knowledge will the applicant need to perform the job well? What personality characteristics are helpful in dealing effectively with any unusual conditions of employment, such as time pressures, extensive travel, or a hazardous environment? In this stage of the selection process rational hypotheses or hunches are formed about what the applicant must bring to the job to be successful. We use the word "hypotheses" because the extent to which specific skills, knowledge, and personality characteristics actually contribute to successful job performance is not fully known at this stage of the selection process. Their relationship to job performance needs to be confirmed, as we will discuss later in this chapter.

Set Out Job Specifications ▬ At this point in the selection process the first potential predictors of job performance are chosen. These are *job specifications*, the employee qualifications required for successful job performance. Job specifications (also called paper qualifications) are typically expressed in terms of educational requirements or years of experience in a related job. For example, the job specifications for the job in Exhibit 9.2 are two years clerical experience, including typing of narrative and statistical information, filing and record systems maintenance, use of adding machine/calculator, and one year of work experience operating IBM System 8100 or equivalent word processing equipment. The job specifications must relate directly to the knowledge and skills identified in the second step. A college degree should not be required if the necessary knowledge and skill could be developed in high school. Five years of related work experience should not be required if two years will suffice. Line managers and human resource professionals need to resist the temptation to unnecessarily elevate job specifications because by doing so they can screen out qualified applicants, increase recruiting costs, and hire overqualified applicants, who may have a higher turnover rate.

Assessment Phase

Once the job to be filled has been clearly defined and appropriate job specifications have been established, the selection process moves into the phase of assessing applicants for the job. If applicants have been recruited through the methods described in Chapter Eight, the next two steps will already have been completed. For internal applicants and walk-ins, however, the assessment phase begins with the review. The assessment phase consists of several hurdles applicants must pass. The goal of each is to eliminate applicants so that only one person is left at the end of the process. That person is the new employee.

However, while the object of this phase is to eliminate all but one application for each opening, the manner in which applicants are turned down is crucial. All applicants, no matter how poorly qualified, should be treated with respect to maintain a positive image of the organization in the labor market. Selection procedures that give all applicants serious and careful consideration also ensure compliance with federal legislation that prohibits discrimination against women and minorities. The assessment phase consists of seven steps.

Review Applicant Qualifications ▬ The assessment phase of the selection process almost invariably begins with a review of the applicant's resume or application form. This step is usually done by a junior member of the human resource department, although in small organizations line managers may be involved. In reviewing this material, one should place emphasis on level of education, degrees, majors, previous jobs, years of related work experience, and specific responsibilities associated with previous jobs, and compare them with the job specifications. In this step the emphasis is on "screening out" all applicants who do not meet the minimal requirements of the job. This review cannot determine *how well* the applicant is likely to perform; it simply passes on those applicants that appear to warrant further consideration and assessment.

Conduct Preliminary Interviews ▬ Applicants who survive the review of their qualifications next undergo a preliminary interview. The primary objectives are the following:

1. To verify material on the resume or application form and fill in any missing items;
2. To collect information from the applicant to determine potential and desire to perform the job;
3. To provide information to the applicant about the job and to promote good public relations.

The first objective is largely a clerical function. Then the matching process begins. The interviewer probes the applicant's background to uncover evidence of knowledge and skill required to do the job in question, as well as the applicant's interest in that kind of work. In addition, the interviewer provides more detailed information about the job, conditions of employment, and employee benefits, and answers any questions that the applicant wishes to raise. Since this interview is the first contact between the employer and potential employee, it has a significant impact on the applicant's image of the hiring organization.

The preliminary interview takes a variety of forms. In large organizations it is usually conducted on site by human resource professionals who may spend as little as five minutes with applicants for lower-level jobs or as much as thirty to forty-five minutes with applicants for more senior jobs. In small companies they may be conducted by a knowledgeable assistant or secretary of the manager of the department with the vacancy. Preliminary interviews are also conducted on university campuses by organizations that hire large numbers of graduating students (see Chapter Eight).

Administer Tests ▬ The next step in the assessment phase provides more extensive examination to determine if the applicant has the knowledge, skills and personal qualities required to perform the job. This is accomplished in many organizations through standardized employment testing. The type of test used for selection depends, of course, on the nature of the job to be filled. Applicants for clerical jobs often take typing and shorthand tests, while tests of mechanical aptitude and dexterity are administered to applicants for small assembly work. Applicants for higher-level jobs are sometimes subjected to more complex personality tests. Those who fail to get minimal scores on these tests are eliminated from the selection process. Great care must be taken to ensure the proper use of employment tests, as we will discuss later in this chapter.

Conduct Selection Interviews ▬ Next, the applicants are interviewed by the people with whom the new employee will actually be working—the immediate supervisor and co-workers. If the previous assessment steps have been done properly, only a few of the most promising applicants will reach this step. For lower-level jobs, relatively brief selection interviews may be conducted by the immediate supervisor only. With more senior jobs, several members of the department may interview the applicant over the span of a day or two.

The selection interview has three major objectives:

1. *Collect information.* As with the preliminary interview, the primary objective is to collect information to determine whether the applicant can and will perform the job successfully. Previous work experience is examined to determine not only *what* job functions the applicants performed before, but *how* they performed them, and *how well.* Similarly, education is examined in detail to learn not only *what* knowledge and skill applicants have acquired, but *how* and *how well* they might apply that knowledge and skill in the job to be filled. Work interests, likes and dislikes, and career plans may also be examined to see if they match the employment opportunities at the hiring organization.
2. *Provide information.* An attempt is also made to inform the applicant about the job and organization. Departmental employees who interview applicants usually focus on the nature of the department and the specific job to be filled. It is important that they present a realistic picture, rather than trying to "oversell" the applicant.
3. *Check personality.* The need to look over a potential employee "person to person" is strong and contributes significantly to the popularity of the selection interview. In this interview supervisors and co-workers can assess each applicant's personal style, attitudes toward work, and many other intangibles that they feel can affect job performance.

All three of these objectives are addressed in the typical selection interview, although the emphasis given to each may vary widely. After all applicants have been interviewed, they are ranked in order of preference by the interviewers.

As we have already mentioned, many organizations first move through these four steps with internal applicants. If no internal applicant survives these steps, applications are solicited from applicants outside the organization. Because of the availability of current employees, these first steps in the assessment phase can often be completed for internal applicants in a week or two. The same steps for external applicants can take considerably longer.

Check References ▬▬ Some organizations routinely contact the previous employers provided by applicants as references to gather additional information about the applicants' potential to perform the job successfully. This can be a good safety check because applicants may include false information about previous employers or educational background on their resumes or application forms that may go undetected in interviews. In recent years, however, employers have grown increasingly reluctant to provide information about employees either in writing or over the phone. Employer reluctance to provide written references is related to federal employee privacy legislation and company policies, which give employees the right to inspect, review, and amend their employee records and ensure that they are not misused (see Chapter Five). Since EEO suits have been won on the contention that letters of reference discriminate against minorities, many employers will provide only factual information such as job title, salary, and dates of employment in response to reference checks. This practice has made it difficult for prospective employers to obtain information about quality of performance through reference checks.

Make Job Offer ▬▬ The human resource professional and the manager of the prospective employee then evaluate the assessments made in the previous three steps and decide which applicant will receive an offer of employment. Organizations differ in their emphasis on interviews, tests, and reference checks, but ultimately all the information must be combined to arrive at a selection decision. Human resource professionals assist in the interpretation of test scores and interviews and make recommendations, but the line manager almost invariably makes the final decisions. The offer is usually made in writing with various conditions of employment indicated such as starting date, monthly salary, and benefits. The written offer may be preceded by an oral offer when the organization is eagerly seeking new employees.

Administer Physical Examination ▬▬ Many organizations have historically included a physical examination in their selection process. The Vocational Rehabilitation Act of 1973 (see Chapter Five), however, restricts organizations with federal contracts and subcontracts from discriminating against physically or mentally handicapped persons for reasons that are not related to their potential to perform a job. To ensure compliance with this legislation, many organizations have attempted to remove any consideration of physical or mental handicap from the selection process until the applicant has been thoroughly examined in the other steps of the assessment phase. In short, they delay the consideration of any potentially job-related handicap until the applicant has passed all other hurdles in the employment process and then make the offer of employment dependent upon the condition that the applicant pass a physical examination.

STANDARDS FOR SELECTION TOOLS

Organizations have shown no lack of creativity in choosing tools to aid in the selection process. In a never-ending struggle to gain information to predict performance, organizations have relied upon a wide range of selection tools, from commonly used tests and interviews to unusual techniques like handwriting analysis and lie detector tests. In all instances, the question is the same. What information can be gathered to predict whether an applicant can and will perform the job satisfactorily?

The importance of each selection decision, coupled with the time and cost of administering the selection process, makes the choice of selection tools crucial. The four standards discussed below provide guidance to line managers and human resource professionals who must choose the tools to be included in their organization's selection process.

Relevance

Simply stated, **relevance** is the *extent to which a selection tool includes a representative sample of job tasks.* Also known as "content validity," this standard is essentially a matter of judgment. For example, a test in which applicants move pegs on a board as rapidly as possible from one position to another may be relevant to a job involving the assembly of small electrical equipment, but its relevance to performance in a sales job would be highly questionable. Similarly, an in-depth interview probing the personalities of applicants might be relevant to a sales job but not to fine assembly work.

relevance

Relevance is the first standard to be used in choosing selection tools. It provides no guarantees that the selection tool will predict job performance; it is merely a hunch. But some hunches are better than others. Selection tools that are chosen on the basis of testimonials or personal preferences (e.g., body signature analysis or lie detector tests) are unlikely to predict job performance. Better choices will result from the preliminary phase of the selection process, which answers the following questions:

1. What specific functions and tasks are involved in the job?
2. What skills, knowledge, and qualities must employees have to perform those functions and tasks?
3. What skills, knowledge, or qualities are measured by the selection tool?

The answers will help identify *potentially* useful selection tools, whose relevance is high.

The use of relevant selection tools also serves an important public relations function. It is important that job applicants perceive an organization's selection tools as appropriate and sensible. Having to take a test that appears totally unrelated to the job opening can be very annoying to an applicant and can hurt the image of the employer. For example, during the 1960s when personality testing was very popular, many tests were used inappropriately, and many applicants objected to employment tests that probed into irrelevant personal matters. The use of seemingly inappropriate selection tools can also undermine the credibility of the organization's human resource professionals. If they recommend selection tools that have little relevance to job performance, they will provide poor service to line managers by screening out the wrong applicants.

Reliability

reliability

Reliability is consistency of measurement. More specifically, **reliability** is the *extent to which a selection tool yields similar results when applied at different times or by different people*. If a tool is used to predict future job performance, it must produce consistent measurements on an applicant. Suppose an applicant takes a motivation test Monday morning and Friday afternoon, and the Monday score is 100 while the Friday score is 125. Which score is accurate? Either the test is faulty and does not produce reliable scores, or it measures something that changes significantly in a short period of time. In either case, the results of the test are so unreliable that it could not be used as a selection tool.

Validity

validity

Validity is the *statistical relationship between scores on a selection tool and a criterion or measure of job performance*. (This standard is also called criterion-related or empirical validity.) Validity is the ultimate standard for a selection tool. A selection tool is valid if it predicts job performance accurately. If it is valid, it can be used in the assessment phase to identify applicants who have the greatest potential to perform the job successfully. If it is not valid, there is absolutely no justification for its use by the organization.

The way to determine validity is to compute the statistical relationship between applicants' scores on a selection tool and a measure of their performance. This relationship is usually expressed as a correlation. Exhibit 9.3 shows the results achieved with three different selection tools.

In A a valid relationship exists between scores on a test of mechanical aptitude and the number of units assembled per hour on the job. Notice that applicants with the highest scores on the test also perform best on this measure of job performance. To ensure that applicants with the greatest potential to perform successfully are chosen, a rational policy would call for selection of applicants with high test scores. Therefore, the cutoff score (score separating accepted and rejected applicants) could be sensibly set at 25.

VALIDITIES OF THREE SELECTION TOOLS

EXHIBIT 9.3

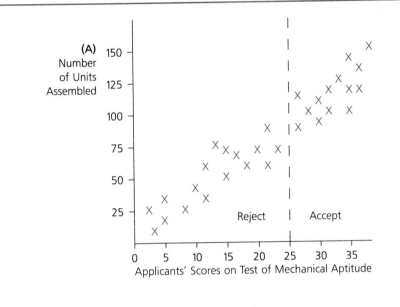

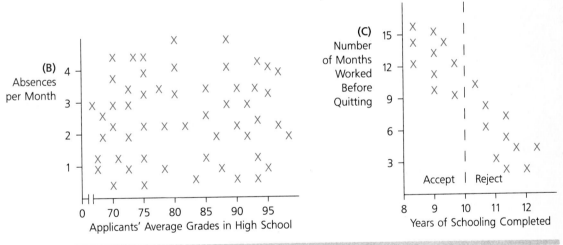

Note: Each applicant's score on the selection tool and measure of performance is represented by an "X."

In B there is no evidence of validity. Some applicants with high average grades in high school are seldom absent and some are often absent. The same is true of applicants with low average grades. Regardless of where the cutoff score is drawn, equal numbers of applicants will be accepted who will subsequently have high or low absenteeism. In short, average grades in high school cannot be used to predict absenteeism.

C illustrates the risk organizations take by not validating their selection tools. Here the selection tool is valid, but there is a *negative* correlation between the selection tool and job performance. The applicants with the lowest amount of formal schooling remained *longest* in the job before quitting, so a policy of hiring *highly* educated applicants would ensure that the wrong applicants were selected. The needs of the organization for low turnover would best be served by a selection policy that rejected applicants with high levels of education. In this case, applicants *below* the cutoff score would be accepted for employment. Without the evidence of this negative relationship, an organization might routinely select the wrong applicants.

Validity can be computed in two fundamental ways. The first is *predictive* validation. The selection tool (e.g., a test) is administered to applicants, who are then hired regardless of their test scores. After several months, employee job performance is measured and is correlated with the test scores to determine validity. If valid, the selection tool is then used in the assessment phase of the organization's selection process. Since this type of validation requires the organization to deliberately hire some applicants who will fail on the job, it is practical only in organizations that hire many applicants and want strong evidence that their selection tools are valid.

The second fundamental way to determine validity is called *concurrent validation*. The selection tool is administered to a group of current employees, and their scores are correlated with job performance measured at the same time. This is a much more practical procedure, although unfortunately it does not necessarily yield a good estimate of predictive validity.

There are many instances in which computing validity would be impossible. For example, many organizations hire only a few employees for a given job in a year and consequently would not have enough for a validation study. Some organizations lack the expertise or the funds to assess validity. In these cases the organization must rely on our first standard, *relevance*, by judging the similarity between the knowledge, skill, or qualities measured by a selection tool and the specific work behaviors and tasks involved in the job. Careful job analysis and close examination of potential selection tools are essential to judge relevance.

Fairness

It would be a waste of human resources and a lost opportunity for the employer if some job applicants were eliminated from the selection process for reasons unrelated to job performance. Therefore, any selection tool must be *fairness* judged by the standard of **fairness,** *the tendency of the selection tool to treat all applicants alike and to provide them with an equal opportunity to gain employment.*

Unfortunately, whether intentionally or not, many organizations have a history of systematically eliminating a portion of applicants from the selection process on the basis of such personal characteristics as sex or color. For example, women have often been omitted from serious consideration for heavy factory work, and blacks from sales and managerial jobs.

Employment practices that discriminate against women and minorities were declared illegal by the Civil Rights Act of 1964 and subsequent equal employment opportunity legislation and court decisions (see Chapter Five). The result was two fundamental restrictions on the selection process. The first prohibits **disparate treatment,** *employment practices that treat individuals differently because of race, color, religion, sex, national origin, age, physical or mental handicap, or veteran status.* This restriction simply requires that all applicants be treated alike in all steps of the selection process. It is usually violated through discriminatory habits, as when a line manager spends only five minutes interviewing a female applicant while conducting forty-five minute interviews with all male applicants. Such practices can be avoided with a careful and comprehensive effort to establish organizational selection procedures that are lawful and are followed by all parties involved in the process.

disparate treatment

The second restriction prohibits **adverse impact,** *the effect of employment practices that screen out a disproportionate percentage of individuals of a protected class for reasons unrelated to job performance.* Adverse impact is a more complex restriction to follow. Suppose 100 male applicants and twenty-five female applicants were considered for employment by an organization. After proceeding through the assessment phase, fifty men (50 percent) and five women (20 percent) were considered suitable for employment. According to this restriction, if the percentage of offers made to members of a protected group was *less than* 4/5 of the percentage of offers made to unprotected applicants, the organization making the offers could be accused of having an adverse impact on the protected group. However, if the organization could show that a selection tool that favored men over women was related to job performance, the claim of adverse impact would be weakened. For example, male applicants may have had better educational qualifications, more related work experience, higher test scores, or better selection interviews than female applicants. If the organization can show that these selection tools predict job performance, then the difference in percentages is justified.

adverse impact

In short, the imposition of the standard of *fairness* by federal legislation has also forced organizations to adhere to the standard of *validity.* Since the use of standardized selection procedures became common in the middle of the twentieth century, human resource professionals have recommended validation procedures as sensible business practice, and professional groups have established guidelines for validation.[2] But the careful, periodic validation of selection tools has unfortunately been overlooked in many organizations. Validity has often been assumed, rather than demonstrated. Recent federal legislation has put increased pressure on organizations to demonstrate fairness of all selection tools through the various validation techniques described in the previous section. Box 9.1 provides an impressive illustration of careful research by Exxon to ensure that its selection tools meet the four standards described above.

DESIGNING AND VALIDATING A SELECTION TOOL

BOX 9.1

Exxon Company, U.S.A. was committed to hiring women into physically demanding jobs in the late 1970s but also wished to ensure that only well-qualified applicants were accepted for employment. Exxon's Personnel Research group therefore set out to develop and validate selection tools for the job of process apprentice at the Baton Rouge Refinery. Evidence of the validity of the selection tools was considered crucial to defend against any charges that the selection process discriminated against women.

The Personnel Research project team began by examining several potential selection tools. An interview resulting in judgments of applicants' physical abilities was rejected because of its subjectivity and the poor ability of interviewers to reliably and accurately assess physical abilities. The requirements of minimum height and weight were also rejected because they clearly discriminate against women. The team decided to develop a number of objectively scored tests of a variety of physical abilities which have been shown to be required for successful job performance.

The project began with a thorough analysis of eleven jobs (including that of process apprentice), and a total of 330 physically demanding tasks were listed. People familiar with the jobs then reduced this list to 133 of the most important and most physically demanding tasks, which represented the job performance to be predicted by the selection tool.

Nine basic physical abilities (e.g., static strength, trunk strength, and gross body equilibrium) were judged necessary to perform the 133 tasks, and measures of the physical abilities were developed. Some measures were work samples; for example, gross body equilibrium was assessed by having applicants walk on a balance beam. This process of careful job analysis and development of work samples produced highly *relevant* selection tools. Objective scoring procedures were also designed to ensure the *reliability* of the selection tools.

A predictive validation study was then conducted with forty-eight male and eleven female applicants. The measures of physical abilities were administered to all fifty-nine applicants, who were then hired regardless of their scores. Supervisors and operators in the refinery observed the apprentices on the job and rated their performance after six months of service. To guard against biased evaluations, between two and four raters independently evaluated each apprentice and then compared their ratings to reach a consensus.

The consensus evaluations of job performance were then correlated with scores on the measures of physical abilities to compute the *validity* of the selection tools. In particular, the measures of strength predicted job performance well. An attempt was also made to assess the *fairness* of the selection tools, although the small number of women prevented a thorough analysis. Preliminary results showed no bias against women.

Exxon's Personnel Research group concluded that the measures of physical abilities showed promise as selection tools for process apprentices. They are continuing to collect data for further validity studies.

The authors wish to thank Personnel Research, Exxon Company, U.S.A. for its kind assistance in preparing this material.

COMMON SELECTION TOOLS

All members of the organization who are involved in selection—human resource professionals as well as line managers and supervisors—can use the four standards discussed above to evaluate and choose selection tools on a continuing basis. *Someone* in the organization must ask, "Is it relevant, reliable, valid, and fair?"

In this section we shall apply the four standards to common selection tools to provide a sense of their usefulness. In assessing each selection tool we have based our conclusions on a huge body of empirical research.[3] We emphasize, however, that individual selection tools must be evaluated in individual organizations before they can be used with confidence to determine whether applicants can and will perform successfully.

Biographical Data

The application form or resume is the first selection tool to be used by many organizations since it forms the basis for *reviewing applicant qualifications*, the first step in the assessment phase of the selection process. Often the information is perused and compared with the job specifications, and applicants who do not possess minimal requirements are rejected. More standardized scoring schemes have also been used with application forms in which specific items (e.g., years of schooling, years of related work experience) are assigned weights and added to produce a total score, which is then used to accept or reject applicants.

Biographical data fare well when assessed with our four standards for selection tools. Their *relevance* is generally good since the information is usually related to job performance. Their *reliability* is high since the information is largely factual and generally completed truthfully by the applicants.[4] Biographical data also have a long history of high *validity*,[5] although validity decreases over time because the scoring weights developed for one sample of applicants may not be accurate for other groups of applicants.[6]

The *fairness* of biographical data is questionable, however, because some information on application forms or resumes clearly identifies applicants as members of protected groups and may contribute to adverse impact.[7] For example, the fact that an applicant attended high school outside the United States could reveal national origin. In conclusion, biographical information is a sound selection tool whose validity is exceeded only by ability tests, especially if data relating to whether applicants are members of protected groups are eliminated from consideration in the selection process.

Standardized Tests

In the preliminary phase of the selection process, skills, abilities, and other personal qualities can be identified as potential determinants of successful job performance. The best way to measure these potential determinants is with standardized tests. There are two major kinds of tests. *Paper-and-pencil tests* include items measuring specific human attributes. Examples are the Wonderlic Personnel test, a measure of general intelligence containing fifty multiple-choice items, and the California Psychological Inventory, a measure of several personality characteristics. The second kind of test is a *performance simulation,* in which applicants must actually demonstrate a skill or ability during the test. A typing test, for example, is often used for applicants for clerical positions.

An immense number of standardized tests measure general intelligence and specific mental abilities, skills, personality characteristics, and interests. Information about their reliability, validity, and scoring procedures can be found in test manuals and published encyclopedias of tests.[8] In general, tests have proven to be very good selection tools when used appropriately. Their *relevance* can be good if they are chosen on the basis of careful job analysis. Tests are generally *reliable* measures and are among the most *valid* of available selection tools.[9] The real weakness of standardized tests is their questionable *fairness.* Members of minority groups often score significantly lower on standardized tests than do whites, especially on so-called culture-bound tests of intelligence and achievement that are based on exposure to white, middle-class cultural values in the United States.[10]

Work Samples

Some selection tools place the applicant in an actual work situation. For example, everyone who has a driver's license passed a work sample when he or she drove a car with a state examiner in the passenger seat. Rather than using a standardized typing test, some organizations have applicants type material they would actually encounter on the job. Work samples are most appropriate for testing skills and abilities directly involved in job performance.

When carefully prepared and scored, work samples are excellent selection tools. They are *relevant* because they are a sample of the job to be filled. Excellent *reliability* and *validity* have also been reported for work samples.[11] Finally, they can be more *fair* than paper-and-pencil tests because they are less likely to be culture-bound.[12]

Assessment Centers

Assessment centers are very elaborate and costly selection tools appropriate in organizations that screen large numbers of applicants for managerial and professional jobs. The centers are generally established and operated by the hiring organization and make use of several tools to examine applicants over two or three days. In particular, they use in-depth interviews, paper-and-pencil tests, and performance tests or work samples with several raters observing and scoring applicants' performance.

Assessment centers have been good selection tools for jobs involving people contact such as management, sales, and police work.[13] They rate highly on the standard of *relevance* since they include many performance tests and work samples. Their *reliability* is also high, but their *validity* varies from moderate to high.[14] Assessment centers have proved to be excellent predictors of promotion (with correlations in the .60s) but their correlations with future job performance have ranged only in the .30s.[15] Evidence on their *fairness* is mixed.[16]

Selection Interviews

For decades the interview has been one of the most commonly used selection tools. Its popularity among members of organizations who screen and hire applicants is in sharp contrast with the conclusions of those who have done research on the effectiveness of the interview as a selection tool. In truth, the interview is a relatively poor device for gathering information to determine whether an applicant can and will perform a job successfully.

One major problem is its lack of standardization. That is, each interviewer conducts the interview differently from other interviewers. This variation in approach strongly affects how the interview measures up to the four standards for selection tools. For example, some interviewers gather information very relevant to the job they are filling, such as previous work experience, education, and career goals, while other interviewers talk about material (e.g., hobbies, sports, and themselves) that has little bearing on potential job performance. Therefore, the *relevance* of the interview varies from excellent to poor, depending on interview content.

A large body of research has shown that the interview has poor *reliability* and *validity*.[17] The culprit is lack of standardization, as each interviewer covers different information or interprets the same information differently. As a result, different interviewers reach different assessments of the same applicant. A more structured approach to the selection interview, in which the same basic content is covered by all interviewers, can improve reliability.[18] Finally, the *fairness* of the interview is also questionable.[19] Many personal characteristics, such as race, sex, age, color, and ethnic background, may be readily apparent to interviewers and can influence their assessments of applicants. While this research evidence is discouraging, all hope is not lost. We shall present some suggestions for improving the effectiveness of the selection interview later in this chapter.

Reference Checks

As a selection tool, reference checks suffer from many of the same problems as the interview; their usefulness varies according to the source of the reference. The *relevance* of the references or letters of recommendation varies widely. Some focus on topics such as specific responsibilities of previous jobs or specific skills and knowledge gained from education that are clearly related to the job to be filled, but others contain only assessments of a series of undefined personal qualities (e.g., bearing, maturity, initiative, appearance, ambition) that are reminiscent of the Boy Scout code and have highly questionable relevance to the job for which the applicant is being considered. The *reliability* and *validity* of references and letters of recommendation vary from low to moderate.[20] Finally, the *fairness* of these selection tools is also likely to be questionable because the race, sex, age, color, and ethnic background of applicants may be apparent to referees and may influence their assessments of the applicants. The popularity of various selection tools is shown in Box 9.2. Note that some of the most widely used selection tools are of poor quality, according to our four standards.

Other Selection Tools

Since even the best selection tools are unable to predict future job performance very accurately, organizations are always on the lookout for new approaches to employee selection. This need, coupled with the lack of information about new selection tools, has led to many fads over the years. Many selection tools currently in use are merely wasting organizations' time and money.

Handwriting analysis, or graphology, is based on the premise that applicants reveal personality characteristics through their handwriting. Approximately 2,000 American firms use handwriting analysis in their selection process.[21] The *relevance* of handwriting analysis is questionable. There is some evidence that graphologists agree in their judgments; therefore, *reliability* of the technique is acceptable.[22] Its real weakness is lack of *validity*. There is no empirical evidence that graphology predicts job performance. Finally, there is no evidence of the *fairness* of handwriting analysis.

Use of another selection tool, the *lie detector test*, or polygraph, is based on the premise that people who tell the truth during the selection process are generally honest. Lie detector tests might therefore appear especially appropriate for jobs that involve handling cash, such as clerks in stores, fast food restaurants, etc. The polygraph is used to measure emotional stress indicated by variations in blood pressure, pulse rate, perspiration, and respiration as applicants respond to questions. Since telling a lie is considered stressful, the stress will be reflected in these physiological responses.

The widespread use of the polygraph provides an excellent example of how some very sound instruments are *misused* as selection tools. The polygraph measures emotional stress, not lying. Many sources of emotional stress unrelated to lying may cause a person to "fail" a lie detector test, and many people can lie without being detected by a polygraph. The *relevance* and *reliability* of the polygraph are poor, and we know of no evidence on its *validity* or *fairness*.

No organization can afford to use a selection tool that has not been carefully checked against the four standards. There is too much at stake. The risk of rejecting an applicant who would have been successful or accepting an applicant who subsequently fails on the job can be minimized through the use of effective selection tools. Exhibit 9.4 summarizes findings on the quality of various selection tools, but it is the responsibility of anyone involved in an

CURRENT SELECTION PRACTICES

BOX 9.2

A survey conducted in May 1983 by the American Society for Personnel Administration and the Bureau of National Affairs examined the selection practices of U.S. organizations of varying sizes and from a wide range of industries. A total of 437 personnel executives reported on the selection tools and validation procedures used in their organizations.

The percentage of organizations that use each selection tool is shown in the graph below. Reference checks and unstructured interviews are most widely used, in spite of their poor quality. Work samples, which are excellent selection tools, are also regularly used, but primarily for clerical jobs. It is somewhat discouraging that standardized tests, known for their excellent reliability and validity, are used by less than 25 percent of the employers surveyed.

The survey uncovered even more discouraging information about the validation procedures in today's organizations. Eighty-four percent of the personnel executives reported that their selection tools had *not* been validated in accordance with federal guidelines. Only 29 percent of the large organizations with more than 1,000 employees reported such validation. Formal evaluations and supervisors' statements are most frequently used as measures of performance in validation studies, followed by

more objective measures such as tenure, production rate, and attendance. Finally, concurrent validation is more common than predictive validation in the organizations surveyed.

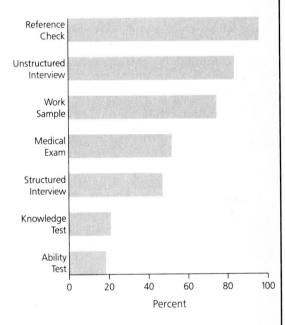

From "Organizational Practice" by Randall B. Dunham, *The Industrial Organizational Psychologist,* February 1984, vol. *21,* no. 2. Reprinted by permission.

EXHIBIT 9.4　　　　*QUALITY OF SELECTION TOOLS*

	Relevance	Reliability	Validity	Fairness
Biographical Data	Good	High	High, but decreases over time	Questionable
Standardized Tests	Good, if test choice is based on job analysis	High	High	Questionable
Work Samples	Excellent	High	High	High
Assessment Centers	Excellent	High	Moderate to high	Questionable
Selection Interview	Varies from excellent to poor, depending on interview content	Low	Low	Questionable
Reference Checks	Varies from excellent to poor, depending on source	Low to moderate	Low to moderate	Questionable
Handwriting Analysis	Poor	Moderate	No evidence	No evidence
Lie Detector Tests	Poor	Low	No evidence	No evidence

organization's selection process—human resource professionals and line managers—to carefully scrutinize selection tools currently in use or new selection tools as they come on the market. Consider the body signature analysis introduced at the beginning of this chapter. It is very likely that some organizations are using it to select or promote employees. How well might it measure up as a selection tool against the four standards?

AFFIRMATIVE ACTION

The Civil Rights Act of 1964 and subsequent legislation not only prohibited discrimination against protected groups but also encouraged employers to take "affirmative action" to counteract discriminatory human resource policies of the past. The Equal Employment Opportunity Coordinating Council, established by an act of Congress in 1972, explained when affirmative action is called for:

> (2) Voluntary affirmative action to assure equal employment opportunity is appropriate at any stage of the employment process. The first step in the construction of any affirmative action plan should be an analysis of

the employer's work force to determine whether percentages of sex, race, or ethnic groups in individual job classifications are substantially similar to the percentages of those groups available in the relevant job market who possess the basic job-related qualifications.

When substantial disparities are found through such analyses, each element of the over-all selection process should be examined to determine which elements operate to exclude persons on the basis of sex, race, or ethnic group. Such elements include, but are not limited to, recruitment, testing, ranking certification, interview, recommendations for selection, hiring, promotion, etc. The examination of each element of the selection process should at a minimum include a determination of its validity in predicting job performance.

(3) When an employer has reason to believe that its selection procedures have the exclusionary effect described in paragraph 2 above, it should initiate affirmative steps to remedy the situation.[23]

Since the middle 1970s affirmative action has become a "way of life" in many organizations. Advertisements for job openings proudly proclaim the organization as an "Equal Opportunity/Affirmative Action Employer." Affirmative action managers who monitor the selection and promotion of women and minorities are common today, especially in large organizations.

Civil rights legislation and affirmative action have had a particularly dramatic impact on the selection process of organizations. The Equal Employment Opportunity Commission requires all organizations to keep specific records concerning their employment practices. When these records indicate potential discrimination, many organizations take affirmative action to reduce it.

First EEOC Reporting Requirement

The EEOC requires that an organization's work force be identical to the relevant labor force from which it draws applicants. Therefore, organizations are required to compute the percentages of women and minorities in the relevant labor market and compare them with the percentages of the same groups in a variety of jobs in the organization. If the percentages of protected groups in the organization are lower than the percentages in the labor force, discrimination in employment practices *may* have occurred.

In response to such a finding, organizations should set goals to increase the number of women and minority employees by increasing the number of applicants from protected groups who are *qualified* to do the job through recruiting and training. Hiring unqualified women or minority applicants benefits neither the applicant nor the organization and is discouraged by the EEOC.

Second EEOC Reporting Requirement

The second requirement is that applicants from protected groups have the same opportunity for employment as other applicants. Therefore, employers must keep records of the percentage of applicants from protected groups who are offered employment. A selection rate for a protected group that is less than 80 percent of the selection rate for other applicants constitutes evidence of adverse impact. In such cases the employer must demonstrate that its selection process does not discriminate against women and minorities.

The only evidence that an organization can produce to refute the charge of adverse impact is the validity of its selection tools. The organization can demonstrate this validity through predictive or concurrent validation procedures, described earlier in this chapter, or by comparing the content of the selection tools with the tasks and responsibilities of the job to show relevance. Unfortunately, a selection tool can be valid (i.e., predict future job performance) and yet be unfair to women or minority applicants. For example, if the selection tool is valid for male and nonminority applicants but does not predict future job performance of applicants from protected groups, evidence exists of differential validity. The selection tool may be valid when applied to some job applicants but not others. If those others are women or minorities, the selection tool is considered unfair. Research has shown that differential validity is quite rare.[24]

The second, more common, type of unfairness occurs when an employer uses a valid selection tool on which applicants from protected groups score lower than other applicants. For example, if a high school education is required for employment, a smaller percentage of black applicants will qualify than whites because fewer blacks complete high school. Similarly, some intelligence and achievement tests are unfair to ethnic minorities because they are based on the knowledge and experiences of middle-class white America. Low test scores by minorities may reflect not low intelligence or achievement, but lack of exposure to middle-class values and experiences. In such cases, selection tools cannot be considered fair to minorities.

The appropriate affirmative action in a case of unfairness is to use other selection tools that are not unfair to women or minority applicants. For example, Exhibit 9.5 shows how disadvantaged applicants can be treated differently than those without a disadvantaged background. In the exhibit, applicants who do not have disadvantaged backgrounds are rejected if they have not completed high school, but disadvantaged applicants who do not have a high school diploma can qualify for employment if they pass Test A. In addition, different employment tests are used for each type of applicant. The objective of such a selection process is to use for each group of applicants only those selection tools that are fair and valid.[25]

The examples of affirmative action discussed in this section are consistent with the ultimate objective of human resource management—namely, to achieve the optimal degree of fit between the individual, job, organization, and environment. It has always been in the organization's best interests to seek out and select employees with the greatest potential to perform the job

ALTERNATIVE SELECTION TOOLS

EXHIBIT 9.5

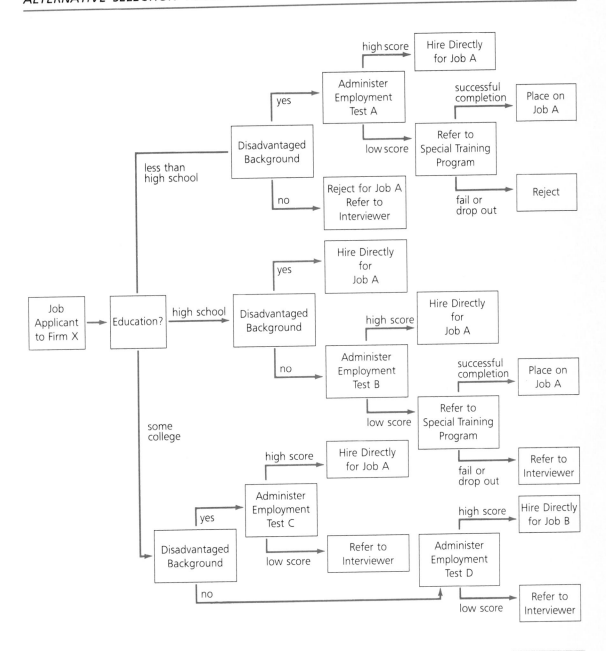

SOURCE: From Figure, "Flow Chart Showing Hypothetical Program Emphasizing Individualized Personnel Decision Strategy" by M. D. Dunnette, p. 62. Reprinted with permission of the Free Press, a Division of Macmillan Inc., from *Integrating the Organization* ed. by Howard Fromkin and John Sherwood. Copyright © 1974 by the Free Press.

successfully. Affirmative action provides the organization with applicants that may have heretofore been overlooked or screened out unfairly.

WEAKNESSES OF THE SELECTION INTERVIEW*

The interview is one of the most commonly used selection tools.[26] Although academic researchers have questioned its effectiveness for decades, practitioners still strongly endorse the interview as a selection device, and its popularity continues to grow.

The effectiveness of the interview as a selection device is relatively low. It did not fare well when measured against the four standards earlier in this chapter. In spite of these weaknesses, the selection interview continues to be used, and it is often considered the most crucial tool in the organization's selection process. In view of this, how can the interview be improved as a selection device? Let's begin by examining its weaknesses in more detail.

The many problems of the selection interview have four major causes, shown in Exhibit 9.6.

Poor Planning

Many selection interviews are simply not carefully planned. With their hectic schedules, human resource professionals often find themselves facing an applicant before they have had time to think carefully about the interview they are about to conduct. Because they see job applicants infrequently, line managers and supervisors may also take little time to plan a selection interview.

The interview is likely to fail if interviewers do not know their objectives and have not developed a plan to meet them. Lack of planning usually leads to a relatively unstructured interview in which whatever comes up automatically becomes the content. This can undermine the relevance of the interview. Also, the less structured the interview is, the less reliable it will be. Furthermore, the less interviewers know about the job to be filled, the less qualified they are to examine an applicant's potential to perform that job successfully and to make a valid selection decision.

Psychiatric Approach

A major weakness in the selection interview stems from the way human beings evaluate each other. All too often interviewers try to assess an applicant's basic character in half an hour. Judgments are made about the applicant's personality, skills, and knowledge. Indeed, some interviewers place

*From James G. Goodale, *The Fine Art of Interviewing*, © 1982, pp. 24-37. Adapted by permission of Prentice-Hall, Inc., Englewood Cliffs, N.J.

IMPROVING THE INTERVIEW

EXHIBIT 9.6

Weaknesses	Causes	Solutions
Poor Planning	Interviewers do not know their objectives. They do not plan and structure the interview. They do not know the job for which the candidate is applying.	Plan properly. Know objectives. Plan an interview format to meet these objectives. Know as much as possible about the job.
Psychiatric Approach	Interviewers assume the role of amateur psychiatrist. They judge applicants on inappropriate criteria.	Evaluate applicants in job-related terms. Evaluate the applicant's potential to perform specific job tasks. Assess the applicant's willingness to do the job.
Fallible Interviewers	Personal attitudes and stereotypes abound. First-impression bias and jumping to conclusions are apparent. Interviewers forget.	Build a better interview. Tailor the interview to a specific job. Systematically cover job-related topics in the interview. Record evaluations and supportive documentation.
Violation of EEOC Guidelines	Interviewers raise prohibited topics. Evaluations are based on irrelevant information.	Make interviews meet EEOC guidelines. Tailor the interview to the job. Systematically cover job-related topics. Evaluate applicants in job-related terms. Record evaluations and supportive documentation.

SOURCE: From James G. Goodale, *The Fine Art of Interviewing* © 1982, pp. 24-37. Adapted by permission of Prentice-Hall, Inc., Englewood Cliffs, N.J..

great emphasis on the assessment of such characteristics as maturity, initiative, aggressiveness, and confidence. This evaluation of traits has become institutionalized in many organizations through the use of interview rating forms that require interviewers to evaluate the personalities of applicants. Line managers and supervisors as well as human resource professionals often are unqualified to make such assessments. Further, since they are poorly defined and subject to interpretation, evaluation of personality traits reduces the reliability of the interview. This approach can also lead to futile attempts by interviewers to trick applicants into revealing their true character by asking "psychological" questions, such as, "If you could be any animal in the forest, what animal would you be?" or "What one word would you use to describe yourself?"

Fallible Interviewers

Everyone judges people in unique ways with reference to unique standards, and this leads to unreliability in the assessment of applicants. The primary problem with selection interviews is the interviewer, who is susceptible to a number of influences that can bias judgments and therefore undermine the interview's reliability and validity.

The attitudes and background of interviewers contribute to low reliability by affecting the interviewers' interpretation of what applicants say and their subsequent evaluation of the applicant.[27] Many interviewers have relatively well-defined stereotypes of the ideal applicant. Since these stereotypes differ with the interviewer, the information to which interviewers attend also differs.[28]

Individual biases are complicated by the human tendency to jump to conclusions. Research indicates that interviewers make global evaluations of candidates very early in the interview—as early as the first four minutes.[29] Initial impressions are often based on information that has questionable relevance to job performance (e.g., dress, firmness of handshake, hairstyle, sex, race). This research suggests that after interviewers have formed an initial impression, they seek out information that is consistent with that impression and ignore inconsistent information. This process is most likely to occur in an unstructured interview.

Forgetting is another important source of error in interviews.[30] Interviewers simply forget much of what they hear. If two interviewers remember different information about an applicant, their evaluations of that applicant can differ.

Violations of EEOC Guidelines

Organizations abound with horror stories about interviewers who have pet questions that violate EEOC guidelines and expose the employer to charges of discrimination. Questions asked of female, but not male, applicants about marital status, family plans, or child care are prohibited, as are questions about any applicant's religious beliefs and ethnic background. In addition, interviewer bias against members of a protected group is unlawful.

WAYS TO IMPROVE THE SELECTION INTERVIEW

Plan Properly

There are many ways the interview can fail as a selection tool. But fortunately, many of its problems can be addressed, and improvements made.

Proper planning can increase the selection interview's relevance and reliability. Specific objectives need to be set and a format to meet them needs to be developed. Since the interview's primary objective is to predict job performance, selection interviewers need to know as much as possible about the job to be filled. This knowledge keeps their questions focused on job performance. To ensure proper planning, interviewers can take two key steps before an interview.

1. *Start with the job.* Preparation for a selection interview should begn with the identification of the major tasks of the job to be filled. This set of tasks provides a focus for the interview and also represents a basis for evaluating the applicant.
2. *Review the resume or application form.* Review of the applicant *on paper* before the interview is a cardinal rule for the interviewer. This review provides the basis for small talk as the interview begins and enables the interviewer to identify areas in the applicant's background to be examined in more detail during the interview. Interviewers should look for previous work experience and training in the tasks of the job to be filled. Finally, this preliminary review can uncover potential problems such as gaps in work history or reasons for leaving previous jobs, which need further examination in the interview.

Evaluate Applicants in Job-Related Terms

The two fundamental questions to be answered during the interview are "Can you do the job?" and "Will you do the job?" The selection interviewer's main objective is to gather information to predict whether the applicant *can* perform the job to be filled. To meet this objective one must first know the job performance to be predicted. A crucial starting point, therefore, is to divide the job into a manageable number of major tasks. Then information can be collected during the interview to assess the applicant's potential to perform each task.

An interviewer can assess an applicant's potential to perform specific tasks by gathering information from three basic sources:

1. *Previous work and nonwork experience.* This answers the question "Has the applicant performed the task before?"
2. *Previous training or education.* This answers the question "Has the applicant learned how to perform the task before?"
3. *Actual applicant behavior during the interview.* This answers the question "Is the applicant demonstrating job-related skills in the interview?" (e.g., communicating clearly and concisely; handling stress well).

Thus, interviewers can probe what applicants *have done* before (on or off the job), what they *have learned* to do, and what they *are doing* during the interview. Both approaches to evaluating applicants in Exhibit 9.7 begin with these three sources of information, but the way the interviewer assesses the information differs significantly. The psychiatric approach involves assessing the applicant in terms of personality traits: "What kind of person is this? What are his or her basic personality characteristics?" These assessments are often irrelevant and unreliable.

EXHIBIT 9.7   **ALTERNATIVE APPROACHES TO EVALUATING APPLICANTS**

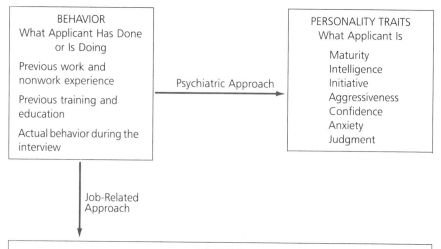

SOURCE: From James G. Goodale, *The Fine Art of Interviewing,* © 1982, pp. 24-37. Adapted by permission of Prentice-Hall, Inc., Englewood Cliffs, N.J..

An alternative is to evaluate applicants in terms of potential to perform specific tasks, such as those of the entry-level accountant's job in Exhibit 9.7. The job-related approach asks, "On the basis of what the applicants are saying and doing, can they perform the required tasks? How will her previous experience help her perform these tasks? Has he had any training and education that he can apply in this job?" The applicant's potential to perform these specific tasks can then be recorded on an interview rating form.

The answer to the question "*Will* the applicant do the job?" is related to the potential employee's interests, intentions, likes, and dislikes. The interviewer examines the potential fit between the job, working conditions, and career opportunities, and the applicant's desires for work and a career. Questions about the applicant's interest in the company and the job to be filled test this fit. Comparing the applicant's career goals with the organization's career opportunities can help to predict the applicant's satisfaction with a new employer. Evaluations of an applicant's work interest and motivation can be recorded on an interview rating form.

This job-related evaluation process is likely to lead to selection interviews with higher relevance. Since job tasks are more clearly defined than personality traits, agreement between interviewers is likely to increase, thereby improving the interview's reliability. Finally, since interviewers are striving to assess applicants' previous experience, training, and interest in specific job tasks, questions are more likely to be job-related, thereby improving the interview's validity and fairness.

Build a Better Interview

As long as people conduct interviews, the problems of stereotyping, jumping to conclusions, forgetting, and other forms of bias will persist. The only solution is to "build a better interview" by designing each interview for a specific job and assessing applicants in terms of the potential they show to perform that job. This puts emphasis on the job-related approach to evaluation. A structured interview encourages interviewers to systematically cover job-related topics, in spite of personal biases and stereotypes. Forgetting can be reduced if interviewers record their assessments of the applicant immediately after the interview. A six-point format for a structured, job-related interview provides guidance to interviewers but still allows flexibility:

1. *Establish rapport.* Many interviewers begin by introducing themselves, referring to the job that is open, and welcoming the applicant warmly. Next, a little small talk about some common ground—a school, part of the country, or hobby—is useful to break the ice.

2. *Set the agenda.* The interviewer should explain briefly the objectives of the interview. Providing a short outline can also help to relax applicants by letting them know what's coming and also puts the interviewer in control of the interview by providing a road map to be followed.

3. *Gather relevant information.* Interviewers should spend the bulk of their time probing applicants' backgrounds for evidence of potential and willingness to perform specific job tasks.

4. *Describe the job and organization.* The interviewer should outline the job duties, the nature of the department and organization, and present information applicants need to assess this employment opportunity.

5.   *Answer applicant's questions.* This portion of the interview allows the applicant time to collect additional information about the job and organization before leaving the interview.

6.   *Terminate.* Thanking applicants for their time and telling them what will happen next (e.g., "We'll be interviewing for the next two weeks and will telephone you with our decision within three weeks") is a straightforward and comfortable way to end the interview.

Make Interviews Meet EEOC Guidelines

The problem of violating EEOC guidelines can be remedied relatively easily through the improvements already discussed. With a properly planned, job-related interview, interviewers are less likely to raise prohibited topics or base their evaluations on irrelevant information. Training can also clarify what questions they can and cannot ask applicants. EEOC guidelines can be particularly intimidating to line managers because they prohibit the discussion of so many topics. A more positive way of viewing these guidelines, however, is to ask what possible relevance topics like race, color, religion, sex, and age have to job performance. If the objective of the interview is to identify people who can and will do the job, EEOC legislation places no restrictions on any *job-related* source of information. The key is to ask questions in job-related terms. For example,

1.   Don't ask a female applicant if she is married; ask her if she can relocate, travel, etc.

2.   Don't ask an applicant his religion; ask him if he can work Saturdays and Sundays.

3.   Don't ask where an applicant was born; ask for proof of qualification to work in the United States (citizenship or permanent residence visa).

4.   Don't ask if a female applicant has child care problems; ask if she can work late on short notice.

Finally, if interviewers record their evaluations of applicants on rating forms, they can document the fairness of their selection decisions.

REASONS FOR SELECTION ERRORS

Of all the functions of human resource management discussed in this text, selection presents the greatest challenge. Many decades of practice and research have shown that choosing the best applicant for a job is very difficult. Selection errors are common. Every working day, hundreds of applicants are hired in the United States who will ultimately fail to meet minimal standards of job performance, and hundreds of other applicants who would have performed well are turned away.

There are three basic reasons for selection errors and an understanding of these three can suggest ways human resource professionals and line managers can substantially improve the selection process.

The Unpredictability of Human Behavior

Human beings are extremely adaptable creatures with a great capacity to change over time. They develop new interests, new skills, new knowledge, and new preferences as time passes, and with these changes come the desire and potential to do new things. While this capacity to change makes life interesting and varied, it creates headaches for anyone who is trying to predict performance. For example, if a company hires a number of entry-level engineers with nearly identical degrees, knowledge of engineering, grades, and career goals, how can anyone identify who will become disenchanted with engineering and quit within two years and who will perform well and move into management in ten years? The personal or work-related factors that cause some employees to suffer a drop in performance, develop a dislike for their work, quit a job, or change careers are very difficult to anticipate as selection decisions are being made. Consequently, a certain degree of error in selection is inevitable. The other two causes of selection errors can be addressed effectively.

Poor Definition of Job Performance

A distressingly common reason for selection errors is a lack of precise definition of what an applicant is *to do*—namely, job performance. Human resource professionals often interview an applicant for a job that the interviewers do not understand fully and therefore make a poor assessment of the applicant. Even line managers and supervisors sometimes make selection decisions without a clear definition of the job to be filled. Every selection decision is a prediction of future performance. When an applicant is rejected, someone has concluded that the applicant will fail to perform specific tasks at an acceptable level. The more line managers and human resource professionals know about job performance, the greater their chance to predict it accurately. A precise definition of the *target* of selection—job performance—is an essential first step in the selection process outlined in this chapter.

Poor Assessment of Applicants

The third source of selection errors is the lack of precision in assessing applicants. A major portion of the selection process consists of the organization's attempts to determine applicants' potential and willingness to perform the job successfully. If care is taken to ensure that selection tools meet the standards of relevance, reliability, validity, and fairness, the accuracy of selection decisions can be increased.

KEY POINTS

■■■■ The selection process begins with a careful analysis of the job to be filled and the knowledge, skills, and personality characteristics required for successful job performance. Then applicants are assessed through interviews, employment tests, and reference checks to determine whether they can and will perform the job effectively.

■■■■ Human resource professionals and line managers can minimize selection errors by examining the relevance, reliability, validity, and fairness of all selection tools used in their organization.

■■■■ Compliance with legislation mandating equal employment opportunity and affirmative action for women and minorities requires evidence that an organization's selection tools are valid and fair.

■■■■ In spite of its many weaknesses, the selection interview continues to be widely used and trusted. Many of its weaknesses can be overcome through proper planning and structuring of the interview and assessing applicants in job-related terms.

■■■■ The inherent unpredictability of human behavior makes selection errors inevitable, but they can be reduced through precise definition of job performance and accurate assessment of applicants' potential and willingness to perform the job.

ISSUES FOR DISCUSSION

1. Outline the ten steps in the selection process used by most organizatons. Which do you think are the most crucial to successful selection decisions? Explain why.

2. Define the four standards for assessing the effectiveness of selection tools and discuss the feasibility of using each in an organization.

3. What requirements do equal employment opportunity and affirmative action legislation place on organizations? Discuss whether these requirements are fair to women and minorities and to other job applicants.

4. Summarize the major weaknesses of the selection interview. What can be done to improve its relevance, reliability, validity, and fairness?

5. Discuss the involvement of human resource professionals and line managers in the selection process. How can they work together to make better selection decisions?

NOTES

1. *Houston Post*, August 28, 1982, p. 4AA.

2. American Psychological Association, American Educational Research Association, and National Council on Measurement Used in Education (joint committee). "Technical Recommendations for Psychological Tests and Diagnostic Techniques," *Psychological Bulletin*, 1954, *51*, pp. 201–38.

3. Major reviews of the usefulness of various selection tools include: M. D. Dunnette, *Validity Study Results for Jobs Relevant to the Petroleum Refining Industry* (Washington, DC: American Petroleum Institute, 1972); J. E. Hunter and R. F. Hunter, *The Validity and Utility of Alternative Predictors of Job Performance* (Washington, DC: U.S. Office of Personnel Management, Office of Personnel Research and Development), 1983; R. R. Reilly and G. T. Chao, "Validity and Fairness of Some Alternative Employee Selection Procedures," *Personnel Psychology*, 1982, *35*, pp. 1–62; and R. Vineberg, and J. N. Joyner, *Prediction of Job Performance: Review of Military Studies* (Alexandria, VA: Human Resources Research Organization, 1982).

4. W. F. Cascio, "Accuracy of Verifiable Biographical Information Blank Responses," *Journal of Applied Psychology*, 1975, *60*, pp. 767–69.

5. M. D. Dunnette, and W. C. Borman, "Personnel Selection and Classification Systems," *Annual Review of Psychology*, 1979, *30*, pp. 477–525.

6. Hunter and Hunter, op. cit.

7. L. A. Pace, and L. F. Schoenfeldt, "Legal Concerns in the Use of Weighted Applications," *Personnel Psychology*, 1977, *30*, pp. 157–66.

8. *The Eighth Mental Measurements Yearbook*, ed. O. K. Buros (Highland Park, NJ: Gryphon, 1978).

9. E. E. Ghiselli, *The Validity of Occupational Aptitude Tests* (New York: Wiley, 1966).

10. R. L. Flaughter, "The Many Definitions of Test Bias," *American Psychologist*, 1978, *33*, pp. 671–79.

11. Dunnette and Borman, op. cit.

12. F. L. Schmidt, A. L. Greenthal, J. E. Hunter, J. G. Berner, and F. W. Seaton, "Job Samples Versus Paper and Pencil Trades and Technical Tests: Adverse Impact and Examinee Attitudes," *Personnel Psychology*, 1977, *30*, pp. 187–97.

13. Dunnette and Borman, op. cit.

14. D. W. Bray, R. J. Campbell, and D. L. Grant, *Formative Years in Business: A Long-Term Study of Managerial Lives* (New York: Wiley, 1974); G. Boehm, "Assessment Centers and Management Development." In K. M. Rowland and G. R. Ferris, eds., *Personnel Management* (Newton, MA: Allyn and Bacon, 1982), pp. 327–62.

15. B. Cohen, J. L. Moses, and W. C. Byham, *The Validity of Assessment Centers: A Literature Review* (Pittsburgh, PA: Development Dimensions Press, 1974).

16. N. Schmitt, and T. E. Hill, "Sex and Race Composition as a Determinant of Peer and Assessor Ratings," *Journal of Applied Psychology*, 1977, *62*, pp. 261–64.

17. R. Wagner, "The Employment Interview: A Critical Summary," *Personnel Psychology*, 1949, *2*, pp. 17–46; E. C. Mayfield, "The Selection Interview: A Reevaluation of Published Research," *Personnel Psychology*, 1964, *17*, pp. 239–60; L. Ulrich, and D. Trumbo, "The Selection Interview Since 1949," *Psychological Bulletin*, 1965, *63*, pp. 100–16; N. Schmitt, "Social and Situational Determinants of Interview Decisions: Implications for the Employment Interview," *Personnel Psychology*, 1976, *29*, pp. 79–101; and R. D. Arvey, and J. E. Campion, "The Employment Interview: A Summary and Review of Recent Research," *Personnel Psychology*, 1982, *35*, pp. 281–322.

18.   R. E. Carlson, P. W. Thayer, E. C. Mayfield, and D. A. Peterson, "Improvements in the Selection Interview," *Personnel Journal*, 1971, pp. 268–75, 317.

19.   R. D. Arvey, "Unfair Discrimination in the Employment Interview: Legal and Psychological Aspects," *Psychological Bulletin*, 1979, *86*, pp. 736–65.

20.   P. M. Muchinsky, "The Use of Reference Reports in Personnel Evaluation: A Review and Evaluation," *Journal of Occupational Psychology*, 1979, *52*, pp. 287–97; and Hunter and Hunter, op. cit.

21.   R. Levy, "Handwriting and Hiring," *Dun's Review*, 1979, *113*, pp. 72–79.

22.   Reilly and Chao, op. cit.

23.   Equal Employment Opportunity Coordinating Council. "Policy Statement on Affirmative Action Programs for State and Local Government Agencies," *Federal Register*, September 13, 1976, *41*, p. 38814.

24.   J. E. Hunter, F. L. Schmidt, and R. Hunter, "Differential Validity of Employment Tests by Race: A Comprehensive Review and Analysis," *Psychological Bulletin*, 1979, *86*, pp. 721–35.

25.   M. D. Dunnette, "Personnel Selection and Job Placement of the Disadvantaged: Problems, Issues, and Suggestions," in H. L. Fromkin and J. J. Sherwood (eds.), *Integrating the Organization* (New York: The Free Press, 1974).

26.   This material is adapted from J. G. Goodale, *The Fine Art of Interviewing* (Englewood Cliffs, NJ: Prentice-Hall, 1982).

27.   E. C. Webster, *Decision Making in the Employment Interview* (Montreal: Eagle, 1964).

28.   M. D. Hakel, T. D. Hollman, and M. D. Dunnette, "Accuracy of Interviewers, Certified Public Accountants, and Students in Identifying the Interests of Accountants," *Journal of Applied Psychology*, 1970, *54*, pp. 115–19.

29.   Webster, op. vit.

30.   Carlson, Thayer, Mayfield, and Peterson, op. cit.

ANNOTATED BIBLIOGRAPHY

American Psychological Association, Division of Industrial-Organizational Psychology. *Principles for the Validation and Use of Personnel Selection Procedures* (second edition), Berkeley, CA: APA, 1980.

> This booklet contains practical guidelines to assist human resource professionals and line managers in the choice, development, and evaluation of selection tools. Its authors are twenty-six leading experts in the field of selection and validation procedures.

BUROS, O. K., Ed. *The Eighth Mental Measurements Yearbook.* Highland Park, NJ: Gryphon, 1978.

> This encyclopedia of tests includes extensive information on the reliability and validity of employment tests. It is an invaluable source for employers who are currently using or considering using tests in their organization's selection process. If a test is not favorably reviewed in Buros, it should very likely be avoided.

GUION, R. M. *Personnel Testing.* New York: McGraw-Hill, 1965.

This is an excellent source of technical information on selection and validation procedures. It provides evaluation standards for both selection tools and measures of on-the-job performance. Also included are reports of the effectiveness of standard employment tests.

McCULLOCH, K. *Selecting Employees Safely Under the Law.* Englewood Cliffs, NJ: Prentice-Hall, 1981.

This is a practical EEOC guidebook that details how to avoid any type of discriminatory practices in hiring, firing, promotion, or terms and conditions of employment. It presents problems encountered by line managers or human resource professionals and describes how to apply the law.

Uniform Guidelines on Employee Selection Procedures. Federal Register, Part IV, August 25, 1978.

These guidelines were adopted by four federal agencies (Equal Employment Opportunity Commission, Civil Service Commission, Department of Labor, and Department of Justice) to clarify the impact of the Civil Rights Act of 1964 and subsequent legislation on the selection process. This publication is the most comprehensive and authoritative source on federal regulations concerning equal employment opportunity and affirmative action and the obligations of employers.

CHAPTER TEN

ORGANIZATIONAL ENTRY

The selection process has been completed and Rosa Sanchez is reporting for work. Entry is under way. Rosa and her new boss, Mike Collins, have differing views of Rosa's first day on the job.

Ms. Sanchez has just graduated from high school, and this is her first full-time job. She is the only new employee in Mike Collins' department. The other fifteen people have been there from four to seventeen years and have developed good working relationships and a high degree of group cohesion. The daily pressures of work are high, and on this day, like most others, department employees are absorbed in their own job activities.

As she enters the building, Ms. Sanchez is aware of many feelings: "What a big, sterile, impersonal building . . . I hope my boss likes me . . . I wonder what the people in the department will be like . . . Will they be hard to get to know . . . I wish the pay were a bit higher . . . I wonder what I'll be doing today?"

As Mike Collins sits in his office, he too is aware of several feelings: "Man, we've got to get the Jenkins report out today. But today we've got that new technician coming in. What will I do with her? Damn! That'll probably take half my morning! Maybe I can have Earnie take care of her. He's good at breaking in new people."

Thus, there is quite a difference between the way Ms. Sanchez views her first day with the company (anxiety, anticipation, excitement) and the way Mike, the manager, sees it (something to be sandwiched into an already crowded schedule). Small wonder, then, that in many cases, the orientation of new employees is done in a fairly casual way. It is simply not a high-priority activity for most managers. It is, however, an extremely high-priority activity for the new employee. The new job is probably the most important aspect of the new employee's life in those first few days on the job. The initial assignment and first year with the company will have a potent effect on the new employee's later performance, success, and decision to remain with the company or to go elsewhere. And since the cost of replacing an employee can be as much as the person's annual salary, it is definitely to the company's advantage to do a good job orienting and developing the new employee.

ORGANIZATIONAL SELECTION AND ENTRY

Organizational entry is such a common occurrence, few people examine it carefully. We tend to think of it as something that organizations and people do naturally, like making love and being a parent. However, we are finding that even natural abilities can benefit from better understanding and skill, and the same is true for matching up people and organizations.

According to the leading expert in this area, John P. Wanous, **organizational entry** is *the process of moving from the status of "outsider" to the status of "insider."*[1] **Effective entry** is a *matching process by which two important kinds of fit are achieved:* A fit between the staffing needs (skills requirements) of the organization and the talents of the individual, and a fit between the needs of the person and the opportunities for work challenge and satisfaction available in the organization. Traditional staffing, recruitment, and selection activities tend to be limited to the first type of fit, which deals with the organization's requirements. Indeed, much of the recruitment and selection material covered in Chapters Eight and Nine, respectively, is concerned with establishing a good match of talent and organizational requirements. And there is good reason for this emphasis, as this type of fit has a strong impact on a person's later work performance. Much less attention has been given to the second type of fit (human needs vs. organizational opportunities). It is this fit, however, which has the greatest impact on the person's satisfaction and likelihood of remaining in the organization.

These two matching processes imply that there are two types of selection at work before a person enters an organization: 1) the organization selects an individual from a pool of applicants to receive a job offer, and 2) the person selects an organization to join, after exploring various job alternatives. Thus, "matching up" is a mutual person-organization decision process. Previous chapters on staffing, recruitment, and selection have focused primarily on the organization's decision process. In this chapter, we will examine the individual's choice processes.

organizational entry

effective entry

Stages in the Individual Choice Process

Individuals tend to select those jobs and organizations which provide the greatest potential for providing a good fit for need satisfaction. Several research studies have assessed the individual's expectancy that an organization would offer various rewards, as well as the valence (attractiveness) the person attached to those rewards. When reward expectancies were multiplied by the valences of the rewards, an index of organizational attractiveness was obtained. This attractiveness index, in turn, was an excellent predictor of later job choices. In one study, 76 percent of the people picked the organization which scored highest in this index,[2] and other studies have obtained comparable results.

The process of selecting an organization takes place in three steps.[3]

1.   *Initial attractiveness of the organization.* At this point, the person has an image of what rewards the organization would provide but does not have much first-hand information.

2.   *Attempts to join a particular organization.* Based upon an initial assessment of alternatives, the person narrows the field and develops a job search strategy for getting a job offer from a particular organization. The person tends to "zero in" on the organizations which offer the greatest attractiveness.

3.   *Choice among job offers.* After the organization has made its selection decision and has offered the person a job, the person in turn must select from among various job offers. Most people choose the organization which offers the greatest likelihood of providing valued rewards.

Reality Shock

Once the person makes a selection from among competing job offers, there are two separate fluctuations in perceived attractiveness. Immediately after making a choice, the person tends to rate the chosen alternative as even more attractive than before making the decision. This appears to be a post-decision dissonance-reduction process,[4] in which people selectively seek positive information about the chosen alternative to help *justify* the decision.

Then just after the employee enters the organization, the perceived attractiveness of the organization tends to decrease. It appears that prior to the entry process, the person develops inflated, unrealistic expectations as part of this choice justification process, and after encountering the actual experience

reality shock

of being in the organization, reality shock sets in. **Reality shock** is *the process by which prior expectations are not fulfilled in the actual job situation.* For example, M.B.A. students tend to have "glowing" expectations of life in an organization before they enter (often based on recruiters' claims), and their expectations decline to more realistic levels as they become insiders.[5] A similar decline in perceived attractiveness was found for new AT&T managers over the first seven years of employment. Other research has shown that over very long time periods (say, ten years or more), satisfaction with the organi-

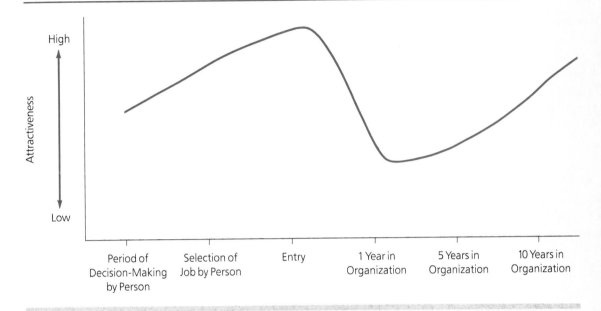

EXHIBIT 10.1

EMPLOYEE SATISFACTION WITH THE ORGANIZATION

zation again increases with time. A graph of these trends in employee satisfaction with the organization is shown in Exhibit 10.1.

Employee expectations do not appear to be unrealistic in all respects. Reality shock appears to occur the most for *intrinsic* rewards (e.g., challenge, status, self-fulfillment), which are most subjective and most difficult to describe objectively. There is less likely to be reality shock on *extrinsic* factors, such as pay or location. These extrinsic factors are more objective, more quantitative, and easier for the person to learn about in advance.

But, the irony here is that the intrinsic rewards are the ones that are most important to people. These are the factors that are most likely to lead to *turnover* if these are lacking. And these are precisely the factors about which prior expectations are likely to be unrealistic—and thus to cause reality shock. And these intrinsic features are the most difficult to describe accurately, because they are the most abstract.

THE SOCIALIZATION PROCESS

Once the person has entered the organization, the next step is socialization. **Socialization** is *the process by which the person learns how to operate effectively in a new culture through the acquisition of information, values, and behavioral skills associated with one's new organizational role.*[6]

socialization

Moving into a new organization, the new employee is immediately struck by the ambiguity and unfamiliarity of the new environment. No matter how experienced the person may be in a particular line of work, every organization has its own unique culture, its own norms, language, traditions, rules, and rewards. The new employee must *make sense* of this new environment. From the individual's perspective, then, socialization is the process of making sense of a new culture and of defining and mastering one's role in it.

The newcomer wants desperately to be accepted and to become an "insider," and is highly motivated and receptive to environmental cues at this time. This is a critical period, for what is learned at this point will probably become the core of the new employee's organizational identity.[7]

Like most parts of a person's life and career, the process of socialization into a new organization occurs gradually. Daniel Feldman has identified three distinct stages, each representing a different set of activities and learning tasks: anticipatory socialization, accommodation, and role management.[8]

Anticipatory Socialization

anticipatory socialization

Anticipatory socialization is the *learning and change which take place before the person joins the organization, in anticipation of entry.* At this point, the person is developing expectations about what life in the new organization will be like. The person may begin to feel like a member of the organization, may begin to modify his or her self-image, and may start to act like a member of that organization. For example, a study of Roman Catholic priests revealed that assistant pastors, in anticipation of being elevated to the role of pastor, begin to acquire the values and self-images of pastors as far as five years in advance.[9]

Two important processes can help a person move smoothly through the stage of anticipatory socialization: realistic expectations, and congruence between the organization's resources and the individual's needs and skills. Both realism and congruence measure the initial match between the person and the organization. The better the fit between person and organization, the greater will be the person's satisfaction and propensity to remain.

Accommodation

accommodation

Accommodation is *the process by which the person, after joining the organization, attempts to become a functioning member of it.* This is the person's initial encountering of the organization as a full-fledged member. The "honeymoon" of the recruiting and selection process is over, and the day-to-day realities of the job begin to sink in. New employees may be very aware of the contrast between their initial expectations and their actual experiences. This clash of expectations and experiences is the *reality shock* we discussed earlier.

As a result of reality shock, the person begins to come to terms with organizational life in several ways (see Exhibit 10.2). First, there is a change from *idealism* to *realism* in one's expectation about the world of work. For example, the new physician or priest may move from a "save the world" ori-

CHANGES DURING REALITY SHOCK

EXHIBIT 10.2

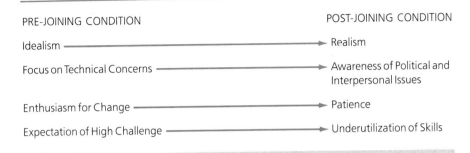

PRE-JOINING CONDITION		POST-JOINING CONDITION
Idealism	⟶	Realism
Focus on Technical Concerns	⟶	Awareness of Political and Interpersonal Issues
Enthusiasm for Change	⟶	Patience
Expectation of High Challenge	⟶	Underutilization of Skills

entation to a "do today's job well" perspective. This is not necessarily a shift from idealism to cynicism, but a realization that even lofty, idealistic goals are long-term objectives which can only be achieved through the mastery of everyday tasks and problems.

Second, there is increased awareness of the *interpersonal* or *political* aspects of organizational life. In contrast to school, where the focus is often on the technical aspects of the person's future work, real jobs exist in organizations, which are *social* systems. Any job, no matter how technical or autonomous, must be done in cooperation with other people—supervisors, peers, subordinates, clients, suppliers, etc. The new member learns quickly that having good ideas and being technically competent are only half of the job. The other half consists of being able to influence people with significant decision-making power.

A third change is the shift from *enthusiasm* to *patience* regarding change. A great source of frustration for the new member is that "there are better ways to do things around here." The new employee may wonder why certain "obvious" problems are tolerated and why improvements can't be made quickly. After a few unsuccessful head-on attempts at change, the new person learns that change is more likely to occur and to be lasting only if other key people are involved (which takes time). Or sometimes, if a key person is blocking change, one has to learn to work around that person. Or perhaps one can find out why that person opposes the change and can learn to reduce the person's resistance instead of putting on more pressure.

Finally, there is a move from expecting high *challenge* to *underutilization of skills*. This feeling that the job is far beneath the new person's ability and training is probably the most important component of reality shock. Studies of recent graduates have found low job challenge to be the major cause of turnover in the first year of employment.[10] This phenomenon is found among teachers, nurses, management trainees, production workers, priests, and many other groups. For example, in one study, a young parish priest reported that his assignment consisted of hearing confessions and saying masses on weekends and supervising bingo games during the week. He described the situation this way:

Priest:

I think one of the great frustrating areas today is . . . where there would be priests involved in work that isn't priestly. It's just as frustrating as having a guy come out of medical school and go through a year of internship and years of residency and have him handing out aspirins. I mean, this is—what a waste! Like using your tape recorder for a door stop.

Interviewer:

Not related to its natural function.

Priest:

Yeah, it'll work, but so would the Hope Diamond. What a waste![11]

Four processes enable a person to progress through this accommodation stage: Initiation to the task entails mastering a job and becoming a productive work partner. Initiation to the group is the social aspect of becoming integrated in the organization. The task here is developing good interpersonal relationships and becoming accepted and trusted by one's co-workers. Role definition involves making sense of the new work role and reaching agreement with others (either explicitly or implicitly) about one's task activities, priorities, time allocations, and other behavior. And finally, congruence of evaluation occurs when the new person's role has been defined and employee and supervisor are in agreement about the employee's strengths, weaknesses, and overall progress in the organization.[12]

Role Management

role management   The third stage of socialization is role management. **Role management** is the *ability to cope with the inevitable role conflicts that occur in any job.* In particular, two types of conflict must be resolved. First, resolution of outside life conflicts is necessary. This coping involves the need to develop decision rules to resolve conflicts between home and work (such as the need to work late, to bring work home, or to have an occasional day off for personal needs). These outside conflicts tend to become greater during a major career transition such as entering a new organization.[13] Resolution of conflicting work demands is the second form of coping necessary. This is the process by which the new person learns to deal with conflicts between groups of role-senders at work (e.g., the way a production employee satisfies the supervisor's demand for high output without appearing to be a "ratebuster" in the eyes of fellow workers).[14]

Feldman has identified two important outcomes that result from successful socialization: *mutual influence* (the amount of control over work that the person feels) and *general satisfaction* (the overall level of satisfaction or happiness with work that the person experiences).[15]

Socialization is complete when the person has moved through all three stages. People who have achieved complete socialization tend to have higher levels of mutual influence and general satisfaction than people whose socialization is not complete. In other words, as a result of socialization, a person

DEVELOPMENTAL TASKS ASSOCIATED WITH ORGANIZATIONAL SOCIALIZATION

EXHIBIT 10.3

Stage:	Anticipatory Socialization	Accommodation	Role Management	Outcome
Developmental Tasks:	Establishment of person-organization congruence. Development of realistic expectations.	Initiation to the task. Initiation to the group. Congruence of evaluation. Role definition.	Resolution of conflicting demands. Resolution of outside-life conflicts.	Mutual influence. General satisfaction.

SOURCE: Adaptation of figure from "A Contingency Theory of Socialization" by Daniel C. Feldman, *Administrative Science Quarterly*, Vol. 21, 1976, Reprinted by permission.

becomes a more fully functioning, satisfied member of the organization. These stages of socialization and their outcome measures are shown in Exhibit 10.3, and a short-form measure of the socialization is shown in Box 10.1.

REALISTIC JOB PREVIEWS

One way to reduce the inflated expectations of new employees is the **realistic job preview** (RJP), *a process by which job applicants are presented with a balanced view of the positive and the negative features of work in a particular organization.*[16] In contrast, the traditional preview attempts to "sell" the job by presenting only favorable information. Exhibit 10.4 shows a traditional (unrealistic) advertisement for the U.S. Navy, while Exhibit 10.5 shows a realistic preview from the Prudential Insurance Company.

realistic job preview

As another example, a traditional recruiting film for telephone operators might depict the work as exciting, important, and challenging. A realistic film would show both positive aspects (e.g., it can be satisfying helping customers, the work is lively and fast-paced) and negative features, such as lack of variety, routine in the job, close supervision, little freedom, limited opportunity to make friends, criticism for bad performance, but no praise for good performance, and the fact that the job is initially challenging but seems easy and unchallenging as it is learned.[17] Additional examples of types and timing of RJPs are shown in Exhibit 10.6.

What are the effects of a realistic job preview? One of management's initial concerns is, "My God! If you tell people the *bad news* about working here along with the good news, nobody will accept our job offers." Such concern is unfounded; most studies have found that realism does not adversely affect the rate of acceptance of job offers.[18] If anything, people seem to respect an organization's candor. Instead, the major effect of an RJP is to lower inflated expectations. This is the unanimous conclusion of all the studies that have examined the effects of RJPs upon expectations.

MEASURING SOCIALIZATION

BOX 10.1

The following questions help to assess the extent to which an employee has passed through the various stages of socialization. They are from a longer questionnaire by Feldman and are only a rough approximation of what the complete questionnaire measures.

Realism
What did you expect your job to be like before you started to work? What did you think were the biggest advantages of that particular job? Disadvantages? Were your expectations confirmed? Disconfirmed? In what ways?

Congruence
In what ways do you think there is a good fit between you and your job? Did you sometimes feel that the job was not the right job for you, or you might not be the right person for the particular job you do?

Initiation to the Task
If you could get more training, what are the areas you would like to get it in? Do you feel the need for more training? What do you feel others think of your work?

Initiation to the Group
What was it like trying to get accepted by other department members? To what extent do people confide in each other? How about you?

Congruence of Evaluation
What kind of procedures are there for performance evaluations? Do you feel you are doing a better job than you're getting credit for?

Role Definition
Do people feel job descriptions are accurate? How about yours? Are there jobs you routinely do that you feel should be part of someone else's work? Can you do anything about it?

Resolution of Conflicting Demands
When there is a conflict with another department, how do you handle it?

Resolution of Outside-Life Conflicts
Do you feel your job interferes with your outside life? How much? In what ways?

General Satisfaction
Overall, how satisfied are you with the job? Where do you think you'll be a year from now?

Mutual Influence
How much opportunity do you have to influence the way things are done around your department? If you had an idea about improving the ways jobs are done around here, how likely do you think it is you could change something?

Adaptation of excerpts from "A Contingency Theory of Socialization," by Daniel C. Feldman, *Administrative Science Quarterly*, Vol. *21*, 1976, Reprinted by permission.

AN EXAMPLE OF TRADITIONAL ADVERTISING

EXHIBIT 10.4

The young men and women of today respond to the same call to adventure that has brought sailors to the sea for generations.

Today's Navy offers an exciting challenge—one that can take you around the world—to new places, new people, and a new life.

Navy Life. It's Not Just a Job, It's an Adventure.

You'll soon be making one of the most important decisions of your life. Deciding what you'll be doing after graduation. It's not easy. In fact, very few students really know what career they want to pursue after high school. It's the smart high school student who will change his or her mind many times before making a final decision. That's because you're constantly growing—physically as well as mentally—and each day you're becoming aware of new career choices. What seems like an attractive choice one day is replaced by a more appealing choice the next. So what may seem like indecisiveness is really very smart thinking on your part. . . .

If you've ever looked at the classified ads in your daily newspaper, you've probably noticed two important qualifications necessary for the good paying jobs—experience and schooling. In the Navy, we'll give you both.

We have more than 60 important skills for you to choose from. And most of them offer schooling and training. So at the very least, you'll learn a skill you can put to good use for the rest of your life—whether you decide to stay in the Navy or return to civilian life.

If You're in High School.

The most important piece of advice we can give you is simply: stay in. A high school diploma opens many doors. If you want to get ahead in a civilian or military job, you'll need your high school diploma. In the past, some high school students have decided to drop out of school to join the Navy. We now have a program that encourages you to complete your education but allows you to sign up while still in school.

It's called the *Delayed Entry Program*. This program allows you to sign up for the assignment, job, and training you want, while still in school. You'll then be given up to 12 months before reporting for duty. The Delayed Entry Program guarantees the job you want. Lets you earn your high school diploma. And gives you another summer vacation before starting your enlistment.

College Bound?

Great! We wish you all the success you'll need in the years ahead. But while you're in college, we'd ask you to look into the *Naval Reserve Officer Training Corps*. This program allows you to qualify for a commission while attending certain colleges.

SOURCE: *National Observer*, April 23, 1977.

The effects of RJPs on satisfaction and performance were mixed: in half the studies the effects on attitudes were positive, and in half they had no impact. Performance is not affected at all, which is not surprising, since the target of the RJP is expectations and retention, not performance.

The most important effect of an RJP is on the *job survival of newcomers*. In nine out of twelve studies which examined job survival, job survival was

EXHIBIT 10.5   **A REALISTIC JOB PREVIEW**

> The following material is from a booklet given to prospective new insurance agents at Prudential Insurance to give them a more balanced view of what work would be like.

The Path To Opportunity

Success is sometimes due to luck. One hears stories about the star discovered in a drug store, the farmer who hits oil under the cornshed, and the one-time lottery player who wins the jackpot. However, successful people don't depend on luck.

Professional men and women, such as doctors, accountants, and lawyers, set career goals, evaluate what they must accomplish to achieve these goals, and then work to meet their objectives. Their success depends on study, a period of internship with experienced people in their profession, locating and contacting men and women who can use their services, and, of course, dedication and commitment to the people they serve.

The Prudential Agent must also follow a similar path. Therefore, to help people meet the goals and standards they must achieve as a professional in the life insurance industry, Prudential has developed the Agent Career Path.

The Career Path is multi-faceted guide for Agents, almost a job description, founded on a fundamental principle—the professional insurance Agent must serve the client, not the product. Success flows from this principle, known as client centered marketing.

The Prudential Agent assists clients in three broad financial areas—Wealth Creation, Wealth Accumulation, and Wealth Protection. The Agent must work with clients to identify their wants and needs in these areas, to help them establish priorities, and then propose solutions which do not exceed their financial capabilities. It is a valuable service which benefits a broad spectrum of people.

It is necessary, however, to establish goals. Oftentimes goal setting is difficult—both for people who just enter a business and for people who have been in a profession for quite a while. Based on the client centered marketing philosophy, the Agent Career Path offers Prudential Agents a well-defined guide for establishing goals.

First, a model projects the number of people an Agent must see in order to reach a target number of sales. Next, based on this level of activity, it illustrates the potential earnings an Agent could reach over a period of ten years. Third, the Career Path includes supervisory tools to help the Agent accomplish these objectives. In short, the Agent Career Path is a complete system of activity objectives, sales tools, and training tools which the Prudential Agent can use to establish a place in the top ranks of the insurance profession.

Prudential offers Agents the Path to Opportunity. It's up to Agents to determine how far they will go on that Path.

SOURCE: From "The Path to Opportunity" in *Agent Career Path Program* booklet, produced by The Prudential's Ordinary Agencies marketing department. Copyright © 1985 by The Prudential Insurance Company of America. Reprinted by permission.

longer for recruits who received the realistic preview than for others. It appears that the realistic preview is effective because it lowers prior expectation to a realistic level, so that reality shock does not occur. As a result, newcomers have more positive attitudes toward the organization.

RJPs tend to work best when they are given early in the entry process, to stop expectations from becoming inflated. And, finally, it is important not to provide excessive negative information.

METHODS OF PROVIDING REALISTIC JOB PREVIEWS
EXHIBIT 10.6

Group Receiving Preview	Preview Method	Timing of Preview
Cadets at the U.S. Military Academy at West Point	Booklet containing positive and negative information about the Academy, based on information from interviews with cadets and officers	After cadets were accepted, but before entry and oath
New Marine Corps recruits	Eighty-minute videotape of recruit training with "voice over" comments of interviews with recruits	After recruit was in the Marines, but before training
Checkers and baggers in a midwest retail chain	Thirty-minute oral presentation as part of two-hour orientation	After accepting job offer, but one month prior to first day at work
Telephone operators at Southern New England Telephone Company	Fifteen-minute realistic film, based on survey of interviews with, and observations of, operators and supervisors	After job offer, but prior to formal acceptance of it
Operators at Texas Instruments	An "anxiety reduction" session on the first day, given orally, as part of standard two-hour orientation	After acceptance of job offer, during first day on the job

SOURCE: John P. Wanous, *Organizational Entry* (Reading, MA: Addison-Wesley, 1980), pp. 64–70.

BUILDING COMMITMENT

Once the person has entered the organization and has been socialized, the process of building commitment to the organization unfolds over time. Several personal characteristics tend to be associated with increasing commitment to the organization. The first is age (older workers may be more committed). A high need for achievement is also related to commitment, as is a good fit between the person's needs and the climate of the organization. Traditional "work ethic" values and personal values that are congruent with the goals of the organization are also strongly linked to commitment.

A number of job and organizational factors are also important. Free choice in entering and remaining and high job challenge (especially in the first year) are critical factors. Satisfying career experiences (such as job-satisfaction, supportive work colleagues, and good future career prospects) are also important. Long service in the organization and high involvement in the work group (if the group's attitudes toward the organization are positive) are also associated with strong commitment.[19]

In sum, the same factors which lead to employee satisfaction also lead, over time, to growing employee commitment to the organization. The major difference between the process of becoming satisfied and the process of becoming committed is time: commitment involves the employee's concluding that the future prospects for continuing to experience these satisfactions are promising.

moral commitment

A person can develop three specific types of commitment over time. **Moral commitment** *is the strong identification of the person with the goals and mission of the organization.* The person becomes linked to the organization because it reflects his or her values, needs, and self-image. The person might be willing to make great sacrifices (financial and others) to remain. For example, a bright young lawyer might take a job with a public interest research group (i.e., a Ralph Nader-type organization) because of a belief in its mission, even though a Wall Street law firm is offering many times more money.

calculative commitment

A second form of commitment is **calculative,** in which *the rewards, inducements, and personal investments associated with the organization make it difficult, when the employee views them rationally, to leave.* For example, an executive who was promoted to a high-paying vice-president's job at a relatively young age might find it very hard to leave if no other firm would match that salary.

alienative commitment

A third, less positive form of commitment is **alienative,** *the perception of very few alternatives in the external job market, which makes one feel forced to remain.* For example, a "plateaued" manager who is dissatisfied with the organization, but has three years to go until retirement, may feel trapped.

Commitment probably does not have a great effect on individual performance, unless the person is in a job where individual effort is of critical importance or one in which the person's attention to quality is important. However, many jobs are designed so as not to require "extra effort" for successful performance.

At the individual level, two types of employee withdrawal are consequences of low levels of commitment: high absenteeism and high turnover. If people are not committed to the organization, they will not make the extra effort to come in to work if they feel slightly ill or if the weather is poor. For example, when budget cuts forced massive cutbacks of personnel in the Boston Police and Fire Departments, morale and commitment plunged. In the Fire Department, the number of sick days shot up; small on-the-job injuries that fire fighters used to "shake off" resulted in sick days.

In another example, during a blizzard in Chicago several years ago, transportation was so poor that Sears employees were told they need not report for work (they would be paid), but the stores would remain open. Sears conducts periodic employee attitude surveys, and personnel researcher Frank Smith has store-wide data on average levels of employee commitment for the stores in the snow area. He collected data on the percentage of employees who braved the elements to come in to work and found that *the higher the average level of employee commitment in each store, the larger was the percentage of employees who defied the snow to report for work.*[20]

The same principle applies to turnover. Most employees encounter a range of frustrations in their jobs, and most perceive a range of outside job opportunities. However, the more committed a person is to the organization, the less likely these frustrations and opportunities are to lead to an exit from the organization.

ORIENTATION

As new employees go through various steps to adjust to the organization, the organization takes steps to orient new employees.

orientation

Orientation is the *process of introducing the new employee to the organization*. The first distinction to make is between formal and informal orientation activities. A formal orientation is planned in advance, where groups of new employees go through the same program (either sequentially or as a group), and where specialized training personnel may conduct the orientation. An informal orientation is one in which the new employee is introduced to the new work environment and it is left to the supervisor and co-workers to provide whatever information is required. An orientation program could be as short as ten or fifteen minutes for people performing routine assembly operations or as long as a year for management trainees. Generally, an orientation will cover such areas as company history and current activities (products and services), the role of this plant or office in overall corporate operations, job responsibilities and expectations of the new employee, compensation and benefits, and personnel policies.

Basically, the orientation reflects the company's understanding of its "psychological contract" with the new employee. The **psychological contract** is *a usually implicit set of expectations which company and employee have of each other*. The company expects certain activities and contributions from employees in return for the pay, benefits, and other inducements it provides. The employees, in turn, expect certain rewards, working conditions, satisfactions, and other contributions from the company in return for their services. As long as both parties feel that they are receiving at least as much value as they are giving, the relationship will continue and will be satisfactory to both. If one or both parties feel that they are getting less out of the relationship than they are putting in, termination of employment might occur.

psychological contract

APPROACHES TO NEW EMPLOYEE TRAINING

In contrast to orientation, in which the main goal is to introduce the new employee to the company, **training** is *the process of helping the employee develop specific skills and knowledge necessary for effective job performance*. Companies tend to use six general strategies to train new employees.[21]

training

Sink or swim entails giving the person an unclear job assignment and little guidance or support from the boss. The new entrant is expected to define the task independently and to work out solutions. The key to success here is the way the organization deals with success and failure. This approach is most likely to be successful under the following conditions:

- If the person is *not punished* for failure,
- If the person is given clear *feedback* on the degree of success or failure attained,

▪ If the person is later helped to see *why* he or she succeeded or failed,

▪ If the person is helped to see *what should be done* about failure (if it occurred).

The *upending experience* is designed to "unfreeze" the person; that is, to show the entrant that there is a need to learn from the supervisor or trainer. The method used is to give the person an assignment at which failure is assured. After failure, any initial cockiness (not to mention self-esteem) is gone, and the person is more receptive to learning.

In *on-the-job training*, the person is given regular assignments, perhaps even challenging ones. The demands of the job itself provide the learning. On-the-job training is most effective when someone more experienced is available to provide coaching and support when necessary (so it doesn't feel like sink-or-swim). The success of the method also depends on the job's being challenging.

In *working while training*, the person is assigned to a full-time training program and is rotated through a series of short-term job assignments. Between job assignments, the employee may spend full time on special training experiences. Such a working-while-training program generally lasts three to twelve months, after which the person is assigned to a permanent job.

Full-time training is a fairly common approach in which special assignments are created for training purposes. Not surprisingly, they are often seen as not "real" jobs and are considered of little consequence to the organization. Sometimes trainees are assigned to particular locations to observe activities; such trainees often report that the main "learning" consists of picking up office gossip. The idea behind rotational training programs is to give the person a broad view of the organization, but they are experienced often as "make-work" or "Mickey Mouse" jobs.

Finally, with the *integrative approach*, the person's training needs are first diagnosed through initial job performance or an assessment center. The person is then put in a simulated job situation where his or her job skills are observed. (More information about assessment centers is found in the next section.) Then a training program is developed to provide skills in the areas most needed.

EARLY ASSESSMENT OF CAREER POTENTIAL

assessment

As part of the integrative approach to training, a growing number of organizations are using an *assessment of career potential* as an early career experience for employees. **Assessment** is *a process of measuring various dimensions of ability and motivation which are related to career effectiveness in a particular organization*. The reasons for doing assessment early in the person's career are 1) to identify people with high potential for advancement quickly so they can be given special development experiences, and 2) to give the individual early developmental feedback on strengths, weaknesses, and career motivation so needed changes can be made in time to pursue attractive career opportunities. The first reason relates to the organization's need for early identification of high-potential managers, and the second relates to the person's need for feedback for development.

Increasingly, organizations are designing early assessment processes which will accomplish both of these purposes, although usually one is primary. For example, if an organization, such as AT&T, has used assessment mainly for early identification of talent, the trend is to add on a developmental component, which includes detailed feedback and coaching for the employee, along with a plan for follow-up developmental activities later on the job.

There are several possible methods for conducting an assessment. Some of the more common ones are discussed below.

Assessment centers. This is perhaps the method most frequently associated with assessment. An **assessment center** is *a one-half- to three-day group experience consisting of simulation exercises, paper-and-pencil tests, interviews, and decision-making tasks which measure skills and motivations which predict managerial success.* Assessment staff members are usually a combination of human resource specialists and specially trained line managers. Staff members observe the behavior of the participants and poll the data from the multiple measures and multiple raters to form judgments of each person's skills and motivation. While time consuming and expensive, assessment centers do provide valid predictions of later success in management.[22]

assessment center

Self-assessment. As the term indicates, this is a method in which the person conducts his or her own assessment. This may involve analysis of past job and other experiences (to identify career-related skills and interests), test of values, interests, and needs, and obtaining feedback from others. This can be done either individually, with workbooks and tape cassettes, or in a group workshop setting. Self-assessment is used more for developmental purposes than for identification of potential.

Management ratings. In this procedure, managers (either individually or in groups) review the past performance of an individual against a set of managerial skills and arrive at a rating profile on these dimensions. Like the assessment center method, management ratings are based on the fact that one of the best predictors of future behavior is past behavior. Whereas the assessment center is using simulated behavior in the evaluation, management ratings employ actual behavior on the job.

Clinical assessments. In this process professional psychologists employ various tests and interview methods to develop a profile of strengths and weaknesses. These can be in-house human resource specialists, but more often they are external consulting psychologists. This method tends to be the one most oriented toward identification and least oriented toward personal development. Because of the high cost, it tends to be used for people in more senior positions.

EXHIBIT 10.7   **EARLY IDENTIFICATION ASSESSMENT**

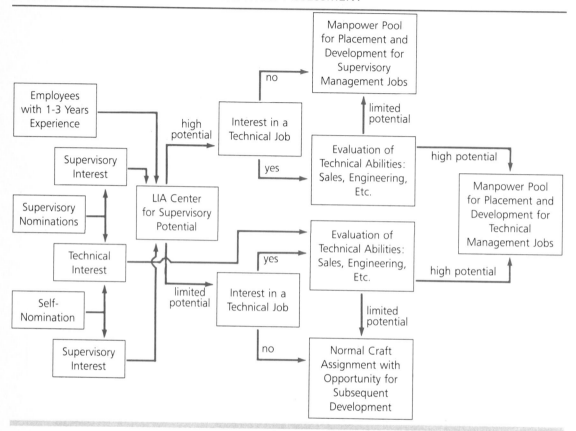

SOURCE: From "Assessment and Management Development," by Boehm and Hoyle from *Applying the Assessment Center Method* by Moses and Byham, eds., 1977, p. 220. Reprinted by permission of Pergamon Press, Inc.

An example of how one organization employed an assessment center for early identification of management potential was AT&T's Guidelines for Manager Development (GMD). This is a first-year development program for newly appointed management trainees and incorporates an assessment center to identify people with potential to reach middle management. As a key link in this development process, the boss receives training in conducting an initial orientation, setting stretching objectives, providing challenging work assignments, conducting performance reviews, and providing career feedback and coaching. At the end of the first year, the new employee attends the assessment center, and the results of the assessment are used to help determine second-year job assignments and longer-term career goals. Exhibit 10.7 illustrates how AT&T's early identification assessment feeds into the process of grooming people for either management, technical management, or craft positions.

FORD EMPLOYEE SELF-ASSESSMENT WORKSHOP OUTLINE

EXHIBIT 10.8

Day 1 Morning

1. Introduction and description of workshop, focus, and model
2. Clarify expectations for workshop
3. Identify participant expectations
4. Context and perspective
       Concept of career at Ford
       How concept of career is changing
       How this change affects individual careers
5. Layout of rest of workshop

Afternoon

1. Introduction and restatement of model, focusing on individual aspect
2. Values clarification and interpretation
3. Skills inventory interpretation
4. Facilitation of combining these two instruments
5. Using the information constructively; discussion of principles of feedback
6. Goal-setting introduction and practice
7. First day wrap-up and assignments (Skill Development Guide)

Day 2 Morning

1. Filling out a short-term development plan, discussion with others
2. Role of other individuals (if I choose to discuss this with others)
3. What to expect and how to approach a discussion of goals
4. Working development goals into performance objectives
5. Coping with realistic feedback
6. Introduction to longer-term perspective (lateral moves)
7. Exposure to Career Information Resource materials

Afternoon

1. Setting tentative longer-term goals in a long-term development plan
2. Using others in the workshop as an initial reality check on these plans
3. Coping in a corporate system; some practical suggestions (informational and interviewing skills)
4. Choosing the next steps beyond the workshop
5. Learning guidelines for evaluating personal progress toward goals

SOURCE: Dr. Phyllis C. Horner, "Career Development Programs in Traditional Manufacturing Firms," presentation at Careers Division Workshop, Academy of Management Meeting, Boston, August 1984.

An example of a self-assessment process, to be used for personal development rather than identification, is the Career Assessment and Development Program developed by Dr. Phyllis C. Horner at Ford Motor Company.[23] The core of the program is an employee workshop (outlined in Exhibit 10.8) designed to help employees conduct a realistic self-assessment, to confront issues related to pursuing a career at Ford, and to establish realistic and attainable career goals. The program also contains a supervisory workshop (to train supervisors in coaching and other skills to support employee development), career information resources, an employee guide with suggested methods of development, and the formulation of management policies to support employee development (e.g., support for lateral transfers).

DEVELOPMENTAL JOB EXPERIENCES

As a final area in which the entry of the new person can be facilitated, great potential lies in the *job itself*. In particular, three characteristics of the job and work setting have strong impact on the person's successful performance and integration into the organization.

Initial job challenge. One of the most reliable predictors of early career success and satisfaction is the challenge of the initial assignment. Wherever possible, new employees should be put on jobs that will stretch and test their abilities. Training supervisors in the skills of job enrichment is another way to accomplish this goal. Eliminating short-term job rotation and putting new people on real jobs would be a minimum requirement in this area.

Developmental bosses. The boss is an important factor affecting the amount of challenge in the first assignment. It is important that new employees be assigned to the better managers, those who are known to be the best developers of talent. It is also extremely valuable to *train* managers in the skills of employee development and to *reward* them for successful development of subordinates.

Performance appraisal. One of the major problems often reported by new employees is a lack of feedback on performance. This feedback is especially important in the first year, when the employee is "learning the ropes" and developing standards of performance. Many managers avoid giving appraisals because they lack the necessary skills and thus feel uncomfortable. Thus, appraisal training for supervisors is another means of aiding the entry process.

Other facets of the work environment, such as the peer group and formal training activities, also have a strong impact on the entry process, but the above factors are probably the most critical. And, since they are all part of a well-managed organization, they do not require anything extra to be used to facilitate entry. In most organizations, however, practices such as appraising performance, giving challenging initial assignments, and consciously assigning new employees to developmental bosses are not utilized to the extent they could be and, thus, represent a great source of untapped potential for effective organizational entry.

KEY POINTS

- Organizational entry (moving from the status of "outsider" to the status of "insider") is a critical phase of a person's career in an organization, since early success is one of the best predictors of later success, satisfaction, and likelihood of remaining in the organization. Unfortunately, many managers neglect this period, with the result that entry is often not a consciously managed process.

In the process of choosing an organization, a person often develops unrealistically high expectations after making the decision. Then, immediately after joining the organization, the person tends to experience reality shock (the process by which prior expectations are not fulfilled in the actual job situation).

Realistic job previews (providing job candidates with a balanced view of the positive and negative features of organizational life) are an effective way to make expectations more realistic, increase initial job satisfaction, and increase retention of new recruits.

Several factors in the work environment (job challenge, developmental supervisors, and effective feedback) tend to increase the person's commitment to the organization and to facilitate the process of entry.

ISSUES FOR DISCUSSION

1. What was your most recent experience with organizational entry? How did your experiences compare with the process described in this chapter?

2. What do you think would be the most promising methods for reducing reality shock?

3. What do you think about the idea of organizations trying to increase the loyalty and commitment of their members?

4. What are the pros and cons of an early identification of potential program?

5. Have you ever had any of the developmental job experiences described in this chapter? Discuss how this aspect of your job affected your attitudes and performance.

6. What can you do, when you are a manager, to give a new employee, such as Rosa Sanchez, the entry assistance she needs?

7. How might the entry process for a 35-year-old going into his or her third job differ from that of a 21-year-old starting the first job? In what ways might the entry process be similar? What can a person learn from entry experiences to make the process more positive?

NOTES

1. John P. Wanous, *Organizational Entry: Recruitment, Selection, and Socialization of Newcomers* (Reading, MA: Addison-Wesley, 1980).

2. Victor Vroom, and Edward Deci, "The Stability of Post-Decision Dissonance: A Follow-Up Study of Job Attitudes of Business School Graduates," *Organizational Behavior and Human Performance*, 1971, 6, pp. 36–49.

3. Wanous, op. cit.

4. Peer O. Soelberg, "Unprogrammed Decision Making," *Industrial Management Review*, 1967, 8, pp. 19–29.

5. Wanous, op. cit., and Douglas T. Hall, *Careers in Organizations* (Glenview, IL: Scott, Foresman, 1976), pp. 37–38.

6. David E. Berlew, and Douglas T. Hall, "The Socialization of Managers: Effects of Expectations on Performance," *Administrative Science Quarterly*, 1966, *11*, pp. 207–23.

7. Ibid.

8. Daniel C. Feldman, "A Contingency Theory of Socialization," *Administrative Science Quarterly*, 1976, *21*, pp. 433–52.

9. Douglas T. Hall, and Benjamin Schneider, *Organizational Climates and Careers: The Work Lives of Priests* (New York: Academic Press, 1973).

10. Hall, op. cit.

11. Hall and Schneider, op. cit., p. 188.

12. Feldman, op. cit., p. 435.

13. Janina C. Latack, "Career Transitions Within Organizations: An Exploratory Study of Work, Nonwork, and Coping Strategies," *Organizational Behavior and Human Performance*, 1984, *34*, pp. 296–322.

14. Ibid., p. 435.

15. Ibid., p. 436.

16. Wanous, op. cit.

17. Wanous, op. cit.

18. This summary of research on RJPs is based on Wanous, op. cit., pp. 83–84.

19. Sam Gould and Douglas T. Hall, "Organizational Commitment: A Review of the Theory and Empirical Research," San Antonio, TX: University of Texas at San Antonio, Working Paper, 1981.

20. Frank J. Smith, "Work Attitudes as Predictors of Attendance on a Specific Day," *Journal of Applied Psychology*, 1977, *62*, pp. 16–20.

21. Edgar H. Schein, "How to Break in the College Graduate," *Harvard Business Review*, 1964, *42*, pp. 68–76.

22. Douglas W. Bray, Richard J. Campbell, and Donald L. Grant, *Formative Years in Business* (New York: Wiley, 1974).

23. John Turner, "Coping with Career Development in an Industry in Transition," contribution to symposium entitled "Meeting the Challenge of the Plateaued Worker in Maturing and Retrenching Organizations," Robert H. Ketchum (Chair), Academy of Management Meeting, Dallas, 1983; and Phyllis C. Horner, "Career Development at Ford Motor Company," Workshop presentation, Careers Division, Academy of Management, Boston, 1984.

ANNOTATED BIBLIOGRAPHY

BAILYN, L. "The Slow Burn Way to the Top: Some Thoughts on the Early Years of Organizational Careers." In C. B. Derr (ed.), *Work, Family, and Career: New Frontiers in Theory and Research*. New York: Praeger, 1980, pp. 94–106.

This is a discussion of the issues involved in early career advancement patterns. Based upon research by M.I.T. alumni, Bailyn identified the *slow-burn* career path, in which a person advances more gradually. The "fast-track" and "slow-burn" paths may both lead to the same destination, but the latter extends career growth over a longer time period, so that total growth may be greater. The article discusses the implications of this alternative career path for corporate career management practices.

BRAY, D. W., CAMPBELL, R. J., and GRANT, D. L. *Formative Years in Business: A Long-Term AT&T Study of Managerial Lives.* New York: Wiley, 1974.

This is a classic study of entry and early career experiences of young managers at AT&T. It describes the early career assessment centers developed at AT&T and reports detailed research on predictors of early managerial success. It also reports on the life and work themes which develop over time as people enter and move through the organization. This is one of the most carefully documented corporate studies of the entry process in the management literature.

FELDMAN, D. C. "A Socialization Process That Helps New Recruits Succeed." *Personnel,* 1980, 57, pp. 11–23.

This article is an extension of Feldman's socialization model, which is presented in this chapter. It focuses on the stages of adjustment to the new organization and describes practical ways that managers and human resource specialists can help ease the entry process.

MOSES, J. L., and BYHAM, W. C. (eds.). *Applying the Assessment Center Method.* Elmsford, NY: Pergamon Press, 1977.

This edited volume contains chapters by the leading researchers and practitioners of assessment methods. Of particular interest are several chapters which focus on new employees and programs organizations use for early career assessment of skills and motivation.

WANOUS, J. P. *Organizational Entry: Recruitment, Selection, and Socialization of Newcomers.* Reading, MA: Addison-Wesley, 1980.

Wanous is the leading researcher on the topic of organizational entry, and this book is the best single source on the topic. It describes in detail the studies on organizational selection and entry, as well as research on realistic job previews and other methods to facilitate entry. It also contains many examples of specific organizations and the programs they have developed to integrate new members.

I N T E R V I E W

MANAGER OF SELECTION AND PLACEMENT, IN A MEDIUM-SIZED PETROCHEMICAL COMPANY

▬▬ *What are your major responsibilities?*

I am responsible for candidate source identification, selection, and employment of personnel within our company. As a member of the Personnel Department, I have two exempt recruiters, three non-exempt recruiters, a coordinator, and a manager reporting to me.

▬▬ *What steps make up the selection and placement process?*

The process begins when a position opens as a result of the resignation or termination of an employee, an internal promotion or transfer, or the creation of a new position due to company growth. We then identify sources of job applicants, recruit and screen the applicants, and recommend acceptable candidates to the hiring manager, who makes the final employment decision.

▬▬ *How do you become aware of a job opening?*

Company policy requires that a requisition for personnel be approved before anyone can be hired. We assist management in the preparation of the requisitions.

▬▬ *Then what happens?*

We help the hiring manager define his or her needs and then find the best possible candidate for a specific job. To accomplish this, a recruiter meets with the manager and asks specific questions to learn about the job and department and updates the job description and job specifications. Since we assign recruiters to given departments for about one year, they have the opportunity to become familiar with the culture of the department and the work style of its members.

▬▬ *What happens next?*

We begin to identify sources of potential applicants. Since we emphasize promotion in our company, we begin with current employees. Through our computerized and manual Human Resource Information Systems, we search for employees with the desired work experience, education, salary history, skills, and performance record. We post all openings for non-exempt positions and review internal applicants before we consider any external applicants. For exempt positions we usually conduct internal and external searches simultaneously.

How do you find external applicants?

We begin with our most cost effective source, applicants on file. We review our file of application forms and also post the job opening as part of our employee referral program (employees who refer successful applicants receive a bonus). Finally, we ask recently hired employees and hiring managers for referrals. If necessary, we then advertise the job opening and also seek assistance from employment agencies and search firms.

What happens if the same applicant responds to your ad and is also referred by an agency?

When we first contact an employment agency, we explain that we are advertising concurrently and pay a fee only if the agency is our sole source of an applicant.

How do you proceed once you have identified a number of potential applicants?

We screen the application forms or resumes of internal and external applicants to eliminate those who do not meet the minimal qualifications for the job. We may also conduct preliminary interviews by phone. The recruiter working on the opening then meets with the hiring manager, discusses the qualified applicants, and schedules a number of one-day visits during which each applicant will be interviewed by the recruiter and three to five members of the hiring department. Members of the hiring department discuss each applicant and make the final employment decision.

How does college recruiting fit in?

That's a whole separate program that we use to fill our entry-level positions. We visit college campuses in the fall and spring. Planning for college recruiting begins with annual discussions between my group and department managers to estimate projected needs for new employees. We base the projections on turnover rates for each hiring department, which we analyze, and the department's projected growth. We then schedule the campus visits and send department employees to conduct preliminary interviews with students. We try to interview students one semester or even one year before graduation to interest them in our company before they see other potential employers. At the appropriate time, we schedule visits to the hiring department.

■■■ *Where do EEO and Affirmative Action fit in?*
At the beginning of the process. The requisition for personnel is reviewed not only by my office but also by our company EEO group. The EEO representative reviews the makeup of employees in the hiring department (percentage of blacks, females, etc), and we discuss these statistics and company affirmative action goals with the hiring manager. This information is considered at each step of the selection and placement process.

■■■ *You have emphasized throughout our discussion that you provide a service to hiring managers. How do they view your group and what steps have you taken to build good relationships with them?*
We have seen a steady improvement in our relationship with hiring managers. We confer closely with them at each step of the selection and placement process. Especially important is the initial discussion between a recruiter and a hiring manager to clearly define the job and the climate of the department. The better we understand their needs, the better we can meet them. We also gain credibility by screening out all but the best applicants for hiring managers to see. Finally, we must help them fill job openings quickly.

■■■ *How quickly do you fill the typical opening?*
We fill non-exempt positions in three to four weeks. Our goal for exempt positions is six weeks, and recently our typical placement has taken thirty days.

■■■ *What about the quality of the applicants you supply?*
We use two criteria to judge our success: the job performance and the promotability of new employees. We stress to hiring managers that new employees should reach performance goals during the first year and begin to show potential for promotion during the second year of employment. If the applicants we find and recommend meet these criteria, the company is successful and the credibility of my group increases. We touch base with hiring managers six weeks and six months after a new employee is hired to see how he or she is doing.

■■■ *You stressed promotion from within when discussing sources of applicants and again in measuring the quality of your selection and*

296

placement process. How many job openings are filled by internal applicants?

In 1983 we filled 60 percent of the non-exempt and 73 percent of the exempt openings with internal applicants. Comparable figures for 1984 (40 percent and 59 percent) were somewhat lower because our business grew considerably in 1984 and we added many new positions.

■■■■ *Once you have hired new employees, how do you make them feel at home and increase their likelihood of staying with the company?*

We conduct a formal half-day orientation session with all new employees. Beyond that, we encourage hiring managers to help new employees to learn the job and become contributors during the first year and to position them for additional responsibility or promotion during the second year.

EMPLOYEE DEVELOPMENT AND PERFORMANCE

Once the staffing process is finished and the person has entered the organization, the difficult process of managing performance begins. It is at this point that the dual responsibilities of the line manager and the human resource professional become most clear and most important. First it is the job of the human resource organization to design and deliver programs and systems to help managers to manage employee performance. It is also the responsibility of the human resource organization to train managers so they can use these performance management programs effectively. The best-designed performance appraisal program in the world will not work if managers do not know how to use it.

Second, it is the responsibility of line managers to implement these performance programs. Again, the world's best program will have no value if managers do not use it.

Part Four begins by discussing how a basic strategy for development is determined (Chapter Eleven), thereby providing the basis for specific development and performance management activities. The employee's immediate need, following entry, is for training in those skills necessary to perform the new job, and this is the topic of Chapter Twelve.

Longer-term development takes place in the context of a life-long career. Chapter Thirteen discusses the process associated with career development, while Chapter Fourteen discusses specific programs which organizations use to facilitate employee career development.

Perhaps the most difficult single job for a manager is to monitor and provide feedback on employee performance. One of the reasons this task is so difficult is that the manager often lacks the necessary skills and training. Chapter Fifteen discusses the issues involved in measuring performance and spells out a step-by-step method for conducting an effective appraisal.

Traditionally, managers have thought of the process of leaving the organization as being the employee's concern, but not the organization's. Now, however, progressive organizations find it is fruitful to manage the process of employee exit. Not only is this a more humane way to treat employees, but it also gives the organization more control over the size of its work force, and aids the morale of the employees who remain. Chapter Sixteen, a novel chapter for a human resource text, describes contemporary methods of managing employee exit.

CHAPTER ELEVEN

STRATEGIC HUMAN RESOURCE DEVELOPMENT

Let us return to the experiences of Rosa Sanchez, whom we met earlier in Chapter Ten, Organizational Entry.[1] Ms. Sanchez went through a three-day training program, during which she acquired the knowledge and skills necessary to perform her job. Within two months she became the top performer in her department. She has been in this job for two years and is beginning to think about a move to a better one. Although she has been able to broaden the scope of her responsibilities through initiative, hard work, and solid results, she feels she has reached the limits of the challenge this job can provide.

She knows that marketing is a high-priority area for the company, as it is developing new products rapidly and is entering new and highly competitive markets. Technical sales staff are difficult to find and recruit, and turnover is running around 50 percent. Right now, 20 percent of the firm's sales slots are open.

Ms. Sanchez has asked several people (her boss, the personnel representative, and a company vice-president) how she might prepare herself for a transfer to a sales position. In all three cases she received the same response: ''We do not transfer people from other departments into sales. We only hire experienced sales people, and we always hire from the outside.''

Ms. Sanchez's company has a problem. It is not managing its human resource process in a strategic way and as a result it is falling into the old trap of having to be *reactive* in the human resource area. It is *reacting* to the tight market for sales people (spending huge sums on recruiting, search firms, travel expenses to interview applicants and to relocate new employees, etc.). As we saw in Chapter Two, strategic human resource management is the process of setting organization objectives and deciding on comprehensive programs of action which will achieve those objectives.

In this organization, a more strategic approach to sales staffing problems would be to set a specific objective for desired sales performance or market share and then to develop a human resource program to get an effective sales force to deliver those sales. And one promising method to create this sales staff would be to develop and transfer present employees from other departments in less tight labor markets to the sales department. The main human resource objective here is to create a high performing, stable sales force; the objective is not necessarily to maintain the practice of hiring experienced sales people from the external labor market.

Unfortunately, however, human resource development is rarely used in this strategic way. Development is seldom seen as a strategic alternative to external recruitment for critical positions, both at lower and more senior levels of the organization. Frequently, organizations have had to go outside to hire a vice-president because, in the opinion of the president, no one inside the organization was qualified, even though there were several high potential (but undeveloped) candidates at the next lower level.

In most organizations, "development" is usually interpreted as training (giving people the knowledge and skills necessary for effective performance in the current job). Development rarely is done with a longer time span and critical business objectives in mind. Therefore, much of this chapter will deal with *what should be* rather than *what is* in the case of human resource development.*

WHAT IS STRATEGIC DEVELOPMENT?

Strategic human resource development is *the identification and growth of needed employee skills and experience for the intermediate and long-range future to support explicit corporate and business strategies.* Let us examine each of the component parts of this definition in turn.

strategic human resource development

The critical element of strategic development most often missing is the linkage of development needs and activities to an explicit organizational mis-

*From "Human Resource Development and Organizational Effectiveness" by Douglas T. Hall, Chapter 11 in *Strategic Human Resource Management* ed. by Charles J. Fombrun, Noel M. Tichy and Mary Anne Devanna. Copyright © 1984 by John Wiley & Sons, Inc. Reprinted by permission.

sion and strategy. Many organizations invest considerable resources to train and develop, but never really examine how training and development can effectively promote organizational objectives, or how development activities should be altered in light of business plans. Even rarer is a recognition that business plans should be altered in relation to expected future employee capabilities. On the contrary, most organizations view training and development as either a necessary evil, something nice to do, or an employee benefit.

This confusion over the meaning and purpose of employee development can work against the objectives of the organization. Consider tuition reimbursement programs as a case in point. Many organizations routinely reimburse employees for tuition for courses that are work-related (e.g., MBA courses), as a matter of corporate policy. Such reimbursement is costly and often is not associated with corporate developmental plans or a career development plan for the person. Employees, however, see university course work as very much a part of their development. When work for a degree is completed, the organization is expected to treat the person differently, perhaps with a new assignment. But in the view of the organization, the person is no different. The problem comes from two different meanings attached to tuition reimbursement: the employee sees it as career development, the organization sees it as an employee benefit.

Another hindrance to strategic development in many organizations is that the time span development is concerned with is often too short. The focus is frequently on skill requirements in new or present assignments rather than on requirements for positions five or ten years into the future. In short, training and development activities are actually much training and little development.

Finally, inadequate energy is devoted to *identification* of future skill needs. Training and development seem to entail more action ("Let's develop a new three-day seminar.") than thought and diagnosis. To be strategic about development means to analyze future business opportunities and plans and to think deductively about the future employee skills which will be necessary to implement these plans. Examples of how some firms in the securities industry link development to new business strategies are shown in Box 11.1.

development

career

In reality, **development** is a *process of enhancing an individual's present and future effectiveness*. Here we are viewing effectiveness in the context of the employee's career. By **career** we mean *the individually perceived sequence of attitudes and behaviors associated with work-related experiences over the span of the person's life*. Thus, career development entails changing both *perceptions* and *behaviors* (or skills).

Outcomes of Development

More specifically, the target of development is the four *outcomes* which measure career effectiveness: performance, attitudes, identity, and adaptability. These outcomes can be broken down in two ways, by time frame and by learning outcome, as shown in Exhibit 11.1.

LINKING DEVELOPMENT TO NEW BUSINESS STRATEGIES

BOX 11.1

Daniel C. Quigley, an assistant vice-president in E. F. Hutton & Co.'s Washington office, recently got an unusual request: to work out a personal budget for a man who earned more than $100,000 per year but found himself chronically short of cash. After reviewing the customer's assets, Quigley recommended selling a sailboat that was expensive to maintain. The client took the advice. "Five years ago, I probably wouldn't have been asked to do that," Quigley says.

As a result of extreme competition in the financial services industry, the broker's role has changed. It now involves more than simply selling stocks and bonds. There is a whole new set of financial products to be marketed: life insurance, IRA's, money market funds, etc.

The tremendous need to develop new brokers to keep up with the rapidly growing market for financial products is also driving brokerages to create or expand entry-level training programs. For example, Dean Witter Reynolds Inc., which is rapidly expanding its sales force, will raise expenditures on training 17 percent this year. Shearson/American Express Inc. had no training program until last fall. Instead, it relied on raiding or acquiring competitors to recruit brokers. . . .

However, the number of experienced brokers available is declining. Concomitantly, the salaries needed to hire them away are climbing. Thus, internal development will be necessary for Shearson to increase its sales force by 17 percent in 1985. Retraining of experienced brokers is becoming the name of the game.

Wall Street experts say E. F. Hutton has set the industry standard in advanced training. Beginning training is available to anyone who wants to learn the basics in, say, real estate tax shelters. Intermediate and advanced courses, however, are available only to those who have shown they can sell the products they have taken an interest in.

At each Hutton office there are "product coordinators"—account executives who are experts in a specific product line. . . .

These coordinators provide coaching and advice to other brokers. They receive extra pay in the form of "overrides" (based on the total sales of the products in their specialty area). Hutton finds this extra pay for coordinators aids recruitment.

Industry executives concede that some brokers who have prospered recommending and selling stocks and bonds resist pressure to learn much about anything else. Some who have left Hutton, for example, criticize their former employer for placing too much emphasis on nontraditional products. Nonetheless, companies are betting that pressure from increasingly sophisticated consumers will force brokers to learn new tricks. "If a broker doesn't offer or doesn't want to deal with what a client wants," says Hutton's Quigley, "that money is going to go elsewhere."

Business Week, September 19, 1983, pp. 97, 101.

EXHIBIT 11.1 OUTCOMES OF DEVELOPMENT

Target of Learning

	Task	Self
Short-Term	Performance	Attitudes
Long-Term	Adaptability	Self-Identity

Time Span

Performance and *attitudes* both concern the present: attainment of present work goals and present feelings about the career, such as involvement, commitment, conflict, etc. *Adaptability* is the extent to which the person is preparing to meet future career demands. *Identity* is a measure of the congruence or integration of the person's self-perceptions over time (i.e., a measure of how the person sees the parts of the career fitting together or "making sense").

Any activity which enhances one or more of these four career outcomes constitutes development. Training and coaching programs, motivational activities, individual efforts to increase job performance are development. Socialization, job experiences, counseling, peer interactions, and other activities which improve or clarify career attitudes are development. Job assignments, education, and other learning which broadens the person's skills and abilities enhance adaptability and thus also are development. And finally, self-examination, self-assessment, feedback and counseling, and other activities which clarify and focus self-identity are also development. Too often, however, organizations define development as working only on short-term, task-related skills. Too seldom are attitudes, adaptability, and self-identity the focus of plans for development.

Let us return briefly to the distinction between training and development. Training is a learning experience aimed primarily at employee knowledge and behavior to enhance the person's job skills to improve present job performance. However, development is aimed at the enhancement of skills for future as well as present job performance, as well as the other three outcomes of attitude, adaptability, and identity change.

Strategies for Different Development Outcomes

In addition to considering the four career outcomes as *goals* of developmental activities, we shall examine various *strategies* for attaining these goals. Wexley and Latham[2] propose three basic developmental strategies. The first strategy is *cognitive*, which involves altering thoughts and ideas. The second, *behavioral*, entails attempts to change behavior directly. In the third, *environmental*, interventions are aimed at altering the immediate work environment of the individual.

If we combine the career outcome goals and these three basic developmental strategies, we obtain the matrix of possible combinations of developmental strategies aimed at particular career outcomes, as shown in Exhibit 11.2. (Since the performance category is so important, it has been subdivided into *technical, interpersonal,* and *conceptual* skills.) The activities listed are not exhaustive, and some cells may represent difficult combinations (i.e., cognitive approaches to developing interpersonal skills). Furthermore, several activities are found in more than one cell, as a given activity can produce multiple outcomes.

It appears that excessive reliance in the past has been placed upon the cognitive strategies, especially formal, in-class seminars. While these might be useful to aid performance (especially technical and conceptual), such activities do little for adaptability, attitudes, and identity. The more potent interventions for attitudes, adaptability, and identity are strategies aimed at behavior and the work environment. Furthermore, environment-based activities may be the most potent producers of changes in important skills, attitudes, self-conceptions, and ability to change. And cognitive interventions may be the least potent. For example, there is nothing quite so "stretching" for a person as a new job assignment in a new functional area. The job will simply *demand* that the person acquire new skills. Unfortunately, environmental changes are the most difficult to create and cognitive activities the easiest, which is why so much "development" takes place in classroom settings.

The cognitive activities (e.g., books, films, training programs) are all basically forms of *communication of information* (either one-way or two-way), where the strategy is to alter the person's knowledge of ways of thinking. The distinction between behavioral and environmental strategies is a bit more subtle. Behavioral approaches attempt to change the employee's behavior within a particular environmental setting (e.g., behavior modeling or role-playing); the behavior changes but the environment is unchanged. In environmental approaches, either the person is moved to a different environment (e.g., job rotation) or the target of change is the environment (e.g., team building).

The basic process by which new skills and attitudes are developed can be shown by the *psychological success cycle*.[3] This cycle is shown in Exhibit 11.3. In this growth process, the person works toward a challenging, stretching goal, achieves it through independent effort, realizes, with feedback, that he or she has performed at a high level, receives intrinsic (satisfaction) and extrinsic (pay, recognition, promotion, etc.) rewards, and becomes more involved in and motivated for future goal-related activity. Thus, "success breeds

EXHIBIT 11.2 DEVELOPMENTAL STRATEGIES TO ATTAIN DEVELOPMENT GOALS

	Goals					
Strategies	Performance Technical	Performance Interpersonal	Performance Conceptual	Attitudes	Adaptability	Identity
Cognitive	Basic knowledge in specialty (entry)	Self-improvement reading Films Inspirational lectures and speeches	University seminar in basic discipline University functional courses Sabbatical Industry boards	Orientation training Retraining programs Company career information Sabbatical	University training programs Career planning seminar Company career information Sabbatical	Self-assessment Seminar for personal interests University training programs
Behavioral	On-the-job training Apprenticeship	Role-playing Apprenticeship Behavioral modeling Assessment centers	Role-playing	Socialization Phased retirement Flex-time Flex-place	Outplacement Career counseling Early retirement Flex-time Flex-place	Assessment centers Outplacement Career counseling Phased retirement
Environmental	Job challenge Job feedback Job autonomy Technical ladder Peer interaction	Team building Organization development Matrix management Project teams Task forces	Matrix management Project teams Task force Employee exchange Employee exchange programs	Matrix management Project teams Job challenge Job feedback Job autonomy Technical ladder Internal consulting Outside consulting Employee exchange Recognition for career specialists Downward moves	Job rotation Temporary assignments Job variety Downward move Employee exchange programs	Job challenge Job autonomy Technical ladder Internal consulting Downward move Outside consulting Recognition for career specialists

success." We will provide the greatest detail on factors at the strategic level which affect development, since strategic development is the topic of this chapter. However, we will comment later on influences or development at the managerial and operational levels, as well.

THE PSYCHOLOGICAL SUCCESS CYCLE

EXHIBIT 11.3

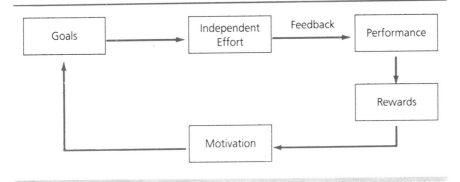

SOURCE: Adapted from Douglas T. Hall, *Careers in Organizations* (Glenview, Ill.: Scott, Foresman and Company, 1976), p. 41.

IMPLEMENTING STRATEGIC HUMAN RESOURCE DEVELOPMENT

Human Resource Policies

At the strategic level, the most important influence on development is human resource policies. **Human resource policies** are *the broad guidelines and corporate strategies which direct the management of human resource activities.* Unfortunately, many organizations do not have explicit formal policies related to people, even though clear human resource policies, formulated and practiced by top management, are the most important element in developing human resources.[4]

human resource policies

Promotion from Within ——— The most critical policy for successful development is a clear organizational commitment to the development of internal candidates for job openings. Such a policy promotes development, if only because there must be a pool of developed employees available to step into openings in higher-level positions. Also, the knowledge that the organization will replace from within motivates employees to develop themselves for promotional opportunities. On the other hand, nothing demotivates an employee as strongly as being qualified but then passed over in favor of an external candidate.

The key point is that the promotion-from-within policy must be strong, clear, and *practical*. In many cases, such a policy is espoused but not practiced widely. The result is that managers often feel forced to "go outside" because no one inside is sufficiently qualified. However, there may have been qualified insiders that the assessment system failed to identify. Or someone inside may have had the potential but not the proper training or experience.

If the policy were truly operative, the necessary assessment and developmental activities would have been in place.

Companies with promotion-from-within policies (such as Sears, AT&T, and Eli Lilly) tend to hire younger people with less education than companies which recruit externally for middle- and upper-level positions. In part, this is true by definition, since promoting from within means *not* hiring more senior people. However, this policy also may lead to *not* hiring people with graduate (e.g., MBA) degrees, as these firms prefer to "grow their own" talent. Thus, the policy of promotion from within creates more systematic employee development. It also leads to more loyal employees, as a result of long organizational socialization and the development of a rich network of social relationships in the organization.

Employment Security ▬ Many organizations with promotion-from-within policies also have a policy of employment security for employees. This is a commitment to provide continuing employment for all employees who have been in the organization more than a specified number of years (e.g., two years at Procter and Gamble, ten in a heavy equipment manufacturing company). This policy does not mean employees will not be fired for poor performance or for disciplinary infractions, but that they will be protected from layoffs due to economic downturns. In some organizations, such as Borg-Warner, employment security is not a guarantee of employment, but a top management commitment to run the business in such a way that layoffs will be used only as a last resort in dealing with business downturns. Other companies with various forms of employment security policies are Johnson Wax, Hewlett-Packard, and Cummins Engine.

Perhaps one of the best-known employment security policies is that practiced by IBM. For over forty years, no IBM employee has lost pay due to a lack of work. This policy started in the depression of the 1930s, when top management decided that skilled employees would be crucial to future corporate growth and effectiveness. Even though the company was suffering through one of the worst economies in business history, it invested in a "stockpile" of human talent. Later, when the new Social Security Administration needed enormous quantities of business equipment, IBM was the only company with the human resources to meet this demand.

At Hewlett-Packard, management rejected large government contracts in its early years, fearing that the unpredictable source of business would lead to large fluctuations in business, requiring frequent layoffs and rehiring. During the 1970 recession, the company cut the work hours and pay of all employees (from the chairman of the board on down) by 10.7 percent, rather than lay people off. (People did not work every other Friday.)

Other methods of "buffering" the work force in full-employment firms are using temporary workers, instituting hiring freezes (letting work force reduction occur through attrition), subcontracting work during peak periods (avoiding the hiring of new permanent employees), encouraging unpaid leaves of absence, transferring employees to maintenance, custodial, community, or

COSTS AND BENEFITS OF A FULL-EMPLOYMENT POLICY

EXHIBIT 11.4

Costs	Benefits
Extra payroll and payroll-related expenses:	Flexibility to reassign workers
• Training costs	Productivity advantages because of high employee morale
• Extra overtime because of reluctance to hire	Greater acceptance of changes in methods and technology
• Possible temporary red circle rates	Lower unemployment insurance costs
• Extra costs of any special early retirement plans	Savings of training costs due to layoffs
Extra employment costs associated with extreme selectivity in hiring	Favorable image in the community and recruiting advantages
Productivity losses associated with people assigned to different jobs	
Moving expenses	
Extra financial charges because of larger-than-necessary inventories	
Possible slower delivery schedule	
Possible slower rate of change in methods or technology due to need to avoid displacing permanent employees	

SOURCE: Reprinted by permission of the *Harvard Business Review.* An exhibit from "How Top Nonunion Companies Manage Employees" by Fred K. Foulkes (September/October 1981). Copyright © 1981 by the President and Fellows of Harvard College; all rights reserved.

other nonessential activities during slack periods, encouraging work sharing, providing early retirement incentives, and offering voluntary severance/outplacement programs. (See Chapter Sixteen, Organizational Exit, for more details on the latter activities.) The costs and benefits of these full-employment policies are shown in Exhibit 11.4.

Such a policy forces the organization to plan carefully, and to link its business plans with its human resource plans. For example, the hiring of a new employee takes on much more significance when one considers that the organization may be, in effect, granting lifetime "tenure" to the person, perhaps forty years' worth of income, a commitment of over a million dollars, assuming an annual salary of $25,000. Management will plan carefully how to develop and deploy that resource, and will be less likely to let that person become obsolete or "deadwood" when it is not possible to let the person go.

As an illustration of the strategic use of an employment security policy, consider the case of Borg-Warner, a large manufacturing company closely tied to the auto industry. The chairman (and C.E.O.) of the company, James Beré, was an interested follower of Japanese management practices and was convinced that the commitment of certain Japanese firms to lifetime employment forced them to develop and manage people effectively. He appointed a task force, comprised of three plant managers, the comptroller, the employee relations manager, and an outside consultant, to study the experiences of American companies with full employment policies and to make a recommendation.

The task force concluded that the most important benefit of employment security was the incentive (indeed, *demand*) it created for managers to treat employees as assets, as investments, to be carefully managed and developed. Because hiring was often more controlled and limited in such firms, managers saw employees as very *scarce* resources which had to be recycled (trained, developed) when necessary, as they could not be discarded. Thus the full employment policy was deemed to be an effective way to motivate line managers to promote employee development.

Most organizations underestimate the full costs of large-scale firing and hiring, including administrative costs, unemployment payments, lowered morale, recruiting expenses, and training. Weyerhauser once computed the expense of cutting personnel costs through layoffs and attrition and found the latter to be less expensive. Thus, the costs of an employment security policy may not be as great as managers might imagine.

Cross-Functional (or Rotational) Movement

While many companies have traditionally promoted people up through one department, function, or operating unit, there is a new trend toward greater cross-functional movement. Experiences in different parts of an organization force an employee to develop a wider range of skills, a wider network of relationships, and more of a company-wide perspective. An executive from Heublein described its change to greater use of cross-division transfers:

> We were a holding company until the 1950s, and you could count on your fingers the number of people who moved from division to division. You grow up in a division, and you get about four miles tall but not very broad . . . Everybody had sneered at lateral transfers. Now, they can point to us. I feel this gives me a chance to see the whole business.[5]

Cross-functional movement (sometimes called rotational movement) is not as straightforward as the above comments might indicate, however. First of all, such movement produces generalists rather than specialists. It may be necessary, however, to produce specialists in technical areas, so the amount of within- and between-function movement must be planned carefully in relation to future staffing requirements.

Another possibility is a mixed model with specialist-generalists. In this system, a person might spend a period of time, perhaps five years, developing as a specialist within a particular function. After that time, the person would be rotated through different functions and become more of a generalist. In this way the person's needs to broaden and prepare for general management could be met, while the organization's need for specialists could also be satisfied. (A hybrid form of this system is the second specialty model, where

COMMON TYPES OF CROSS-FUNCTIONAL MOVEMENTS

EXHIBIT 11.5

Type of Rotation	Objectives
New Employee Exposing new employees to a number of jobs before placing them in a permanent position	Provide understanding of operations in different areas Test skills Determine appropriate placement
Personal Growth Moving employees temporarily to jobs they have not undertaken in the past	Learn variety of skills Learn new skills Opportunity for advancement
Executive Development Moving managers or managerial candidates to various units of the organization	Opportunity for lateral moves Assess managerial potential Understand total organization Determine next move
Revolving Door Shifting employees back and forth between jobs at predetermined intervals	Reward for level attained Broaden skill base Alleviate boredom of doing same job Provide depth of talent through cross training
Continuing Reassignment Reassigning employees to different units or geographic locations at set intervals	Geographic relocation Facilitate new ideas through diversity Prevent employees from getting stale in one place Use employee talents in diverse settings

SOURCE: Beverly L. Kaye, *Up Is Not the Only Way: A Guide for Career Development Practitioners*, © 1982, p. 197. Reprinted by permission of Prentice-Hall, Inc., Englewood Cliffs, N.J.

several years are spent in one specialty and then the employee rotates to, and remains in, a second specialty.)

Some of the more commonly used means to accomplish job movement are shown in Exhibit 11.5, along with the objectives sought.

Policies about movement have potent effects on what kinds of skills are developed. In many organizations, movement policies survive out of tradition, rather than out of a strategic plan to develop certain types of businesses and people.

Minimum and Maximum Incumbency Times ▬ Whether it is a cross-functional move or a within-function change, nothing creates learning opportunities as effectively as a new job assignment. Many organizations, however, have no policies governing how long a person should remain in a particular position. Mobility tends to be greatest in the early career years and then to level off in mid-career, so that the person reaches a career plateau. In

one chemical company, it was not unusual to find people who had been in the same job for ten, fifteen, or twenty years. As one person seriously remarked, "After twenty years in this same job, things get to be a little repetitious."

In their research on R & D scientists and engineers, Pelz and Andrews found it was useful to remain in one problem area for five to ten years.[6] In other occupations this time might vary with the amount of on-the-job learning and experience required for effective performance. For example, a right-of-way negotiator for a gas pipeline company, whose inclusion of an apparently insignificant contingency in a contract might save the company millions of dollars, indicated in a recent seminar that it may take well over five years to reach peak effectiveness in this position.

A company policy that no person should be in a given position more than a certain number of years (which might vary by position) would be a way to force management to assess the skills and placement needs of each employee. If an employee were difficult to move anywhere else because of narrow skills, this would force retraining. And movement to a new assignment would produce on-the-job development.

In practice, a min-max incumbency policy could specify that no person with less than the minimum time in position could be moved without the consent of the division manager or the president. The policy could also state that whenever an employee reached the maximum number of years in a position, the personnel record system would trigger an assignment review, conducted by the human resource department, the boss, and the employee. The person might remain in the present position, but not without good reason.

Successor Training Before Promotion ▬ Another corporate policy to promote development by managers of their subordinates is a requirement that no manager be considered a candidate for promotion until a subordinate is ready for promotion. The employee need not be developed specifically for the boss's position, but organizations need people who can assume increased responsibility somewhere in the organization. Managers are often reluctant to develop subordinates because there seems to be little incentive to do so. Linking the manager's career development with the subordinate's provides a powerful inducement in this direction.

Understaffing ▬ Some organizations by policy are somewhat understaffed, perhaps by 10–20 percent. People Express, for example, has built a highly successful airline based on "lean" staffing. Many organizations came out of the 1982 recession with a new stress on "lean and mean" low staffing levels (e.g., Ingersoll Rand, Monsanto, Polaroid, Ford Motor Company). In addition to producing a more efficient operation, understaffing also stretches or challenges employees and develops a wide range of skills, since employees are called on to perform many tasks. Also, if staffing and hiring are tight, managers will devote more attention to the "care and feeding" of their people.

Of course, a risk of understaffing is that a manager might tend to "hoard" talent and prevent people from moving cross-functionally. Development in place might be achieved at the expense of development through movement. In this case, understaffing should be combined with a strong commitment to internal employee mobility and a human resource system which will assure managers that for each good employee they give up, they will receive a good person in exchange from elsewhere in the organization.

Other Development Policies ▬▬ Other corporate policies that affect employee development can also be developed. For example, one important policy issue is how low in the organization a professional or management trainee should start. In some organizations, the policy is for all trainees to start at the operating level so they can truly understand the business (e.g., Procter and Gamble and Vicks products management trainees all start off with a sales territory). In other cases, the person starts off with managerial or professional responsibilities to provide greater initial job challenge (e.g., in AT&T).

Other policies affecting development pertain to the amount and timing of corporate vs. field experience, the amount of geographic relocation, the assistance provided for spouse employment and relocation and the expected rate of advancement ("fast track" vs. "slow burn"). All of these, as well as the policies discussed earlier, have profound effects on employee development. Often, however, such policies are operative but are not stated explicitly. The more aware and the more clear the organization is about development policies, the more effectively it can control employee growth. A summary of these policies which promote employee development is shown in Exhibit 11.6.

Structural Effects on Development

The organization's structure has a profound effect on employee development. Again, like policy, structure is rarely considered a strategic variable to be used to affect development. The structure of the organization not only is a way to arrange the performance of needed work roles, but also contains the array of future *opportunities* available to the employee.[7] There are two ways in which structure can be employed for strategic development. First, strategic plans for the ways employees will be moved through various positions and between various units (divisions, companies, departments) can be developed. For example, at Sears it was possible to construct job progressions, based upon job evaluation points, which could produce various types of career paths.[8] (See Box 11.2). Few organizations take advantage of their corporate structure for strategic development. They usually fill positions based solely on organizational requirements, rather than considering individual development needs.

The second way structure can be employed for strategic development is more extreme: the structure can be modified to provide different developmental outcomes. Perhaps the most common way structure is modified is through the creation of additional grade (and pay) levels for a particular job area to provide additional incentives and opportunities for upward mobility. For example, the position of associate partner was added to the structure of a

EXHIBIT 11.6   HUMAN RESOURCE POLICIES FOR EMPLOYEE
DEVELOPMENT

Policy	Benefits
Promotion from within	Forces top management to plan for employee development, since outside hiring for supervisory and managerial positions is not permitted.
Employment security	Forces management to take a long-term view of lifelong employees' development. Hiring is more difficult, making development more attractive as a way to obtain needed skills.
Cross-functional movement	Forces employees to learn new skills in order to perform effectively. Also provides better understanding of the value and problems of the new area, producing higher interdepartment understanding and cooperation.
Minimum and maximum incumbency times	Prevents employee from getting "stuck" in one job, unless desired, for an excessive time period.
Successor training before promotion	Ties boss's career opportunities to his or her development of subordinates.

public accounting firm to provide advancement opportunities during what was seen by junior accountants as a long wait before they were considered for promotion to partner.

Another way levels often are added is through the development of a "dual ladder" concept, which provides two advancement paths, one into the management ranks and one into higher grades of professional responsibility. Often the technical side plateaus faster than the managerial side, which has led many organizations to add higher grade levels to the technical side. This concept was originally developed in research and development organizations, where the technical side included engineering and scientific job categories. Now the concept is being applied to a wide range of professional specialist positions, such as finance specialists in banks, information specialists in computer companies, and a range of staff specialists in other business organizations.

The Use of Strategic Development to Affect Structure

Not only does structure affect development, but development can affect structure. Specific patterns of development can create effects similar to those of the formal structure. For example, if an organization has a decentralized structure with few formal communication mechanisms, a strong policy of promotion from within and cross-functional mobility can, through employee so-

USING STRUCTURE TO PROMOTE DEVELOPMENT

BOX 11.2

In the mid-1970s Sears, Roebuck realized it needed to manage the career growth of its management trainees more precisely. On the one hand, there was a need to groom high-potential people, minorities, and women more quickly for store manager positions. Current "wisdom" at the time said it took at least fifteen years to "grow" a store manager, and the company's affirmative action goals simply did not permit that much time to develop underrepresented groups. On the other hand, being a flat organization (i.e., decentralized, with few levels), Sears did not have many promotions available for many experienced employees, yet these people needed to be developed in some way.

About that time Sears was implementing the Hay system to evaluate jobs to determine compensation levels. The Hay system scores each job on three main skill dimensions (know-how, problem-solving, and accountability), as well as on several subdimensions. There is also a total point score for each job, to determine the compensation for that position.

Director of Human Resources Harry Wellbank felt that in addition to its use for job evaluation and compensation, the Hay system could also be used to indicate development needs and to plan career paths. Whenever a person was promoted or transferred to a new job whose Hay points on one job skill dimension were a certain percentage (usually 15 percent) more than the former job, this indicated the person needed training in that skill area.

Developmental career path planning for a starting store manager's job began with the Hay point profile. A computer model was used to construct rational sequences of job moves that would gradually advance a person to a store manager's position from a trainee's job, with no change being a jump of more than 15 percent in Hay points. A number of paths were identified, some of which would get a person to the store manager's job in six or seven years (fast tracks). Most of those paths had never actually been used but were quite feasible. And, in fact, by using logical, nontraditional job progressions, Sears was able to grow store managers in well under ten years.

In a similar way, it was possible to identify lateral and even downward moves that would develop the person in one or more skill areas. Even though the total Hay points might be lower for a lower-rank job, the skill profile could be different enough so that the points in one particular skill area could be significantly higher than those for certain higher-rank jobs. For example, a senior technical specialist's job might score high on know-how and problem-solving but low on accountability. A lower-ranked supervisory job might score lower on the former two dimensions but much higher on accountability. If demoted into the supervisor's role, the professional specialist would be "stretched" to develop accountability skills.

cialization, "program in" an organization-wide perspective, integration of corporate goals, and smooth communication. These promotion-from-within and mobility policies have been found to be effective integrative devices in organizations as diverse as the U.S. Forest Service and the Roman Catholic Church.[9]

Galbraith and Edstrom explained how organizational transfers are part of an organization's verbal information system:

> Briefly, we believe that transfer changes managerial behavior; and that, collectively, changes in behavior change organization structure. More specifically, we hypothesize that transfer influences verbal contact with colleagues in other units and therefore amounts to designing the organization's verbal information system. The result is believed to be greater local control in the presence of interdependence.[10]

Thus, if structure is an attempt to provide rational control over organizational activities, the strategic development (i.e., socialization) of individuals is another way to achieve the same objective.

Strategic Development Through Other Human Resource Activities

One of the most powerful ways to facilitate employee development is to develop human resource systems for the achievement of other objectives, with the full knowledge that improved development will be an important spin-off benefit. Human resource functions do tend to be interdependent, and these interdependencies can be employed strategically.

The two human resource functions which probably have the strongest impacts on development are *rewards* (especially performance appraisal) and *succession planning*. Each of these topics is considered in detail elsewhere in this text, but they cannot be separated from the development process.

The Use of Rewards ▬ When employees receive clear feedback on their performance, when rewards are tied to performance, and when performance expectations are stated in clear behavioral or goal-related terms, the employee's first question after asking, "How did I perform?" will be, "How can I perform better?" Learning to perform better requires acquiring and sharpening knowledge and skills—in short, development. Therefore, if a new performance appraisal/reward system is put in place, the natural next step is a system for long-term performance improvement and skill development. In many organizations, the performance appraisal form has a reverse side which covers development (strengths, weaknesses, and a plan for development).

Strategically, then, one of the best ways for an organization to stimulate development is to start with the performance appraisal system, either creating one, if there is none, or improving it, if one currently exists. This will impress managers and employees with the need for performance improvement and will lead to a natural need for planned development. Another implication of this performance-development link is that if there is not currently an effective performance/reward system, the organization should *not* initiate a development system until the reward system is in place. It makes no sense to work on future performance if present performance is not well managed.

The Use of Succession Planning ▬ Succession planning is another human resource activity which requires planned corporate-wide development activities. A typical human resource forecasting form, from the Ontario Ministry of Transportation and Communications, is shown in Exhibit 11.7. In forecasting and succession planning, future demands, based on strategic business plans, are compared to sources of people. To assess "sources," there is a review by top management of incumbents and identification of back-ups, as well as expected losses from retirements, transfers out of the function, and resignations. These factors result in an equation of supply and demand which indicates any existing personnel imbalance. If a shortage exists, strategies for development and recruitment must be devised. If a surplus exists, strategies such as redeployment (transfer out), "stockpiling" of surplus people, attrition, outplacement, and accelerated retirement might be considered. Many of these strategies, especially redeployment to different functional areas or operating units and outplacement, require a considerable developmental component. Thus, an effective forecasting and succession planning system necessarily leads to strategic development as well.

Why bother attacking development indirectly, as a spin-off of other systems such as rewards and succession? Again, the issue is a strategic one: managers, especially middle managers, who are the primary implementers of any management system, are more concerned about activities which help them attain their business objectives (activities like performance improvement and succession planning) than about individual employee development *per se*. So, it may be difficult to motivate managers to work on employee development, because their rewards may be questionable. It is far clearer to managers how they will benefit from performance improvement and succession planning. In short, to the manager, organizational needs are more pressing than individual employee concerns, and the manager often sees development as only a concern of the employee. The more that development can be linked to the achievement of business objectives, the more that development will take place.

Perhaps the most important factor needed to ensure strategic development is the participation of top management in the process. Since top management is the strategic level of the organization, and represents strategic *business* planners, it should also include human resource planners. Top management should plan and execute employee development activities. Box 11.3 is an example of how the systematic development of people was used strategically, as an alternative to external recruiting.

Development should *not* be the responsibility of the human resource function. Human resources should act as a third party and assist/monitor the development process, but actual development decisions and strategies should be the responsibility of top management. The active involvement of management in development at organizations as diverse as Citicorp,[11] Southern New

EXHIBIT 11.7   A REPRESENTATIVE HUMAN RESOURCE FORECASTING FORM

| Job Level | Current Strength | Losses | Back-up | Future Demand | Imbalance | | |
					Surplus	Shortage	Promotionally Blocked

Source: Human Resource Inventory	*Sources:* Current job incumbents Retirement Transfers out of function Resignations	*Sources:* High-potential people Mobility and career development preferences, from managers and employees	*Source:* Strategic and operational business plans	*Action Plans:* Development Recruitment Reassignment

SOURCE: Adapted from "Succession Planning in the Ministry of Transportation and Communications, Province of Ontario," by L. J. Reypert, *Human Resource Planning*, 1981. Reprinted by permission of the Human Resource Planning Society.

England Telephone Company,[12] the Province of Ontario,[13] the Arizona Public Service Company,[14] and General Electric[15] was critical to the success of development in each. When the president and chairman of an organization meet monthly or biannually to review succession plans, back-ups, and developmental plans, planned, strategic development is actually accomplished.

STRATEGIC WORK FORCE PLANNING AT SUNCOAST ELECTRIC

BOX 11.3

Suncoast Electric is an electric power company employing over 14,000 people. The blue-collar work force of its power stations is completely unionized, and their jobs are classified according to the levels of skill and responsibility required. Clearly defined career paths have been established for employees to move from one job classification to another, and up to six years are needed for new employees to progress from entry-level apprentice jobs to the most senior jobs in the power stations. Because of the unique nature of most jobs in electric power stations, experienced applicants are in very short supply in the labor market. To match people with jobs, Suncoast must either recruit experienced employees from the power stations of other regional utilities or hire inexperienced applicants and train them over a period of years. As a result, the human resource department must anticipate the company's long-term needs to fill specific types of jobs, monitor the supply of potential employees, and make long-range plans to train the required types and numbers of employees through the process of strategic human resource development. In short, Suncoast has to create its own internal labor market through apprenticeship and training programs.

Two basic kinds of information are essential for successful strategic human resource development at Suncoast. First, the supply of potential employees for each job classification must be estimated. This information is derived from an automated data base that projects turnover of current employees grouped by job, age, sex, or years with the company. These projections give the human resource department a relatively accurate estimate of the work force available to the company one, two, three, four, and five years into the future. The second essential piece of information is a projection of the number of jobs that will have to be filled a specified number of years into the future. This information is estimated through the process of strategic business planning.

Strategic planners at Suncoast Electric estimate regional power needs from city, county, and state projections of population and industrial growth up to twenty years into the future. With this information the company projects the need for new power plants in its region and makes detailed plans for the construction and staffing of new plants over the next five to ten years. The human resource department is actively involved in the planning and scheduling of new plant construction in order to coordinate the completion date with the availability of needed employees. Human resource specialists use their projections of attrition and employee movement through various training programs to estimate the supply of essential employees at various dates. In some cases the timetable for construction of a new plant must be extended until prospective employees for senior jobs are in good supply.

The involvement of the human resource department in strategic planning at Suncoast has enabled the company to estimate its supply of unique employees up to five years into the future, project its future demand for those employees, and take steps to train and develop current employees to staff power plants years before they are opened for operation.

This is a real case. The name of the company has been disguised.

EXHIBIT 11.8 **INDIVIDUAL AND ORGANIZATIONAL LIFE STAGES**

Individual	Organization			
	Birth	Growth	Maturity	Decline
Exploration/Entry	X			
Establishment/Advancement		X		
Maintenance			X	
Disengagement				X

DEVELOPMENT DURING THE ORGANIZATIONAL LIFE CYCLE

It is becoming clear that organizations and individuals have developmental life cycles, with each stage having distinctive needs and concerns.[16] Basically, both people and organizations are human systems, with biological-type growth and decay curves: birth, growth, maturity, and decline. In a new and growing organization, personal development occurs naturally because corporate growth provides a wide range of opportunities for the individual. The risk, though, is that the employee will be drawn into areas of organizational priority which are not of the greatest personal interest or long-term benefit. During organizational maturity and decline, opportunities become more limited, and greater planning is required if individual growth is to continue.

A diagram showing combinations of personal and organizational life stages is shown in Exhibit 11.8. There is a tendency for individual and organizational life stages to be congruent: young, fast-growing employees gravitate toward young, fast-growing organizations. Mature, stable organizations tend to have older employees. These congruent combinations are marked by "X's" in Exhibit 11.8.

One promising avenue for strategic development, however, would be to encourage *intentional misfits*. In other words, assuming a "go-go" manager (in the establishment and advancement career stage) would fit naturally in a growing organization, a counter-intuitive development strategy might assign that person to a mature part of the organization to develop budget-management and administrative skills. Or, perhaps that employee might be assigned to a declining organization to develop planning, conflict-management, cost-reduction, and interpersonal abilities, all of which would be severely tested in such an environment.

Similarly, a plateaued administrator (in a maintenance career stage) might be placed in a fast-growth unit to revitalize skills and attitudes. And a person whose career is nearing its end (the disengagement stage) might be highly effective as a mentor for people in new or growing organizations by passing on the knowledge and expertise necessary to succeed in new, growing systems.

Strategic misfitting can be a means to promote organization development, as well. A mature manager in a fast-growth environment can add needed stability and organization. On the other hand, a rapidly moving manager can revitalize a mature, "middle-aged" organization.

One risk of strategic misfitting is that the impact of the manager may be so great that it alters the course of the organization's development. For example, a young, aggressive manager hired by a declining organization to help it die gracefully might instead develop new products and markets, putting it back into a growth stage. Such an outcome could be welcomed at the corporate level, or it could be a problem if that business simply did not fit with the firm's overall business plans. Implication: corporate expectations must be extremely clear to the misfitted manager. And rewards would have to be uncoupled from the performance of the business unit (i.e., the manager assigned to "wind down" a business could not be compensated with a bonus plan tied to the profits of that business).

Along with clear expectations, great care must be exercised to communicate clearly the reasons why the manager is being placed in an intentionally imperfect fit. If this is not done, the manager, employing traditional means of evaluating the move, might misinterpret the organization's future plans for him or her. To illustrate, in a large commercial bank, an aggressive, advancing loan officer with a bright future was put in charge of the controller's division, traditionally seen as a non-mainstream area in the bank and definitely *not* a career-enhancing place to be assigned. The assignment was to "shake up" the division, to make it more responsive to the lending areas and to stimulate creativity and productivity in the development of new information systems. Unfortunately, though, the loan officer was not adequately (or convincingly) informed of the reasons for the new placement. The first two months in the job were spent moping around the bank and worrying about the message top management was sending—time that should have been spent initiating major organizational changes. Implication: when misfitting people, tell them extra clearly why they are being put where they are, *especially* if it is "good news."

DEVELOPMENT AT THE MANAGERIAL AND OPERATIONAL LEVELS

The key to strategic development is activities and polices at the strategic level of the organization, and that has been where most of our attention has been devoted in this chapter. However, if supportive systems and practices are not in place at lower levels, strategic plans will not be executed.

At the managerial level, the critical factors are training for managers and rewards for those who are developing subordinates. To do development, the manager must see a personal payoff. Including development as part of a manager's job objectives and making development of subordinates a prerequisite for promotion are two important ways to provide rewards. Managers need skill training in job design, career coaching, succession planning, assessment of potential, and feedback to be more effective developers of talent.

Inter-unit cooperative arrangements are also necessary to facilitate movement throughout the corporation. Since managers are understandably wary of accepting unknown transferees, career brokers or internal placement managers are often necessary. A good way to give power to these internal brokers is to have them manage the corporate management training program. In this way, the broker can say to the reluctant receiving manager: "You want some of our good trainees this year? You can have them if you accept some transfers from other departments as well."

Strategic development is at its weakest at the managerial level in many organizations. Often there is a strong commitment to development at the strategic level, coupled with specific programs and systems to aid individual employees at the operational level (e.g., career planning workshop, job posting systems). But there is often no attempt to communicate downward the top-level strategy in the form of objectives for development so that managers are encouraged (or required) to develop their own strategies to implement these organization-wide objectives. The problem here is that strategy is often seen as the exclusive domain of the senior levels of the organization, so that middle managers are not held accountable for strategic planning at their level. Then, in turn, the managers do not hold their operational-level subordinates responsible for planning sub-strategies at their level.

Richard Vancil describes how this downward "cascading" of strategy can integrate the planning of all levels in the organization.

> A personalized strategy is feasible in a complex organization if the statement of strategy is drafted carefully. As discussed earlier, the superior manager devises his strategy and expresses it in the form of constraints on the scope of the activities of his subordinates. However, he should take care to leave them some discretion as to how they will operate within these constraints. Each subordinate manager will then accept (or challenge) those constraints, devise "his" strategy within them, and in turn express his strategy to his subordinates in the form of constraints on their activities. The resulting series of progressively detailed statements of strategy are personalized in the sense that each manager can see his imprint on his part of the series. Furthermore, they are integrated throughout the organization as a whole because each statement is consistent with the constraints imposed by higher authority.[17]

Vancil points out two advantages to this cascading approach: lower managers become personally involved in the planning process and come up with high-quality, creative strategies, and this involvement produces a greater commitment on the part of the managers to these strategies.

With this process of top-down communication about strategy (where the strategy at the higher level becomes the set of objectives to be achieved for the lower level), many of the reasons why managers resist developing subordinates vanish. Consider a few of the reasons managers give for not spending time on subordinate development:

> There are no rewards for developing subordinates. In fact, we are punished for it, since when we develop people, they are often rotated out to another department.

This cascading policy-process becomes an effective way to link the manager's development strategy to the boss's objectives. In this way the boss is paying attention to development and is more likely to recognize the subordinate manager's performance in this area.

> There is no time to develop our people.

There's a role modeling effect here, as well. If top-level people spend a lot of time on strategic development, managers will find time for it as well.

> Top management doesn't care about my career. Why should I care about my subordinates' careers?

Again, if the top level is doing its own strategic planning for development, a prime target group for its activities will be people at the managerial level. This reasoning can then be reversed, for if the top level is concerned about their managers' development, then the managers will be inclined to think that it's only fair that they should attend to the development of their subordinates.

> My career advancement has slowed down. Why should I be expected to help my subordinates advance if I can't move up?

First, strategic development makes advancement opportunities more rational, more based on performance and potential at *all* levels, and thus helps managers continue advancing. Second, even if a given manager does not advance further, development is now part of his or her expected performance and will affect other rewards, such as pay and recognition.

> I don't have sufficient company career information and skills in feedback and coaching to help subordinates.

This moves us on to the operational level. If developmental strategy is being communicated and implemented logically up and down the organization, one predictable result will be the need for operational career development information and training programs for managers.

At the operational level, specific employee development activities are necessary. These include career development seminars and workshops, assessment centers to identify potential, career monitoring and coaching, challenging assignments, and all the other activities discussed earlier in relation to different career stages. Perhaps the most critical factor at the operational level is specific *programs* and *systems* to permit organization-wide development policies and practices. Activities such as AT&T's Initial Management Development Program (IMDP) give formality and visibility to the development effort. (IMDP was a program, based on considerable company research, to place new college graduates into challenging initial assignments, to assign them to the best bosses, to assess the recruits' management potential through assessment centers, and to track and support their development through the early years of their careers.) Human resource information systems, often computerized, effectively help to identify high-priority developmental needs and match job assignments and candidates. The role of human resources is probably greatest at the operational level, in developing and managing development programs and systems.

A problem with an organization's engaging in development activities *without* taking a strategic approach is that it may start with a general, vague expression of commitment from the top, which gets too quickly translated into very concrete operational activities. For instance, in the Ford Motor Company in the mid-1970s, a massive program to train first-line supervisors (a *sizable* group) in career counseling skills was initiated and guided by a three-word directive from the executive committee in the course of a discussion of affirmative action and career development: "Let's do something." At Continental Insurance a key vice-president, the head of the Property and Casualty Division, by far the largest division in the company, initiated an effort to improve employee development and managerial succession planning. Responsibility for developing and implementing a division-wide program was immediately delegated to an entry-level training specialist. The specialist did a nearly miraculous job of developing the commitment of the various management levels between the specialist and the initiating vice-president, a process which would have been unnecessary if the initiator had taken a strategic approach. The staff person's energies then could have been used as intended to design and deliver the development program.

Exhibit 11.2 contains a detailed list of developmental activities. Some of the more promising strategies for development at the operational and managerial levels are summarized below.

Job rotation. Job rotation should continue throughout an employee's career. It should *not* be used only for younger employees on the way up. Lateral moves, cross-functional moves, and moves to operating companies can all be useful. However, geographical movement seems neither desirable nor necessary. Other types of mobility, such as temporary assignments, "trouble shooting," consulting assignments, task forces, and project teams, can be useful alternatives to permanent moves.

A professional placement function. One good way to promote systematic strategic movement is through a specific human resource function with the responsibility for professional placement. The person charged with this function ideally would be a well-respected individual who knew the corporation well and was able to act as a "broker" to place employees internally and to "free up" employees to be moved. Outplacement could be another part of this person's responsibility. Often an operating unit's human resource director might be charged with this internal staffing function. This internal placement role is becoming more common as rotational moves are given higher priority.

Career counseling and exploration. Many employees would be more open to various kinds of job moves *if* the moves were part of a formal career plan and were career-enhancing. Employees need to be encouraged to do more exploration of career alternatives.

Increased company career opportunity information. The *most important* career development need for many employees is improved information about career opportunities in other parts of the organization. Several ways to communicate this information are employee career manuals, seminars and workshops with personnel specialists and executives familiar with the total corporation, informational interviews in other parts of the organization, job posting, and position descriptions from other areas.

Improved career feedback. Increased feedback to the employee regarding his or her own career is needed. Feedback could be part of a career counseling discussion with the immediate supervisor and would provide frank, realistic information about the person's career prospects, strengths, weaknesses, and steps needed to increase career mobility.

Permission for outside consulting (for professionals). Some organizations now find that motivation of professionals is enhanced if they have an opportunity to do consulting and other types of work on their own time for other organizations. Obviously, this must be done carefully, with concern for possible conflicts of interest and other potential problems. However, it can be a valuable way to provide more variety in work, more recognition, more external visibility, and more opportunity to explore second-career options. Some companies let professionals do outside consulting on their vacation time, while others permit unpaid leaves of absence which can be used for outside work.

Recognition for career specialists. Many professionals feel fulfilled in their present specialist role but also feel that the organization does not value those who devote their careers to a professional specialty (as opposed to supervision or management). A task force of committed professionals and managers might "brainstorm" ways for the organization to provide more recognition and rewards for career specialists.

Slower early-career advancement: enrichment of lower-level jobs. Part of the problem of career plateauing is the immediate result of a company's use of rapid early promotion to develop and retain young professionals. What the young professional needs most is *challenge*, but the most challenging jobs are often at higher grade levels.

Some organizations have successfully enriched entry-level and lower-level jobs in order to satisfy the growth needs of younger employees, so that fast promotions are less necessary. This is best done in the context of a general strategy for employee development. Many Japanese firms use this approach with success.

KEY POINTS

▪ Strategic human resource development is the identification of needed skills and the active management of employee learning for the long-range future to support explicit corporate business strategies. Thus, strategic development is different from training (development of performance-related knowledge and skills) in that the former has a longer time span, is explicitly related to business objectives, and aims at changes in attitudes, adaptation, and identity, in addition to the employee's performance.

▪ Strategies for development can focus on either cognitive changes (new knowledge and insights), new behaviors, or changes in the environment (which will in turn develop the person).

▪ A number of human resource policies can be effective strategies for developing people on an organization-wide basis: promotion from within, employment security, cross-functional movement, limits in job incumbency, successor training before promotion, and understaffing.

▪ The structure of the organization represents the set of career opportunities available to employees. Thus, the structure can be used strategically to foster development.

▪ Rewards and succession planning are two human resource activities with especially important effects on employee development.

▪ An organization's employee development needs will vary systematically with its life-cycle stage. In the early growth stage, development opportunities occur naturally and planning is necessary to best utilize these opportunities. In more mature stages, more effort is needed to create growth opportunities for the person.

ISSUES FOR DISCUSSION

1. Why do so few organizations engage in the strategic development of human resources?

2. Can you think of an organization that did take a strategic approach to development? Describe how it was done and what was accomplished.

3. Selection of managers and executives from outside the organization is an alternative to the development of the firm's own people for these higher-level positions. What are the pros and cons of outside selection vs. internal development as strategies for staffing key positions?

4. Which of the development-promotion policies described in this chapter would be most difficult to "sell" to top management in contemporary organizations? Why? How would you go about gaining acceptance for this policy? (Specify first whether your role would be as a senior line manager or a senior human resource executive.)

5. Is it more effective to develop people to "fit" the characteristics of their organization's current life stage or to allow some people to be strategic "misfits?" Why? Can you cite examples of people who were successful fits or misfits?

6. In what stage in the organizational life cycle do you think you would operate most effectively? Why?

NOTES

1. This chapter is a revised version of Douglas T. Hall, "Human Resource Development and Organizational Effectiveness," in Charles J. Fombrun, Noel M. Tichy, and Mary Anne Devanna, *Strategic Human Resource Management* (New York: Wiley, 1984), pp. 159–81.

2. Kenneth N. Wexley and Gary P. Latham, *Developing and Training Human Resources in Organizations* (Glenview, Ill.: Scott, Foresman, 1981).

3. Douglas T. Hall, *Careers in Organizations* (Glenview, Ill.: Scott, Foresman, 1976).

4. Fred K. Foulkes and Henry M. Morgan, "Organizing and Staffing the Personnel Function," *Harvard Business Review*, 1977, 55, pp. 142–154.

5. *Business Week*, July 14, 1975, pp. 82–84.

6. Donald C. Pelz and Frank M. Andrews, *Scientists in Organizations* (Ann Arbor, Mich.: Institute for Social Research, the University of Michigan, Revised Edition, 1976).

7. Rosabeth M. Kanter, *Men and Women of the Corporation* (New York: Basic Books, 1977).

8. Harry Wellbank, Douglas T. Hall, Marilyn A. Morgan, and W. Clay Hamner, "Planning Job Progression for Effective Career Development and Human Resources Management," *Personnel*, 55, March–April 1978.

9. Douglas T. Hall and Benjamin Schneider, *Organizational Climates and Careers* (New York: Academic Press, 1973).

10. Jay Galbraith and Anders Edstrom, "Creating Decentralization Through Informal Networks: The Role of Transfer," in L. Pondy, R. Kilmann, and D. Slevin (eds.), *Managing Organization Design* (New York: American Elsivier Publishing Co., 1977), pp. 289–310.

11. Daniel A. Saklad, "Manpower Planning and Career Development at Citicorp," in Lee Dyer (ed.), *Careers in Organizations* (Ithaca, N.Y.: New York State School of Industrial and Labor Relations, Cornell University, 1976), pp. 31–35.

12. Douglas T. Hall and Francine S. Hall, "What's New in Career Management?" *Organizational Dynamics*, 1976, 5, pp. 17–33.

13. L. J. Reypert, "Succession Planning in the Ministry of Transportation and Communications, Province of Ontario," *Human Resource Planning*, 1981, 4, pp. 151–56.

14. J. K. Wellington, "Management Succession at Arizona Public Service," *Human Resource Planning*, 1981, 4, pp. 157–67.

15. Stewart D. Friedman with Theodore P. Levino, "Strategic Appraisal and Development at the General Electric Company," in Fombrun et al., op. cit., 1984, pp. 183–201.

16. John R. Kimball, Robert H. Miles and Associates, *The Organizational Life Cycle* (San Francisco: Jossey-Bass, 1980).

17. Richard Vancil, "Strategy Formulation in Complex Organizations," *Sloan Management Review*, Winter 1976, pp. 4, 5.

ANNOTATED BIBLIOGRAPHY

ANDERSON, J. C., MILKOVICH, G. T., and TSUI, A. "Intra-Organizational Mobility: A Model and Review." *Academy of Management Review*, 1981, 6, pp. 529–38.

This is a comprehensive review of the literature on the operation of internal labor markets, the mechanisms by which people are moved around organizations and developed. The authors also present their own stochastic model for analyzing the likelihoods of movement between various positions, which is useful for understanding the main flows of personnel within an organization.

BRAY, D. W. "Management Development Without Frills." *The Conference Board Record*, September 1975, pp. 47–50.

This useful paper is written by a pioneer in the field of management assessment centers. Based upon extensive research in AT&T with its Management Progress study, it describes a clear, straightforward strategy for more effective development of managerial talent.

DIGMAN, L. A. "How Well-Managed Organizations Develop Their Executives." *Organizational Dynamics*, 1978, 7, pp. 63–80.

This is an analysis of the development strategies of a number of effective organizations. The author describes how the process of development is performed in these organizations. In most of the methods identified, employee development is not a separate staff activity but a part of operating the business.

KANTER, R. *The Changemasters*. New York: Simon and Schuster, 1983.

This is a study of a number of successful innovative corporations (e.g., Wang, Honeywell). The author gives special attention to the role of organizational entrepreneurs ("changemasters") who have a vision of creative new methods and products, as well as the organizational influence to actualize that vision. The book discusses organizational and personal strategies for developing these entrepreneurial skills in the organization.

SCHEIN, E. H. *Career Dynamics: Matching Individual and Organizational Needs*. Reading, Mass.: Addison-Wesley, 1978.

In addition to its excellent material on the processes of individual career development, the second half of this book describes a total system for human resource planning and development. It does an excellent job of showing how individual (micro) career development processes tie in with organizational human resource planning systems.

WALKER, J. W. *Human Resource Planning*. New York: McGraw-Hill, 1980.

In addition to his work on the overall human resource planning process, Walker is also widely known for his work on individual career planning and management development. This book is an extremely practical guide to the process of pursuing employee development in a strategic way.

CHAPTER TWELVE

TRAINING

After earning a bachelor's degree in business administration, Betty Collins began her career in banking as a credit analysis trainee in the Commercial Credit Department of Grandview Bank and Trust.[1] Although she had majored in finance, Betty realized that she had much to learn before she could function as a lending officer. She was eager to begin a two-year training program with a group of twenty other new employees.

Betty was attracted by Grandview's philosophy of on-the-job training, which enabled her to learn while working. The program began with three weeks of intensive orientation to the bank's lending operations. Each day consisted of a two-hour classroom presentation by the credit department staff, self study of a training manual, and practice exercises. After three weeks, trainees had been introduced to credit and collateral documentation, techniques of statement spreading and loan pricing, and a variety of information sources used by bank management and lending officers to evaluate credit applications. In the fourth week, each trainee applied this training by analyzing a commercial loan application and preparing a recommendation to a lending officer. The manager of the credit analysis program then discussed it with the trainee.

Twelve months of on-the-job training followed, with each trainee analyzing credit applications and recommending credit decisions to lending officers. The credit analysis trainees were assigned loan applications from lending groups throughout the bank to ensure their exposure to all lending functions within one year. The manager of the training program and the lending officer reviewed and discussed each credit analysis and recommendation with the trainee to provide feedback and instruction. Trainees also attended two seminars a month on current developments in the banking industry.

During their second year, the trainees became interns of their preferred lending group in the bank. They assumed the full responsibilities of a lending position in the group and worked closely with a lending officer, much as an apprentice works with a journeyman in the skilled trades. After six to twelve months, the trainees became lending officers.

As Betty progressed through the training program at Grandview Bank and Trust, she was impressed with the responsibility she was given, her exposure to all banking operations, and the amount of feedback she received on her work. Upon completing the program, she felt she was ready to be a lending officer.

Of all the human resource functions included in this book, organizations probably spend the most time on training. Virtually all employees experience some form of training and development as they begin each new job and at many other times during their careers. Training can be quite extensive, such as in the bank described above, or it can be a brief set of instructions given by a supervisor to a new employee. Because of its pervasiveness, training is more likely than other human resource functions to affect employees significantly during their work lives. Furthermore, training can have a direct and lasting effect on individual employees, for in training the employees themselves are actually changed.

The responsibility for training is often shared by human resource professionals and line managers. At Grandview Bank, for example, the training director from the bank's human resource department and the vice-president of commercial lending consulted extensively to design the credit analysis training program and choose the training methods. They developed the training manual and the content of the classroom presentations, and they selected and trained the manager of the training program as well as other members of the credit department who made the presentations. The vast majority of the classroom and on-the-job training was then done by credit department staff.

training

Training is a *planned effort by an organization to facilitate the learning of job-related knowledge and skills by its employees to improve employee performance and further organizational goals.*[2] Training is one of the methods used to achieve the optimal degree of fit between the employee, job, and organization as outlined in Chapter Two. In training, the job and organization are viewed as relatively stable, and the individual is changed.

Three points in this definition will be developed throughout this chapter. First, training is *planned* by the organization. It does not just happen. Planning implies a process of analysis, consideration of alternatives, and decision making. Any discussion of training, therefore, must begin with an analysis of the need for training and a specific plan. Second, training involves the learning of *job-related knowledge and skills*. New knowledge and skills are of little use to the organization if they are not directly related to job performance. Third, training is intended to *improve employee performance and further organizational goals*. Again, this implies a process of planning. First the goals of the organization must be identified, and then the kind of performance that enhances these goals must be isolated. At that point, the type of training can be selected to change employee performance in the desired way.

THE NEED FOR TRAINING

Training is needed whenever organizational goals can be furthered by improved employee performance. As we stressed in Chapter Eleven, training is one of the major ways in which employers develop employees to meet organizational objectives and business plans. In short, training is big business. Business and industry now spend nearly $60 billion a year on corporate-run training and education, which is comparable to the cost of all the four-year colleges and universities in the U.S.[3] According to recent surveys, about 70 percent of organizations have formal training programs, and the majority have plans to expand the training function.[4] In addition, over 90 percent of the organizations refunded tuition for job-related training outside the organization. Indeed, expenditures on training are even maintained in many companies during business slowdowns resulting from recessions.[5]

There is a growing demand for firms that design and conduct training for the business community.[6] The American Management Association, a giant in the training business, increased its annual income for training from $11 million to $60 million in a recent ten-year period. Other training firms such as Xerox Learning Systems, Wilson Learning, and Forum Company report annual growth rates of 30 to 45 percent.

Although training is widespread and growing, human resource professionals and line managers must be able to judge when training is preferable to the other means of achieving an optimal degree of fit between employees and jobs (e.g., increased recruiting efforts or higher selection standards). There are four specific conditions under which the need for training is particularly great.

The base rate is very low. The base rate is the percentage of employees who are adequately qualified to perform a job at an acceptable level. If the base rate is very low, an organization will encounter difficulty finding enough people who can enter the job and immediately meet desired performance standards. This will very likely be true in spite of extensive recruiting and high selection standards. Consequently, there is a need to select the best available applicants and then immediately train them until they become fully qualified to perform the job. A good example of this occurs in public accounting firms that hire business school graduates with accounting majors. Most new employees immediately embark on a training program to become certified public accountants.

Selection is unsuccessful or selection errors are costly. Even the most rigorous selection procedures invariably result in errors because of the inherent unpredictability of human performance. When unqualified applicants are chosen, they become unqualified employees. Faced with unqualified employees, the organization must either fire them or attempt to increase their capacity to perform the job successfully through training. Organizations must also avoid hiring unqualified applicants for jobs in which the cost of ineffective performance is prohibitive. For example, the mistakes of astronauts, airline pilots, bus drivers, or operators of very sophisticated or expensive equipment are so costly in human or dollar terms that employers go to great lengths to avoid selection errors. Consequently, applicants who meet very high selection standards may immediately enter training programs which, in the case of astronauts, can last a number of years.

Job functions or performance standards change. In this age of very rapid technological growth, jobs are constantly changing, and employees must also change to maintain acceptable levels of performance. In some cases, the basic nature of the job may change. For example, a new computer system may require programmers to use a new language, a new bookkeeping system may create new procedures for clerical staff to follow, or a recent unionization of a plant may demand more sophisticated knowledge of labor law and negotiating tactics from plant supervisors and managers. In each case, a change in the functions of a job creates the need for new kinds of performance. This need can be met through training that provides employees with new knowledge and skills.

Similarly, while the basic nature of the job may remain the same, performance standards may be changed. For example, a need for higher productivity in an organization may lead to increases in the sales quotas of the sales staff. Marginal performers may need training to meet the new standards. In another illustration, as the staff grows in size and education, a supervisor's unsophisticated management skills may require upgrading if higher standards of supervision on the job are to be met.

There is high variability in job performance. The final condition that suggests a necessity for training is one of relatively large differences in the performance of several employees in the same job. In jobs where a few employees clearly outperform all others, some fundamental questions should be asked: "What knowledge or skill do these few have that makes them do so well? Can the others learn it?" Answers to these questions may lead to training that substantially raises the performance of the rest of the employees.

These conditions are described in the case of Ron's Krispy Fried Chicken (Box 12.1). Since very few newly hired employees know how to manage a fast-food store, the base rate was low and selection errors were reducing company revenues. The job of store manager changed as the company grew larger and more sophisticated and there was great variability in the performance of store managers. An effective training program was designed to meet the training needs at Ron's.

GENERAL APPROACHES TO TRAINING

In this society with its strong orientation toward career development, training programs exist to teach employees practically anything. All of these programs fall into one of four basic categories, based on who assesses the training need and who actually does the training.

On-the-Job Training

The most common and often the least formal approach to training takes place while the employee is performing the job. In many cases, the need for training is discovered by the employee, the employee's boss, or a co-worker, and the boss or co-worker actually conducts the training. Several basic steps in training should take place even in the most informal on-the-job training. A

TRAINING STORE MANAGERS AT RON'S KRISPY FRIED CHICKEN

BOX 12.1

Ron's Krispy Fried Chicken of Houston, Texas, was expanding rapidly in the late 1970s, and John White, the training director, realized that some action was essential to staff their thirty-five fast-food stores with effective managers. Like most small companies, Ron's had developed an informal approach to training new employees, but ten days of on-the-job training were no longer enough to produce the number of new managers Ron's now needed. In 1980 and 1981, between 80 and 100 percent of new store managers quit or were terminated during their first six months of employment, and gross sales were suffering. Furthermore, new company financial and inventory control policies added to the manager's job. Since few applicants were familiar with how to manage a fast-food store, White concluded that more extensive training was necessary.

He began to design the training by identifying his target—the performance of successful store managers. They were responsible for supervising all employees, overseeing the preparation of food, and completing paperwork to maintain inventory and prepare monthly profit-and-loss statements. They also cooked food and waited on customers, as needed. White's training objectives were to expose trainees to all jobs in the store, to let them perform all jobs with guidance and feedback, and to teach the entire business cycle of a store, from the arrival of raw chicken each day to the completion of a monthly profit-and-loss statement.

White chose a combination of on-the-job and classroom training and selected a regular store to serve as the corporation's training store. One to three people were trained at a time. They spent their first three weeks at the training store, where they functioned as a fry cook, sales person, and eventually as a co-manager, completing paperwork and bookkeeping, under the close tutelage of the store manager. Their last week of training consisted of classroom instruction in basic and advanced bookkeeping, performance appraisal, human relations, and positive management.

Recent statistics show the dramatic results of the training. Of the forty-five applicants hired as store manager trainees during 1982, forty-three completed the training and were still on the job after six months. After twelve months, thirty-three of the original trainees were still with Ron's, six had quit, and four had been terminated. In spite of this significant improvement over turnover figures for 1980 and 1981, John White feels that the training still needs adjustment. It provides excellent technical preparation but needs more emphasis on the management of people. In particular, the trainees spend only three days as co-managers during on-the-job training, and they have no time to practice the skills they learn in the classroom before they move into a store as a full-time manager. Therefore, White plans to place more emphasis on management training and also to precede on-the-job training with classroom training.

The authors wish to thank Mr. John White for his cooperation in preparing this material.

need should be assessed, a plan should be made, training should be done, and results should be observed and assessed. But supervisors must resist the temptation to do the work themselves, rather than to train an employee.

Other kinds of on-the-job training are much more extensive and formal. Some entry-level employees are trainees for months and are continually trained and monitored. The case of Betty Collins illustrates this approach. A major task of the supervisor is to train new employees and evaluate their progress.

Internal Training Courses by Company Personnel

A second type of training occurs inside the company but off the job. These training courses or programs are designed and conducted by company personnel, usually through the coordination of human resource professionals. A company trainer may conduct the course, or a line manager or other employee with expertise in the subject.

New knowledge or techniques in a field may suggest a clear need for training, or line managers may notice an area of consistent weakness in their employees' job performance and request a course. Finally, employees themselves may ask to learn new job-related skills or knowledge via internal training courses. The courses are then designed, and appropriate company personnel are selected to conduct the training.

Internal Training Courses by External Consultants

Training courses may also be designed and conducted by an outside consultant. Often company personnel lack the expertise or credibility of a consultant who specializes in a specific area of training. This is particularly true in small companies in which the need for a training course arises too seldom to justify keeping a trainer on staff. Although these courses are conducted by external consultants, they can be tailored specifically to the needs of the company and the trainees.

External Training Courses

The final approach to training is simply for the employee with the training need to attend a training program that is designed and conducted by a consultant and held outside the trainee's organization, perhaps with employees from other organizations. These training courses can range from part-time degree or certification programs (e.g., executive MBA or CPA courses) to one-day seminars on a specific topic. They can be sponsored by universities, professional associations, or private consultants who specialize in a particular kind of training.

EXHIBIT 12.1

THE TRAINING PROCESS

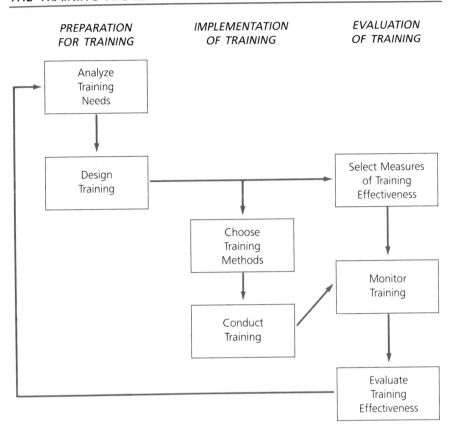

External training courses have advantages and disadvantages. Their great strength is that they allow employees to learn from experts in a given field. They also allow employees to share views with people in similar jobs from other organizations. However, the training may not address the needs of a particular employee. In the seminar business, it is truly "buyer beware." To avoid disappointment participants can check the credentials and reputation of the presenters and sponsors and carefully review the content of the seminar.

THE TRAINING PROCESS

The training process consists of three major phases, shown in Exhibit 12.1. Both human resource professionals and line managers should be involved in all three phases. The process begins with preparation. Employees, jobs, and the organization are carefully analyzed to establish the need for training, and then a training program is designed to meet that need. The next phase is implementation. Training methods are selected and training is conducted. The final phase, often overlooked in today's organizations, is evaluation. Measures of training effectiveness are chosen, and then training is carefully monitored to ensure it is proceeding as planned. Finally, changes in employee knowledge, skill, and performance are measured to determine the effectiveness of the training. This information can also be used to analyze future training needs, and the training process then begins again.

PREPARATION FOR TRAINING

Training is an expensive investment for any organization. The cost of obtaining internal training staff or external consultants is high, but the greatest cost is the time lost from productive work by the trainees themselves. Every hour in a training course is an hour of lost productivity. A two-day training program for forty supervisors may cost the company $1,500 in the consultant's fee and $8,000 in salaries for two days' pay for forty employees. To be a wise investment, the training must return at least $9,500 worth of increased productivity.

To provide an adequate return on investment, a training course must produce results that exceed its costs. Given finite training budgets, human resource professionals and line managers must make difficult trade-offs to determine which type of training will produce the greatest return for the organization. The potential for such a return on investment begins with careful and informed preparation. This preparation begins with an analysis of the need for training.

Analysis of Needs

The most obvious requirement of training is that it should meet a need, but this is sometimes overlooked. There are many wrong reasons for doing training:

1. This course has been given for the past three years.
2. There is $10,000 left in the training budget.
3. A friend said it was a great seminar.
4. Any training course held in Bermuda in May is worth attending.
5. The company next door is heavily involved in this new XYZ training and we don't want to be left behind.

But there is only one right reason: to improve employee performance and further organizational goals by increasing employees' job-related knowledge and skills.

Establishing the need for training takes time. Since training is one way to achieve an optimal individual-job-organization fit, a starting point is to analyze the three components of that fit. Of course, much of this information is collected as a starting point for many human resource functions covered in this book. Let's examine the specific kinds of analyses that are required for effective training.

Five basic questions must be answered in preparation for a training course:

1. Who is to be trained?
2. In what are they to be trained?
3. By whom are they to be trained?
4. How are they to be trained?
5. How are the results of the training to be evaluated?[7]

These are simple questions, but they cannot be answered simply. Answers can only be derived through three basic analyses described by McGehee and Thayer. They are organization analysis, job analysis, and person analysis.[8]

Organization Analysis

By definition, training is intended to further the goals of the organization. Therefore, an assessment of training needs must begin with an examination of the organization.

Information about the organization that is relevant to training falls into four categories, which we shall examine in some detail.

Goals of the Organization ▬▬ Goals can be analyzed for an entire organization or for an organizational unit such as a department or division. Information on the goals and objectives can be used to identify the scope and content of the training (see Chapter Eleven). For example, to meet the goal of increased sales, training in new product knowledge and new customer development may be needed.

Quality of Human Resources ▬▬ Another essential step in the organization analysis is to assess the employees available to meet organizational goals. This analysis is comparable to an analysis of physical equipment and materials commonly done in organizations and leads to a human resource inventory and a skills inventory. The human resource inventory contains such information as the number of employees in a job and the number of employees needed in this job, potential replacements for this job within the organization and outside the organization, and training time required for potential replacements and for a novice.[9] This information suggests whether training of current employees is feasible, or whether selection of new employees is a better way to fill this job (see Chapter Seven). Similarly, a skills inventory provides information about the number of employees with specified knowledge and skills, their levels of that knowledge and skill, and the time needed to train employees in that knowledge and skill.[10]

Degree of Goal Achievement ▬ A critical piece of information is the degree of goal achievement, the extent to which current employees are performing well enough to achieve organizational goals. There are a number of indicators: productivity, accidents, waste, quality of product or service, and employee performance.

Organizational and Human Factors That Interfere with Goal Achievement ▬ A fourth factor is the *symptoms* of poor performance in the organization and potential *causes* of that poor performance. For example, analysis of the organizational climate may identify problems in an organization that adversely affect employee morale and performance. Direct measures, such as the amount of turnover, absenteeism, sick leave, grievances, and strikes, can be interpreted as symptoms of a positive or negative organizational culture. In addition, employee attitude surveys, exit interviews, and analysis of employee suggestions can uncover factors that interfere with employee performance. Once the symptoms have been identified, one should try to identify the likely *causes*. For example, poor employee morale may be traced to the ineffective supervisory skills of a number of managers; this would indicate a need for training.

Job Analysis

job analysis

Job analysis is the *systematic study of the tasks and responsibilities included in a job, its relationship to other jobs, the conditions under which work is performed, and the personal capabilities required for satisfactory performance.* As we have stressed throughout this text, a clear understanding of the job is the starting point for all human resource functions. This is particularly true for training because in job analysis the specific content of a training program is identified.

Specialists in human resource management (sometimes called "job analysts" in large organizations) typically conduct job analyses in close consultation with job holders or their immediate supervisors. There are a number of ways to collect the information required in job analysis.[11] The first is through *observing* or *interviewing* employees performing the job. Observation is especially useful to analyze jobs involving repetitive physical work with tools and materials (e.g., assembly work), whereas interviews are useful for jobs involving more mental activity. The second is through *group interviews* with job holders and their supervisors. The third is through more structured techniques, such as *questionnaires* or *checklists,* which include specific questions for the job analyst to ask or lists of work activities for the job analyst or job holder to check as part of the job. Structured techniques (e.g., the *Position Analysis Questionnaire,* developed by McCormick and his associates at Purdue University) are based on general categories of work activities, such as decision making and reasoning, information processing, use of physical devices, interpersonal relationships.[12] The fourth method of job analysis is *crit-*

ical incidents, in which supervisors enumerate employees' work behaviors that contribute to particularly successful or unsuccessful job performance.

The information collected in job analysis may be either *task-oriented* or *employee-oriented*, depending on the human resource function for which the information is needed. Task-oriented job analysis focuses on the tasks and responsibilities of the job, its relationship to other jobs, and working conditions, and produces a *job description*, which is vital to the selection process (see Exhibit 9.2). Employee-oriented job analysis focuses on the knowledge, skill, and personal traits required for successful performance and results in a list of *job specifications*. Employee-oriented job analysis is especially crucial to training because it identifies the characteristics that are essential for successful performance.

In organization and job analyses, detailed information about what is to be achieved on a given job, and how, can be determined. This information can be used to identify the knowledge and skill to be taught and the training procedures. But still unanswered is the question of who is to be trained. This can be answered only through the analysis of current employees.

Person Analysis

Person analysis is the *assessment of employee performance and the knowledge and skill necessary to reach that level of performance.* McGehee and Thayer outline two ways to analyze current employees.[13] The first is a *summary person analysis* in which an assessment is made of how well each employee is performing a given job. Objective indicators of employee performance, if available, are very useful. Examples are productivity, quality of products and services, customer complaints, waste, accidents, and down time. In many cases, more subjective measures must be used, such as rating scales, critical incidents, and checklists (see Chapter Fifteen).

person analysis

The second type of analysis, *diagnostic person analysis*, is much more crucial in determining training needs. In this analysis, the levels of knowledge and skills that lead to successful job performance are measured in each employee, and required increases are estimated. This information can be collected in two ways. The first is through observation and interviews. Supervisors can observe employees in action or interview them in detail about how they do their jobs and the knowledge and skill they use. Similarly, employees can observe and record their own performance and related knowledge and skill by keeping diaries. A second approach is through various forms of structured testing. Paper-and-pencil tests of very specific knowledge can be administered. Various work simulations can test specific knowledge and skills. Examples are role plays, case studies, various business games, or activities at assessment centers. All of these techniques give employees the opportunity to demonstrate specific knowledge and skills that are necessary for successful job performance.

Additional Considerations

The information generated by three basic analyses of training needs is very useful in the preparation of training programs. At first glance, however, the amount of time and effort involved in these analyses may appear great. Few organizations conduct these three analyses thoroughly before planning and conducting training programs, even though much of this information is routinely collected and readily available. As we stressed in Chapter Two, regular analysis of the organization, jobs, and employees is a fundamental first step in many of the human resource functions described in this book. Organizational and departmental goals are often set by line managers, job descriptions and job specifications are established for recruiting and selection purposes, and employee performance is periodically evaluated as a part of the performance appraisal process. Therefore, training needs analysis can begin with information that already has been compiled. Then, additional information not routinely collected (e.g., tests of specific knowledge and skills) can be gathered with a reasonable amount of time and effort.

A second major consideration is that a clear deficiency in performance, as established in a training needs analysis, may not necessarily indicate the need for training. The key here is the difference between symptoms and causes. The discrepancy between actual and desired performance of a number of employees is a symptom that may be caused by lack of employee knowledge or skill. If so, training would be advisable. But employees' performance often suffers for reasons other than their own capabilities. For example, the employees may be poorly supervised, and a training program for the supervisors, not the employees, may be necessary. Still other causes of poor employee performance are totally unrelated to training, such as unclear job responsibilities and performance standards or unfair organizational pay policies. The organization analysis is necessary to identify potential causes of poor employee performance that cannot be addressed via training. It must always be remembered that training changes only the trainee, not the work situation. For example, no amount of training in motivation and team spirit will raise the morale of employees who are unfairly paid. Therefore, the analysis of training needs should be comprehensive and thorough. Only then can organizations determine when training is really needed.

Designing Training

Once the need for training has been established through the analyses described above, human resource professionals or line managers determine the content of the training and the training method. In short, the questions of *what* is to be taught, and *how*, must be answered.

Although there are various theories of instruction and categories of learning, answering these questions is as intuitive as it is scientific. Even in a relatively short training program of two or three days, an extremely large degree of detailed planning and decision making must be done by someone.

OBJECTIVES OF A CREDIT ANALYST TRAINING PROGRAM

EXHIBIT 12.2

Knowledge	Skills	Job Performance
Knowledge of the operations of all major credit groups in the bank.	Skill in reviewing financial statements, business trends and prospects, and the character of the credit applicant.	Successfully performs loan collateral documentation reviews.
Knowledge of techniques for credit and collateral documentation, statement spreading, and loan pricing.	Skill in identifying potential problems and raising questions about a credit application.	Prepares loan proposals with appropriate analysis and recommendations.
Knowledge of credit information sources, such as trial balance and activity journals, financial analyses, and bank policy and procedure manuals.	Skill in organizing and summarizing information from a credit application into a clear, well-documented recommendation for a credit decision.	Assists in the daily servicing of credit customers to the satisfaction of the lending officer.

What content will be included? In what order? What words will the instructor use to present the material? What instructional aids, such as slides, printed material, films, and demonstrations, will supplement the spoken words? What kind of practice will the participants receive (e.g., case studies, role playing, short exam) and when will the practice sessions occur? What form of feedback will be included so trainees will know how much they have learned? These questions become even more complex when a training program of several weeks or months is designed. And there is no research or theory that provides clear answers to these questions. But they can be answered with some degree of confidence if they are approached systematically, as shown in the four steps outlined below.

Job analysis. The first step in determining what the training will include is to analyze the job and identify the knowledge and skill required to perform the tasks involved. This is done in the analysis of training needs, primarily in the job analysis. The result of this analysis is a detailed job description, with not only the specific tasks identified, but the knowledge and skill necessary to perform them.

Training objectives. Next, a set of objectives must be established. These are the desired results of the training—namely, an acceptable level of job performance and indications that trainees have learned important knowledge and skills. Exhibit 12.2 outlines key objectives of the credit analyst training program at Grandview Bank and Trust.

Training content. Once objectives are set, the *means* to reach these ends are selected. Training content is the material that participants are taught. The credit analyst program includes information about bank policies and procedures, analytical techniques, information sources, and approaches to organizing and writing credit recommendations.

Training method. The final step in the process is to determine how the content will be presented. What procedures will be used—lecture, self-study, discussions, cases, programmed text, demonstrations? Perhaps a more appropriate question is, what *combination* of training procedures will be used? Seldom is a training course conducted with only one method. It is crucial that the training method fits the content. Some trainers become enamored of one technique (e.g., role playing, group discussion, or behavior modeling). It is preferable to clearly establish training content, and then select appropriate methods. In the credit analyst program, for example, lectures, self-study, discussions, and case study were used.

IMPLEMENTATION OF TRAINING

Analysis of training needs and design form an essential foundation, and if *not* properly done, no degree of skill by the trainer will make the training effective. But obviously, the foundation is just the beginning of a successful training program. To have any impact on employee performance, training must be implemented.

There are many ways to conduct training programs and there are numerous training techniques that can be combined in a variety of ways. How, then, can anyone decide which methods to use to conduct a training program? The relative merits of training techniques (e.g., lecture versus case study; classroom versus on-the-job; home study versus role playing) have been discussed in business organizations and universities for decades, but there is no compelling evidence favoring any one method because the effectiveness of a training method is dependent on the training situation.

Three major components of the training situation are the *trainer*, the *training content*, and the *trainees*. Trainers differ in knowledge of the material, communication skills, ability to respond to questions and challenges, and ability to motivate trainees. Therefore, some trainers are more effective than others with specific training methods. Training content also strongly influences the appropriateness of a training method, and some trainees are more receptive to specific training methods than others. For example, university students are so accustomed to a classroom setting that even the rather unpopular lecture method works on them. Time-conscious executives with years of practical experience, however, would probably respond more positively to case studies or business games.

Requirements for Effective Training

While there are no clear-cut rules for choosing one training method over another, there are guidelines that can be used. Wexley and Latham have presented four requirements for effective training, which can be used to evaluate the potential of various training methods.[14]

Goal Setting ▬▬ One very important consideration is that participants know the goals of the training. What expected changes should occur in trainees' knowledge, skill, and performance? The clarity and relevance of the goals strongly influence motivation of the trainees. A training program without specific goals endorsed by participants is unlikely to motivate participants to learn. Since motivation is a vital prerequisite for effective training, trainee participation in establishing training objectives is worthy of consideration. For example, the Life Office Management Association, supported by insurance companies, presents trainees with a list of objectives to rate in terms of importance to their training needs.[15]

Meaningful Material ▬▬ A fundamental requirement for effective training is that the material learned be applied on the job. Transfer from training to the job occurs when material is meaningful to the trainees. The credit analyst training program meets this requirement well since all training content is relevant to the job of lending officer. This requirement makes it important for trainers to talk the language of their audience, to illustrate concepts with relevant examples, and to present material in an organized and logical manner. In *skill* training Wexley and Latham emphasize the importance of *showing* trainees examples of desired performance through a technique called *behavioral modeling*, in which trainees view taped or live demonstrations of the skill being taught.[16] For example, trainees might watch the trainer discipline an employee in a brief simulation of a persistent work problem, or view a demonstration selection interview on videotape.

Practice ▬▬ Effective training requires practice. This involves the trainees' attempts to demonstrate their newly acquired skill by *doing*. They may land an airplane in a simulator or conduct an interview in a role-playing situation. In training to acquire new knowledge, practice involves repetition, clarification, and testing. Questions during lectures and small group discussions are useful for clarifying new knowledge. Finally, structured examinations provide further opportunity for practice as trainees review material in preparation for exams and demonstrate their knowledge or skill in the exams.

The amount of practice is a key consideration. Too much practice will bore trainees, and too little will inhibit learning. The degree of concentration of practice is also important. In general, distributed practice (two hours a day for four days, rather than eight hours one day) is preferred in the acquisition of complex or difficult material and also in skill training to prevent fatigue.

Feedback ▬▬ The fourth requirement for effective training is feedback or knowledge of results. Learning would be impossible without feedback because trainees would never know whether they had done something right or wrong. In training, the main focus of feedback is *when* and *how* trainees have done something properly.[17] Feedback may be either intrinsic or extrinsic. For example, a bookkeeper receives intrinsic feedback after several unsuccessful attempts to balance a set of books. Extrinsic feedback is received from others, such as a trainer or other trainees. In general, training is most effective when feedback:

1.   Follows trainee performance as soon as possible,
2.   Is both intrinsic and extrinsic,
3.   Is specific, and
4.   Is both positive and negative (but not so negative that it threatens trainees' self-esteem).

Training Methods

There are many different methods of training. Each has strengths and weaknesses and must be selected to fit the training content, the trainer, and the trainees. To be effective, each must meet the four conditions outlined in the previous section. Some of the major training methods are summarized below.[18]

On-the-Job Training
In on-the-job training a new employee is typically assigned to a supervisor or experienced co-worker who is responsible for teaching the newcomer. Emphasis is on learning by doing. The trainee first watches the trainer perform the job, receives explanation and instruction, and then attempts to perform actual job duties. Feedback is particularly important as the trainer reinforces what the new employee does correctly and makes suggestions for changes and improvements.

Occurring in the work setting, on-the-job training is relatively inexpensive and realistic, and its goal is clear. Conditions for learning transfer are excellent since the training occurs in a real job situation and the material is relevant. This method also provides opportunity for practice and immediate feedback.

In spite of obvious advantages, much on-the-job training is ineffective, primarily because of the trainers. Employees who act as trainers must be given sufficient time from their regular responsibilities to spend with trainees; they must also be selected on the basis of their training skills and their willingness to convey knowledge and skill to new employees.

On-the-job training takes various forms. Three of the more common are apprenticeship training, job rotation, and coaching.

As the most lengthy and formal variety of on-the-job training, *apprenticeship training* occurs in the skilled trades such as plumbers, electricians, brick layers, and carpenters. Classroom instruction is used to teach work principles and techniques, but the bulk of the training occurs on the job under the direction of a fully qualified employee who assigns the trainee specific tasks and provides guidance and feedback.

In *job rotation*, employees move from one part of the organization to another, assuming specific assignments and job responsibilities at each location. Assignments can last from a few days or weeks to a year or more. The goal is to provide employees with a broad understanding of the relationships among functions within a department. For example, an accountant in a financial controls department might spend twelve to eighteen months working in the general accounting section, reports and budgets, governmental reports, and treasury in a job rotation program.

The shortest and least formal type of on-the-job training, *coaching* can occur any time a supervisor feels that an employee's work needs improvement. Coaching usually consists of feedback on past performance and follow-up instruction and guidance. It frequently occurs in conjunction with the performance appraisal process, in the form of follow-up (see Chapter Fifteen).

Off-the-Job Training ▬▬ Other training methods occur off the job. They are used in internal training courses by company personnel and external consultants, as well as in external training courses. In all of the following methods, meaningful material and good transfer of training are major concerns, since the training situation differs from the job situation.

Every student is familiar with the weaknesses of the *lecture*. Communication is primarily one-way, there are no allowances for individual differences in ability to understand material, and the material presented can be irrelevant, poorly organized, and boring. Training directors rate it as almost universally ineffective.[19] But when new material must be presented, the lecture is an inexpensive and effective technique. Lectures should be brief, well organized, and supplemented with printed material for future reference. Coupled with questions and discussion by trainees, the lecture is an effective device for transferring knowledge from trainer to trainees.

With the advent of television and video games, trainees have become used to seeing as well as hearing. Consequently, the use of audiovisual techniques has grown dramatically in the training field. Slides, movies, and videotapes have the advantages of permanence and repeatability (dear to the heart of any trainer who has delivered the same lecture five days in a row). They can also be shown simultaneously to several audiences. Audiovisual aids can supplement lecture material by providing vivid illustrations. They are also excellent in developing skills via taped demonstrations for guidance and via tapes of trainee practice sessions for feedback.

A training technique used primarily in managerial training is the *case study*. A "case" or written description of a work problem is given to trainees to study individually and to identify the causes of the problem and the appropriate solution. The case is then discussed in a group session conducted by the trainer. The assumption is that trainees will learn diagnostic skills and discover underlying principles concerning the causes and solutions of work problems. The main problem is the lack of control over what trainees learn. Since trainees teach themselves, some may develop incorrect insights. In addition, cases may have little relevance to a trainee's work situation, thereby minimizing transfer of training. This method is most effective if the cases are clearly relevant to trainees' work situations and if the trainer clearly draws central ideas and principles from the case discussion.

Role playing is particularly useful in skill training because trainees learn by doing. A problem situation is presented in written form (e.g., a conflict between two department heads) and trainees assume the roles of people in the situation and respond in ways they feel are appropriate. Role playing is almost invariably used with other training techniques such as lecture with discussion or demonstration tapes. Its primary strength is that it enables trainees to practice and receive feedback, either from observers or from videotape playback of the role playing.

Programmed instruction is based on "operant conditioning," in which people learn through responding and receiving positive feedback. In programmed instruction trainees typically receive a printed manual containing material divided into small, organized segments. The material is presented in discrete sentences and paragraphs, followed by questions to test the trainee's learning of the material, followed by answers. This cycle is repeated throughout the manual. Programmed instruction offers the advantages of well-organized material, self-pacing by trainees, active responding, and immediate feedback. Research has also shown that it decreases the time required for training.[20] Its primary disadvantage is cost. An organization must train numerous people to justify the cost of preparing a manual for programmed instruction.

One need only watch computer commericals on television or browse through toy departments to discover the growth of *computer-assisted instruction*. Much of what has appeared in programmed instruction manuals can now be incorporated into computers, with the trainee receiving and sending information through a terminal. Computer-assisted instruction is excellent for self-paced knowledge acquisition. This technique is also useful in motor skills training. The computer simulates the responses of a piece of equipment (say, an airplane) and displays them on a screen, while the trainee operates controls. The clarity of the training goals, the realism of the situation, the opportunity for practice, and the immediate and dramatic feedback (e.g., a simulated airplane crash) nicely meet our four requirements for effective training. Computer-assisted instruction offers the same advantages of on-the-job training without the disadvantages of ineffective or reluctant trainers. This effective, although costly, training method should flourish in the future.

At the risk of appearing old fashioned, we wish to describe one more training method, *self-instruction*. People often learn *in spite of* other training methods. Certainly, studying written material and doing homework is an integral part of all training methods. Studying material of one's own choosing and at one's own pace can produce dramatic results. Box 12.2 illustrates the effectiveness of self-instruction in an industrial setting. All four requirements for effective training were met in the training program described. The proposed test provided training goals. The material on the union contract was clearly meaningful to the foremen. Practice and feedback occurred spontaneously as the foremen discussed the material and tested and corrected one another. One final point. This was not a "non-training course" as Thayer and McGehee assert. It was simply an excellent use of self-instructed training.

THE SELF-INSTRUCTION TRAINING METHOD

BOX 12.2

The events described below occurred during the summer of 1953 at the Fieldcrest Mills, Incorporated, plants in North Carolina. The authors, Thayer and McGehee, were told that this anecdote was the kind of thing students should, but never do, hear about.

During 1953, McGehee was under increasing pressure from various mill managers to fulfill his role as training director by holding a course for foremen on the union contract. The problem, the managers contended, was that the union stewards knew the contract from beginning to end. The stewards constantly challenged the foremen's authority to assign specific jobs and to discipline employees.

McGehee was concerned that any standard course on the contract would be ineffective. Careful observation of mill managers and foremen suggested that the stewards' behaviors were a problem for the managers, not the foremen. While competent instruction, suitable classrooms, materials, and time were available, one essential condition for learning was missing—motivation.

It was suggested that some baseline data be gathered by giving foremen a test to reveal what they already knew about the contract. A shorter course would result, and boredom would be avoided. Since foremen could consult their pocket editions of the contract on the job, the exam should be of the open book type. Thayer got the job of preparing the test.

As an incentive for test-taking, the company president agreed to host a steak dinner for the foreman who submitted the most correct answers in the shortest time period. He also promised that foreman's manager the same.

In the meantime, McGehee suggested to the various mill managers that other managers were willing to wager that more of their foremen would score higher than foremen at other mills. In short order, bets were being placed at all levels among plants, from foreman to manager. Thayer prepared the most difficult and comprehensive multiple-choice exam possible. While only one alternative was correct for each question, a good deal of hairsplitting was done to create the incorrect responses.

The stage was now set for the non-training course. Exams were delivered simultaneously to all mills at exactly 8:00 A.M. Immediately, managers and chief foremen began holding joint exam-taking sessions before work, during breaks, at lunch, after work, at home, etc. McGehee made sure that everyone knew who the test author was. At 8:05 A.M., Thayer's phone began to ring. It did not stop for a week. Everyone protested that there were two, three, and even four correct answers to various questions.

Within a week, all exams were in and all were perfect or near perfect. Two weeks later, the president hosted a steak dinner for seventy-five foremen and their managers.

During the dinner, Thayer was surrounded by indignant foremen who quoted sections of the contract verbatim to support contentions of the unfairness of certain exam questions.

Did the non-training course work? Behavior at the dinner suggests it did. At least as important, pressure for a course disappeared.

Essential learning conditions must exist. Do we look at those conditions first before—or instead of —building a course?

Adaptation from "Comments on the Effectiveness of Not Holding a Formal Training Course" by Paul Thayer and William McGehee, *Personnel Psychology, 30,* 1977. Copyright © 1977 by Personnel Psychology, Inc. Reprinted by permission.

EVALUATION OF TRAINING

The final step in the training process is evaluation. Once the need for training has been carefully assessed and training has been designed and implemented, there is only one way to demonstrate the effectiveness of this entire process. Evidence of the training's impact must be gathered.

To determine what evidence is needed, let's return to the original definition of training: a planned effort by an organization to facilitate the learning of job-related knowledge and skills by employees to improve employee performance and further organizational goals. Therefore, evidence of learning that improves employee performance and furthers organizational goals is necessary to evaluate the training.

Demonstrating that training has led to changes in employee performance and furthered organizational goals is difficult. Indeed, in one survey, 75 percent of the organizations admitted to having no formal procedures to evaluate training effectiveness.[21] Often it is assumed that the benefits of training are intangible or cannot be converted into dollar terms for cost/benefit analysis. Certainly in the area of training evaluation, there is a wide gap between the formal evaluation techniques described below and business practice.

In some cases this gap is not completely unjustified. For example, line managers who give brief instruction and coaching to their employees hardly need formal procedures to evaluate training effectiveness. They *see* the changes in employee performance almost immediately. But when training is designed and conducted more formally, as with more extensive on-the-job training as well as internal and external training courses, systematic evaluation is highly desirable.

There are four basic kinds of evidence that demonstrate training effectiveness: *reaction, learning, behavior,* and *results.*[22] Each contributes some information about the impact of training. Comprehensive evaluation, however, includes as many kinds of evidence as possible.

Reaction

Many training departments use questionnaires to collect reactions to training (Exhibit 12.3). Participants record their responses to the quality and relevance of the content, the method of training, quality of training aids (e.g., handouts, cases, role-playing scenarios, videotaped presentations), and effectiveness of the trainer. In on-the-job training, reactions often are given orally as the trainee responds to the supervisor. Evaluation forms are typically filled out after the training has been completed.

Reactions to training provide little information about how effective training has been, but they do suggest whether the training achieved *minimal* requirements for success, or if it failed. Trainee motivation is the key factor. If trainees evaluate a training program as irrelevant or rate the trainer a poor communicator or unknowledgeable, their motivation will be low and learning will be poor. On the other hand, glowing comments about content and pre-

SAMPLE TRAINING EVALUATION FORM

EXHIBIT 12.3

Name of Course or Seminar: _____

_____

Organization Presenting Program: _____

Training Dates: _____ To _____

Hours of Actual Training: _____

Location of Training: _____

Place an "x" on each scale to reflect your opinion of the training:

1. How much will this course help your current job performance?

    Not at all   0   5   10   Significantly

2. To what extent did this course add to your knowledge?

    All new material   10   5   0   No new material

3. How much will this course prepare you for achieving your career goals?

    Not at all   0   5   10   Very much

4. How was the training time used?

    Much time wasted   0   5   Efficiently   5   10 Too much material for allotted time

5. How would you rate the presentation of the material?

    Very disorganized   0   5   10   Highly professional

6. Did instructor(s) seem to be knowledgeable of subject matter?

    Clearly inadequate   0   5   10   Obviously an authority

7. To what extent did the course meet your expectations?

    In every respect   10   5   0   In no respect

8. What important topics were left out of the course?

    _____

    _____

9. Additional comments: _____

    _____

Would you recommend future participation by company? _____

Which departments or employees would benefit most from this program? _____

_____

_____   _____

     Employee Number   Employee Name

_____

Supervisor Verification of Training

(Outside Schools Only)

sentation do not necessarily indicate learning. Training content can be fascinating and contribute little to job performance, and trainers can be entertaining but ineffective.

In spite of their limitations, trainee reactions can help to revise a training program. They provide detail about what was taught, how, and by whom and can suggest making content and presentation changes before the training is repeated. Evaluation forms are most often completed immediately after training, but follow-up evaluations several months after can add information that may be more indicative of learning and actual changes in performance.

Learning

The second kind of evidence of training effectiveness is learning. Evidence of learning can be collected in a relatively objective way by measuring knowledge and skill *before* and *after* training and noting the increase. In many cases, pre-training information can be routinely collected during the diagnostic person analysis, which identifies the level of knowledge and skill of employees eligible for the training and aids in the selection of those to be trained. Testing employees' knowledge and skill after training provides a measure of learning.

Learning can be measured with tests or with actual demonstrations of knowledge and skill. A line manager training employees on the job often tests learning by asking specific questions or reviewing work assignments. Training programs designed to build skills frequently include several exercises during the training. A good example is Tenneco's program on effective presentation for managers and executives, in which all trainees make seven speeches during a three-day program and receive feedback and coaching after each. A comparison of the videotapes of the last and first speeches provides a graphic illustration of learning.

Behavior

Learning is of little use to the organization if it is not applied. Changes in job behavior, the third kind of evidence of training effectiveness, are too often overlooked. While organizations rarely overhaul machinery without checking its subsequent performance, they often invest hundreds of thousands of dollars to train employees without checking their subsequent performance.

Translating learning into performance is a major challenge for the trainee. It is easier to pass a test or incorporate new skills into a role-playing case than it is to apply new knowledge and skill on the job. Several conditions can facilitate changes in behavior after training:

1. *Employee motivation*. As we have already noted, motivation during training is necessary for learning. But after the challenge and excitement

of training have passed, the motivation to try new knowledge and skill back on the job is essential for behavioral changes. To change job performance, employees must want to improve by applying what they learned in training.

2. *Recognition of weaknesses.* Employees need to know *how* to change their behavior. They must know what they are doing right and wrong on the job before they can make appropriate changes.

3. *Opportunity to experiment.* Employees must have an opportunity to try out new knowledge and skills in the work situation. First, the job must provide opportunities to apply what has been learned. Obviously, a training program on accounting procedures will have no immediate impact on the job performance of employees whose jobs do not involve accounting. Similarly, the behavioral changes stimulated by training must be consistent with the goals and climate of the trainee's department and organization. Newly learned behaviors that conflict with the behavioral norms of the organization will be quickly unlearned. As a result, there will be no evidence of changes in job performance.

4. *Supportive feedback.* Employees must have feedback from supportive and knowledgeable supervisors and colleagues in order to change job performance. Feedback and coaching enhances the likelihood that new knowledge and skills will be put into practice.

If these four conditions are met, the likelihood that training will lead to changes in behavior is high. But the only convincing evidence that training has changed behavior is provided by measuring job performance before and after the training. The measurement of changes in on-the-job behavior is usually done through observation. Employees can use self-reports to record changes in their job performance. For example, supervisors trained in how to delegate work might keep track of assignments given to their employees and the amount of detailed technical work they still take on themselves. Superiors, peers, and subordinates may also observe and record changes in trainees' job performance. For example, does the boss who recently completed meeting effectiveness training behave any differently in meetings? These observations can then be passed on to human resource professionals formally evaluating the training.

Results

Results are the ultimate evidence of training effectiveness. Did training affect sales, dollar volume, absenteeism, turnover, or productivity? Did training in selection interviewing result in higher acceptance rates and lower failure rates for new employees? Did technical training lead to reductions in waste and failures in quality control? Did training in employee motivation decrease employee turnover? To measure the impact of training on results, it is necessary to record results before and after the training has occurred.

EXHIBIT 12.4 **EVALUATION OF TRAINING EFFECTIVENESS**

Evidence	Measure	Example
Reaction	Questionnaire	Specific questions on the quality of instruction and usefulness of the material
Learning	Knowledge	Theory X and Y styles of management
		Contingency theory of leadership
	Skill	Ability to diagnose the supervisory situation
		Ability to adjust supervisory style to the situation
Behavior	Supervisory style	Degree of consultation with staff
		Amount of delegation
		Flexibility in supervising staff
Results	Employee satisfaction	Number of absences and tardinesses
		Employee complaints
		Employee turnover
	Employee performance	Group productivity
		Quality of work

A Final Note on Training Evaluation

To summarize, most organizations have no formal procedures to evaluate training effectiveness, and those that do frequently rely on questionnaire measures of employee reactions. To document the impact of training more conclusively, organizations must gather additional evidence of learning, behavior, or results.

Our initial analysis of training needs listed five questions to be answered. If the fifth question—How are the results of training to be evaluated?—is raised at the outset, a giant step can be taken toward improved evaluation of training effectiveness. The first step is to choose the kind of evidence needed to evaluate training—reaction, learning, behavior, or results. Next, the *measure* is chosen. Reactions can be measured with a questionnaire, learning by the amount of knowledge or skill acquired, behavior by appropriate on-the-job performance, and results by the significant organizational result that occurs.

Exhibit 12.4 is an example of a training program designed to teach supervisory effectiveness. Trainees' reactions were gathered by questionnaire after the training. The knowledge and skill taught in the training were selected as measures of learning. Specific on-the-job performance (e.g., consultation and delegation) was the measure of behavior, and the results of the training were measured with indicators of employee satisfaction and performance. In this example *as the training was being planned*, four kinds of evidence were selected to evaluate training effectiveness.

The final decision in planning for training evaluation is to determine when to measure the evidence. If learning, behavior, or results are used,

EXHIBIT 12.5

GUIDELINES FOR TRAINING EVALUATION

	Before Training	Training	After Training
Measure before and after			
Training group	T1	X	T2
Compare with another group			
Training group	T1	X	T2
Control group	T1		T2
Control for learning how to take the test			
Training group 1	T1	X	T2
Control group	T1		T2
Training group 2		X	T2

trainers must decide whom to measure, and when. There are three major guidelines to follow.

Evidence of change in learning, behavior, or results requires that measures be taken *before* and *after* the training. For example, a test administered to supervisors before and after training would demonstrate increased knowledge of theory X and Y styles of management. Similarly, lower employee turnover after training would indicate positive results. What is needed is a plan for training evaluation. In Exhibit 12.5, T1 is the measure taken before training and T2 the measure taken after training. The training is designated as X.

Secondly, changes in the training group should be compared with changes in the same measures for a group that did *not* receive the training. The use of a *control group* is not difficult, but it does require planning. For example, in the person analysis, many employees could be tested for knowledge and skills. Those not selected for training could be tested at the same time as those who completed the training (T2) and could be used as a control group.

The third guideline is to control for learning *how to take the test*. If trainees are tested for knowledge or skill before and after training, two factors can cause a rise in the second test score. Test scores may rise because trainees learned new knowledge or skill during the training. But test scores may also rise because trainees who took the test *before* training became familiar with certain material in the training that they may focus on to score better on the test *after* training.

For example, suppose a group of crusty, authoritarian supervisors answered a questionnaire on participative management style before training. Questions about delegation to employees and participation in decision making in the test might alert them to similar material in the training program.

Hence, they might answer all the questions in the questionnaire differently after the training, primarily because they learned how to take the test. But they might also have no intention of changing their supervisory style.

The possibility of learning how to take the test can be controlled for with a more complex plan for training, outlined under the third guideline in Exhibit 12.5. In addition to a training group and a control group, another training group can be added that is tested *only after training* and thus has no opportunity during training to learn how to take the test.

These three guidelines for training evaluation require some planning but little extra work. Measures of knowledge or skill, behavior, and results should be taken during the analysis of training needs; training evaluation requires that they be taken after training, as well. In addition, we strongly recommend the use of a control group in training evaluation. Relatively little time is required to measure employees who are *not* trained.

Evaluation of training effectiveness needs more attention in nearly all organizations. Employee reactions to training are useful, but more evidence is needed. Evidence of learning, behavior, and results is the ultimate measure of training effectiveness. This evidence can be gathered practically and efficiently.

EEO AND TRAINING

Training, like other major human resource activities discussed in this text, is governed by federal legislation. Since the equal employment opportunity legislation presented in Chapter Five prohibits discrimination in "terms, conditions, and privileges of employment," it applies to all training policies and decisions. Consequently, employers must ensure that training programs do not have an adverse impact on minorities and women.

Avoiding Adverse Impact

Two major policies associated with training may lead to discrimination. The first concerns how employees are chosen to participate in a training program. In practice, many organizations select trainees in highly subjective or arbitrary ways (e.g., through supervisory recommendations or according to which employees volunteer for the training) and may therefore discriminate on the basis of race, color, age, sex, etc. The second policy concerns the use of successful completion of training as a *prerequisite* for a specific job (e.g., all clerk typists must successfully complete a training course in word processing and shorthand before they can be promoted to the job of secretary). This policy establishes the training program as a selection tool (Chapter Nine). Since training enhances employees' knowledge and skills, it often qualifies them for promotions. But if the most successful employees in a training program, and therefore the most likely to be promoted, are predominantly white males, the training has an adverse impact on women and minorities.

One way employers can reduce the occurrence of these forms of discrimination is to prepare training programs according to the principles presented earlier in this chapter (see Exhibit 12.1). The key is to make the policies and decisions mentioned above clearly *job-related*. The choice of trainees should be based on a complete analysis of training needs, especially the summary person analysis and diagnostic person analysis. These analyses identify the employees whose current levels of job performance, knowledge, and skill indicate they need the training most or are most likely to benefit from it. Using the successful completion of training as a selection tool should be based on a thorough job analysis, and accurate job descriptions and job specifications. The training can then be designed to teach the specific knowledge and skills needed to perform the job successfully. Evidence of the similarity of the knowledge and skills taught during training and the knowledge and skills required for successful job performance demonstrates the *relevance* of the selection tool (Chapter Nine).

To demonstrate empirically that a training program does not discriminate against women and minorities, the *validity* of the training program must be computed. Remember that a selection tool that screens out a disproportionate percentage of individuals in a protected class is not necessarily discriminatory *if it is related to job performance* (Chapter Nine). Therefore in organizations where employees must successfully complete a training program to be promoted, human resource professionals should compute the statistical relationship between measures of success in training and subsequent job performance.

Affirmative Action

As we noted in Chapters Eight and Nine, many organizations routinely take affirmative action to enhance the employment opportunities of women and minorities through their recruitment and selection programs. Federal contractors and subcontractors are required to take affirmative action, and many other organizations do so voluntarily. The training process provides an excellent means for employers to promote and retain female and minority employees, and many court decisions have required organizations guilty of discrimination to make special efforts to train members of protected groups (see the historic settlement between the EEOC and General Motors in Chapter Five).

Affirmative action is appropriate when the proportion of women and minorities in a particular job is less than the proportion of potential female and minority employees available in the labor market. For example, if only 2 percent of a company's sales force is black, compared with a labor supply that is 5 percent black, the employer can take affirmative action by qualifying more blacks for the job of salesperson through a sales training course.

To take affirmative action through training, an organization must amend the two training policies discussed above. First, the employer may increase the number of women and minorities selected to participate in the training. This policy reduces the number of white males who can receive training, and it can be argued that the employer is now discriminating against white males. Brian Weber, a white laboratory analyst, brought charges of "reverse discrimination" against Kaiser Aluminum and Chemical Corporation and the United Steelworkers of America in 1974 because he was denied admission to a company training program that would qualify him for a promotion. The company and union had included this training program in an affirmative action plan to promote more minority employees into skilled jobs held primarily by whites and had adopted a policy of admitting one minority employee for each white employee who was admitted. Consequently, a black employee with less seniority than Weber was accepted into the program, while Weber was rejected. In 1978 the Supreme Court made a historic ruling against Weber although the court admitted that the training program favored black employees. This decision endorses voluntary affirmative action training programs designed to correct racial imbalance in jobs.

The second policy that may be amended to promote affirmative action is the use of successful completion of a training program as a selection tool. As we noted earlier, an organization is not necessarily guilty of discrimination if it uses a *valid* selection tool to screen out a disproportionate percentage of women and minorities. But if members of protected groups consistently perform poorly in training and therefore fail to qualify for promotion, it is in the organization's best interests to redesign the training program. Wexley and Latham cite examples in which women and minorities had difficulty completing training programs successfully because the training materials had been designed for white males.[23] The companies took affirmative action by altering the training materials. For example, a chemical company lowered the reading difficulty of its training manuals (which had been more difficult to read than on-the-job materials) to accommodate Hispanic trainees, and AT&T redesigned its pole-climbing gear so female trainees could use it successfully. Through affirmative action in training, both employers effectively met their needs for qualified employees. If these types of revisions can make training less difficult for members of protected groups *without lowering their subsequent job performance below acceptable standards*, both the organization and the trainees benefit.

KEY POINTS

▬ Training is a method through which human resource professionals and line managers ensure an optimal fit between employees, jobs, and the organization by enhancing employees' job-related knowledge and skills to improve their performance and further organizational goals.

▬ To ensure training effectiveness, the need for training must be established through the careful analysis of the organization, job, and employee. Only then can training be properly designed and implemented.

▬ Training programs can best be designed by analyzing the tasks of a given job, setting training objectives, choosing the material to be learned, and selecting the best methods for presenting the material.

There are many ways to conduct training programs, and each has its strengths and weaknesses. The success of any training method is dependent on the trainer, the training content, and the trainees.

Since training is so rarely evaluated, the majority of organizations have no evidence of the effectiveness of costly training programs. The benefits of training can be demonstrated only through evidence of employee reactions, or changes in learning, behavior, or results.

Equal employment opportunity legislation governs the way employees are chosen to participate in training programs and the actions taken after employees have completed training. Training is often used by organizations to meet affirmative action goals.

ISSUES FOR DISCUSSION

1. The university course you are currently taking is comparable to a training program. Evaluate it in terms of whether it meets the four requirements for effective training, the teaching methods used, and the evidence gathered to demonstrate teaching effectiveness.

2. Imagine yourself as the new vice-president of human resources in an organization that has a long history of conducting training programs without analyzing training needs or evaluating training effectiveness. What steps would you take to make training more effective in the organization?

3. Think of an informal or a formal training experience in which you have been involved as either trainer or trainee. What specific factors contributed to its effectiveness or ineffectiveness?

4. Suppose the training department of your organization wanted to include twenty of your employees in a week-long training program that you thought was a useless fad. How would you convince the training department to exclude your employees?

5. What training policies may lead to violations of EEO legislation? How can policies be established to avoid adverse impact against protected groups?

6. How can training be used to achieve affirmative action goals? Do you think the Supreme Court decision on the Weber case was fair to minorities? To white males? Why?

NOTES

1. Based on a real organization with a disguised name.

2. Adapted from K. N. Wexley and G. P. Latham, *Developing and Training Human Resources in Organizations* (Glenview, Ill.: Scott, Foresman, 1981), p. 3.

3. E. B. Fiske, "Booming Corporate Education Efforts Rival College Programs, Study Says," *New York Times*, January 28, 1985, A10.

4. H. Z. Levine, "Consensus: Employee Training Programs," *Personnel*, 1981, 58(4), pp. 4–11; ASTD National Report, Business Poll on Education/Training, November 28, 1983, p. 3.

5. *Wall Street Journal*, February 2, 1982, p. 1.

6.   J. Main, "The Executive Yearn to Learn," *Fortune*, May 3, 1982, 234–48.

7.   W. McGehee and P. W. Thayer, *Training in Business and Industry* (New York: Wiley, 1961), pp. 22–23.

8.   Ibid.

9.   Ibid, p. 33.

10.   M. L. Moore and P. Dutton, "Training Needs Analysis: Review and Critique," *Academy of Management Review*, 1978, 3(3), 532–45.

11.   See E. J. McCormick, "Job and Task Analysis," in M. D. Dunnette (Ed.), *Handbook of Industrial and Organizational Psychology* (Chicago: Rand McNally, 1976).

12.   E. J. McCormick, P. R. Jeanneret, and R. C. Mecham, "A Study of Job Characteristics and Job Dimensions as Based on the Position Analysis Questionnaire (PAQ)," *Journal of Applied Psychology*, 1972, *56*, pp. 347–68.

13.   McGehee and Thayer, 1961.

14.   K. N. Wexley and G. P. Latham, p. 77.

15.   D. Fast, "A New Approach to Quantifying Training Program Effectiveness," *Training and Development Journal*, 1974, 28(9), pp. 8–14.

16.   K. N. Wexley and G. P. Latham, p. 77.

17.   Ibid, p. 61.

18.   This is a brief summary of the strengths and weaknesses of various training methods. For more information, see I. L. Goldstein, *Training: Program Development and Evaluation* (Monterey, Calif.: Brooks/Cole, 1974); and Wexley and Latham, 1981.

19.   S. J. Carroll, Jr., F. T. Paine, and J. J. Ivancevich, "The Relative Effectiveness of Training Methods—Expert Opinion and Research," *Personnel Psychology*, 1972, *25*, pp. 495–510.

20.   Wexley and Latham, 1981, p. 137.

21.   W. H. Wagel, "Consensus: Evaluating Management Development and Training Programs," *Personnel*, 1977, *54*(4), pp. 4–10.

22.   D. L. Kirkpatrick, "Techniques for Evaluating Training Programs," *Journal of the American Society of Training Directors*, 1959, *13*, pp. 3–9, 21–26; 1960, *14*, pp. 13–18, 28–32.

23.   K. N. Wexley and G. P. Latham, pp. 24 and 25.

ANNOTATED BIBLIOGRAPHY

MCGEHEE, W. and THAYER, P. W. *Training in Business and Industry*. New York: Wiley, 1961.

     This classic text was written by two practitioners for those who have staff responsibilities for training as well as managers who instruct and guide their employees. The authors view training as a management tool that requires careful planning, design, and implementation. They emphasize the necessity of organization, task, and person analysis to establish the need for training and the importance of incorporating learning principles into training. They also describe and evaluate various training methods and present techniques to evaluate training effectiveness.

Training and Development Journal

Published monthly by the American Society for Training and Development (ASTD) this journal is an excellent source of current developments in training, career development, and related topics. Both academic researchers and practitioners contribute to the journal. Each issue also contains book reviews and descriptions of new training tools. ASTD is an educational society for persons engaged in the training and development of business, industry, education, and government personnel. It serves more than 23,000 members and is divided into seven regional associations, which hold annual conventions, as well as 132 local groups, many of which meet monthly. ASTD holds annual conventions, conducts annual institutes for training professionals, compiles statistics, and operates a member inquiry service. It also publishes many books and journals.

WEXLEY, K. N. and LATHAM, G. P. *Developing and Training Human Resources in Organizations*. Glenview, Ill.: Scott, Foresman, 1981.

This book provides practical and comprehensive coverage of training, with special emphasis on training methods. It begins with a discussion of the training director's job, the identification of training needs, and the conditions for maximizing learning. It describes and evaluates several types of on-site and off-site training methods and approaches to management development. Also included are techniques for measuring training effectiveness.

CHAPTER THIRTEEN

CAREER DEVELOPMENT PROCESSES

As the drinks were being served on the plane bound for Phoenix, the controller for the manufacturing department of one of the largest computer companies in the United States began to talk with the passenger in the next seat about the purpose of his trip.

"I have to decide whether to let the plant marketing and finance managers in Phoenix switch jobs," he explained. "Neither of them wants to leave Phoenix, and the plant manager wants to make the lateral move so he can develop the two of them. They are both very excited about the idea; in fact, it was originally their idea, and they sold it to the plant manager.

"I can't count on the corporate personnel department for help on this one. They have enough trouble just getting the pay checks out! If I need help, I'll talk to the plant personnel manager. He knows them both and can give me a good reading. I'll also talk to the subordinates in each area, to assess the competence and credibility of each person. I also want to see how the subordinates' motivation will be affected by bringing in a new boss from outside their function. What effect do they think this would have on their own career opportunities? My hope is that we will be making more of these developmental cross-functional moves in the future and that the subordinates will see this kind of move opening up more options for them, too.

"In fact, I just went through a cross-functional move myself. Three months ago I moved from the marketing department to manufacturing. I see it as a good opportunity to grow and learn another angle of the business. I hope that when our CEO wakes up to the need for a divisionalized structure, I'll be ready to be a division general manager. A big percentage of my time is spent learning, not really performing. I'm just hoping nothing major comes up for a while so I don't really screw up!"

The sentiments of this controller reflect several important characteristics of organizational careers today. First, managers, not human resource professionals, often make staffing decisions (like this one) which have major impacts on employees' careers. Human resource managers might advise, but the final decision is often the manager's. Managers must be able to assess both the employee's ability to perform in a new job and the developmental value of these moves. Managers must also consider the career concerns of subordinates.

More and more, managers can see the career-enhancing importance of job assignments, particularly in new functional areas, which stretch the employee to develop new skills. And, finally, managers are also concerned about their own careers. Many have just recently gone through a major transition themselves when they are required to make important decisions that affect subordinates' careers.

Career development is a major concern of employees in contemporary organizations. Concerns about future advancement are especially strong in organizations experiencing slow growth and large numbers of established employees entering midcareer (i.e., members of the "baby boom" generation).

Even Snoopy, of "Peanuts" fame, shares those concerns. In one recent strip, he complained, "Yesterday I was a dog. Today I'm a dog. Tomorrow I'll probably be a dog. There's just so little hope for advancement."

Perhaps there isn't much hope for Snoopy, but there is cause for optimism in the case of the controller and the managers in his organization. In many organizations the career development of employees has become a pressing personnel problem, and career development programs are springing up everywhere. In this chapter we will examine some basic concepts and issues associated with career development—why careers are important, what a career is, how people make career decisions, and how careers develop. In the following chapter we will examine career development programs and practices in work organizations.

WHAT IS A CAREER?

The term "career" has multiple meanings. To some people, career denotes *advancement*. By this definition, jobs offering little chance for advancement would not be careers. A less common way to view careers is to associate them with *certain occupations* (especially the professions). Thus, higher status occupations are careers, while lower status occupations are merely jobs. A sociological view considers a career as a *lifelong sequence of jobs*, regardless of occupation or job level. The broadest definition is *career as life*. Organizations which use this definition sometimes allow employees to participate in life planning exercises, which deal with family, community, and personal planning, as well as one's work activities.

Combining some of these approaches leads to the following definition of career: A **career** is *an individually perceived sequence of attitudes and behaviors associated with work experiences and activities over the span of the person's life.*[1] Like the career-as-life approach, our definition deals with life histories and processes, but only as they relate to work. "Attitudes and behavior," include both the subjective and objective (job history) aspects of the career. We assume nothing about what is "up" or "down" for a given person and nothing about the type of work in which the person is engaged.

career

CAREER ROLES AND IDENTITIES

Perhaps the most obvious career development changes occur in the person's occupational skills, attitudes, goals, and plans. However, at a more fundamental level the most important changes in career development involve the person's sense of *identity*, the person's sense of who one is and how one fits into the social environment.

There are two important aspects of identity. The first is the person's awareness of those qualities which make him or her a unique human being: values, interests, abilities, and so forth. The clearer and more integrated (or consistent) this self-awareness is, the clearer the person's identity is.

A second aspect is the fit between one's past, present, and future selves. Because people constantly change (and hopefully develop), they often feel like different people at different stages of their lives. One's self-concept may be quite different from one's sense of who one was five or ten years ago; a strong identity does *not* require remaining the same person over time. However, a person needs to see some relationship between the "old self" and the "new self."

One's sense of identity, then, is a measure of the wholeness of one's life. It is a self-concept which indicates how the parts of a person's life fit together in the present, and how the present is linked to the past and the future.

THE CAREER DEVELOPMENT PROCESS

A major task for the person and the organization is to achieve a fit between the person and the occupational role. People's needs can change to become more (or less) compatible with the opportunities for satisfaction in their jobs. Similarly, interests and personal orientations can also change over the course

THE PSYCHOLOGICAL SUCCESS MODEL
OF CAREER DEVELOPMENT

EXHIBIT 13.1

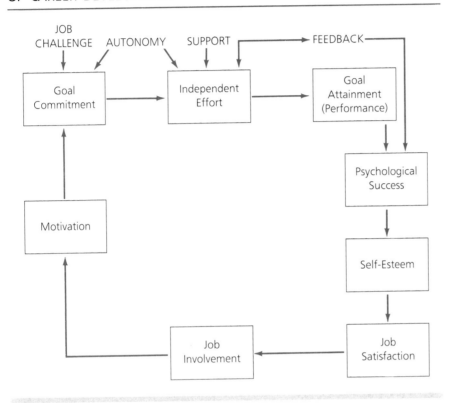

SOURCE: Reprinted from D. T. Hall, *Careers in Organizations* (Glenview, Ill.: Scott, Foresman and Company, 1976), p. 126.

of a forty-five-year career. People can become more or less identified with and involved in an occupation. What influences these changes in the person's career orientation and makes the person more or less involved in a career? In this section we will explore possible answers to this question.

Psychological Success

As careers develop changes occur in the way people relate to their jobs and in their attitudes toward work. The process by which involvement increases is summarized in Exhibit 13.1.[2]

Generally when people work on a task, they do so in response to certain *plans, intentions,* or *goals.* Often these goals are not very explicit, and the person may not even think of them as goals—e.g., "Now I am going to start drilling holes on my drill press." But usually the person does have some intention or "plan of attack" when doing a job.

The amount of challenge necessary to meet these goals affects the amount of *effort* the person will expend on the task.[3] And autonomy is necessary so that the person sees success as coming from his or her independent efforts. In addition, the clarity of the goal will have an important relationship to effort. The more effort put forth, assuming the person has the necessary ability and support to guide those efforts, where necessary, the better *performance* will be.

psychological success

Performing well and achieving a challenging goal provide the person with a feeling of intrinsic satisfaction or **psychological success,** *a sense of personal accomplishment and fulfillment.* This feeling is enhanced if *feedback* on performance is received from the boss, peers, or the task itself. Feedback is important because in many jobs performance is hard to measure objectively. Therefore, to assess one's own performance accurately, it helps to have external feedback to confirm (or disconfirm) one's own perceptions.

Psychological success is satisfying because it represents the enhancement of one's present skills or competencies, or the development of new, previously unexplored skill areas. It is associated with identity growth, which increases the person's self-esteem—something all people crave. It tends to increase *involvement* in the work which led to the success experience. This, in turn, may lead to the pursuit of *further goals*, perhaps on a higher level.

For example, more successful young managers tend to become more involved in their careers over a five- to seven-year period, while less successful managers maintain the same level of involvement. School children tend to become more involved in work activities in which they experience success, and business students become more involved (and set higher goals) in management simulations in which they achieve higher performance levels. Simply put, the success cycle is a process by which "success breeds success." And research has shown that this experience of psychological success is even more important than salary levels (e.g., earning one's age, i.e., $30,000 at age 30) as an overall measure of career success.[4]

Career Stages

career stage

A career usually unfolds in phases or *stages.* **A career stage** is *a period marked by relative similarity of career experiences which is set apart from other periods in the career by role transitions, crises, or other turning points.* Career stages are influenced by personal development processes, organizational career patterns, family development, physical aging, and social aspects of aging. A graph representing the net effect of all these influences is shown in Exhibit 13.2.

The first phase of the career is *exploration.* This starts in childhood, with fantasy exploration of a wide range of occupations (e.g., the five-year-old trying to decide whether to become Batman or a fireman). Later, options become more realistic. During the period of realistic exploration the person grapples with issues of personal identity—what are my capabilities and values, what do I want to do with my life, etc.? Levinson et al. indicate that the central developmental task during exploration is to make the transition from

STAGES IN CAREER DEVELOPMENT

EXHIBIT 13.2

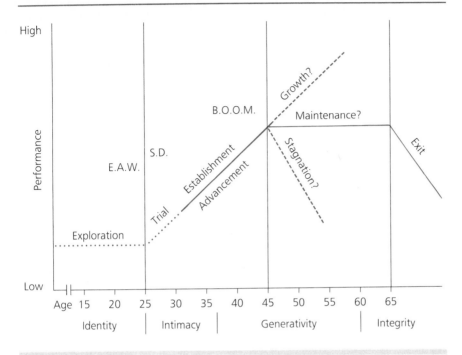

SOURCE: Adapted from D. T. Hall, *Careers in Organizations* (Glenview, Ill.: Scott, Foresman, 1976), p. 57.

home and parents to the work world, or "Entering the Adult World" (E.A.W.).[5]

After exploration, the next stage is a *trial* work period. This may be a series of jobs and employers in which attempts are made through trial and error to find a good fit between the person's own identity and a work role.[6] The main developmental task here is "settling down," according to Levinson et al.[7] The outcome being sought is intimacy.[8] Intimacy means becoming involved and forming attachments, not just on the interpersonal level, but also in a work role.

After the person has gone through a trial period and found a niche, the next stage is *establishment and advancement* in the chosen work role. Once the person is *in* a field, the developmental task is to move *up*. This is a time to become independent from sponsors or mentors, and to become one's own man (B.O.O.M., according to Levinson et al.).[9] At this time the workings of the psychological success cycle and great increases in work involvement may be most evident.

Around the 40s the person reaches midlife and *midcareer*. Physical aging becomes apparent, children grow up, organizational advancement slows down, and many people enter a 15- or 20-year midcareer plateau. Super calls this a period of maintenance, when work continues at a competent level, but no new ground is broken.[10] For some people this is a time of questioning ("Do I want to do this same thing for the next twenty years?" "Is this all there is?") Some people switch jobs or occupations, some go back to school, and some make major changes in lifestyle. A marriage counselor once remarked, "Between the ages of 40 and 50 people either change jobs or spouses." For some this is a period to explore new areas and to grow personally. Even the underworld has its midcareer transitions, as indicated in Box 13.1.

For others, midcareer can bring organizational security with the opportunity to become less involved in work, and perhaps to allow performance to slip (stagnation). (A professor once commented, "We have a term for this in universities: we call it tenure.")

In midlife the person's main developmental need is to achieve a sense of generativity: to produce something of true value to leave behind for future generations. The concern is not just achievement, but accomplishment of something *worthwhile* to other people, to leave one's mark on the world, thereby achieving a form of immortality.

The final stage of the work career is *exit*, the decrease in one's involvement in the work role and the re-investment of oneself in other areas of activity—a second career (or third or fourth), a retirement community, volunteer organizations, more family activities, etc. This may not be just an ending, but also a beginning of another cycle of trial, establishment, etc., in one's next life stage. Erikson views this stage as one where the person strives for a sense of *integrity*, comes to terms with one's one and only life cycle and values it as a pretty good life, all things considered.[11]

Alternative Career Patterns

Obviously, not all people stay in one occupation and go through such a neat progression of stages. People often change fields and go through several cycles of exploration, trial, and establishment. Some people never hit a plateau, and some never really hit a decline, or they decline far later than age 65.

Some of the variations on these traditional career stages are shown in Exhibit 13.3. For purposes of comparison, the traditional pattern is shown in simplified form in graph 1. A "fast-track" version of the traditional model is shown in graph 2, "the American dream." (This person also is termed a "water walker," "five-percenter," etc.) The problem with the fast track is that there are relatively few people in such careers (as organizations have eliminated layers of management and slowed down career advancement), but many people still see the fast track as society's ideal (but not necessarily their own). It has become the standard of comparison, against which very few people compare favorably. Consequently, most people feel like relative failures when judged against such an unrealistic standard. And, furthermore, in view of the new work values reported in Chapter Three, the fast track is not the personal ideal for many employees; they just feel that social norms value it highly. Thus, many people feel trapped competing against a fast-track standard which is often impossible to attain, and which they do not personally value.

BOX 13.1

MIDCAREER TRANSITION
IN THE UNDERWORLD

Nearly half the men who begin criminal careers in their youth drop out of crime by the time they reach the age of 40, a Justice Department survey showed yesterday.

The study, based on questioning 843 male prisoners over the age of 40 in 1979, found 47 percent were in prison for the first time, and nearly two-thirds had at some point participated in an alcohol abuse program.

It is said there are more than 274,000 male criminals over age 40 in state prisons.

Two-thirds of those questioned were imprisoned for violent crimes: murder, manslaughter, and rape. Few were repeat offenders. About 10 percent had been imprisoned before, during middle age, at the time of their interview the survey said.

The study, conducted by the department's Bureau of Justice Statistics, was entitled "Career Patterns in Crime."

Patrick Langan, one of two bureau statisticians who wrote the study, said the men who dropped out of criminal life earliest were least likely to return. Only 1 percent of the over-40 prisoners had been jailed in adolescence.

He said 92 percent of those who committed crimes in adolescence continue their criminal career into young adulthood, but only 14 percent are chronic offenders who continue to enter prison in middle age.

The high dropout rate, he said, may mean "there is a long-term deterrence effect associated with punishment." He said middle-aged criminals in another study had said the criminal justice system had "worn them down."

The study said the typical middle-aged prisoner had "had repeated difficulties" in life. Almost 41 percent had little education; 26 percent had at least one family member who had also been imprisoned; and more than 22 percent were unemployed at the time of their imprisonment offense.

Adaptation of "Many Careers in Crime Said to End by 40" from Boston Globe, July 25, 1983. Reprinted with permission of United Press International, Inc.

EXHIBIT 13.3 ## ALTERNATIVE CAREER PATH MODELS

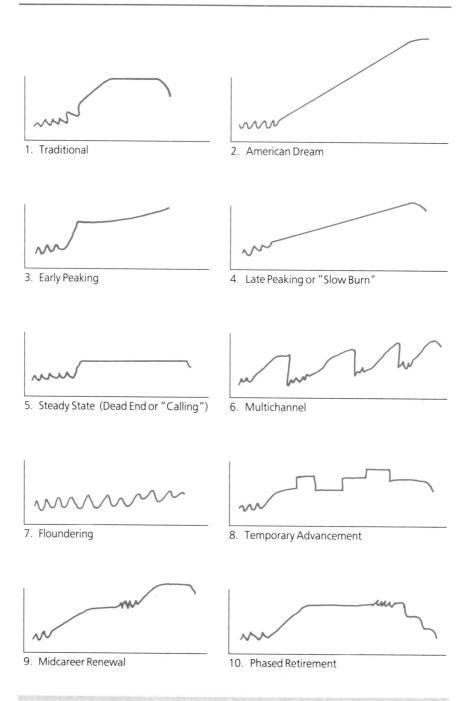

1. Traditional

2. American Dream

3. Early Peaking

4. Late Peaking or "Slow Burn"

5. Steady State (Dead End or "Calling")

6. Multichannel

7. Floundering

8. Temporary Advancement

9. Midcareer Renewal

10. Phased Retirement

SOURCE: D. T. Hall, "Alternate Career Paths," Working Paper, Boston University, 1985.

Because organizations have "bought" the idea of this fast track (and, as we saw in Chapter Four, a value for rapid early promotion characterizes U.S. business, compared to Japanese firms), many organizations do try to promote people quickly in their first few years on the job. However, because there are relatively few higher-level positions open, the fast track often ends abruptly after three to five years. The result is early peaking (graph 3). People are now becoming plateaued in their 30s instead of 40s or 50s.

One alternative to the fast track is the slow-burn career (graph 4), which is more characteristic of the Japanese system. The human resource development strategy here is to use more lateral movement and to leave people in positions longer so they develop social networks and technical expertise. People are moved up gradually to the ultimate attainment level, with the final promotion coming, say, in their late 50s, rather than 30s. If this rate of promotion becomes the norm, no one will feel like a failure. A study of the career patterns of store managers at Sears, Roebuck found that opportunities for growth through lateral or even downward moves can be built into job progressions through careful use of job analysis.[12]

Another career path which is coming back into style is the "steady state" (graph 5) career.[13] Here the person stays in one role for most of the career (for example, an engineer or salesperson). Being stuck in a dead-end position can result in such a lifelong career experience. The other possibility is that the work is truly loved and seen by the person as a true vocation or "calling." This was the case in a study of Roman Catholic priests.[14] Their calling was to be a priest, not to "advance" to be a bishop or cardinal. The career was the role of priest. Similarly, many professionals want simply to be engineers or lawyers or dentists or teachers. One important task of human resource development is to find ways to legitimize and reward people who aspire to a steady-state career. This will be an important step toward progress in dealing with career plateauing.

In the multichannel pattern (graph 6) the person makes fundamental career shifts from time to time. Michael Driver calls this type of person a "spiral," one who becomes bored after five to ten years in a particular career area, and moves on to something different.[15] The term "spiral" suggests the person is in a continual psychological success growth cycle and moving up to greater levels of competence.

A less fortunate outcome is the person who never really gets established in any one area and keeps floundering (graph 7). Such a person might always be job-hopping or be periodically unemployed. From a more positive view, the person may have made personal life the number one priority and works only as long and as often as necessary to provide money to support a preferred life-style.

The temporary advancement (graph 8) pattern is being seen more often as an antidote for the "Peter Principle" (people rising to their level of incompetence and staying there) and for career plateauing. In this pattern, a person is given a *temporary promotion*, say to department manager, for a fixed period of time, say three years. Then the person moves back to his or her previous position. The Lawrence Livermore Laboratory in Livermore, California, effectively uses this method to staff management positions in some areas, with good results. An excellent opportunity to retrain exists after the move back, since the person could not be expected to keep pace with technological developments while in the manager's role. Bell Telephone Laboratories also uses this process in certain areas, since it is the only way some of its professionals will accept a managerial position. Another model is universities, which routinely rotate professors in and out of department chair and dean positions.

Midcareer renewal (graph 9) is increasing as organizations do more career retraining, career management, and lateral, cross-functional movement. When put into an assignment which demands new skills, the person is forced to grow. This growth of skills often leads to new career self-identity and involvement. This process returns the person to the psychological success cycle in midcareer.

For example, one human resource specialist in the same personnel researcher job for twenty years, was bored, frustrated, and plateaued. When the organization introduced a quality of work life program, he was given major responsibility for the effort. The program literally saved the company from bankruptcy. The specialist went from research technician to highly respected, skilled internal change agent, at age 53. In the words of one colleague, "He's become a new man."

The final variation is a process of gradual or phased retirement (graph 10) which more organizations are using to help people adjust to their withdrawal from the organization. One way to phase withdrawal is to let people take longer vacations or unpaid leaves of absence later in the career. These periods of time away can be used to explore second careers or retirement living. Some organizations give people one more week of vacation time after a certain age (say, 60) to force them to learn to manage personal time better. Other firms let technical people "buy off" their time to try doing outside consulting, to start up their own business, or to explore other options. Other firms offer early retirement in the mid-fifties, often with outplacement assistance, which usually leads to a second career or to part-time employment, in which the person is essentially semi-retired. Thus the drastic shock caused by a sudden shift from being employed to not being employed is avoided. Since work is the major element in the personal identity of most people, as we saw earlier, it is helpful to make the withdrawal from the organization an orderly, planned process so that there is a sense of meaning and purpose in the person's next role.

THE MANAGER'S ROLE: MENTORING AND OTHER DEVELOPMENTAL RELATIONSHIPS

As we saw in the discussion of career stages, the developmental needs and strengths of the young person in the trial or establishment stages of a career are quite different from those of someone (such as the person's manager) in midcareer. Not only are the career needs and resources of these two stages

EARLY-CAREER AND MIDCAREER NEEDS AND RESOURCES

EXHIBIT 13.4

Early Career Employee		Midcareer Employee	
Resources	Needs	Resources	Needs
Cutting-edge technical knowledge			To keep up with cutting-edge technical knowledge
Energy, enthusiasm, motivation			To maintain energy, enthusiasm, motivation
Fresh outlook, openness to new ideas, desire to innovate			To avoid tendency to resist change
Optimism	To overcome naivete	Realism	To avoid cynicism
	To obtain assistance in becoming established in one's career		To help younger people develop (generativity)
	To attain organizational status and power	Organizational status and power to innovate	
	To learn and develop political skills	Experience and skills in organizational politics	
	To learn to "sell" new ideas	Ability to "sell" ideas	
	To learn patience in creating change	Maturity and patience	

different, but they are *complementary*. And this complementarity of needs is what makes mentoring possible and effective.

The mentor is often the person's manager, although the mentor could be an older peer (or even a subordinate, as in the case of the senior sergeant and the green second lieutenant). For the purposes of our discussion, we will consider the mentor to be an older person in a managerial role.

Complementarity of Career Stage Needs and Resources

In what ways are the developmental needs of the two stages complementary? The manager or other midcareer person has a need for generativity (to help the younger generation develop), which will help satisfy the younger person's need to get established (Exhibit 13.4). The young person possesses the latest technical knowledge; the older person may need updating. The young person may be full of energy and enthusiasm; the older one may have slowed down. The junior colleague may want to innovate, to question why things are done as they are. The midcareer person may want to continue to do things the way they have been done and may resist change.

Although midcareer managers may have less motivation to create change, they have more resources to do so: more organizational power, political skills and experience, greater (learned) ability to sell ideas, and greater maturity and patience. The younger person has a need to learn and attain these qualities. And, the young person may be optimistic and a bit naive in outlook, while the midcareer person may be more realistic and somewhat cynical.

As Exhibit 13.4 shows, the young person tends to have resources which the midcareer person needs, and vice versa. If you put these two people together, wouldn't they make a great team? Putting the early career person and the midcareer person together as a team is what mentoring is all about.

Mentoring Functions

mentoring relationship

As defined by Kathy E. Kram, **mentoring relationship** is *a relationship between a junior and senior colleague that is viewed by the junior as positively contributing to his or her development.*[16] Two types of functions contribute to the development of the junior person.[17] First are a range of *career advancement activities:* sponsorship, coaching, exposure and visibility, protection, and challenging work assignments. All these activities are ways the senior person facilitates the task accomplishments and organizational recognition the young person needs to advance.

A second set of mentoring functions deals more with *personal support* and the development of the junior member's sense of *personal identity:* role modeling, counseling, acceptance and confirmation, and friendship.

When both these sets of functions, the task and the personal, are present, there is a very complete and significant mentor relationship. However, for many people a subset of these functions may be present in a junior-senior developmental relationship. The range of functions which are present in the relationship may depend upon factors such as the individuals' backgrounds, attitudes, skills, occupational structure, organizational culture, formal roles, and physical proximity. And, over the course of a career, a person might have a developmental relationship with several people. In her research, Kram finds that these developmental relationships have a limited duration, they are unavailable to many people who need them, and they can become destructive to one or both parties under certain conditions.[18]

Facilitating Mentoring

If mentoring is usually helpful in the growth of both the junior and senior person, how can these relationships be facilitated? Three conditions are necessary:

1. Opportunities for frequent and open communication between people at different hierarchical levels must exist.
2. Members of the organization must possess necessary *interpersonal skills* to cultivate developmental relationships, and *positive attitudes* toward mentoring.

3. Certain features of the organization must *reward* developmental relationships and view them as essential to achieving organizational objectives: organizational reward system, task design, performance management system, and organizational culture.[19]

To illustrate the last point, if the reward system stresses "bottom line," end results to the exclusion of organizational *processes* such as relationships, mentoring will be seen as a costly distraction for senior people and will be done infrequently. When jobs are "solo" tasks, not done in teams, there is less likelihood of mentoring. If performance management systems, such as performance appraisal, management by objectives (MBO), or career development do not include relationship building or relationship training, and if the corporate culture does not value mentoring, then seniors will lack the incentive and skills to develop juniors. At this point, mentoring becomes one of those "nice to do" activities that never gets done.

Interventions to Promote Mentoring

An organization faces a dilemma in planning interventions to facilitate mentoring. While naturally occurring mentoring can be helpful to both parties, it is difficult to artificially create a good relationship. Some organizations use *educational intervention*, seminars which train managers in the skills of effective mentoring and which encourage them to attempt to become mentors to their subordinates.[20] However, not all managers are interested in mentoring. Also, if the organizational rewards, task design, performance systems, or culture are not compatible with mentoring, the effects of the mentor training will be likely to fade quickly. These educational interventions are most likely to be successful when top management takes the lead in doing and rewarding mentoring.[21]

The other strategy to promote mentoring is what Kram calls *structural intervention* aimed at the reward system, task design, performance management systems, and culture. For example, using as a criterion for promotion the ability to develop subordinates would be a powerful way to reward mentoring. At some development-oriented organizations like IBM and AT&T, managers will not be considered for promotion until they can demonstrate that they have prepared one or more subordinates for promotion. At Sears, Roebuck store managers who are known to be excellent people-developers often are assigned the most promising management trainees. (This not only helps the growth of the younger person but also gives the store manager the best talent for his or her management team, which improves store performance, which improves the manager's salary increases.)

Work experiences can be enhanced by systematically using age composition as a criterion in the selection of personnel for group tasks, such as project or product teams, task forces, and committees. Performance management systems can be modified by adding "subordinate development" to the performance appraisal form or to the MBO system, or by making job assignments in a career development program based in part on who the manager would be.

As a general rule, it is probably easier and more productive to reward and encourage mentoring where it already exists naturally than it is to try to create it where it does not exist. It is fortunate that mentoring is as wide-spread as it is, considering that it is not often rewarded, and it is unfortunate that it is actively discouraged and even punished in some places. If an organization could simply stop discouraging mentoring, these relationships would spread rapidly, because, as was indicated at the beginning of this section, mentoring satisfies important personal needs and is *intrinsically rewarding* to the mentor and to the protege.

WOMEN AND MINORITIES

The processes involved in career development are universal. Influences which facilitate the career growth of one kind of person can also affect the development of a different type of person. Thus, the basic career growth factors for groups which are underrepresented in management and professional positions (especially women and minorities) are not really different from those for majority members (i.e., white men). However, there is ample evidence that underrepresented groups have less access to career-enhancing experiences than do majority members.[22]

For example, mentor-protege relationships enhance career development. However, senior people (usually white men) tend to develop mentor relationships with people similar to themselves (usually white men). Unless minority members go out of their way to cultivate developmental relationships (through networking and the support of the few senior minority people), they will lack this important developmental opportunity. Thus, we see outcomes such as lower salaries and slower advancement for minorities than for whites with comparable training.[23]

As another example, consider the psychological success cycle described earlier. Initial job challenge is critical to career success, but often management does not trust underrepresented groups sufficiently to give them a great deal of responsibility early in their careers.[24] Thus, white men may be given the most challenging jobs, while women may be given staff or "assistant-to" positions. Minority employees may be channeled into "minority positions," such as community relations or affirmative action.

In addition to lacking the challenging goals so necessary for the psychological success process, underrepresented groups are less likely to get the necessary feedback on their performance. It is difficult enough for a superior to give feedback to anyone, but it is much more difficult to do so with a person who is "different" and with whom the supervisor may not feel comfortable.

A major culprit in unequal opportunities is simply the low numbers of women and minority group members. Many of the problems just discussed relate to the issue of being "different." As Rosabeth Kanter shows with her

"Story of O," consider what stands out in the following set of characters:

XXXXOXXXXXX

Obviously, the O stands out, because it is different. And if there were two Os, they would still stand out. Kanter shows that an O can be anyone: a black, a woman, an Asian, a young person, a particular nationality group, a newcomer, etc. Probably everyone has had the experience of being an O at one time or another. And as long as Os exist in small numbers, problems of unequal opportunity will exist.[25]

How do organizations increase the numbers, then, if the low numbers create forces against increased representation? Some of the following activities have been used with positive results:

- *Networking by similar Os.* This is a self-help process in which peers and the few available senior Os create support systems to provide opportunities, feedback, and rewards which might otherwise be lacking.
- *Tailor-made career development programs.* Recognizing that many career-facilitating factors were lacking for Os, many organizations have created special career development programs for underrepresented groups. These entail special recruiting and assessment efforts, training for supervisors, careful tracking of career progress, and rewards for line managers for successful development of Os.
- *Appointment of Os to corporate boards.* While it may take decades to increase the representation of Os in top management, it is quite feasible to make rapid increases in their numbers at the very top, the board of directors, simply by appointing them. While in some cases this can be a token move, where management is sincerely open to change the board can be a critical place to start.
- *General career management programs.* One lesson learned from the last decade of career development and affirmative action programs is that the two are not as different as was once thought. A well-planned career development program will open up more growth opportunities for all employees, both Xs and Os. Similarly, many tailor-made programs for Os have been so successful or visible that Xs began to ask to be included. In many organizations affirmative action has now become an integral part of the main-stream corporate career management program.

PLATEAUING AND MIDCAREER TRANSITIONS

Because of the staffing reductions or slow growth experienced by many organizations in recent years, coupled with great numbers of "baby boom" employees entering midcareer, the problem of midcareer stagnation and plateauing is often a serious one. Employees may be either *personally plateaued* by choice or because they have reached the limits of their potential, or they may be *organizationally plateaued*, with potential for upward mobility but with no promotional opportunities available in the organization.

There are two types of plateaued employee.[26] One is the strong performer who is seen as having little potential for advancement. This person is often called the *solid citizen*. The low-performing, nonpromotable person is often labeled *deadwood*. Performance coaching and/or termination have reduced the incidence of deadwood in many contemporary organizations. Thus, the main issue in plateauing in many organizations is how to provide continuing motivation and growth for the solid citizen.

Many methods can be effective in dealing with plateauing. First, *recognition* for the established performer is critical. This is the number one career deficiency experienced by plateaued employees.[27] *Cross-functional, lateral job moves* are being used to provide novel, stretching experiences, as we saw in the opening case about the controller. *Job redesign* can be a way of adding more challenge and responsibility to the present job. *Temporary moves* and *internal consulting or trouble-shooting assignments* can be ways to both meet real organizational needs and to give the plateaued employee a new experience and an opportunity to utilize valued skills. *Career planning workshops* (see Chapter Fourteen) are an important way for the person to come to terms with being plateaued and to explore possible career changes. *Project type assignments* can also be a powerful way to keep the person involved in always-new task areas, yet provide a sense of task completion and success.[28]

The process of making a midcareer change involves getting out of a "career routine" that often occurs as the person enters the maintenance stage of the career. Many experiences can trigger a change in the career routine: entrenchment (e.g., a plant closing), personal life changes, being in a growth-promoting environment, a job or organization change, having positive role models (such as mentors), not being under immediate performance pressure, or being in a job that requires the acquisition of new skills over time (e.g., project work; see Exhibit 13.5).[29] Personality factors (such as flexibility, independence, dominance, and others) can also lead the person to self-initiate change.

Trigger events can interrupt a career routine and create an awareness of choice for the person; support and feedback can also enhance this awareness of choice. At this point the person begins to explore career opportunities and the present job and career. Career information and coaching can aid this exploration process. Next the person tries some changes; the learning from this trial activity enhances the exploration process. Next the person makes a choice, perhaps very tentatively. This leads to a transition, a change in the person's sense of identity. Transition entails leaving the old role and moving into a new one. The person now begins the process of becoming established in the new role. From this experience with change, the person probably comes to feel more adaptable and has a heightened sense of being the agent (in control) of his or her own career.[30]

EXHIBIT 13.5 FACTORS IN CAREER ROUTINE CHANGE

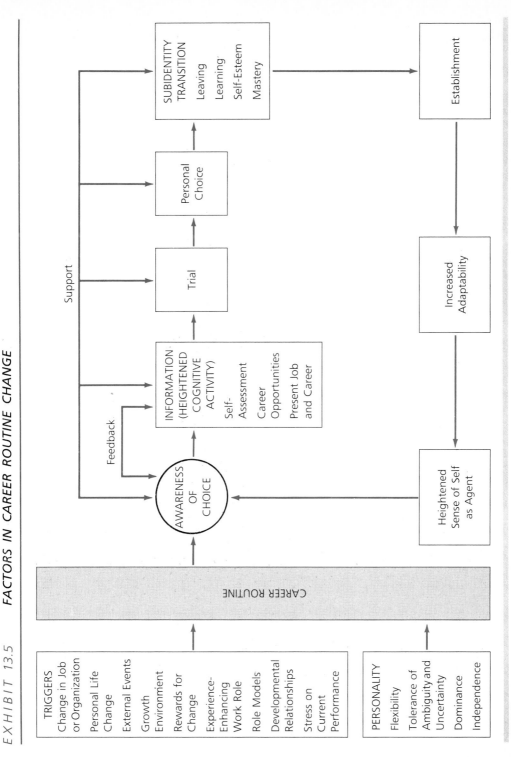

SOURCE: D. T. Hall, "Midcareer Choice and Subidentity Development," in D. T. Hall and Associates, *Career Development in Organizations* (San Francisco: Jossey-Bass, 1986) in press.

TWO-CAREER COUPLES

If it is challenging to manage one career effectively, it is far more difficult to manage two careers, a loving relationship, and possibly a family. This is the situation facing a two-career couple.

Initially the two-career phenomenon was stimulated in part by the woman's desire for fulfillment in a work role outside home, at least for college-educated professional couples. Women in blue-collar and clerical jobs often worked out of economic necessity, but now even professionals are more likely to report that they work out of necessity. It is estimated that by 1990 ninety percent of all married couples will be two-career couples. This is a phenomenon which affects greatly both the couple and the company.

Couples at Different Stages

First, let us consider the different types of two-career couples in the work force. Hall and Hall, in their studies of couples and companies, described several types of couples based upon their career stage: early career and mid-career.[31] The characteristics of these types are summarized in Exhibit 13.6.

Early-Career Couples ▬▬ The first type of couple—frequently encountered—is in the *trial stage*. Both parties have just started their careers. The big issue here is to find two good jobs in the same geographic area. Often one might have to sacrifice job quality to accommodate the other. (Unfortunately, even in the era of supposed equality, it is still the woman who is most likely to do the accommodating.)

The second type·is the young couple on the way up, in the *establishment and advancement stage*. Here the most common issue is how can each accept the necessary geographic job moves and promotions and still live with the partner? This is the point at which the employing organization really begins to worry about two-career issues. Issues of *whether or when to start a family* are salient at this point, as well. This is another issue with major implications for employers, as evidenced by the incidence of corporate child care assistance activities.

There are several common characteristics of couples at this early stage. They tend to have the same career needs—challenging jobs, job movement, recognition, and a need to establish themselves. Their best career opportunities may take them in opposite directions, and their career commitment is extremely high. They are relatively naive about how to plan and manage a career and how to resolve conflicts in their relationship and in their organizations. They are not secure enough yet to ask for help or flexibility from the organization to deal with their career-home conflicts. But the good news here is that since the couple is just starting out in the relationship and in their careers, they are willing to be flexible and to make sacrifices in both areas.

TYPES OF TWO-CAREER COUPLES

EXHIBIT 13.6

Early Career

I. Couple at entry (trial stage)

II. Advancing careers (establishment/advancement stage)
Common characteristics
- Similar career stage needs
- Conflicting career path alternatives
- High commitment to career goals
- Lack of preparation for career planning
- Lack of experience in conflict resolution (at work and at home)
- Reluctance to approach company
- High personal flexibility

Midcareer

III. Established vs. delayed career needs

IV. Two established careers and a family

V. Multiple careers (his, hers, children's)
Common characteristics
- Career stage needs conflict with life/family needs
- Alternative career paths viewed as viable
- Clearer couple and family priorities
- Greater family responsibilities
- Better prepared to plan and cope
- Less reluctant to influence company
- Acceptance of family as "given," career as flexible

VI. Midcareer stress vs. spouse career needs

SOURCE: From *Types of Two Career Couples* by F. S. Hall and D. T. Hall, pp. 41–55. Copyright © 1979 by Addison-Wesley Publishing Company, Inc. Reprinted by permission.

Midcareer Couples ▬ For older couples a wider range of types is seen. In Type III the career has been delayed (often the woman's) to start a family (through either working part time or taking time off) while the spouse has continued in the career and become established. Here the issue is often *how can the delayed-career person remain competitive in her (or his) profession, in spite of lower career involvement?* This can be a problem, since in many organizations top management assumes that less-than-full-time work involvement means less-than-full career commitment.

In Type IV both have continued their careers and also raised a family. There are heavy demands from multiple roles: job responsibilities, growing children, home and community. There can be more routine here, since careers and family are all established, but the level of role pressure is high. Here the issue is how can we survive the stress of "having it all"? It is hard. Type V is a slightly older version of Type IV, where the children have grown and their interests take on a "career" status of their own. Examples would be the high school world-class figure skater whose mother took a job in Colorado (the father stayed in Wisconsin) so her son could prepare for the Olympics with his skating coach, or the Chicago high school senior drama star whose father turned down a promotion-and-relocation with Ford so the son could complete his senior year with his long-time drama coach. (The father was subsequently offered the same promotion two years later and accepted, so there is a happy ending.) The issue here is often how can we give family needs greater priority in relation to career demands?

Some of the common elements of Types II–V deal with this issue of family work *balance*. The conflicts between work and family grow at this stage, but the couple is open to a wider range of career options than before. The family priorities have become much greater; the career is not the be-all and end-all. Family commitment and responsibility are higher; aging parents as well as maturing children increase the total range of family obligations. Fortunately, the couple's planning and coping skills are greater, as is their willingness to negotiate personal demands with the employer, and to plan their careers around the family, rather than vice versa.

The seventh type is that in which one member (often the man) is going through a difficult midcareer transition. The spouse also has strong career needs, perhaps being at an earlier advancement stage. The latter may be in a rapid-growth stage, which may serve to heighten the career frustrations of the former. Often this couple consists of a fast-rising wife and a bored or plateaued husband. The issue here is how can I provide the support, recognition, and enthusiasm which the other requires when my own career needs are so self-consuming?

Human Resource Issues for the Company

So much for the couple's problems. What issues does the two-career couple raise for managers in the employing organization (see Exhibit 13.7.)? A survey of companies reported that *recruiting* is made more difficult if there is a career partner in the picture; often, networks of human resource recruiting specialists will help one another by hiring spouses. There are also problems with *work schedules*, although as we have seen in Chapter Four, flextime and other forms of flexible scheduling ease these problems greatly. The main problem is *relocation*. It can be extremely difficult to move someone geographically if the spouse cannot move. Or if one partner is moving to a new place, the firm representing the other partner may not have a place for their employee in the new location. Again, informal corporate human resource networks are helpful here. And firms sometimes use their own outplacement services to assist the spouse in relocating. This restriction on movement also makes *promotions* more difficult, as these often require a move. The higher the person advances in the pyramid, the fewer and farther between the avail-

IMPACT OF DUAL-CAREER COUPLES ON HUMAN RESOURCE MANAGEMENT

EXHIBIT 13.7

1. Recruiting: need to integrate two sets of career needs
2. Scheduling: need to be flexible
3. Transfers and relocation: need to deal with this number one problem
4. Promotions: less upwardly mobile career couples
5. Travel: need to manage demands on family life, especially families with children
6. Benefits: need to provide maternity/paternity leaves, leaves without pay, personal days
7. Conflicts of interest: need to manage confidential information at home
8. Career development programs: need for new career paths
9. Plateauing and deadwood: need to deal with possible result of lower aspirations, resistance to relocation, etc.
10. Career bargaining: need to add assistance to spouse to total "package" of inducements

SOURCE: From *Types of Two Career Couples* by F. S. Hall and D. T. Hall. Copyright © 1979 by Addison-Wesley Publishing Company, Inc. Reprinted by permission.

able jobs are. *Travel* can be a strain, especially if there are children. *Benefits*, such as parental leaves and flexible benefits (if, for example, one person does not need health insurance but wants to trade it for more time off) are becoming an area of great innovation. If the couple works in similar fields (e.g., management consulting), conflicts of interest can be stressful.

Because of problems with mobility, firms are re-examining their traditional career-development paths. Is it really essential that the young oil company manager move from Houston to Stillwater, Oklahoma, for three years to acquire production experience? Would a temporary two-month assignment produce the same learning? Can a Houston-based assignment have the same effects?

As couples make decisions in favor of family over career, there is the risk of plateauing, deadwood, and burnout. People may have been willing to make career sacrifices at one point, but they may have regrets later. And, finally, more couples are becoming comfortable engaging in *career bargaining* with their employers: "I'll go to San Francisco if you help my husband find a good job there in his field."

PROTEAN VS. TRADITIONAL CAREER

When we combine the orientations of young people toward careers (concerns for freedom, mobility, personal fulfillment, shared authority) with the rumblings which are being heard from mid-career executives and professionals (re-examination of career goals, switching fields), there appears to be a new

---

EXHIBIT 13.8   FEATURES OF PROTEAN AND TRADITIONAL CAREERS

Issue	Protean Career	Traditional Career
Who's in charge?	Person	Organization
Core values	Freedom, growth	Advancement, power
Degree of mobility	High	Low
Important performance dimensions	Psychological success	Position level; salary
Important attitude dimensions	Work satisfaction; professional commitment	Work satisfaction; organizational commitment
Important identity dimensions	Do I respect myself? (self-esteem)	Am I respected in this organization? (esteem from others)
	What do I want to do? (self-awareness)	What should I do? (organizational awareness)
Important adaptability dimensions	Work-related flexibility	Organization-related flexibility
Current competence	Measure: marketability	Measure: organizational survival

SOURCE: D. T. Hall, *Careers in Organizations* (Glenview, Ill.: Scott, Foresman, 1976), p. 202.

career ethic emerging. To describe this new ethic succinctly, the term protean career has been employed.[32]

protean career

The **protean career** is a *process which the person, not the organization, is managing*. It consists of all the person's varied experiences in education, training, work in several organizations, changes in occupational field, etc. The protean career is *not* what happens to the person in any one organization. The protean person's own personal career choices and search for self-fulfillment are the unifying or integrative elements in his or her life. The criterion of success is internal (psychological success), not external.

In short, the protean career is shaped more by the individual than by the organization and may be redirected from time to time to meet the needs of the person.[33]

In the traditional career, once the person commits to a career ladder in an organization, a more passive role can be taken in managing the person's career. In the protean career greater responsibility for one's choices and opportunities goes along with the greater personal freedom. This can entail greater feelings of insecurity and fear of failure than would be found in the traditional career. The protean person knows that he or she cannot depend too heavily upon the employing organization for direction and security. These features of protean and traditional careers are summarized in Exhibit 13.8. An illustration of how the protean career concept is being incorporated in career planning at Ford Motor Company is shown in Box 13.2.

ENCOURAGING PROTEAN CAREERS AT FORD MOTOR COMPANY

BOX 13.2

The following comments were presented in a paper at the Annual Meeting of the Academy of Management in 1983.

Since the 1979 recession we find ourselves in a less stable, less favorable environment with a rapidly changing technology. In order to be effective it is necessary to move from a mechanistic organization to a smaller more organic, efficient organization, characterized by flatter structure, broader spans of control, responsibility focused at lower levels, and a participative management style (which we call "Employee Involvement").

This change in management style and organization structure affects our personnel systems and our views of career progress and career planning. First, we want to establish a climate of openness and trust, with decisions based on shared information. Our personnel systems must be consistent with this or the climate itself will not persist. With respect to career planning we must:

- Encourage employee participation in the management of their own careers.
- Provide information on organizational trends and developments that will facilitate career planning.
- Define criteria for success in various areas and provide extensive feedback to individuals on where they stand in relation to those criteria.
- Implement supportive practices.

The reduction in overall number of employees and the reduction in structure (levels of management and numbers of positions) forces a change in the way we look at career development.

- Fewer positions means fewer promotional opportunities.
- Broader spans of control—delegated responsibility—means more people with more breadth of experience to manage the organization.

The previously held ideal of rapid upward movement is no longer viable. Instead we must look at career as a life-long sequence of job experiences to be ordered by the individual's own needs and interests and coupled with as complete a picture of organizational reality as possible. Careers will be characterized more by lateral movement or no movement than by upward movement.

From the individual's perspective there is need to understand the factors affecting their own careers. From the company's viewpoint there is a need to encourage broad-based development to provide future managerial and professional personnel . . . . There is also a need to signal to employees, especially high-performing individuals, that while there has been a change in orientation toward careers, there are still viable options within the company.

The Ford Career Planning Program is based upon the following beliefs:

- Individuals have the right and responsibility to participate in the management of their own careers.
- The Company has the right and responsibility to provide information to individuals and to act on individual plans consistent with the needs of the organization.

John Turner and Dr. Phyllis C. Horner "Coping With Career Development in an Industry in Transition." Reprinted by permission.

Research has found that one important aspect of the protean style, career mobility, was not related to self-concepts, health, or general attitudes toward life. However, protean-type employees were more self-assured than comparable less mobile people. Furthermore, the protean people were more satisfied with their marriages, but less satisfied with friendships and nonwork activities. This suggests that the sense of stability the protean person (like any person) needs is found in the family, not in the ever-changing environment.[34]

CONCLUSION: CAREERS AND HUMAN RESOURCE MANAGEMENT

What implications does the protean career pattern have for the structure of human resource management systems? Because of the need for organizations to mirror to some extent the characteristics of their members, and vice versa, the fluidity of the protean career calls for increased flexibility on the part of managers and for better self-management of careers by individuals. If individuals are going to feel less commitment to organizations, they will look for opportunities to further their personal development, and if they are more independent of organizational constraints, then managers must gear themselves to a more mobile, independent work force. In short, organizations will have to adapt to the changing orientations of employees, and they will have to be able to individualize jobs somewhat to accommodate a range of people with quite different concerns and needs. To an extent, then, the organization will have to be "humanized" or "individualized" to better meet the needs of employees.

There are two ways in which organizations have become more individualized, and these reflect the line management/human resources partnership concept on which this book is based. It is the responsibility of human resource executives to work with line executives to formulate new strategies for career development, based upon new types of employees (e.g., more women, more baby boomers, more two career couples). It is also the task of human resource managers to design career programs and systems and to oversee the implementation of these programs. (The design and development of these career programs will be covered in Chapter Fourteen).

On the other hand, it is the responsibility of line executives to recognize these changing career needs of the contemporary work force and to work with senior human resource executives to formulate new strategies and policies for career development. Senior executives are also responsible for providing support to human resource professionals as they design and implement new career development programs. And, finally, executives and managers at all levels need to develop their own subordinates through periodic career planning discussions, and through everyday activities such as job assignments, mentoring, and career coaching (as we saw with the controller at the beginning of this chapter). More detail in the design and implementation of career programs and in the respective responsibilities of line managers and human resource professionals will be provided in the following chapter.

KEY POINTS

▬ A career is the individually perceived sequence of attitudes and behaviors associated with work experiences and activities over the span of the person's work life.

▬ The career unfolds in a series of stages: exploration, trial, establishment and advancement, midcareer (either growth, maintenance, or stagnation), and exit. A variety of alternative career paths is now seen, representing variants of these basic stages.

▬ The large numbers of working women and two-career couples have required major adjustments in organizations' recruiting and career management practices.

▬ The process of mentoring is one way people in different career stages can meet their own career stage needs while also meeting a colleague's needs. A mentoring relationship is a relationship between a junior and senior colleague that is seen as developmental by the junior member.

▬ The protean or self-directed career is becoming a more common organizational phenomenon, calling for increased flexibility in human resource management systems.

ISSUES FOR DISCUSSION

1. Why is it necessary for a manager or human resource specialist to worry about the concept of career? Isn't the career just the employee's own private concern?

2. Examine the definition of "career" at the beginning of this chapter. Note that there is no mention of advancement or upward mobility. Why not? Where does upward mobility fit in?

3. How does the concept of psychological success help to explain people's career decisions? Can you think of one or two examples (perhaps in your own career) where a particular decision was motivated by psychological success considerations?

4. What can a manager do to motivate an employee in each of the various career stages? What stage would you put yourself in? What motivates you right now?

5. Are you, or do you plan to be, part of a two-career couple? If the answer is yes to either part of the question, what do you see as your major immediate concern in this area? What issues do you anticipate five years from now?

6. How can managers deal with the effects of career plateauing in subordinates? In themselves? How can the plateauing of midcareer employees affect the careers of younger people in the organization?

NOTES

1. D. T. Hall, *Careers in Organizations* (Glenview, Ill.: Scott, Foresman, 1976), p. 4.

2. From Hall, op. cit. For another description of the success cycles, see Marilyn Machlowitz, *Whiz Kids* (New York: Arbor House, 1985).

3. E. A. Locke, "Toward a Theory of Task Motivation and Incentives," *Organizational Behavior and Human Performance*, 3, 1968, pp. 157–89.

4. Hall, op. cit.; and Beth Brophy, "Success: Satisfaction with Job," *U.S.A. Today*, November 5, 1984, p. 3B.

5. D. J. Levinson, et al., *The Seasons of a Man's Life* (New York: Knopf, 1978); and E. Erikson, *Childhood and Society* (New York: Norton, second edition, 1963).

6. D. J. Power and R. J. Aldag, "Soelberg's Job Search and Choice Model: A Clarification, Review, and Critique," *Academy of Management Review*, 1985, *10*, pp. 48–58.

7. Levinson, et al., op. cit.

8. Erikson, op. cit.

9. Levinson, et al., op. cit.

10. Donald E. Super, *The Psychology of Careers* (New York: Harper and Row, 1957).

11. Erikson, op. cit.

12. H. L. Wellbank, D. T. Hall, M. A. Morgan, and W. C. Hamner, "Planning Job Progression for Effective Career Development and Human Resources Management," *Personnel*, 1978, 55, pp. 54–64.

13. M. J. Driver, "Career Concepts and Organizational Change," in C. B. Derr, (ed.), *Work, Family, and the Career* (New York: Praeger, 1980), pp. 5–17.

14. D. T. Hall and B. Schneider, *Organizational Climates and Careers: The Work Lives of Priests* (New York: Academic Press, 1973).

15. Driver, op. cit.

16. K. E. Kram, *Mentoring at Work* (Glenview, Ill.: Scott, Foresman, 1984).

17. K. E. Kram, "Phases of the Mentor Relationship," *Academy of Management Journal*, December 1983, *26*, pp. 605–25.

18. Kram, *Mentoring at Work*, op. cit.

19. K. E. Kram, "Creating Conditions That Encourage Mentoring in Organizations," paper presented at the IEEE Careers Conference, Palo Alto, California, October 27, 1983; and K. Kram, "Mentoring at Work: Agenda for Research and Practice," in D. T. Hall, (ed.), *Organizational Career Development* (San Francisco: Jossey-Bass, 1986), in press.

20. L. Phillips-Jones, *Mentors and Proteges* (New York: Arbor House, 1982); L. Phillips-Jones, "Establishing a Formalized Mentoring Program," *Training and Development Journal*, February 1983; and E. Lean, "Cross-Gender Mentoring—Downright Upright and Good for Productivity," *Training and Development Journal*, May 1983.

21. Kram, "Creating Conditions . . ." op. cit.; L. Baird and K. Kram, "Career Dynamics: Managing the Superior/Subordinate Relationship," *Organizational Dynamics*, Spring 1983, pp. 46–64.

22. F. S. Hall and M. H. Albrecht, *The Management of Affirmative Action* (Santa Monica, Calif.: Goodyear, 1979).

23. H. A. Brown and D. L. Ford, Jr., "Employment Progress and Job Satisfaction of Minority Candidates," paper presented at the Association of Social and Behavioral Scientists Meeting, Charlotte, N.C., 1975.

24. R. M. Kanter, *Men and Women of the Corporation* (New York: Basic Books, 1975).

25.   Ibid.

26.   T. P. Ference, J. A. F. Stoner, and K. E. Warren, "Managing the Career Plateau," *Academy of Management Review*, 1977, *2*, pp. 602–12.

27.   D. T. Hall, "Midcareer Plateauing and Development," in D. T. Hall (Ed.), *Organizational Career Development* (San Francisco: Jossey-Bass, 1986), in press.

28.   D. T. Hall, "Project Work as an Antidote to Career Plateauing," *Human Resource Management*, 1985, in press.

29.   J. C. Latack, "Career Transition Within Organizations: An Exploratory Study of Work, Nonwork, and Coping Strategies," *Organizational Behavior and Human Performance*, 1984, *34*, pp. 296–322.

30.   D. T. Hall, "Midcareer Plateauing," op. cit.

31.   F. S. Hall and D. T. Hall, *The Two-Career Couple* (Reading, Mass.: Addison-Wesley, 1979). See also J. H. Greenhaus, and N. J. Beutell, "Sources of Conflict Between Work and Family Roles," *Academy of Management Review*, 1985, *10*, pp. 76–88.

32.   Adapted from Hall, *Careers in Organizations*, pp. 200–04.

33.   Hall, op. cit., pp. 201–02.

34.   J. M. Brett, "Job Transfer and Well-Being," *Journal of Applied Psychology*, 1982, *67*, (4), pp. 450–63.

ANNOTATED BIBLIOGRAPHY

BOLLES, R. *What Color Is Your Parachute?* Berkeley, Calif.: Ten-Speed Press, 1985.
This is *the* book to read for individual career planning. It provides a wealth of practical information, tips, and skills for assessing one's own interests, needs, and skills; for finding and assessing career opportunities; for developing goals, plans, and strategies; and for overcoming obstacles to reaching those goals. The "Quick Job-Hunter's Map" is an excellent way to map your skills onto various career fields. This book has been on the best-seller list for years.

HALL, D. T. *Careers in Organizations.* Glenview, Ill.: Scott, Foresman, 1976.
This is a general overview of the literature on organizational careers. It examines the varied meanings of the term "career" and discusses the reasons a manager should be concerned about careers. It reviews the ways researchers have attempted to study career choice, a major issue in the area of careers. It treats in detail career stages and the predictors of four major career outcomes: performance, identity, attitudes, and adaptability. It identifies the various organizational intervention points to facilitate career development and the strategies for career self-management. Finally, it examines major career issues, such as equal opportunity, a new definition of success (psychological success) and the emerging self-directed or *protean career.*

KAYE, B. *Up Is Not the Only Way: A Guide for Career Development Practitioners.* Englewood Cliffs, N.J.: Prentice-Hall, 1982.
This book is a kind of road map (as the author describes it) for the career development practitioner who is designing a career program for an organization. It identifies six distinct stages in such an undertaking: *preparation*, the often unnoticed, often behind-the-scenes informal activities involved in gaining support

and developing a strategy; *profiling*, helping employees identify and assess their skills for realistic career planning; *targeting*, helping people explore and specify ways to move; *strategizing*, coming up with the most appropriate action plans; *execution*, advising employees of the options for acquiring the tools and skills they will need to implement their plans; *integration*, finding ways to evaluate and reward employees who have grown in, and managers who have facilitated, this process.

KRAM, K. E. *Mentoring at Work.* Glenview, Ill.: Scott, Foresman, 1984.

This is a thorough examination of the processes involved in mentoring in organizational settings. Professor Kram views mentoring as a mutual exchange, in which both the mentor and the protege can experience career growth. The book identifies the various functions at work in such a relationship, the stages through which it passes, the career needs of both the junior and senior members, organizational conditions that hinder or facilitate mentoring, intervention strategies to facilitate mentoring, and special issues, such as cross-gender mentoring. The book is both a good theoretical treatment of the subject and a practical guide to promoting mentoring in work settings.

LONDON, M. and STUMPF, S. A. *Managing Careers.* Reading, Mass.: Addison-Wesley, 1982.

This book provides an overview of managing careers from the twin perspectives of the individual and the organization. It is a good summary of theory and research in careers, as well as a good guide to individual career planning and organizational career program development. For individuals, it examines how to assess one's own skills, interests, and potential, how to identify realistic career objectives, and how to obtain necessary training and experience to prepare for future career opportunities. For organizations, it discusses staffing procedures to fill positions with the most qualified personnel, providing challenging job opportunities to "grow" people, and assisting individuals in career planning and development. Cases, individual career management exercises, and real-company illustrations are useful features of the book.

SCHEIN, E. H. *Career Dynamics: Matching Individual and Organizational Needs.* Reading, Mass.: Addison-Wesley, 1978.

Edgar Schein is one of the "founding fathers" of the field of organizational career development, and this book is the result of years of research, theory development, and practical experience. The concept of *career anchor* (a complex of needs, interests, and values which pull a person toward a certain area of work) is described in detail, as are issues such as career stages, dual careers, and career programs. A major contribution of the book is the model of human resource planning and utilization which forms the basis for much of the second half. It provies a more "macro" approach to the topic than the other works described here.

CHAPTER FOURTEEN

CAREER DEVELOPMENT PROGRAMS

Brenda Johnson has worked in the engineering department of Amalgamated Industries, a medium-size manufacturing firm, for four years. She is active in the local branch of a professional engineering society and is known to senior engineers and managers in other area companies. She has had several "feelers" about job possibilities with other companies, but has never felt the need to pursue them.

Recently, a colleague with a competitor approached Brenda about a project manager's position which was about to open up. Brenda has had some experience coordinating large projects, but she has never held the title of project manager. The salary would be 20 percent above her current rate. She was interested, but she also thought her prospect for promotion to project manager at Amalgamated might be reasonably high, too. If so, she would prefer to stay.

To explore her future at Amalgamated, she asked her boss, Jane White, for an appointment to discuss her work. Brenda was unclear about where she stood with Jane and with the company. Jane was up against a tight deadline for completing a proposal on an important new project, but she suggested they meet for lunch the next day.

The lunch meeting took place in the company cafeteria, a small, spartan room in the basement, with a tile floor, vending machines lining the walls, and plastic furniture. Jane's morning meeting ran late, and she arrived breathless at 12:30 for the noon appointment. She told Brenda she would have to leave at 12:50 for a 1:00 management briefing.

After initial pleasantries, Brenda said she has been doing some thinking about her future and would like some feedback on where she might go next at Amalgamated.

Jane, who felt she was overdue for a promotion herself, was a bit irritated with the question. In fact, Jane knew that Brenda was seen by top management as a high potential candidate for management. Jane also realized how much she relied on Brenda for crucial activities like this proposal.

Most of the conversation consisted of Jane's trying to convince Brenda that her present position was a challenging, rewarding one, and that it was essential to the smooth functioning of the engineering department. She told Brenda that the most important thing to do was to maintain her good performance, and *then future opportunities would come her way. The message seemed to be, "Just be patient." Jane never asked Brenda what she would like to do in the future or if she were talking to other firms. The information about the competing offer never came out.*

The next week, Brenda announced that she was taking the job with the other company. Everyone in management was shocked at the news, and no one could understand why someone with such a bright future in the company would leave.

Cases like Brenda Johnson's are extremely common. Because managers lack the time and skills to do good career coaching and counseling, many employees leave organizations in which they would prefer to remain. Others fail to receive corrective feedback on career-related skills and never achieve to the level of their potential. And others, without a good assessment of their skills and potential, aspire too high or too low, and experience great frustration in the process. What can organizations do to provide more effective career guidance for employees?

A growing number of organizations are creating career development programs to prevent situations like this. Since the early 1970s, career development activities have become part of the standard "technology" of human resource management. The positions of "career development specialist," "manager of career development," and others related to facilitating employee growth have become accepted components of the human resource department. In this chapter, we will examine the various systematic methods organizations use to help employees plan and manage their careers, as well as the process by which an organization might start up a career program if none now exists. In addition, we have included a "Career Planning Paper Assignment" in the appendix of this text that we suggest you get started on as soon as possible.

WHY THE INTEREST IN CAREER DEVELOPMENT PROGRAMS?

A number of forces have converged to produce the recent impetus for career development activities in work organizations. In the early 1970s, external pressure for affirmative action and equal employment opportunity led to special recruiting and development programs for women and minorities which, over time, were expanded and made available to all employees. Also, new employees were more interested in career fulfillment and self-direction, as we saw in Chapter Three. An increasing number of two-career couples made career planning necessary to permit the balancing (or juggling) of career and home demands. Greater employee concern for quality of life and personal freedom in work also led to more interest in career planning. And then, as the economy slowed in the late 1970s and early 1980s, it became clear that career planning was essential simply to find and maintain employment. Finally, as more of the post-World-War II "Baby Boom" generation moved into middle age, they felt a growing need for career planning to avoid career plateauing and obsolescence.

In the 1980s, career management has become essential for organizations as a way to cope with an economy that swings between near-depression and very slow growth. Through careful career management and human resource planning, the organization can be kept "lean and mean," but still ready to seize upon emerging business opportunities. An organization can no longer afford the luxury of excess "inventories" of human talent, nor can it afford to be short of qualified people when business picks up.

Walter Storey, who developed highly respected career programs at General Electric, lists the following goals of career development programs:

- identify and develop high-potential employees,
- facilitate orderly succession planning,
- improve the fit between the employee's career interests and organizational needs,
- respond to environmental changes and government regulation,
- increase employee productivity,
- increase employee retention,
- provide career opportunity information,
- ensure a supply of professional, managerial, and technical talent (i.e., to create an internal labor market),
- enhance the adaptability of employees,
- enable managers to facilitate the career development process.[1]

Obviously not all these results occur in all organizations with career development programs, but when such a program is working all these outcomes are possible. The reason is simple: effective **career development** is *the appropriate, long-term utilization and development of human talent in the work setting.*

career development

STRATEGIES FOR CAREER DEVELOPMENT

There are two basic strategies available to an organization initiating career development activities, each representing one facet of career growth. The first is to focus on the *individual employee* and to help the employee plan his or her career in a personally satisfying and productive manner. The second is to focus on *organizational human resource planning* needs and engage in activities that will effectively select, assess, assign, and develop employees to provide a pool of qualified people available for future corporate needs. This individual-level approach is often called career planning, while the organizationally focused strategy is termed career management. **Career planning** *is a*

career planning

EXHIBIT 14.1   SPECTRUM OF CAREER DEVELOPMENT ACTIVITIES

Organization-Centered Career Management			Mutual Focus Manager-Assisted Career Planning		Employee-Centered Individual Career Planning		
Corporate succession planning	Corporate talent inventories	Development assessment centers (with feedback)	Manager-employee career discussions (Includes separate training for managers)	Corporate seminars on organizational career	Company-run career planning workshops	Self-directed workbooks and tape cassettes

Note: This is a sample of program activities to illustrate different points on the continuum between career management and career planning. This is not a complete list of possible career development activities.

*career
management*

deliberate process of becoming aware of self, opportunities, constraints, choices, and consequences, identifying career-related goals, and programming work, education, and related developmental experiences to provide the direction, timing, and sequence of steps to attain a specific career goal. **Career management** *is an ongoing process of preparing, implementing, and monitoring career plans undertaken by the individual alone or in concert with the organization's career systems.*[2]

According to Gutteridge and Otte, a balanced approach to organizational career development includes the use of both approaches.[3] The two strategies complement and reinforce each other; if individual employees haven't planned well for their own development, they may not be ready or willing to respond to opportunities presented through organizational career management activities. Similarly, no amount of individual career planning and preparation will be effective if organizational opportunities for career movement are not available.

THE RANGE OF CAREER DEVELOPMENT ACTIVITIES

Before we discuss career development activities actually used, let us consider the range of activities possible. These activities range from career management at the organization-centered end to career planning at the employee-centered end, as shown in Exhibit 14.1. On the individual side, career planning is an attempt to increase a person's *career skills.* John Crites has identified five skills necessary for effective career planning: self-assessment, assessment of career opportunities, goal-setting, planning, and problem-solving.[4]

The first two skills are necessary in order to get a good match between the person and his or her needs, interests, training, skills, etc., on the one hand, and the demands and opportunities of the work organization on the other. Having goals is important to achieving goals, and skills are required to know how to set goals that are challenging but attainable, specific and concrete, quantifiable, and short- or intermediate-range.

Having goals does no good if the person does not plan well to achieve them. Therefore, knowing how to work logically from goals to a clear, operational plan for goal attainment is also critical.

And, finally, since nothing ever goes completely according to plan, it is important to recognize and solve unforeseen problems as they arise. This may entail soliciting the help of other people, knowing whom to ask, and thinking creatively about possible solutions.

Therefore, to do an adequate job on the individual career planning side, an organizational career program should help a person work on all five of these career skill areas. If the program does not directly aid the employee in these areas, it should train someone (such as managers or human resource specialists) to help employees work on these five career competencies.

On the organizational side, many elements in the internal and external environment affect the individual's opportunity to apply career skills: job opportunities and career paths, labor market conditions, organizational policies and practices, developmental supervisors and managers, human resource planning systems, selection and recruitment systems, performance and potential appraisal systems, assessments of managerial potential, career planning activities, training and developmental activities, staffing decisions, staffing and support systems.[5] Some of these organizational factors are the responsibility of line management (e.g., performance appraisal), while others are handled by human resource specialists (e.g., training and development, human resource planning systems). Other factors are under no one's control, but must be carefully taken into account (e.g., labor market conditions, organizational type).

CAREER DEVELOPMENT PRACTICES

We have just reviewed the range of individual and organizational characteristics which might relate to a career development program. How does this compare with *actual practices?* A survey of 225 member companies of the American Management Association by James Walker and Thomas Gutteridge suggests what these organizational practices are.[6] In addition to asking what the firms are doing, it also asked about planned activities, discontinued activities, and those which had never been done.

As Exhibit 14.2 shows, the most common form of career development activity involves *career counseling* by human resource staff or supervisors. Career counseling is also done by specialized staff counselors and outside career specialists. (Since respondents were able to check as many activities as they wished, some of these categories could overlap; for example, the specialized career counselors could be members of the human resource staff.)

EXHIBIT 14.2   **CAREER PLANNING PRACTICES**

Practice	Doing	Planning	Discontinued	Never Done
Informal counseling by human resource staff (n = 222)	89%	5%	1%	6%
Career counseling by supervisor (n = 217)	56	18	0	27
Workshops on interpersonal relationships (n = 213)	49	12	2	37
Job performance and development planning workshops (n = 210)	42	21	0	36
Outplacement counseling/related services (n = 212)	37	2	2	59
Psychological testing and assessment (n = 221)	35	8	19	38
Workshops and communications on retirement preparation (n = 212)	34	24	0	43
Testing and feedback regarding aptitudes, interests, etc. (n = 208)	33	10	14	44
Referrals to external counselors and resources (n = 209)	29	4	4	63
Training of supervisors in career counseling (n = 212)	25	32	1	43
Career counseling by specialized staff counselors (n = 210)	21	8	1	71
Individual self-analysis and planning (n = 211)	16	19	1	64
Assessment centers for career development purposes (n = 213)	15	17	4	64
Life and career planning workshops (n = 210)	11	17	1	71

Bases of percentages vary with responses. Nonresponses are excluded from percentage calculations.

Thus, it appears that human resource staffs bear much of the responsibility for career planning in work organizations. Activities performed by the individual alone (16 percent) and in life and career planning workshops (11 percent) are relatively rare. A considerable amount of career-related work is also conducted in specialized workshops, which would generally be the responsibility of the human resource department: interpersonal relationships, job performance and development, and retirement preparation. And, in an era of staff reductions, outplacement counseling (37 percent) has also become an important part of the human resource function.

The type of activity most often cited in new corporate career development plans is the training of supervisors in career counseling skills. This is important, as training the supervisor is a way to build career development into the everyday job environment. If the employee has to take the initiative to go to the human resource department for career assistance, that action is far less likely to occur. Walker and Gutteridge quote a human resource executive from a large electric utility on the importance of involving managers and supervisors in the career development process:

> To the extent that supervisors and managers take it on themselves to accomplish the task, [career planning] is somewhat successful. Most supervisory personnel are weak in this area and shy away from the one-to-one encounters. Very little training has been directed at this subject [so far].[7]

In a similar vein, a representative of a diversified chemicals company reported:

> In the future, we will have a corporate commitment to annual in-depth career discussions between manager and subordinate. My guess is that we will concentrate on providing better data to supervisors about job behaviors and requirements for success and on doing a more effective training job.[8]

Developmental assessment centers can also help to gain top management support for a corporate career development program. Since the main purpose of most traditional assessment centers is to help identify high-potential management candidates, these centers meet a critical management succession need. Furthermore, successful managers usually participate in the assessment center as staff members, which builds management commitment. And, when an attempt is made to provide constructive developmental feedback to participants, this usually leads to an enthusiastic evaluation by participants and requests by other employees to attend such a center.

SPECIFIC CAREER PROGRAM AUDIENCES

Many companies do not apply their career programs "across the board," but rather target special employee groups for specially designed career programs (see Exhibit 14.3). The most common audience in Walker and Gutteridge's study was *management trainees*. Closely related were *fast-track management candidates*. These programs often involved creating special records showing the interests, experience, education, and skills of these future managers. The programs often included assignment to especially challenging jobs with successful bosses, setting career and job objectives, tracking progress, and moving rapidly from job to job. This is obviously an elite group in many organizations, and a considerable amount of time, energy, and resources are devoted to them.

Next most common were special programs for women and minority employees. Such programs focused on specially selected job assignments, the

EXHIBIT 14.3

AUDIENCES FOR CAREER DEVELOPMENT PROGRAMS

Management trainees	66%
Fast-track management candidates	62%
Women employees	38%
Minority employees	36%
Pre-retirement employees	27%
Midcareer employees	19%
Handicapped employees	5%
Older employees	4%
Other (professional trainees, senior employees)	9%

SOURCE: Reprinted by permission of the publisher of *Career Planning Practices: An AMA Survey Report* by James W. Walker and Thomas G. Gutteridge, pp. 11 and 12. Copyright © 1979 AMACOM, a division of American Management Associations, New York. All rights reserved.

skills needed to perform them, issues unique to minorities, and future development opportunities.

Pre-retirement employees were a target group found in over one-quarter of the responding firms. And, as we will see in Chapter Eighteen, more firms are planning programs to help employees deal with issues such as financial management, insurance, health care, second-career planning, developing leisure interests, and changing marital relationships. Financial, health, and emotional aspects should all be covered in an effective pre-retirement program. Often, only the financial issues receive adequate attention.

Midcareer employees, a rapidly growing group, were the target of special programs in 19 percent of the firms. Some of these activities involved refresher training, and some complete *retraining* in a new career field. Some focused on the issue of career plateauing and ways to develop oneself in the absence of upward mobility.

Handicapped and older employees were the least frequently identified special groups. However, as the proportion of older employees grows over the years, they will probably receive more attention. Also, since the definition of "midcareer" in many organizations is quite broad, older employees may be included in midcareer programs, as well.

ASSIGNING RESPONSIBILITY FOR CAREER PLANNING

Walker and Gutteridge found that human resource staffs were most often seen as the primary responsible parties in career development activities. In less than a quarter of the responses, career development was seen as the primary responsibility of line managers and supervisors.[9] Indeed, "career development manager" has become a standard job title in the human resource staffs of many contemporary organizations.

PROS AND CONS OF VARIOUS APPROACHES

Each career development approach has advantages and disadvantages. Individual activities are the least expensive, but are dependent on the person's motivation, and do little to tie in with the organization's human resource planning.

Professional counseling can be highly effective, but not very cost-effective since it is labor-intensive, conducted on a one-on-one basis. Also, the counselor may not know much about company career opportunities. Counseling by the boss can be productive *if* the boss is well-trained and the relationship is based on trust.

Developmental assessment centers yield much rich information, but can be expensive and threatening to participants because of the objective personal feedback they provide. Management support is critical here.

Life and career planning workshops have moderate costs, but sometimes provide little information about career opportunities in the organization. However, if attempts are made to include career opportunity information, workshops can be useful and cost-effective.

A more detailed listing of pros and cons for each method is shown in Exhibit 14.4.

TYPES OF CAREER DEVELOPMENT ACTIVITIES

Now that you have an overview of general career development practices, we shall describe career development activities in specific companies. We will start with activities aimed at individual career planning and work our way up to organization-level programs for career management. (In terms of Exhibit 14.1, we will move from right to left on the spectrum of career development activities.)

Career Planning Workbooks

Probably one of the most widely used self-directed career planning activities is found in a series of career workbooks for individual use, the Career Dimensions system developed by Walter Storey at the General Electric Company.[10] Career Dimensions I and II are designed to be used individually by employees, with optional inputs from the supervisor. The focus is on assessment of one's own interests, values, skills, etc., and of where these personal qualities might fit best in a work environment. Although developed at General Electric, the workbooks can be applied generally and are used in a variety of organizations. (Career Dimensions III and IV are not directed at the individual employee; we will discuss them later.)

In contrast to career workbooks, most of which are aimed at lower-level employees, AT&T developed a Career Planning Instrument (CPI) to be used by middle-level managers being considered for fifth-level (assistant vice-pres-

---

EXHIBIT 14.4   *CHARACTERISTICS OF CAREER PLANNING ACTIVITIES*

Activity	Potential Advantages	Potential Disadvantages
Individual Planning		
The person plans with the possible aid of self-help materials.	For persons with strong motivation and adequate sources of information, this may be adequate for goal setting. Cost is minimal.	Most people need interpersonal feedback to develop a complete and accurate self-evaluation. No built-in mechanism exists to check completeness of information on occupational opportunities or to correct distorted views of self. No opportunity exists to explore new occupational possibilities.
Counselor-Client Activities		
Guidance counselor administers vocational interest and aptitude tests and feeds data back to client. Helps client assess own career needs.	Test results and information supplied may be new and of considerable value to client.	Such activities are usually expensive. Client has no way to test validity of counselor's views or test results. Interpersonal feedback is likely to be minimal.
Boss as Counselor or Coach		
Superior regularly or periodically assesses subordinate's career strengths and weaknesses and provides feedback and suggestions for improving performance and/or career opportunities.	Superior may have an excellent opportunity to observe subordinate's behavior in a number of work activities. Superior knows career opportunities within the organization. Superior can provide assignments to expand subordinate's capabilities and can help employee transfer to a new job.	Superior's power can be highly threatening; could cause subordinate to be defensive, cautious, and closed to feedback. Superior's first loyalty may be seen to be the interests of the organization, not subordinates.

ident) positions in various operating companies. (This was done when AT&T still owned the Bell System operating companies.)

The CPI was developed to be used as part of a high-level assessment center, called Advanced Management Potential Assessment (AMPA). In contrast to most of the AMPA activities, which were geared toward an organizational assessment of the participants, the CPI was an attempt to help the participant engage in *self-assessment*.

The instrument contained several elements. First, self-directed activities measured the skills developed to date and personal career orientation

Activity	Potential Advantages	Potential Disadvantages
Group Activities		
Assessment Center: Usually conducted by employer. Employee given tests, situational exercises, and interviews, where performance is observed and evaluated. Evaluators are often managers trained in the technique. Psychologists design center and interpret test results.	Substantial amounts of data can be developed quickly. Multiple judges on panel and results of several tests provide variety of perspectives for candidate. Moderate cost is usually borne by employer.	High threat situation: Employee is likely to feel anxious about results. Center serves interests of employer first. Primary emphasis is not on setting of personal goals. Data generated is primarily applicable to career with employing organization only.
Life Planning Workshop: Conducted either inside or outside the organization. A set of semistructured experiences are presented which encourage participants to assess their values, situation, etc., to set goals, and to develop greater self-awareness through interpersonal interaction with other participants.	Can be of little or no cost to participant. Personal goal setting is encouraged. Wide exploration of self and needs is encouraged. Supportive environment: Other participants are frequently valuable source of information on career alternatives.	Normally does not provide occupational information, especially for careers outside of the organizations. Provision for periodic follow-up is probably necessary to maximize value to most participants. Participants may not be encouraged to explore changing jobs or careers.

SOURCE: Adapted from "Career Planning for Employee Development" by Donald D. Bowen and Douglas T. Hall, *California Management Review,* Winter, 1977. Copyright © 1977 by the Regents of the University of California. Reprinted by permission of the Regents.

(e.g., willingness to engage in certain activities required in fifth-level positions). Next, the person was examined for *gaps* between required fifth-level activities and the participant's present skills and personal orientation. Third, the person was informed about developmental experiences and knowledge seen by fifth-level executives as necessary for advancement. Next, fifth-level executives compiled a list of satisfactions associated with moving to that position. Finally, the person developed goals and plans. Based on all the above inputs, participants then identified their most important developmental needs, and their goals or objectives in each need area.

It was not unusual for participants to decide, after this realistic career preview, that they were not interested in making the trade-offs necessary to advance to fifth level. For the company, this sort of early *self-selection* was far superior to a person's coming to that realization after having invested several years attempting to reach fifth level.

Most workbooks are developed for a particular company and can be completed in one or two sessions. In contrast, the workbook *Self Assessment and Career Development* was developed by Clawson, Kotter, Faux, and

McArthur for use in a semester-long course on careers, but can also be used as a free-standing, self-directed career planning workbook.[11]

The first part takes the reader through an extremely detailed self-assessment. From these self-assessment data, the reader develops *themes* which put the data into meaningful categories which describe him or her. Typical themes might be "social relations," "freedom," "balance between work and play," "need for achievement," "importance of money to lifestyle," etc. Also the reader is asked to identify the *implications* of these themes for career planning.

Next the reader goes through a search process in which career options are explored (published sources of career information, informational interviews, etc.). Based on this search and the self-assessment material, the individual develops a career plan, which is written up as a paper.

This process is time-consuming. It can be done as a self-directed exercise, but is more often done during a career planning workshop or course covering several weeks.

Perhaps the best-known, most successful career workbook in history is Richard Bolles' *What Color Is Your Parachute?*[12] Not necessarily intended to be gone through in sequence, *Parachute* is more like an encyclopedia or cookbook through which people can browse to find particular exercises or information they need. It is updated frequently so that its information is always current. The "Quick Job-Hunter's Guide" at the end helps to identify the particular skills one has, as well as to match those skills with specific jobs. This book is a classic for individual career planning.

Career Planning Workshops

One of the dilemmas in company-based career development activities is how to provide company support and encouragement for career planning while maintaining the employee's choice about whether to participate or not. One way is to have career workshops available to any employee who is interested, perhaps on company time, perhaps off company premises, and not to make an issue of who attends and who doesn't. Also, a fairly nonintensive introductory workshop, aimed primarily at providing company opportunity information, can be a good way to start.

A typical employee-oriented workshop might look like the one summarized in Exhibit 14.5. This workshop was developed by a department manager in collaboration with an external consultant. The manager saw a need for his specialized professionals to get some realistic information on career opportunities in various parts of the company and to conduct a realistic assessment of their own career interests and skills. Most of them, in their late 20s, had focused on developing professional skills and had not thought much about later career moves and issues such as interdepartmental transfers and moving into management. Similar employee workshops have been used at Continental Insurance Company, Gulf Oil Company, Ford Motor Company, Xerox, Prudential Insurance, and numerous other organizations.

EXHIBIT 14.5

ONE-DAY CAREER PLANNING WORKSHOP FOR EMPLOYEES

Morning

9:00–10:00	Introduction to career concepts (career and life stages, career planning skills, etc.)
10:00–11:00	Career opportunities in this organization: Panel of senior executives (including a senior personnel manager)
11:00–12:00	Small group discussion of company career opportunities, based on panel

Afternoon

12:00–1:00	Lunch
1:00–2:00	Career self-assessment exercise
2:00–3:00	Career counseling sessions in pairs (each participant with one personnel specialist)
3:00–4:00	Exercise: Development of own career action plan
4:00–5:00	Conclusion: Group discussion of action plans with personnel staff

Career Coaching Workshop for Managers

Supervisors and managers need training in the skills of counseling and coaching subordinates about their careers. However, before managers can be motivated to help subordinates with their careers, they need to discuss their own careers, which they often feel are stagnating. Thus, a career workshop for managers might look like the one summarized in Exhibit 14.6.

Often in such a workshop, managers will discuss issues related to their own careers as well as their subordinates'. Especially for established midcareer managers who are feeling plateaued, this may be the first opportunity they have had to discuss midcareer stagnation with senior executives and human resource staff. If the senior people are receptive and responsive, the workshop can also be a useful form of upward feedback and organization development.

Once the managers in a workshop have had a chance to express concerns about their own careers, they are generally willing to examine ways they could aid the development of their subordinates. In fact, they are usually eager to develop better skills in order to respond to employees' concerns about their careers. Many have had the experience of Jane White, whom we met at the beginning of this chapter, and have lost good people because of an inability to be a good career coach and counselor. The career coaching role provides a chance to practice important skills, and the ensuing discussion enables managers to share experiences and learn from each other how to deal with difficult employee career situations. Workshops like these have been used by numerous organizations, including Prudential Insurance Company, Ford Motor Company, United Gas Pipe Line Company, and Eli Lilly. The

EXHIBIT 14.6   **CAREER COACHING WORKSHOP FOR MANAGERS**

Morning

9:00–10:00	Career development concepts
10:00–11:00	Small group discussion: Major career issues for managers in this organization (results are summarized for each group and posted on large sheets)
11:00–12:00	Discussion of career issues with a panel of executives and senior personnel staff

Afternoon

12:00–1:00	Lunch
1:00–3:00	Career coaching role plays (role plays of manager-employee career discussions, developed by personnel staff to tap familiar career issues in the organization)
3:00–4:00	Role-play debriefing (comparison of various ways of handling different employee problems)
4:00–5:00	Action planning (developing a plan for helping subordinates "back home" on career issues)

process is enhanced greatly if the organization uses a combination of employee career planning workshops and career coaching workshops for managers.

Handbooks for Managers and Human Resource Specialists

Walter Storey's Career Dimensions III workbook is a guide for managers on how to coach employees and deal with difficult career issues. He describes some of the difficult employee career questions addressed to a manager:

- I have an offer. (Should I take it?)
- What is my potential?
- How can I move?
- Why was I passed over?
- Where to next? (What's my career path?)
- How come so-and-so is . . . and I . . . ?
- What's available?
- Where's the business going?

To assist managers in responding to these questions, Storey provides rules for the manager.

- Help thyself, manager. (Be aware of your own career needs and get your career planned before helping others.)

- Deal with the employee as a person. (Try to understand what his or her particular values and interests are.)
- Listen for meaning and tell what you understand, and ask what was meant. (Test for understanding; don't just assume you are hearing the person correctly.)
- Teach responsibility (Help the employee to see that the ultimate responsibility for career is his or hers.)
- Act on realistic career plans for the next step. (The step is the first part of the career future.)

Several thousand G.E. people and many outside G.E. have used this system. The results have been positive. Managers report they feel less threat and emotion in holding career discussions, more comfort and effectiveness in helping employees, and more acceptance by the employee of his or her responsibility for the career planning process.[13]

Talent Inventories

With the advent of computerized human resource information systems, it is possible for an organization to construct a data bank containing information on the career histories, skill evaluations, and career preferences of its employees. Input information might include education, previous positions held, performance ratings, potential assessment ratings, career goals (from the employee), desired next assignment (from the employee), and other relevant information, such as family status and geographical preferences.

When a job opening occurs, or is about to occur, the human resource placement officer or the hiring manager can get a printout of all employees with the desired personal qualifications, and use this list as the starting point in the recruiting process. Sources such as manager referrals and self-nominations can still be used, but the talent inventory can give a wide range of employees an opportunity to be considered without their continually searching out leads and poring over job postings. A talent inventory in operation at RCA is described in Box 14.1.

Succession Planning and Executive Development

When companies develop people for managerial and executive positions, the focus is mainly career management and the needs of the organization. A primary concern is how to develop and identify acceptable candidates for senior management positions for future organizational growth. Succession planning is discussed in detail in Chapter Seven, "Strategic Staffing." In this section we will focus only on the career development issues involved. The core of succession planning is the review of key positions, the incumbent, and the development of a list of backup candidates. These candidates are identified through a comprehensive assessment of potential mangerial and professional

RCA'S TALENT INVENTORY

BOX 14.1

Some 7,500 managers in RCA's nine major divisions want to know where they stand with the company. So, for that matter, does RCA, which maintains for just that purpose a management Talent Inventory.

The system was designed to provide reliable and valid performance data, to achieve high credibility with the company's managers, and to enhance administrative efficiency.

RCA has found that assessment by five to seven individuals who have a substantial work relationship with an employee is a more reliable predictor of potential than appraisal by one supervisor, and provides a more complete view of a manager's performance.

The Talent Inventory system relies on the employee under evaluation to suggest appropriate raters. From this list, the employee's immediate supervisor, following clear guidelines, selects two or three superiors, two or three peers, and one or two subordinates.

Rater anonymity is guaranteed in order to encourage candid and accurate evaluations. Precautions are also taken to eliminate raters who are close friends of the subject or who are known for their severity, leniency, or rigid middle-of-the-road approaches to rating.

Specific managerial qualities are assessed through a list of over forty concrete performance practices called "Critical Incidents." The list was developed by managers from each RCA division based upon incidents known to them to have led in the past to success or failure.

The practices deal with everything from creativity to analytical ability to dedication to cost control. Supervisory skills are broken down into

such categories as the ability to criticize constructively, to lead a group, to balance autonomy with delegation, to acknowledge and support subordinates, to create challenges, to direct meetings, and to treat all subordinates without bias.

The incidents also deal in specifics with such personal character traits as reliability, initiative, integrity, optimism, flexibility, poise, responsibility, and general grace under pressure. Communication skills include articulate speech and writing and receptive listening.

Finally, the responses are factored and adjusted for bias through comparisons with other responses to the subject and with general responses within the division, and are printed out as a range of assessments rather than one overall judgment.

The Talent Inventory indicates training, both in-house and outside, which might further career goals.

Jay N. Nisberg, director of management and organization development, estimates that raters spend perhaps five working days once or twice a year evaluating managerial potential and that ten or fifteen raters to a group, with a counselor to answer questions and urge objectivity, works best. He admits that the system sounds complex but maintains that it takes less time than traditional systems and costs about half as much.

"RCA's Talent Inventory" adapted from *The Career Development Bulletin*, 1980, *2*(1), pp. 2-3. Reprinted by permission.

talent throughout the organization. At Exxon, for example, 50,000 managers and professionals from thirteen organizations in 100 countries are reviewed, each by four different superiors. There is "amazing consistency" in these ratings, according to Frank Gaines, Jr., Exxon's Executive Development Coordinator. "Potential is hard to define but easy to recognize. Our objective is not to waste time arguing."[14]

Along with the assessment rating of each manager or professional, there is usually some sort of recommendaton about future development, such as training or educational activities, future job assignments, and developmental tasks on the current assignment. Personal considerations, such as having children in high school or an employed spouse, are also taken into consideration in planning moves for future executive talent.

One by-product of succession planning in recent years has been *outplacement and other activities to facilitate exit.* With promotion opportunities becoming scarcer as growth slows and layers of managerial positions are pruned, it is in the organization's best interests to give people straight feedback if their promotion prospects are slim, even if it means losing those people. As companies like Exxon have found, it is important to *let go of talent* when the firm is heavy in talent and light on opportunity. In this situation, "You can kill more talent than you lose," says Exxon's Gaines. If the company doesn't let people go, career paths get clogged, and "then the best ones quit, and the rest get flabby," he concludes.[15] Seeing a well-developed management development and outplacement activity tends to reassure new recruits that their own careers will keep moving, either inside the firm or elsewhere.

ISSUES RAISED IN CAREER DEVELOPMENT PROGRAMS

Who Should Participate in Career Development?

Several issues tend to arise as an organization creates formal career development activities.[16] A primary issue to be faced in doing career development is the *audience* to be covered. Should all employees have access to career development? Or is this an activity for specific groups, such as managers and professionals? If the company's goal is career management, the audience may more likely be managers and professionals (to meet corporate needs). If the focus is more on individual career planning, the audience then would tend to be all interested employees.

Of course, it is possible to have two types of career development programs: a career planning workshop for any employee who wants to participate, and a management development program for managers and high potential management candidates. There seems to be a growing tendency for companies to provide both types of career facilitation to meet both organization and individual needs.

Does Career Planning Raise Expectations?

A survey of companies with career development programs found that, when problems did occur, the major difficulty with such programs was the development of unrealistic employee expectations.[17] However, in many organizations this was *not* a problem. The critical factor was that when the program included giving employees *realistic feedback* on their skills and their prospects for promotion, there was no problem with unrealistic expectations.

Do Problems Arise in Giving Feedback on Potential?

Problems can arise in giving straight feedback, but the risks of telling people where they stand are far less than the risks of not telling them. If employees are unhappy with the feedback, they might leave if they are competent performers and have external options. This may be the best option for the person and the organization. If they stay, they may look for ways to improve their ratings or to move to a different assignment and boss who might rate them differently. Again, the result might be a better fit.

The most serious risk is that a person might remain, demotivated, in the current assignment. The answer, in this case, is to have an effective performance appraisal system to maintain strong performance (or to detect and deal with sagging performance).

How Does the Organization Deal with Management Resistance?

There are many reasons why a manager might resist employee career development. One of the most effective means to increase a manager's commitment to career development is to *make it available for the manager as well as the subordinate.* Once the manager's career is attended to, he or she will be more supportive of career development for employees. The second critical factor is to *reward managers for development of subordinates* (e.g., as part of the manager's performance appraisal). In this way, there is something in it for the manager as well as the employee.

How Can an Organization Do Career Planning when Promotion Opportunities Are Diminished?

Career development programs are *most* critical when there are fewer promotion opportunities. Through career planning a more realistic picture of personal skills, weaknesses, and promotion prospects can be developed by employees. Employees can learn to be best positioned to take advantage of lateral move opportunities and whatever promotional opportunities do exist.

The career development program can also give the organization a relatively nonthreatening opportunity to provide outplacement services to help some employees leave the organization. Thus, in many ways, career development programs can serve as a "safety valve" for the increased employee pressure on limited promotion prospects.

GENERAL PRINCIPLES FOR EFFECTIVE CAREER DEVELOPMENT PROGRAMS

In this chapter, we have examined many ways to facilitate career development, ranging from very person-centered to highly organization-centered. To conclude, let us see what general principles apply regardless of the program or approach used.

Start Small and Build on Existing Human Resource Systems

Career development is a perfect example of where "less is more." Nothing is more likely to fail than a career development effort which tries to do everything at once: individual planning, talent inventories, etc. The result is often an "integrated system", beautiful on paper but never implemented due to its complexity and resistance from everyone except those who planned it.

A far more effective strategy is to start with the human resource systems already in place and build on those. The system most likely in place is a performance appraisal process. It is quite simple to add another step to this process, a discussion between boss and employee of the employee's strengths and weaknesses, plans for the next job, and ways to increase the individual's strengths to best qualify for that desired next step. If there is a succession planning process or centralized staffing activity operating, it is not difficult to add an individual career planning activity. Succession planning is an excellent trigger for a more complete career development activity, since top management cares so deeply about the growth of future generations of leaders for the organization. It is a short step from grooming top executive talent to providing development opportunities to all employees. The idea is to determine what human resource activities are available and then to build on them.

Focus on the Manager as the Career Development Agent

Since most development is provided by the job itself, and since the job is largely defined by the boss, the immediate supervisor is the most promising agent for career development. It is much more efficient to get the boss to coach and counsel employees than it is to attempt to provide one-on-one or group career planning through the human resource department. The boss knows the employee best and has the "clout" to help motivate an employee to improve skills and to make a job move, if necessary, for career growth. Using the boss as the agent of career development means, as we have seen, providing training for managers in employee counseling and coaching, performance appraisal and feedback, mutual goal setting, and job redesign (to provide in-place development). These skills are general management skills, not just employee development skills, so the organization ends up with more effective managers and more developed employees when this approach is used.

Use Human Resource Staff as Third-Party Agents

The line management/human resource partnership is especially important to career development. If managers are to be the primary agents of employee development, then human resource specialists and managers must facilitate the manager's activities. This entails *training* managers in the necessary skills, *monitoring* the process as managers work with employees, *consulting* with managers and employees on special career problems, and *informing* managers and employees of career opportunities in the organization. Perhaps most important, the human resource staff is usually responsible for *designing the overall career development program.*

Provide Realistic Organizational Career Opportunity Information

Employees need information on career opportunities beyond their own particular part of the organization. However, most managers also lack this information. It is useful for human resource personnel to provide information on possible career paths, number of positions at various levels and divisions of the organization, job descriptions for those positions, skills and experience required, etc. Career information manuals can provide this information, as can career resource centers. Also, company-sponsored programs to assist employees in conducting information interviews with employees in different parts of the organization can be a way to develop search skills, so employees can obtain needed information for themselves. For example, employees may feel awkward about exploring career possibilities in another department, but if the human resource department conducted a "Take a Manager to Lunch" program, the barriers to such career exploration would be reduced. Also, periodic career seminars, in which panels of executives from different divisions and departments discuss career paths in their units, can be another powerful way to disseminate career information.

Information extremely useful to an employee is some input on the organization's business directions, so that the person can develop realistic career plans in harmony with the organization's strategic plans. These do not have to be detailed accounts of sensitive, proprietary information, just general trends on where the future growth of the organization will most likely occur. Such information is probably already available to competitors, so there would be little business risk in sharing it with employees.

Focus on All Types of Career Movement

The goal of a career development program is a good fit between the person and the work being performed, so that employee productivity, satisfaction, and growth take place. The ultimate objective is not promotion (which is neither realistic nor desired for many people), but rather to help the person determine what would be a good fit for him or her. This being so, all types of movement become viable: lateral movement, a change in responsibilities within the current job, downward movement, exit, and upward movement in some cases. Most people begin career planning thinking the only sign of success is advancement. Through personal and professional exploration, they usually become aware of a much wider range of options for career fulfillment.

Provide for Individual Differences in Career Needs

As organizations develop more experience with career planning, they realize that the needs of employees change greatly as they move through different career stages. For the person in the trial stage just starting out, there is a need to experience different types of jobs to see where he or she would like to settle down. For the person in the establishment stage, it is important to develop a wide range of skills and to get visibility and exposure for his or her performance. The person in midcareer, on the other hand, may want to rethink career direction and review the relationship between career and personal involvements. All of this means that a range of career development activities is necessary, and these activities need to be tailored to the unique needs of employees in different career stages. There is also a growing number of specialized career programs for people in different life stages and personal situations, such as seminars for two-career couples and working parents. For an example of how one successful organizational career development program has demonstrated these principles, see the description of the Goddard Space Flight Center's program in Box 14.2.

The most important point to remember about career development activities is that they are an ideal way to integrate the needs of the employee with the goals of the organization. The person has need for challenge, job satisfaction, and growth. The organization needs to tap the creative potential of all its employees to a far greater extent than ever before. In the move to a postindustrial service- and knowledge-based economy, organizations need to hire minds, not hands. Career development is an important way to utilize a vast supply of untapped human resource potential.

CAREER DEVELOPMENT AT GODDARD SPACE FLIGHT CENTER

BOX 14.2

What contributes to the success and institutionalization of a career development effort? Few programs have existed long enough to make that kind of analysis, but the longevity—seven years—of the program at NASA's Goddard Space Flight Center offers that opportunity.

A brief description of the organization points to the following characteristics: an R&D organization employing primarily engineers and scientists, with approximately 3,300 employees. When Goddard turned to the University of Maryland for help with career development, it was faced with the following issues: a changing mission, a decline in the growth of the organization, rapid changes in technology, and an aging work force.

The following elements of the program have contributed to its long-term success:

- *Response to organizational problems*—Many programs, such as short-term rotational assignments, were designed to respond to the set of problems described above.
- *Balanced effort*—Interventions continually have been designed which provide employees with information about the organization so they can plan their careers in concert with organization realities.
- *Involvement of first-line managers*—A major programmatic effort has been to provide managers with coaching and counseling skills.
- *Specialized approaches for key target groups*—Different programs and interventions are designed based on the needs of key target groups. For example, a workshop helping engineers considering a move into management is offered. Such a workshop differs greatly from the workshop designed to help clericals consider a move into a professional job.
- *Visible products*—Career development is an intangible process. Constant effort is made at Goddard to design visible products such as planning guides, bulletins, and resource centers.
- *Integration with other training/HRD activities*—Planning and coordination of career development activities and other human resource activities exists. Cooperative programming, rather than a duplication of effort, is the norm.
- *Evaluation and monitoring*—Continual evaluation and assessment of all activities provides data for making program changes. Results are widely publicized.
- *Long-term commitment and involvement of top management*—Top management at Goddard has been visibly committed and involved with the employee development effort. Management was willing to commit a long-term return on its investment, rather than push for only short-term and less substantive results.

Success characteristics of a career development effort such as Goddard's could serve to aid in the design of other career development programs which will endure.

Excerpts from "Career Development at Goddard Space Flight Center—A Long Term Commitment" by Zandy Leibowitz, *Career Development Division Newsletter,* American Society for Training and Development, November 1983, p. 5. Reprinted by permission of the author.

KEY POINTS

▪ There are two basic approaches an organization might take to career development. At the individual level, *career planning* is a deliberate process of becoming aware of self, opportunities, constraints, choices, and consequences; identifying career-related goals; and programming work, education, and related developmental experience to provide the direction, timing, and sequence of steps to attain a specific career goal. At the organization level, *career management* is an ongoing process of implementing and monitoring career plans undertaken by the individual alone or in concert with the organization's planning systems.

▪ Most organizations engage in some sort of career development activities, with the most common being career counseling (either by supervisors or by human resource staff), career planning workshops, and job performance/developmental planning workshops.

▪ The primary audiences for career development activities are management trainees and fast-track management candidates, followed by women employees and minority employees.

▪ A range of issues arise in career programs that include concerns about limiting employee participation, raising employees' expectations unrealistically, providing feedback on career potential, overcoming managerial resistance, and providing career planning under conditions of reduced organizational opportunities.

▪ Principles for effective career development programs include: start small, building on existing human resource systems; focus on the manager as the primary agent of career development; use human resource staff as third-party agents; provide realistic organizational career opportunity information; focus on all types of career mobility; and provide for individual differences in career needs.

ISSUES FOR DISCUSSION

1. What are the two sides of career development? Give an example of each.

2. What employee groups have been the primary beneficiaries of formal career development programs? What are the pros and cons of this focus?

3. What specific approach to career development do you think is most useful? Why?

4. What are the major issues in career development programs?

5. What is the most appropriate role for human resource staff to play in career development? Why?

6. What is the manager's role in career development? Why do you think an organization should take an interest in an employee's career development?

7. How would you build upon the career programs discussed in this chapter to design a program to assist two-career couples with their career planning? What do you think is the appropriate role for the employing organization in assisting couples with career planning?

NOTES

1. Walter D. Storey, *A Guide for Career Development Inquiry: State-of-the-Art Report on Career Development*, ASTD Research series, Paper No. 2. (Washington, DC: American Society for Training and Development, 1979). See also Jeffrey Pfeffer and Yinon Cohen, "Determinants of Internal Labor Markets in Organizations," *Administrative Science Quarterly*, 1984, *29*, pp. 550–72.

2. Thomas G. Gutteridge and Fred L. Otte, *Organizational Career Development: State of the Practice* (New York: American Society for Training and Development, 1982).

3. Gutteridge and Otte, op. cit.

4. John O. Crites, *Theory and Research Handbook, Career Maturity Inventory* (Monterey, CA: McGraw-Hill, 1973).

5. Manuel London and Stephen A. Stumpf, *Managing Careers* (Reading, MA: Addison-Wesley, 1982).

6. James W. Walker and Thomas G. Gutteridge, *Career Planning Practices: An AMA Survey Report* (New York, NY: AMACOM, 1979).

7. Ibid., p. 12.

8. Ibid.

9. Ibid.

10. Walter D. Storey, *Career Dimensions* I, II, III, and IV. (Croton-on-Hudson NY: General Electric Company, 1976).

11. James G. Clawson, John P. Kotter, Victor A. Faux, and Charles C. McArthur, *Self-Assessment and Career Development* (Englewood Cliffs, NJ: Prentice-Hall, 1985).

12. Richard Bolles, *What Color Is Your Parachute: A Practical Manual for Job-Hunters and Career Changers* (Berkeley, CA: Ten Speed Press, Rev. Ed., 1984).

13. London and Stumpf, op. cit.

14. "Succession Planning at Exxon," *Career Development Bulletin*, 1980, *2* (1). p. 1.

15. Ibid., p. 2.

16. A somewhat different and very practical approach to the development of career programs is found in Beverly L. Kaye, *Up Is Not the Only Way: A Guide for Career Development Practitioners* (Englewood Cliffs, NJ: Prentice-Hall, 1982).

17. Marilyn A. Morgan, Douglas T. Hall, and Alison Martier, "Career Development Activities in Industry: Where Are We and Where Should We Be?" *Personnel*, 1979, *56*, pp. 13–30.

ANNOTATED BIBLIOGRAPHY

The Career Bulletin. New York: Graduate School of Business, Columbia University.
   This is a quarterly publication of the Center for Career Research and Human Resource Management at the Columbia University Business School. It contains sections on new practices, recent research, and special reports on topics of current interest (e.g., exit incentives, performance appraisal). Information can be obtained by calling or writing the Career Center Bulletin, Uris Hall, Columbia University, New York, NY 10027, telephone 212/280–2830.

Career Development Division Newsletter. New York: American Society for Training and Development (ASTD).

> This is also a quarterly publication containing news of current activities by ASTD members and member companies. It describes a variety of career-related activities provided by or through ASTD. It is an excellent way for someone with professional interests in the field of career development to become "connected" with others in the field. The *Newsletter* is sent to members of the Career Development Division of ASTD (600 Maryland Avenue, S.W., Suite 305, Washington, DC 20024).

GUTTERIDGE, T. G., and OTTE, F. L., *Organizational Career Development: State of the Practice.* New York: American Society for Training and Development, 1982.

> This is an excellent survey of corporate practices in the area of career development. It describes what is being done, how career programs are started, and what issues arise as the programs are in operation.

KAYE, B. L. *Up Is Not the Only Way: A Guide for Career Development Practitioners.* Englewood Cliffs, NJ: Prentice-Hall, 1982.

> This is an excellent source of ideas for designing and implementing career development programs. An extremely practical, useful handbook for practitioners, it is based upon six stages in program development: preparation, profiling, targeting, strategizing, execution, and integration. Numerous boxes and exhibits provide concrete organizational examples.

ROTHENBACH, W. F. "Career Development: Ask Your Employees for Their Opinions." *Personnel Administration*, November 1982, pp. 43–51.

> This is a national survey of 1,293 employees in a national manufacturing organization to identify issues and needs employees perceived in relation to their careers. The study identified perceived inequities in the career advancement process, relatively little concern by managers for employee career development, and a general lack of awareness by employees of career opportunities. Perceptions also differed by age and sex. Although the data were from only one company, the results seem to be a representative view of employee career needs related to career programs.

CHAPTER FIFTEEN

PERFORMANCE APPRAISAL

When David Stein reported to his manager's office at 9 A.M., he suspected they would discuss David's performance during the past year. He was aware that Ms. Brewster had had several closed-door meetings with her staff in the past two weeks, and recent office gossip had confirmed his hunch that performance appraisal time had arrived again this year. Since David had joined the Marketing Department ten months ago, he was quite excited about receiving a formal assessment of his work and discussing his future with the company.

"David," Doris Brewster began, "I suppose you know that my department follows company policy and completes performance appraisal forms on all employees once a year. Please read through your form and let me know your reactions."

David quickly scanned the boxes checked under Quality of Work, Quantity of Work, Initiative, Attendance, and Maturity and then moved on to the section, Main Strengths and Improvements Needed. "Why is my rating only average in Attendance?" he asked.

"Oh, that category applies only to non-exempt employees, so I gave an average rating to all of my exempt employees," replied Ms. Brewster.

When David questioned his rating of average on Initiative, Ms. Brewster told him he hadn't been around long enough to show much initiative, but she expected more of him next year. A brief discussion followed about the rationale for the other ratings and the few words in the Strengths and Improvement section. Then Ms. Brewster informed David that he would receive a 6 percent salary increase and asked him to sign the form. David left after only twenty minutes, feeling disappointed and uncertain about the quality of his work and his future with the department.

Adrian Bentley was also aware that it was time for performance appraisal in her organization because her manager, Ken Rickets, had called her and arranged an appointment for next week. He requested that Adrian review the work goals they had set a year ago and rate her success in achieving them, and outline her main job responsibilities and note any changes that had occurred in them during the past year. He also asked her to prepare a list of her work goals for the upcoming year, her training needs, and her long-term career objectives.

Mr. Rickets began the meeting by summarizing the purpose of performance appraisal in his department and then asked Adrian for her input. In the ensuing hour *and a half, Adrian raised the points she had prepared and her boss probed for her rationale and gave his reactions. By the end of the discussion, Adrian had revised some of her evaluations of her success in achieving work goals, discussed and amended her work and developmental goals for the following year, and received Mr. Rickets's endorsement of the changes she had made in her job duties. She left the meeting with a thorough understanding of her boss's evaluation of her work, a clear plan for next year, and a strong sense of commitment to the department.*

*I*t is through performance appraisal that employees learn what the boss thinks of their work. **Performance appraisal** is *the process through which the organization assesses the quality of the work of its employees and attempts to improve their performance.* This process affects employees significantly. It affects their pride in their work and even their self-esteem. People who are committed to their careers, such as Adrian Bentley, can be thrilled and motivated by a positive assessment of their work and just as deeply disappointed and hurt by a negative or unclear assessment, as in the case of David Stein. The process of performance appraisal strongly affects how employees feel about their employer and themselves.

performance appraisal

Performance appraisal also has a powerful influence on what happens to employees in their careers. It is the basis of many important decisions such as salary increases, transfers, and promotions. Many a career has received an early boost through the recognition and appreciation of excellent performance, while others have come to an abrupt halt because of poor performance.

The systematic measurement of employee performance is an essential step in the operation of an organization. All employees are hired by organizations to produce goods or services, and to survive and prosper, organizations must monitor the performance of employees to ensure that they are producing at acceptable levels.

The assessment of employee performance is also a crucial step in the process of human resource management. Performance is one of the major results of the optimal fit between the individual, job, organization, and environment, and performance appraisal is the tool through which the quality of the fit can be assessed and improved. It provides information that can be used to assess the effectiveness of some key human resource functions discussed in this book. Successful performance is what is being predicted with various selection tools, and it is a desired result of employee training and career development. Performance appraisal also provides the basis for line managers to help employees improve their performance by identifying the causes of poor quality work and taking appropriate action (coaching, training, motivating, planning) to increase quality.

THE ROLE OF THE LINE MANAGER

Of all the human resource functions discussed in this book, performance appraisal probably requires the most involvement of line managers. Performance appraisal is basically a tool that supervisors and managers use to assess and improve employee performance. Human resource professionals can design a technically sound appraisal process, with the best available rating forms, policies, and procedures, but if line managers do not *implement* the system well, it is doomed to failure.

The performance appraisal process takes two fundamental forms. The first, *supervisory feedback*, is very informal and occurs spontaneously in contacts between manager and employee. As line managers see their employees in the work setting, they observe the manner in which the employees are performing and the results of their performance. For example, one employee fails to follow instructions and produces a faulty product, another works too slowly, a third performs assigned tasks consistently well, and a fourth does everything fast and well and asks for more. As line managers interact with their employees, they are continually observing, assessing, and taking steps to influence employee performance.

The second kind of performance appraisal, *performance review*, is the more formal interaction between manager and employee that occurs one or more times a year, in which the boss evaluates the employee's performance and has a discussion to help him or her improve. Performance review is common in large organizations and requires line managers to follow standardized procedures for observing and recording employee performance with various methods we will discuss later in this chapter. Then, line managers conduct interviews with their employees to inform them of their performance review and to discuss plans for improvement.

These two forms of performance appraisal clearly complement one another. Systematic supervisory feedback provides essential raw material for the annual performance review, and regular interaction between manager and employee enables them to carry out and monitor work plans made in the annual review. Many small organizations have no formal system of performance review and rely entirely on supervisory feedback to monitor and improve employee performance. In larger organizations both types of performance appraisal are used.

OBJECTIVES OF PERFORMANCE APPRAISAL

As any line manager can testify, assessing employee performance and discussing it with an employee is often difficult and time-consuming. It can be stressful for manager and employee alike. Indeed, recent surveys have indicated that between 30 percent and 50 percent of employees believe that formal performance reviews are ineffective. A Psychological Associates, Inc., survey of 4,000 employees in 190 companies found that 70 percent of employees claim that performance appraisal interviews did not give them a clear idea of what was expected on the job, and only 50 percent said that their managers helped them set work objectives.[1] In another major study, "Supervision in the '80s: Trends in Corporate America," Opinion Research Corporation reported that first-line supervisors and middle managers lack skills to supervise others, and few communicate effectively.[2]

But if properly designed and implemented, the performance appraisal process can be very beneficial to both employees and employers. A starting point often overlooked in organizations is the explicit consideration of the objectives to be achieved in performance appraisal. The choice of objectives strongly affects how formal performance appraisal systems are designed and implemented. Performance appraisal has two primary objectives, which we shall now examine.

Human Resource Decisions

One fundamental objective is to provide the basis for decisions about individual employees. For example, which employees should be promoted, transferred, left in their current jobs, or terminated? Who should receive salary increases or bonuses? Certainly, an assessment of employee performance should enter into these decisions.

Similarly, performance appraisal provides information to evaluate the effectiveness of major human resource functions. Assessments of performance are useful in measuring the effectiveness of training programs (Chapter Twelve) and in validating selection tools (Chapter Nine).

Employee Development

The second fundamental objective is to provide assistance to employees so they can develop in their work lives and reach their potential as working people. Performance appraisal provides the following:

1. *Feedback and recognition*—Most employees want to know how they're doing on the job and to be recognized for their performance. Systematic

performance appraisal can provide them with this information and satisfy their need for recognition.

2.   *Personal development*—Performance appraisal can help reveal the causes of good and poor employee performance. Through discussions of the assessment with individual employees, a line manager can discover why they perform as they do and what steps can be taken to improve their performance. One employee may need to have the job more clearly defined, another may need special training, a third may need more autonomy and responsibility, and a fourth may need some coaching and encouragement. Changes in the employee, the job, or the entire work situation (including the manager's behavior) may improve the employee's opportunity to perform well.

3.   *Goal setting*—Once the causes of employee performance have been identified, specific plans must be made that will lead to desired changes in performance. This can take place in a discussion in which the manager and employee set out specific, shared goals to be addressed in the next appraisal period. Goals may be set to achieve results on the job (e.g., a 5 percent increase in sales volume), or to improve job performance (e.g., more planning to help the employee organize time and work better). They may also be *developmental* goals that increase the employee's potential to perform successfully (e.g., attending a training course in time management).

4.   *Career development*—Long-term planning may also occur in connection with performance appraisal. In addition to short-term goals for the next appraisal period, the manager and employee may discuss plans for a three-to-five-year period. This discussion addresses basic questions that most employees have asked themselves at one time or another, such as, What kind of work can I do best? What kind of work do I prefer doing? Where am I heading in this organization? What steps do I have to take to get there?

Notice that all four of the purposes served by the objective of employee development require discussion with the employee. If one fundamental objective in performance appraisal is to develop employees, then feedback and planning are essential steps in that process. Therefore, we will address the performance appraisal interview as an integral part of the appraisal process later in this chapter.

Choice of Strategy

As Exhibit 15.1 shows, the objective the organization chooses to emphasize in performance appraisal (human resource decisions or employee development) affects both the method of appraisal and the policies and procedures line managers follow to implement the appraisal system. For example, some organizations view performance appraisal primarily as a way to evaluate employees and award salary increases according to each employee's contribution to the firm. Therefore, elaborate policies are established to ensure that the

EXHIBIT 15.1

PERFORMANCE APPRAISAL STRATEGY BY OBJECTIVE

	Communicate Human Resource Decisions	Develop Employees
Appraisal Forms:	Designed to evaluate overall performance and rank-order employees.	Designed to evaluate performance, to identify causes of poor performance, and to set goals for improvement.
Timing:	Appraisals are done when salary increases are awarded.	Appraisals are done as often as necessary to improve employee performance.
Distribution:	Evaluations are reviewed and forced into a distribution which approximates a desired salary distribution.	Less emphasis is placed on the distribution of evaluations.
Interviews:	Appraisal interviews focus on justifying salary increases and other decisions.	Appraisal interviews focus on employee performance and goal setting.

distribution of employee evaluations approximates the distribution of planned merit increases (e.g., a policy of "forced distribution" which requires managers to place 10 percent of their employees in the lowest performance category, 20 percent in the next, 40 percent in the average category, 20 percent above average, and 10 percent in the highest category). Appraisal interviews are done when salary increases are given and focus on justifying the size of the increase.

Organizations that emphasize the objective of employee development usually use a more complex appraisal form that not only documents the level of employee performance but also includes sections on employee strengths and weaknesses and developmental plans and work goals for the coming year. Appraisal interviews are held as often as necessary and concentrate on feedback and goal setting.

THE PERFORMANCE APPRAISAL PROCESS

The process of performance appraisal is planned, designed, and implemented through a series of steps outlined in Exhibit 15.2. All nine steps should be followed in organizations that plan to use formal systems of performance review, and most of the steps also need to be included in organizations where informal supervisory feedback is the only form of performance appraisal. Note

EXHIBIT 15.2 **PERFORMANCE APPRAISAL PROCESS**

Prior to Appraisal Period	During Appraisal Period	After Appraisal Period
1. Identify Objectives and Establish Policies and Procedures	5. Observe Employee Performance and Results	7. Evaluate Performance and Results
2. Analyze Jobs	6. Document Performance and Results	8. Discuss Appraisal with Employee
3. Design Measures of Performance		9. Follow-up: Observe Employee Performance and Results
4. Communicate Performance Standards to Employees		

that the first four steps in the process take place prior to the appraisal period, the period of time during which employee performance is observed and assessed (one year in the cases of David Stein and Adrian Bentley).

Let us examine these steps in some detail.

1. Identify objectives and establish policies and procedures. As we have already noted, a crucial first step in establishing a system of performance appraisal is for senior managers and human resource professionals to decide on the objectives the organization will emphasize and to establish the appropriate appraisal forms, policies, and procedures they wish line managers to follow.

2. Analyze jobs. Next, human resource professionals analyze jobs or review existing job descriptions to identify the types of performance to be assessed in the organization. It is often useful to involve line managers in this step because they are familiar with the jobs in their department and can specify the key performance categories they wish to assess and improve in their employees. Often similar jobs are grouped (e.g., all exempt jobs or all semi-skilled jobs), for which different measures of performance are designed.

3. Design measures of performance. Next, human resource professionals design or select measures of performance, which form the basis for the organization's performance appraisal system. In David Stein's organization the measures were rating scales, while Adrian Bentley's department used work goals to assess performance. As in the previous step, line managers can make useful suggestions about the kinds of performance they wish to evaluate and the sections they wish to include in the appraisal form.

4. Communicate performance standards to employees. Line managers are responsible for the remaining six steps. Prior to the appraisal period, they communicate performance standards to employees to ensure that all employees know the level of performance they are expected to attain. It is useful to review appraisal forms with employees and check to see if they understand their job responsibilities and work goals.

5. Observe employee performance and results. Direct observation of either on-the-job performance or results during the appraisal period is essential. This has implications for who is *qualified* to appraise an employee's performance. A rule of thumb is that the person who *knows an employee's work best* should appraise that employee's performance. This usually means that the employee's immediate supervisor is responsible for the employee's performance appraisal.

Most line managers directly observe the performance and results of their employees in their daily or weekly interactions with them. There are some instances, however, in which a manager may have minimal employee contact for weeks or even months. This is particularly likely to occur with employees who work away from the office. Periodic location visits by the boss in such a situation are essential to establish a sound basis for performance appraisal.

6. Document performance and results. Probably the most serious error in the process of performance appraisal occurs at this stage. Some documentation of employee performance and results is crucial for several reasons. First, it can be used as evidence against charges that the organization's appraisal process discriminated against employees protected by civil rights legislation (Chapter Five). Second, it offsets the tendency of line managers to remember recent and unusual events and to forget instances of routine, acceptable job performance. Documentation insures that the appraisal will be based on a representative sample of employee performance during the appraisal period. Third, documentation is especially important to the feedback phase (to be addressed shortly) in which managers discuss their appraisals with employees. With documentation, they can provide instances of employee performance on which the appraisal was based.

Routine documentation can be incorporated into the performance appraisal process without a great deal of additional time and effort from managers. Results are routinely recorded in most organizations, so managers can merely seek them out before appraising employees. Managers can systematically record employee performance by keeping a diary of specific instances of performance.

7. Evaluate performance and results. Once the employee's performance and results have been observed and recorded, they must be evaluated against some standard. Observation and documentation take place throughout the appraisal period; evaluation occurs as the manager fills out the appraisal form. Evaluation is, and will always be, subjective. There is no way to remove some element of subjectivity from the performance appraisal process. Even objective results (e.g., sales, units of production, waste) or objective indicators of performance (lateness or absences) *must be interpreted* in the context of some standard. But the subjectivity can be minimized with good measures of performance and sound instruction in the use of the measures.

8. Discuss the appraisal with the employee. Some discussion is necessary to explain decisions (salary increases, promotions, and transfers) that are based on the appraisal and to make plans to improve employee performance. This discussion occurs in the performance appraisal interview.

The performance appraisal interview can be a difficult experience for employee and manager alike. It requires a high degree of skill from the manager, but unfortunately the vast majority of line managers receive no training in how to conduct this interview.

9. Follow-up: observe employee performance and results. The primary objective of performance appraisal is to develop employees so they perform their jobs better, and to coach and guide them as often as necessary *after the performance appraisal interview* to assist employees in making changes. In the final phase of the appraisal process, managers monitor and reinforce employee performance and provide guidance when needed. This follow-up of a given appraisal period overlaps with the observation phase of the next appraisal period.

Designing the Performance Appraisal System

As we have already noted, the partnership between human resource professionals and line managers is particularly important in performance appraisal. Once senior management has decided which objectives (human resource decisions or employee development) to stress in performance appraisal, then human resource professionals take the major responsibility for designing the appraisal system, consisting of the *forms* and *procedures* which line managers use to assess and improve the performance of their employees.

Designing the system is very important, for if the organization's measures of employee performance are flawed, all hope of successful implementation is lost. Two fundamental decisions have to be made in the design of a performance appraisal system, what performance to assess, and how to measure that performance. The choice of the performance to be assessed sets the tone for the entire organization. For example, the choice of poorly defined personality characteristics like initiative and maturity in David Stein's organization contributed to the ambiguity and mystery of the appraisal process, while the use of job-related objectives in the case of Adrian Bentley created a more positive tone. This choice says to all employees, "This is what we expect of you, this is how we want you to develop yourself, and this is the basis of all the rewards you will receive from this organization." Human behavior on the job is very complex, and job performance can be broken down into a large number of "pieces" or dimensions. Selecting a relatively small number of dimensions of job performance to assess is the first step in designing a performance appraisal system.

The next step is to decide how to measure the dimensions of performance selected. Suppose "quality of output" is chosen. How is it to be measured? What about maturity, innovation, profits, or teamwork? What objective or subjective measures can be used to measure them?

Standards for Measures of Performance Appraisal

Certain standards can be used as guidelines for the two fundamental choices of what performance to assess and how to measure that performance.[3] The first two standards apply to the choice of what dimensions of performance to include in the performance appraisal system. They are relevance and accountability.

Relevance ▬▬ **Relevance** is *the relationship between each dimension of performance and some important personal or organizational goal.* In short, the chosen dimension should be worth evaluating and developing in employees. Relevance is largely a matter of judgment about how much a particular dimension contributes to success on a given job. For example, accident rate may be judged as an important dimension of performance on a factory floor, but not so in an office setting. Leadership effectiveness may be included in the performance appraisal for supervisors, but not for clerical employees. Thorough job analysis is necessary to judge the relevance of any dimension of performance.

relevance

Accountability ▬▬ **Accountability** is *the extent to which a dimension of performance can be attributed to a specific employee.* It is a judgment of how much influence the individual employee has over the performance being assessed. For example, should team leaders be held accountable for the effectiveness of their five team members? Probably yes. But should a departmental manager be held accountable for the turnover rate among the 200 departmental employees? Perhaps not, because the relationship between the manager's performance and employee turnover is not very clear. If important decisions concerning salary and promotion are based on a dimension of performance, then its accountability should be high.

accountability

Once the decision has been made to include a number of dimensions of performance in an organization's appraisal system, then accurate measures of these dimensions must be found. This is not as simple as it may sound. How can quality of output, leadership effectiveness, accident rate, or sales volume be measured? Are these measures fair to all employees and practical for line managers to use? These questions can be answered with the four standards below.

Reliability ▬▬ **Reliability** is *the extent to which the measure of performance yields consistent results when applied at different times or by different methods.* Of course, all employees vary somewhat in peformance from month to month, but most people perform relatively consistently over a period of time. Consequently, a reliable measure of performance taken at different times produces similar assessments. Reliability also refers to how consistently a measure of performance is applied to the same employee by different appraisers. For example, a subjective measure of performance, such as a rating scale of supervisory style, would have low reliability if a manager received a low rating on supervisory style from one executive and a high rating from another.

reliability

Validity ▬▬ **Validity** is *the extent to which the measure of performance actually reflects that performance.* Validity can be determined by comparing a given measure of performance with other measures of the same performance. But even the most obvious measures may lack validity because they are contaminated by other influences. For example, dollar volume of sales may reflect not only the performance of a sales person, but also regional busi-

validity

ness conditions, past records of sales and service to customers, and the influence of a competitor's sales force.

fairness

Fairness ▬ **Fairness** is *the extent to which measures of performance differentiate among employees solely on the basis of differences in performance.* Assessments on a fair measure are therefore not influenced by such personal characteristics as age, sex, race, and religion. The same government regulations that apply to employee selection (see Chapter Nine) also apply to performance appraisal. In short, any measure of employee performance that discriminates against employees of a protected class is unlawful.

As we will discuss later in this chapter, government regulations have had a significant impact on the methods used in organizations to appraise employee performance. Many methods that were used routinely in the past have been found by federal courts to discriminate against protected groups.[4] The courts have found performance appraisal methods to be discriminatory under the following conditions:

1.   They were not based on job analysis.
2.   They contained subjective, undefined, global measures of performance.
3.   They may have been affected by sexual or racial bias.
4.   They were not validated to demonstrate their relevance to job performance.
5.   They were not collected and scored under standardized conditions, thus compromising their reliability and validity.

It is likely that many, if not most, performance appraisal systems currently in use would fare very poorly if subjected to close scrutiny by the courts.

practicality

Practicality ▬ The final standard is **practicality,** *the extent to which measures of performance can be used without undue time and effort.* Organizations do not exist for the sake of complex, esoteric performance appraisal procedures, but instead, performance appraisal exists to serve the organization in its quest for employee productivity and satisfaction.

There are several aspects of practicality. The benefits of sound measures of performance should clearly outweigh the costs in managers' and employees' time and effort. The measures must also differentiate between good and poor performers; an appraisal procedure that yields nearly identical evaluations for all employees serves no purpose. Finally, the performance measures must provide useful input for good human resource decisions and employee development.

WAYS TO MEASURE EMPLOYEE PERFORMANCE

What measures of employee performance should be included in an organization's performance appraisal system to meet the dual objectives of good human resource decisions and employee development? The large number of potential measures fall into three main categories, shown in Exhibit 15.3.

PERFORMANCE APPRAISAL MEASURES

EXHIBIT 15.3

	Traits	On-the-Job Performance	Results
Information Collected	What Employee Is	What Employee Does	What Employee Achieves
Methods Used	Narratives of Employee Strengths and Weaknesses, Rating Scales	Checklists, Behaviorally Anchored Rating Scales, Behavioral Observation Scales	Management by Objectives, Work Planning and Review

SOURCE: James G. Goodale, *The Fine Art of Interviewing*, ©, 1982, p. 72. Adapted by permission of Prentice-Hall, Inc., Englewood Cliffs, N.J.

Traits

One very common approach to performance appraisal is to assess the personal characteristics and abilities of employees that presumably *cause* them to perform successfully or unsuccessfully. For example, consistently good performance under stressful conditions may be attributed to an employee's dependability and maturity. Another employee's success as a manager may be attributed to superior intelligence and personality. Similarly, a technical employee may succeed because of creativity and initiative. Other employees may be viewed as unsuccessful because of a poor attitude, poor organizational ability, or low motivation.

Traits such as the examples above are typically assessed in one of two ways. One approach is to have the manager write a brief *narrative* about the traits of a particular employee that influence his or her work performance positively or negatively. Such an appraisal frequently leads to a discussion of employee strengths and weaknesses. The second approach is through the use of a rating scale. The trait rating scale is still the most commonly used measure of employee performance in today's organizations, though its use may be on the decline.[5] Rating scales come in many sizes and shapes, but they all consist of the characteristic to be assessed and a series of numbers or phrases representing different *levels* of the trait (examples appear in Exhibit 15.4). The rater simply marks the level on the scale that best describes the employee being assessed.

The widespread use of measures of personal traits is puzzling, because they are clearly the *weakest* of the three approaches outlined in Exhibit 15.3. First, the relevance of employee traits (e.g., maturity, dependability, initiative, personality, and attitude) to successful job performance and the attainment of organizational goals is at best questionable. It can be argued that the kind of people employees are inevitably affects their behavior in any setting, but the relationship between general personal characteristics and performance on a specific job is unclear.

The accountability of measures of traits must be considered high because personal characteristics can certainly be attributed to individual employees. Employees may be unable to change some of their personal charac-

EXHIBIT 15.4   *TRAIT RATING SCALES*

PERFORMANCE APPRAISAL REPORT (CONFIDENTIAL)   APPRAISAL DATE_____

Name   Title   Time in Present Position

Division/Department   Employment Date   Last Review Date

Appraised by   How Long Have You Supervised Employee?

Rate each factor below. Base ratings on overall performance during total period since last appraisal. "Comment" sections are provided after each factor to allow remarks of qualification regarding a particular rating. Attach evaluation to salary review sheet; direct both to Personnel Group. Recommendation: Discuss appraisal with employee after report has been returned to you from Personnel Group.

(CIRCLE APPLICABLE NUMBERS)

	1 *Poor; Definite improvement needed*	2 *Fair; Meets minimal job standards*	3 *Good; Consistently meets standards*	4 *Excellent; Usually exceeds standards*	5 *Superior; Consistently exceeds standards*
Initiative	1	2	3	4	5
Comments. _____					
Maturity	1	2	3	4	5
Comments. _____					
Creativity	1	2	3	4	5
Comments. _____					
Diligence	1	2	3	4	5
Comments. _____					
Attitude	1	2	3	4	5
Comments. _____					

teristics, such as mental and physical abilities, aggressiveness, and tolerance for stress, but they can be held accountable for the characteristics they reveal on the job.

The reliability of measures of traits is low. On most scales, the trait to be rated is not defined, and the levels are indicated with ambiguous terms such as "poor," "fair," and "consistently exceeds minimal requirements." This forces managers to define the traits themselves, and the result is about as many different definitions of the trait as there are managers. The reliability of rating traits is further lowered by four common rating errors. The so-called *halo* error occurs when a manager forms a general impression of an employee and then gives the employee similar ratings on a number of specific traits that may not be related to one another. The other three rating errors involve concentrating evaluations within certain ranges of the rating scale. A manager committing the *leniency* error rates most employees above average, while another shows the *severity* error by rating most employees below average. Finally, the error of *central tendency* involves concentrating all ratings toward the middle of the rating scale.

Validity of measures of traits is also low because traits cannot be directly observed but must be inferred from behavior. This indirect measurement is therefore very subjective and makes it difficult to demonstrate with any precision what is being measured.

Measures of traits for performance appraisal also fail to meet the standard of fairness. Trait rating scales have been found by the courts to be particularly susceptible to managerial bias against protected groups because they have no clear relationship to job performance.

Practicality of evaluations of traits is mixed. Trait rating scales are quick and easy to construct, but they are very difficult to complete because of their extreme ambiguity and questionable relevance. Their susceptibility to the four rating errors interferes with their differentiating between good and poor performers. Finally, trait rating scales produce feedback of questionable use to employees who wish to change their performance because of the ambiguity of the feedback.

On-the-Job Performance

A second approach to performance appraisal is based on incidents of actual on-the-job performance. Managers are asked to observe and record what employees *do* on the job and then to transform the recorded incidents into an evaluation. These appraisal methods may be subjective or objective. In a common subjective method, the boss or employee makes a list of the employee's major responsibilities (a job description is sometimes used) and the boss judges how well the employee has performed each responsibility. The number of errors made by a typist, number of products assembled in an hour, and number of instances of tardiness or absence are objective indicators of job performance that can be counted and recorded. At appraisal time, evaluations are based on the number of errors, products, times tardy, or absences recorded for a given employee.

Another technique that measures performance is a *behavioral checklist*[6] made up of "critical incidents." A group of managers with good job knowledge prepares a comprehensive list of specific incidents of on-the-job behavior critical to successful or unsuccessful performance. To appraise a given employee, a manager checks the critical incidents that he or she has observed the em-

EXHIBIT 15.5 **BEHAVIORAL OBSERVATION SCALE**

This behavioral observation scale was used in an organization's Strategic Planning Group (SPG) to assess the job performance of managers. Supervisors circled the number that most closely represented the frequency with which the manager demonstrated each behavior. Total score represented the manager's rating on the dimension of performance.

Team Playing

Invites the input of SPG managers on issues that will directly affect them before making a decision

    Almost Never   0   1   2   3   4   Almost Always

Explains to SPG the rationale behind directives, decisions, and policies that may or will affect other divisions

    Almost Never   0   1   2   3   4   Almost Always

Keeps SPG informed of *major* changes in the department regarding people, policies, projects, construction, etc.

    Almost Never   0   1   2   3   4   Almost Always

Continually seeks input of SPG as a group on capital policy and plans rather than engaging primarily in interactions with individual managers

    Almost Never   0   1   2   3   4   Almost Always

Is open to criticism and questioning of decisions from SPG members at SPG meetings

    Almost Never   0   1   2   3   4   Almost Always

Supports SPG decisions

    Almost Never   0   1   2   3   4   Almost Always

Generates new ways of tackling new or ongoing problems

    Almost Never   0   1   2   3   4   Almost Always

Solicits comments from SPG members on the effectiveness of the structure of the organization

    Almost Never   0   1   2   3   4   Almost Always

SOURCE: Adaptation of "Team Playing" from Appendix B, pp. 234–35 in *Increasing Productivity Through Performance Appraisal* by Latham and Wexley. Copyright © 1981 by Addison-Wesley, Reading, Massachusetts. Reprinted with permission.

ployee engaged in. The items checked are combined to compute a numerical appraisal.

Recent adaptations of the critical incidents technique are *behavioral observation scales* and *behaviorally anchored rating scales*.[7] Although they are forms of rating scales, their focus is on performance, rather than traits.

An example of a behavioral observation scale is shown in Exhibit 15.5. It consists of a dimension of performance and a number of behavioral examples of that dimension. Each behavioral example is accompanied by a five-point scale of frequency of occurrence. In the appraisal process, managers check the frequency with which they have observed an employee performing each behavioral example. Total ratings are then computed on each dimension of performance.

Behaviorally anchored rating scales are similar in form to the trait rating scale shown in Exhibit 15.4. Both are headed by the concept being evaluated, and both have a rating scale consisting of a series of numbers and phrases that represent various levels of the concept being evaluated. But the behaviorally anchored rating scale differs substantially from the trait rating scale in its focus and meaning. The concepts being evaluated, such as communicating or applying technical knowledge and skill, are dimensions of performance, and can therefore be directly observed. In addition, the levels of performance along the rating scale are defined with examples of on-the-job performance, rather than by vague adjectives such as poor, average, excellent, etc. Clearer definition of both the dimension of performance being evaluated and the levels along the scale aids managers in their interpretation of what they are to appraise.

The relevance of these three measures is good because they evaluate actual on-the-job performance that is related to success on the job. The selection of the dimensions of performance to be included in each method is based on thorough job analysis and is made by managers of the employees to be appraised.

The accountability of measures of performance is also high. Employees can clearly be held accountable for their specific behavior on the job and can be rewarded accordingly.

One way to improve reliability and validity is to provide the manager doing the appraisal with a clearly defined measure. In general, behavioral observation scales and behaviorally anchored rating scales are somewhat more valid and reliable than trait rating scales, although the research results are by no means clear-cut.[8] Validity and reliability are increased when:

1. The concepts being rated are observable dimensions of performance, rather than traits.
2. The concepts being rated are clearly defined.
3. The phrases along the rating scales that define levels of performance are carefully developed.
4. Managers are trained in their use.

The superiority of measures of on-the-job performance is most evident when measures are assessed by the standard of fairness. Measures of performance can be designed to comply very precisely with legislation prohibiting discrimination in employment practices.

1. They can be based on job analysis and input from managers who know the job well.
2. The dimensions of performance are observable, specific, and well defined.
3. They are less likely to be affected by sexual or racial bias.

others, manage people, and follow directions. Results represent the *ends* that employees strive for in their work. They make the sale, produce the product, prepare the report, and meet the deadline.

No appraisal system is complete without some measure of on-the-job-performance. Objective measures should be used if they are available, but in most cases subjective measures will be necessary. The choice of format—checklist, behavioral observation scale, or behaviorally anchored rating scale—is largely a matter of preference, for no format has clear superiority over the others. The more important matter is that the appraisal method be *comprehensive* and represent the dimensions of performance that are relevant to the work of the employees being appraised. The dimensions of performance should be selected on the basis of thorough job analysis, and they should be clearly defined.

The appraisal system should also include the assessment of results that can be recorded and evaluated. A results-oriented approach to performance appraisal encourages a future orientation in that achievements of the last appraisal period are reviewed and goals for the next appraisal period are set. The advantage of a results-oriented appraisal system is its flexibility. That is, results and goals can be chosen that apply to a given job or employee.

This dual approach—measuring on-the-job performance and results—is especially effective in meeting the objective of employee development. In the performance appraisal interview, it is useful to focus not only on *what* was achieved, but *how* it was achieved. If a manager fails to reach a goal of reducing turnover, feedback on performance that affected that goal (e.g., supervising employees, planning and organizing, communicating) is useful. A discussion of the *ends* achieved and the *means* to those ends provides comprehensive feedback.

Developing and Implementing a Performance Appraisal System

The performance appraisal system, which includes measures of performance and policies governing their use, needs improvement in most organizations. Many have been developed via the "arm chair" method in which a human resource specialist sits in the office and creates an appraisal form consisting of trait rating scales. The forms are then mailed to managers with minimal guidance on how to use them. Since the appraisal process is vital to any organization, the performance appraisal system should be carefully designed and introduced. After senior management has selected the goals to be achieved through performance appraisal, there are six steps involved in designing and implementing the system. We recommend that human resource professionals and line managers work together in each of the following steps:

1. Conduct a thorough analysis of all the jobs in the organization to be covered by the performance appraisal system. Since job analysis is an essential first step in a number of the human resource functions described in this text, up-to-date job descriptions may be available.

2. Combine the jobs into a few relatively homogeneous clusters. It is sometimes necessary to develop more than one appraisal system in an organization that contains clearly different groups of jobs. Different systems may be developed for exempt and non-exempt employees or for supervisory and non-supervisory employees. For example, the measures of performance included in Box 15.1 were used only for oil-field production employees.

3. Identify the dimensions of performance to be included in the appraisal system and develop objective or subjective measures of those dimensions. It is especially important to involve line managers who will actually use the appraisal tool in this step. Their input will likely increase the relevance and validity of the measures, and their involvement will generate increased commitment and better implementation of the appraisal system.

4. Hold orientation meetings to introduce the new performance appraisal system to all employees in the organization. Appraisal forms, policies, and procedures should be introduced and explained at this time.

5. Hold training sessions for all supervisors and managers who will use the new appraisal system. Too often steps 4 and 5 are omitted, and new appraisal forms and manuals are merely distributed to line managers. A technically superior appraisal system will achieve nothing if it is not properly implemented, and training is a crucial step.

6. Test the reliability and validity of the new measures of performance. Test-retest reliability can be examined by correlating evaluations of employees done on two different occasions. It may also be possible to have some employees evaluated by two people (e.g., supervisor and co-worker or supervisor and manager) and correlate the two sets of appraisals to estimate inter-rater reliability. Validity can be computed by correlating ratings of performance with results attained by a group of employees.

These six steps take time, but they can produce an excellent appraisal system for line managers to use and thereby improve the performance appraisal process in an organization. Box 15.1 illustrates how the first five steps were followed in a division of Gulf Oil Corporation.

THE PERFORMANCE APPRAISAL INTERVIEW

The performance appraisal interview is a discussion between an employee and his or her immediate supervisor that focuses on that employee's performance during the past appraisal period and also includes some planning for changes in future performance.[11] As we have said, this interview requires a great deal of skill. Managers who have a good day-to-day relationship with employees often see that relationship severely strained during this formal interview. A poorly handled performance appraisal interview, such as the one involving

DESIGNING AND INSTALLING A PERFORMANCE APPRAISAL SYSTEM

BOX 15.1

Prior to 1980, the Production Department of the Western Division of Gulf Oil Exploration and Production Company had no formal training programs for non-exempt field jobs such as roustabout, lease operator, instrument technician, and well tester. Industry and commercial schools were evaluated and found to be inappropriate for the company's use. In the early 1980s, the Production Department began to train full-time employees for these field production jobs. A two-year training program was designed to provide on-the-job and classroom training for both new and older employees as they progressed from the entry-level job of roustabout to more senior positions.

Members of the Human Resource Department and the Production Department decided to design a performance appraisal system for the non-exempt field jobs so that promotions of new employees to more senior jobs could be based on a sound measure of performance. They also planned to use the appraisal system to measure the effectiveness of the training program. They were particularly interested in the number of months of training needed to produce employees who reached acceptable standards of performance on the job.

They began the project by reviewing and revising the job descriptions of all non-exempt field jobs. Then a group of experienced field supervisors identified ten dimensions of on-the-job performance that were present in all the field jobs and could be directly observed and assessed:

- Following instructions,
- Following safety requirements,
- Maintaining equipment and facilities,
- Working independently,
- Housekeeping,
- Recording and communicating,
- Planning and organizing time and work,
- Working with others,
- Applying job knowledge,
- Supervising Gulf and contract employees.

The supervisors then defined the dimensions and wrote examples of poor, moderate, and good performance on each to develop a set of behaviorally anchored rating scales.

A manual describing the objectives and procedures of the new performance appraisal system was distributed to all field supervisors in one-day orientation sessions. During the sessions, the origin and purpose of the new system were outlined, and all participants filled out rating forms for one of their own employees. In addition, they practiced performance appraisal interviewing with role-playing cases. The main objective of the orientation sessions was to ensure that the new appraisal system was implemented consistently and effectively throughout the Production Department.

This experience at Gulf illustrates a sound procedure for designing and installing a new performance appraisal system. The procedure began with job analysis of a relatively homogeneous cluster of field jobs. Then supervisors who would use the new system played a major role in designing the measures of performance. Finally, the new system was introduced through orientation and training sessions to ensure proper implementation.

The authors wish to thank Mr. F. H. Martin for his assistance in preparing this material.

PERFORMANCE APPRAISAL INTERVIEW

EXHIBIT 15.7

Weaknesses	Solutions
Multiple Objectives	*Specific Objectives*
Conflict exists between communicating human resource decisions and developing employees.	Focus on employee development.
	Tailor interview objectives to the employee.
Objectives require the interviewer to assume multiple roles.	
Poor Measures of Performance	*Avoid Ambiguous Measures*
Many measures are highly subjective.	Use measures of on-the-job performance or results.
Feedback is not useful to the employee.	
	Make feedback useful to the employee.
Poor Approach to the Interview	*Approach the Interview Properly*
Managers do not have a well-considered approach.	Choose an approach to enhance employee development.
No one approach works with all employees.	Adapt the approach to the individual employee.

SOURCE: James G. Goodale, *The Fine Art of Interviewing* ©1982, pp. 69–70. Adapted by permission of Prentice-Hall, Inc., Englewood Cliffs, N.J.

David Stein, can confuse and demoralize an employee. On the other hand, an effective interview can be a very exhilarating and motivating experience for the manager and the employee.

Weaknesses of the Performance Appraisal Interview

Conducting performance appraisal interviews may be the most difficult assignment that line managers and supervisors are asked to carry out by human resource professionals. Three major weaknesses of the interview and their solutions are summarized in Exhibit 15.7. Let's begin with the weaknesses.

Multiple Objectives ▬▬ Attempts in one interview to communicate human resource decisions based on assessments of employee performance and also to develop employees often lead to difficulties.[12] The discussion of human resource decisions tends to take precedence over the objective of enhancing employee development. In many cases, as soon as the discussion turns to the percentage of salary increase or the denial of a desired promotion, goal setting and upward communication are lost in the shuffle. If the employee is unhappy with the raise, he or she may ask the boss to justify the decision. At this point the boss may present the appraisal in defense of the decision, and the employee may counterattack. The discussion can degenerate into a rather heated debate in which little actual listening occurs. This atmosphere is hardly conducive to a positive discussion of employee development.

Furthermore, the two basic objectives of performance appraisal require that line managers assume two quite different roles during the interview. In one role, managers are primarily giving information to their employees. They have to do a good deal of talking to communicate salary decisions and give employees feedback on their performance. As they discuss the causes of employee performance, set work goals, and discuss career plans, managers assume a more passive role of seeking information and listening. These two roles require a high level of skill from the interviewer.

Poor Measures of Performance ■■■ As discussed earlier, since the most common measure of performance is the trait rating scale, most organizations' performance appraisal systems are seriously flawed. Ratings of personal traits are highly subjective, have low relevance to job performance, low reliability and validity, and violate federal guidelines.

Such poor measures create special problems in the interview. Managers have difficulty justifying decisions about promotions and salary increases on the basis of highly subjective assessments of initiative, maturity, and attitude. Furthermore, ratings of ambiguous traits provide feedback that is of little use to employees who wish to improve their job performance.

Poor Approach to the Interview ■■■ Discovering an approach to conducting the performance appraisal interview that works for them is often difficult for line managers and supervisors. Simply proceeding as they usually do in their daily contact with employees is not likely to work. The performance appraisal interview is more formal and important than everyday interactions between a boss and an employee.

Managers often begin these interviews simply by telling the employee of their evaluation of his or her performance and making suggestions for improvement. Such a beginning almost invariably leads to one of two fundamental approaches to the performance appraisal interview: *Tell and Sell* or *Tell and Listen*.[13] In the first approach, the manager's main intention is to tell the employee what is right and wrong with his or her performance and what changes are necessary in the future. The manager then strives to convince the employee to accept this judgment. The manager assumes the role of an all-powerful and all-knowing judge and uses various persuasive techniques to get the employee to accept the judgment. Employees often become defensive in the interview and resent the one-sided nature of the discussion. This approach rests on the questionable assumptions that the manager's assessment of the employee's performance is complete and accurate and that the employee does not wish to contribute to the discussion. Consequently, this approach often fails to produce a plan to improve employee performance that is endorsed by both parties.

In the Tell and Listen approach, the manager also serves as a judge and tells employees what is right and wrong with their past performance. This approach is based on the assumption that the boss has all the answers and need only communicate them to the employees. After the telling is done, however, the manager does not press employees to accept this judgment, but allows them to vent feelings of disappointment and defensiveness. The manager allows employees to complain about how they were evaluated and remains understanding and sympathetic during this phase. The assumption is that if employees are allowed to express their feelings, they will be more likely to accept the manager's judgment ultimately. Note that there is more upward communication in this interview than in the Tell and Sell, but the employees still contribute nothing to the manager's evaluation of them; hence a successful interview is rare.

Improving the Performance Appraisal Interview

The key to effective appraisal interviews is careful preparation. Managers must consider their objectives, the nature of feedback, and the way they wish to approach the interview.

Plan the Interview to Meet Specific Objectives ▬▬▬ The complex objectives and roles assumed by the interviewer prompted Herbert Meyer and his colleagues (who were then at General Electric) to recommend that the two major objectives—communicating human resource decisions and developing employees—be addressed in separate interviews.[14] Although recent research, also done at General Electric, has indicated that employees want to learn about decisions concerning salary increases and promotion during the performance appraisal interview,[15] we think that Meyer's original recommendation that line managers place emphasis on *either* employee development *or* human resource decisions in the interview is still sound. If an organization's primary objective in performance appraisal is to develop employees, then policies can be established to support that objective. For example, many organizations conduct *performance appraisal interviews* before salary budgets have been set for the coming year. These interviews are aimed primarily at employee development and can be conducted several times a year. After each department receives its final salary budget and salary increases are determined, a second set of annual *salary review interviews* are conducted to communicate and justify human resource decisions. This practice not only separates the difficult discussion of salary from the performance appraisal interview, but also prevents managers from working backward (i.e., deciding on a merit increase and then appraising employee performance to justify the increase). Since this practice of conducting two separate interviews appears to be on the rise in organizations, the remainder of this section will focus on the performance appraisal interview dealing primarily with employee development.

One more point on objectives should be addressed. The objective of employee development contains four components: feedback and recognition, personal development, goal setting, and career development. Before conducting a performance appraisal interview, managers need to review these four components to determine which are appropriate for a given employee. All four may apply to new, career-oriented employees, but with seasoned employees who have reached their peak in an organization, managers may wish to limit the interview to giving feedback and recognition and setting goals for the next year. It is important that managers have a clear plan for which components are most suitable for each employee before conducting an interview.

Avoid Ambiguous Measures ▬▬▬ The solution to faulty performance measures is to develop measures that focus on performance and results, not on personal traits. Employees should be evaluated in terms of what they do and what they achieve, not what they are. Relevant, reliable, and valid measures also contribute to successful appraisal interviews because they provide employees with *useful feedback*. Useful feedback is behavioral, specific, balanced, and future-oriented.

First, as we have already discussed, feedback should be given about what employees *do* or *achieve*, not about what they are. Personal feedback makes employees defensive. Feedback from trait rating scales passes judgment on the basic character of employees and threatens their esteem. They are likely to argue with assessments of their personality and attitude and be insulted by ratings of their maturity and initiative. In addition, personal feedback is not useful because it provides too little information to employees who wish to change their job performance. However, if a boss gives feedback on what employees *do* on the job that leads to the conclusion of a poor personality or a bad attitude, the employees will find this feedback more useful. They have more control over how they behave. If a boss says to a particular employee, "You frown and interrupt customers when they raise reservations about our product," "You doodle and do paperwork when others are speaking in sales meetings," or "You push clients too hard when trying to close a sale," the employee can use this feedback. He or she may not like what the boss has said, but he or she can stop frowning, interrupting, doodling, and pressuring clients.

Second, feedback in performance appraisal interviews should be specific. Telling employees that they are doing an adequate job and asking them to do better probably will not improve their performance. This is not because the assessments are incorrect, but because the feedback is too general to give employees enough detailed information about what they have done that needs to be changed.

Instead, line managers and supervisors need to give employees detailed feedback that specifies the behaviors to be altered on a daily or weekly basis, and the behaviors to be maintained at a high level. Feedback that is specific and behavioral is more likely to have a positive effect on how employees perform in the future.

One of the cruel realities of performance appraisal is that praise is often given in general terms, but criticism is almost always specific. For example, an employee may be told, "We're very pleased with your performance in the technical area. This is a strength that has stood out in your work ever since you joined the company." This general praise may encompass over 50 percent of the employee's job responsibilities, but it says very little about what he or she is doing well. Consider the negative feedback:

> . . . and you simply must pay more attention to detail. Remember that shipment you sent to Birmingham, England, rather than Birmingham, Alabama? Do you realize how much that cost the company? $1,352.43! We just can't tolerate that kind of mistake.

This brings us to the third characteristic of good feedback, balance. Because praise is typically general and criticism specific, time spent on criticism is often much greater than time spent on praise. Many performance appraisal interviews are characterized by a "sandwich" approach. They begin with a minute or two of general praise, followed by that telltale word "but" or "however." Then comes twenty-five minutes of discussion about problem areas and ways in which the employee needs to improve, followed by a brief dose of reassuring praise. The result is an interview in which most of the time is spent on what the employee has done wrong, even though the employee may be performing acceptably on most facets of the job.

It is important to maintain a balance between positive and negative feedback in the performance appraisal interview. This balance will be achieved if line managers give specific, behavioral feedback about not only the job facets in which employees must improve, but also the facets in which they are doing well.

Fourth, good feedback is future-oriented. The past is dead and should not be belabored in a performance appraisal interview. Rather, it should serve as a springboard to plan the future. It is important, therefore, that line managers turn their attention to the future and set some goals before completing the interview. These goals are most likely to be achieved if they are *specific*. General goals such as "doing my best" or "trying harder" are less likely to lead to improved performance. Like New Year's resolutions, they are easily set and just as easily forgotten. Furthermore, general goals provide unclear targets. Employees may be highly motivated to change, but general goals like "being more cooperative," "improving my attitude," or "working harder to meet the sales quota" are too vague to specify where employees should direct their energies.

Finally, whenever possible, goals should also be endorsed by both the manager and the employee. People tend to form a stronger commitment to goals they set for themselves than those they are instructed to achieve. Therefore, a performance appraisal interview in which employees set their own specific goals is most likely to lead to changes in performance.

Approach the Interview Properly ▬▬ To improve the success of the performance appraisal interview, Maier suggests a problem-solving approach, in which the role of the manager shifts from judge to helper.[16] The manager's intention is to allow employees to evaluate their own performance, identify their own problems, and set their own goals for improvement in the future. The boss begins the interview by asking employees to evaluate their own performance. During this discussion the manager uses non-directive skills such as paraphrasing ideas and feelings, asking for elaboration and clarification, and summarizing to draw out the employee's ideas and evaluation. There is a strong orientation toward the future in this interview, as the employee is encouraged to set goals for improved performance and to identify steps necessary to meet these goals. These steps may include informal assistance from the manager or more formal training courses or even changes in job responsibilities.

As Maier points out, the problem-solving approach has its pitfalls. When asked for a self-appraisal, the employee may say very little or may fail to raise the problems the boss wishes to address. When asked for goals, the employee may have none to offer. Such employees may respect the boss and want to be told how they are doing and what changes to make. Another risk is that the employee may have plenty to say, but it may not be what the manager wants to hear. The employee may evaluate his or her performance quite differently than the manager has evaluated the employee. The employee may also propose goals which the manager feels are inappropriate.

What is needed is an approach to the performance appraisal interview that enhances employee development and can be adapted to the individual employee. Our recommendation is a composite of the problem-solving and telling types of interviews. Beginning with a telling approach will make it almost impossible to shift in the same interview to a problem-solving approach. If the interview begins with an overwhelming flood of downward communication, there is little likelihood that much upward communication will follow. Therefore, managers should begin with problem-solving and then shift to telling if necessary in an approach called problem-solve and tell.[17]

Conducting the Performance Appraisal Interview

Careful preparation is essential prior to the interview. Line managers and supervisors must assess the performance of their employees and give some thought to developmental plans for each. This preparation will enable them to enter the interview with an agenda containing an assessment of each employee's past performance and ideas of how he or she may change.

The basic premise of the problem-solve and tell approach is to allow the employee to raise as much of the manager's agenda as possible in the interview, thereby minimizing the amount of "telling." To maximize potential upward communication in the interview, employees need to do some preparation, too. Prior to the interview, managers should encourage them to do some thinking about their performance in the past year and their work and career goals for the coming year. The nature of the employees' preparation depends on the organization's performance appraisal system. In a system of manage-

EXHIBIT 15.8

FEEDBACK GUIDE

	Positive Feedback	Negative Feedback
Employee Aware	I	III
Employee Unaware	II	IV

ment by objectives or work planning and review, employees will review past goals and set new goals for the future. In a system where performance is evaluated formally, employees may rate their own performance on a checklist or rating scale. It is important that employees enter the interview having looked both to the past and to the future.

This preparation for the interview by both manager and employee will generate two agendas, with some degree of overlap. The matrix in Exhibit 15.8 summarizes the information about the employee's past performance that is contained in the agendas of the two parties. Employees come to the interview with an awareness of some facets of the job they perform well and those in which improvement is needed. This information is contained in quadrants I and III. Employees may be unaware of their manager's assessment of other facets of their job performance. For example, a salesperson may attribute decreased volume to economic conditions, whereas the sales manager attributes lost volume to the salesperson's ineffectiveness in promoting a new product line to customers. Similarly, an employee may think little of his or her informal training sessions with new employees, but the boss views them as a very positive feature of the employee's performance. This kind of information falls in quadrants II and IV of Exhibit 15.8. The key to success in the problem-solve and tell approach is for the manager to draw from quadrants I and III *extensively* before adding information from quadrants II and IV. To do so, line managers and supervisors can follow a seven-point interview format outlined below.

Restate the purpose of the interview. The employer can begin the interview by saying that the time has come to meet with employees to discuss how they have performed during the past year and to hear their plans for the next appraisal period.

Get the employee talking about past performance. The goal during this early stage of the interview is to encourage the employee to raise points from quadrants I and III. Open-ended questions such as, "How would you assess your own performance over this past year?" "What goals do you feel you have achieved during this past year?" or "What achievements have given you a particular sense of satisfaction at work during the last twelve months?" are useful. As the employee responds, managers need to listen very carefully for points to pursue.

Focus on quadrant I and add items from II. The real tone of the interview is set here. Managers must resist the temptation to jump to the "telling" portion of the interview or to focus only on their agenda items. Instead, patience is required to probe for what the employee has to contribute. If, for example, an employee's assessment of his or her performance is, "I think I've done fine," the ball is very abruptly back in the boss's court. He or she can come back with a more specific question to keep the employee talking. For example, "Well, I'm pleased to hear that you feel that way. Can you name some of the things you've done that you are particularly pleased with?"

As the employee raises topics, managers must remember them and bring each up later for discussion. The discussion should begin with a positive topic from quadrant I, as the manager probes into *how* the employee performed in that area. This questioning uncovers the causes of successful employee performance. For example, "So you feel you've been particularly successful this last year in developing your juniors. What steps have you taken to bring them along so well?" or "You mentioned your improvement in servicing customers during the last several months. How have you changed your approach?" Then managers can add some of their own topics from quadrant II for discussion.

Focus on quadrant III: probe for how and why. After discussing a number of the more positive aspects of an employee's performance, managers can turn their attention to the areas needing improvement. They should try to begin with negative feedback of which the employee is already aware. If employees raise disappointments or concerns in response to initial questions, managers can raise them at this point of the interview with questions like, "You mentioned earlier that you were concerned about your working relationship with the service group. What has led to your concern?"

If employees do not raise any negative points in response to initial open-ended questions, managers can encourage them to raise some negative assessments at this point in the interview by asking, "From our discussion so far, it sounds as if you feel pretty satisfied with the past year. Are there any areas in which you feel you need to improve?" Then listening and learning become crucial. Managers should probe into the specifics of *how* the employee has approached a facet of his or her job and *why* the problems have arisen.

Add items from quadrant IV, if necessary. It is at this juncture in the interview that managers can add negative feedback that has not already been addressed. In some interviews there may be nothing to add, while with other employees the boss may need to raise major weaknesses in performance. In the discussion of the negative feedback, managers should probe for the causes of unacceptable performance through questions of how the employee approached the job and why the failures occurred.

Set specific goals. On the basis of the discussion to this point, the manager and employee are now ready to set goals that are as specific as possible and are ideally endorsed by both parties. Some of these goals may have already emerged in the earlier discussion, but this is the time to restate and record them.

Propose follow-up. Plans for change may be discussed in the fervor of the moment and quickly forgotten. It is useful to conclude the interview by setting the timing and nature of the follow-up to monitor the employee's proposed goals. Through this follow-up, managers can also assess whether the goals are appropriate or feasible. If, for example, an employee sets a goal that is not compatible with company policy or is beyond the employee's personal capabilities, quick follow-up will enable the supervisor and employee to revise the goal.

ORGANIZATIONAL CULTURE, APPRAISAL STYLE, AND SUPERVISORY STYLE

The way in which employees respond to the performance appraisal process depends on two major factors. The first is the recent history of performance appraisal in the organization. A kind of culture evolves from the emphasis an employer places on objectives (employee development and human resource decisions), appraisal methods, policies and procedures that govern the appraisal process, and the way feedback is given. In some organizations managers view the annual rating forms as annoying paperwork, while in others they complete the forms with great care. Some employees believe that favoritism and politics lead to salary increases and promotions, while others perceive clearly the link between evaluations of performance and organizational rewards.

The second factor is the way managers conduct the appraisal interview. Although we recommend the problem-solve and tell approach for most situations, line managers and supervisors must conduct the interview in a way consistent with their style of supervision. For example, an autocrat who tries to adopt this approach will be viewed with suspicion or even disbelief. Such a boss is probably better off with a tell-and-sell approach. Managers who practice a consultative or participative style of supervision, however, will find the problem-solve and tell approach quite compatible.

Employers have typically not addressed the two factors discussed above in a comprehensive way. Instead, they have focused on the evaluation form or the policies and procedures for filling it out and awarding salary increases.[18] Performance appraisal is more likely to contribute significantly to organizational effectiveness if human resource professionals and line managers focus on the *entire* process in Exhibit 15.2.

EEO AND PERFORMANCE APPRAISAL

Like other major human resource activities, performance appraisal is governed by federal equal employment opportunity legislation. Title VII of the Civil Rights Act of 1964 prohibits discrimination in terms, conditions, and privileges of employment, and the 1978 Uniform Guidelines on Employee Selection Procedures clearly specify that EEO legislation applies to employment decisions such as "promotion, demotion, retention, and transfer . . . and other decisions [that] lead to any of the decisions listed above."[19] In sum, any formal or informal assessment of employee performance that leads to human resource decisions (e.g., promotion, transfer, salary increase, or participation in employee training and development activities) is subject to charges of discrimination against protected groups.

In our earlier discussion of *fairness*, one of the standards for measures of employee performance, we noted some of the conditions under which federal courts have found performance appraisal methods to be discriminatory. Since the early 1970s, over 100 court cases have generated a considerable body of case law that provides practical guidelines concerning the design and implementation of performance appraisal systems that comply with EEO legislation.[20]

Design

Several guidelines affect the way the appraisal system is designed and measures of employee performance are chosen:

1. Gain support for the appraisal system by conferring with top management and other supervisory personnel to identify its major objectives.
2. Conduct job analyses or review and revise current job descriptions for all jobs covered by the appraisal system and identify common dimensions of performance and results that contribute to organizational goals.
3. Select or develop measures of job performance or results that meet the standards of relevance, accountability, reliability, validity, fairness, and practicality. Avoid global measures of personal traits.
4. Design appraisal forms and establish policies concerning the timing and frequency of performance appraisals.
5. Provide an appeal process for employees who disagree with their supervisor's evaluation of their performance or human resource decisions based on that evaluation.

Implementation

Once an appraisal system that can be defended in court has been designed, a number of guidelines will contribute to its fair and effective implementation and reduce the likelihood of complaints from minority and female employees:

1. Ensure that line managers discuss objectives of the appraisal system, performance standards, appraisal forms, and policies and procedures with their employees.
2. Train line managers how to observe and evaluate employee performance to reduce common rating errors and the effects of personal bias,[21] and how to conduct appraisal interviews.
3. Carefully document and store appraisals of employee peformance for use in making human resource decisions and in responding to EEOC inquiries.

4. Ensure that line managers conduct performance appraisal interviews to discuss employee performance and set developmental and performance goals with employees.

5. Ensure that line managers continue to systematically observe employee performance and results to determine whether developmental and work goals are being met.

These guidelines are consistent with earlier discussions of the performance appraisal process and the standards for performance appraisal measures. If human resource professionals and line managers work together to follow them, they will produce a performance appraisal system that not only conforms to EEO legislation, but is also technically superior and likely to be endorsed by managers and employees alike.

KEY POINTS

- Performance appraisal, the process of assessing and improving the quality of employees' work, provides input to develop employees and make decisions about salary increases, promotions, and transfers.

- Employee performance is assessed with measures of personal traits, on-the-job performance, or results. In spite of their poor quality, trait rating scales continue to be the most widely used measure of employee performance.

- Performance appraisal is a joint responsibility of staff and line personnel. Human resource professionals take the lead in designing appraisal measures and procedures, and line managers and supervisors appraise performance and discuss the appraisals with their employees.

- The performance appraisal interview often fails because the supervisor concentrates on telling employees what is right and wrong with their performance and how they can improve. More two-way problem-solving communication is the key to successful appraisal interviews.

- To avoid discriminating against women and minorities, employers must ensure that their performance appraisal system is designed and implemented according to equal employment opportunity guidelines.

ISSUES FOR DISCUSSION

1. Outline the nine steps in the performance appraisal process. Which do you think are most crucial to successful performance appraisal? Why?

2. If an organization chooses to stress the objective of employee development in its performance appraisal system, what kind of appraisal forms and policies is it likely to develop? What kind of appraisal forms and policies are common in organizations that place more emphasis on the objective of facilitating human resource decisions?

3. Define the six standards for assessing the quality of performance measures. Summarize the quality of the three measures of employee performance, using these standards.

4. What are the major weaknesses of the performance appraisal interview and what can be done to improve its effectiveness? Discuss your personal experience in a performance appraisal interview and its impact on you.

5. Suppose you joined an organization in which trait rating scales were the sole measure of employee performance. As a line manager, what steps would you take to improve the appraisal process for your employees?

6. How does equal employment opportunity legislation apply to the performance appraisal process? What guidelines can an organization follow to avoid discriminating against protected groups?

NOTES

1. C. Hymowitz, "Bosses: Don't Be Nasty (and Other Tips for Reviewing a Worker's Performance)," *Wall Street Journal*, Jan. 17, 1985, p. 29.

2. J. Guyon, "Performance Reviews," *Wall Street Journal*, August 28, 1984, p. 1.

3. These standards are adapted from: R. M. Guion, *Personnel Testing* (New York: McGraw-Hill, 1965); P. C. Smith, "Behavior, Results, and Organization Effectiveness: The Problem of Criteria," in M. D. Dunnette (ed.), *Handbook of Industrial and Organizational Psychology* (Chicago: Rand McNally, 1976), pp. 745–75.

4. W. F. Cascio and H. J. Bernardin, "Implications of Performance Appraisal Litigation for Personnel Decisions," *Personnel Psychology*, 1981, *34*, pp. 211–25; L. S. Kleiman and R. L. Durham, "Performance Appraisal, Promotion and the Courts: A Critical Review," *Personnel Psychology*, 1981, *34*, pp. 103–21; D. B. Schneier, "The Impact of EEO Legislation on Performance Appraisals," *Personnel*, 1978, *55* (4), pp. 24–34.

5. A. H. Locher and K. S. Teel, "Performance Appraisal—A Survey of Current Practices," *Personnel Journal*, 1979, *56*, pp. 245–47 and 254; T. Rendero, "Consensus: Performance Appraisal Practices," *Personnel*, 1980, *57* (6), pp. 4–12.

6. J. C. Flanagan, "The Critical Incident Technique," *Psychological Bulletin*, 1954, *51*, pp. 327–55.

7. G. P. Latham and K. N. Wexley, "Behavioral Observation Scales for Performance Appraisal Purposes," *Personnel Psychology*, 1977, *30*, pp. 255–68; P. C. Smith and L. M. Kendall, "Retranslation of Expectations: An Approach to the Construction of Unambiguous Anchors for Rating Scales," *Journal of Applied Psychology*, 1963, *47*, pp. 149–55.

8. P. O. Kingstrom and A. R. Bass, "A Critical Analysis of Studies Comparing Behaviorally Anchored Rating Scales (BARS) and Other Rating Formats," *Personnel Psychology*, 1981, *34*, pp. 263–89; F. J. Landy and J. L. Farr, "Performance Rating," *Psychological Bulletin*, 1980, *87*, pp. 72–107; G. P. Latham and K. N. Wexley, *Increasing Productivity Through Performance Appraisal* (Reading, MA: Addison-Wesley, 1981).

9. For details on procedures for the development of behaviorally anchored and behavioral observation scales, see: J. G. Goodale; "Behaviorally Based Rating Scales: Toward an Integrated Approach to Performance Appraisal," in W. C. Hamner and F. L. Schmidt (eds.), *Contemporary Problems in Personnel*, 2nd ed. (Chicago: St. Clair Press, 1977), pp. 246–54; Latham and Wexley, "Behavioral Observation Scales for Performance Appraisal Purposes."

10. G. S. Odiorne, *Management by Objectives: A System of Managerial Leadership* (New York: Pitman, 1965); H. H. Meyer, E. Kay, and J. P. R. French, Jr., "Split Roles in Performance Appraisal," *Harvard Business Review*, 1965, *43*, pp. 123–29.

11. Much of this section is adapted from J. G. Goodale, *The Fine Art of Interviewing* (Englewood Cliffs, NJ: Prentice-Hall, 1982), pp. 68–96, 169–85.

12. Meyer, Kay, and French.

13. N. R. F. Maier, *Psychology in Industrial Organizations*, 4th ed. (Boston: Houghton Mifflin, 1973).

14. Meyer, Kay, and French.

15. E. E. Lawler, III, A. M. Mohrman, Jr., and S. M. Resnick, "Performance Appraisal Revisited," *Organizational Dynamics*, Summer 1984, *13*, pp. 20–35.

16. Maier, op. cit.

17. Goodale, op. cit., p. 89.

18. E. E. Lawler, III, A. M. Mohrman, Jr., and S. M. Resnick, "Performance Appraisal Revisited," op. cit.

19. "Uniform Guidelines on Employee Selection Procedures," *Federal Register*, Part IV, August 25, 1978, Section 2B.

20. For a synopsis of major cases, see H. J. Bernardin and R. W. Beatty, *Performance Appraisal: Assessing Human Behavior at Work* (Boston: Kent Publishing, 1984), pp. 42–61; H. S. Feild and W. H. Holley, "The Relationship of Performance Appraisal System Characteristics to Verdicts in Selected Employment Discrimination Cases," *Academy of Management Journal*, 1982, *25*, pp. 392–406; G. P. Latham and K. N. Wexley, *Increasing Productivity Through Performance Appraisal*, pp. 13–35.

21. H. J. Bernardin and M. R. Buckley, "A Consideration of Strategies in Rater Training," *Academy of Management Review*, 1981, *6*, pp. 205–12; W. C. Borman, "Format and Training Effects on Rating Accuracy and Rater Errors," *Journal of Applied Psychology*, 1979, *64*, pp. 410–21.

ANNOTATED BIBLIOGRAPHY

BERNARDIN, H. J. and BEATTY, R. W., *Performance Appraisal: Assessing Human Behavior at Work*. Boston, MA: Kent Publishing Company, 1984.

This text offers comprehensive coverage of its topic to students, researchers, and practitioners in human resource management. The authors stress the importance of job analysis in developing appraisal systems and also include legal considerations. Drawing on extensive research, they review performance appraisal methods and formats and evaluate their effectiveness. Also included are detailed recommendations and flowcharts for developing performance appraisal systems.

LATHAM, G. P. and WEXLEY, K. N., *Increasing Productivity Through Performance Appraisal*. Reading, MA: Addison-Wesley, 1981.

Written for human resource managers and business students, this book stresses the importance of developing high-quality measures of performance and training supervisors to use them properly. The strengths and weaknesses of various measures are discussed, and detailed guidelines are included for designing and implementing performance appraisal systems.

MAIER, N. R. F., *The Appraisal Interview*. New York: Wiley, 1958.

This classic book introduced the three basic approaches to performance appraisal interviewing—tell and sell, tell and listen, and problem solving. The assumptions, gains, and risks of each approach are discussed, and interview transcripts from a role-playing case are included. Detailed analyses of the transcripts point out the skills required by supervisors and the reactions of employees to each type of interview.

CHAPTER SIXTEEN

ORGANIZATIONAL EXIT

When Betty Alexander was given a "golden handshake" (an attractive cash bonus for voluntarily retiring early), she said that, at 43, she was "too young to retire." So instead, she will use the separation bonus from Metropolitan Life Insurance Company to help finance a career switch she had already been planning. Her retirement pension will be held for her until she reaches age 55, although the payments will be lower than they would have been if she had stayed with the company, and her bonus will be equal to one and one-half years' salary based on twenty years of service for the company. She will use the money to complete a masters degree in social work. "Now I can go to school full time," she commented happily.[1]

A co-worker, Dorothy Antonium, who at 49 also had two decades' service with Metropolitan, made the opposite decision and stayed with the company. She did not think that the reduced pension and risk of unemployment were worth the sizable bonus. "Waiting to age 55 to pick up 72 percent of my pension didn't satisfy me," she said.[2]

The cases of Ms. Alexander and Ms. Antonium represent a new issue being faced by more employees and employers: making choices about how and when an employee will leave an organization. These cases also indicate some of the creative new arrangements under which people are leaving organizations.

Even in Japan, known for long-term employment security, organizational exit is becoming more common (see Box 16.1). In recent years, there has been a marked increase in the number of ways a person can leave an organization. In the past, people generally remained with one organization until they retired, occasionally switching companies to improve their career prospects. If their performance was poor, and the organization was willing to make difficult decisions, they might be fired. However, in many organizations, managers were reluctant to confront poor performers, especially if they were approaching retirement age, so that "good old Joe" was often carried on the payroll for years, perhaps after being "put on the shelf" (transferred to a nonessential job).

EXECUTIVES PAID TO SIT BY WINDOW

BOX 16.1

In Japan they're called the "tribe that sits by the window." They're middle-aged executives working mostly for large companies who get paid for doing almost nothing.

Given various prestigious but meaningless titles, these white-collar workers are assigned desks by the window where they can bask in the sun and read newspapers all day. For this routine they often draw salaries of $4,000 a month or more. Many have access to lavish expense accounts.

In the United States, they are known as "deadwood" and often are the targets of corporate purges.

In Japan, they are known as "madogiwa zoku"—the window tribe. They rose to management positions during the heyday of Japan's economic boom. Under Japan's traditional lifetime-employment system they normally cannot be fired, except for serious misdemeanors. This has caused a "corporate headache" in Japan's business world.

How to get rid of them is a problem faced by personnel managers among top companies like Mitsubishi, Mitsui, Marubeni and Nissho-iwai.

"Officially, we don't have any," said Mutsua Sato, public relations manager for the giant Mitsui Co.

But he estimated about 700 of the company's 11,000 employees belong to the window tribe.

Beginning April 1, the company will offer certain employees 30 million yen (about $150,000) if they will retire early. That amount, which includes a special allowance, is about three times as much as the retirement allowance usually granted employees when they retire at 57.

The new system is to be applied to male employees between 48 and 52 years old, but the company expects only two to three people to take advantage of the system initially. The firm has the backing of the labor union, somewhat unusual in this country where firms expect total devotion in exchange for complete job security.

"By shelling out such large sums we're saving money, believe it or not," Sato said in an interview. He said an employee working until normal retirement age could expect to earn nearly $500,000 in his last ten years at work.

"We have to restructure the system, that is very clear. The seniority system will remain up to the age of 40, along with annual pay hikes. After that, people will be judged solely on their merits."

Adapted from "Executives Paid to Sit by Window" by Richard Bill, *Fort Myers News-Press*, March 18, 1979. Reprinted by permission of The Associated Press.

Many forces have altered these practices, with the result that more people now change employers more frequently. As a result of corporate human resource management strategies to improve productivity and prune costs, more marginal performers are being fired (or, to use the human resource jargon, "terminated"). As a result of changes in the laws on mandatory retirement, companies are less willing to carry "good old Jane or Joe" until age 70 (rather than 65, as was the previous retirement age in many places). As a result of tight economic conditions, many companies have cut expenses by "reducing head count" (i.e., cutting staff), an understandable move since in most companies the largest single expense item is wages and salaries.

Head count reductions or "reductions in force" ("RIFs," a term used more in government organizations) can be achieved in several ways. One is to put a *freeze on hiring* and allow attrition to cut employment; as people leave for the normal reasons, they are simply not replaced. Another common method is the *layoff*, in which people are dropped from the payroll, with the least experienced leaving first. The understanding is that, when conditions improve, they will have the opportunity to be rehired in order of seniority.

Several innovations related to retirement have expanded the options for older employees. *Early retirement programs* make it possible to retire before the normal age, with certain reductions in benefits. *Voluntary severance programs* provide cash incentives (usually linked to length of service) for leaving the organization. *Flexible or phased retirement* provides ways to make a gradual transition from work to retirement. In short, the traditional "pink slip" is now coming in different shapes and colors. In this chapter, we will examine the variety of ways a person can leave an organization.

CONSTRAINTS ON THE FREEDOM TO FIRE

Twenty years ago the bulk of this chapter would have dealt with how to fire or discharge an employee. Now, however, it is becoming increasingly difficult and costly for an organization to unilaterally let an employee go, which is one reason for the focus on voluntary separations.

One factor curtailing the freedom to fire is the threat of discrimination suits. Many employees now belong to at least one protected group: women, racial minorities, handicapped persons, older workers (40–70 years of age), etc. If an employee in one of these groups is fired and sues the organization for discriminatory treatment, unless the firm has evidence that the action was impartial and performance-related, the organization could have a difficult case on its hands. And the fact is that many organizations simply do not have performance records on employees adequate to support termination.

In unionized firms, the labor contract provides another set of constraints on management's ability to fire employees.

A third and rapidly growing factor curtailing the freedom to fire is legislation that would prohibit employers from firing workers except for just cause. Bills to outlaw unjust firings have been introduced in California and Michigan. In Massachusetts, Governor Michael S. Dukakis is supporting legislation to regulate plant closings, to require a minimum advance notice period, and to require employers to assist employees in retraining and job search.

Research indicates that when employees do have ways to appeal firings, such as through union grievance procedures, half of the firings are overruled. Since about three million people in the United States fired each year have no access to an appeal process, it can be argued that over a million people are fired annually without just cause.

To make the anti-firing bills more acceptable to employers, the appeal process would be arbitration instead of more costly litigation. Also, the bills would rule out punitive damages, awards with no upper limits. (For example, in thirty-two jury trials in California between 1980 and 1984, six workers won awards exceeding $600,000.) The proposed bills generally tend to award job reinstatement and lost pay to employees who have appealed their terminations.

At the same time, many employers have taken steps to limit arbitrary firing. In a study of 2,000 large companies, almost 900 already have a voluntary appeal process for dismissals. It is apparent that the increased interest in legislation has greatly increased companies' interest in voluntary programs, and that it is important that companies have a system to deal with internal complaints fairly.[3]

TOWARD A SHARED DECISION TO EXIT

The line between voluntary and involuntary exit from an organization is becoming increasingly blurred. On the one hand, people who perform poorly are often counseled about their work and may decide the real problem is a poor job fit and decide to leave on their own. Perhaps they sense that if they do not resign they might soon be fired. Even people who are fired are often offered the face-saving option to resign. People being fired also find that they may have a considerable amount of bargaining power to negotiate the conditions of their own termination (due to a variety of factors such as the employer's sense of fairness, guilt, or desire to avoid conflict).

On the other hand, in the case of employees thinking about leaving a job because of dissatisfaction or the desire to seek added opportunities elsewhere, the employer is now more likely to play an active role in the employee's decision process. One option here is through a career counseling program, where organizational specialists, usually housed in the human resource department, help the employee arrive at the decision that is best for him or her. Or a "deal" may be struck, such as that offered by certain Big Eight accounting firms. The organization agrees to help the person find another job if the employee agrees to stay until an agreed-upon date (after the busy tax season). For organizations with busy peak periods, such as accounting firms tied to government tax schedules, the ability to plan for and depend upon proper staffing is crucial. It is in the firm's interest to help even the most valued employees leave—if they agree to leave at the right time. More and more, companies are also assisting employees to make decisions about retirement. One way is to offer the person extra inducements either to remain longer or to retire earlier. Pre-retirement career/life planning workshops to give employees a realistic preview of retirement life, to explore the range of post-retirement work and lifestyle options, and to provide financial counseling, are another form of assistance. (Career workshops are discussed in detail in Chapter Fourteen, Career Development Programs.)

Just as plans and decisions throughout the career cycle are being managed more by both the employee and the organization, so is the process of leaving the organization. The organizational exit is becoming part of the self-directed or "protean" career as well as an area for which the organization feels more responsibility.[4]

It may seem reasonable that the employee would care about the exit process, but why should the organization be concerned? Enlightened companies find there are many benefits to managing the exit process. First, the easier and more mutually satisfying it is for an employee to leave the organization, the easier it is for the organization to use the exit as part of its human resource management strategy. If there are no standard procedures to reduce the work force other than regular turnover, firings, and retirement, managers will go to great lengths to avoid terminating people because it is so difficult and unpleasant.

Second, the more control the organization exercises over people's leaving, the more options it has to hire and develop people. The manager who knows that he or she may be stuck with a new employee for life will be much more cautious in hiring people. If a manager knows that he or she will be held accountable for how he or she deals with an employee who is being fired, that manager will be more careful to hire employees with a strong likelihood of succeeding. The manager will attempt to reduce risk and carefully select people who will fit, rather than hiring in a more casual manner.

A third reason to manage exit is that the way the organization treats departing people affects the people who stay. Exit procedures have a tremendous impact on an organization's climate. When a new manager immediately executes a "house cleaning," the event leaves a lasting imprint on the "organizational memory." On the other hand, if employees see that people leave the organization in planned ways, ways that help them develop, and ways that are personally satisfying, then the climate is characterized by a sense of security and organizational support.

Finally, managers who know they are expected to terminate poor performers and to handle terminations in a way that leaves the employee feeling fairly treated (a *large* double order) are forced to become better managers. First, managers will work harder to counsel and develop employees with performance problems to reduce the likelihood of termination. The effective manager will also enlist the support of co-workers to assist low-performing employees. The manager will be forced to communicate clear and specific performance goals and expectations. And if termination is necessary, the manager should be able to avoid legal problems by documenting the causes for termination while helping the employee through the process and while increasing his or her own sense of comfort.

The three major forms of managed exit organizations employ are termination, outplacement, and retirement. Often, termination and outplacement are combined. Let us consider each form of exit now in more detail.

TERMINATION AND OUTPLACEMENT

Termination

termination

As we have been saying, with increasing pressures on managers caused by productivity concerns, quality pressures, budget tightening, head count controls, and retirement changes, performance and organizational staffing needs have received closer scrutiny. It has become far more common for an organization to terminate employees because of either poor performance or the elimination of positions. **Termination** is the *decision by the organization to end a person's employment.* According to Donald Sweet, an expert on what he calls "decruitment" (the management of the exit process), there are several reasons why managers need assistance from human resource professionals in order to facilitate the exit process.

Managers often are unwilling to admit they have made a mistake in hiring a person and thus tend to tolerate an incompetent person and take the easy way out. Also, some companies have too little turnover during economic boom periods because they hired incompetent people who are not attractive to other employers. Selection procedures should be examined to see if the best people are being hired.

Most organizations do not have human resource programs capable of both hiring and terminating in a planned, professional manner. A company is more likely to have a policy for selection than for termination. The need for special programs for termination is heightened by the fact that many employees may be incapable of adapting to job changes and corporate reorganizations, as the organization adjusts to new technologies, economic fluctuations, new products, and new competition. This inability can be due to either limited skills or a personal unwillingness to change.[5]

According to Sweet, the guilty party is the organization itself:

> In the final analysis, the real culprit in turnover and layoffs is the organization when it allows fat to develop and incompetence to flourish. How many times have you seen a job grow into a group, then into a department? Some individual gets hired and then the growth process

begins and the accoutrements evolve: secretary, equipment, assistant, etc. Then additional help is hired to handle some of the work they create. This is the perfect example of the bureaucratic syndrome. It may sound ridiculous but it's unfortunately true and happens almost every day, when business is good. Avoiding the growth of bureaucracy has to be one of the best arguments for asking some questions and instituting some strict control on hiring. Although controls are not "popular" in good times, the discipline of having them makes the bad times easier.

The organization is the "culprit" also in the sense that it condones managers who do not, or will not, understand that jobs change as the organization changes, and that many people cannot adapt and should be moved to a more compatible environment (internally or externally). Unfortunately, in a majority of cases the individual employee, through complacency or whatever, does not make the decision to get out if the situation isn't right. Widespread knowledge of the decruitment program may ease this problem for the individual—he or she may be a little more prone to take the initiative. If not, the burden is on the organization to get realistic and take the necessary action.[6]

The *dual-responsibility* concept is especially important in managing exit. In the termination process, *line managers* should do several things, the first being to devote a certain percentage of time to developing and moving people, using techniques and information received from the human resource staff. Next, they should develop plans to improve the work environment to reduce unwanted turnover. An understanding of the financial importance of people decisions is vital, as is assuming major responsibility for head count controls. And finally, they should be actively involved in decruitment planning, as in all human resource planning. Above all, managers need to stop thinking that turnover is all negative.[7]

The *human resource department*, on the other hand, should assist in human resource planning and staffing controls and assist in policy development, administration, and revision relative to decruitment. They can also assist in providing necessary economic and administrative controls for the total decruitment process and educate the organization about it. Human resource professionals have a special responsibility to ensure that the decruitment process conforms to legal requirements, especially those that are EEO- and age-related. The human resource department also can provide supportive services to manage exit by training individuals in methods of decruitment, providing day-to-day guidance, consulting, and counseling to managers and employees affected, and providing job-hunting information and assistance. Human resource staff can also cultivate a network of third-party contacts to assist employees in the job-hunting process, provide group workshops in self-assessment, career planning, and job-hunting techniques, and maintain the necessary records and reports related to decruitment.[8]

The *performance appraisal policy* of the organization becomes critical when terminations are involved. Everything we said about performance ap-

EXHIBIT 16.1

TERMINATION PAY POLICY

Guidelines

The termination pay policy should be *designed* to guarantee equitable treatment for the terminated employee who has to leave because of job elimination, work force reduction, economic downturns, and other factors beyond his or her control. People who are discharged for poor performance should not receive termination pay.

Termination pay should be based on length of service. There should be a minimum of X weeks' pay plus Y weeks' pay for each year of service. A maximum should also be stipulated.

The classification of employees who are eligible will be a management decision, influenced by relevant collective bargaining agreements. Pay may be granted in lieu of notice. However, if notice is given, the period of notice should be deducted from the eligibility period.

Termination pay will not be made if an equal job is offered and refused elsewhere in the organization.

A process for handling exceptions or disputed cases should be provided. Guidelines should be considered for allowing for special early retirement.

SOURCE: Excerpt adapted from *Decruitment and Outplacement: A Positive Guide to Termination* by Donald Sweet. Reprinted by permission of the author.

praisal in Chapter Fifteen applies here. Also, since termination is a form of selection (de-selection), the concepts of selection in Chapter Nine apply here as well. In particular, it is crucial that the organization's appraisal and selection policy ensure the establishment of the following: *valid* job-related objectives and performance standards for each employee (independent of age and gender), a realistic time frame to evaluate performance, clear communication between manager and employee so that performance standards and objectives are clearly understood and agreed upon, and periodic appraisal discussions as a fair and objective method to evaluate performance and make termination decisions.[9]

The organization also will need a clear *termination pay policy*. Suggested guidelines are shown in Exhibit 16.1.

Once the termination decision has been made, the handling of the *termination interview* is critical to the establishment of an effective exit process. All the qualities of a good interview (e.g., empathy, effective listening, confronting performance information and company needs openly, avoiding stereotyping, etc.) are especially important here.

The termination interview should be conducted in privacy by the responsible manager in an informal and pleasant environment, preferably not with the interviewer behind a huge desk. Phone calls or other interruptions should not be allowed. The primary purpose of the interview is to communicate to the employee that an irrevocable decision has been made to terminate his or her employment and why.

The time the interview is held is also important. It should be scheduled with nothing pressing at either end, so as much time as necessary is available. It should not be conducted at the start of a holiday or vacation. Not only would this ruin the employee's personal time, but it would give him or her a long time to brood about the termination without being able to take any action. It is important to time the interview so that the self-appraisal and job search process can start right away.

The interviewer plays a dual role in this process. On the one hand, he or she should be a *good listener* and focus on hearing and understanding the employee. On the other hand, the interviewer also represents the organization and must *evaluate* the validity of the information received.

The termination interview can be extremely volatile (just think how it would feel to be suddenly told "you're through" after twenty-two years with a company). The primary purpose of this meeting is to *inform* the employee that he or she will no longer be employed by this organization and to *begin the exit process*. The objective is to minimize defensiveness and hostility and to maximize constructive communication and positive, forward thinking.

The interviewer should do the following:

- Explain clearly what happened and why. The person needs to know the reasons for him- or herself, as well as for friends and family.
- Do not blame the termination on higher management. Give the person the specifics he or she will need to get the next job and to perform effectively.
- Know all of the *facts* of the situation to be able to document and explain them in specific, concrete terms.
- Be alert to his or her (i.e., the interviewer's) own prejudices and biases. This is especially important for an employee whose style or personality has caused difficulties in the past.
- Know the organization and its people. Each part of the organization and each person is different and requires different handling.
- Be sure to be a good listener. Get the employee's side of the story.
- Be as helpful and constructive as possible, even if the circumstances or employee's behavior are negative.

The employee's behavior may make the interview more difficult as it moves along. The interviewer should be prepared for certain normal employee reactions. The interviewee may expect the interviewer to be on the defensive, because of discomfort and guilt, and may attempt to take advantage of it. Or, the employee may use threats—e.g., "You know I'm 45 years old" (people 40–69 are in a protected age group). The employee may question the fairness of the performance appraisal process or challenge every piece of information the interviewer provides (e.g., "Can you be more specific?"). The interviewee may be super-alert to illogical or conflicting information, since the issue is so important to him or her. And finally, the interviewee may get very upset with meaningless generalizations. He or she needs and wants honest, objective statements.

Outplacement

outplacement

Once an employee has been informed about termination, the person or people responsible should start the counseling and job-search phase of the process as quickly as possible, if the organization is providing outplacement assistance. **Outplacement** is *the process by which an organization provides financial and professional support to help a terminated employee find a satisfactory position in another organization.* The more the organization can assist terminated employees to find other jobs, the less difficult future terminations are. The morale of the people who remain is enhanced considerably as well.

There are two ways an organization can provide outplacement: *in house,* where the firm's own human resource staff members provide counseling and job-search assistance, and through *external outplacement consultants,* who provide these services for a fee paid by the organization. With the recent stress on productivity and work force control, outplacement has come to be a standard part of the human resource "tool kit," just like recruiting, training, and compensation. Outplacement was used by more than 75 percent of the Fortune 500 firms in 1983.[10]

It is important for the outplacement specialist to help the employee establish the proper *attitude* about the transition he or she is about to go through. This attitude consists of accepting several basic facts. First, a business decision has been made, like it or not. There is no way to alter this fact. Second, employees lose jobs every day; this situation is not unique. Losing a job is always difficult, but it is not the end of the world. Third, objectivity and realism must be the guide words. A change of environment may be the best thing that ever happened. A new boss, a new environment may add up to a whole new world. And finally, reflective, honest self-appraisal and objective soul-searching will pay off in preparing for job hunting.[11]

According to outplacement specialist Lawrence Stybel, a terminated person goes through predictable stages of reaction. These five stages are remarkably similar to those experienced by terminally ill patients:

1. *Denial:* This isn't really happening to me. There must be some mistake.
2. *Grief and mourning:* Why me? I've played by the rules. This isn't fair.
3. *Bargaining:* Can't we talk this over and work something out? If I can just (keep this job) (live), I promise I'll always be a model person.
4. *Anger:* They can't do this to me! I'll show 'em just how well I can do. And *then* they'll be sorry!
5. *Acceptance:* What's done is done. No point dwelling on the past. What's important is planning and preparing.[12]

According to Stybel, each stage is necessary, and part of the task of the outplacement counselor is to help the person move through each one. It is especially important to help the person move quickly through the grief stage. A certain amount of grieving is necessary, as it helps the person make the separation from the previous job, organization, and identity, but it can be too easy for the person to wallow in self-pity, and this interferes with getting on with the task at hand: the job hunt.

The counselor can help the person use anger effectively in the job search process. The employee should be "fired up" to go out and find a fantastic job and to be extremely successful at it, to show the people who terminated him or her what a terrible mistake they made. There are four steps in the outplacement process which the counselor can help the person through:

- *Counseling.* The counselor must help the employee develop the right frame of mind, prepare a financial evaluation and a psychological self-assessment to identify where he/she is now and where he/she wants to go, obtain references, develop a resume, and develop job interview skills.
- *Establishing contacts and following up.* Here the task is to establish a "network" of people who can be helpful, through informational and employment interviews. Special attention is paid to learning how to develop "high quality," effective contacts.
- *Being interviewed.* This may be difficult, because a person may have spent the last twenty years on the other side of the desk and not had to practice the skills of selling himself or herself. This task of making a good impression is made even more difficult by the reduced self-esteem caused by job loss.
- *Evaluating prospects and selecting the right job.* This is an important step that many people overlook in their initial panic about finding a job. After putting all their energy into the job search, they suddenly find themselves confronted with a few offers. If they have not previously thought through what would constitute a "good fit" for them, they run the risk of heading into another failure.

If these outplacement services are not provided by the organization, they can be obtained from a wide range of career counseling firms. The tight job market in recent years has led to a proliferation of these firms, and they must be selected with care. Unfortunately, the person who has just lost a job is often easy prey to wild promises and ends up paying thousands of dollars for nothing more than resume assistance. Even if the organization does not provide outplacement assistance, it should at least be prepared to refer the employee to competent, reliable professional counseling from external sources.

What are the results of outplacement? Obviously, they vary with the quality of the specialists, with the economy, and with the employee. However, as a result of careful self-assessment, counseling, and conscious attempts to find a better fit in the next job, outplaced individuals usually report greater satisfaction in their new job than in the old one. And, as an added bonus,

EXHIBIT 16.2   **SUCCESS RATES OF OUTPLACEMENT PROGRAMS**

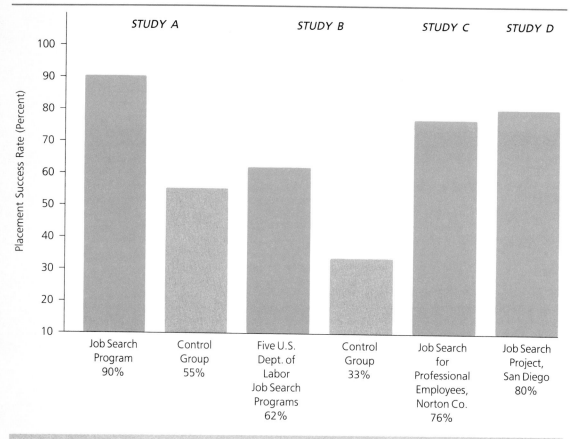

some consulting firms which do outplacement, such as Drake-Beam & Associates, report that the employee usually makes a higher salary in the new position as well.[13]

There have been several studies of the success of outplacement job search activities to help people find jobs, as reported by Lawrence Stybel.[14] The results of these studies are illustrated in Exhibit 16.2. Study A was composed of 120 adults, half of whom were given structured job search assistance while the other half (a control group matched in age, work experience, and education level) were given no assistance. Three months later, 90 percent of the people in the job search program had found jobs vs. 55 percent of the control group. As an added bonus, salary levels averaged 36 percent higher for the group in the job search program.[15]

The second study was conducted by the U.S. Department of Labor. It consisted of 1,000 people assigned to either job search programs or control groups. Again, the job search group was almost twice as successful in job placement (62 percent vs. 33 percent).[16] Two other studies without control groups also reported successful placement records (76 percent and 80 percent).[17]

WAYS TO MANAGE A LAYOFF

After voluntary measures, such as voluntary severance programs and early retirement, have been employed, and there is still a need to reduce the work force further, there may be no alternative but to lay people off. A few simple procedures can greatly minimize the negative consequences of involuntary termination.[18]

Plan for the Reduction

The most important ingredient in a well-managed layoff is a contingency plan for how to deal with a layoff. This should be done before the need arises, when business and the economy are strong. A personnel data base system is recommended, along with the prior identification of existing personnel surpluses. This plan should be developed by top management, both line and human resource executives.

Communicate the Plan

The procedure to be followed in the event of layoffs should be published as part of company policy. Procedures for redeploying personnel, job bumping, and identifying candidates for layoffs should be stated in advance. (Recent court decisions have tended to uphold seniority as the basis for layoffs, overriding affirmative action considerations.)

Once a decision is made to lay off particular people, they should be informed as quickly as possible. This reduces unnecessary uncertainty and gives employees time to adjust emotionally and to start a job search. Direct one-on-one discussions between the employee and the immediate superior are recommended.

Some of the "do's" and "don't's" are as follows:

- Try to break the news on Friday. This gives the person the weekend to think things over and empty his or her office. Friday also tends to be a day when the boss is most likely to have free time to discuss the matter with the discharged person.
- Don't mince words in the decision. It is not possible to soften the blow of dismissal, and attempts to do so could lead to misunderstanding.
- Do not go into detail about the person's performance in the dismissal interview. The purpose here is simply to inform the person in a firm but supportive way that his or her career with the organization is over. Discuss performance later.
- The severance package should be a signed agreement covering cash and non-cash compensation, written references, outplacement services pro-

vided, and the employee's obligations regarding previously signed non-disclosure and noncompetitive agreements.

- Cash settlements should be handled on an individual basis, with the objective being to get the person in a new job as quickly as possible. Free the person from job demands as much as possible while he or she works out his or her remaining time with the organization, to permit time for the job search. Provide office space and secretarial help.
- Agree in writing what the letter of reference will say, and treat this agreement as "gospel." This will be the foundation of the employee's job search.[19]

After the laid-off employees have been informed, the remaining employees should be notified. They should be given information such as the reasons for the work force reduction, the basis of the reduction method (e.g., seniority, performance, job category), the date the terminations will take place, the geographic locations and job levels to be reduced, and the efforts the organization will make to assist discharged employees to relocate. Remaining employees should also be given the opportunity to express their feelings about the terminations (to "grieve" for their terminated co-workers) and to ask questions.

A Humanistic Approach

Considerate treatment of all employees—those terminated and those remaining—after the layoff is critical. Outplacement can effectively convert a devastating experience for the laid-off employee into a career growth experience, perhaps a career switch. Simply maintaining good communication with affected employees is very important, although managers and fellow employees tend to feel uncomfortable and tend to reduce communications just when they are needed most.

For the "survivors," there may be morale problems. These can result from the sense of loss of valued friends and colleagues, as well as from increased work loads and stress resulting from reduced resources. Meetings with the remaining employees to involve them in planning can be a useful source of ideas and motivation. Also, the more information provided to respond to employees' anxieties about future layoffs, the better.

THE EXIT INTERVIEW

exit interview

For both the voluntary and involuntary terminatee, an exit interview is usually held before the person leaves. The **exit interview** is a *discussion between a representative of the employing organization* (usually a human resource professional) *and a person who is about to leave.* Its purpose is to identify characteristics of the organization and the work environment which might cause high turnover and to uncover features of other organizations which attract employees. For obvious reasons, the exit interview is most useful, and probably most valid, for employees who are leaving voluntarily.

The topics to be covered depend upon the situation, but at a minimum they should include the following:

- *Orientation and training at entry.* This is especially important for younger and newer employees. How was the person introduced into the department? How clear and challenging were job expectations? How much instruction and training was there?
- *Work itself.* How much of the employee's skills and training did the job require? How much autonomy, variety, and feedback were there? How significant and meaningful was the job?
- *Supervision.* Was there conflict with the boss? Did the boss recognize and reward good work? Did the boss delegate? How much feedback was there?
- *Performance appraisal and employee development.* Was the employee's work recognized? Were rewards fair in relation to performance? Did the employee and the boss discuss career development?
- *Company benefits and policies.* How did the employee evaluate his or her salary? Benefits? Working conditions? Hours and overtime?

The Format of the Interview

The exit interview is semistructured. Although the approach to the interview is flexible, the following basic format forms the skeleton of the interview with the employee who is leaving voluntarily:

- *Set the ground rules.* Remember the employee is doing the company a favor by agreeing to be interviewed. Thank the person and explain that the purpose of the interview is to learn why he or she decided to leave the organization.
- *Discuss the employee's new job.* This starts the interview off on a positive, future-oriented note. Showing interest in the new job will help create a positive atmosphere in the interview.
- *Examine the employee's reasons for leaving.* This is the time to cover the five topics described above. Remind the employee that his or her remarks are confidential; nothing said here will be placed in the employee's file nor will it affect any reference the company will give for the employee. It is important to encourage the employee at this stage of the interview to speak candidly.
- *Give thanks and wishes for success.* Express gratitude and best wishes for success and happiness in the new job.

A summary sheet from one company's exit interview is shown in Exhibit 16.3

EXHIBIT 16.3   **SEPARATION—POST-INTERVIEW SUMMARY**

Employee Name _____

Title _____ Department _____

Date Hired _____ Date Separated _____

Interviewer's Initials _____ Date _____

I. Description of Future Plans

_____

_____

_____

II. Factors Related to Employee's Separation

    Category   Description of Factors

_____

Job

work itself _____

benefits _____

compensation _____

Work Setting

environment _____

supervision _____

training _____

Organizational Setting

career _____

management _____

communications _____

III. Points Needing Immediate Attention

_____

IV. Under What Scenario Could the Employee Have Been Retained?

_____

V. Other Observations

    Category   Description

Job

_____

_____

_____

Work Setting

_____

_____

_____

Organizational Setting

_____

_____

_____

VI. Summary Interpretation by Interviewer

_____

Don't's of Exit Interviewing

It is important to avoid three common traps in the conduct of the exit interview:

- *Don't defend the employer.* It will be natural to feel a desire to defend the organization as the employee presents the reasons for leaving.

    Don't try to justify the employer's actions.

    Don't ask leading questions that attempt to elicit positive comments (e.g., "Don't you understand why the company's salary raises were so low this year?").

- *Don't attack the employee's views or choice.* Even though the employee's statements may seem wildly distorted,

    Don't argue with the employee's views.

    Don't criticize the new employer.

- *Don't attempt to "rescue" the employee.* By this time, the employee has made up his or her mind, and reopening the issue would be unsuccessful, and might make the employee uncomfortable and defensive.

    Don't try to change the employee's mind about leaving.

    Don't do career counseling.

Do's of Exit Interviewing

To complete this discussion on a positive note, here are some things to be sure to do:

- *Do listen 80 percent of the time.* If the company representative is talking, he or she is not listening. And by not listening, the person learns nothing about the employee's decision.

- *Do rely heavily on nondirective techniques.* Maintain good eye contact, reflect ideas and feelings, and summarize occasionally.

- *Do listen for sensitive topics and feelings to be probed.* Small cues, such as a change in the tone of voice or inconsistencies in statements, might indicate important feelings related to why the person is leaving.

- *Do cover topics on the interview checklist.* Although the interview is flexible, be sure to cover all the possible reasons for leaving that were included in the interview plan.

- *Do keep the interview constructive.* At times the employee may keep repeating the same frustrations or criticisms. It is important to prevent the interview from becoming a "bitch session." One way to do this is to ask the employee for positive suggestions for ways to deal with these problem areas.

After the Interview

To draw useful information from the interview, what happens afterward is just as important as what happens in it. The interviewer should record the employee's reasons for leaving, validate employee comments against other information, analyze many exit interviews for general trends, identify general problem areas, and take corrective action in problem areas identified.[20]

RETIREMENT

Retirement has traditionally been thought of as the end of the person's career. However, in recent years, retirement from a particular employing organization is seen more as a transition than as an end point. By **transition** we mean *a point at which the person goes through a career shift of some sort, a point at which the person's work and other activities change course.*

transition

Two transitions are involved in retirement because there are two types of retirement. The first is retirement from the organization, and the second is retirement from employment. Retirement from the organization is often made at an earlier age than the second, and for some people the second type never occurs at all (consider comedian George Burns's remark in his late 80s about when he plans to retire: "Never!"). **Retirement from the organization** occurs when *the person has reached (or passed) the contractually agreed-upon age and/or length of service at which he or she is permitted to exit the organization and receive retirement benefits.* Following organizational retirement, the person may start a "second career,"—a continuation of the career in a different organization or a different field. To be precise, a second career is a career change or career shift. **Retirement from employment** is the *cessation of paid employment activities.*

retirement from organization

retirement from employment

This distinction is more than just a matter of semantics. The term "second career" implies that the work done later is less important than that of the "first career." This perception could be a severe disadvantage if the new employer views the "second career" person as less committed, less competent, and less needing and deserving of organizational rewards (such as pay raises and promotions). Because the "second career" person receives retirement benefits, the new employer may allocate rewards instead to those employees whose income is not supplemented from other sources. This is discriminatory treatment because rewards are not related to performance.

Organizational Retirement

Organizational retirement is becoming increasingly distinct from employment retirement for several reasons. First, as life spans increase, more people want to continue working for the structure, meaning, and sense of identity it provides; also, more people are likely to be healthy enough to enjoy working. The importance of paid work as part of a person's self-identity and self-esteem cannot be overestimated. Donald Super's description of a recently retired man and his wife, a full-time homemaker, illustrates this point.

> His wife . . . still has a job. The home is still there to be taken care of, dusting and straightening must be done. . . . She has already adjusted

to a reduction of roles, for the children left the home when she was in her forties. As she goes about her daily routines, the husband is occasionally in her way, and both of them become uncomfortably conscious of the fact that she belongs there, that—whereas she has a role to play and ideas as to how she should play it—he does not belong there; he has no role to play. His role has changed from that of breadwinner to that of do-nothing, while his wife is still a homemaker. The self-concept which goes with the role of do-nothing is not a comfortable one to try to adopt after thirty-five years of working and being a good provider.[21]

A second reason people continue to work for pay after organizational retirement is financial need. Because of inflation, many people fear that their pensions might not be adequate to support them for very long.

Third, social norms about the role of older people are changing. It is becoming more socially acceptable for a retired person to accept a "low status" post-retirement job, such as a bagger in a supermarket. Employers often find that retirees in low-level, low-paying jobs are more dependable and productive than younger employees in the same jobs.

A fourth reason for post-retirement employment is a major one: more organizations are designing early retirement programs. For example, some organizations have "thirty and out" programs, under which the person can retire with full pension and other retirement benefits after thirty years of service with that organization regardless of age. This policy is common in the auto industry, and rubber workers have "twenty-five and out." Many state and local government organizations have such programs, and in the U.S. military, a person can retire with pension, health, and other benefits after twenty years of service. When a person "retires" around age 40, continuation of the career is almost mandatory.

ERISA ▬▬ In the early 1970s the concept of retirement began to change in the United States. Before that time people who had thought that their private pension coverage was quite adequate were often shocked to find that they were either not covered or were poorly covered because of financial mismanagement, complicated company eligibility rules, insufficient funding, or company insolvency. In response to these concerns, the Employee Retirement Income Security Act (ERISA) was passed in 1974 to ensure that employees covered under private pensions would receive the proper benefits.

ERISA does not require employers to have pension plans (in fact many employers terminated their pension plans after ERISA was passed, to avoid the new regulations), but if the employer has a plan, the act establishes minimum standards for its administration. Concerning *eligibility*, employers were prohibited from using eligibility requirements of more than one year of service. Previously, long waiting periods had been required, effectively shutting out many newer employees.

An important element of ERISA affected *vesting* (the right to participate in the plan and to receive rights to benefits even if employment is terminated). Previously, many employers had long vesting periods, so that employees with ten or fifteen years' service might not have received benefits if they left the organization at that point. Now the employee has three vesting options from which to choose. First, the employee could receive 100 percent vesting after ten years' service. Or the employee could choose 25 percent vesting after five years, graded up to 100 percent after fifteen years. And a third option provides 50 percent vesting when the sum of the person's age and years of service is forty-five (with a minimum of five years' service), and this amount increases up to 100 percent vesting five years after that point.

Portability (the right to transfer pension credits from one employer to another) has also been made available under ERISA, as a voluntary option of the employee and employer. *Funding* arrangements were also made more stringent under ERISA to ensure that funds to cover payments would actually be available upon retirement. Other provisions to increase the security of pension funds and the quality of investment decisions are contained in ERISA as well. ERISA gives the employee greater flexibility to plan for job change and retirement, and provides greater security for the financial future. The provisions of the act do create greater administrative costs for employers, however.

ADEA ▬▬ Prior to 1979, many corporations had retirement policies which made retirement mandatory at age 65. As of January 1, 1979, under the amended Age Discrimination in Employment Act (ADEA), it became illegal for organizations to force retirement on or otherwise discriminate in employment against employees between the ages of 40 and 69. The idea of a prescribed age at which retirement benefits might start is still perfectly legal, so that companies may still use 65 as the "normal" retirement age. The major difference is that no employee may be forced to retire before 70.

In some organizations, normal retirement is determined by adding the person's age to his or her length of service to establish a minimum number of "points" for retirement (often either 85 or 80). For example, at Monsanto employees are eligible for full retirement benefits when they reach 80 points, with at least 55 years of age and twenty-five years of service.

According to James Walker and Harriet Lazar, with changes in the corporate retirement policies and in Social Security provisions, the most common age for retirement has dropped to 62 (reduced Social Security benefits can be collected at 62; full benefits start at 65). They quote a Conference Board survey of executives which said that over 50 percent of employees were retiring early. Finally, Walker and Lazar report that executives are more likely to retire earlier than other groups, due, in part, to their greater financial resources.[22]

Buy-outs ▬▬ In addition to lowering their normal retirement age, many companies now offer special inducements for even earlier retirement. One popular concept is "buy-outs": cash inducements for early retirement. Under these "voluntary severance programs" the person is offered an earlier-than-normal opportunity to collect retirement benefits, plus a cash payment determined by his or her salary level and length of service. In addition, there is a "window" time period during which employees must make the decision, after which time the company reserves the right to start making involuntary terminations, if necessary.

A detailed examination of one company's (Polaroid) voluntary severance program is shown in Box 16.2. Many other firms, such as Monsanto, AT&T, Continental Insurance, Firestone Tire and Rubber Co., and Sears, Roebuck, have offered similar programs. There have been so many of these early exit incentive programs, in fact, that they have become a relatively routine form of human resource activity.

A voluntary "buy-out" program is often seen by employees as a prelude to layoffs or forced terminations, which may make the program a bit more than purely voluntary. For example, in an early retirement program for Sears executives (all of whom were seen as good performers), 60 percent (or 1,484) of the 2,474 eligible people accepted the offer (vs. an earlier company estimate of 28 percent). Of the people who left, 50 percent said they felt the company wanted them to leave.[23]

Similarly, Firestone's offer to 59-year-old N. J. "Bud" Laube was one he felt he could not refuse. The early retirement offer came after 1982s second quarter earnings had fallen 81 percent from their 1981 levels, and Laube's staff (he was manager of college recruiting) had been reduced to just one secretary, plus himself. There were plans for further cutbacks. As Laube said, "There wasn't any guarantee my job would continue." He accepted the buy-out bonus of sixteen months' pay for his thirty-two years of service, with plans to invest the money to make up for the reduction in his pension.

Another option being utilized more frequently is *flexible* or *phased retirement*. Under this approach the person makes a gradual transition from full-time employment in the organization to full-time organizational retirement. This is accomplished through a reduced workweek for older workers, say a four-day week for a period of time, then a two- or three-day week for a year, and then full retirement. Or the reduction could consist of a shorter workday with a full workweek. Or the employee might shift to a part-time job during the last few years.

In other organizations, employees over a certain age are given increasingly long vacations, to help them learn to plan large blocks of personal time. For example, in one firm, when an employee reaches the age of 60, vacation time is increased by one week each year. Leaves of absence are another way to give people large blocks of free time.

The line between employment and retirement is also "blurred" through consulting activities. This is usually most feasible for professional and managerial employees. In *pre-retirement consulting*, the employee is permitted to take time off from work (usually without pay) to perform consulting services for other organizations. Often it is necessary to establish policies to deal with issues of corporate propriety rights and conflicts of interest. This is a valuable way for the older professional to put a career's worth of experience and ex-

A VOLUNTARY SEVERANCE PROGRAM AT POLAROID

BOX 16.2

At Polaroid, faced with a 40 percent drop in sales of amateur cameras from 1978 to 1981, sizable reductions in the work force were necessary. If layoffs had been used, under the company's policy that only people with less than 10 years' service could be let go, it was estimated that perhaps a quarter of the work force might have shifted jobs as a result of seniority "bumping" privileges (where displaced senior workers can apply for open positions in other areas). The voluntary severance program (VSP) was seen as a gamble, since no one could predict who would leave, especially in critical skill areas such as marketing. Severance payments could range from $5,000 for a 45-year-old camera assembly operator with ten years' service earning $10,000, to $316,000 for the executive vice-president of marketing.

At this time, neighboring high-technology firms were also laying off large numbers of people: Honeywell (1,150 people), GTE (197), Nixdorf Computer (250), Raytheon's Data Systems (250). The economy was at a low ebb. Despite the bleak job market, 970 people left Polaroid, with another ninety taking a more modest program for employees with less than ten years' service. The average age of those leaving was 54, with an average of eighteen years' employment. One-third was salaried, two-thirds hourly. The work force in 1983 was down 11 percent from the start of 1981. Company management described the program as a great success, and employees used terms such as "noble," "gracious," and "hitting the lottery."

The program was, however, expensive. The company had set aside a $30.4 million pretax reserve to pay for VSP, which all but wiped out fourth-quarter earnings. Some employees in critical skill areas (e.g., the executive vice-president of marketing) were lost, and some outside hiring was necessary, but many of the jobs that needed to be filled could be staffed with current employees. After the program was completed, 400 jobs were declared "surplus." As a result of positions vacated by VSP, there were good prospects for redeploying the people in those surplus jobs elsewhere within the company.

The following incident reflects personal reactions to VSP:

One day while the program was running, an employee called the Polaroid public relations office. The man's wife did not believe his description of the program and he wanted Polaroid to explain it to her on the telephone extension. The wife came on the line and the program was explained.

"What a nice company that is to work. for," she exclaimed. "Maybe I should work for Polaroid."

"Polaroid isn't hiring," her husband reminded her, gently.

Adaptation of "Developing a Labor Cutback" by Joan Fitzgerald, *Boston Globe*, March 16, 1982. Reprinted courtesy of the Boston Globe.

pertise to work where they are truly needed (which may not be in the person's own company). The rewards in terms of recognition and self-esteem can be tremendous. This sort of pre-retirement consulting option can also "test the waters" for a possible career shift into full-time consulting work after retirement.

In *post-retirement consulting* the person is hired back to provide consulting services to the former employer. Again, this might be on a part-time basis, to provide a gradual transition *after* the formal organizational retirement. Another variant is for the organization to create a separate consulting firm, such as Control Data's Business Advisors, made up of former employees, which sells its services to its parent firm and other companies. This is an excellent way to utilize the skills of older employees and at the same time reduce the psychological barriers to retirement.

Pre-retirement planning programs are another way companies can assist employees with the transition into organizational retirement. Most large corporations (e.g., AT&T, Citicorp, TRW, Zenith, Ampex) now have such programs, reflecting corporate awareness of the responsibility to help employees plan their lives after organizational exit. At a minimum, retirement preparation workshops provide information on finances and benefits, especially health insurance plans. More complete programs provide general counseling and life and career planning activities. One specific pre-retirement program is described in Box 16.3.

Employment Retirement

The decision to retire from employment is, in effect, a double decision (to leave the company and to leave the work force). The second decision, however, is less likely to be irrevocable: many people initially cease working when they retire, then start job hunting after a few months of full-time golf, fishing, and soap operas. One survey of retired managers found that two-thirds were engaged in post-retirement work, paid or unpaid.[24]

Several factors influence an employee's decision to retire from employment.[25] Health (more specifically, poor health) seems to be the most important factor affecting early retirement in the absence of an incentive program: in one survey, of all the people who retired before 65, 54 percent listed poor health as the reason. For those who retired at 65, only 25 percent listed health as the reason for leaving.[26] Under a buy-out program, however, only 13 percent listed poor health as a factor at Sears.[27]

Financial status is the other major factor that affects the desire to retire from employment. One important part of this is the individual's own financial resources (pension, Social Security, savings, insurance, etc.). Another critically important part is the person's perceptions of prospects for future inflation. The greater the expected inflation, the more the person would fear an erosion of those carefully planned resources, and thus the more likely he or she would be to continue working. Cost-of-living adjustments in retirement benefits are becoming more common as a means of dealing with inflation.

PRE-RETIREMENT PLANNING

BOX 16.3

Like many people approaching retirement, 56-year-old Frank Salmon, a mechanical engineer at Duquesne Light Co., long worried about being "put out to pasture" without enough money to maintain his middle-income way of life. Then he heard about an adult-education class in pre-retirement planning sponsored by his alma mater, the University of Pittsburgh. He and his wife, Jean, enrolled.

During the five-week workshop, the couple learned how to calculate their retirement needs in today's dollars and to calculate their tax bracket in retirement. They learned of ways to reduce or do away with life-insurance premiums. They learned the pros and cons of lump-sum pension-plan distribution and retirement annuities. And they learned how to set and meet investment objectives geared to offsetting taxes and inflation. Today, after several big changes in family money management, the Salmons think they will be able to retire early on an income of $2,000 to $3,000 a month—in today's dollars—with no wrenching retrenchment in life-style.

Planning for retirement is hardly novel, and many companies for years have given some kind of individual retirement counseling to high-income executives to guide them through the labyrinth of stock options, pension distributions, and insurance the executives customarily were provided. But more companies nowadays are offering such counseling to employees of all income levels . . . .

Changes in tax and other legislation affecting employee benefits and investments generally have made retirement-planning decisions trickier than before. That's one reason why corporate employers are turning to outside counselors to assist employees. Too many personnel managers lack the legal and financial expertise to provide proper counseling, and in some cases employers may be legally vulnerable for giving employees improper financial advice. Some corporations offer pre-retirement counseling to encourage older workers to retire earlier to make room for younger employees. But inflation, many retirement planners say, has given the biggest boost to retirement planning. The prospect of living on a fixed income when inflation erodes the dollar's value "gives a lot of people facing retirement a sense of insecurity," says Woodrow Hunter, former president of the Institute of Gerontology at the University of Michigan and himself a pre-retirement counselor.

The evening seminars at the University of Pittsburgh are typical "rehearsals." Nina Gowell, director of the university's program, says it was designed specifically to help the retiring employee and spouse to "handle the massive adjustment demanded by the retirement experience." Although a ten-hour seminar offers much that is useful to householders of any age, Miss Gowell says that workers within ten years of retirement benefit the most. The university seminar has been oversubscribed each time it has been offered, she says . . . .

Corporate employers typically pick up between one-half and all of the cost of pre-retirement sessions that the companies sponsor, although retirees themselves foot the bill for outside seminars such as those offered by the university . . . .

INDICATORS OF ECONOMIC UNCERTAINTY
FOR THE INDIVIDUAL INVESTOR

EXHIBIT 16.4

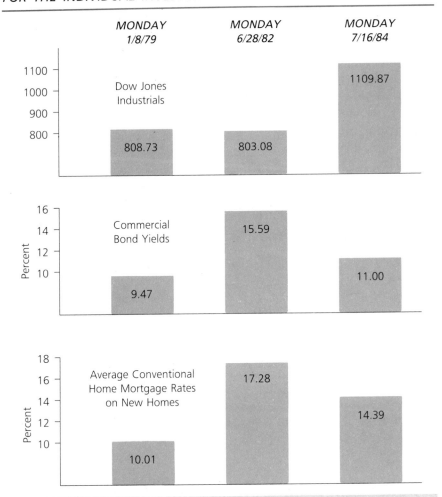

SOURCE: Excerpts from *Wall Street Journal,* January 8, 1979, June 28, 1982, and July 16, 1984.
Copyright © 1979, 1982, 1984 Dow Jones & Company, Inc. All rights reserved. Reprinted by
permission.

Financial worries also interact with health concerns, through the threat that a
serious, costly illness might cut deeply into one's savings. Exhibit 16.4 illustrates the financial fluctuations that heighten uncertainty.

Another major factor related to the retirement decision is, logically
enough, the person's attitude toward retirement. If the person sees work as
the main source of meaning and purpose in life, then retirement will be
viewed as tantamount to death. Consider the following response by a 64-year-
old employee warily discussing retirement with a 64-year-old co-worker:

Question: Why should you want to keep on working?

Answer: Why? I'll tell you, last year a man I know reached 65. Then, they had to retire, even the big shots. But he told the foreman he wanted to go on working. The foreman told him, "Why the hell should you go on working? You have a house, a car, the family, the money— why don't you want to quit?" He answered, "Sure I have the money and the car, but I'm used to working. If I quit, I'll die in a little while." The foreman told him he had to quit anyway, and three months later he was dead. When a man's used to exercise and work, he can't just quit and do nothing. The only way to stay alive is to keep working.[28]

For other people, retirement is a way to live the way one has been wanting to live and represents a welcome change. This positive view of retirement is more likely to exist when the person has retired by choice (and has not been pushed by the company or poor health) and has leisure activities which he or she values and a plan for retirement.[29] People who make the most satisfactory transition into retirement are those who have planned their post-retirement activities and life.

Feelings about the job are a major influence on a person's views of retirement. The more dissatisfied a person is with work, the more likely he or she is to want to retire. Satisfied employees, to the extent that they want to retire, want to do so more out of an attraction to the other things they can do in retirement.

With changes in legislation affecting mandatory retirement and age discrimination (i.e., the Age Discrimination in Employment Act of 1967, amended in 1978), employers are giving more attention to the performance of older workers. While this attention promises more rewards for the productive employee, it may put more pressure on weaker performers. According to Walker and Lazar, many older employees retire voluntarily when they feel their performance is unsatisfactory, rather than go through the unpleasant experience of a negative performance appraisal.[30]

Factors affecting the decision to retire from employment are summarized in Exhibit 16.5. As the figure illustrates, this decision is determined by several competing factors. Since these opposing forces can cause severe conflict, the need for organizational assistance with the retirement decision is obvious. For many people, this is the only time in their lives when they have a real choice about whether to be employed or not. They are choosing identities for the rest of their lives.

Retirement Styles

As a large proportion of our society ages and we see more variation in the life-styles of older people, different styles of retirement are beginning to emerge. A survey conducted by the human resource consulting firm of Towers, Perrin, Forster, & Crosby (TPF&C) identified four such styles:

FACTORS AFFECTING DECISION TO RETIRE
FROM EMPLOYMENT

EXHIBIT 16.5

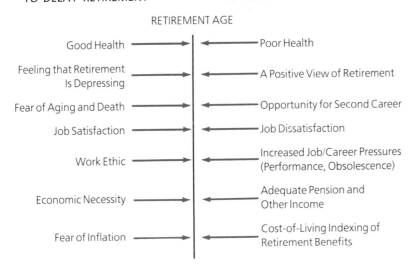

FACTORS THAT TEND TO DELAY RETIREMENT	FACTORS THAT TEND TO ACCELERATE RETIREMENT
RETIREMENT AGE	
Good Health ⟶	⟵ Poor Health
Feeling that Retirement Is Depressing ⟶	⟵ A Positive View of Retirement
Fear of Aging and Death ⟶	⟵ Opportunity for Second Career
Job Satisfaction ⟶	⟵ Job Dissatisfaction
Work Ethic ⟶	⟵ Increased Job/Career Pressures (Performance, Obsolescence)
Economic Necessity ⟶	⟵ Adequate Pension and Other Income
Fear of Inflation ⟶	⟵ Cost-of-Living Indexing of Retirement Benefits

SOURCE: From *The End of Mandatory Retirement: Implications for Management* by James W. Walker and Harriet L. Lazer. John Wiley & Sons, 1978. Reprinted by permission.

1. *Reorganizer.* These are the people for whom employment retirement is a transition from one type of active life to another. Voluntary activities, the management of their sunbelt condominium, or retirement community organizational activities occupy their time. Their health is good, they plan ahead, and they tend to be in good financial condition.

2. *Holding on.* This is another active group, in good health, who continue working after retirement, in another job. Many feel they need to work to earn money. This group tends to be active in influencing state and federal legislation dealing with retirement and age-related issues.

3. *Rocking chair.* This group represents the stereotyped view of retired people. They prefer a reduced level of activity, tend to retire "on time," and move gracefully into a slower-paced life.

4. *Dissatisfied.* These people have not adjusted to retirement (they may not have been satisfied with employment, either). They tend to have poor health and low incomes, and are inactive and apathetic.[31]

In a sample of 1,341 retirees, the most common style was the traditional "rocking chair."[32] The percentages of people showing the various styles were as follows: Rocking chair, 44 percent; Reorganizer, 24 percent; Holding on, 19 percent; and Dissatisfied, 13 percent. One interpretation of these percentages is that the traditional view of retirement has some validity. However, since 43 percent (Reorganizer and Holding on) would prefer *not* to slow their pace in retirement, the "low energy" and the "high energy" approaches to retirement seem to possess equal validity.

One can conclude from these statistics that there are great differences among people in their preferences for later-life activities. A well-managed exit process not only helps the organization plan better, but also extends the employee's career planning into important late-career transitions.

KEY POINTS

- In the past, turnover and termination were taboo topics and were not managed well. Organizations find it in their own best interests to help employees leave the organization to aid in work force reductions, to increase flexibility in hiring and developing people who remain, to enhance morale, and to stimulate managers to manage human resources more effectively.

- Outplacement has become an important way to assist people who are terminated for economic reasons and has been shown to be an effective means to facilitate job placement.

- By mastering the "do's" and "don't's" of the exit interview, the organization can learn much about why people leave voluntarily.

- Early retirement incentive programs are now an important type of human resource activity.

- Retirement is becoming a gradual, phased process for many employees, calling for careful career and life planning before retiring from an organization.

ISSUES FOR DISCUSSION

1. How has the climate relative to leaving an organization changed in the last twenty years?

2. If an organization must lay off employees, what steps should be taken to make this an effective process?

3. What are the customary benefits included in a voluntary severance program? What kind of experience have organizations had with these programs?

4. What activities are involved in a formal outplacement program? What have been the results of outplacement?

5. What are the two types of retirement? What affects an employee's decision to retire?

6. How can the exit process affect the "input" process of recruitment, selection, and entry? How are new employees affected by the way in which people leave the organization?

7. Do you know of someone who has been fired (or retired) recently? How would you describe their experiences? What did their employer do well? What should the employer have done differently?

NOTES

1. J. Bittner, "Companies Seek to 'Buy Out' Older Workers; Paying for Early Retirement Is Spreading," *Wall Street Journal*, June 29, 1982, p. 34.

2. Ibid.

3. Further information on this subject can be found in "Curtailing the Freedom to Fire," *Business Week*, March 19, 1984, pp. 29, 33.

4. For further discussion in career management of older employees, see J. Sonnenfeld, "Dealing with an Aging Work Force," *Harvard Business Review*, November-December 1978; and B. Rosen and T. H. Jerdee, *Older Employees: New Roles for Valued Resources* (Homewood, IL: Dow Jones-Irwin, 1985).

5. D. H. Sweet, *Decruitment and Outplacement: A Positive Guide to Termination* (Reading, MA: Addison-Wesley, 1975).

6. Ibid., pp. 11, 12.

7. Ibid., p. 39.

8. Ibid., pp. 40, 41.

9. Ibid., p. 52.

10. W. Buchanan, *Career Planning and Adult Development Newsletter*, November 1980, *2*, pp. 1–2.

11. Sweet, op. cit., p. 104.

12. L. J. Stybel, "How Managers Deal with the Trauma of Dismissal," paper presented at Annual Meeting of Academy of Management, 1981. For more on the process of job loss and job search, see H. G. Kaufman, *Professionals in Search of Work* (New York: Wiley, 1982); and S. Fineman, *White Collar Unemployment: Impact and Stress* (Bath, Avon, U.K.: Pitman Press, 1983).

13. G. C. Dinas, New York Office, Drake-Beam & Associates, personal communication, 1980.

14. L. J. Stybel, "Does Outplacement Really Work?" *Business*, October-December 1983, pp. 55–57.

15. N. Azrin, et al., "The Job-Finding Club: A Group Assisted Program for Obtaining Employment," *Behavior Research and Therapy*, February 1975, *13*, pp. 435–533.

16. R. Wegmann, "Job-Search Assistance: A Review," *Journal of Employment Counseling*, April 1979, *12*, pp. 197–225.

17. Ibid.

18. From D. A. Benton, "A Guide to Work Force Reductions Planning," *Personnel Journal*, April 1980, 59 (4), pp. 281–84, 316.

19. Based on the comments of L. J. Stybel, "What to Do, What Not to Do," *Boston Globe,* September 21, 1982, p. 55. See also L. J. Stybel, R. Cooper, and M. Peabody, "Planning Executive Dismissals: How to Fire a Friend," *California Management Review,* Spring 1982, *24* (3), pp. 73–80.

20. This section was adapted from J. G. Goodale, *The Fine Art of Interviewing* (Englewood Cliffs, NJ: Prentice-Hall, 1982), pp. 169–89.

21. D. E. Super, *The Psychology of Careers* (New York: Harper & Row, 1957), p. 159.

22. J. W. Walker, and H. L. Lazar, *The End of Mandatory Retirement* (New York: Wiley, 1978).

23. F. J. Smith, "Reaction to Early and Normal Retirement Among Managers," paper presented at 42nd Annual Meeting of the American Psychological Association, New York, August 1982.

24. W. S. Wilistrom, *The Productive Retirement Years of Former Managers* (New York: The Conference Board, 1978).

25. Walker and Lazar, op. cit.

26. L. T. Smedley, "The Patterns of Early Retirement," *AFL-CIO Federationist,* January 1974, pp. 1–6.

27. Smith, op. cit.

28. Friedman and Havighurst, quoted in Super, op. cit., p. 95.

29. Smith, op. cit.

30. Walker and Lazar, op. cit.

31. J. W. Walker, K. F. Price, and D. C. Kimmel, "Retirement Style and Retirement Satisfaction," paper presented at the Western Meetings, American Institute of Decision Sciences, San Diego, CA: 1978.

32. Ibid.

ANNOTATED BIBLIOGRAPHY

Human Resource Management, Winter 1983, 22 (4).

This is a special issue on managing organizational decline. It contains one of the best collections of theoretical, empirical, and practical readings available on this topic. Articles cover retrenchment, work force reduction, matching corporate strategy to conditions of decline, organizational death, managing job insecurity, and employee involvement in a declining organization. This journal is published quarterly and is a good general reference on human resource management.

JACOBSON, B. Y. *New Programs for Older Workers: Case Studies in Progressive Personnel Policies.* New York: Van Nostrand, 1980.

This is a practical guide, full of concrete corporate examples, of actions taken by successful companies to hire, retrain, and provide more options for older employees. The book covers six areas: new work arrangements (part-time work, phased retirement, and second-career training), reentry workers, secondary organizations (employers who hire retirees), organizational redevelopment programs (e.g., outplacement, downward movement), second careers for older workers, and assessment and advising of employees (with a special focus on job redesign for older workers). With cases ranging from banking and high technology to school systems and government, this book provides numerous creative ideas for managing older employees.

ROSEN, B. and JERDEE, T. H. *Older Employees: New Roles for Valued Resources.* Homewood, IL: Dow Jones-Irwin, 1985.

This book offers strategies for maximizing the contributions of senior employees. Building on a foundation of psychological and legal knowledge (on issues such as age stereotyping, health, obsolescence, and age discrimination), the authors provide guidelines for assessing the performance and potential of older workers. A model program for combatting obsolescence is presented, and younger managers are shown how to overcome communications barriers with older employees.

SWEET, D. H. *Decruitment and Outplacement: A Positive Approach to Terminations.* Reading, MA: Addison-Wesley, 1975.

This is one of the earliest and most authoritative books on the process of employee termination from a practitioner's point of view. Sweet, who was formerly Director of Employment for Celanese Corporation, is now a human resource consultant specializing in outplacement. The book covers recruitment, appraisal, exit interviews, and job search. The advice is aimed at both the individual and the organization and shows how both parties can gain the most positive advantages from an initially negative situation.

WALKER, J. W. and LAZAR, H. L. *The End of Mandatory Retirement: Implications for Management.* New York: John Wiley & Sons, Inc., 1978.

The authors, noted consultants and authors in the area of human resource planning, examine the implications for management of the legal issues involved in corporate retirement programs. Contents include retirement issues, flexible retirement strategies, appraising older employees, aging and retirement, helping employees plan for retirement, and resources and references. This is an excellent guide not only on retirement, but also on the whole general topic of managing older employees.

INTERVIEW

ROBERT RIPSTON, VICE-PRESIDENT, HUMAN RESOURCES, INGERSOLL-RAND

▬▬ When did you know you would have to lay off large numbers of people?

We first began to realize layoffs would be necessary by our monthly forecasting. The year 1981 had been a record year, but by mid-1981 we could see some deterioration. Certain sections were hit first, notably the tool business. There was widespread deterioration in world markets in terms of orders and profitability. We were surprised by the depth of the recession.

▬▬ What was your strategy for cutting costs?

Inventory is the first place to look. The quickest way to reduce inventory is to reduce people. But we needed to cut back our production rate. We began by looking at direct labor, then at indirect labor and support people. If you think that business will be coming back, you keep people on, and try to cut down on indirect and overhead expenses. Material handlers, stockroom people, and quality control go first, then supervisory and management people, foremen and supervisors. The plant is restructured, support people are taken out.

▬▬ How did you go about restructuring the company?

If it becomes clear that the problems are long-term, the question becomes, "How do you significantly restructure the business, reduce staff in coordination with what is occurring in the economy?" As successive cuts become worse, you have an industrial depression.

We reduced our staff from 48,000 to 38,000. Our department, the Human Resources Department, established policy, devised game plans, played a role in organization planning, and worked with executives on how best to handle the layoffs. As much as possible, we tried to move people around in the corporation, but of course we soon exhausted the possibilities. We tried shortened weeks and temporary shutdowns, until it became clear that layoffs were a necessity.

▬▬ How did you manage the layoffs?

With the hourly employees, seniority and qualifications provide the criteria for who stays and who goes. There is a bumping process. For example, if you have ten tool makers, and need to lay off two, these two can bump the machinists with lowest seniority and so on down the line. The unions generally go along with it.

With salaried people, seniority is less important. Performance appraisal is much more important. Marginal performers are reduced first. What if Joe is a marginal performer but has been with the company for thirty-five years?

Performance comes first, seniority second. The higher you go, the more you consider performance.

We considered the demographics of the salaried people. We had a certain number over 55 who had retirement benefits. We knew that we needed 20 percent of these people to retire. These were the higher paid people. Pension plans were utilized to encourage people to retire early. Windows were opened up in the pension plans to provide incentives. We gave people from April to September to decide; anyone who wanted to retire got a bonus, a proportion of a week's pay for each year of service. The career bonus went into the pension, so it also boosted the pension base.

The strategy was to help people preserve their dignity. We made the plan positive. We had to be careful about age discrimination—people cannot be fired because of their age. The first go-around with this plan we reached 90 percent of the group we were aiming for. After that, we got tougher. Ultimately we had to give some employees the choice of leaving or taking a lower-level position. There were some who chose to stay on those terms.

In order not to lose essential people, we excluded certain classes. We were all right with ERISA laws as long as we did not discriminate against lower level people to the advantage of higher level employees.

How did you deal with employees during this process?

An important issue throughout this process was communication. First we prepared a communication plan. We wrote a letter describing the situation to the top managers. The letter was fairly widely distributed, the management communicated verbally. From there, rumors got out, and we prepared news releases. Concurrently, we pulled people together in groups to explain what was happening. It's important to prevent panic, and to be as honest and direct as possible. Explain what and why, and what groups will be affected. Never say the layoffs are over. We worked with managers on how to best conduct the layoffs. For instance, it is our policy to never conduct a performance appraisal during the layoff. People need to be supported for their strengths at that time.

We worked to help people through the trauma. Almost all of the people we laid off have found jobs, and often better jobs.

What did you learn from this experience?

There are some things I would have done differently. We would have given the laid-off employee only a week or two to stay around. We would try to forecast better. I would bring down the retirement age to 60 or 62.

It's been the toughest year of my life. It's like Eisenhower at D-Day. For the good of the company you have to accept some losses. But it's awful. You try to be as humane as possible.

PART FIVE

HUMAN RESOURCE SYSTEMS

In the previous part we examined the relationship between the employee and the organization—in particular, the methods by which employee performance and development were managed. Now we turn to the more formal systems associated with the human resource function. These represent some of the more specialized areas of activity in this field. Effective systems for managing human resources are generally designed at the managerial level of the organization, and thus represent a key link between strategy and implementation.

First we consider one of the most important forms of employee rewards: compensation, one of the most difficult problem areas in the practice of human resource management. As in other parts of this book, we begin with the strategic context of compensation (Chapter Seventeen). The more the organization can manage compensation in a strategic manner, the more motivational "mileage" it will derive from the salaries and wages it pays.

Chapter Eighteen covers the specific methods organizations use to set wage and salary levels and to administer compensation systems. Methods of dealing with issues such as equity and comparable worth are also discussed. The key here is to design compensation systems that not only fit with the external labor market but also promote strong performance and support the strategic direction of the enterprise.

As has been evident in industrial catastrophes in recent years (e.g., the Union Carbide gas leak in Bhopal, India; Manville's declaration of bankruptcy because of asbestos-related cancer claims; the Three Mile Island nuclear reactor's malfunction), the issue of industrial safety has become a major public issue and it is apparent that line management is being held accountable for the health and safety of the work environment it provides. Chapter Nineteen discusses these issues.

A theme of this book has been the needed proactive role of the human resource function. An important part of the human resource function's consultative role is the process of facilitating communication between the institution and its various stakeholders: employees, shareholders, customers, the general public, and various government entities. Chapter Twenty describes the methods by which human resource professionals develop strong communications with employees and external stakeholders. Communication is an emerging role of the human resource function, and thus chapters on this topic have not traditionally been found in human resource management texts.

CHAPTER SEVENTEEN

STRATEGIC COMPENSATION

Bill Johnson, a man in his early 30s, asked to see the president of a small manufacturing firm. He had been with the firm for six years and had performed very well since joining the sales group two years ago. He was aware that he was going over his sales manager to see the president, but in this small business the president maintains a personal relationship with all employees.

"Mr. Jackson," said Bill, "I need your help. Janet and I really want to move into a larger house, now that our fourth child has arrived. We also have to buy a new car because our old one is six years old and won't make it through another winter. I just don't know how we can make it on my current salary. How about a salary review?"

"Bill, I certainly know how personal situations can change and create financial pressure. I can't promise you anything, but I'll talk to your boss and see if we can work something out."

In a discussion with the sales manager, the president learned of Bill's excellent performance in sales for the past six months. Equally important, he learned that Bill has caught the interest of sales managers of two major local companies. The president decided to give Bill a 20 percent salary increase.

Jane Cooke, an accountant with a large corporation, faced a similar problem. Her husband had been laid off indefinitely by his employer, and they suddenly found themselves in a financial pinch. Knowing that her last raise was six months ago, she approached her boss and asked if another raise would be possible. As expected, she was told that salary increases are given once a year and although her recent work was excellent, she must wait six months before her salary could be reviewed. Jane reluctantly began to look for another job and four weeks later took one with another company for 18 percent more money.

These two cases illustrate two approaches toward compensation. In the first, the compensation policy is informal and can be adjusted to meet the needs of a specific employee, and in the second, a formal far less flexible policy prevails. Which company's compensation policy is better for the individual employee who wants to adjust his or her salary or benefits? Which is fair to the employee's co-workers? Which is better for the entire corporation?

These are not easy questions to answer. The rationale behind the salaries and benefits that employees receive is often confusing or elusive. (See Exhibit 17.1.) The President of the United States currently earns an annual salary of $200,000, but many professional athletes earn over $1,000,000 per year. Why? A survey by the Administrative Management Society showed that the average base salary of sales managers increased 13.7 percent during the first three quarters of 1981, while the average plant manager's salary grew only 6.3 percent.[1] Why the difference? Finally, union employees who earned approximately $20,000 a year were asked by management at one company to accept a wage freeze in their 1982 contract negotiations. (This was a common occurrence during that recession year.) In anger, the union pointed to the $650,000 salary of the company's chief executive for whom no pay freeze was planned. Is this fair?

This chapter is about **compensation,** *the money and benefits that organizations give employees in exchange for work.* All employees, of course, are familiar with the compensation that they receive in actual wages or salaries. But few employees are aware of the amount of compensation they receive in benefits such as paid vacation and holidays, various forms of insurance, employer contributions to social security, and even subsidized lunches and employee health club memberships. In many organizations, the largest item in the budget is wages and salaries. It is not unusual for total compensation expenses to amount to 60 or 70 percent of an organization's total operating expenses. Compensation is also significant at the level of the total economy, as well. Salaries and wages represent about 60 percent of the total gross national products of the United States and Canada.

compensation

Compensation is one of the most complex functions of senior line executives and human resource executives. It involves strategic, managerial, and operational issues of job worth, social and legal issues of equitable, fair treatment of all groups of employees, motivational issues of rewarding excellent performance, and external issues of competing in the local labor market. At the strategic level, an effective compensation system should ideally accomplish the following objectives:

link compensation policies and practices to the strategic business objectives of the organization,

EXHIBIT 17.1   **SALARIES IN VARIOUS JOBS**

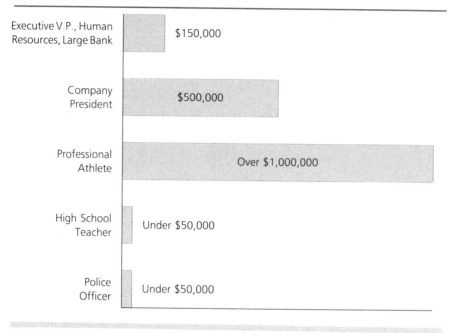

provide fair treatment for all employees, resulting in equal pay for equal or comparable work, through systematic job evaluation,

link financial rewards to clear, objective measures of outstanding performance,

maintain equity between compensation levels in the organization and compensation rates in the external labor market,

provide sufficient flexibility so that the mix of pay and benefits provides the type of rewards which employees need and value the most,

deliver compensation in a way that, in addition to the above functions, is also maximally cost-effective and controlled (particularly in escalating areas such as health insurance).

In this chapter we will discuss these general strategy issues, and in Chapter Eighteen we will discuss methods to accomplish these difficult objectives. These two chapters, considered together, represent the dual responsibilities of line and human resource management. The strategy issues covered in this chapter deal with the responsibilities of line management and senior human resource management. The compensation methods discussed in Chapter Eighteen are more the responsibility of middle and first level human resource managers.

SOCIAL TRENDS AND COMPENSATION

Senior executives must consider first what compensation means to employees. What do employees want, and how do those wants relate to pay? As we discussed in Chapter Three, workers tend to value opportunities to do something that makes them feel good about themselves, to accomplish something worthwhile, to learn new things, and to develop their skills and abilities, as well as the amount of freedom they have on their jobs. In many surveys of rewards valued most by employees, pay ranks around number five or six, but rarely does it rank number one or two. Therefore, while pay may be important, intrinsic rewards, such as job satisfaction, seem to be more important.

To further complicate the picture, the work force is more *differentiated*. Compared to twenty years ago, there is a more even mix of men and women in particular jobs; no longer are all secretaries or nurses women, nor are all engineers or telephone installers men. Furthermore, women constitute a greater proportion of the work force than they did a decade ago. There are more older workers, as retirement laws and policies change, and as work force reductions cut down the number of recently hired employees. There are also more two-career couples, more working mothers, more single parents, more minority groups, more handicapped—in short, a much more diversified work force within any one organization. It is more difficult to apply uniform policies and practices to all employees. Organizations now find it necessary to provide more *individualized treatment* in areas such as compensation.

Not only does this more diverse work force have more varied personal circumstances, but many employees now expect to have *more influence* over decisions that affect their careers. This means they expect more consultation on career decisions and in the way their compensation dollars are divided between salary, various types of benefits, and other forms of reward. As we said earlier, attitudes toward authority have changed, and employees are far less willing to assume that the organization will act in their best interest in making decisions about these rewards.

Employees are also more concerned about *privacy* and *leisure time*. Thus, not only is freedom on the job more important than ever, but freedom *from* the job is of great concern. One critical potential reward that few organizations have taken seriously is increased free time, perhaps traded off for money.

A related issue is increased concern for *employee rights* and *due process* within the organization. The "Employee Bill of Rights" described in Chapter Three concerns the employee's right to privacy in his or her personal life and to freedom from discriminatory job treatment. A less dramatic way in which employees' desires for fair and equitable treatment are being seen is in the area of compensation. Today's employees are more likely to challenge performance appraisal ratings and the resulting organizational actions on salary increases.

All of these characteristics of the "new work force" mean a great increase in the demands placed upon an organization's compensation system. If we add to these factors an organizational economic environment with increased competition for cost and quality, slow economic growth, and more service jobs (and therefore more people-intensive activities), this means the financial resources available for compensation will be very scarce indeed. Thus, with more demands being placed upon a diminishing pool of financial resources, compensation systems must be managed much more carefully, strategically and creatively to tap their full potential.

According to Edward Lawler, all of these forces ensure that future compensation systems will possess the following characteristics:

1. *Individualization.* Perhaps the most important implication of the trends mentioned above is the need for compensation systems to become more flexible so that they can be tailored to different employees. This does not mean devising a unique system for each person, but offering enough different types of compensation options so that employee needs and life styles can be addressed.

2. *Open, Defensible Decision Process.* To provide a connection between employee-perceived performance and rewards that will produce a fair and motivating compensation system, there must be open communication about the compensation system, and the system must be fair and rational. Growing concern about employee rights has increased legal pressures to make compensation systems more open and equitable.

3. *Performance-Based Compensation.* Compensation systems must become better motivators of employee performance. To better motivate, compensation must be closely linked to good performance and employees must be able to see the connection between their level of performance and their compensation. Better, more creative performance-based compensation systems are needed.

4. *More Egalitarian Reward Systems.* One barrier to the more participative, employee-involved culture which many organizations seek is the intricate system of status differentials and "perks" which have been built up over the years. Special dining rooms, elevators, parking lots, office floors, office sizes, and office furniture are a few of the ways used to differentiate between senior and lower levels.

    One status differentiator is the compensation system. Often lower-level employees are on hourly pay (and are thus labeled "hourly people"). Higher-level (and higher status) people are salaried. Executive-level personnel may have a bonus system or a stock-option program, or some other performance-based incentive.

    As senior management redesigns jobs to bring employees more into the decision-making and problem-solving process, these status differentials will need to be reexamined.[2]

An organization with all these features is discussed in Box 17.1.

THE WAY THAT WORKS AT LINCOLN

BOX 17.1

Two years ago, when the Lincoln Electric Company's sales were sagging because of the recession, fifty factory workers volunteered to help out.

After a quick sales training course, they took to the road, their only compensation 18½ cents a mile for expenses, with no money for lodging or meals. Their objective: to help sell the company's Model SP200, a small welder introduced a couple years earlier for use in small machine shops and auto body shops.

An unusual scenario, perhaps, in American industry where, often as not, a company and its workers are at odds. But from its earliest years, 90-year-old Lincoln has charted a unique course in worker-management relations—featuring high wages, guaranteed employment, few supervisors, a lucrative bonus incentive system, and piecework compensation.

The company, the world's largest maker of arc welding equipment, has 2,650 employees in the United States, the bulk of them blue-collar workers. There are no unions. . . .

Workers have shared in the company's fortunes. Under an employee stock purchase plan, about 75 percent of the workers own about 40 percent of the stock, which must be sold back to the company when an employee quits or retires. Most of the rest of the stock is owned by members of the Lincoln family.

Many innovative management practices set Lincoln apart. Guaranteed employment is provided for all full-time workers with more than two years' service, and no mandatory retirement. No worker has been laid off in more than forty years, except for some temporary workers at the end of World War II.

High wages are paid, which include a substantial annual bonus based on the company's profits. While the average Lincoln worker earned about $44,000 in the industry's last good year, 1981, half of that was bonus. In 1983, a troubled year in which employees worked thirty hours a week under the company's traditional work-sharing plan that means no one had to be laid off, average pay was about $20,000—half in bonus.

Lincoln has never had a strike and has not missed a bonus since the system was instituted in 1934 to spur production and to enable it to pay more to its workers, hard-pressed by the Depression.

More than half of Lincoln's production workers are paid by piecework, i.e., according to what they produce, rather than an hourly or weekly wage. If a worker is sick, he does not get paid. Workers with serious illnesses must use state workers' compensation, personal insurance through a plan administered by the company's employee association, or income protection insurance. . . .

While the company insists on individual initiative—and pays according to individual effort—it works diligently to foster the notion of teamwork. Long before the Japanese became known for emphasizing such concepts, Lincoln stressed that its workers throughout their lives were part of what it called "the Lincoln family."

If a worker is overly competitive or (in the words of Mr. Richard S. Sabo, manager of publicity and education) "playing dirty" with fellow employees, the worker is rated poorly in terms of cooperation and team play on his semiannual rating reports. Thus, that worker's bonus will be smaller.

Adaptation of "The Way That Works at Lincoln" by William Serrin, *New York Times*, January 15, 1984. Copyright © 1984 by The New York Times Company. Reprinted by permission.

STRATEGIC COMPENSATION

These characteristics of the "new compensation system" suggest that organizations must be far more *strategic* in designing future systems. There is a need for more explicit use of the compensation system to achieve organizational objectives. This implies a strong role for senior line executives in formulating the organization's compensation strategy.

Functions of Compensation

Compensation is an extremely powerful organizational reward affecting employee behavior in profound ways. The problem is that many of these effects are unintended and undesired. There are several functions money performs in an organization.

Money helps attract and retain people. Pay and benefits are very important tools in recruiting talented people to an organization. Although not always the most important factor in a person's job decision, the overall compensation package is almost always near the top of the list. Similarly, when a person is considering leaving a job, improved salary and other financial inducements are often effective ways to influence him or her to stay.

Money satisfies a wide range of needs. In expectancy motivation terms, money has very high valence for most people. However, the reason for that high valence varies widely from person to person. In terms of Maslow's hierarchy of needs, money can certainly provide the means (housing, food, clothes, transportation, etc.) to meet physiological needs. Money can provide a sense of safety and security. Moving up the need hierarchy, money can provide social interaction (e.g., memberships in clubs, free time to spend with friends), ego and esteem rewards (a big salary is a major ego-related "scorecard" for many people), and self-fulfillment (money can signal the achievement of important personal goals). Perhaps one of the most important rewards associated with money in work organizations is *recognition*, the ego/self-esteem boost one receives from being seen as a valued contributor to the organization. Often the *symbolic* value of money is far more important than the dollars themselves.

Money can reward good performance. Another very critical function of money is its role as a potential motivator of excellent performance. In order for money to be a motivator, however, it must be linked to performance in a way that is clear to employees. As we will see later, this link is not easy to establish. Using money as a motivator also requires specifying exactly what type of performance the organization is trying to motivate.

Money can influence organizational structure and culture. The pay system can reinforce and define both the structure and culture of an organization. For example, the Ford Motor Company has four hierarchical levels which are defined and referred to by the compensation system:

Top level: Executive compensation roll,

Upper middle level: Bonus compensation roll,

Lower middle level: Salaried compensation roll,

Lower end: Hourly compensation.

Thus, the forms of compensation have been deeply embedded in the culture of the organization. Furthermore, a pay system that rewards new products and services and market growth will produce an innovative culture. A pay system that rewards meeting budgets will produce a very low-risk culture, etc.[3]

Although money can serve all of the above functions (and usually does), the functions are usually met in unplanned ways that may conflict with each other. For example, rather than being based on a well-thought-through strategic compensation plan, salary increases are often made on an ad hoc, case-by-case basis, as when a key performer like Bill Johnson (whom we met at the beginning of this chapter) is about to leave and his pay is raised 20 percent. This action aids *retention*, but it may kill the *motivation* of his coworker, who may be an equally strong performer but has not tested the external job market (yet). Thus, we need to consider how the pay system can be used in a more internally consistent, strategic way.

Strategic Planning for Compensation

In examining how compensation might be used strategically, let us refer again to the model (in Chapter Two) in our integrated approach to human resource management. The first step is to work out the overall strategic corporate business plans. These must then be translated into human resource plans. This includes forecasting and staffing to secure the right people and to design the proper organization and job structure in which these people can function effectively.

In considering compensation, it is most important to know what sort of performance is needed from these people to best attain corporate objectives. It is necessary as well to translate organizational and job requirements into compensation which will promote these requirements. And compensation must be linked to the desired performances. (We will talk more specifically about ways to establish these linkages in the next chapter.)

First, however, senior management must develop its overall philosophy in relation to pay. Such a philosophy provides a common set of beliefs and principles, which add stability and coherence to the pay system. A pay philosophy must deal with issues such as:

Goals of a compensation system. Which function(s) of compensation does the organization want to emphasize?

Communication policy. How will top management communicate with employees about pay, and how *open* or *closed* will the pay system be?

Decision making. What process will be used to make pay decisions?

Desired pay levels in relation to the market. Does the organization seek to maintain a certain level of salaries in relation to the industry or community, such as being in the top quarter or top half?

Centralized vs. decentralized systems. Is the goal to have uniform organization-wide pay policy and administration, or should different locations or divisions develop their own?

Cash vs. benefits. What is the desired mix in the total compensation system between cash and benefits?

Role of performance-based pay. Is a merit pay system desired, and if it is, how is it best attained?

Performance appraisal. What performance is expected, and how clear is the performance feedback process?

Fit of compensation policy with management philosophy. Are those elements both clear? And is the compensation policy consistent with the management policy?

Management of change in the pay system. Whatever change process is desired in other areas of company management (e.g., participative management), is the pay system managed and changed in the same way?

Many of these issues associated with developing a compensation strategy revolve around the issue of the congruence of the pay system with other management processes and systems. It makes no sense to develop an open pay system where employees participate in evaluating the performance of their peers and in determining their salary increases and where salary levels are public information if the basic management style in the organization involves top-down control and secrecy. Similarly, it would be foolish to attempt to use pay as a motivator if jobs were designed in such a way that the employee's behavior had little impact on performance. Therefore, looking at pay strategically is a way top management can force itself to integrate its approach to pay with the other facets of running the business.

Strategic Issues in Comparable Worth

comparable worth

A major policy issue that will face employers in the coming decade will be that of **comparable worth:** *the idea that men and women should get equal pay for doing different jobs which have the same level of difficulty and require equivalent levels of skill.* Women's pay has traditionally averaged only about 60 percent of men's (although that figure dropped to 57 percent in 1973 as women began to enter the labor force in larger numbers, mainly in the lower-paying service sector, and it rose to 64 percent by 1983).[4] Comparable worth has become an important issue in the process of addressing this pay differential between men and women. A major reason why women's pay averages less than men's is that women tend to work in lower-paying occupations, and it has been argued that the main reason these jobs are lower-paying is that they are traditionally female-dominated. Comparable worth is seen as one way to get out of this self-perpetuating cycle.

The issue here is not the unequal pay of men vs. women within a job category, but the pay discrepancies between workers in different jobs. If the difficulty and skill levels of different jobs can be assessed, then the pay of, say, truck drivers (mostly men) and secretaries (mostly women) could be made more equitable.

This issue first came into focus in *American Federation of State, County and Municipal Employees v. Washington State* in September, 1979, when U.S. District Judge Jack Tanner awarded $140 million to some 15,000 employees of the state because of inequities between salaries of female-dominated jobs and those in male-dominated jobs. Since then comparable worth has been more of an issue in the public sector than the private sector, for several reasons.[5] First, the public sector employs people in a broader range of jobs than do private companies, which opens the possibility of greater pay discrepancies. Second, it is easier to gather information about compensation in the public sector, because by law such data are usually a matter of public record. Third, pay equity is usually a matter of public policy in most public organizations, as a result of laws against discrimination in employment. Finally, the growing strength of organized labor in the public sector, often led by women, has led to numerous bargaining victories over comparable worth. To date, unions have won over sixty-five bargaining victories, and thirty states have enacted comparable worth laws or have begun to do so. National legislation in this area has been enacted in Britain and Australia.[6] This issue will undoubtedly become increasingly important in the private sector in the years ahead.

In the following chapter we will discuss specific methods to deal with comparable worth (mainly centered around job evaluation methods). The main point here is that, rather than wait for employees to take action, it is in the organization's best interest to take a *proactive* stance and formulate its own policy regarding comparable worth. Even though theoretically the concept of comparable worth should be applied to the entire economy, for practical purposes the comparability test will probably be applied within a particular organization.

Many executives in the private sector have tried to ignore comparable worth, however, on the grounds that no one can explain exactly what it means (and it is, in fact, still an unclear concept, as we will see in the next chapter). However, this is just a way of evading the issue. The editors of *Business Week* point out, "As far as employers are concerned, comparable worth means what unions and women's groups want it to mean, and they want it to mean higher pay for women."[7]

In Britain, the comparable worth law is administered by local three-person industrial tribunals which hear and decide cases. In the U.S., Sharon Spigelmyer, associate director of human resources and equal opportunity for the National Association of Manufacturers, argues that "what employers don't want is some court or government agency playing God."[8] This is a key example of how a clear *strategy*, formulated by line management, is essential to the *design* and *implementation* of effective human resource activities. Therefore, a strong statement of policy endorsing comparable worth and equal pay for equal work, supported by appropriately designed compensation programs, is a critical element in the establishment of a fair compensation system.

EXHIBIT 17.2

TOTAL COMPENSATION FOR A $25,000 PER YEAR EMPLOYEE

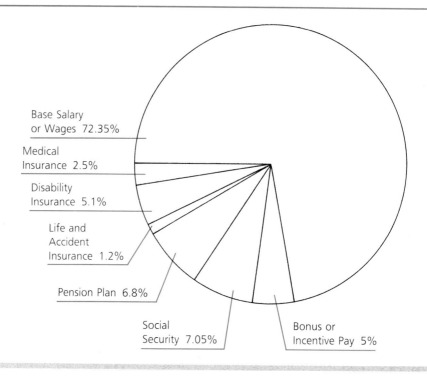

Base Salary or Wages 72.35%

Medical Insurance 2.5%

Disability Insurance 5.1%

Life and Accident Insurance 1.2%

Pension Plan 6.8%

Social Security 7.05%

Bonus or Incentive Pay 5%

Forms of Compensation

Several forms of compensation can comprise a person's total "compensation package" (see Exhibit 17.2 for the breakdown of compensation components for a typical employee).

Time-based pay: salaries and wages. The basic component of an employee's compensation is the direct cash compensation paid for the performance of services. The basis of payment is usually a unit of time. "Wages" are usually thought of as being paid by the hour, whereas "salary" is usually tied to longer time periods, such as weekly or monthly increments of service. When pay is determined on an hourly basis, the person is usually entitled to *overtime* pay for time beyond the basic 35 or 40 hour work week, whereas salaried employees generally do not receive overtime pay.

Performance-based pay. Another basis of compensation is the volume of output that the employee produces. Some examples are a stamping machine operator's payment for parts produced which pass inspection, a salesperson's commission of 5 percent on each sale, and an artist's income based upon the number of paintings sold.

benefits

Benefits are the *wide range of indirect (or supplementary) forms of compensation usually provided to make employment more attractive.* In a unionized organization the total benefit package is the result of the collective bargaining process.

Insurance. Insurance is an important way to provide a true sense of security to the employee—security from financial worry in the event of an accident or illness. The most common forms are health insurance (regular and major medical), dental insurance, life insurance, accident insurance, and personal disability insurance.

Because health care costs have been growing so rapidly in recent years (see Box 17.2), business organizations are supporting legislation (and other attempts) to limit health costs in various ways, such as "caps," or limits on annual budget increases of hospitals, medical reimbursement based on standard costs for particular kinds of treatment (e.g., X dollars per appendectomy), and payments to employees for second and third opinions.

Health maintenance activities. In another attempt to slow down the rapid increases in health insurance costs, many organizations have established fitness (or "wellness") programs and facilities to help employees stay in good physical condition. For example, Ford Motor Company bought the old Edison School in Dearborn, Michigan, within blocks of the Ford world headquarters and other company facilities. The main part of the school has been converted into a corporate training center, and the gyms and pool have become an employee fitness center (which is employee run and costs only $90 a year to join).

Vacation, holiday, sick, and personal time. There are presently a variety of ways in which organizations can provide employees with time off the job. At lower levels, employees are usually allowed a certain number of paid sick days, in addition to vacation and holiday time. At higher levels, salaried employees may have fewer restrictions on sick days, but for managers and executives the norm against work absence is so strong that the concept of "sick days" may be meaningless. Many employees, especially working parents, tend to take sick days to attend to personal or family matters. To make it unnecessary for employees to misrepresent the reasons for absence, some organizations have combined sick days with personal days into a single category, "personal time." Also, to encourage better attendance (since paid time off does reduce productivity), some organizations have developed incentives to encourage employees not to use all available personal days. For example, by reimbursing employees for personal days not used (at a rate below the full cost) both the employee and the organization gain financially.

Retirement benefits. One important retirement benefit is a pension plan, toward which the employer usually pays the major share, if not the full amount. The 1974 Pension Reform Act (the Employee Retirement Income Security Act, or ERISA) established maximum "vesting" periods (i.e., the time by which the employee is entitled to the full amount of the employer's

SKYROCKETING HEALTH CARE COSTS AT CHRYSLER CORPORATION

BOX 17.2

Health care insurance is the fastest-rising business expense in the United States today. Joseph Califano, former secretary of Health, Education, and Welfare, and later a member of the Board of Directors of the Chrysler Corporation, predicts that total corporate health care costs could add up to $1 trillion per year by 1993, if current inefficiencies are not corrected. In 1982, the health care costs of the Fortune 500 companies (over $80 billion) were greater than the profits of those firms.

Put in terms of cost per employee, the cost of health care insurance at Chrysler was $6000 per worker in 1983 (compared to $850 in 1972). The cost of employee health care per car was $600, or 10 percent of the price of a Dodge Omni or Plymouth Horizon automobile. In 1983 Chrysler's health insurance premiums were $373 million, "making Blue Cross-Blue Shield our biggest suppliers," according to Califano.

INSURANCE PREMIUMS PER ACTIVE EMPLOYEE

1964	Company Pays Full Benefits for Active and Retired Employees	$ 295
1969	Drug Plan Added	482
1974	Dental Plan Added	1,157
1977	Vision and Hearing Plans Added; Dental Plan to Retirees	2,044
1979	Benefits Improved; Vision Plan to Retirees	3,154
1983	Rapid Health Care Inflation; Smaller Work Force; More Retirees	6,000

HEALTH CARE COSTS*

	Insurance Premiums	Premiums per Hour Worked	Hourly Wage	Premiums per Vehicle Produced
1970	$ 81	$ 31	$ 4.27	$ 55
1973	141	.45	5.25	73
1976	230	.90	7.00	127
1979	350	1.93	9.81	287
1982	331	3.30	11.13	458
1983	364	2.74	10.47	346

*Cost breakdown for premiums in millions of dollars. Hourly wages of Chrysler assemblers in December of each year from United Automobile Workers. Other data from Chrysler Corporation.

From "Chrysler, Hit Hard by Costs, Studies Health Care System" by David E. Rosenbaum, *New York Times,* March 5, 1984. Copyright © 1984 by The New York Times Company. Reprinted by permission.

contributions to the pension), which make pensions more "portable," or easier to transfer from one employer to another. The employer must also make contributions to Social Security for each employee.

Educational benefits. As the work force gets older, employers will probably assume greater responsibility for the continuing education and development of their employees. Various in-house training and development activities are being expanded, as are programs administered with local colleges and universities. For example, the Ford Fitness Center is staffed with physical education majors from a local community college. Perhaps the most common form of education benefit is tuition reimbursement, in which the employer pays part or all of the employee's tuition for certain work-related courses and programs (e.g., evening MBA courses). New kinds of retraining are also being offered, as the need to redeploy workers to newly emerging areas becomes more urgent.

Employee assistance programs (EAPs). Employee assistance programs enable employees to deal with personal or emotional problems which may affect job performance. The most common are alcoholism programs, which grew from six programs in 1945 to 4,400 in 1979–80.[9] Help with other types of drug dependency is also part of many EAPs. Newer forms of assistance include personal counseling in relation to career problems, family problems, and other sources of personal stress. The EAP may be delivered by either in-house specialists (e.g., psychologists, social workers) or outside agencies and firms. These programs can be justified quite easily in terms of reduced absenteeism, accidents, turnover, and medical expense, and they are seen as highly valued benefits by the employees who participate in them.[10]

Unemployment benefits. Employers are able to contribute to an employee's basic sense of security in many ways. Through contributions to unemployment insurance and supplemental unemployment benefits, the financial costs of job loss are reduced. (Unemployment insurance is the employer's legally mandated contribution to government-provided unemployment payments. Supplemental unemployment benefits are additional payments, which can vary by employee and are often set through collective bargaining.) Some organizations also provide assistance in insurance coverage during a layoff.

Special termination benefits. As explained earlier in Chapter Sixteen, when an employee is fired, an employer may provide certain benefits to ease the pain of moving to a new job. There may be *severance pay* to help the person during the job search period. The company may also provide outplacement assistance (career counseling and job search assistance), as well. Early retirement, to provide a bridge between the age of early retirement (often 55) and the customary retirement age (62 or 65) when the person starts Social Security, is another benefit which facilitates voluntary exit.

Parental leave. As numerous couples combine careers and parenting, the concept of a paid leave of absence for childbirth and postnatal care is becoming more popular. Even though traditional sex-roles are changing, this leave is still seen as maternity rather than paternity leave, but it is becoming more available to men.

Relocation assistance. An important benefit offered employees assigned to new geographic locations is relocation assistance. In addition to moving expenses, this could include assistance in buying and selling houses, personal and family counseling and orientation related to the process of moving, mortgage and cost-of-living differentials, and, in some cases, assistance in job relocation for an employed spouse.

Bonus compensation plans. For higher level managers and executives, various forms of extra-income plans are frequently made available. They may be year-end bonuses, stock-options, special tax-advantaged deferred compensation plans, or other forms of increased income, usually related to performance of either the person, the unit, or the total organization.

"Perks". A wide range of perquisites (or "perks") can be offered to make employment in an organization more attractive. These could include free (or reserved) parking, a company car, a corporate day care center or a child care subsidy, free lunches in a company dining room, first-class air travel for executives, a company-sponsored country club, or a host of other offerings. They all cost the company money and should be considered part of the total corporate compensation package.

401K retirement plans. These are plans, sometimes called CODAs (for cash-or-deferred arrangements), which have become very popular in recent years. They permit employees to contribute pretax income to company savings plans, often with the company matching all or part of the employees' contributions. The money earns interest tax free, and when it is withdrawn (when the person is presumably in a lower income bracket), it qualifies for ten-year forward income averaging (i.e., the withdrawal is treated as if it were received over the next ten years, rather than all in one lump sum in one year).

This list by no means exhausts the forms of compensation provided by organizations today. New inducements for joining, for staying, and for performing are being devised all the time. This area represents a creative convergence of compensation management and human motivation.

Tax Considerations

A subject of great controversy and uncertainty is the tax status of employee benefits. Traditionally, benefits such as company contributions for education, health insurance, group term life insurance (up to $50,000 coverage) and 401K plans have been tax deductible for the employer and untaxed for the employee. However, the recent trend has been to make these benefits part of the employee's taxable income, which makes them less attractive. As the nation moves toward a major restructuring of the tax system, these changes will have major impacts on an organization's compensation policies.

PERFORMANCE-BASED COMPENSATION

One of the "hottest" issues in management circles is that of merit-based pay. A survey of 305 major compensation plans revealed that in 77 percent "pay for performance" is increasing, and in 66 percent there is declining use of across-the-board increases.[11] Hours of debate are almost guaranteed when employees are asked to what extent pay is based on performance in their organization. Most people believe in principle that merit pay is a good idea, and the main disagreement is over whether it is used, and how best to strengthen the link between pay and performance.

Reasons for Linking Pay to Performance

Why should an organization link performance to pay? At least four advantages of a merit-pay system can be identified:

1. *Motivation.* When pay is based on performance, then pay can be a good motivator of effective performance.
2. *Attraction.* A merit pay system attracts entrepreneurial and achievement-oriented employees.
3. *Retention.* In merit pay systems strong performers are paid more than marginal performers, and thus are motivated to remain, while marginal performers might be motivated to look for employment where they can make more money. When pay is not limited to performance, weak performers tend to stay and strong performers leave.
4. *Satisfaction.* Individuals tend to be more satisfied with pay when compensation is tied to performance. This improves employee quality of work life, which is another factor which aids retention.[12]

Issues in Merit Pay Plans

As we move from the issue of "should we have merit pay?" to "how do we do it?" we immediately become aware of the complexities involved. We will consider a few of the more important ones.[13]

Level of Aggregation ▬ At what level should merit pay be awarded: individual, work group, department, plant, division, or organization-wide? Or should there be combinations, as at Lincoln Electric, where a bonus pool is determined by company performance and distribution of the pool is based on individual performance?

The problem with larger aggregation levels is that the perceived link between the person's performance and his or her ultimate reward becomes weaker. That is, one individual cannot always control the conditions of performance. On the other hand, individual plans run the risk of fostering competitive behavior between employees. Generally, Lawler argues that individual plans may be most appropriate under the following conditions:

- Independent, simple technology,
- Good trust in superior-subordinate relationships,
- Large organization or subunit (where the person might feel lost in an organization-wide plan),
- Good information system for measuring individual performance,
- Nonunion organization, providing greater flexibility for individual plans.

On the other hand, aggregation to a larger unit (group, plant, department, or total organization) might be more appropriate under the following circumstances:

- Complex, interdependent tasks,
- Good employee trust in organization; good organization-wide communication,
- Small subunit size; employee relates his or her performance to that of the unit being rewarded,
- Good measures of information available only at group or plant level.

Number of Plans ▬ Should there be just one company-wide plan or different ones for different units or levels? A variety of plans (e.g., one for executives, one for managers, and one for workers) can create barriers between levels and work against overall cooperation and teamwork. However, as organizations move into more specialized, differentiated markets and industries, it may be necessary to use different plans based on what is appropriate for each industry. For example, at Continental Bank, the leasing division competes for employees with other sales-oriented financing firms (e.g., GMAC), and thus a strong incentive-pay system is necessary. Other divisions, like the controller's area, have accountants and systems people who are accustomed to straight salary, so that incentives are not used (except for senior executives).

Plans can also differ based on short-term vs. long-term payout periods. Generally, the long-term payout is more appropriate for higher-level people, since the time span of their job activities is longer.

Salary vs. Bonus ▬ How should the merit-based reward be given—as a salary increase or as a bonus? The problems with salary increases are that they become, in effect, annuities, since they become a permanent part of the person's salary, and if they are spread out over the entire year's pay checks, they may lose visibility and impact. Also, the salary increase may include some market or cost-of-living factors, making it even more difficult for the person to see the merit component. A bonus, on the other hand, can be a one-shot reward for excellent work, with no commitments to future payouts.

Size of Merit Pay ▬▬ How large should an increase be to be motivational? Lawler argues that it should be a *noticeable increment,* and he offers a minimum of 3 percent of present pay as a rule of thumb. If the amount of a "good" increase is less than 3 percent, it is probably not worth the administrative expense involved.

The other critical element is *potential.* Individuals must see the pay plan as able to produce a noticeable change in their pay if they perform at a high level.

Measures of Performance ▬▬ As we saw in Chapter Fifteen, the issue of measuring performance is a complex one. In a merit pay system, it is important that the measurement of performance be seen as equitable and clear to employees (so they know why they were rated as they were, as well as how to improve).

Should the ratings be objective or subjective? Objective ratings may be clearer but they may not always be equitable if they do not take all relevant factors into account. Subjective measures have the twin advantages that they can be more inclusive and they make data collection easier. If there is a high level of trust in management, subjective ratings can be quite effective.

Frequency of Payout ▬▬ How often should a payout be determined? On a piece rate system, the payment may be hourly, whereas in a top-executive performance plan, the period may be five or ten years. As we will see later, many incentive compensation plans have been criticized for being too short-term oriented, resulting in various activities to drive up current performance (e.g., earnings per share) at the expense of longer-term investment and growth. However, if the time period is too long, the person may lose sight of the potential payoff. In many organizations, the result of these competing considerations is a decision to award bonuses and salary increases annually.

Choosing a Merit Pay Plan

All things considered, what sort of plan makes the most sense—individual, group, or organizational? It really depends upon the objectives of the pay plan, as we said earlier in the chapter. There are advantages to each type, just as there are problems. Or, as Edward Lawler commented, "You tell me what kind of problem you want to have, and I'll tell you which pay plan to use."

However, Lawler has offered us some guidelines. Exhibit 17.3 is a summary he compiled showing ratings for various pay plans (industrial, group, and organizational). These three types are further broken down into plans where the performance measure taps productivity, cost effectiveness, or superiors' ratings.

The criteria used to evaluate the various plans are:

▬▬ Is the plan, in fact, perceived by employees to link pay to performance?

EXHIBIT 17.3   RATINGS OF VARIOUS PAY INCENTIVE PLANS

Salary Reward	Measure Used	Ties Pay to Performance	Produces Negative Side Effects	Encourages Cooperation	Is Accepted by Employees
Individual plan	Productivity	4	1	1	4
	Cost effectiveness	3	1	1	4
	Superiors' rating	3	1	1	3
Group plan	Productivity	3	1	2	4
	Cost effectiveness	3	1	2	4
	Superiors' rating	2	1	1	3
Organizational plan	Productivity	2	1	3	4
	Cost effectiveness	2	1	2	4
Bonus					
Individual plan	Productivity	5	3	1	2
	Cost effectiveness	4	2	1	2
	Superiors' rating	4	2	1	2
Group plan	Productivity	4	1	3	3
	Cost effectiveness	3	1	3	3
	Superiors' rating	3	1	3	3
Organizational plan	Productivity	3	1	3	4
	Cost effectiveness	3	1	3	4
	Profit	2	1	3	3

On a scale of 1 to 5, 1 = low and 5 = high.

SOURCE: Adapted from *Pay and Organizational Development* by Edward E. Lawler, fig 6.3, p. 94. Copyright © 1981, Addison-Wesley, Reading, Massachusetts. Reprinted by permission.

- Are there unwanted negative side effects, such as peer hostility toward outstanding performers, employees' faking of performance information, etc.?
- Does the plan encourage employee cooperation?
- Is the plan likely to be accepted by employees?

Certain trends are apparent. For tying pay to performance, individual plans seem to work best, but they also can produce negative side effects, such as conflict between employees. Group and organizational plans seem to facilitate cooperation more effectively. In general, bonus plans tend to be rated higher than pay raise and salary increase plans, since a bonus makes it possible to vary a person's pay greatly from time period to time period. And, in general, objective performance measurement seems preferable to subjective measures (e.g., superiors' ratings).

Regarding employee acceptance, most of the plans seem to rate rather low, especially individual bonus plans, probably because of perceived problems with fairness and the feeling that management may raise the standards if people make too much money from the plan. As you might expect, employees tend to prefer salary increases to bonuses, since the salary increase becomes a permanent part of the person's pay.

Stress on Long-Term Performance

One problem with performance-based pay programs is that they focus mainly on short-term performance. This has been especially a problem in the area of executive compensation. Senior executives are supposed to be concerned about the long-term growth of the organization, yet many executive incentive plans have been based on short-term indicators, such as quarterly or annual earnings per share.

There are two problems with such indicators. First, one year is a short time in the development of the organization, and important activities undertaken to promote long-term growth may not show up within a year. Second, earnings (profits) per share are an accounting concept subject to various legal forms of manipulation. Different forms of depreciation, different ways of handling inventory charges, and other accounting practices can affect reported earnings.

To encourage longer-term activities by managers, companies are rewarding them for increases in the *value* of the business, as opposed to earnings. Rewards tied to measures such as asset growth or stock price are becoming more attractive. New types of stock options (e.g., book value stock options) are ways to motivate executives to engage in action that increases the overall value of the company, as reflected in the price of the stock. David Larcker found that companies with long-term performance plans such as these had higher levels of long-term activities, such as investment, than did firms lacking such plans.[14] Many organizations are creating these long-term financial inducements to encourage more development by managers and executives.

Conditions for Effective Merit Pay Plans

Overall, the following conditions are necessary for an effective merit pay plan:

1. Rewards must be high enough to be worth working for,
2. Rewards must be allocated differentially, based on performance,
3. Performance must be measured validly and inclusively,
4. Information must be communicated clearly to employees regarding how rewards are given,
5. Trust in management must be high,
6. Employees must accept the performance-based pay plan.[15]

If these conditions are not all present, installation of a merit pay system may not only be ineffective, but could increase employee mistrust of management and lead to a breakdown in communication (e.g., "It's all a trick to get more work out of us for less money"). If these conditions do not exist, it is better not to try to use pay as a motivator.

The Portfolio Approach to Compensation

As organizations move toward a more strategic approach to management of the enterprise, they also stress the concept of differentiated strategies for particular business units. It is possible to identify different types of strategic business units (SBUs), based upon the size of their market share and their rate of growth:

- *Stars:* high growth, high market share,
- *Cash cows:* low growth, high market share,
- *Wildcats:* high growth, low market share,
- *Dogs:* low growth, low market share.[16]

The strategy used to manage each type of unit depends upon the firm's objectives for that unit. A *build* strategy represents an attempt to improve market share, which requires a net inflow of cash. Such a strategy might be used to drive a "dog" or to maintain the growth of a "wildcat" or "star." A *hold* strategy involves maintaining and protecting current position. *Harvest*, as the term implies, involves maximizing short-term earnings and cash flows without strong concern for possible market slippage. The harvest strategy implies a decision to withdraw from a particular business area through divestiture or termination of that operation (one approach to "dogs").

If top management is going to manage SBUs in different ways, it makes sense that different forms of compensation would be important to motivate managers to focus on different criteria of performance. And, in fact, research has shown that if a strategic business unit is to perform effectively, differential reward systems are important.[17] In particular, it was found that incentive bonuses for managers in "build" units were based on long-term criteria (sales growth, market share, new product development, and political/public affairs). Furthermore, this relationship was even stronger for more effective units than for less effective units. On the other hand, short-term criteria (e.g., operating profits) were less likely to be used with a build strategy than with the others. As one might expect, preference for short-term profits over sales growth was more common for "harvest" units than for "build" units.

The *form* of performance assessment also differed by strategy. Judgmental estimates (superiors' ratings, as opposed to objective quantitative measures) were considered to be more important in build units than in other types. Furthermore, the stronger the judgmental ratings were in build units, the more effective were those units. And, finally, to encourage growth, bonuses were a much larger proportion of the manager's total compensation in build units.

Not only is a differential reward strategy useful to reinforce strategic business objectives, but the approach is also consistent with the individual differences among managers likely to be attracted to or selected for each type of unit. The growth-oriented entrepreneurial person found in a build unit (such as a star or a wildcat) would probably thrive on the high risk-high payoff of a large bonus component in his or her pay check. The budget-oriented

FORMS OF COMPENSATION IN RELATION TO BUSINESS STRATEGY

EXHIBIT 17.4

Business Strategy Measures	Bonus/Salary Ratio	Bonus Criteria	Subjective or Quantitative Ratings
Build	High bonus component	Long term (e.g., new product development)	Subjective
Hold	Moderate bonus component	Intermediate term (e.g., product improvement, cost reduction)	Quantitative
Harvest	High salary component	Short term (e.g., operating costs, profit margins)	Quantitative

manager of a harvest unit would probably be more interested in a higher fixed-salary component. And, finally, the external labor markets competing for each type of manager would probably offer this sort of congruent compensation, as well. These relationships between strategy and compensation are summarized in Exhibit 17.4.

Scanlon and Other Gain-Sharing Plans

With increased concern for productivity and employee involvement in job-related decision-making, there is also a growing desire to find ways to share the fruits of increased productivity with employees. Various forms of financial gain-sharing have grown in popularity. Gain-sharing is different from a simple bonus or incentive system. It is based more on actual organization profit or productivity improvements and is part of an overall corporate philosophy of participation and organization development.

Some classic examples of gain-sharing are the Lincoln Electric Plan, the Scanlon Plan, and the Rucker Plan. Of these, the Scanlon Plan is probably the most widely used. The underlying principle of any gain-sharing approach is that there is a vast reservoir of untapped potential creativity and experience in an organization's work force. If this potential were properly tapped, productivity would be dramatically improved.

The Scanlon Plan, a group-based incentive system, has two components for tapping this potential—a financial bonus and a mechanism for employee participation. The bonus is based on actual savings in payroll costs, as compared to the historical ratio of payroll costs to sales value of production. The actual computation formula for the bonus can be quite technical (all the more reason to have employees participate), but the basic idea is to provide an incentive for employees to find ways to reduce labor costs—this is generally *not* a goal of employees in a traditional organization and in a traditional compensation system.

After an organization sets aside a portion of the bonus pool to cover deficit periods, the Scanlon bonus is paid to all employees as a percentage of base pay. Improved productivity is accomplished by the employee's involvement in decisions related to his or her own job, and a system of employee committees to process suggestions for improvements at the department levels.

Change agents who have helped implement the Scanlon Plan emphasize that it is a *process*. It is not just an incentive system to involve employees in management and to develop an identity between employees' goals and those of the organization. Also, strictly speaking, there is no such thing as *the* Scanlon Plan. Because of the participative process by which the plan is designed, each company develops its own unique system. Again, the essence of the Scanlon approach is the participation process which is used.

What makes for success with a Scanlon Plan? Based on a study of twenty-three organizations with Scanlon Plans, Kenneth White came to the following conclusions:

1.　Most importantly, a high degree of *employee participation* is strongly related to Scanlon Plan success.
2.　Company *size* seems to be unrelated to success (at least based on the size range in his study, 23 to 3,000 employees).
3.　The more positive *top management's attitudes* toward participative decision-making, the more successful the Scanlon Plan was.
4.　The *longer* the company has had the plan, the greater was its success.
5.　Favorable (but realistic) initial *expectations* are related to success.
6.　*Sponsorship* of the plan by a high-level executive is required if it is to be successful.
7.　The type of *technology* employed does not appear to be a factor in the success of a Scanlon Plan.[18]

More complete details on the Scanlon Plan can be found in Lawler[19] and Frost, Wakely, and Ruh.[20] As we have said, if top management wants employees to participate more in decision-making to improve productivity it is only fair (and consistent) that the compensation system allow employees to share in the rewards from productivity gains.

PROCESS ISSUES IN COMPENSATION

The process by which a compensation system is created and administered is *at least* as important as the type of system employed. The two most critical process issues here are the nature of information about compensation and the degree of employee participation in the compensation system.

Open Information

There is a tendency toward secrecy in most organizations. For some reason, compensation is treated almost like sex—a "hush-hush" matter that is considered improper to discuss openly. There are functions to secrecy, to be sure.

If there are inequities in the system, then open communication would bring those inequities to light and cause dissatisfaction. Open posting of individual salaries would probably make some people quite uncomfortable and would require a high level of trust in the organization. (But the practice is followed successfully in some well-managed, high-trust firms.)

Far short of the extreme of posting individual salaries, however, is the practice of communicating openly about the pay system itself, the salary grades at different organizational levels, and the ranges within each grade. This information is often provided to employees. And information on officers' salaries in publicly owned firms is public information by law.

Another type of information sometimes provided is the size of annual salary increases at different levels of the organization. This information is extremely useful for people to use in a comparative way, so they can determine how well or poorly they did with their own pay raise.

Lawler has found that secrecy about pay raise information can actually negatively reinforce good performance.[21] Surveys have found that, in the absence of valid information, employees tend to overestimate the average pay increase at their level. Thus, if people do not have any official information and believe the "grapevine," they might think that the average raise was 10 percent, when it was actually only 6 percent.

And what if the raise was 8 percent? Because the employee thought the average was 10 percent, he or she would think that the raise was subpar. Yet, in fact, an 8 percent raise was one-third more than the actual average of 6 percent. The employee is an above average performer, yet thinks he or she is receiving below-average rewards. Thus, this secrecy results in negative reinforcement for good performance.

The ultimate example of how ludicrous secrecy about pay rewards can be was reported by an engineer in a large manufacturing firm. He was called in by his boss, congratulated on his outstanding performance, and informed that he would receive the company's Outstanding Achievement Award. This prestigious honor carried a sizable financial bonus. The engineer was understandably ecstatic. After more praise from the boss, the engineer turned around to leave. The boss's parting words were, "By the way, don't tell anyone but your wife about this award. We don't want other people getting jealous." As the engineer later complained, "What's the point of getting a nice award if you can't brag about it afterward?"

If more information about pay is desirable, what sort of information should be provided? Lawler reports the following results of a survey of managers regarding a bonus plan:

More information should be given about the bonus plan	92 percent
The size of the bonus plan should be made public	60 percent
The range of bonus rewards should be made public	57 percent
Individual bonus awards should be made public	5 percent[22]

Thus, complete information about individual pay raises is not desired, although Lawler sees some trends in this direction. However, it is clear that many people would like more aggregate data to determine how their rewards compare with those given to others. For pay to be an effective motivator of performance, people need to assess accurately the connection between performance levels and pay raises received.

Participation

When employees help to create their own pay plan, there is less resistance and the plan is more likely to be a successful motivator than one imposed by management.[23] Often employee participation occurs through employee *task forces* that help design and plan the new system. There are several reasons why employee participation is helpful in designing compensation systems:

1.   Employees know what factors motivate them most and are able to "design in" the most effective incentives (thus maximizing "bang for the buck").
2.   They gain more information about the realities of the compensation process.
3.   They are committed to the plan because it is theirs.
4.   They have control.
5.   They trust the system.

However, the decision to use a participative method to design a new pay system should not be made lightly. This method is effective only when there is a general philosophy of participative management and a climate of reasonable organization trust. Also, participation takes time—perhaps six months to a year with task forces. If trust and time are limited, a more top-down method might be more appropriate.

KEY POINTS

▬ Compensation systems are becoming more individualized (tailored to individual needs), more open, more performance-based, and more egalitarian.

▬ The strategic compensation process explicitly designs and utilizes the compensation system to achieve important organizational objectives.

▬ The total compensation package may include base wages or salary, incentive pay, and benefits such as insurance, health maintenance activities, vacation, holiday, sick and personal time, retirement contributions, educational payments, unemployment contributions, employee assistance programs, special termination payments, parental leaves of absence, relocation assistance, and "perks," such as parking and cafeteria privileges.

▬ Many organizations attempt to link pay to performance, and a variety of plans are available, aimed at either individual, group, or organizational performance. Each method has advantages and disadvantages, which means that top management must decide which would best fit the organization's strategic direction.

- In general, openness about average pay increases and reasons for individual pay raise decisions increases the motivational impact of compensation.

ISSUES FOR DISCUSSION

1. What is the meaning of the term "strategic compensation"? How can strategic planning be applied to compensation?
2. What are the functions of pay? How can a manager determine what pay means to a particular employee or to a group of employees?
3. What does "comparable worth" mean? What would a clear, simple policy related to comparable worth be?
4. What are the different forms of compensation? How could an employer determine which were most important to his or her employees?
5. Why should pay be linked to performance? What are some methods of tying pay to performance? Considering all the pros and cons involved, which do you think is most effective?
6. How can secrecy about pay reduce the motivational value of a salary increase?
7. Think of a time when you felt especially satisfied about a salary increase you received. Now think of a time you felt especially dissatisfied. Discuss these experiences in relation to the concepts of strategic compensation in this chapter.

NOTES

1. *Houston Post*, February 4, 1982, p. 5.
2. E. E. Lawler, III, *Pay and Organizational Development* (Reading, Mass.: Addison-Wesley, 1981), pp. 223–29.
3. Ibid., pp. 31–33.
4. "Women at Work," *Business Week*, January 28, 1985, p. 80.
5. R. L. Brady, L. N. Persson, S. E. Thompson, and D. Cadrain (eds.), *Comparable Worth Compliance: A Wage and Salary Handbook* (Madison, Conn.: Bureau of Law and Business, Inc.), 1984.
6. "Women at Work," op. cit.
7. Ibid., p. 140.
8. Ibid., p. 83.
9. U.S. Department of Health and Human Services, *Fourth Special Report to the U.S. Congress on Alcohol and Health* (Washington, D.C.: U.S. Government Printing Office, 1981).
10. For more on EAPs see D. C. Walsh, "Employee Assistance Programs," *Health and Society*, 1982, *60*, pp. 492–517.
11. F. Kiefer, "Salaries, Benefits Undergoing Numerous Changes," *Houston Post*, October 10, 1983, p. 5.

12. E. E. Lawler, III, *Pay and Organizational Effectiveness: A Psychological View* (New York: McGraw-Hill, 1971).

13. E. E. Lawler, III, *Pay and Organizational Development,* op. cit.

14. D. F. Larcker, "The Association Between Performance Plan Adoption and Corporate Capital Investment," Working Paper No. 81–1, Evanston, Ill.: Accounting Research Center, J. L. Kellogg Graduate School of Management, Northwestern University, 1981.

15. Lawler, *Pay and Organizational Development,* p. 100.

16. B. O. Henderson, *Perspectives on the Product Portfolio* (Boston, Mass.: Boston Consulting Group, 1970).

17. A. K. Gupta and V. Govindarajan, "Business Unit Strategy, Managerial Characteristics, and Business Unit Effectiveness as Strategy Implementation," *Academy of Management Journal,* 1984, 27 no. 1, pp. 25–41.

18. J. K. White, "The Scanlon Plan: Causes and Correlates of Success," *Academy of Management Journal,* 1979, 22, pp. 292–312.

19. Lawler, *Pay and Organizational Development,* op. cit.

20. C. F. Frost, J. H. Wakely, and R. Ruh, *The Scanlon Plan for Organization Development: Identity, Participation, and Equity* (East Lansing, Mich.: Michigan State University Press, 1974).

21. Lawler, *Pay and Organizational Development,* op. cit.

22. Ibid., p. 113.

23. E. E. Lawler, III and J. R. Hackman, "The Impact of Employee Participation in the Development of Pay Incentive Plans: A Field Experiment," *Journal of Applied Psychology,* 1969, 53, pp. 467–71.

ANNOTATED BIBLIOGRAPHY

FROST, C. F., WAKELY, J. H., and RUH, R. *The Scanlon Plan for Organization Development: Identity, Participation, and Equity.* East Lansing, Mich.: Michigan State University Press, 1974.

> This is an excellent statement of the theory and research behind the Scanlon approach to incentive compensation. The book also stresses the importance of the process by which a pay plan is designed and implemented. Many practical corporate case examples are included.

LAWLER, E. E., III. *Pay and Organizational Devlopment.* Reading, Mass.: Addison-Wesley, 1981.

> Lawler is one of the foremost scholars in the area of the psychological and motivational aspects of compensation. This book provides a detailed discussion of how to manage the compensation system in a strategic way. It also provides many examples of innovative company pay practices, as well as how to design compensation programs for participatively managed firms.

NASH, A. and CARROLL, S. A., Jr. *The Management of Compensation.* Monterey, Calif.: Brooks/Cole Publishing Co., 1975.

> This is an excellent resource for information on specific methods of administering wage and salary systems. It deals more with specific operating-level issues than Lawler's book, and less with strategic issues.

CHAPTER EIGHTEEN

COMPENSATION METHODS

If nothing else, the case may prove that curiosity can kill the state kitty.* Sometime ago an official of the Washington Federation of State Employees asked then Governor Daniel Evans to examine the wages paid to public employees. Evans commissioned a study and found that jobs that tended to be filled by women systematically earned twenty percent less than comparable jobs held by men. Later, the union took the state to court on the basis of the findings, and a federal judge in Tacoma declared that 15,000 Washington state employees were entitled to immediate raises and back pay to remedy years of discriminatory treatment. The cost to the state: possibly more than $800 million.[1]

Nationwide, working women earn roughly 60 percent of what men do, in part because they have been confined to employment ghettos—clerical, cleaning, or cooking—that traditionally pay less than equally low-level jobs held by men. Evans had proposed remedying that with graduated raises. His successor, Dixie Lee Ray—the state's first woman governor—killed his plan.

But the union hadn't forgotten. It went to court, charging that the state's pay patterns violated federal and state antidiscrimination law. The state legislature had previously approved a ten-year plan to resolve the "comparable worth" problem—but appropriated only $1.5 million for the first year. That clearly was not enough to buy off the union.

At the trial, union counsel Winn Newman called Evans as a witness. Evans testified that while the state had not intentionally discriminated against women, there were "gross disparities" between the sexes. Lawyers for the state explained that the public salaries merely mirrored private industry and contended that Washington was being punished for being in the "vanguard" on the comparable-pay issue.

U.S. Judge Tack Tanner gave the state pleas short shrift. Relying in part on the 1974 study, he found that the state had violated the Civil Rights Act of 1964. He later ruled that the state must pay both increased wages and back pay to an estimated 15,000 workers—men or women—who hold jobs that had traditionally been dominated by women. He conceded that his order might put a severe dent in the recession-ridden state treasury but insisted the remedy "has to be disruptive because you're changing past practice. . ."

To raise the money, the legislature would have to lay off state employees, slash programs or hike taxes. But before the state scours its cupboards for funds, it will likely tie up Tanner's decision for several years on appeal. The stakes could not be higher; one lawyer for the state claimed Tanner's decision could "jeopardize the pay scheme of every employer in the country." That, of course, depends on how higher courts rule. In the meantime, few states or private employers are likely to repeat Washington's impulse to study and denounce their wage scales.

How does one determine what is "fair" for particular jobs, such as the ones in question in the state of Washington? Because of the subjective nature of concepts such as the "worth" of a job, it may not be possible ever to provide a completely satisfactory answer to this question. However, there are methods to evaluate the content of a job in terms of required skills, knowledge, experience, responsibility, and other attributes, which represent a first step toward an answer. In this chapter we will examine methods and issues involved in job evaluation. We will also consider in more detail the issue of "comparable worth" which was raised by the state of Washington case.

DETERMINING FAIR COMPENSATION

Employee Worth

The amount of compensation received by a given employee should reflect the worth of the employee to an organization. Everyone wants to be paid according to his or her ability to perform for the organization. In a free-market society people are able to place a value on their services and offer them to the highest bidder. Similarly, an organization needs to place a value on the services of each of its employees to establish a level of compensation for the employees. Three major factors affect the level of compensation employees receive for their services: worth of the job, worth of employee performance, and employee supply. These three factors are highly interrelated, but we will discuss each separately.

Worth of the Job ▬ Jobs vary significantly in their difficulty, complexity, and challenge. Some require high levels of knowledge and skills while others can be done by almost anyone. Jobs are evaluated in terms of the demands they place on employees and their contribution to organizational goals. Jobs that involve simple, routine tasks that can be done by many people with minimal skills receive relatively low pay. On the other hand, jobs that involve complex, diverse tasks that can be done by few people with high-level skills tend to receive high pay.

Worth of Employee Performance ▬▬ Certainly the quality of an employee's work affects that person's worth to an employer. The belief that those who work hard and achieve will reap their rewards is a part of our traditional work ethic, and almost all organizations endorse the concept of "pay for performance." Exhibit 18.1 illustrates the relationship between the worth of the job and the worth of employee performance. Notice that as the job becomes more complex, the worth of the job increases. Furthermore, as job worth increases, the relative importance of the individual employee's performance in the job increases even more. Therefore, compensation for high-level jobs may be as dependent on the worth of the employee's performance as it is on the worth of the job.

Employee Supply ▬▬ In terms of labor economics, employees are a commodity in the marketplace that can be acquired by employers. The worth of the job and worth of employee performance determine the *demand* for this commodity, and the higher the demand, the more the employer will usually pay for a prospective employee. But another important factor that affects compensation is the *supply* of that employee in the marketplace. If the demand for a commodity is low and the supply is high, its value will be driven down. If, on the other hand, the demand is high and supply is low, competition for the commodity will be brisk and its value will increase. While we do not wish to equate human beings with commodities that are bought and sold in the marketplace, the compensation that employees receive is influenced by the need of organizations for employees and their availability in the labor market. For example, during the 1982 recession, demand for semiskilled factory workers was low and wages shrank accordingly. Many unions accepted pay cuts in exchange for job security. On the other hand, the 1980/1981 boom in the U.S. oil and gas industry produced a high demand for engineers and geologists. This resulted in stiff competition among firms for a relatively small supply of these employees and extremely high starting salaries.

Methods of Job Evaluation

The first step in assessing employee worth is to determine the worth of that employee's job.[2] **Job evaluation** is *the process of determining the worth of jobs and ranking them in order of their worth.* Job evaluation is the foundation of any organization's compensation policies because salaries cannot be assigned until jobs have been evaluated. The assignment of salaries to jobs results in a salary curve or salary structure (Exhibit 18.2), which is essentially a graphic representation of the compensation policies of an organization. For

job evaluation

EXHIBIT 18.1   **COMPONENTS OF JOB WORTH**

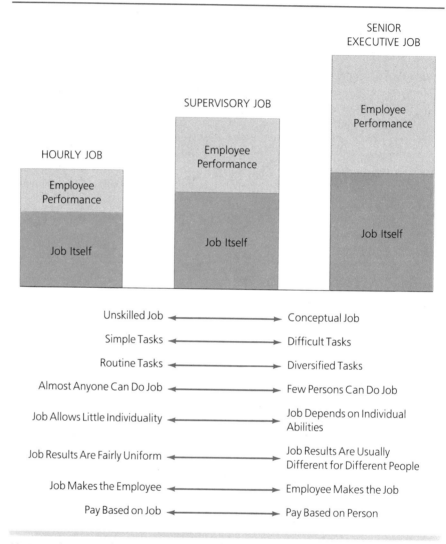

SOURCE: Adapted from *Wage and Salary Administration*, 2nd. by Zollitsch and Langsner. Copyright © 1970, by South-Western Publishing Co. Reprinted by permission.

each job level there is a salary range, and the salary curve intersects each salary range at its *midpoint* (e.g., points A and C in Exhibit 18.2). The *base salary* is the bottom of the range and is the salary paid to a new employee who has all the qualifications to perform a given job. Employee salaries can be increased in three ways. First, the entire pay curve can be moved upward

COMPANY SALARY STRUCTURE   *EXHIBIT 18.2*

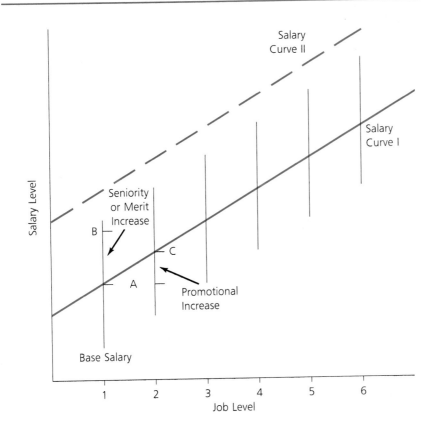

to increase all salaries by a constant value (e.g., a shift from salary curve I to salary curve II in Exhibit 18.2). In most cases the midpoint for each job level is increased by a given percentage to adjust for inflation; this is a cost-of-living adjustment (COLA). The second kind of salary increase is given to individual employees. On the basis of seniority or performance, they may move up in the salary range (from A to B in Exhibit 18.2). The third type of increase, also for individual employees, occurs when an individual is moved from one job level to another, and to the appropriate higher salary (A to C).

The size of the salary ranges and the slope of the salary curve are determined by organizational policies. A wide salary range allows for many salary increases to be awarded to employees who perform well, and provides incentive for excellent performance, while a narrow range allows for few merit increases because the employee's salary quickly reaches the top of the range. The slope of the curve also reflects compensation policy. A steep curve provides a financial incentive for promotion to a higher-level job, while a flatter curve can discourage promotion because employees being paid at the top of a salary range might take a reduction in salary if they accept a promotion and move to the midpoint of the next salary range. (In practice, however, salary reductions in such cases are rare. Usually the present salary is maintained or "red-circled" without an increase until inflation brings the lower salary range up to that salary level.)

But salaries cannot be assigned and the salary curve cannot be drawn until jobs have been ranked in order of their worth. It is important to remember that job evaluation is concerned with the worth of jobs, *not* with the worth of employee performance. So if all the jobs in an organization are considered and employees are temporarily forgotten, how might job value be determined? One option is to consider the worth of the *work output* of each job and focus on its importance to the organization's success. While work output is conceptually very appealing as a basis for job evaluation, it is very difficult to measure and convert to a dollar value. How might a value be placed on the products and services of jobs such as clerk typist in the shipping department, market research analyst, assistant controller, and vice-president of production? (This gets at the issue of "comparable worth," which will be discussed later.) Work output can be used as a measure of worth of a few very senior jobs, but it is not a feasible basis for evaluating all jobs in an organization.

A far more common basis for assigning value to jobs is *work input*. This option focuses on the demands that the job places on employees. Work input such as the level of education, experience, and skill required to do the job, the level of responsibility for people and funds involved in the job, and even physical working conditions are often used to evaluate jobs. The greater the demands of the job, the greater its worth. In terms of the actual techniques employed to evaluate the worth of a job, there are two basic approaches— non-quantitative and quantitative—and each approach includes two methods. The non-quantitative approach includes *ranking* and *job classification*, while the quantitative includes *factor comparison* and the *point* method. Job descriptions of duties, working conditions, and qualifications for all jobs to be evaluated are a necessary starting point for each method.

Ranking ▬▬ Ranking is the simplest way to evaluate jobs and is used today primarily in very small organizations. Usually a committee of senior managers reviews all job descriptions and ranks them in order of their importance or worth. The ranking method is simple, easy to understand, and inexpensive, but it is highly subjective because no explicit components of the jobs (e.g., level of education required, experience, skill, responsibility) are used for comparison. Furthermore, a simple ranking of jobs gives no information about the distances between jobs, and therefore gives no rationale for precise differences between salary levels assigned to each job ranked.

Job Classification ▬▬ Job classification is a complex ranking method. The first step is to select a number of factors common to all the jobs, such as the following:

1. Difficulty of work (simple, routine, varied, complex),
2. Volume of work (small, average, great),
3. Responsibility (little to great in dollars, number of people in unit, etc.),
4. Degree of supervision given or received (none, limited, general, close),
5. Experience required (none to ten years or more),
6. Special knowledge necessary (none, some, normal, highly technical),
7. Judgment involved (none, limited, shared, independent).

All jobs are then judged on the factors and grouped according to the findings. These groupings are then *ranked* in importance. For example, suppose a job classification system had the following rank order:

1. General management,
2. Departmental management,
3. Supervisory/technical,
4. Highly skilled,
5. Semiskilled,
6. Unskilled.

All of the jobs in an organization would be placed into one of these six grades, and then salaries would be assigned to each grade, and in some cases, to individual jobs in each grade.

The largest user of the job classification method of job evaluation is the U.S. Government. Its General Schedule (GS) Job Classification, containing grades ranging from GS-1 to GS-18, is prominently displayed on the ID cards of federal employees, along with the salaries for each GS level. The job factors used for classification and the various levels are shown in Exhibit 18.3.

The job classification method makes it possible to rank a large number of jobs by combining them into groups. It has some disadvantages, however. As more technical and staff jobs are created, there is an increasing probability that many jobs may fit into more than one group. Furthermore, job grouping is done on the basis of relatively few factors, which does not allow for the possibility that additional factors (such as interpersonal skills) could make the job more complex. Finally, the ranking of job groups is highly subjective, and differences between grades may not be clear to employees. For example, in Exhibit 18.3, one questions the difference between "attainments of high order," "marked attainments," "unusual attainments," and "exceptional attainments," representing GS-12 through GS-15.

Factor Comparison ▬▬ The factor comparison method is more popular than the non-quantitative methods and is particularly appropriate for blue-collar jobs. The evaluation of jobs is most often based on five factors:

1. Mental requirements,
2. Skill requirements,

EXHIBIT 18.3   *U.S. GOVERNMENT GENERAL SCHEDULE (GS) JOB CLASSIFICATION*

Number	Difficulty	Responsibility	Qualifications
GS1	simplest routine work		
GS2	routine work		some training or experience
GS3	somewhat difficult	somewhat responsible	working knowledge
GS4	moderately difficult work	moderately responsible work	moderate training, good working knowledge
GS5	difficult work	responsible work	considerable training, broad working knowledge, college graduate
GS6	difficult work	responsible work	broad working knowledge, special and complex subject
GS7	considerable difficulty	considerable responsibility	comprehensive and thorough working knowledge
GS8	very difficult	very responsible	comprehensive and thorough working knowledge
GS9	very difficult	very responsible	administrative experience, sound capacity for independent work
GS10	highly difficult	highly responsible	somewhat extended administrative experience
GS11	marked difficulty	marked responsibility	marked capacity for independent work
GS12	very high order of difficulty	very high order of responsibility	leadership and attainments of a high order
GS13	work of unusual difficulty	work of unusual responsibility	leadership and marked attainments
GS14	exceptional difficulty	exceptional responsibility	leadership and unusual attainments
GS15	outstanding difficulty	outstanding responsibility	leadership and exceptional attainments
GS16	unusual difficulty and national significance	unusual responsibility and national significance	leadership and exceptional attainments involving national significance
GS17	exceptional difficulty	exceptional responsibility	exceptional leadership attainments
GS18	outstanding difficulty	outstanding responsibility	outstanding leadership

3.   Physical requirements,
4.   Responsibility,
5.   Working conditions.

     With this method the first step is to select a number of key jobs that represent the entire range of jobs to be evaluated. Key, or benchmark, jobs are ones which are well known in the organization and are, in the opinion of the evaluators, thought to be fairly paid. These jobs are ranked independently on factors like the five above. Consequently, a key job that received a high rank on physical requirements (strength, height, weight) may be ranked low on mental requirements and moderate on working conditions.

RANKINGS AND MONEY VALUES   *EXHIBIT 18.4*

Factor Rankings and Rates

Key Job Titles	Hourly Wage Base Rate	Mental Requirements		Skill Requirements		Physical Requirements		Responsibility		Working Conditions	
		Rank	Rate	Rank	Rate	Rank	Rate	Rank	Rate	Rank	Rate
Pattern-maker	$8.40	1	$2.46	1	$3.04	7	$0.94	2	$1.44	9	$0.52
Machinist	7.10	3	1.50	2	2.26	5	1.28	3	1.34	7	0.72
Pipe Fitter	6.96	4	1.18	4	2.08	4	1.40	4	1.18	4	1.12
Poleman	6.92	8	0.76	8	1.18	2	2.48	8	0.90	2	1.60
Painter	6.60	5	1.12	5	2.04	6	1.26	6	1.12	5	1.06
Substation Operator	6.00	2	1.80	3	2.10	10	0.24	1	1.62	10	0.24
Drill Press Operator	5.80	6	1.04	6	1.86	9	0.76	5	1.16	6	0.98
Rammer	5.60	10	0.34	9	0.50	1	2.52	9	0.56	1	1.68
Carpenter's Helper	5.20	7	0.94	7	1.72	8	0.88	7	1.04	8	0.62
Laborer	5.00	9	0.64	10	0.36	3	2.10	10	0.50	3	1.40

SOURCE: Adapted from *Wage and Salary Administration,* 2nd. by Zollitsch and Langsner. Copyright © 1970, by South-Western Publishing Co. Reprinted by permission.

Next, each factor is assigned a weight on the basis of its relative importance. Then each key job is assigned a dollar value for each factor (based on its rank on that factor and the importance of the factor), and the sum of the five dollar values becomes the hourly wage for the job. An example is shown in Exhibit 18.4 for a variety of craft jobs ranging from an unskilled laborer up to a machinist and a pattern-maker. The key jobs and their dollar values for each of the five factors become the standards against which all other jobs are evaluated. The factor comparison process is complete when all jobs have been ranked on each of the five factors and assigned a dollar value.

The major strength of the factor comparison method is that it enables evaluators to break each job into factors, rank the jobs on each factor, and then compute a wage for each job on the basis of ranking on the factors. This makes it very clear what specific attributes are the basis for its level of compensation. This method also allows for differential weighting of the factors to reflect their relative worth. Its major disadvantage is that the numerical value of each job is in terms of actual hourly wages, and the entire wage structure will require revision in times of high inflation.

EXHIBIT 18.5   POINTS ASSIGNED TO FACTORS AND DEGREES

Factors and Subfactors	%	Points						Weight in Percent
		1st Degree	2nd Degree	3rd Degree	4th Degree	5th Degree	6th Degree	
Skill	50							
1. Education/Experience		12	24	36	48	60	72	12
2. Experience/Training		24	48	72	96	120	144	24
3. Initiative/Ingenuity		14	28	42	56	70	84	14
Effort	15							
4. Physical Demand		10	20	30	40	50	60	10
5. Mental and/or Visual Demand		5	10	15	20	25	30	5
Responsibility	20							
6. Equipment or Tools		6	12	18	24	30	36	6
7. Material or Product		7	14	21	28	35	42	7
8. Safety of Others		3	6	9	12	15	18	3
9. Work of Others		4	8	12	16	20	24	4
Job Conditions	15							
10. Working Conditions		10	20	30	40	50	60	10
11. Unavoidable Hazards		5	10	15	20	25	30	5
TOTAL	100%	100	200	300	400	500	600	100%

These data are hypothetical and are used for illustrative purposes.

Point Method ▬▬ The most widely used method of job evaluation is the point method. This method contains fundamental characteristics of factor comparison, with some refinements that add flexibility and practicality. The point method is based on a set of factors that can be assigned differential weights according to their importance. Each factor includes a number of degrees, and each job to be evaluated is given a rating on each factor.

Consider the example in Exhibit 18.5. Four factors—skill, effort, responsibility, and job conditions—are divided into eleven subfactors on which each job is to be evaluated. Each subfactor has been assigned a weight (far right column) according to its importance. Each subfactor has also been divided into six degrees. To evaluate a number of jobs in an organization, a committee studies job descriptions and judges which degree of each subfactor is involved in a given job. The appropriate number of points on each subfactor is then assigned to the job. For example, a job involving the third degree of "Initiative and Ingenuity" receives 42 points. The points on all subfactors are summed to determine each job's relative worth in the organization. The highest evaluation in this example would be 600 points for a job rated at the 6th degree on all eleven subfactors.

The point method has many strengths. The factors with their degrees and points provide relatively clear standards for the evaluation of jobs. Zollitsch and Langsner report greater consistency among raters using the point method than with other job evaluation methods.[3] The method also allows the evaluation of jobs to be done independently of salary or wage levels. Consequently, total points can be converted to any salary level that is competitive in the labor market. The major disadvantage of the point method is its complexity. It is difficult to install, and it is difficult for employees to understand. And in some organizations it is difficult to identify key jobs, which are the basis of this method.

EFFECTIVE JOB EVALUATION IN TODAY'S ORGANIZATIONS

A sound job evaluation system is the cornerstone of a successful compensation program in any organization and it must be properly developed to meet organization and employee needs. But the most technically valid compensation program will fail if it is not understood and perceived as fair by employees. Managers and supervisors, as well as human resource specialists, will be sorely pressed to defend a program that they or their employees feel is unfair. Developing and maintaining a valid job evaluation system is essential for effective compensation policies and procedures.

Developing the Job Evaluation System

Three elements are essential in a job evaluation system:

1. *Complete and current job analysis and job descriptions.* As in all major personnel functions discussed in this text, job evaluation begins with good job analysis, leading to a carefully written set of job descriptions. When a job evaluation system is developed or updated, all jobs included in the system must be carefully analyzed to ensure that accurate job descriptions are available. (Job analysis, you will remember, is the process of collecting data about and making judgments about the nature of a job, as we saw in Chapter Two. Job evaluation goes further and assesses the relative worth of each job in terms of its contribution to organizational effectiveness.)

2. *Team approach.* In most organizations job evaluation is done by a committee made up of one or more human resource specialists and a number of managers representing major disciplines throughout the organization. All four basic approaches to job evaluation require judgments, and the committee making these judgments should represent a wide range of job knowledge and viewpoints.

3. *Simple job evaluation system.* A rule of thumb to promote employee acceptance is to keep the job evaluation system as simple as possible. If a ranking method will suffice, use it. If four or five factors are sufficient in a factor comparison or point system, do not use seven. One organi-

zation used nineteen factors in its point system; the result was mass confusion among the compensation manager who administered the system, the managers who provided input for job evaluations, and employees throughout the company. Similarly, one university had used such a complex point system for its staff and support employees, that there were over 500 different job titles and point totals for a mere 1,000 employees. According to the job evaluation system, there were, on average, no more than two employees performing any given job in the university.

Maintaining the Job Evaluation System

Once a valid and fair job evaluation system has been developed, it must be introduced, installed, and regularly updated. This involves two major steps. The first is to promote employee understanding and acceptance. Compensation policies and procedures, and the job evaluation system on which they are based, will not succeed without employee acceptance. Two groups in the organization whose understanding and acceptance must be sought are the supervisors and managers (who implement compensation policies by making salary offers to prospective employees and raises to current employees) and all other employees of the organization (whose salaries are determined by the compensation policies). Two basic approaches can be taken to deal with these groups. The first is a compensation handbook that describes the job evaluation system, the salary structure, and all compensation policies. The second is a series of orientation meetings to introduce the organization's compensation program to all employees. The orientation meetings include all the material usually covered in a handbook but add the opportunity to discuss specific issues.

The second step is to keep the system current. Once the job evaluation system has been developed and installed, it must be regularly updated. In most organizations this is an ongoing enterprise. Employees often take on additional responsibilities as jobs expand with the growth of a department or the entire organization, and the result can be a substantial increase in the worth of the jobs. The usual procedure is for supervisors or managers to update job descriptions and submit the jobs to the organization's compensation committee, which may, in turn, reevaluate the jobs. Employee salaries can then be adjusted accordingly.

Environmental Changes That Affect Job Evaluation

In today's world of work, major changes have occurred that have had direct impact on job evaluation and compensation. Jobs and employees have changed dramatically in relatively short periods of time, and recent fluctuations in the supply of and demand for employees, as well as periods of high inflation, have required organizations to make major adjustments in their job evaluation systems and salary structures.

Changing Jobs ▬ With changing technology many changes in jobs in American business have occurred. New jobs are continually created, and old jobs are often altered. Many secretaries and clerk typists have become "word processor operators" or "display writer operators," computer programmers and operators are working with a new generation of languages and equipment, and gene-splicing technicians are completely new. All of these jobs must be placed into existing job evaluation systems and salary structures. Furthermore, as the work force becomes more highly educated and trained, individual employees greatly exceed the minimal educational requirements included in job evaluation systems and expect their jobs to be upgraded accordingly. A job evaluation system that is not regularly updated to incorporate these changes in jobs and employees will lead to dissatisfaction with pay.

External Equity Versus Internal Equity ▬ The second major element of change that represents a constant difficulty for compensation programs is the fluctuation of salaries in the marketplace. This problem is particularly severe when there is a scarcity or overabundance of available employees in a particular field, and salaries increase more or less than anticipated. For example, if engineers and geologists are scarce, companies must adjust starting salaries upward to attract and retain them. But these changes in the market value of specific groups can disrupt the "internal equity" of a compensation system. As we explained earlier, the object of job evaluation is to order jobs according to their worth. **Internal equity** is *the high positive correlation between salary level and job level that exists in an organization when salaries are assigned to jobs according to their worth.* In other words, the jobs judged to be worth the most receive the highest salaries, etc.

    External equity is *the compensation of jobs in one organization at the same level at which they are compensated in other organizations.* The salary level for a given job is also dependent on the supply of people in the labor market who are able to perform that job. If demand for these people is high and supply is low, their worth will rise. As a result, the prevailing salaries for certain types of employees may be artificially high, higher than a job evaluation might indicate.

    A problem arises if the salary on an organization's salary curve is not competitive in the labor market. Suppose the jobs of accountant, engineer, and geologist have been judged to be nearly equivalent in worth according to an organization's job evaluation system. These jobs fall in the same job grade and have been assigned the same salary. But due to high demand and low supply, the prevailing starting salary, as determined by area salary surveys, for engineers and geologists is much greater than that for accountants, and falls well above the salary range for grade seven. The organization must decide whether to maintain its internal equity and pay engineers and geologists at the same rate of all other jobs in grade seven, thereby making its salaries

internal equity

external equity

for these scarce employees uncompetitive, or raise salaries for engineers and geologists to be competitive, thereby creating an imbalance in salaries within the organization. This is the classic dilemma of external versus internal equity. In practice, many organizations are forced to maintain the external equity of their compensation programs by adjusting salaries to remain competitive in the marketplace.

For example, assume that engineer A joins an oil company in the fall of 1981 at a starting monthly salary of $2,300. In fall 1982, she receives an 8 percent cost-of-living increase and a 5 percent merit increase. Her 1982 salary is then $2,300 + 184 + 115 or $2,599. But in the fall of 1982, the company raises its starting salary by 12 percent to attract scarce engineers. Hence, engineer B receives a starting salary of $2,300 + 276 or $2,576, a mere $23 less than engineer A, who has one year of excellent work experience. Successive years of high increases in starting salaries can artificially compress the difference between the salaries of experienced and inexperienced employees. This form of inequity can be very demoralizing for experienced employees.

The dilemma of choosing between internal equity and external equity forces organizations into some unsatisfactory practices. Some simply maintain internal equity and try to attract good employees in spite of relatively low salaries by stressing non-financial features such as security, the nature of the work, and attractiveness of the organization. Other organizations adjust salaries to market conditions but try to suppress employee perceptions of the resulting internal inequity through various tactics. One tactic is to reevaluate high demand jobs to raise them to a level in the job evaluation system that is more consistent with their prevailing salary levels. In essence, the job evaluation committee chooses a salary level for a job and then reinterprets the worth of the job so that it reaches the desired level in the job evaluation system. This practice weakens the validity of the job evaluaton system and can undermine employee acceptance of the system.

Another tactic to suppress employee perceptions of internal inequity is secrecy about an organization's job evaluation system and salary structure. Information about job grades, salary ranges, and salary increases is often withheld from employees to prevent informed comparisons that would reveal internal inequity. As we said in Chapter Seventeen, however, this secrecy does little to instill employee trust in the organization's compensation policies, and it tends to decrease employee motivation.

individual equity

Individual Equity ▬ To complicate the issue, there is a third type of fairness involved in a compensation system: **individual equity,** *the extent to which an individual's pay is linked to that individual's contributions to the organization.* The two most common types of employee contribution would be years of service to the organization (i.e., seniority) and the person's level of performance (as measured by the performance appraisal process). Even if the firm's pay structures meet the test of external and internal equity, if individual pay levels or pay raises are not related to some measure of employee contribution, there will be significant feelings of inequity (and dissatisfaction)

THREE FORMS OF EQUITY

EXHIBIT 18.6

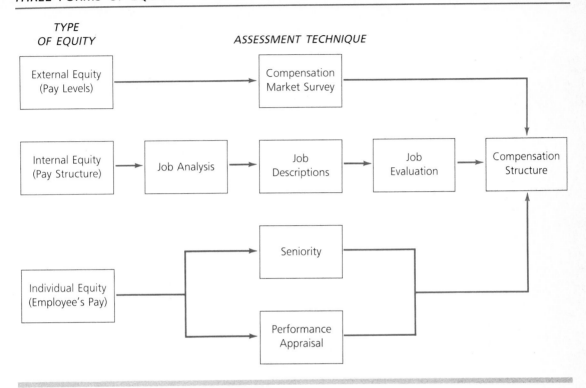

TYPE
OF EQUITY   ASSESSMENT TECHNIQUE

SOURCE: Adapted from "Compensation System: Basic Concepts, Components and Objectives" from "The Emerging Debate" by George T. Milkovich in *Comparable Worth: Issues and Alternatives,* 2nd. edition, E.R. Livernash, ed. (Washington, D.C., Equal Employment Advisory Council, 1984), p. 27. Reprinted by permission.

on the part of employees. (Chapter Seventeen discussed the strategic issues involved in linking pay to performance, and Chapter Fifteen gave details on how to measure performance objectively.) A summary of the three forms of equity, and the techniques for assessing them, is shown in Exhibit 18.6.

Comparable Worth

Let us now return to the court case described at the beginning of this chapter. On the average, women earn 60 cents for every dollar earned by men in the United States. Even when influences on pay which might explain such a discrepancy (influences such as age, education, and years of experience) are taken into account, a large disparity still exists between the salaries of men and women.

The notion of equal pay for equal work was central to the Equal Pay Act of 1963. However, the concept of "comparable worth" goes beyond equal pay for equal work. Court interpretations (see the *Gunther* case, described below) of Title VII of the 1964 Civil Rights Act extended the concept of equity to include equal pay for work of comparable worth (i.e., different jobs that require comparable levels of knowledge, skill, effort, and responsibility). The former Chair of the Equal Employment Opportunity Commission (EEOC), Eleanor Holmes Norton, has called equal worth the dominant women's issue of the 1980s, one to be litigated under Title VII, and one whose scope would be comparable to school busing.

The Gunther Case ▬ Before the late 1970s, there was debate about whether or not Title VII incorporated the *equal work* requirement of the Equal Pay Act (i.e., the idea that a person could only claim wage discrimination in the case of unequal pay for substantially equal work, as in the case of a female executive secretary's pay compared to that of a male executive secretary). The main debate was focused on the Bennett Amendment to Title VII: "It shall not be an unlawful employment practice . . . to differentiate on the basis of sex . . . if such differentiation is authorized by the provisions of the Equal Pay Act."

Lawyers opposed to the equal work interpretation of Title VII argued that this narrow interpretation would give no recourse to the great majority of potential plaintiffs, since, because of the high degree of sex segregation in the work place, most women would not be able to compare their pay with that of men in similar jobs.

The U.S. Supreme Court settled this debate on June 8, 1981, in the case of *County of Washington v. Gunther,* No. 80–429, when it interpreted the meaning of the Bennett Amendment. The Court ruled that Title VII is not restricted to the "equal pay for equal work" standard of the equal pay act.

Thus, after *Gunther,* employees may make claims of sex discrimination in pay under Title VII even if the job is different. To prove sex discrimination a woman must show that she is a member of a protected class (i.e., a woman); she works in a sex-segregated job, primarily held by women; her pay is less than a primarily male-occupied job classification; and the jobs are similar enough in required skill, effort, responsibility, and working conditions to be considered "comparable" to the employer. In addition, under Title VII a woman can compare herself to a man working in a different establishment of the same employer.[4]

Problems in Assessing Job Worth ▬ On the surface, it would seem to be quite straightforward to measure the worth of a job: simply use one of the job evaluation procedures described earlier in this chapter. However, the inadequacy of traditional job evaluation in this case is that job evaluation is used to determine how a particular job should be assessed in relation to the existing structure of market wage rates. Thus, a job evaluation rating for a particular position is based not only on the intrinsic worth of that job but also upon the external market value of the skills and other employee attributes required for that job. The true societal worth of a job, then, and the labor market's determination of that job's worth (based upon supply and demand) are not necessarily the same thing.

A large part of the controversy about comparable worth comes from the subjective nature of "worth." Within a society, different groups or individuals would undoubtedly disagree sharply about the value of work produced in different jobs. How would you compare the work of a fire fighter with that of a company president? Does a professional athlete produce more "worth" than a nurse or airline pilot?

Another approach has been to study ways to improve job evaluation so that it can take more explicit account of the perceived intrinsic worth of various jobs. One recommendation is that the federal government fund job analysis research related to pay equity.[5] This recommendation also calls for "relevant professional organizations to establish an authoritative set of minimum standards for competent job analyses and job evaluations which are needed to establish equitable compensation procedures."[6] Box 18.1 illustrates how job evaluation data were used in the *Washington State* case.

Another alternative would be a two-step process which explicitly attempts to use both job evaluation and market factors. The first step would be to build the best possible job evaluation system. To permit comparison of quite different types of jobs, a point or factor comparison system would probably be most effective. The next step would be to adjust the resulting job levels to fit market conditions (i.e., to achieve external equity). These two steps would be an attempt to balance internal and external equity. The key here is to realize that any attempt to achieve both internal and external equity will involve compromise and *knowing* when internal equity is violated for pragmatic market conditions.

As a final note on the complexity of the comparable worth issue, consider the effects of political and personal characteristics and other environmental factors, as discussed by industrial relations expert Donald Schwab:

> [Compensation] policies are implemented within a political as well as an economic environment. The former often attempts to modify and shape pay policies to serve other than organizational goals. Thus, state and/or federal regulation legislates minimum wages, or requires or regulates indirect compensation as through Old Age Survivors and Disability Insurance, as well as reallocating direct pay through income and social security taxes. Union pressure exercised through the collective bargaining process also serves as an environmental parameter that shapes organizational pay setting process and outcomes. Taken together, economic and other environmental factors serve as constraints that must be accounted for as compensation administrators attempt to develop pay policies.
>
> Thus the pay obtained by any individual will ordinarily reflect not only the job he or she holds but also personal characteristics such as past performance levels and service with the organization. If individuals are aggregated into groups, such as by sex, and a difference is observed, the source of the difference could be due to job and/or individual pay variation.[7]

VALUING JOBS IN WASHINGTON STATE

BOX 18.1

The chart [below] is a "scattergram"—a pictorial device that is endlessly onstage in the comparable worth debate and supposedly tells you whether there's discrimination in a given job universe. The universe shown here consists of seventy-five job categories monitored by the state of Washington's personnel department in 1974—the year in which the state began doing job evaluations. The chart depicts only jobs that were predominantly (70 percent or more) male or female, and it reflects the logic by which the state satisfied itself that it was discriminating.

Scattergrams show the extent to which jobs are paid more or less than their evaluated worth. In an ideal world, workers' pay (vertical scale) would precisely reflect the evaluation point scores (horizontal scale), and all the plot points would fall on one straight line. Nobody expects this to happen in the real world, where such complications as seniority, unionization, and plain measurement errors are bound to scatter the plot points, leaving some jobs with more dollars per evaluation point than others. But suppose you drew a "fair pay" line that best expressed the trend of the plot points. And suppose it turned out that virtually all the "overpaid" jobs (those above the line) were predominantly male, while those below the line were just about all female. As you can see, that happened in Washington and encouraged a federal judge to find the state had violated the Civil Rights Act.

However, it is far from clear that purely statistical measures like scattergrams prove anything about discrimination. Women were not, after all, barred from the higher-paying job categories above the line; indeed, the state had affirmative-action programs designed to encourage their entry into those jobs. Nor were the majority of women paid less than the minority of men in the categories below the line. In effect, the state was paying market wages for all the jobs depicted and usually finding it possible to fill "women's jobs" more cheaply.

Excerpt from "But Does it Prove Discrimination" from *Fortune*, May 14, 1984, p. 134. Copyright © 1984 Time Inc. All rights reserved. Reprinted by permission. Scattergram from *Fortune*, May 14, 1984, p. 134. Reprinted by permission of the artist, Nino Telak.

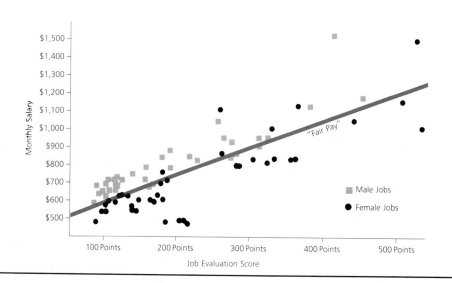

Guidelines for Employers ▬▬ Although court decisions are still evolving and shaping the definition of comparable worth, it is possible at this point to pull together some guidelines for employers to follow. Cases in the private sector (e.g., *Taylor v. Charley Brothers, Power v. Barry County, Mich.*) indicate that underpayment alone is not sufficient for an employee to win a lawsuit; there must also be evidence of intent to discriminate in pay. Therefore, the following steps are suggested:

1. *Eliminate sex-segregated job categories.* Do not deny female employees access to particular job categories. Similarly, attempt to integrate more *men* in jobs primarily staffed now by women.

2. *Consider qualified applicants of both sexes for all jobs.* Even if you feel a certain job may be unsuitable for one sex or another, let that choice be the employee's. In *Taylor* and *AFSCME*, part of the reason the court ruled against the employer was the employer's practice of channeling the sexes into particular jobs, independent of the preferences and abilities of the applicants.

3. *Avoid wage differentials within a job classification that are based upon built-in biases of the external labor market.* Unequal pay for equal work is a clear violation of the Equal Pay Act, as well as a possible violation of Title VII. Within-job differentials based on sex still exist in many organizations and represent easy targets for employee suits. Employers should be proactive and identify and rectify these inequities.

4. *Examine closely any other sex-related wage differentials that reflect market conditions.* Since there will probably be more legal action on comparable worth in the future, it is worth examining differentials between comparable positions. Can they really be justified by the economic realities of the labor market, or does there in fact appear to be some indication of international sex discrimination?

5. *Use the results of job evaluation or document why it is not accurate.* Part of the problem the employer had in the *Washington State* case was that the state had actually convicted itself by having conducted its own job evaluation study which showed that female workers were significantly underpaid in relation to males and by then failing to act to equalize salaries. This point has also been made in *Gunther* and other cases. Thus, ignoring the results of the employer's own job analysis is asking for trouble.[8]

NEW TRENDS IN COMPENSATION

The All-Salaried Work Force

As we said earlier, one function of a pay system is to reinforce the structure and culture of the organization. One of the strongest elements of structure and culture in many organizations, especially traditional manufacturing organizations, is the distinction between salaried and hourly employees. In many cases this is in effect a two-class system, in which hourly employees have to punch time clocks, lose pay if they punch in late, have prescribed times for breaks, and may have little sick or personal leave. Salaried employees, on the other hand, generally do not punch time clocks, have more flexibility, do not lose pay if they are late, and may have more sick or personal leave.

Many organizations in recent years have eliminated the time clock and put all employees on a salaried income. In many cases this is part of a move toward more participatory management. It is a way to remove status barriers between management and operating employees. It shows management's trust in the maturity and responsibility of employees.

As part of this move to an all-salaried work force (a practice employed by IBM and Gillette since the 1950s), firms may also introduce new terms to replace the old "hourly worker." Terms like "manufacturing specialist" or "associate" are often used. Such general terms are also useful because of changes in job design which have combined old jobs or resulted in more rotation of workers between various jobs.

There has been little union support for this all-salaried idea, perhaps because of a fear that it may be a union-avoidance strategy, or may lead to increased employee identification with management. There has been little evaluation of the impact of an all-salaried system on absenteeism and tardiness, and there could be problems in this area without some sort of supervisory or peer discipline. However, organizations such as IBM have found that where there is good management, these problems do not exist.

Skill-Based Job Evaluation Systems

In most cases, a person's pay is determined by the position which he or she holds. The salary or hourly wage usually falls within a range established for that position, with some individual variation based upon performance, length of service, market factors, and other considerations.

"paying the person"

In contrast to paying the job, the idea of paying the person is growing in popularity. **"Paying the person"** means *basing pay on the number of skills the person possesses, rather than paying on the basis of the position the person holds.* This is seen most often in connection with job redesign, where the person is encouraged to learn new skills as the jobs are enriched. It may take several years to acquire all the skills in a particular plant, and when that point is reached, the person would be at the top pay rate. This "topping out" has been a minimal problem in new plants such as the Topeka General Foods plant and Rockwell's Battle Creek, Michigan, facility because of the selective movement of people through various skill areas and the fact that not all employees want to learn all skills. However, such plans require a high investment in training and strict controls so that employees do not move on to learn new jobs until they have thoroughly mastered the present jobs. Also, setting pay rates can be difficult, since it is hard for an employee to know whose pay their pay should be compared with. Overall, though, skill-based plans are associated with increased satisfaction with pay and quality of work life, and with decreased absenteeism and turnover.[9]

Lump Sum Salary Increases

In most organizations, when employees receive salary increases, the amount of the increase is spread over the entire year in the employee's regular paycheck. After tax and other deductions are made, the person may see very little change in the weekly or monthly amount.

To get more impact from pay increases, Lawler indicates that some organizations (such as B.F. Goodrich, Timex, and Westinghouse) have started lump sum increase programs that give employees the choice of when and how to receive raises (including in one lump at the beginning of the year, although some firms charge interest on the money when taken this way).[10] If the employee quits before the end of the year, the unearned part of the increase is treated as a loan to be paid back. Such lump-sum plans can be a useful way to see pay-raise dollars more clearly and to be able to buy more with them.

Flexible Benefit Programs

Perhaps the most widespread of the new compensation plans is the flexible benefit system. Often called a "cafeteria" benefit plan, it gives the employees a choice in selecting the combination of benefits they will receive. In contrast to most benefit packages, in which all employees receive the same set of benefits, the flexible plan permits the employee to apply the employer's contributions toward specific benefits, based on his or her life-style, life stage, and needs. For example, older employees might want more of their company-provided benefit money to be used for medical or life insurance. Younger employees might prefer to have that money in the form of cash. Working parents might prefer to have it in the form of more free time (e.g., more personal days or vacation time). In this way, by letting the employees choose benefit combinations that they value most, the company gets more return in employee satisfaction for its benefit dollar.

One possible problem is that the cost of certain benefits, such as insurance, is based on the number and age composition of people who take them. If a smaller number of people and predominantly older people opted for them, the costs could rise. However, in larger organizations there are enough employees who would probably opt for any component so that this would not be a problem. In small companies, enough experience would eventually accumulate so that the number of participants could be estimated accurately, and the components priced appropriately.

Another problem here is the potential taxability of benefits. The Revenue Act of 1978 and the Deficit Reduction Act of 1984 were major factors in the establishment and definition of "cafeteria compensation," as it is called legally. The trend is to increase the taxability of benefits, and this may hinder the growth of cafeteria plans.

A major issue for many organizations is the administrative cost to provide different options for different people. With computerized personnel systems becoming more advanced, this problem may diminish over time, but it is a real one. However, organizations can minimize these administrative costs. A fixed set of options might be provided, rather than an infinite number of

EXHIBIT 18.7   NEW PRACTICES IN COMPENSATION

	Major Advantages	Major Disadvantages	Favorable Situational Factors
All-salaried work force	Climate of trust; increased satisfaction and job attraction	Possible higher costs and absenteeism	Supervisors who will deal with absenteeism problems; a participative climate; an involved, responsible work force; well-designed jobs
Skill-based evaluation	More flexible and skilled work force; increased satisfaction; climate of growth	Cost of training; higher salaries	Employees who want to develop themselves; jobs that are interdependent
Lump-sum salary increases	Increased pay satisfaction; greater visibility of pay increases	Cost of administration	Fair pay rates; pay related to performance
Flexible benefits	Increased pay satisfaction; greater attraction	Cost of administration	Well-educated, heterogeneous work force; large organization; good data processing

SOURCE: Adapted from *Pay and Organizational Development* by Edward E. Lawler, fig. 5.1, p. 77. Copyright © 1981, Addison-Wesley, Reading, Massachusetts. Reprinted by permission.

combinations. In many cases, employees are allowed to modify their package only once a year, which cuts down on the administrative burden.

Another way to simplify the flexible system is to use a single benefit as "currency" against which employees can trade off other benefits. For example, at Continental Bank, benefits can be traded for time off. If a person does not want or need the company's medical coverage, for example, because of the spouse's coverage elsewhere, he or she can take the equivalent value in increased personal days. (The time off is a particularly attractive benefit in this organization, with so many members of two-career marriages, particularly women.)

A summary of these new approaches appears in Exhibit 18.7. The major advantages seem to be increased satisfaction and job attractiveness, and to some extent decreased turnover, absenteeism, and tardiness. In general, lump sum increase plans and cafeteria benefits are most appropriate where present pay rates are fair, and the all-salary approach works best with a participative management style. For that difficult situation in which present pay rates are not fair, a skill-based plan might be worth trying, since it gives the opportunity to drastically revamp the pay system.

CURRENT ISSUES IN SALARY ADMINISTRATION

If one asked a human resource executive what the three or four most pressing human resource issues currently were in his or her organization, regardless of the year—1950, 1975, or 1990—chances are the executive would mention something about compensation. Pay is simply a very important issue in managing any organization, and there seems to be no end to the problems related to compensation. For example, a survey of the Human Resource Council of the American Management Association in 1983 found executive compensation to be the number one human resource issue at that time.[11] What follows are some of the important compensation issues organizations are currently facing.

Swings in Inflation

A well-designed pay system can be totally stymied by inflation unless it is designed with inflation in mind, and in times of price stability a system based on inflation can have problems. For example, if a merit pay plan lets people earn up to a 10 percent increment and inflation is running at 13 percent, a person may feel that the best he or she can do is come near to breaking even. Or if a firm has been paying 13 percent increases over the years to match cost-of-living increases and the inflation rate drops to 3 or 4 percent, how can management convince employees that 7 percent is a good raise? (This is what happened during 1982 and 1983 when the inflation rate dropped sharply. In 1982 raises in executive compensation were down to 5.4 percent, from 13 percent in 1981, according to a survey by consultants Towers, Perrin, Forster, and Crosby.)[12]

One implication of this is the need for a compensation system that is flexible and can handle large changes in the proportions of merit and cost of living. It is also necessary to have a good communication process, so that employees always have current information on the meaning of their increases.

Bonus Expectations During a Recession

One of the problems faced by many firms with well-functioning bonus systems during the 1982–83 recession was the frustrated expectations of employees who survived the staff reductions. By definition, these survivors tended to be the more effective performers; they were people top management cared about keeping. Initially the survivors were pleased just to have a job, after seeing what had happened to some of their co-workers. However, in time they became acutely aware that their rewards had diminished. Many organizations were slow to pick up and people were not receiving bonuses or other forms of incentive pay. For executives, as much as half of their pay was in the form of bonus, which meant that they faced the prospect of going several years with their pay cut in half. The result was that many of the good performers left for "greener pastures" (where a bonus was not a major part of their total compensation) during this period.

Health Care and Benefit Cost Containment

In a survey of 305 chief executive officers, 83 percent cited rising benefit costs as the greatest single obstacle to designing compensation systems which reinforce corporate values.[13] As we said earlier, health care is the fastest growing expense in running a large business today. Although Joseph Califano estimated that the Fortune 500's medical bill would hit $1 trillion by 1993, the present problems in the health care system will probably not be allowed to continue, so that figure may not be reached by 1993. By 1984, in fact, the rate of increase in health costs, while still high, had begun to drop.[14]

Companies are restructuring their health insurance programs. Whereas many firms once paid all bills, they may now have a $500 front-end deductible. Or they may require greater employee contributions to the program. For example, it is not unusual for an organization to offer health insurance with a health maintenance organization (HMO) as one option. The employee might pay about one-third of the cost, while the employer pays two-thirds. HMOs are growing rapidly in response to this need to contain medical costs.

Some medical plans are being discontinued. Dental coverage, very popular a few years ago, is being cut back.

Companies are using different methods to restrain the rise in medical costs. Many are attempting to educate their staffs in effective and efficient use of benefits. Corporate subsidies for second and third opinions are another effective way to keep costs down. Companies are using their "clout" to control the cost of health care delivery. For example, Continental Bank established a policy to restrict charitable donations only to hospitals with budget increases below a particular level, thus rewarding those which help keep down the cost of health care.

The federal government is working toward health cost reductions, as well. By instituting taxes on employee health benefits (e.g., by treating health insurance benefits as income), the government is making the individual employee more conscious of health costs and their tax implications.

The Need to Resist Compression

One unfortunate consequence of years of inflation in the 1970s and early 1980s was a tremendous compression of salary levels from entry level positions to lower and middle management. In the past it was not unusual to see a manager earn four times as much as a starting person (e.g., $60,000 vs. $15,000). Now the ratio may be as low as 2 to 1 ($70,000 vs. $35,000 for some new MBAs). In universities, the ratio between the top and bottom of the faculty pay scale used to be around 4:1 ($40,000 to $10,000) in the late 1960s. Now it ranges around 2:1 ($50,000 vs. $25,000).

The main reason for this compression is the escalation of starting salaries, due to inflation, and the competition for entry-level people. With inflation lower, and with the labor market a bit looser, companies are seeking ways to keep starting salaries down. Here are some approaches:

- One chemical firm cut the starting salary for chemical engineers by $4,000, and increased its stress on the company's quality as a career environment in its recruiting. Its success in recruiting top candidates did not suffer.
- Some companies start new employees in non-exempt positions at salaries below the going rate, but give the guarantee of *overtime pay*, to increase overall compensation.
- Some companies start new employees at relatively low base salaries but provide "perks" such as company cars, club memberships, liberal relocation allowances, and even bonuses for signing.
- Some companies make low starting salaries more palatable by reviewing the person's salary and giving an increase after six months, rather than the customary one year review. (See Box 18.2 for an example of a creative compensation package for a professional football player.)

As organizations have gone into specialized new businesses and developed a more differentiated set of occupational specialties among employees, the problem of internal equity has grown greatly. For example, accountants and computer science specialists often are paid more than sales and personnel people because of outside market competition for computer people and accountants. This salary differential for people at the same level creates an internal inequity and feelings of friction between the two groups. Two methods are used to deal with these market anomalies:

- One-time adjustments can be made in the salaries of employees who are not in high-demand disciplines to improve equity.
- Several different pay scales may be set up based on the same job evaluation system. That is, everyone may have the same grade in the job evaluation system, but a grade 20 is converted to several different salary scales, depending on market conditions for the various disciplines. This maintains equity within a discipline and maintains external equity for each discipline. It does, however, create inequities between disciplines.

Services as Employee Benefits

As organizations attempt to cut back on expensive benefits, such as medical insurance, there is increased interest to explore alternative benefits which will have high value to employees yet low cost to the organization. One such service is *financial and investment assistance*. This can be either individual financial advice and consultation, or simply investment seminars to provide financial education. These services can be provided by either outside firms or members of the internal financial staff.

Child care information networks are another example. Rather than provide a day care center or even a child care subsidy to the employee, some

HOW TO HAVE HIGH COMPENSATION AND "LOW" PAY

BOX 18.2

Quarterback Tony Eason signed with the New England Patriots for a $2.225 million four-year package. While the package is indeed generous, his yearly salaries were relatively low. The package breaks down as follows:

Signing bonus	$800,000
Low-interest loan worth	200,000
Salary: year 1	200,000
year 2	250,000
year 3	325,000
year 4	450,000
TOTAL	$2,225,000

In addition, the contract provides for creation of a scholarship to Eason's high school and contributions to a Boston charity for each Patriot victory.

For the Patriots, this was a way to maintain salary equity with their starting quarterback, Steve Grogan. The *Boston Globe* reported how both the Patriots and Eason's goals were met:

"As the (negotiation) talks come down to the final hours, the overriding factors on both sides become clear.

"For Eason, it was the size of the total package and the fact that he had always wanted to play for the NFL. For [Patrick] Sullivan [the Patriots' general manager], it was making sure that Eason did not come to New England as the highest-paid player on his roster.

"Both goals were achieved Tuesday night and, after a fitful night's sleep, Eason agreed to terms.

" 'His starting salary was very important to them,' said Leigh Stanberg, Eason's agent. 'All that mattered to us was the total package.' "

Note the tension here between external equity (the outside market for Eason's services, such as the then thriving U.S. Football League) and internal equity (Eason's annual salary vs. Steve Grogan's, the senior quarterback). In this solution, both types of equity were maintained.

This settlement is also an example of the concept of "integrative bargaining" described in Chapter Six (Labor-Management Relations): a "win-win" situation was found in which each party could achieve its most important goals, while providing room to the other party to do the same. (This is in contrast to distributive, or "win-lose" bargaining, in which one party achieves its goals at the expense of the other.) With increased restrictions on compensation, from a variety of factors—financial pressures, internal equity, external equity, comparable worth, etc.—the creativity of integrative bargaining has become increasingly important in salary negotiations for key employees, such as star athletes, senior executives, and outstanding technical professionals.

Adaptation of "How to Have High Compensation and 'Low' Pay" by Ron Borges, *Boston Globe,* May 26, 1983. Reprinted courtesy of The Boston Globe.

organizations have one child care coordinator who maintains a file of quality child care services and provides advice and counseling to employees about what form of child care is appropriate to their needs.

Legal services plans are another growing benefit. This benefit is becoming a more popular ingredient in union contracts. These plans provide routine personal legal services for employees on matters that cover such diverse areas as divorces, wills, and real estate transactions, with the fees paid by the employer.

KEY POINTS

- Fair compensation should be based upon the worth of the employee and the worth of the employee's job to the organization. Job evaluation is a systematic process to assess the worth of the job.
- The main non-quantitative methods of job evaluation are ranking and job classification. The most common quantitative methods are factor comparison and the point method.
- Three steps are involved in setting up a job evaluation system: developing current job descriptions, using employee teams to evaluate jobs, and keeping the job evaluation system simple. Maintaining the system entails employee acceptance and frequent updating as jobs change.
- In working toward equal pay for jobs of comparable worth, employers are advised to eliminate sex-segregated job categories; consider qualified applicants for all jobs, regardless of sex; avoid wage differentials within a job classification based on built-in labor market biases; examine any other sex-related wage differentials caused by the market; and use the results of job evaluations, if they are being conducted.
- New trends in compensation include the all-salaried work force, skill-based job evaluation systems, lump-sum salary increases, and flexible work programs.
- Current issues which organizations must address are inflated employee expectations during a recession, health care cost containment, salary compression, and employee services as benefits.

ISSUES FOR DISCUSSION

1. How does employee worth change as a job becomes more complex? Why? Can you give an example of this tendency, based on organizations where you have worked?

2. How do the quantitative and the non-quantitative methods for conducting job evaluation differ from each other?

3. What are internal, external, and individual equity? Why is it difficult to maintain all types of equity simultaneously?

4. What is comparable worth? Why is it so difficult to arrive at equal pay for jobs of comparable worth? What ideas can you suggest to help solve this problem?

5. What are the major current issues in compensation? Which one do you think is most important?

NOTES

1. Adapted from Doug Underwood, "Women Win One in Washington," in *Newsweek*, December 12, 1983, p. 43.

2. H. G. Zollitsch and A. Langsner, *Wage and Salary Administration*, Second Edition (Cincinnati: South-Western, 1970).

3. Ibid.

4. R. L. Brady, L. N. Persson, S. E. Thompson, and D. Cadrain, *1984 Comparable Worth Supplement, Comparable Worth Compliance: A Wage and Salary Handbook* (Madison, Conn.: Bureau of Law and Business, Inc., 1984), p. 15. See also *Public Personnel Management*, "Special Issue: Comparable Worth," N. E. Reichenberg (Ed.), *12*(4), 1983.

5. L. D. Eyde, "Testimony for Congressional Pay Equity Hearing," *The Industrial-Organizational Psychologist*, August 1983, *20*(4), pp. 13–16.

6. Ibid., p. 16.

7. D. Schwab, "Job Evaluation and Pay Setting," *The Industrial-Organizational Psychologist*, August 1983, *20*(4), p. 18. For a more critical review, see D. Seligman, " 'Pay Equity' is a Bad Idea," *Fortune*, May 14, 1984, pp. 133–40.

8. Brady et al., op cit., pp. 24, 25. Similar ideas, as well as male-female differences in perceived causes and cures in pay discrepancies, are found in B. Rosen, S. Rynes, and T. Mahoney, "Compensation, Jobs, and Gender," *Harvard Business Review*, July-August 1983, pp. 170–90.

9. E. E. Lawler, III, *Pay and Organizational Development* (Reading, Mass.: Addison-Wesley, 1981).

10. Ibid.

11. E. Croissant, AMA Human Resource Council Chair, *Personal Communication*, April 1983.

12. Labor Letter, "A Special Report on People and Their Jobs in Offices, Fields and Factories: Top Officers' Pay Raises Slowed in 1982, but Fringes Abound," *Wall Street Journal*, April 26, 1983, p. 1.

13. W. M. Mercer, "Employee Attitudes Toward Compensation Change and Corporate Values," *Career Development Bulletin*, 1984, *4*(2), p. 5.

14. "Health Costs up 6.1%, a Slight Decline," *New York Times*, January 28, 1985, pp. 1, 13.

ANNOTATED BIBLIOGRAPHY

NASH, A., and CARROLL, S. A., Jr. *The Management of Compensation*. Monterey, Calif.: Brooks/Cole Publishing Co., 1975.

> This is an excellent resource for information on specific methods of administering wage and salary systems. It deals with ways to link compensation with other management systems, and is a practical, how-to treatment of the topic.

SCHWAB, D. P., "Job Evaluation and Pay Setting: Concepts and Practices," in E. R. Livernash (Ed.), *Comparable Worth: Issues and Alternatives*. Washington, D.C.: Equal Employment Advisory Council, 1980.

> This chapter provides a detailed discussion of organizational practices in setting pay levels. It discusses the "real world" factors which make it difficult to set pay levels in terms of systematic increases in job worth (such as market rates, political factors, union agreements, and individual employee differences).

SELDON, C. *Equal Pay for Work of Comparable Worth: An Annotated Bibliography*. Chicago: American Library Association, 1982.

> This is a useful collection of materials related to the legal issues involved in comparable worth. Copies may be obtained for $4.40, prepaid, from the American Library Association, Office for Library Personnel Resources, 50 East Huron Street, Chicago, IL, 60611.

ZOLLITSCH, H. G. and LANGSNER, A. *Wage and Salary Administration*. Cincinnati: South-Western, 1970.

> This is a detailed treatment of ways to do job evaluation and set pay levels. For those who want to learn "how to do it," this is the book to use.

CHAPTER NINETEEN

EMPLOYEE HEALTH AND SAFETY

Just after graduation from high school in 1962, Danny Jones went to work in a parts plant of a heavy manufacturing company. The first day on the job, he was given a brief physical examination and issued a hard hat and steel-toed safety shoes. He then proceeded down a long corridor toward the time clock where he was to punch in and out every working day. As he walked along, he noticed a long line of footprints leading from the work area. They were outlined in red paint and the front third of each footprint was missing. This was a vivid and grisly reminder to wear safety shoes at all times in the work area. This was the only safety orientation or training he received during his five years with the company.

During the next two decades, Danny worked for several companies and progressed to his current job of shift superintendent of Carter, Inc.'s largest assembly plant.[1] Things have changed in many ways during those twenty years. Danny recently walked into the cafeteria of Carter's Employee Center and saw several of his young employees selecting lunch from three types of menus (regular, low calorie, and special diet). The calories of each item appeared on the menus, and several dining areas in an atrium were filled with beautiful greenery and the soothing sound of falling water. Also available was a fully-equipped health club with jogging track, exercise areas, racquetball courts, and weight equipment. Employees brought their own athletic shoes and selected from an array of shorts, tops, and socks. Complete exercise programs could be planned for each employee, and progress could be monitored on each visit with the aid of a computer.

Down the hall the safety manager of the plant's human resource department conducted a safety awareness program for a group of new employees. The company also offered mandatory refresher training every year for all equipment operators to reinforce correct operating procedures and prevent accidents. Safety equipment throughout the plant was also regularly inspected to maintain safety standards.

*T*he years between Danny's first and current jobs reflect the dramatic change in emphasis that organizations and individual employees place on employee health and safety. In this chapter we will discuss the role of the human resource department, supervisory personnel, and employees to maintain the health and safety of all members of the organization.

THE NEED FOR EMPLOYEE HEALTH AND SAFETY

Before the Industrial Revolution, work injuries were relatively rare, but with the arrival of large factories and complex machinery, occupational accidents increased dramatically. Recent statistics show the importance of employee health and safety today. The number of work-related accidents and the resultant costs in U.S. organizations are awesome. As Exhibit 19.1 shows, there were 10.5 cases of work-related injuries in 1972 for every 100 full-time workers, and nearly one-third of these cases resulted in lost workdays. Although the incidence of occupational injuries has declined in the past decade, time lost from work has remained relatively constant. Additional figures released by the U.S. Department of Labor in 1984 are as follows:

1. Work places employing eleven workers or more in the private sector recorded 3100 work-related deaths in 1983. Nearly 30 percent of these fatalities resulted from car and truck accidents.
2. Nearly 4.75 million job-related injuries and 106,000 occupational illnesses were reported in 1983.
3. About 36 million lost workdays resulted from work-related injuries in 1983.

Ten times more workdays are lost every year because of injuries than because of strikes. The National Safety Council estimates the direct cost of

EXHIBIT 19.1   OCCUPATIONAL INJURY INCIDENCE RATES

	Total Cases	Lost Workday Cases	Lost Workdays
1972	10.5	3.2	46.3
1975	8.8	3.2	54.6
1978	9.2	4.0	62.1
1981	8.1	3.7	60.4
1982	7.6	3.4	57.5
1983	7.5	3.4	57.2

Rates per 100 full-time workers.

SOURCE: U.S. Department of Labor

work-related injuries at more than $21 billion per year, and with health care costs expected to double from 1983 to 1989, organizations are actively seeking new ways to control these costs.[2] As sobering as these figures are, they represent only part of the hazards of working in today's organizations. These figures include only *work-related injuries,* which in themselves are a major threat to employee safety. But they do not include the incidence of *illness and disease* attributable to work-related hazards, whose costs are difficult to estimate because the symptoms of diseases like black lung and asbestosis may appear only after years of exposure to contaminants in the work place. Work-related illnesses can also lead to the additional, sometimes prohibitive, costs of lawsuits against a company. For example, in 1984 the Manville Corporation filed for protection under Chapter 11 of the federal Bankruptcy Code because of the volume of lawsuits from individuals claiming health damage from exposure to asbestos produced by the company. By January 1985, nearly 3,500 claims, totaling over $1 billion, had been filed against Manville.[3]

As early as 1902, physicians studying the health hazards of the work environment recommended standards to prevent illness and diseases caused by working conditions.[4] More recently the link between poor physical and mental health and employment has stimulated concern not only to keep employees safe from accidental injury, but also to keep them in good health. Studies of the relationships between emissions of the manufacturing process (e.g., dust, fibers, and chemicals) and the incidence of disease have raised serious questions about the effects of the physical work environment on employee health. According to government estimates, about 21 million U.S. employees face known health hazards on the job, and up to 40 percent of cancer cases may be caused, at least in part, by work place exposure.[5] Similarly, the link between job stress and high blood pressure, strokes, and heart attacks has directed attention to employee life-style and the psychological hazards of being employed. The Centers for Disease Control have estimated that eight of the ten leading causes of death in the U.S. are related predominantly to life-style (Exhibit 19.2) and can be prevented in part by proper diet and weight, regular exercise, and moderation of alcohol and tobacco use.

THE INFLUENCE OF LIFE-STYLE ON TEN LEADING CAUSES OF DEATH

EXHIBIT 19.2

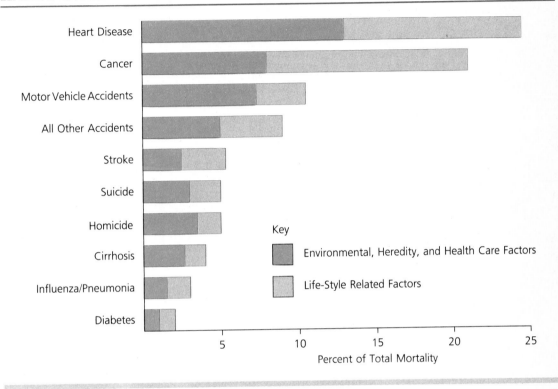

SOURCE: From "Handling Health Costs by Reducing Health Risks" by James E. Bernstein, copyright November 1983. Reprinted with the permission of *Personnel Journal*, Costa Mesa, California; all rights reserved.

There is much concern about the well-being of employees in today's organizations. More and more organizations are not only taking steps to prevent work-related injuries, but are also encouraging employees to reach and maintain a state of good health.

RESPONSIBILITY FOR EMPLOYEE HEALTH AND SAFETY

The responsibility to ensure employee health and safety is shared by human resource professionals, line managers, and the employees. Although the employee certainly assumes some of the responsibility for his or her own health and safety, tradition and government regulations have placed the ultimate responsibility for employee health and safety with the employer. The employer has the greatest degree of control over working conditions that can lead to injuries and disease. In addition, the employer influences the psychological hazards that contribute to stress at work, although, as we will see later, employees have some control over their own responses to psychological hazards.

Top management frequently takes the lead by setting health and safety *objectives* and developing *plans* to achieve those objectives. Certainly, support and funding from senior managers are essential for major health and safety strategies that include employee centers like the one at Carter, Inc., wellness programs, employee assistance programs, and regular safety training.

The responsibility to *design* and *monitor* health and safety programs rests primarily with human resource professionals in today's organizations. Throughout this century, this responsibility has been so assigned as much by chance as by design. Ensuring safe working conditions was regarded as a staff function and was therefore delegated to a staff department. The human resource department was a sensible choice, since orienting new employees to safety policies and practices could be viewed as part of the selection and entry process, and preparing and conducting safety training courses was a part of employee training and development. As state and federal legislation on employee health and safety was passed, the need arose for centralized policies and practices as well as record keeping and reporting to government agencies, and the human resource department was a logical agent to meet these needs. Therefore, employee health and safety has evolved as a human resource function.

Implementing employee health and safety programs is the responsibility of every member of the organization. Human resource professionals or safety specialists engage in many activities such as conducting safety courses and stress management seminars, monitoring the impact of various programs, and completing safety reports. Line managers communicate and enforce organization-wide safety policies and procedures by instructing employees and disciplining offenders. They may also diagnose problems and refer employees to employee assistance programs or reorganize work to reduce stress. Finally, employees are responsible for following safety rules and regulations.

Safety committees, consisting of safety specialists, line managers, employees, and union representatives (where appropriate), are common in organizations that strongly endorse employee health and safety. The committees recommend policies to top management, conduct inspections, monitor the impact of current rules and regulations, and design safety training.

APPROACHES TO ENSURE EMPLOYEE HEALTH AND SAFETY

The maintenance of employee health and safety in today's organizations is a complex and highly regulated function. To understand current health and safety standards and practices and the rationale behind government regulations, it is useful to trace the historical development of this function.

As already noted, hazards to employee health and safety increased sharply with the Industrial Revolution. The working conditions in factories of this era were dangerous indeed. Long work days (and resultant fatigue, a major cause of accidents), poor lighting and ventilation, and noisy and unfamiliar machinery posed very real risks to employees. As time passed, major efforts were made to improve the health and safety of employees. Over time, three general approaches evolved to address hazardous working conditions. We shall examine each in turn.

Retribution and Compensation

The first approach was to compensate employees for job-related injuries or illnesses. The first remedy available to an injured employee was based on *common law;* the employee could bring suit against the employer for losses due to job-related injuries or illnesses. Unfortunately, common law usually favored the employer because the employee assumed a certain degree of risk simply by taking the job, and the employee or a fellow employee may have been partly responsible for the accident.[6] The inadequacy of common law remedies and the prevailing values, which stressed employer prerogatives more than worker rights in the late 19th century, underscored the need for effective accident prevention. Among the main motives to reduce industrial accidents were:

1. A recognition of social responsibility for the welfare of those injured in industrial accidents.
2. A desire on the part of industrial executives to reduce costs associated with accidents.
3. A desire, growing out of the scientific management movement and early work in employment psychology, to reduce industrial waste and inefficiency.[7]

Consequently, greater protection of employees was sought by social activists through state workers' compensation laws.

State workers' compensation laws essentially establish an insurance program that compensates employees or their survivors in the case of work-related injuries or death. Compensation is given for lost income, medical expenses, disability, or death. These laws offer advantages to employees as well as employers. They provide for no-fault insurance, so any claim for job-related illness or injury is covered. There is a limit on the liability of employers, and employers pay premiums to an insurance fund that increase or decrease depending on the number of claims against the employer. A major problem, however, is the inconsistency of coverage from one state to another.[8] Furthermore, the orientation of worker's compensation is *reactive*—it provides compensation after an employee's health or safety has been affected, but it offers very little incentive to prevent job-related injuries or illnesses.

Prevention

Between 1910 and 1920, when workers' compensation laws were first passed by states, a second approach to employee health and safety began to evolve. Its emphasis was on prevention. The efforts to prevent work-related injuries and illnesses were made by four groups.[9] The first included a number of professional safety associations that evolved in the early 1900s to urge employers to take steps to prevent industrial accidents and illnesses. These associations conducted research on the incidence and causes of industrial accidents and established safety codes and promoted their use in their respective industries. These safety activities were the forerunners of those that eventually became a human resource responsibility in modern organizations.

A second major group was the American Society of Safety Engineers, organized in 1915. It focused on the technical side of accident prevention by devising machine guards and safety equipment and devices. The society also promoted the profession of safety engineering from which industrial firms drew specialists to supervise safety functions.

A third major group to emphasize the prevention of job-related accidents and illnesses was made up of physicians who specialized in industrial medicine. Their focus was not only on injury prevention, but also on the control of the work environment to reduce the incidence of illness and disease. It was through this group's efforts that employers adopted standards and practices that we take for granted today, such as health standards, sanitation and environmental control, medical records, physical examinations, workers' compensation investigations to determine causes of accidents and injuries and means of prevention, emergency treatment, and professional nursing service.[10]

The fourth group to promote employee health and safety were labor unions, who have been active throughout this century in pressuring employers to improve working conditions and reduce the risk of injury to their members. In coal mines, meat packing plants, and textile mills, many employers have been slow to acknowledge unsafe conditions, and union pressure has led to many reforms.

Uniform Standards and Enforcement

These pioneering efforts to provide compensation for job-related injuries and illnesses and prevent their occurrence expanded throughout the first half of the 20th century. By 1948, workers' compensation laws existed in every state and many safety practices that had been novel in the 1920s quickly became commonplace. But during the 1960s, concerns were raised about the adequacy of the status quo. Workers' compensation laws provided no real incentive for employers to reduce work hazards, and there were no significant legal penalities for employers who did not adopt health and safety practices. In addition, a dramatic 29 percent increase in the injury rate from 1961 to 1970, with 14,000 deaths resulting from job-related accidents, coupled with the publicity given to major work-site disasters aroused public and government concern.[11] Consequently, the federal government entered the arena of employee health and safety, and in 1970 Congress produced one of the most controversial pieces of legislation in its long history—the *Occupational Safety and Health Act* (OSHA). In essence, OSHA established uniform health and safety standards for virtually all U.S. employers engaged in business that affects interstate commerce (except federal, state, and local governments) and provided the means to ensure that the standards are adopted.

THE OCCUPATIONAL SAFETY AND HEALTH ACT

OSHA was designed to fill gaps left by state workers' compensation laws and voluntary health and safety standards and practices of organizations prior to 1970. In contrast to workers' compensation laws, which become relevant only after an injury or illness occurs, OSHA was intended to reduce hazards and *prevent* injury and illness. In contrast to health and safety practices recommended by professional associations and medical groups and unions, OSHA established *mandatory* standards. Some of the major provisions of OSHA are included in Exhibit 19.3.

Agencies

OSHA established three agencies to administer and enforce its provisions. The main agency, the *Occupational Safety and Health Administration* (OSHAdmin), is empowered to establish health and safety standards, to allow variances from those standards, to conduct inspections of employers' premises, and to issue citations and fines for OSHA violations. The *Occupational Safety and Health Review Commission* (OSHRC) consists of three members appointed by the President to hear employer appeals of OSHAdmin citations. OSHRC findings may be appealed to the federal courts of appeals and ultimately to the Supreme Court. The *National Institute for Occupational Safety and Health* (NIOSH) is primarily involved in research and training. It conducts research on the causes and prevention of work-related illnesses and injuries and provides information on which new standards can be based. NIOSH also trains OSHAdmin inspectors (called *compliance officers*) and other enforcement personnel.

Occupational Safety and Health Standards

Once the act was passed, OSHAdmin quickly attempted to establish health and safety standards for all employers and allowed variances from those standards in cases where compliance was not feasible. One of the major criticisms of OSHA was that standards were set without thorough research, so many appeared arbitrary, trivial, or unrealistic. In many cases industry standards

EXHIBIT 19.3 **MAJOR PROVISIONS OF THE OCCUPATIONAL SAFETY AND HEALTH ACT**

Section 3

(8) The term "occupational safety and health standard" means a standard . . . reasonably necessary or appropriate to provide safe or healthful employment . . . .

Section 5

(a) Each employer

(1) shall furnish to each of his employees employment and a place of employment which are free from recognized hazards that are causing or are likely to cause death or serious physical harm to his employees;

(2) shall comply with occupational safety and health standards promulgated under this Act.

(b) Each employee shall comply with occupational safety and health standards and all rules, regulations, and orders . . . which are applicable to his own actions and conduct.

Section 6

(a). . . the Secretary shall . . . promulgate as an occupational safety or health standard any national consensus standard, and any established Federal standard. . . . In the event of conflict among any such standards, the Secretary shall promulgate the standard which assures the greatest protection of safety or health of the affected employees.

(b)(5) The Secretary, in promulgating standards dealing with toxic materials or harmful physical agents under this subsection, shall set the standard which most adequately assures, to the extent feasible, on the basis of the best available evidence, that no employee will suffer material impairment of health or functional capacity even if such employee has regular exposure to the hazard dealt with by such standard for the period of his working life. Development of standards under this subsection shall be based upon research, demonstrations, experiments, and such other information as may be appropriate.

(b)(6)(A) Any employer may apply to the Secretary for a temporary order granting a variance from a standard or any provision thereof promulgating under this section.

Section 8

(a) In order to carry out the purposes of this Act, the Secretary, upon presenting appropriate credentials to the owner, operator, or agent in charge, is authorized

(1) to enter without delay and at reasonable times any . . . workplace or environment where work is performed by an employee of an employer; and

(2) to inspect and investigate . . . any such place of employment . . . and to question privately any such employer, owner, operator, agent, or employee.

(c)(1) Each employer shall . . . make available . . . such records regarding his activities relating to this Act as the Secretary . . . may prescribe by regulation. . . .

(f)(1) Any employees or representative of employees who believe that a violation of a safety or health standard exists that threatens physical harm, or that an imminent danger exists, may request an inspection . . .

Section 9

(a) If, upon inspection or investigation, the Secretary or his authorized representative believes that an employer has violated a requirement of . . . this Act, . . . he shall with reasonable promptness issue a citation to the employer. . . . the citation shall fix a reasonable time for the abatement of the violation.

Section 17

(a) Any employer who willfully or repeatedly violates the requirements of . . . this Act, . . . may be assessed a civil penalty of not more than $10,000 for each violation.

were adopted as OSHA standards, even though the industry considered them ideals to be aimed for, rather than presently attainable. Stories abounded about seemingly arbitrary standards that required employers to invest vast amounts of money and time. More recently, however, research has accumulated to strengthen the need for some standards, and many of the trivial ones have been eliminated.

Compliance by Employers and Employees

OSHA placed an unparalleled responsibility on employers to *prevent* injury and illness to employees. Section 5(a)(2) requires employers to comply with specific safety and health standards established by OSHA. In addition, Section 5(a)(1) imposes on employers a general obligation to keep employees free from hazards that cause or may cause death or serious physical harm. Through this general obligation, the federal government can require the employer to identify and correct any hazards not included in specific safety and health standards.

Section 5(b) in the act requires that employees comply with all standards that apply to their work setting. However, the burden of employee compliance rests with the employer. OSHA does not penalize employees for noncompliance, and accident investigations place much greater emphasis on violations by employers then by employees. In short, OSHA requires relatively little of employees, and employers must find other means to ensure that employees follow health and safety practices at work.

OSHA Inspections and Penalities

Sections 8 and 9 of the act authorize the federal government to enforce compliance with occupational safety and health standards. These sections empowered OSHAdmin to conduct unannounced inspections and investigations on employers' premises and to require employers to report on their compliance with OSHA. Furthermore, employees may request an inspection if they feel they are working in unsafe conditions. In 1978, however, the Supreme Court upheld the contention that OSHAdmin's unannounced inspections violate the right of employers to be free from warrantless search under the Fourth Amendment,[12] and now compliance officers must obtain a warrant in court before they can inspect a worksite, if the employer requests a warrant. Finally, in Sections 9 and 17 punitive procedures are established to require employer compliance through citations and fines.

When requiring compliance, the federal government's primary consideration is *feasibility*. Can the safety standard be attained given the current technology of the industry? In some cases, a temporary or permanent variance may be granted to an employer by OSHAdmin if compliance is not immediately feasible. The cost of compliance, however, has not been given significant consideration by the agency in granting variances. As a result, compliance with OSHA has been very costly to American business.

Reporting Requirements

Also costly to American business have been the time and effort to keep the records required by OSHA. One investigation of a medium-sized manufacturing company showed that personnel managers at the typical plant spent 20 percent of their time on OSHA paperwork.[13] OSHA requires employers to keep a general log of each injury or illness, supplementary records of each injury or illness, and an annual summary of the log.

Success of OSHA

How much has OSHA contributed to the safety and health of American workers? The evidence on OSHA's success is mixed, at best. U.S. Labor Department statistics in Exhibit 19.1 show a decline in the total number of occupational injuries since 1972, although an increase in lost workdays since 1972 suggests that injuries have become more serious. Opponents of OSHA point to the high costs of compliance versus the small number of lives saved. In an excellent discussion of the effectiveness of OSHA, Ledvinka notes that work-related accidents are caused by an interaction of "people" problems and "thing" problems.[14] OSHA does very little to address people problems, such as employee fatigue and poor health or failure to follow safety procedures. He also argues that OSHA's approach to thing problems is inadequate because of its emphasis on *specification* standards (e.g., types of facilities and equipment to be used) rather than the *performance* of those standards (e.g., strength of a railing). One conclusion is inescapable. Organizations must do more than merely comply with OSHA if they are to achieve high levels of employee health and safety. In the remainder of this chapter we will discuss how approaches to employee health and safety have broadened in the past decade and describe health and safety practices in today's organizations.

THREATS TO EMPLOYEE HEALTH AND SAFETY

employee safety

Employee safety is *the absence of injuries due to the interaction of the employee and the work environment.* An injury may result from an accident caused by employee behavior (e.g., failure to wear a hard hat) or from a hazard in the work setting (absence of a railing on a walkway twenty feet above the floor). **Employee health** is *the absence of illness or disease resulting from the interaction of the employee and the work environment.* For example, a healthful work environment is free of hazardous chemicals, fibers, and dust that lead to disease or illness.

employee health

The Physical Environment

The threats to employee safety and health that have received the most attention by employers and state and federal governments are found in the physical work setting. This includes safety hazards, such as dangerous equipment and machinery, as well as threats to employee health, such as noise, chemical emissions, fibers, and dust. While the hazards of equipment and machinery are immediate, the damage that some chemicals and fibers do to employee health can go undetected for as long as twenty years after exposure.

The Psychological Environment

Much attention has been given in the last decade to the effect of work-related stress on employee health. **Stress** is *the physiological or emotional response to an external event or condition called a stressor.*[15] Many common stressors, such as great responsibility, challenge, conflict, support, and time pressure, make up the psychological environment. Thus, the psychological environment is an employee's *perception* of the characteristics of the job and work setting. The physiological and emotional responses to these stressors (e.g., high blood pressure, ulcers, job dissatisfaction, low self-esteem) are definite symptoms of poor physical or emotional health.

stress

Of course, not all stress is bad. Hans Selye has noted that stressors may cause distress or eustress (good stress), depending on the individual.[16] Each employee has an optimal range of stress, caused by stressors like moderate challenge and realistic deadlines, that produces healthy physiological and emotional responses. Levels of stress over or under that optimal range, however, can be unhealthy.

The Employee

A third potential threat to employee health and safety are employees themselves. Employees interact with the physical work environment eight hours a day, and can be influenced by the psychological work environment every waking hour and even during their sleep. Whether that interaction is safe or hazardous depends a great deal on the individual. Physical and emotional health is important. Employees who are so obese that they cannot see their feet are likely to trip over something at work and cause an injury. Those who smoke and drink heavily may develop high blood pressure under stress. Similarly, the employee who is generally unhappy and angry at the world is likely to respond negatively to stressors by being dissatisfied with the job and abusive with co-workers.

Another characteristic of employees is the importance they place on being physically and mentally healthy. A healthy life-style can certainly affect employee health and safety. For example, non-smokers are five times less likely than smokers to take early disability retirement.[17] Many employees take time out at work to do relaxation exercises to deal more effectively with stressors. In short, a concerted effort on the part of employees to stay healthy can increase their level of health and safety at work.

A final factor is the employee's attitude toward safety. Some employees faithfully follow company safety procedures while others deliberately violate them. Some employees are very cognizant of potential safety hazards and avoid or correct "accidents waiting to happen," while others drift obliviously through the work site. By being conscientious about their personal safety, employees can reduce accidents and injuries on the job. They may develop a positive orientation on their own as a part of their personal life-style, or they may be encouraged to do so through company-sponsored health and safety programs. Whatever the sources of the employee's orientation, it will have a significant impact on that employee's health and safety at work.

AN INTEGRATED APPROACH TO EMPLOYEE HEALTH AND SAFETY

There are many different ways in which employers attempt to keep their employees safe and healthy. To succeed, however, employee health and safety programs must control the physical work environment, the psychological work environment, and employee attitudes and behavior.

Various approaches to controlling the physical and psychological environment are summarized in Exhibit 19.4. The physical environment, at the top of the exhibit, can affect both employee health and safety (e.g., emissions can cause illnesses and lack of machine guards and handrails can cause injuries). It ranges from entirely safe to extremely hazardous.

The psychological environment, at the bottom of Exhibit 19.4, consists of stressors that can lead to emotional and physical illness. It ranges from optimal to very high or low to reflect Selye's assertion that some level of stress is essential for humans to function, and that extremely high or low levels of stress cause negative responses. For each employee, therefore, there is an optimal level of psychological stressors (e.g., work load, performance standards, deadlines) that lead to excellent health. At the other extreme is the psychological environment in which the stressors are very high or low.

The effects of various types of physical and psychological environments on employee health and safety are also shown in Exhibit 19.4. They are based on the seven stages of development of stress-related diseases proposed by Pelletier.[18] In an entirely safe environment there is no risk of injury or illness. At Stages 2 and 3 some degree of risk is present, but no actual health and safety problems have occurred. For example, harmful chemical emissions may be present in a processing plant but no clinical signs of illness have yet appeared. Stages 4 through 7 represent the range of injury or illness that can result from the physical environment.

Seven comparable stages of response to the psychological environment are shown in the lower portion of Exhibit 19.4. The optimal level of stressors represents no risk to employee health. As the level of stressors moves away from that optimal level, Stages 2 and 3 are reached, and employees are under stress but exhibit no obvious symptoms. As the psychological environment becomes even more stressful, Stages 4 through 7 are reached. Stage 4 may be characterized by moodiness or a feeling of tension, followed by symptoms of stress such as high blood pressure in Stage 5. Actual illness and eventual death can occur in Stages 6 and 7.

INTEGRATED APPROACH TO EMPLOYEE
HEALTH AND SAFETY

EXHIBIT 19.4

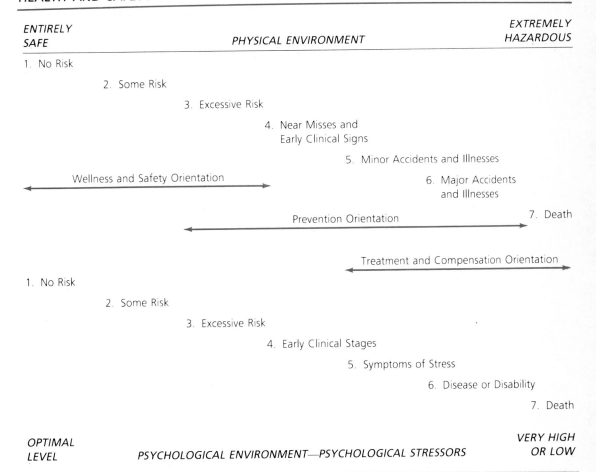

ENTIRELY
SAFE

PHYSICAL ENVIRONMENT

EXTREMELY
HAZARDOUS

1. No Risk

   2. Some Risk

      3. Excessive Risk

         4. Near Misses and
            Early Clinical Signs

              5. Minor Accidents and Illnesses

Wellness and Safety Orientation
                  6. Major Accidents
                     and Illnesses

Prevention Orientation
                      7. Death

Treatment and Compensation Orientation

1. No Risk

   2. Some Risk

      3. Excessive Risk

         4. Early Clinical Stages

           5. Symptoms of Stress

              6. Disease or Disability

                7. Death

OPTIMAL
LEVEL

PSYCHOLOGICAL ENVIRONMENT—PSYCHOLOGICAL STRESSORS

VERY HIGH
OR LOW

SOURCE: Excerpted from the book *Mind as Healer Mind as Slayer* by Kenneth R. Pelletier. Copyright © 1977 by Kenneth R. Pelletier. Reprinted by permission of *Delacorte Press/ Seymour Lawrence* and Robert Briggs Associates.

All attempts by employers to ensure that their employees remain safe and healthy can be grouped into three basic orientations—treatment and compensation, prevention, and wellness and safety. Treatment and compensation are effective only in Stages 5 through 7. Once an employee has been injured at work or actual symptoms of illness have appeared, an organization can respond with the necessary medical care, and employees or their families can also be compensated in the case of lost time from work, permanent disability, or even death.

    Prevention begins with the recognition of excessive risk (Stage 3) and can be appropriate in situations as extreme as Stage 6. For example, OSHA requires all employers to take preventive measures if excessive risk is present in the physical environment. Preventive measures can include employee training in the use of safety equipment. An example of preventive action in Stage 6 would be to reduce the workload and institute physical therapy for an employee who is recovering from a heart attack brought on by the combination of a high level of stressors, heavy smoking, and obesity.

The third approach to employee health and safety places emphasis on remaining healthy and safe at work. Unlike the first two approaches, which are triggered by excessive risk or actual symptoms, this approach is not reactive. Rather, it is an orientation toward a life-style and work style of safety and good health. Much of this approach's attention is on the employee's emotional and physical condition and behavior at work. Carter, Inc.'s, Employee Center reflects this orientation. A regimen that employees follow to exercise regularly and watch their weight and diet and the use of safety awareness programs are typical of the wellness and safety orientation that has grown in popularity in recent years.

Treatment and Compensation Orientation

In spite of the preventive measures taken, some injuries and illnesses will always result from exposure to the work environment. It is therefore necessary for organizations and governments to provide for appropriate treatment and compensation.

Compensation and Treatment ▪▪▪ State workers' compensation laws

provide for some degree of compensation for the treatment of work-related injuries and illnesses and for time lost from work. This compensation is superior to the coverage provided by company group health insurance plans, so it is to the employee's advantage to file a claim under workers' compensation. Employers provide varying degrees of treatment on their premises and at their expense. The most common form of treatment is given in response to Stage 5 of Exhibit 19.4—minor accidents and illnesses resulting from a hazardous physical environment, or symptoms caused by a stressful psychological environment. Many organizations provide a small clinic on site with a nurse to administer first aid to employees suffering from minor injuries and illnesses.

Employee Assistance Programs (EAPS) ▪▪▪ Increased awareness of

the psychological environment's impact on employee health has led to the creation of "employee assistance programs" to treat diseases or disabilities that result from psychological stressors (Stages 5 and 6). **Employee assistance**

employee assistance programs

programs are *employer policies and procedures to identify, treat, and rehabilitate employees whose job performance has deteriorated because of alcohol or drug abuse.* Employees are usually referred to social agencies or physicians outside the work place for treatment and rehabilitation, although some large corporations operate their own treatment facilities.

The roots of these programs can be traced back to the 1940s when employers initiated attempts to salvage alcoholic employees.[19] E. I. duPont de Nemours & Company was one of the first corporations to begin an employee assistance program in 1942 with a few company doctors. The program is now staffed by sixty company and sixty contract physicians. United Technologies became the first company to operate its own halfway house, where employees report six mornings a week for up to eight hours of intensive therapy and return to their homes each evening.[20]

Efforts of the National Council on Alcoholism and the National Institute on Alcohol Abuse and Alcoholism triggered rapid growth of employee assistance programs during the 1970s, and their scope broadened to include treatment for drug abuse. About 57 percent of Fortune 500 corporations had some form of employee assistance program in 1979.[21]

Roman provides a summary of the underlying assumptions of employee assistance programs:

> First is the assumption [by the employer] that deteriorating job performance frequently results from behavioral problems of the individual employee. A second assumption holds that these behavioral problems cannot be effectively dealt with through means typically available in the workplace and that only intervention by professionals can prevent an inevitable course of continued deterioration. It is also assumed that employees' personal problems have sapped productivity in work organizations for many generations, but that these problems have remained untreated. The final assumption is that such inattention has exacted heavy costs because employers have lacked strategies to deal effectively with these problems.[22]

The many activities in an employee assistance program are summarized in Exhibit 19.5. They are grouped into three major phases. Phase 1 includes documentation of the need for assistance and referrals. Assessment and treatment are included in Phase 2, and Phase 3 is concerned with follow-up to document the effectiveness of treatment.

Notice that several people may refer an employee to an employee assistance program, including family members, co-workers, and the employee himself or herself. In addition, the employee's union or the employer's medical department may refer the employee directly to an assessment interviewer. The process through which an employee's supervisor makes a referral is more complex. A supervisor would typically identify a troubled employee by a drop in job performance that appears to be linked to psychological stressors. The supervisor's emphasis should be on attendance and performance, rather than on the underlying personal problem. In cases of suspected alcoholism or drug abuse, diagnosis of the cause of the problem is best left to professionals. If the employee refuses to accept the existence of a problem and his or her job performance continues below standard, standard procedures for dealing with poor performance are followed. If the employee refuses to accept the existence of a problem but is able to improve job performance, then participation in a costly employee assistance program is unnecessary.

EXHIBIT 19.5   **AN EMPLOYEE ASSISTANCE PROGRAM**

PHASE 1

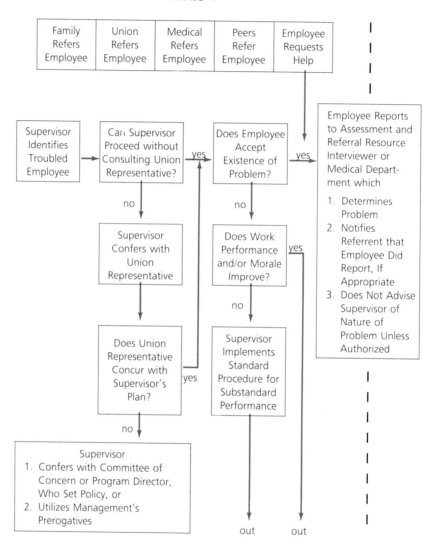

NOTE: The term "out" means that the employee is no longer in the employee assistance program. He/she has either improved work performance to an acceptable level and successfully completed the program or has not accepted or responded positively to the program and standard procedure for substandard performance is implemented. The point is that no one stays in the program indefinitely. They move one way or the other.

PHASE 2   PHASE 3

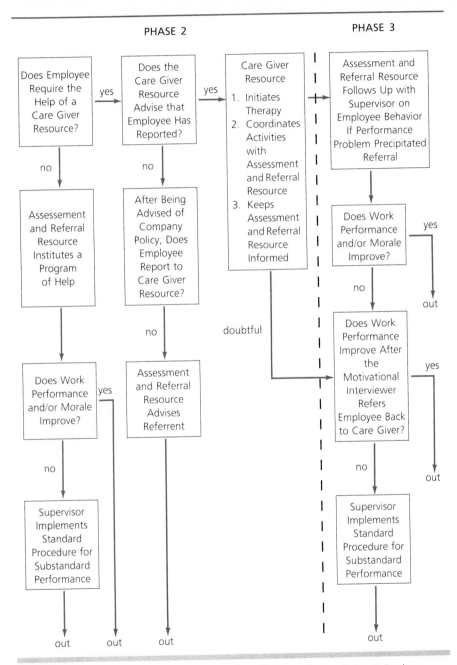

Phase 1 ends with a professional assessment to determine the necessary treatment while maintaining employee confidentiality.

Phase 2 includes various ways to treat the problem that has caused the employee's drop in performance. Treatment can range from detoxification for alcohol or drugs to career counseling or guidance to manage stress. Finally, in Phase 3 follow-up is made to assess the effectiveness of the treatment and resultant changes in work performance.

Participation in an employee assistance program is often a constructive alternative to dismissal on the grounds of poor performance. Pressure is put on employees to cooperate and make the most of the treatment. This orientation is reflected in Exhibit 19.5 by the number of arrows leading to "out" or to "supervisor implements standard procedure for substandard performance." Employees who do not agree to participate in the program and to take full advantage of treatment will find themselves out of the program and perhaps out of a job.

How effective are employee assistance programs? Much research has been done on the number and nature of organizations that offer such programs as well as their operational characteristics and costs. It is apparent that these programs are growing in popularity. The number of EAPs in Fortune 500 corporations more than doubled between 1972 and 1979,[23] and the number of programs for alcoholics is estimated at over 5,000 nationwide.[24] Some studies have shown that employee assistance programs have positively affected retention rates, absenteeism, and job performance, although much more research is needed.[25] Wrich suggests focusing evaluation research on measurable outcomes, such as access to and utilization of the program, assessment and referral resource effectiveness, treatment results, and changes in the severity or impact of the employee's problems in the work place and in personal affairs.[26] The approach to evaluating human resource programs described in Chapter Twenty-Three can also be applied to employee assistance programs.

Prevention Orientation

The prevention orientation spans Stages 3 through 6, beginning with the recognition of excessive risk and ending with disease or disability caused by psychological stressors, or major accidents and illnesses resulting from the physical environment. Traditionally, many of the efforts that employers have made to ensure employee health and safety have been preventive in nature.

The Physical Environment A physical work environment that is free of hazards is an obvious objective of any organization's approach to employee health and safety. As we have already discussed, compliance with industry and OSHA standards is a major concern and responsibility of all employers to ensure employee health and safety. Employer efforts often go beyond compliance with standards, since a healthful and safe work site is in the best interests of all members of the organization. Safety specialists continually examine and test equipment and facilities to identify potential health and safety hazards before minor accidents and illnesses occur.

The Employee ▬ Accidents result from a combination of "thing" problems and "people" problems. Employees can become injured or ill in a physical work environment that contains all feasible preventive measures. All the employees must do is violate health and safety policies and practices, such as not wearing safety equipment, taking dangerous shortcuts to save time, or ignoring posted warning signs. It is therefore necessary for employers to control employee behavior so that employees do not become hazards to themselves.

Government regulations add to the pressure on employers because they place the responsibility for safe employee behavior squarely on the shoulders of employers. For example, injured employees receive workers' compensation even if they caused the injury. Similarly, OSHA will not penalize employees for non-compliance, and OSHA investigations place much more emphasis on employer violations than employee violations. As a result, line managers and supervisors, as well as human resource professionals, must take steps to ensure that employees behave safely in the work place.

The many ways in which employers control employee behavior to ensure health and safety fall into three basic categories: Awareness, Training, and Discipline.

In order to comply with organizational health and safety policies and practices, employees must be *aware* of them. A safety manual, safety posters, warning signs, a prominent sign recording the number of days since the last work-related accident resulting in lost time, and even painted footprints in the corridor leading to the work area can be used to raise employees' awareness of how to keep themselves healthy and safe. These attempts to make employees aware of health and safety practices are typically initiated by human resource specialists, but line managers and supervisors play a major part in monitoring employee behavior and enforcing the practices. Through positive feedback for safe practices and negative feedback for unsafe practices, they can alter employees' awareness of and compliance with health and safety practices.

Training employees in how to operate equipment and machinery safely has a long history in industrial settings. Much technical training includes an emphasis on safety, whether it deals with how to handle a wrench without skinning one's knuckles or how to prevent an oil well from blowing out. Many organizations use safety training as a form of preventive maintenance. For example, a city transportation department was aware that city bus drivers became careless and prone to accidents about one year after their initial training on the vehicles. Therefore, refresher safe driving courses were made mandatory for all bus drivers every six months to sharpen their awareness and skill *before* accidents were likely to occur.

The ultimate step to control employee behavior is to *discipline* employees who do not follow health and safety practices. This is particularly necessary in view of OSHA's lack of provision for penalities for employee non-compliance. As with any other form of unacceptable performance, careful observation and documentation by the supervisor are necessary, and feedback and training may be used to alter employees' unsafe behavior. In extreme cases, suspension without pay or even dismissal may be necessary.

Box 19.1 illustrates one company's efforts to prevent accidents at work. HYDRIL's safety coordinators substantially reduced the number of accidents by altering the work environment and training new employees in safe work procedures. Incentives and training were also included to encourage supervisors to stress safety.

The Psychological Environment ▬ Awareness of the relationship between psychological stressors and employee health has grown dramatically in the past two decades, and employers have taken steps to treat stress-related problems through employee assistance programs, discussed above. But many stress-related problems are never treated in employee assistance programs because they are manifested as physical illnesses such as coronary disease, ulcers, and migraine headaches. The personal and organizational costs of stress-related illnesses are terribly high, and some authors have argued that stress contributes to 80 percent of the deaths in the United States.[27] Many of these deaths can be postponed if the impact of psychological stressors is reduced.

Major efforts are now underway in organizations to prevent stress-related illnesses. Preventive measures are triggered by Stages 3 through 6, ranging from awareness of excessive risk to disease or disability. Remember that stress is a physiological or psychological response that people make to an external stressor. To minimize stress, therefore, either the stressor must be altered or the person's response to the stressor must be changed.

A model for understanding stress, shown in Exhibit 19.6, includes many potential causes and many common symptoms of stress. The first column includes major sources of work-related stress. Exposure to extremes of light, noise, and temperature in the physical environment can be stressful. In addition, specific characteristics of an employee's job, work group, organization, and career can produce stress. For example, less than a year after the announcement of the reorganization of AT&T, medical directors throughout the Bell System reported higher levels of anxiety among employees taking routine physical examinations.[28] A likely source of this stress was the announcement of the pending reorganization of AT&T, which was to significantly affect organization structure, job titles and duties, and entire methods of operation throughout the giant corporation. The final group of stressors in Exhibit 19.6 includes family, community, and financial matters outside the work place that can generate conflicts and stress at work.

There is little doubt that the same stressors affect different employees in different ways. Some people thrive on pressure, while others find it intolerable. Some prefer routine, while others find it stupefying. Therefore, Exhibit 19.6 also includes a number of personal and hereditary characteristics

BOX 19.1

EMPLOYEE SAFETY AT HYDRIL

Phil Edwards, Manager of Industrial Relations and Training at HYDRIL, has been actively involved in employee safety for over fifteen years, first as a supervisor and later as a human resource professional.

HYDRIL, a privately owned oil field equipment manufacture and service company, has plants in which employees operate lathes to machine tubing and casting joints for use in tubes and pipes that convey oil and gas. Because the lathe operators had a history of minor injuries to their hands, feet, and eyes, HYDRIL initiated a comprehensive effort to reduce the occurrence of accidents.

Prior to the passage of OSHA, HYDRIL took conventional steps to ensure employee safety through safety manuals and films, but after 1970 top management took several additional steps to strengthen the company's safety orientation. First, safety coordinators at each plant conducted safety audits to identify potential hazards. Second, supervisors were required to fill out detailed accident reports and submit them to the safety coordinator within twenty-four hours of the accident. Safety coordinators were to be notified immediately of major accidents. Third, safety goals were added to the production and quality goals of the bonus program of each plant, so supervisors could increase their bonuses with a good safety record.

Minor eye injuries had been common among HYDRIL workers, and careful examination of accident reports revealed that many of the injured workers had removed their safety glasses when they had become cloudy from the heat and humidity of the plant. "Dirty safety glasses can be more hazardous than none at all," says Edwards, "so we kept the glasses clean by installing fans above the workers to keep them cool. Again, the accident rate dropped."

Of course, many injuries cannot be eliminated by altering the work area. Analysis of HYDRIL accident reports indicated that most accidents occurred within the first six months of employment. Edwards set out to design a program that would make new machine operators more safety conscious. He explains:

I wanted to avoid safety films and lectures, which often have little impact, so I included safety practices in the films we made to teach machine operation. We showed operators cleaning and checking their safety glasses and inspecting and cleaning their tools as a normal part of machine operation. Consequently, new employees learned only one way to operate their machine—the safe way.

HYDRIL also provides safety training for supervisors and has an award program in which employees receive a portion of the costs that are avoided when accident rates are reduced.

The authors wish to thank Mr. Philip S. Edwards for his assistance in preparing this material.

EXHIBIT 19.6   **FRAMEWORK FOR UNDERSTANDING STRESS**

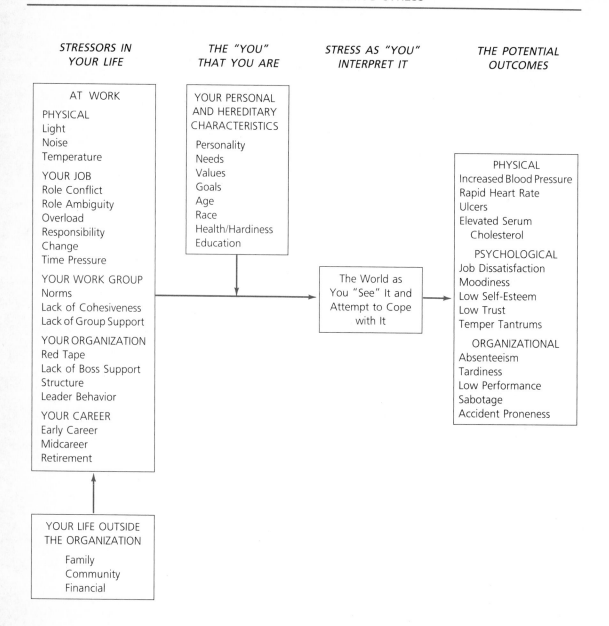

| STRESSORS IN YOUR LIFE | THE "YOU" THAT YOU ARE | STRESS AS "YOU" INTERPRET IT | THE POTENTIAL OUTCOMES |

AT WORK

PHYSICAL
Light
Noise
Temperature

YOUR JOB
Role Conflict
Role Ambiguity
Overload
Responsibility
Change
Time Pressure

YOUR WORK GROUP
Norms
Lack of Cohesiveness
Lack of Group Support

YOUR ORGANIZATION
Red Tape
Lack of Boss Support
Structure
Leader Behavior

YOUR CAREER
Early Career
Midcareer
Retirement

YOUR PERSONAL AND HEREDITARY CHARACTERISTICS
Personality
Needs
Values
Goals
Age
Race
Health/Hardiness
Education

The World as You "See" It and Attempt to Cope with It

PHYSICAL
Increased Blood Pressure
Rapid Heart Rate
Ulcers
Elevated Serum Cholesterol

PSYCHOLOGICAL
Job Dissatisfaction
Moodiness
Low Self-Esteem
Low Trust
Temper Tantrums

ORGANIZATIONAL
Absenteeism
Tardiness
Low Performance
Sabotage
Accident Proneness

YOUR LIFE OUTSIDE THE ORGANIZATION
Family
Community
Financial

that may influence how people respond to stressors. For example, the relationship between personality and heart disease has received much recent attention. Competitive, success-oriented people who place themselves under great time pressure have been classified as "Type A" personalities, who are highly susceptible to stress-related symptoms.[29]

A third major determinant of stress is the individual's perception of the world and the way he or she copes with it. Whether a *stressor* becomes *stressful* depends very much on how people perceive it. Do they perceive a traffic jam as an infuriating interruption in their schedule or as an opportunity to relax and listen to the radio? Do they set expectations and goals so high that they are never satisfied, or do they try to make the best of every life experience? These three factors—stressors, personal characteristics, and perceptions—combine to create the physical, psychological, and organizational symptoms of stress.

Stress Management ▬ Awareness of the causes and symptoms of stress has given rise to employers' and employees' efforts to *manage* stress. These efforts are aimed at adjusting the fit between the employee and the work environment to reduce stress to a level that is nearly optimal for the individual employee. To reach this optimal level, either the work environment or the employee must be changed.

Altering stressors in the work environment to prevent symptoms of stress is difficult because each individual responds differently to the stressors. It is very difficult to find routine, standard approaches, analogous to those used to prevent illnesses and injuries in the *physical* environment. However, stressors can be adjusted to levels that are suitable to the tolerance and needs of individual employees. The first step is early detection of symptoms of stress. This can be done by individual employees or their immediate supervisors. At AT&T, for example, group meetings were held to discuss the various sources of stress and methods of coping. More formal procedures can be initiated by medical or human resource personnel. Matteson and Ivancevich propose a series of questionnaires that can be scored to derive the level of stress caused by such stressors as administrative policies, inadequate group support, work overload, responsibility for people, and time pressures.[30] Questionnaires that assess personal life-style (exercise, nutrition, alcohol, drug and tobacco use, personal relationships, health and safety awareness) and thorough physical examinations also help to detect symptoms of stress. The next step is to alter the stressors that create the symptoms. Job-related stressors can be changed by an individual supervisor (e.g., update an employee's job description and clarify his or her duties and goals to reduce role ambiguity) or by the human resource department (e.g., enrich a job that was characterized in a survey as boring and unchallenging by several employees). More comprehensive programs for physical fitness, weight loss, and better nutrition can be initiated to alter personal life-style.

Of course, many stressors in the psychological environment simply cannot be changed, so employees must learn to tolerate a certain degree of stress. To do so, they must alter the way they respond to stressors. The first step is awareness. Two kinds of information are essential to this form of stress management: employees' personal characteristics (the second column in Exhibit 19.6) and their perceptions of the world (the third column). Employees need to know about themselves and how they respond to stressors. For example, would they characterize their personalities as "high-strung and anxious" or "easy-going and relaxed"? Do they strive for wealth and luxury, or do they just want to be comfortable? Are their goals unrealistically high or attainable? Similarly, employees need to consider their perceptions of the world. Do they view the world as basically unfair and unfriendly, or fair and cordial? Do they feel that what happens to them in life is under their control or that there is little they can do to influence what happens to them? Because of their personal characteristics and perceptions, some people are much more likely than others to develop symptoms of stress that can lead to major medical problems.

Once employees become aware of their personal characteristics and perceptions, the next step is to alter the characteristics and perceptions that can be changed and reduce negative responses to stressors. This can be done through individual efforts. For example, people who are constantly in a hurry to achieve more and more in less and less time can slow down periodically or choose a time to do relaxation exercises every day. Training programs sponsored by employers can also be helpful. For example, in "stress inoculation training"[31] employees learn to deal more effectively with stressors. Trainees use a series of questions which help them to prepare for the stressors, confront the stress, cope with stressful feelings, and reinforce themselves in order to deal with the stressors. Considering the growing uncertainty in modern life and the accumulating evidence that links emotional health and major physical illnesses, such as high blood pressure, coronary disease, ulcers, and even cancer, this form of stress management is particularly appealing. Making changes in their personal characteristics and perceptions is a fruitful way for employees to reduce stress in life and to avoid major medical problems.

Wellness and Safety Orientation

The third approach to ensure employee health and safety spans Stages 1 through 3. This orientation differs somewhat from the preventive in that it is appropriate even when employees are perceived to be at no risk at all. Its emphasis is not to avoid risk, but to stay safe and healthy even under conditions of no risk. The wellness and safety orientation is analogous to preventive maintenance with equipment and machinery, long recognized as a valuable practice. Now the value of preventive maintenance with *human resources* is also recognized, and Exhibit 19.7 presents a compelling case for its widespread practice.

Regular training in safety practices for experienced employees is a common illustration of the wellness and safety orientation. Annual mandatory re-

PREVENTIVE MAINTENANCE AND PREVENTIVE HEALTH MANAGEMENT GUIDELINES

EXHIBIT 19.7

Preventive Maintenance Protecting Physical Resources	Preventive Health Management Protecting and Preserving Human Resources
Equipment should not be overworked or mistreated.	Workers should not be manipulated, overloaded with work, or ignored.
Regular lubrication and checkup of parts is necessary to maintain high-level efficiency.	Regular exercise and periodic checkups are necessary to keep workers healthy.
When work parts are worn or defective, corrective action must be taken.	Through physical exams future problems or weaknesses can be detected and programs to minimize or eliminate the risks can be directed by the physician.
Older equipment needs more careful monitoring.	Older workers need to be monitored more frequently than younger workers.
Operators should assume some responsibility for maintaining equipment.	Each individual worker must assume some responsibility to maintain good physical and mental health.
Operators should be made aware of the risks and costs of downtime or failure.	Workers should understand the risks and costs of becoming ill.
Operators should be trained to determine symptoms of equipment malfunctions or when action must be taken.	Workers need to identify symptoms of stress or person-environment discrepancies. Self-awareness is an important step.
Vibration, friction, or corrosion should be immediately checked by the operator and management and some action taken before major breakdown occurs.	Constant tension, insomnia, headaches, or irritability are symptoms that the worker and his manager must both be on the lookout for before a health breakdown occurs.
Effective preventive maintenance costs money, but it is dollars well spent.	Although effective preventive health management will cost money, the dollars spent may reduce the expenses involved in the recruitment, selection, training, and replacement of premature personnel losses.
Preventive maintenance programs are more effective when supported by top management.	Preventive health management programs are more effective when supported by top management.

SOURCE: Reprinted by permission of the publisher, from "Optimizing Human Resources: A Case for Preventive Health and Stress Management" by John M. Ivancevich and Michael T. Matteson, *Organizational Dynamics*, Autumn 1980, p. 12. Copyright © 1980 AMACOM, a division of American Management Associations, New York. All rights reserved.

fresher training for all equipment operators at Carter, Inc., is another example. Similarly, many metropolitan transportation departments require bus drivers to take drivers' training courses every year, regardless of their accident records, to maintain the high levels of skill necessary to avoid accidents.

More recently, organizations have begun to actively encourage employees to take better care of their minds and bodies through more healthy lifestyles. Rising health care costs, often assumed by the employer, and the physical fitness boom have combined to encourage company efforts that promote good health as a wise investment.

Promoting wellness is a four-step process.[32] It begins with educating employees about health-risk factors such as poor nutrition, lack of exercise, smoking, drinking and drug abuse, and being overweight. Next, individual employees receive information about their own health risk factors through life-style assessments and physical examinations. Then plans are developed for them to reduce risk through healthier life-styles. Finally, employees receive assistance to maintain changes in their life-style through continued monitoring and evaluation.

Wellness programs vary markedly from the distribution of educational material to company-sponsored lunchtime exercise classes to fitness centers on company premises. Shaklee offers an indoor track, weightlifting equipment, bicycles and workout clothes to its employees and reports reductions in absenteeism, smoking, and excess weight. Pepsico attributes fewer visits to the company medical department to its swimming and golf facilities for employees.[33] Control Data's "Staywell" program, described in Box 19.2, is a major investment in the health and safety of employees. It is based on the following premises:

- Life-style has a major effect on illness and life spans.
- People can change their habits, with appropriate help.
- The work place is the most effective place to help people change, because people spend so much of their time there.
- Companies have a major stake in promoting a healthier life-style for their employees, due to potential benefits of reduced insurance costs, decreased absenteeism, improved productivity, and better morale.

The program is available free to all company employees and their spouses. The program begins with an orientation session and a physical examination. Then participants complete a questionnaire on their medical and family history, life-style, and mental outlook, and a health-risk profile is computed to show the difference between their chronological age and "risk" age. Next come courses on health awareness, health education, and life-style change. Finally, specific activities to change life-style and improve health are planned for each individual. Approximately 22,000 Control Data employees and spouses currently participate in the Staywell program in fourteen American cities and employee enrollment ranges from 65 to 95 percent.[34]

Positive results of wellness programs include 50 percent reductions in sickness rates and absenteeism, increases in job performance and attitudes toward work, improved stamina, sounder sleep, and weight loss.[35] Similar improvements have also been converted into reductions in health care cost claims at Control Data. Statistically significant ($p < .05$) reductions have been associated with discontinued cigarette smoking, regular exercise, and lack of hypertension. Decreases in absenteeism and lost time due to illness were also associated with an increase in the number of health habits developed by employees in the Staywell program.[36]

CONTROL DATA'S "STAYWELL" PROGRAM

BOX 19.2

George O'Neill, a 50-year-old manager at the Control Data Corporation facility in San Diego, had been feeling less than well in recent years. He knew he was overweight and that his diet wasn't the best. But as O'Neill stated it, "I attributed it to lack of exercise, long hours at the desk, things like that." Two years ago, he found out it was worse than he thought. A blood test given him as part of a new CDC "wellness" program revealed a dangerously high blood-sugar level. O'Neill was diabetic.

O'Neill was in the pilot group in the fall of 1979 for the new program, called "Staywell," that eventually will be offered free to all Control Data employees and their spouses. The results so far at CDC have been striking.

Society in general and industry in particular are embracing the concepts that to stay well is less costly than to get well, that to prevent is more rational than to cure, and that a healthy life-style enhances the chances for improved health, longevity, and quality of life.

In 1979, a Staywell program consisting of health-risk profiling, medical screening, health education and life-change activities was offered to CDC employees in San Diego and New York. Since then additional sites have been added.

Participation is on a voluntary basis and both employees and spouses are included. All activities are provided at the work site and time off is made available to attend an orientation session, the risk profiling activity, and a subsequent group interpretation meeting. Those who sign up are weighed and measured and have their blood pressure taken and a blood sample drawn. They also fill out a questionnaire on their medical outlook. The screening and questionnaires are used to provide a computerized health-risk profile of each participant. The profile compares the employee's chronological age with his or her "risk age" and shows how the risk age can be improved if certain behaviors are changed.

On completion of this phase, participants are encouraged to select from a group of one-hour health awareness courses. These range from "How to Utilize the Health Care System" to breast self-examination and substance abuse. Of greater personal interest to the participants have been the multi-session behavior and life-style change programs which deal with specific high-risk areas, such as smoking, fitness, nutrition/weight control, hypertension, and stress.

Of vital importance to the entire effort are the various follow-up and support-system programs. The real pay-off to these programs, after all, is compliance, and compliance usually requires a change in the subculture, a change in people's value systems. Thus, the follow-up is important, and one ingredient of the follow-up is the formation of employee groups, groups of individuals interested in or troubled by similar problems.

These form at the end of each of the Education and Life-style-Change Courses. The instructor continues to meet with participants for a period, but then gradually withdraws. They learn to assist one another to maintain and continue to modify their behavior, and practice various techniques and strategies to avoid failure. The peer support, whether it be in the area of weight reduction or smoking cessation, helps to persuade people not only to get with it, but to stay with it.

Adaptation of "Control Data's 'Staywell' Program" by John F. McCann from *Training and Development Journal*, October 1981, pp.39–43. Reprinted by permission of the author.

A FINAL WORD

Employers' efforts to ensure the health and safety of employees are probably more innovative and varied today than ever before. All three fundamental orientations are widely practiced in today's organizations, and many employees are assuming the responsibility to ensure the effectiveness of health and safety policies and practices in their organizations. In consultation with senior management, human resource professionals can take the lead in establishing the policies and practices, and line managers can be highly involved in their implementation. Treatment and compensation of injured and ill employees, required by state legislation, as well as the preventive measures mandated by OSHA, are now commonplace. As health care costs rise and evidence of the effectiveness of wellness programs accumulates, growing numbers of organizations are adopting the wellness and safety orientation and calling upon all employees to participate.

KEY POINTS

- The evolution of the United States from an agrarian to an industrial society has been accompanied by increased threats to employee health and safety. In 1983 over 3,000 employees died from work-related causes, one of every thirteen was injured or became ill, and 36 million work days were lost because of work-related injuries.

- Growing concern in the 1900s produced state laws to compensate injured or ill employees and voluntary efforts by employers to prevent work-related illnesses and injuries. The ineffectiveness of these measures led to federal intervention through the Occupational Safety and Health Act of 1970.

- OSHA established health and safety standards for all employers, set out the requirements for employers and employees to comply with the standards, and created a system of inspections and penalties to ensure compliance. Active debate continues on the effectiveness of this highly controversial law.

- Three basic strategies to protect employees from the physical and psychological work environment are evident today. Treatment and compensation are provided for illnesses, injuries, and death. Prevention is stressed under work conditions of excessive risk. The third strategy emphasizes employees' remaining healthy and safe even under conditions of no risk at work.

ISSUES FOR DISCUSSION

1. Discuss the adequacy of laws applying to employee health and safety and of voluntary company and industry efforts to promote employee health and safety prior to 1970. How did those efforts contribute to the passage of OSHA?

2. What are the major provisions of the Occupational Safety and Health Act of 1970? Name the three agencies established by OSHA and outline the functions of each.

3. As a student, what physical and psychological threats to your health and safety are you aware of? What are you doing to avoid or minimize the impact of the threats?

4. Outline the approach your current or most recent employer took to ensure employee health and safety. Under which of the three major orientations in Exhibit 19.4 does it fall? What impact has it had on you?

5. How personally responsible are individual employees for their health and safety? Discuss specific steps individuals can take to improve their chances for safe and healthy work lives. How can employers encourage employees to take these steps?

6. What are the major stressors in your life? How do you respond to them? What steps can employees and employers take to manage stress more effectively?

7. What three steps can employers take to ensure the health and safety of their employees? How effective is each?

NOTES

1. Based on a real organization with a disguised name.

2. J. E. Bernstein, "Handling Health Costs by Reducing Health Risks," *Personnel Journal*, 1983, 62, pp. 882–87.

3. J. Dahl, "Asbestos Claims Against Manville Exceed $1 Billion," *Wall Street Journal*, Jan. 31, 1985, p. 3.

4. C. C. Ling, *The Management of Personnel Relations: History and Origins* (Homewood, Ill.: Irwin, 1965), p. 209.

5. M. Witt, "Protecting Workers' Safety and Health," *USA Today*, 1980, *109*, pp. 51–52.

6. Ling, op. cit., p. 184.

7. Ibid., p. 185.

8. J. Ledvinka, *Federal Regulation of Personnel and Human Resource Management* (Belmont, Calif.: Wadsworth, 1982), p. 145.

9. Ling, op. cit., pp. 207–24.

10. Ibid., p. 224.

11. Ledvinka, op. cit., p. 163.

12. *Marshall v. Barlow's, Inc.*, 436 U.S. 307 (1978).

13. D. Ignatius, "Paper Weight: Companies Often Find They Must Put Forms Ahead of Substance," *Wall Street Journal*, July 16, 1976, pp. 1 and 19.

14. Ledvinka, op. cit., pp. 193–95.

15. Adapted from M. T. Matteson and J. M. Ivancevich, *Managing Job Stress and Health* (New York: The Free Press, 1982), p. 9.

16. H. Selye, *The Stress of Life*, revised (New York: McGraw-Hill, 1978).

17. W. Cascio, *Costing Human Resources: The Financial Impact of Behavior in Organizations* (Belmont, Calif.: Wadsworth, 1982), pp. 65–78.

18.   K. Pelletier, *Mind as Healer Mind as Slayer: A Holistic Approach to Preventing Stress Disorders* (New York: Dell Publishing Co., 1977).

19.   M. Shain and J. Groeneveld, *Employee Assistance Programs: Philosophy, Theory, and Practice* (Lexington, Mass.: D.C. Heath and Company), 1980.

20.   T. McCarroll, "Workplace Help for Alcoholics," *New York Times*, May 14, 1981, Section 3, p. F11, col. 1.

21.   P. M. Roman, "Medicalization and Social Control in the Workplace: Prospects for the 1980s," *The Journal of Applied Behavioral Science*, 1980, *16*, pp. 407–22.

22.   Ibid., p. 408.

23.   Ibid.

24.   McCarroll, op. cit.

25.   Shain and Groeneveld, op. cit. J. T. Wrich, "Guidelines for Developing an Employee Assistance Program," *AMA Briefing*, 1982.

26.   Wrich, op. cit., p. 72.

27.   M. T. Matteson and J. M. Ivancevich, op. cit.

28.   *Business Week*, May 28, 1979, p. 95.

29.   M. Friedman, and R. Rosenman, *Type A Behavior and Your Heart* (New York: Knopf, 1974).

30.   Matteson and Ivancevich, op. cit., p. 100.

31.   J. M. Ivancevich and M. T. Matteson, "Optimizing Human Resources: A Case for Preventive Health and Stress Management," *Organizational Dynamics*, Autumn 1980, 9, pp. 5–25.

32.   R. W. Reed, "Is Education the Key to Lower Health Care Costs?" *Personnel Journal*, 1984, *63*, pp. 40–46.

33.   *Wall Street Journal*, August 31, 1982, p. 1.

34.   M. P. Naditch, "STAYWELL: Evolution of a Behavior Medicine Program in Industry." In M. F. Catalado and T. Coates, eds., *Behavioral Medicine in Industry* (New York: Academic Press), in press.

35.   R. M. Cunningham, Jr., *Wellness at Work* (Chicago: An Inquiry book, 1982), pp. 26–27.

36.   Naditch, op. cit.

ANNOTATED BIBLIOGRAPHY

CUNNINGHAM, R.M., Jr. *Wellness at Work.* Chicago: An Inquiry book, 1982.

This book traces the development of the wellness movement from the ancient Greeks to the twenty million joggers in the United States today. The wellness programs of pioneers like Xerox Corporation, Continental Bank, and IBM are described, and specific guidelines are offered for starting such programs. Innovative suggestions are made for companies with limited resources to work with hospitals and to obtain health promotion information from Blue Cross and Blue Shield. The impact of many programs on employee health is also documented.

LEDVINKA, J. *Federal Regulation of Personnel and Human Resource Management.* Belmont, Calif.: Wadsworth, 1982.

> Chapters 7–9 of this text provide excellent coverage of major laws regulating employee health and safety. The problems leading to Workers' Compensation Laws are described, and the provisions of the laws are interpreted. The Occupational Safety and Health Act is also covered in detail. The controversy surrounding OSHA, the obligations it places on employers and employees, and its impact are discussed extensively.

MATTESON, M.T., and IVANCEVICH, J.M. *Managing Job Stress and Health.* New York: The Free Press, 1982.

> This practical guide provides a wealth of information about diagnosing and reducing stress. The authors clearly define the sources and symptoms of stress and emphasize its pervasiveness in today's work world. The relationship between individual and organizational personalities and stress is also discussed. Especially useful are the many questionnaires for readers to diagnose their level of stress and numerous practical guidelines to reduce and avoid stress. Various techniques like exercise, diet control, and mental and physical relaxation are also reviewed.

CHAPTER TWENTY

EMPLOYEE COMMUNICATIONS

When problems first began to develop with the Firestone 500 automobile tire, the Firestone Rubber Company insisted there was nothing wrong with the tire. However, there were persistent reports of structural defects leading to auto accidents, personal injuries, and fatalities. There were rumors of internal engineering reports documenting problems with the tire. Management continued to defend and market the tire. Only after years of legal action and investigation did the facts emerge, which confirmed the tire's basic flaws and resulted in a judgment against Firestone. A massive internal corporate cover-up had prevented the facts from being disseminated within and outside the company.

Procter & Gamble responded differently when problems began to develop with its "Rely" tampon. (It was found to be related to toxic shock syndrome in some users.) Procter & Gamble quickly published the results of investigations of the product, pulled the product off the market, and warned women not to use the product if they already had it. As a result, although P&G lost a great deal of money on Rely, its prompt communication has been hailed as a model of social responsibility and public communication. Some observers feel that the direct loss on the product was more than compensated for by the increased good will and customer loyalty to other P&G products which resulted from the company's prompt communication and action.

communication

*I*n this chapter we will examine the various ways communication can operate in an organization. **Communication** is the *exchange of meaningful information*. Information in its "natural" state is not organized in any meaningful way, but rather is presented through various media (verbal, nonverbal, written, electronic, etc.) that need to be perceived and interpreted. Someone must "make sense" of information before it can be used to guide action. To make sense of information and to exchange it with various audiences is the purpose of organizational communication.

COMMUNICATION AND HUMAN RESOURCE MANAGEMENT

What is the relevance of communication to human resource management? Simply put, communication is an important ingredient in the effective management of people. If you asked a group of managers what their most difficult task was in working with people, you would probably hear two areas mentioned most often: communications and motivation.

Most of the human resource functions discussed in this book require communication for their successful implementation. Strategic human resource planning, for example, requires that senior management discuss and agree on strategic business objectives, as well as on ways that human resources can be organized to achieve those objectives. Recruiting involves informing potential employees of the benefits of employment in the organization. Training entails interaction between trainer and trainee to share information, instructions, and feedback on performance. Managing requires communicating well to establish clear, stretching objectives, coach behavior, and reward performance. And so it goes.

Formal organizational communication is often a specific responsibility of a human resource management department. This responsibility may include employee communications (through company newsletters, for example), community relations, labor relations, public relations, stockholder communications, and government relations. Communicating human resource policies to employees is becoming an increasingly critical activity. In some organizations there is a vice-president in sole charge of communications or public affairs (as at Borg-Warner), but in many the V.P. for human resources is also responsible for communications. Even where public affairs is a separate function from human resources, there is a growing trend to integrate the two areas.[1]

If the management of human resources is to be truly a line/human resource partnership, as we have stressed throughout this book, then yet another critical form of communication is that between line managers and human resource professionals. For example, in one manufacturing company, when a business planner showed human resource managers a transparency summarizing business strategy, he was shocked to hear that this was the first time the human resource managers had ever seen this information. Most of the morning was spent discussing the first "review" transparency. As a result of this meeting, a major decision was made to develop ways to communicate this business strategy information within the human resource department.

In another example, the topic of employee benefits as a recruiting tool came up during a meeting of sales managers with the human resource director. The human resource director presented a ten-minute summary of the company's extremely generous and flexible benefit plan.

The sales managers were stunned. Many of them had been with the firm twenty or thirty years, yet were not aware of the overall benefit package. They were tremendously impressed, and agreed that this information would greatly aid recruiting efforts; this was a recruiting resource they had never used before. And again, as in the previous example, action was taken to communicate this information to the other managers and employees of the division. (Note that in the first example, the line organization needed to communicate better with the human resource function, while the reverse was needed in the second example.) Thus, enhanced communication between the line organization and the human resource function is a way to increase the *leverage* of existing human resource offerings.

DIRECTIONS OF COMMUNICATION

If an organization is seen as a pyramidal structure, there are various directions in which communication can occur:

1. In *internal communication*, information flows within the formal hierarchy of the organization. It either flows up and down the hierarchy (as did *not* happen at Firestone in the tire cover-up), or laterally between people or units at the same hierarchical level in the organization. The need for lateral information flow was illustrated in the preceding two examples of communication meetings between human resource staff and line managers.
2. In *external communication*, information flows from the organization to the external environment, and vice versa (as happened with Procter & Gamble in the Rely case).

Of the two types, internal communication is probably more familiar as a human resource function. The relevance of external communication to human resources may be less obvious. However, if we think of human resources as encompassing the organization's activities geared toward people, then we realize that there are a number of other people in addition to employees who are major constituencies or stakeholders in the organization: stockholders, community residents, suppliers and dealers, legislators and regulators, and others. These people in the external environment have a major impact on the functioning and effectiveness of the organization, and are a major target of a proactive organization's communications activities.

The organization's own employees are also a major target of external communication. Employees are extremely concerned about the organization's activities and seek out information about the enterprise which is reported in the press. (In fact, in many cases, the information in the press is more current and complete than that received on the job.) Furthermore, employees are often viewed as agents of external public communications and encouraged to work actively on behalf of the organization, such as through direct contact with their Congressional representatives.[2]

Specific human resource methods are used to communicate with both internal and external stakeholders and we will discuss them in some detail.

INTERNAL COMMUNICATIONS

One problem with naturally occurring internal communications is that information is filtered systematically as it moves up and down and around an organization. In particular, *negative* information is screened out as it moves up the hierarchy. Thus, in the My Lai massacre in the Vietnam War, estimates of civilian deaths, as originally reported by field troops in My Lai, were around 2,000. However, these counts were reduced as they moved up the chain of command, so that the number of confirmed deaths that reached the Joint Chiefs of Staff was around twenty.

This same screening of "bad news" was found in other organizational failures, such as the Watergate affair in the Nixon administration, the Bay of Pigs invasion during Kennedy's term, and the abortive Iranian hostage rescue during President Carter's administration, as well as in the Firestone 500 case discussed earlier. In this section, we will examine some of the methods by which organizations attempt to improve communication between different parts of the hierarchy, from the bottom to the top, and laterally from one department to another.

Importance of Employee Information and Attitudes

Why should top management want to improve the quality of information available to employees? Exhibit 20.1 illustrates the reasons why employee communication is important. First, information is important for its own sake, so that the employee can maximize *job performance*. For example, the clearer an employee is about the basic goals and mission of the organization, the easier it is to direct his or her own job activities in that direction. In one organization that makes paging radios ("beepers"), employees had thought that a high volume of production was the most important objective of management. As a result, people pushed hard for quantity but quality was low. In fact, customer satisfaction was more strongly (and permanently) affected by

EXHIBIT 20.1   **IMPACT OF INTERNAL COMMUNICATION ON EMPLOYEES**

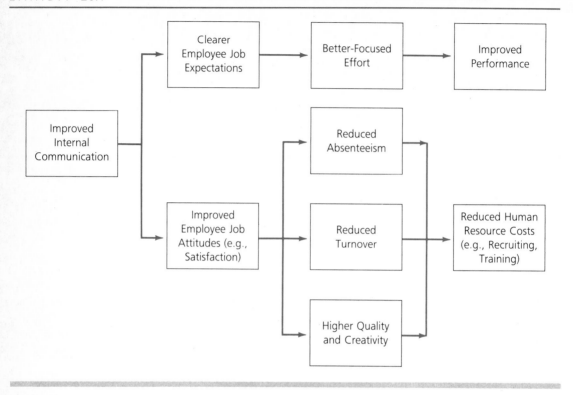

quality than by fast delivery. As a result of a strong human resource communication campaign (e.g., quality circles, company newspaper articles) on the need for and consequences of high quality and on methods of quality improvement, employees were able to redirect their efforts quickly. Quality showed dramatic improvement. Often employees perform below par because they lack information on what the organization expects and needs from them.

A second reason employee information is critical is that it affects the *attitudes and motivation* of employees. As we have seen from research on communications-facilitating human resource activities such as employee involvement and participation programs (see Chapter Four), when employees are in good two-way communication with management, attitudes such as satisfaction are much more positive.[3]

When satisfaction is higher, several human resource benefits are realized. Absenteeism is lower, which means that costly excess staffing or temporary hiring is less necessary. Turnover is lower, which means lower recruitment and training costs, as well as less lost work due to vacant positions.

Quality and creativity are higher, as employees invest more care and energy in their work. All of these human resource benefits of satisfaction result in a significant cost savings to the organization. In fact, through the methods of regression analysis and human resource accounting, it is possible to quantify the relationship between employee satisfaction and human resource costs. In one small bank organization, for example, it was found that an increase in job satisfaction of half a standard deviation would lower total costs by over $100,000.[4] Thus, in addition to the intrinsic value of employees feeling better when they are in fuller communication with management, there are practical business reasons for this process, as well.

Organizational Surveys

One of the most important ways to move information, both negative and positive, from lower-level employees to higher-level, and laterally from one department to another, is the organizational survey. A **survey** is a *systematic, objective, nonevaluative examination of the perceptions, attitudes, and opinions of members of the organization.*[5] Usually paper-and-pencil questionnaires or structured interviews are used to gather the necessary information. Information is collected anonymously to protect the identity of respondents, and the results are presented to higher management in aggregated, statistical form. The data may be aggregated in whatever ways are meaningful—e.g., by department, by age group, by job level. With present computer technology, a personnel staff member can sit at a computer terminal and analyze the survey data in response to virtually any question from line management. For example, the following questions could be easily addressed with a file of survey data:

survey

- How does the job satisfaction of our male managers at levels 37, 38, and 39 compare with female managers at the same levels and with comparable levels of education and experience?
- How do the career needs of engineers who have been in their present positions for over fifteen years compare with the career needs of engineers with less than five years in their current positions?
- How does the success of MBA graduates compare with that of non-MBAs when other relevant factors are constant?

Although the content of surveys varies widely, areas such as policies and practices, compensation, co-worker relations, physical conditions of the environments, promotional opportunities, supervisory skills and relationships, and the amount, demands, and characteristics of work are generally tapped.[6]

An important function of the survey is its use as a human resource *audit* device. Much as a financial audit evaluates different areas of financial performance, the survey can measure different components of the management process. For example, in one study of buyers, assistant buyers, and assistant sales managers at Sears, Dunham found that the following factors explained varying degrees of job satisfaction:

- Individual characteristics: predicted 2 percent of job satisfaction.
- Job characteristics: predicted 12 percent of job satisfaction.
- Organizational environment characteristics: predicted 38 percent of job satisfaction.[7]

Obviously, this suggests that factors in the organizational environment are the high-payoff influence to examine in the attempt to increase employee satisfaction. The organizational environment in this case included factors such as organizational climate, work-group climate, and leadership (task and interpersonal).

Feedback from surveys can also be useful in human resource planning. For example, a survey of perceptions of the compensation system in an insurance company was used to help plan a new compensation system.[8] Survey feedback is also an effective way to evaluate organizational change. In one chemical firm, a major new career planning program was introduced to give employees more information about career opportunities in other parts of the company and to help them develop realistic career goals and plans. Through the use of pre- and post-change surveys, it was possible to demonstrate significant gains in meeting employees' career development needs.

Another important function is *problem solving*. Surveys can help management better understand the reasons behind important organizational problems. Examples of questions which surveys can answer are the following:

1. What factors are associated with career success among engineers?
2. How can turnover be reduced?
3. What factors are associated with employees' desires to join a union?
4. How can satisfaction with supervision be increased?

To answer these questions, the problem or issue to be investigated (e.g., how to promote career success) is surveyed along with a full range of employee attitudes. Then the employee attitudes are correlated with various methods used to work on the problem. For example, one study of Roman Catholic priests in the Archdiocese of Hartford, Connecticut, revealed that the two factors most highly related to staying in the priesthood were satisfaction with supervision and satisfaction with the work itself. Based on this diagnosis, the archdiocese created team ministries in which groups of priests worked as peers with no boss. Later surveys found that this change increased satisfaction with both supervision and work.[9] Other studies have been able to diagnose factors related to important outcomes such as absenteeism, good performance, work quality, and union organizing.

Another function, often overlooked, is *training*. Generally, teams of managers conduct the exploratory interviews to identify the issues to be tapped in the questionnaire. By learning more about the dynamics of job attitudes, by developing the listening skills of a good interviewer, and by hearing firsthand how employees describe good and poor managers, the manager can't help but develop new insights and skills in management. Often managers find themselves listening to employees describe their boss's shortcomings and thinking, "Hey, I do that. That could be *me* he's talking about." So, ironically and unintentionally, some of the organizational feedback collected in the interview is taken as personal feedback by the interviewing manager.

A final benefit of a survey program is that it reflects a *corporate value*. The program is tangible evidence that the organization values the feelings and ideas of its employees. It also provides a way to measure and reward managers' performance in managing their people. At Sears, survey results are tied to a manager's pay; a portion of an executive's bonus is based upon employee attitude results. Thus, if managers are measured and rewarded in part on employee attitudes, this provides tangible evidence to employees that senior management places real value on employees and cares about how they feel about their work.

How Surveys Are Done

If surveys are initiated and used by top management for organizational decision making, they are more likely to be successful than if done without top-level commitment. The type of survey to be conducted will depend upon the needs and goals of the organization; thus, any initiation of a survey should be preceded by a thorough diagnosis of the organization: leadership patterns, structure, work flow, interpersonal relations, physical environment, job characteristics, etc. This diagnosis would probably best be done through interviews with people in different parts of the organization. Based on these interviews, the content of the survey can be identified. Without the initial diagnosis, the right questions may not be asked.

Timing is critical in administering a survey. The best survey is conducted on a routine, periodic basis as part of a regular survey program. For example, at Sears Roebuck, every store is surveyed once every three years. Thus, when the time for the survey comes around, it is not a "big deal."

Special surveys can be conducted to respond to special problems, to help plan major changes, and to provide employee input for the "action agenda" when a new manager or executive of the unit surveyed takes office.

It is illegal to conduct a survey during a union organizing campaign and during contract negotiations. It is unwise to administer surveys during the summer or in other periods when large numbers of employees are likely to be on vacation such as during a major work shutdown (for, say, a model change), a major crisis, or a peak work time (e.g., at tax time in a public accounting firm). Other than these considerations, there are not many poor times to conduct a survey. However, some managers anxious about the results might raise objections about any time period and try to stop the survey because "the time is not right." If the survey is scheduled far enough in advance, if management communicates clearly its nature and purpose, if the administrative arrangements do not interfere with work, and if employees have a choice about whether they will participate, the survey will probably be a very smooth operation.

The next question is, *which employees should be surveyed?* Should all levels in the organization be involved, or just certain groups? The answer will depend upon whether it is important to learn about organization-wide issues or just those related to particular groups. Surveys more typically cover lower-level employees than top executives, but this is usually because the communications gap between top management and operating-level employees is greater than that within the management ranks. However, when Sears conducted a survey of its executives, many new issues of executive concern were uncovered: relocation practices (executives found geographic moves stressful), compensation (the bonus system was seen as unfair), leadership patterns (more interchange with subordinates was needed) and structure (responses to a major reorganization).

A related question is whether to canvass all employees or simply sample a representative subgroup of the target population. If the group is small enough, it may cost little extra to do a complete canvass. An advantage, besides the quality of full representation, would be the psychological effect of giving everyone the opportunity to express an opinion. Usually employees appreciate the opportunity to communicate their ideas and feelings, and if certain people were excluded, they might feel resentful and discriminated against (even with a perfectly random sampling technique). If a sample is to be employed, it is important to sample a large enough subgroup to be truly representative of the target population.

A final important issue is *feedback to employees.* Employees who participate in surveys generally want to learn the results of the study and to see what changes might take place. To maintain employee involvement and commitment, a policy to provide feedback to all participants is strongly recommended. Often, if nothing happens after a survey and there is no feedback, morale drops and conditions may worsen. However, regardless of whether feedback is to be provided or not, it should be clearly communicated to employees at the time of the survey whether feedback will be provided or not. And if feedback is promised, nothing should stop this process from taking place.

If feedback is to be provided, one useful approach is to present the results to managers first and give them a chance to react to the data and discuss their implications. Since managers may be more likely to feel threatened by the results than employees, it is helpful to give them time to deal with the results. Managers may need training in feedback and action planning, as well. Then a useful next step is to have managers present the results to their subordinates for discussion, problem solving, and action planning. In this way, the manager develops more "ownership" of the survey results than he or she would if they were presented by members of the survey staff. This step of feedback and action planning is critical to maximize the benefits of a survey program.

In conclusion, it is important to remember some basic principles of effective survey administration:

1. If possible, survey people at all levels in the organization. This produces greater involvement and acceptance throughout the organization.

2. Deal honestly and in specifics, and cover issues that are important to people.

3. If possible, plan a continuing program. One-shot surveys will produce one-shot results. Regularly scheduled surveys provide ongoing upward communication.

4. Give participants full information about the program. Be sure to say how and when feedback of results will be handled. The feedback report should be honest and complete. Do not claim or imply that the survey will solve all problems.

5. Develop a climate of acceptance for the program. This includes getting support from top management and maintaining anonymity and confidentiality in the results. Do not identify any individual or report any individual's results. Report data in aggregated form in groups large enough so that no individuals can be identified (e.g., if there are only two female vice-presidents, do not report data for female vice-presidents).

6. Use professional procedures and standards to design the issues covered, the instruments, data analysis and interpretation, feedback of results, and organizational interventions. If line managers are involved in survey administration and/or feedback, be sure they follow strict guidelines to ensure uniform conditions of administration.[10]

Mass Media Communications

Much as formal surveys are becoming more professional and more common for upward communication, so are mass media techniques becoming more common for downward communication within the organization. *Communication departments* are being established in many organizations, and they are usually responsible for communication with employees as well as with external groups, such as analysts and shareholders.

Some specific forms of mass media employed inside organizations are the following:

- Employee newsletters,
- Company magazines,
- Letters to employees (sent home),

- Benefit information booklets,
- Benefit films, video, and slide presentations,
- Personalized benefit computer printouts,
- Recruiting booklets,
- Orientation booklets, films, and slide presentations,
- Messages in pay envelopes,
- Company histories and anniversary books,
- Company fact books.[11]

Other innovative communications are becoming more common, as organizations place greater emphasis on employee involvement. *"Speak-up" programs* are named after a process developed at IBM to provide direct, two-way vertical communication with a senior official. These programs all share certain characteristics: employee confidentiality, an independent coordinator, questions and answers sent through the mails, and full access to and support of the CEO. Usually there is some established procedure for response in terms of number of days allowed, a plan for redress if the speak-up was a complaint, or for providing the answer if the speak-up was a question.

Although the employee inputs vary from program to program, they generally break down about as follows, according to Roger Feather:

- Complaints: 55 percent,
- Questions: 40 percent,
- Opinions: 5 percent.[12]

Usually, standard forms are provided for employee inputs. Before they are passed on to the senior person, they are usually retyped and any other identifying material is removed. Inter-office mail is often used. Surprisingly, managers often utilize this communications channel more than lower-level employees.

Breakfast (or lunch) with the president. In some organizations, the president or chairman will be available on a periodic basis (perhaps once a week or once a month) to meet with groups of employees to discuss any matter. This is often done over breakfast or lunch to foster a more congenial atmosphere. Employees generally participate voluntarily, and there are often waiting lists. An example of this kind of program, as well as other processes one organization used to improve vertical communication, is reported in the interview with Barbara James following this chapter.

MBWA. This stands for "Management By Walking Around," a process by which executives and managers walk the halls or shop floor to make themselves available for informal discussions with employees. Although this seems to be an incredibly simple procedure, the facts are that managerial "walking around" is rarely done by most managers, and MBWA produces a gold mine of information for managers and employees. George Labovitz describes MBWA in more detail in Box 20.1.

Meetings. Another simple communications device—and one rarely used—is meetings between managers and groups of employees in their units.

WANT TO FIND OUT WHAT'S GOING ON? TAKE A WALK

BOX 20.1

There are basically two ways for a chief executive to find out what's happening in his organization: the first is to rely on the chain of command; the second is to find out for himself.

John C. Teets of Greyhound tries to spend a day or more each week in the field talking to plant managers, supervisors and production people, asking questions of everyone he meets. He credits the practice with solving a major quality problem in a food division and contributing to a much healthier management climate . . . .

"You can't follow the chain of command and know what's really going on in your company," insists Greyhound's Mr. Teets. "The information that comes in in monthly reports has been screened several times; it often doesn't get to the core of problems." Moreover, he says, "lots of people who surround the boss operate from the assumption: 'If he doesn't ask, don't tell him.' They know nobody likes surprises."

To overcome the bureaucratic filter, Mr. Teets raises questions directly with the people in the best position to answer, rather than going through channels. In his last assignment, as CEO of Greyhound's Armour meat division, Mr. Teets wanted to know why a profitable line of strip steaks had suddenly turned unprofitable. The explanation aides gave him was that raw product costs were up. Unsatisfied, he called the field manager and found that half the cases of strip weren't getting into the production system owing to employee theft and lack of control. "I never would have known if I hadn't asked directly," he says.

To encourage candor, some officials set up one-on-one meetings with line people in addition to the more casual conversations. "I'll ask a plant manager to set me up with two or three people who have a good sense of the place," one executive says. "I'll tell them straight out I want to understand what the company world looks like from where they are . . . ."

It's also important to describe to those who may feel bypassed what the executive will be doing, and why. Stress that his or her efforts are a supplement to, not a subsitute for, the regular chain of command.

Making people feel at ease in the presence of the "big boss" isn't always easy. But the comfort level can be enhanced by emphasizing that the senior person wants to know what ideas they have for making the company better. As a general rule, questions should be work, not personality, oriented, and have a clear business purpose.

It's legitimate in any organization for the boss to ask questions about how to improve quality, productivity or morale, or to inquire about working conditions and professional aspirations. It's highly risky—and usually not desirable—to inquire about union activities, levels of compensation, or the management skills or practices of particular individuals.

How much a boss can learn from wandering around depends on his ability to establish a trusting relationship with those he talks with—and the knowledge of the people he talks with. Says one executive: "You find some people who've been waiting years to be asked for their ideas, and others who never gave it a thought."

For a plant manager with 1000 people, the employees in the meeting might be a representative group. Or, an open meeting might be held in the evening, so that only interested, motivated employees would attend. In these meetings, the manager may begin by reviewing current business activities, problems, or plans, and employees would be encouraged to offer their questions, concerns, and opinions.

Electronic communication.   With the capabilities of electronic communication, it is becoming more feasible for senior people to communicate directly with large groups of employees through computers and closed circuit television. In this way, if a crisis occurs (e.g., a plant accident or an adverse legal ruling), a company representative can have instant communication with the work force, to control rumors. Also through electronic mail, or through the telephone, employees can address questions to specific individuals or to a company "hot-line" and get instant answers. This is an electronic version of "speak-up." Some people have called this use of computers for communications "Compunications." The ubiquity of telephone conversation is illustrated by the story of the credit card that helped win a battle during the U.S. invasion of Grenada.

An army unit was in a house surrounded by Cuban forces. One soldier found a telephone and, using his long distance telephone credit card called Ft. Bragg, N.C., telling Army officers there of the perilous situation. The officers in turn called the Air Force, which sent in AC 130 Spectre gunships to scatter the Cubans and relieve the unit.[13]

Teleconferencing.   Since the late 1960s executives of the Bank of America in Los Angeles and San Francisco have met regularly without the rigors of traveling. Sitting in their own conference rooms, they converse via a high quality audio conferencing system that is a growing form of electronic

teleconferencing

communication. **Teleconferencing** is *interactive group communication through any electronic medium.*[14] While the most common forms of teleconferencing are audio and full-motion video, other forms of communication can be exchanged as well: still video snapshots, keyboarded text messages ("electronic mail"), drawings ("electronic blackboard"), and page copies ("fax").

The group involved can be any size, ranging from three- or four-person groups to mass meetings. (An example of the latter would be political rallies or corporate gatherings where a leader who cannot be physically present addresses followers via wide-screen television.) Question-and-answer follow-ups are also possible in these large group meetings. While most teleconferencing is in "real time," it is also possible to store audio or video communications as well, so that participants can check into the conference at different times. This recorded format is termed an "asynchronous" or "store and forward" conference.

Communications companies are expanding teleconference services. As of 1983, 204 organizations had some form of permanent facilities for teleconferencing.[15] This number includes telephone companies and other vendors in the industry. Johansen and Buller estimate that seventy-five organizations in North America in 1984 had permanently installed audio systems, and twenty had full video (e.g., Boeing, Allstate, Arco, Liberty Mutual).[16] Thus, while teleconferencing is growing, it is not yet a widespread activity and is not growing rapidly. The dominant activity seems to be to hold conferences about teleconferencing. There are many experiments in the field, but most users are what Elliot Gold, publisher of a teleconferencing newsletter, calls "tire kickers."[17]

Surprisingly, it does not appear that teleconferencing is a substitute for travel. Although this is often used to justify the purchase of costly equipment, there is little evidence, based on ten years' experience, of direct travel substitution.[18] Rather, electronic methods may represent simply one *additional* way to exchange information.

Another surprise is that audio systems are more technically difficult than video. Participants will tolerate fuzzy video quality, but not poor audio quality.[19] Some of the advantages and disadvantages of teleconferencing are shown in Exhibit 20.2.

EXTERNAL COMMUNICATION

Traditionally, organizations have been thought to exist in an environment made up of elements such as government bodies, competitors, suppliers, labor unions, emerging technologies, various advocacy groups, the financial community, etc. The environment exerts a potent effect on the organization in the form of uncertainty and change. When faced with a turbulent environment, the most effective response is to be flexible and adaptable so the organization can respond quickly to changes in the demands and opportunities presented by the environment. This traditional view suggests a fairly passive and reactive role for the organization.

A more proactive view of the organization and its environment began emerging in the mid-1970s. It is based on the belief that the organization is able to influence its environment. And the method often used to exert influence on the environment is communication with various components of the environment.

Public Affairs

Formal communication with the environment is often the responsibility of a department with a title such as "public affairs" or "corporate affairs." Such a department handles functions such as public relations, government lobbying, communication with various social action groups, tracking social issues, and developing appropriate response strategies. This has become a critical, high-

EXHIBIT 20.2 POTENTIAL EFFECTS OF TELECONFERENCING

Cost Advantages

Reduces travel expense.

Reduces unproductive time while traveling as well as travel fatigue.

Reduces mistakes made because the "right person" was not at meeting.

Lessens duplication of effort by geographically separated sites.

Shortens business cycles and facilitates important decisions.

Reduces need to update people not at face-to-face meetings and improves accuracy of information at the update.

Reduces equipment downtime when repair person is at another site.

Reduces effects of disruption such as fuel unavailability or political unrest.

Opportunity Enhancement

Allows communication not practical before teleconferencing.

Allows more people to attend a meeting, especially on short notice.

Improves opportunities to prepare for and follow up on face-to-face meetings.

Increases flexibility in frequency and timing of communication.

Improves managerial control over field sites and decentralized offices.

Improves ability to share geographically separate "people resources."

Provides better personnel relations by keeping lines of communication open.

Makes job assignments less dependent on where an employee happens to live.

Provides faster and better responses to emergencies when key people are geographically separated.

Allows new opportunities for chance meetings among people who could benefit from working together.

Encourages consideration of alternative solutions to given problems.

Increases potential for improved computer programs to contribute to the work of teleconference participants.

Alters how employees think about their roles and their relation to organizations.

Negative Effects

Increases unproductive time spent in unnecessary but easily arranged meetings.

Decreases freedom of operation for remote field sites because of too much control by management.

Lowers morale because of decreased personal contact.

Encourages overspecialization and narrowness.

Fosters dependence on technology, creating vulnerability to breakdowns or even sabotage.

SOURCE: Reprinted by permission of the *Harvard Business Review*. An exhibit from "What to Expect from Teleconferencing" by Robert Johansen and Christine Bullen (March/April 1984). Copyright © 1984 by the President and Fellows of Harvard College; all rights reserved.

level function in many firms, with a corporate vice-president in charge. In some organizations, the human resource function has been expanded to include corporate affairs (e.g., Continental Illinois National Bank).

In a study conducted at Boston University, James Post, Robert Dickie, John Mahon, and Edwin Murray found in a survey of 361 large- and medium-sized U.S. business firms, that there is a growing level of public affairs activity.

Post sees the basic role of a public affairs function as "a window out of the corporation through which management can monitor external change, and, simultaneously, a window in through which society can affect corporate policy."[20] Thus, he argues, public affairs is a *boundary-spanning role* through which the organization communicates with its social and political environment. Post and his colleagues found that over one-half of all public affairs units had been created during the 1970s and one-third since 1975.[21] Sixty percent of the public affairs departments covered in the survey reported directly to the company chairman, president, and/or chief executive officer, giving these departments strong access to corporate policy-makers. Over half of the departments had annual budgets that were between $500,000 and $10,000,000.[22]

The scope of public affairs generally includes community relations, government relations, corporate contributions, and media relations (in 70 percent or more of the firms surveyed). To a lesser extent (24–49 percent) public affairs can also incorporate stockholder relations, advertising, consumer affairs, graphics, institutional investor relations, and customer relations. In all of these activities, three main functions are performed by the public affairs unit:

1. *Social and political intelligence.* This function includes issue identification, analysis and prioritization, and position formulation. This intelligence can be used to develop external programs (below). This is the important "window out," by which the organization reads its environment.

2. *External action programs.* These are activities designed to influence various components of the environment: government (e.g., lobbying, political action committees), media (e.g., public appearances), employees (e.g., employee newsletters in company issues), shareholders (e.g., dividend "stuffers"), and the public (e.g., advocacy advertising). This is the "window in," through which the outside world can see the organization's positions more clearly.

3. *Internal communications.* This is the function by which senior management communicates with employees about the demands, constraints, and opportunities presented by the external environment.[23]

Let us consider some specific examples of these three functions of public affairs in more detail.

Issue Tracking

A major form of organizational intelligence activity is issue tracking. **Issue tracking** is a *process of identifying as early as possible those issues in the environment (social, political, economic, etc.) which have a high probability of affecting the firm's business (and employees relations) in the future.* Some issues which many firms have been tracking are the growing number of women (particularly mothers) in the work force, changing work values in the labor force, and increasing consumer demand for product quality.

The idea behind issue tracking is that if the firm can be informed about emerging trends before the trends have their major impact, the organization will have a competitive edge by responding early. The process is a kind of "early warning system," much like a weather forecast which predicts a hurricane far in advance, allowing for effective preventive action.

Obviously, any firm that can spot such trends early in the game is going to have a head start in responding to and capitalizing on them. It is quite true that a problem is an opportunity in disguise. For example, when AT&T was under pressure to take affirmative action for women, top management realized very quickly that there was a tremendous pool of high-potential female candidates for management positions: thousands of female operators, clerks, and other lower-level employees. By opening up career advancement paths and developing better methods to identify and train high-potential people, the organization was able to upgrade its management, provide more fulfilling careers for employees, and meet its legal and moral obligations in the area of equal employment opportunity—all at the same time.

How is issue tracking performed? In many organizations, *issue tracking committees* are used. Such a group is drawn from various parts and levels of the organization and may be supplemented by people from outside the organization. Often an issue-tracking committee reports to a high level in the organization, sometimes to the board of directors. The committee is responsible for monitoring trends and focusing them in action terms for top management, and perhaps for monitoring the organization's responses to these issues.

Advocacy Advertising

As part of a strong public affairs external action program, some companies use a somewhat controversial activity: advocacy advertising. This form of advertising entails taking a position, often political, in advertisements, rather than just attempting to sell the product. This is often done in the belief that the press has communicated inadequately or unfairly about the issue and that there is a need to correct these abuses.

Perhaps the best-known example of advocacy advertising is that of the Mobil Corporation, although other companies such as Union Carbide and LTV are also known for their work in this area. Mobil's issue-oriented ads have been running since the early 1970s and have provoked strong reactions, pro and con. One example of a Mobil advertisement (responding to public reactions to its ads) is shown in Box 20.2. Whereas in the past business orga-

THE CUSTOMERS ALWAYS WRITE

BOX 20.2

From the beginning twelve years ago, Mobil's messages in this space and elsewhere have been intended to stimulate national dialogue on a variety of issues. Judging from our mail, we've succeeded in this basic goal.

Through the years, we've received thousands of letters—many from readers who agreed with our point of view but also some which dispute our messages. Almost all made reasoned points *pro* or *con*, though a few arrived with four-letter words crayoned across the column. Either way, we've read them all. Above all, we're convinced these responses clearly show that more and more people recognize the right of business corporations to speak out on the issues.

Following are some samples of recent vintage:

• *On a message defending corporate Political Action Committees:*

"I applaud you on bringing this truth on business PACs to the public. . . . I contribute *voluntarily* to the Schering-Plough Better Government Fund and watch very closely where our contributions go. I want my contribution to support politicians who share my views on free enterprise, the free market, and who support the best interest of my company."

• *From a reader who disagrees with Mobil's advocacy advertising program in general:*

"I've tolerated your 'issue ads' in magazines and periodicals long enough, but now I hear that they're going on television. I've felt that your *silly, complaining, misguided, self-serving messages* were bad enough when I could just *turn the page.* Now I'll have to turn *my television off.* You, certainly have finally turned a customer off."

• *But, on the same subject, another reader writes:*

"I wish to congratulate you on your public information program in which your printed messages have appeared in various publications. It is my understanding that your attempts to use broadcast media have been stifled, which if true only reinforces my contemptuous attitude toward the 'Gods of Antenna.' As a very small token of my appreciation, please accept this, my first application for a credit card from your company."

• *In response to a message poking gentle fun at the media for criticizing Mobil's attempt to acquire another oil company, this reply from a reader-writer:*

"Look, Mobil, you're entitled to your opinion and you are certainly entitled to all the space your money can buy on the op-ed page. . . . As a reporter for a small-market TV station . . . I am sick and tired of businessmen who whine about getting a raw deal from The Media. I am not The Media. No one I know is The Media . . . Mobil Oil can't seem to tell the difference between the so-called monopolistic press they seem to hate so much and the majority of working journalists who love the truth and would love to report the truth about American business . . ."

• *In response to a message urging the media to adopt and enforce a code of ethics, one reader replied:*

"Unfortunately, many who are in a position to be heard are intimidated by the press's unbridled power and remain silent. Your efforts are extremely important to public service."

• *On a message giving Mobil's views on ways to help steer the nation out of the recession:*

"Awareness is the first step in coming up with possible solutions to correct the issue. The majority of Americans are unaware of the economic situation facing our nation. You've placed an importance on educating the consumer. My hat is off to you. . . . All in all, I am pleased to see Mobil Corporation spending time and money in the area of educating the consumer. Keep up the informative messages."

Thank you. We will.

nizations often shied away from public attention, many firms now attempt to influence the external environment, which in turn affects them so strongly.

Social Responsibility

Issue tracking and environmental scanning are both related to the issue of social responsibility, the organization's moral and ethical obligations as a member of the social community. Meeting social responsibility commitments can include managing layoffs in a humane way, meeting consumer needs for truth in advertising or packaging, providing complete information about product limitations and adverse effects, providing a high-quality environment, and generally being a "good corporate citizen." Often social responsibility is "housed" in the marketing department, since so many of the issues it includes relate to consumer needs. However, since certain aspects of social responsibility relate to hiring and firing practices and the treatment of employees, social responsibility often overlaps with human resource functions in certain ways. And, similarly, public affairs and issue tracking also may cover issues which the firm defines as part of its social responsibility concerns.

Official Public Communications

The final form of external communication we will consider here is formal, official communication made by senior executives speaking on behalf of the organization. Examples include quarterly and annual statements on earnings made by the Chief Executive Officer, speeches by senior officials, press releases, and interviews or statements for the media.

Official public communication has become highly professionalized in many organizations. Business communication has become an important and respected program of study in schools of communication and journalism, and corporations can compete quite effectively with mass media organizations for talented people. Thus, the president's speech, the annual report, the company newspaper, and the chairman's speech to an industry association are all likely to be written by highly skilled professional writers. Furthermore, the official company spokesperson who appears on the six o'clock news on the day of a layoff or plant accident has probably been trained in print and electronic journalism. Also, the corporate line executive who is called on spontaneously to comment on some charge against the company is likely to have been trained to deal with the press.

Consider the simple device used by one corporate vice-president to avoid being televised when a reporter's hostile question caught him by surprise. He agreed to be interviewed at the airport, returning from a tiring trip, on the understanding that the topic would be the trip. As the lights went on and the camera moved in for a close-up, the interviewer said, "Now, Mr. ____, what do you have to say about the affirmative action charges being brought against your firm?" The interviewer was trying to catch him off guard even if the answer was a terse "no comment." At the very least, the interviewer would get the immediate nonverbal (facial) response. There was no time to come up with a suitable "non-answer."

What did the trapped executive do? He pulled out a handkerchief and proceeded to blow his nose as loudly as he could, making it impossible for the reporter to use that material on the air. The executive had been trained in a media communication workshop on how to deal with this sort of surprise question, and he was well practiced in dealing with this and other potentially difficult situations.

In another example of increased professionalism, annual reports have become a highly creative art form. In addition to communicating financial performance information to stockholders and the financial community, they also tell the company's story about its products, its concern for employees, its commitment to social responsibility, and its orientation toward product quality and customer service. Often the message is humanized by focusing on individual employees or customers, to show how their lives are favorably affected by the company.

This discussion by no means exhausts all the ways organizations communicate with their external environments. Customer surveys, follow-up questionnaires following product service, special toll-free "hot lines" (with area code 800 numbers) relating to product service and safety, participation in national surveys of employee values (e.g., the Yankelovich survey program), participation in industry surveys, and use of corporate executives in advertisements are some of the other ways external communication is done.

The main conclusion to be drawn here is that external communication is being done far more frequently now than in the past and is seen as a vital part of everyday business.

KEY POINTS

- With the new involved, participating work force and uncertain, turbulent business environments, information sharing and communication are now more important than ever before.

- Communication is the exchange of meaningful information. Information may be transmitted and shared, but if it is not meaningful (if it does not "make sense") to the receiver, communication has not occurred.

- Human resource professionals and line managers can act as facilitators to improve communication by promoting positive cycles of communication.

- A variety of forms of internal communication are available to organizations: surveys, meetings, MBWA, speak-up programs, mass media, etc.

- The public affairs function is becoming an increasingly common means through which the organization can communicate with its external environment. Many other forms of external communication, such as advocacy advertising and issue tracking, are available as well.

ISSUES FOR DISCUSSION

1. In what ways do you see communications as being relevant to human resource management?

2. How might some of the communications methods described in this chapter have been used to deal more effectively with the Firestone 500 case?

3. How do employee surveys require the active partnership of line managers and human resource professionals?

4. What are some of the different methods of internal communication that a manager might use? What do you think the pros and cons of various types would be?

5. What is the public affairs function? What is your personal opinion about the methods of external communications described in this chapter?

6. What effects do you think telecommunications will have on various human resource management functions (e.g., training, labor relations, recruiting)?

NOTES

1. C. P. Zeithame and G. D. Keim, "How to Implement a Corporate Political Action Program," *Sloan Management Review*, Winter 1985, *26*, pp. 23–31.

2. Ibid.

3. P. C. Richardson, "Courting Greater Employee Involvement Through Participative Management," *Sloan Management Review*, Winter 1985, *26*, pp. 33–43.

4. P. Mirvis and E. E. Lawler, III, "Accounting for the Quality of Work Life," *Journal of Occupational Behavior*, 1984, *5*, pp. 197–212.

5. R. B. Dunham and F. J. Smith, *Organizational Surveys* (Glenview, Ill.: Scott, Foresman, 1979), p. 4.

6. Ibid.

7. R. B. Dunham, "Two Job Evaluation Technologies and Determinants of Pay Satisfaction," paper presented at the convention of the American Psychological Association, Toronto, Canada, 1978.

8. Ibid.

9. D. T. Hall and B. Schneider, *Organizational Climates and Careers: The Work Life of Priests* (New York: Academic Press, 1973), pp. 233–42.

10. Adapted from F. J. Smith and L. W. Porter, "What Do Executives Really Think About Their Organizations?" *Organizational Dynamics*, Autumn 1977, *6* (2), p. 79.

11. R. Feather, "Feedback for Evaluation and Information," in C. Reuss and D. Silvia (eds.), *Inside Organizational Communication* (New York: Longman, 1981), pp. 267–83.

12. Ibid.

13. *Boston Globe*, May 31, 1984, p. 7.

14. R. Johansen and C. Buller, "What to Expect from Teleconferencing," *Harvard Business Review*, March–April 1984, p. 164.

15. *1983 Teleconferencing Directory* (Madison, Wisconsin: Center for Interaction Programs, 1983).

16. Johansen and Buller, op. cit. See also J. F. Magee, "SMR Forum: What Information Technology Has in Store for Managers," *Sloan Management Review*, Winter 1985, *26*, pp. 45–59.

17. Ibid.

18. Ibid.

19. Ibid.

20. J. Post, "Public Affairs: Its Role," in J. S. Nagelschmidt, (ed.) *The Public Affairs Handbook* (New York: AMACOM, 1982), p. 23.

21. J. E. Post, R. B. Dickie, E. A. Murray, Jr., and J. F. Mahon, "Managing Public Affairs: The Public Affairs Function," *California Management Review, Fall 1983*, *26* (1), pp. 135–50.

22. Ibid.

23. Ibid.

ANNOTATED BIBLIOGRAPHY

DUNHAM, R. B. and SMITH, F. J. *Organizational Surveys*. Glenview, Ill.: Scott, Foresman, 1979.

> This is the most complete source available on employee attitude surveys for vertical communication. Dr. Smith, now an independent communications consultant, has for years been responsible for the huge survey program at Sears Roebuck, which serves as an industry model. This book is an excellent source of information on survey theory, research, and practice.

JOHANSEN, R., VALLE, J., and SPANGLER, K. *Electronic Meetings*. Reading, Mass.: Addison-Wesley, 1979.

> This book describes the various sorts of communication made available through electronic and computer technology. It reports practical examples, pros and cons, and ideas on how to use technology most effectively to enhance communication.

NAGELSCHMIDT, J. S. (ed.). *The Public Affairs Handbook*. New York: AMACOM, 1983.

> This is an excellent resource on the emerging public affairs function in business organizations. It contains chapters by respected executives, academics, and public affairs professionals. Areas covered include management of the public affairs function, public policy, government relations, community relations, communications methods, and executive education in managing public affairs.

O'REILLY, C. A., III. "The Use of Information in Organizational Decision-Making: A Model and Some Propositions," *Research in Organizational Behavior*, 1983, *5*, pp. 103–39.

> This is an exhaustive, scholarly examination of communication factors which affect the quality of decision-making in an organization. It is organized in terms of major propositions (e.g., "Proposition 3. Information is more likely to be used

by decision makers if it is: readily accessible; summarized; presented orally; from a source deemed as credible, that is, trustworthy") (p. 19). For each proposition, relevant theory and research are summarized.

SONNENFELD, J. A. *Corporate Views of the Public Interest.* Boston: Auburn Publishing Co., 1981.

This award-winning volume is a detailed analysis of how the concept of corporate affairs unfolds in the forest products industry and provides the beginnings of a theory that relates managerial actions in public affairs to corporate effectiveness. The "meat" of the book (Chapters 8 through 12) is an in-depth look at how various constituencies (various functional departments, different companies, different levels of management, and key stakeholders) view the interactions between company and environment.

INTERVIEW

BARBARA JAMES, A BANK EMPLOYEE-RELATIONS COORDINATOR

▮▮▮▮ *Could you tell us something about your work in communication at your bank?*

Typically, communications are handled by the marketing department. Usually people think of communications as the company newsletter, or as it's sometimes called, the "company rag." I'm involved in a different kind of work. It is employee relations, which brings together different levels of management and employees to create an egalitarian atmosphere.

We have several mechanisms to facilitate communication between different levels of management. One is our "Breakfast with the Boss" program. Three executive managers get together with employees. Each top manager meets once a month with eight employees who have been with the bank for a period of time. They have breakfast for one hour and then tour the executive offices. The officers usually start by asking, "What do you want to talk about today?" It is a chance for the employees to air their concerns—parking, cafeteria, training. Opinions are expressed, unanswered questions are routed through personnel, and answers are provided.

These breakfasts have been extremely well-received. They give the message, "We care about you, whoever you are." The officers are laid back in their approach. The message that we care to listen is important.

We have other structured communications avenues. Once a year we have a company-wide meeting. Large groups of 300 employees come together with top managers and division managers. Questions are taken in advance. Prepared questions come first; then questions can come from the floor. Sometimes these meetings are pretty lively. They serve as a way to keep communications open.

We also have an employees' club. There are four committees: Social Activities, Sports and Recreation, Service to the Community, and Crafts. Officers and clerks work together on events like the Halloween Dance. I guide these things. I make sure all levels of the bank are involved, and that different people share in the leadership of committees. We want the employees to feel that it is their club. We put up the money, but it's their thing.

There are other mechanisms to find out employee concerns. Periodically, we have attitude surveys. I work closely with the people who do the newsletter. I give them information—for example, if a physical fitness class is coming up. My role is to be in the middle of everything.

The grapevine is an important source of information. It's a matter of building up trust. I do a lot of counseling. People know that I don't betray confidences.

An additional feedback mechanism comes at termination. We ask every employee for a termination interview. Employees are usually willing to share things at that time that they would not have risked before.

It's vital to keep lines of communication open. It helps with morale and prevents griping. It also cuts down on back talk about the bank on the outside.

▓▓▓▓ *How would you describe your position? How have you developed your role?*

I am the Employee Relations Coordinator. This job was created when I came. It was felt that there was a need to improve feedback mechanisms, a need for someone to whom people could talk about their concerns, and a need to organize employee activities. I was hired to be a liaison person between different levels.

The first six months were hard. I had to develop visibility. This came initially through the newsletter. I ran a training session where I presented what I do. You keep on repeating yourself. A trust level had to be established. I had to get out and mix and mingle. The counseling function was most beneficial. It helped to get people to know that I was here. If you listen to personal problems without being judgmental, you develop credibility.

Top management had hired me. I had backing from the top, therefore I had backing from the divisions. However, there is fear about my role. Will the employees talk to me about the managers? Is the system going to work for or against them? It's a difficult role being in between. It's getting better. There are more calls from supervisors and managers. When they call themselves, you know it is beginning to work.

I work directly with the managers around the bank. My focus is to assist the employee. I work for managers to help them help their people.

▓▓▓▓ *Where do you see your role going in the future?*

One of my primary goals is to make help more readily accessible for employees. We are starting to do monthly seminars on awareness, how to cope in today's economy, and stress management. I have speakers come to discuss popular topics: two-career couples, working and raising children, dressing for success, etc. In addition, I plan to put out a list of resources, sources of help, twice a year.

One of the problems as a counselor is that people are afraid to use you for personal issues. I want to help create a climate where it's "O.K. to be not O.K." My goal is to expose people to psychological resources, to sensitize people to feel that it's O.K. to seek help. I would like to work more with managers to identify and refer employees for help.

I would like to start a formal employee assistance program. This would help to legitimize our services. It's important to have built-in formal structures. This tends to increase their availability and usage. I'd like to see a twenty-four-hour answering service for problems and questions, anything related to work. I would also see getting into outplacement using my connections with employment agencies.

My biggest job is to keep the function alive and well. My role changes constantly. The economy has gotten strange. Turnover has decreased. It is easier to get qualified people; it's no longer an employee's ballgame. Management can be less concerned about making everyone satisfied. Just because people are not leaving, this is not the time to stop. At a good work place, it's important to have systems in place.

PART SIX

IMPLEMENTING HUMAN RESOURCE STRATEGY

Throughout this text we have demonstrated how human resource professionals and line managers work together to plan, design, and carry out human resource activities that make employees productive and satisfied and also contribute to organizational goals. In these concluding chapters we discuss the crucial "bottom line" of human resource management; i.e., how the human resource function can best be located in the structure of the organization, and how it can be managed and evaluated to maximize its positive impact.

Chapter Twenty-One focuses on decisions such as how to structure the human resource function and where to place it in the organization. These decisions are influenced by factors like the size of the organization and the extent to which it is centralized or decentralized. We compare the choice of a large, centralized corporate human resource department with the choice of a small corporate office and a more powerful human resource department in each division of a large corporation. We also discuss how the design of the department affects the working relationship between line managers and human resource professionals.

Chapter Twenty-Two examines how human resource professionals gain power and influence in their organizations. It describes five stages through which human resource management evolves and the readiness of the organization for sophisticated techniques and procedures at each stage. We also identify the power bases available to human resource professionals and explain how they can use each to gain credibility and influence. Finally, we comment on a formal accreditation program to certify human resource professionals.

Chapter Twenty-Three concludes with the vital topic of evaluation. It begins by acknowledging that human resource practitioners must do a better job of demonstrating their impact on the organization and stresses the need to document the costs and benefits of human resource management in financial terms. Approaches are discussed not only for measuring the impact of human resource programs on employee performance but also for computing the cost and value of these activities. This documentation provides the basis for assigning priorities to human resource programs.

These topics seldom receive sufficient attention in today's organizations by either human resource professionals or line managers, although both parties, as partners in managing human resources, have a vested interest in them. In all three chapters, we point out how the two parties can work together to design, manage, and evaluate the human resource function.

CHAPTER TWENTY-ONE

STRUCTURING THE HUMAN RESOURCE FUNCTION

Prime Computer, founded in 1971 by a group of former Honeywell employees, grew rapidly in the 1970s under the leadership of its CEO, Ken Fisher. Between 1974 and 1979 sales revenues doubled practically every year, as did hiring, and the stock price appreciated approximately 3,000 percent. However, overhead was also growing at an annual rate of 90 percent, and there was a need to "tighten up" the company's management operations.

When Fisher left in the early 1980s, he was succeeded by Joe Henson, a twenty-eight-year veteran of IBM, whose mission at Prime was to establish a more controlled growth rate and to develop a strategic planning focus for the company. Within a year, he had replaced all of the vice-presidents, except for one, with his own people from IBM.

The change in management style and structure was painful. Fisher had been very popular with employees. They had lost their "Big Daddy." But many employees were also stockholders and they saw the need to tighten up.

Under Fisher, Prime had been a family company with a "small" feeling, a people company, with cream rising to the top. With Henson, there was more of a systems approach, more of a professional management orientation. The human resource department was given the charge to develop new management systems for the whole corporation.

One of Henson's aims was to reward people for staying, for building their careers at Prime, as people do at IBM. His philosophy stressed product quality, the customer as the sole source of sales, and respect for the individual employee. He was a strong supporter of the human resource department as an agent to establish this IBM-style culture.

How have these changes in the strategic orientation of the company affected the design of the human resource department? Patricia O'Neill, Manager of Human Resource Systems and Projects, describes the changes:

The Human Resource Function changed in many ways. When Fisher left we temporarily lost our VP. The Human Resource department head became a director and moved down a notch in the organization. With Henson, we have moved back into VP status.

Under Fisher, Human Resources were decentralized and all functions were located in each department—i.e., manufacturing, engineering, marketing, etc. Employee relations (ER) was seen as the power within each individual group. Recruiting, compensation, and planning were seen as the more secondary functions within each group.

Under Henson, Human Resources have been restructured so that functions such as Compensation, Recruiting, Planning, and Development are now centralized corporate functions. Employee relations people have become the brokers for all the functions.

Human Resources are seen as serving the company very differently. There is more of a corporate rather than functional viewpoint. The structure of compensation/incentives, hiring, recruiting, all these jobs have changed. Branch managers used to be paid a percentage of sales. Now they are paid for managing well.

There are more human resource systems. There are systems to control spending. There are systems to help employees maintain a clear view of their work, to give them feedback. There are training programs that bring managers together from different functions.

We are developing core programs, training middle managers first, then supervisors and executives. Affirmative Action has clear goals; there are new incentive systems that will reward managers based on their skillful management of people. The Human Resource department is now seen as the designer of programs and structures for the whole corporation.

The philosophy is not to be more specialized but to become better generalists. This philosophy has been evolving since the reorganization of the department. We are evolving from working in highly specialized, fractionalized kinds of roles into becoming generalists.[1]

Although the changes in other organizations may not be as dramatic as those at Prime, human resource departments have been experiencing profound transformations in recent years. As we saw earlier in Chapters Three and Four, there is both a "new work force" and a "new work place," as well as a new economic situation. In short, today's business environment is so turbulent that strategically planned human resource management is at once extremely difficult and absolutely essential. How can rational planning be performed in the face of such uncertainty? In this chapter, we will consider ways to "build in" human resource planning by designing the structure of the human resource department appropriately.

In Chapter Two we discussed the need to link human resource planning to corporate business planning. The idea is deceptively simple: planning can't be done properly for people (recruiting, staffing, training, compensation, etc.) until business goals and plans are known. However, as simple as this idea is, in many organizations strategic business planning and human resource planning are two totally different functions—they are done by different departments staffed with people from different disciplines (business planners may have finance and economics training, human resource planners often have psychology degrees) and often with no need or way to collaborate with each other. Often, human resource planning consists simply of determining the number of new employees the company will aim to hire during the next year's college recruiting season.

There is also little feedback to the human resource department on the effectiveness of whatever planning it actually does: if too many college graduates were hired, the managers responsible for unnecessarily high salary budgets might know it and the new employees with little real work to do might know it, but there would often be no mechanism to tell the human resource planners that they had overestimated the need for graduates.

In short, what more and more companies need is not just human resource planning, but *strategic* human resource planning—the linking of future human resource activities to the competitive business environment of the organization. In this chapter, we will discuss the ways the human resource department can be designed to increase its integration with line management, as both parties pursue the basic objectives of the enterprise.

DESIGNING THE STRUCTURE OF THE HUMAN RESOURCE FUNCTION

One critical factor in the delivery of effective human resource services remains to be discussed: the structure of the human resource function. One key aspect of strategic human resource planning is planning for the human resource function itself. It is not enough for human resource executives to help the organization plan for the effective management of its human resources; they must start "at home," and give careful thought to the way their own department is organized before that function can most effectively serve the rest of the organization.

There are two important questions about human resource structure, one internal and the other external:

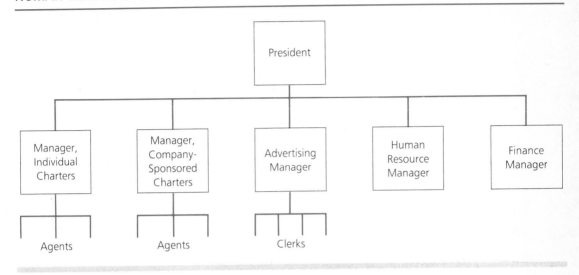

1. How does the human resource department fit into small and large organizations?
2. How is the human resource department itself organized?

We shall consider each in turn.

Human Resources in Small and Large Organizations

The nature of human resource activity in an organization changes as the organization grows and develops. In a small organization, the human resource function would probably be limited to basic activities such as staffing and compensation. In a very small organization there may not be a formal human resource department; there may be an office manager or an administrative assistant who performs human resource activities along with other general business tasks. Or, there may be a small human resource department with a manager who does all the hiring, firing, training, and compensation, perhaps with the aid of one clerk. An organization chart for the human resource department in a small organization, a travel agency with fifty employees, which develops and sells package charter tours, is shown in Exhibit 21.1. The agency demonstrates an early stage of development with just the beginnings of human resource programs and with the major activities being general administrative and technical duties, rather than specialized, human resource functions such as development, compensation, or staffing. (We will discuss general stages in the development of the human resource department in Chapter Twenty-Two.)

A larger organization usually offers a wider range of human resource services, but the structure is not necessarily more complex.

It is interesting to note that in a large organization such as IBM (with over 370,000 employees in over 120 countries), its senior corporate structure is quite simple, with three main corporate groups reporting to the corporate office: finance, operations, and services. Human resources and industrial relations at the corporate level are part of the corporate services staff, along with communications and government programs. IBM's technical human resource development is separate from personnel, reflecting the great emphasis IBM places on employee development. This is consistent with the heavy technical demands on the work force, the fast-changing technology, and the need for career-long education.

Personnel also exists in each of the operating areas. Each division and each national operation has its own human resource department.

At Continental Insurance, another large company, Human Resources is one of six staff areas reporting to the Chief Executive Officer. The operating units are organized in terms of the line of business they represent (property and casualty insurance, international and reinsurance, life and health insurance, investments, etc.).

Organization of the Human Resource Function

"Personnel" vs. "Human Resources" ▬▬ Continental Insurance uses the term "human resources," rather than "personnel." The first term implies a more comprehensive set of activities, including compensation, benefits, development, planning, employee relations, E.E.O., medical services, and even food service. In general, most activities which serve various employee needs are included in human resources.

This difference between "personnel" and "human resources" is more than a matter of semantics, as we discussed in Chapter One. It involves the issue of *how integrated* and *how specialized* the activities will be. There are definite trade-offs here, and there is no best way to structure the functions.

With a more encompassing "human resource" department with all of the activities reporting to one person (usually either a director or vice-president of human resources), there is better coordination of activities. Also, because only one person is ultimately responsible for all these functions, she or he has a "unified constituency," in a sense, and can represent human resource concerns more forcefully than could three or four heads of more specialized units, such as training or industrial relations. Furthermore, with one integrated human resource function, there is a simpler, more direct link from the main line business areas to human resources making it easier to integrate human resource planning into business planning.

On the other hand, there are disadvantages to the integrated "human resource" approach. When the human resource activities are separated, as at

IBM, each function tends to be *more specialized*. This means that each group becomes more professional within its own specialization and develops more expertise. The organization is more likely to have strong human resource specialists. They may have higher levels of formal education and training. For example, many organizations like IBM have people with Ph.D.'s in the behavioral sciences in their corporate service groups. Continental Insurance has few, if any, Ph.D.'s.

Of course, other factors, such as organization size and management support for personnel/human resource activities, will also affect the degree of professional training and specialization the personnel/human resource staff has; IBM is a huge organization with an extremely strong tradition of support for personnel activities. However, the structure of the activities can contribute to specialization as well.

Thus one must often choose between integration with the line business and specialization of human resource activities. Let us consider the pros and cons of each.

Centralization Vs. Decentralization ▬ A critical design issue is where the organization's human resource staff should be deployed. Should there be a large, strong, highly professional central corporate staff? Or should there be a lean corporate staff with more specialists working in the divisions and operating units of the organization? This is a specialization issue. With more focus on a large corporate staff, it is possible to have specialists in particular areas of human resources. For example, there could be one or two highly trained compensation experts who can research "state of the art" salary systems and carefully design a sophisticated compensation system to be applied throughout the corporation. On the other hand, if the organization does not have such strong resources in a corporate staff, and instead has more human resource people on division or plant staffs, each division or plant might have to design its own system. Since those division or plant personnel may have to deal with a wider range of human resource issues in their location, they may not have as much time to research pay systems and to design a state-of-the-art system. On the other hand, the system is more likely to be better tailored to the unique needs of that particular division or plant.

The structure of a typical divisionalized human resource department is depicted in Exhibit 21.2. In such a department the division human resource manager (a director) generally reports directly to the division general manager, but has a coordinating (dotted line) relationship to the corporate head of human resources. This structure represents a *decentralized* human resource function, with responsibility and accountability more clearly at the division level than at the corporate level.

This "dotted line" relationship shows the strain inherent in any relationship between corporate management and a division manager in a decentralized company. In theory, a division manager is a general manager responsible for all functions and facets of his or her business. The business is operated as

EXHIBIT 21.2   **A DIVISIONALIZED HUMAN RESOURCE DEPARTMENT**

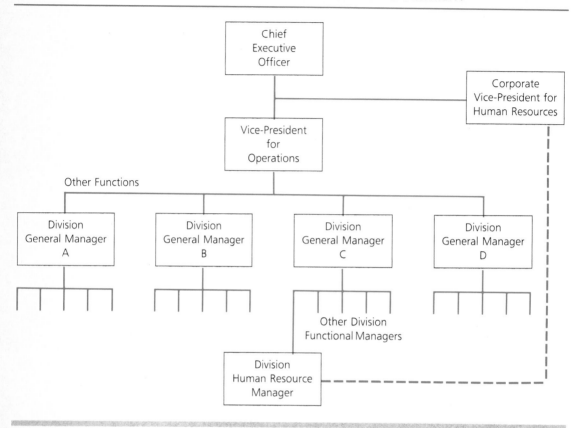

a profit center, and the division manager is "left alone" as long as profit objectives are being met.

In a similar way, the head of a divisional functional area like personnel/human resources has great autonomy in relation to the corporate human resource director. Corporate management would usually communicate corporation-wide human resource policies to the division human resource director (e.g., policies affecting hiring practices, compensation, promotion, benefits). Corporate staff would provide certain types of professional and management training and development, would probably develop corporation-wide systems for employee records, pay, performance appraisal, and succession planning, and might offer certain consultation services. Basically, in such a decentralized organization, the corporate human resource staff members are "staff to staff," meaning they provide a staff function to the division staff (who in turn provide staff services to operating line managers).

This is the way the coordinating relationship works under normal operating conditions. However, the corporate staff may also step in and provide direct assistance and direction in an emergency (such as a strike, a major lawsuit involving employees, illegal employment practices, etc.).

The same concept of decentralization can be applied to human resources at the interface between the division level and the individual plant or office. In the more decentralized approach, there would be a local human resource department with a range of functions (such as compensation, hiring, training, etc.) at the plant level reporting to the plant manager. Again, there would be a dotted line relationship with the division human resource manager.

Division Vs. Corporate Staffs ▬▬ Generally, most divisionalized organizations have both corporate and division human resource staffs, but there is always strain between the two over how much power each will have. The corporate staff is usually responsible for the coordination and integration of human resource systems. To a corporate compensation specialist the prospect of five pay systems for five divisions seems like a nightmare. The division staff, on the other hand, is concerned about the autonomy of its operations, so it can better meet the needs of its division general manager or plant managers. When new systems are developed, there may be great conflict about who will "own" them.

In one large financial services company, for example, there was a race between the corporate human resource department and the staff of the firm's largest operating division to develop a new career management system. The informal decision rule for allocating "turf" between corporate and division staffs was that whoever developed a system first would own it. If a division developed a system that worked well, that division could keep it. However, if the corporate staff developed a system first, all divisions would be expected to adopt the corporate system. Thus, there were constant races between corporate and divisional staffs.

The advantages of strong corporate human resource staffs are as follows:

1. They allow for greater specialization and thus greater competence in those specialized areas.
2. A strong corporate staff can act as *consultants* to the division human resource staffs, so that each division does not have to "discover the wheel anew."
3. Corporate staff members are often "career" human resource professionals, experienced in dealing with human resource matters in that organization. This contributes to greater competence, as well as an enhancement of the history and traditions of the organization.

The advantages of strong divisional human resource staffs are as follows:

1. The division staff is better integrated with the business needs and plans of that division. It can contribute more directly than corporate staff to the attainment of "bottom line" results.

2.   In times of economic recession, the division staff is less vulnerable to being cut than the corporate staff.

3.   The division staff can generally adapt more quickly to changing business needs than the corporate staff because division-level people are closer to these needs and can tailor human resource systems to the unique needs of the division.

4.   The division staff, through its everyday working relationships with line managers, has more credibility than does the corporate staff with line managers, and can more effectively influence managerial actions.

In contemporary organizations, with the great concern for cost containment and improved productivity, there seems to be a tendency to reduce large corporate human resource staffs. Rightly or wrongly, such staffs are often seen by managers as a "luxury," and many firms are reorganizing and downsizing their corporate human resource staffs so the staffs can support local operations more directly. For example, one large manufacturing company reduced its corporate human resource staff from sixty-one professionals in 1980 to eleven in 1985.

matrix human resource structure

The Matrix Structure ▬ The matrix human resource structure is midway between the centralized and decentralized design. The **matrix human resource structure** is a *dual reporting structure in which the human resource function is accountable to both a client group and a traditional human resource department.*[2] The client groups could be divisions (as in a decentralized structure), plant locations, geographical territories, or product groups. The core element would be a *service team* which would provide a full range of human resource services to the client organization. Team members would be drawn from each of the traditional human resource functions (e.g., staffing, compensation, training). For example, in a bank, each branch might have its own human resource team physically located within the branch to provide all necessary human resource services. This matrix approach is especially useful under the following environmental conditions:

▬ when there is pressure for better client service,
▬ when there is pressure for a high level of information processing capability within the human resource function, and
▬ when there is pressure to share resources among human resource groups.

An example of a matrix human resource structure is shown in Exhibit 21.3.

BUDGETING FOR HUMAN RESOURCES

Related to the issue of how the human resource functions are linked to the total organization is the method by which human resource activities are budgeted. In many organizations human resources is treated as an *overhead* expense and is, in effect, charged against the overall corporate operations. Im-

EXHIBIT 21.3   A MATRIX HUMAN RESOURCE ORGANIZATION

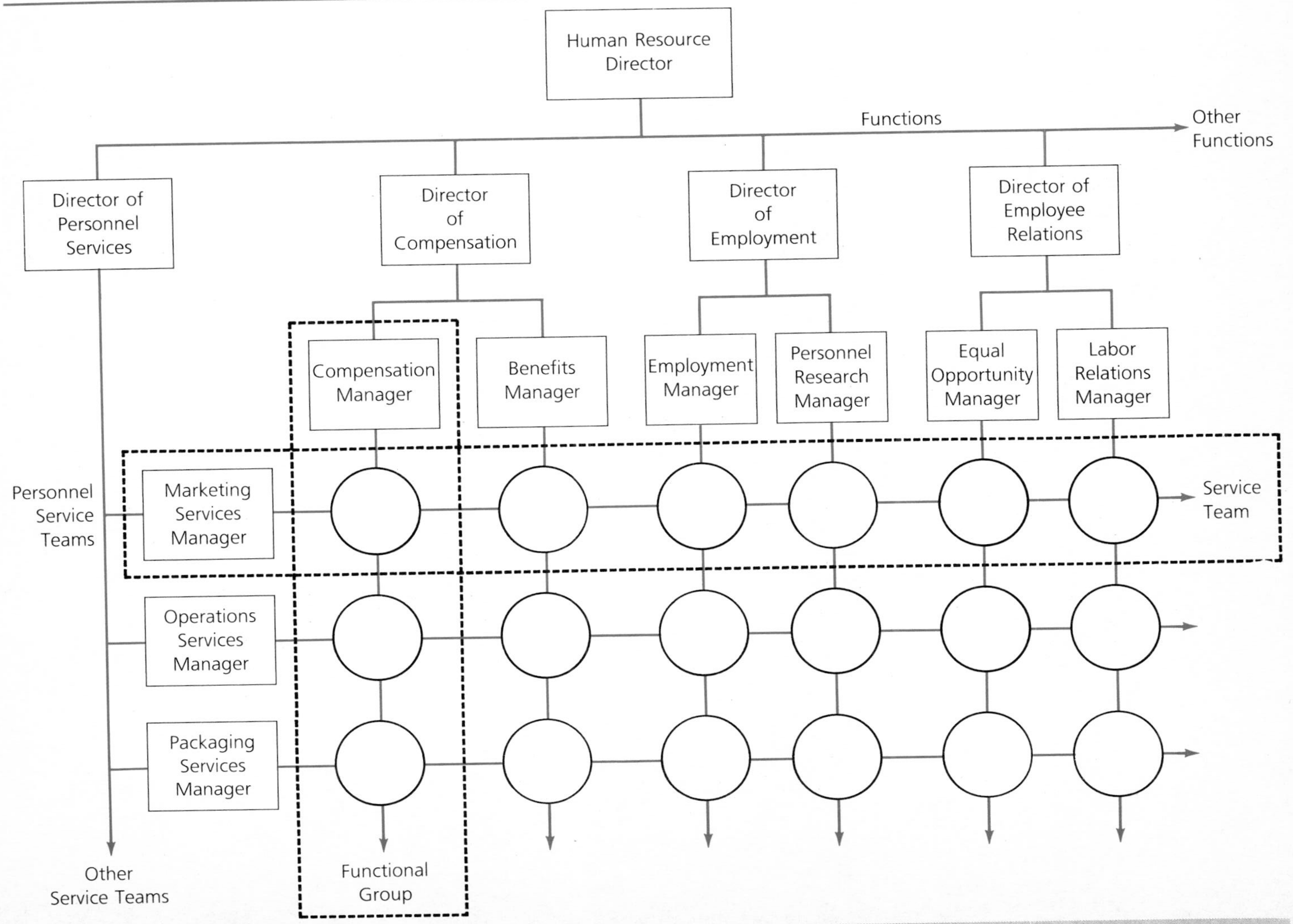

SOURCE: Curtis C. Paulson, "The Matrix Structure in Personnel," unpublished manuscript 1981.

plicit in this approach is the notion that human resources is a general corporate service producing universally shared benefits, much like the company computer, library, research laboratory, and parking lot.

The benefit of this approach is that there is no cost penalty to any manager or operating unit that wishes to make frequent use of services, such as recruiting, training, or special surveys.

A variant of this approach is the use of *charge-backs for special services*. For example, personnel may be corporate overhead charged for general services, but if the manager of a particular unit wants a special activity performed, such as a training program tailor-made for his or her division or a one-shot employee attitude survey, these special charges might be billed directly to that manager's operating budget. The advantage of this charge-back system is that it forces managers to be selective when requesting human resource services. It also develops greater managerial commitment to those services, because the manager has paid for them, and it allows the human resource function to evaluate and justify line management's demand for its services.

When human resources is decentralized, with separate divisional human resource departments, the expense for these departments is usually charged to the divisional operating budgets. This divisional funding clearly indicates that these human resource subunits are there to serve the division manager, and the direct costing again gives that manager a strong incentive to utilize human resource services effectively.

INCREASING THE INTEGRATION AND INFLUENCE OF THE HUMAN RESOURCE DEPARTMENT

Importance of Strategic Human Resource Planning

Why is it that the human resource department in some organizations is very much integrated with line management, as part of the team, while in others it is an isolated unit, unrelated to the mission of the organization? Part of the answer is sheer growth. As an organization employs more people, it is forced to develop more specialized human resource activities to accommodate a larger work force, but growth alone would probably not lead to integration of those services.

Movement to an integrated human resource department can only be achieved through the strategic planning process as described in Chapter Two. (More detail on the growth of the human resource department will be provided in Chapter Twenty-Two.) This requires a clear identification of the corporate mission consistent with the culture of the organization and the environment in which it operates. The corporate strategy must flow logically from its mission. This overall corporate strategy should then influence the strategies of various business units (service or product lines) and corporate functions or departments (such as marketing or production). The strategy of these business units and corporate departments should integrate substrategies for marketing, finance, production, and human resources. For example, a business unit that markets through retail stores would need a compensation strategy for its sales force different from a unit that sells directly to customers.

Based on the overall corporate strategy, the business unit strategies, and the strategies of the corporate functional departments (e.g., marketing), an integrated strategy for human resources can be developed.

The model showing how an integrated human resource strategy is developed is shown in Exhibit 21.4. Baird, Meshoulam, and DeGive describe the interactive nature of this process as follows:

> . . . There is no real starting or finishing point in this integrated plan model. No element dominates the others; rather, they are integrated to develop a consistent and complementary corporate strategy. Each element has a role to play in the development of a human resource strategy because it is not simply a top-down or bottom-up process. Those near the bottom of the organization, in the business unit, are in direct contact with the employees, and have much of the information that's necessary to develop an overall strategy.
>
> The business unit is critical to corporate human resource strategy but it cannot dominate because overall corporate strategy must reflect the overall environment and corporate culture. Strategy formulation must be a process of negotiation and integration; corporation elements must constantly be interacting to develop a strategy that accurately reflects all its components.[3]

An example of this complex interplay between culture, environment, strategy, and structure is found in the process of managing the divestiture of AT&T (Box 21.1).

Negotiation and Influence Methods

Since achieving integration of the human resource department with the other parts of the organization is such an ongoing interactive process, involving negotiation and constant dialogue, what are some of the methods by which this negotation might be carried out effectively?

A study of a large midwestern bank which developed an integrated human resource department over the last twenty years found several leadership requirements to be important in the department's achieving full integration with the line organization.[4]

Ability to Use Personal Power ▬ Whoever the senior human resource person is (e.g., vice-president, director, manager), the more personal influence he or she has, the better are the chances that the department will attain influence. In the case of the bank studied, the senior person, Don

EXHIBIT 21.4   INTEGRATED STRATEGIC HUMAN RESOURCE MANAGEMENT MODEL

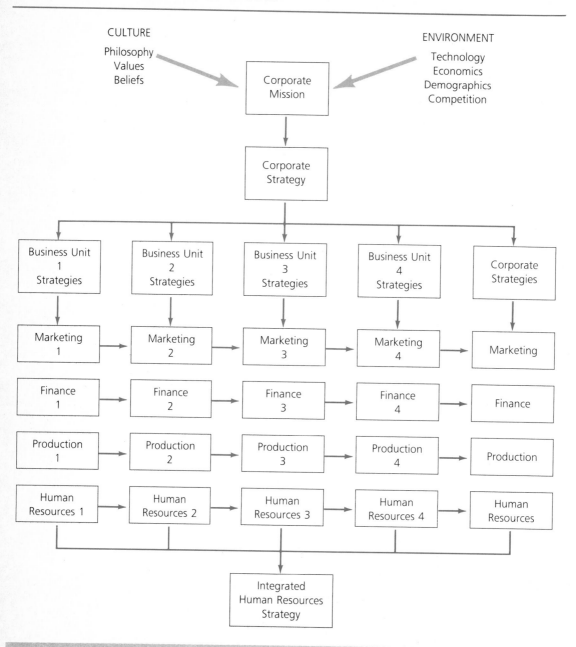

MANAGING CULTURAL TRANSITION AT AT&T

BOX 21.1

On January 1, 1983, the largest organizational change in history took place. The American Telephone and Telegraph Company (AT&T) divested its twenty-two Bell operating companies, which formed seven new regional companies (e.g., NYNEX, Bell South) and a centralized service staff. AT&T also formed, under order from the Federal Communications Commission, a separate subsidiary (AT&T Information Systems) to provide all new customer equipment and "enhanced services" on a detariffed basis.

The new, smaller AT&T was restructured in two important ways:

1. The headquarters staff was drastically reduced. From a predivestiture size of 15,000, its ultimate level will be around 2,000. Former staff members were redeployed to the divested operating companies and to the new operating units of AT&T.
2. Two new large sectors were formed: AT&T Communications (to provide regulated interchange service nationwide), and AT&T Technologies (an unregulated entity combining Western Electric, Bell Labs, and AT&T International).

The magnitude of the structural and cultural change was staggering. As one executive described the process, "It was like taking a 747 apart in mid-air and keeping it flying." The sense of loss and grieving among the highly loyal work force was intense. The process was managed by a task force which set basic policies for the change. The specific implementation methods were then left to each function, using the task force's policies for guidance.

The divestiture brought certain human resource policies under review:

1. What kind of experience should a high-potential manager have as part of grooming for senior management? In the past, movement through an operating company was critical, but now this was unavailable. Will marketing and manufacturing experience be more important in the AT&T executive of the future?
2. What should the company's policy be regarding employment security? The old AT&T was known for having a long-term career orientation among its employees. Should or could this be maintained in the new fast-changing, environment?
3. How should the organization reward risk-taking and competitiveness by employees?
4. What human resource systems will facilitate delegation of decision-making, open communication, and reduced administrative "red tape?"

Many of the details in the organization's new structure can be decided only after some basic human resource policies have been agreed upon. (The authors' predict the company will retain policies based on cultural values attached to a loyal, committed, long-service work force.)

Information for this Box was gathered through discussions with several AT&T executives and from "Cultural Transition at AT&T," W. Brook Tunstall, *Sloan Management Review,* Fall 1983. Copyright © 1983 by the Sloan Management Review Association. All rights reserved. More detail can be found in Richard J. Campbell and Joseph Moses, "Careers from an Organizational Perspective," in Douglas T. Hall and Associates, *Organizational Careers,* San Francisco: Jossey-Bass, 1986, in press.

Cornell (not his real name), executive vice-president, was a "fast tracker," a star in the system. He came from a "hard" background in systems and operations. He had gone to one of the most respected local universities. He was physically attractive, a good listener, bright, dynamic, and tough, when necessary. He could "read" people with great skill. He could diagnose and focus on the interests of his adversaries in negotiations and could generate solutions that would let everyone win.

Ability to Use Relational Power ▬

In addition to Cornell's personal attributes, one of his greatest strengths was his relationship to the chairman/chief executive officer, who was his mentor. The CEO sought his advice on many issues, and Cornell had good access to and support from the CEO when he needed it. Other executives in the bank would make comments like, "Talking to Don is as good as talking to (the CEO)."

Cornell was also well-connected with most other senior executives because of his long service with the bank. Although he was only in his mid-40s, he had started with the bank as a part-time high school employee, so he "grew up" with most of the key leaders in the organization. He was well liked, respected, and trusted.

Ability to Think Strategically ▬

Because of his close relationship with the CEO, Cornell had a clear sense of the corporate mission and strategy, probably a clearer sense than did many of his peers, which further enhanced his influence. Based on the corporate mission, he first developed a strategy for his department, which was to create a personal role and a human resource department which would help build the CEO's vision of the organization of the future.

Second, Cornell developed different substrategies for human resource activities at the three organizational levels described in Chapter Two. At the strategic level, his strategy was to influence the CEO and the top management team to adopt new human resource policies and to incorporate human resource considerations into their business plans. At the managerial level, the strategy was to design and implement modern human resource systems in critical areas like compensation, staffing, and performance management. This was done by assessing the needs of middle managers, designing systems to help them do their jobs better, and securing their participation in the development of the systems.

At the operational level, Cornell replaced many human resource staff members who had been "dumped" in his department either because they had failed in other departments (but no one had the courage to fire them) or because they were "good with people." Cornell recruited people with training in human resources as well as high-potential management trainees on developmental rotational assignments from more mainstream departments, such as commercial lending.

The key activity, however, was to develop the overall corporate strategy for human resources. Whereas many human resource executives fall into the seductive trap of focusing solely on management-level human resource systems (because they are so visible and show quick results), Cornell let his middle managers handle this activity.[5] He spent most of his time with the CEO and top management team going over and over the corporate human resource strategy as it related to strategies for business units, for other departments, and for the corporation as a whole.

Ability to Influence Top Management ▬▬ As part of his strategic definition of his own role as the senior human resource executive, Cornell determined that a major task for him would be to "educate" top management. Much of this was done informally, by injecting the human resource "message" in everyday discussions of business issues with the CEO and other top executives. He also used staffing changes, especially for senior jobs, as occasions to stress the need for a manager to have good skills in managing people (selection, development, etc.). He also made strategic use of outside consultants, not just to solve human resource problems, but also to work with key executives and create enthusiasm for human resource activities.

Cornell cultivated a role as counselor to the CEO. This often meant just being available to listen and to act as a sounding board, often on matters unrelated to human resources. These interactions, over a period of years, greatly enhanced the CEO's respect for and trust in Cornell.

Another way to influence was to involve top management in human resource issues. He created various committees of senior executives to develop human resource policies and select key managers. This was a way to "infiltrate" line management with human resource thinking.

A final method Cornell used to influence top management was to rotate fast-track trainees and managers through the human resource department. In this way, human resources came to be seen as a "plum" assignment, which increased the department's status. Also, over time, most of the key people in senior management had had an assignment in the human resource department, which socialized them to the human resource implications of various business activities.

Ability to Change the Culture ▬▬ The culture of an organization (its pivotal norms and values) permeates the thinking and behavior of all employees. Because he recognized that the traditional culture of the bank would be a barrier to necessary change, Cornell used a series of climate surveys to draw attention to the corporate culture and to the need for change. The survey results for each division and department were given to their respective managers, who were also given responsibility to make desired changes. Through this decentralized "soul searching" process, all managers became change agents. This activity also generated a need for more human resource specialists to act as internal consultants to line managers as they interpreted results and planned action.

The culture was also strongly affected by new staffing and socialization practices. More MBAs and BAs with specialized training were hired, which upgraded the technical skill levels of the work force. More planning went into job assignments, a director of internal placement was appointed, and the "new breed" of specialists changed the organization as they became more senior.

Ability to Change Information Systems

Ability to Change Information Systems ▬▬ At the managerial level, new information systems had a strong impact on the line organization. A new performance appraisal system gave the human resource department influence over a key resource: the administration of rewards. The climate surveys just described were a potent means of drawing attention, through data, to areas needing change. Publications, such as employee newsletters and periodic reports to employees, shareholders, and other stakeholders, became effective ways to promote top management's objectives. The internal placement function described earlier gave human resources control over job moves for professionals and managers. Human resources became a broker for managers seeking people and for people seeking positions, which put the human resource department in a key power position.

Finally, Cornell created a human resource information system. This computerized system provided easily accessible information about the work force, which was invaluable for activities such as top management succession planning, compensation changes, individual career planning, and business planning.

Ability to Incorporate Public Affairs

Ability to Incorporate Public Affairs ▬▬ As the need for the bank to communicate more effectively with the external environment increased, the human resource function was expanded to include public affairs (see Chapter Twenty, Employee Communications). By helping the corporation meet an important need, Cornell was able to further expand the influence of his department.

Ability to Make Strategic Use of Human Resource Activities

Ability to Make Strategic Use of Human Resource Activities ▬▬ As these different human resource activities were being developed, Cornell was very much aware of the need to use them strategically to enhance the future bargaining power of his department. His department's services, when they were offered, were given with the message that human resources was an integral part of running the business. This was accomplished, but not without some initial tension and resentment about the growing power of the human resource department. However, this reaction was counterbalanced by an awareness of the clear benefits which Cornell's department provided to the line organization.

All of these factors, combined with the corporate strategic planning process, resulted in a highly integrated human resource department. A summary of the steps leading to the integration of the human resource department with the line organization is shown in Exhibit 21.5.

EXHIBIT 21.5

REQUIREMENTS FOR INTEGRATING THE HUMAN RESOURCE DEPARTMENT WITH THE LINE ORGANIZATION

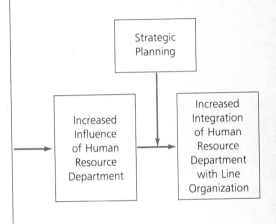

HUMAN RESOURCE DEPARTMENT
LEADERSHIP REQUIREMENTS

Ability to Use Personal Power of Human Resource Leader

Ability to Use Relational Power of Human Resource Leader
    With CEO
    With senior management team

Ability to Think Strategically
    Develop corporate human resource strategy
    Develop human resource strategies at managerial and
    operational levels

Ability to Influence Top Management
    "Educate" CEO and top team
    Impact on staffing
    Outside consultants
    Counselor to CEO
    Involve top management in key human resource issues
    Rotate fast-track managers through human resources

Ability to Change the Culture
    Survey program
    New staffing and socialization practices

Ability to Change Information Systems
    Performance appraisal
    Publications
    Internal placement function
    Human resource information system

Ability to Incorporate Public Affairs

Ability to Make Strategic Use of Human Resource
Department's Activities

Strategic Planning

Increased Influence of Human Resource Department

Increased Integration of Human Resource Department with Line Organization

CONCLUSION

The structure of the human resource function is critical to the effective delivery of its services. Two major obstacles to effectiveness in many organizations have been *inadequate power* and a *lack of integration with the line organization.* As we have seen, both of these issues can be managed in such a way that the human resource department moves toward a more central mission orientation.

At the same time, it is critical to carefully determine how centralized or decentralized the human resource function should be, while realizing that there is never a final "best" position to have on the centralization/decentralization question. From time to time, as business needs change, it might be useful to tighten human resources' connection to field units, while different conditions may demand stronger corporate ties. In general, the direction the line business units take should influence the direction of human resource services.

As we said earlier, human resource planning for the total organization is an activity that is more often preached than practiced. This discrepancy between words and action is even more pronounced when it comes to planning strategically for the structure of the human resource function. It is critical that those responsible for the human resource function have strategic management skills, with a primary focus on the top strategic level of the organization. The process of elevating the human resource function demands nothing more or less than outstanding organizational leadership.

KEY POINTS

▬ The way in which the human resource department is structured has a strong impact on how well integrated it will be with the line activities of the organization.

▬ Decisions about the structure of the human resource department must consider issues such as organizational size, centralization vs. decentralization, and emphasis on divisional vs. corporate human resource staffs. There are pros and cons to the different design alternatives, and there is no "best way" to structure the human resource department.

▬ Developing a human resource function which is integrated with the business units of the organization is an interactive process involving the corporate business strategy, strategies of the various business units, and the strategies of the different functional departments.

▬ Strategic planning and a range of influence methods are key factors in increasing the integration of the human resource department in the line organization. Strong leadership by senior human resource executives is required.

ISSUES FOR DISCUSSION

1. Discuss the changes at Prime Computer, based upon the strategic human resource planning concepts described in Chapter Two.

2. What are the advantages of a centralized human resource department? Of a decentralized department?

3. What is the matrix human resource structure? What would be the pros and cons of such a design for the human resource function?

4. What are some of the ways in which the integration of a human resource department with the line organization can be increased?

5. What have been your experiences in dealing with organizations' human resource departments? Describe and discuss one or two human resource departments you have known and the reasons why you think they were effective or ineffective.

6. Discuss the strategic leadership of Don Cornell. How would you feel about being a line manager working with him? How would you feel about being a human resource professional, with Cornell as your boss?

NOTES

1. The material about Prime Computer is based on an interview with P. O'Neill of that company.

2. C. C. Paulson, "The Matrix Structure in Personnel," unpublished manuscript, 1981.

3. L. Baird, I. Meshoulam, and G. DeGive, "Meshing Human Resources Planning with Strategic Business Planning: A Model Approach," *Personnel*, September–October 1983, *60* (5), p. 22.

4. D. T. Hall, "Human Resource Management," in M. H. Bazerman and R. J. Lewicki (eds.), *Negotiating In Organizations* (Beverly Hills, Calif.: Sage Publications, 1983), pp. 339–59.

5. D. T. Hall, "Human Resource Development and Organizational Effectiveness," in C. J. Fombrun, N. M. Tichy, and M. A. Devanna, *Strategic Human Resource Management* (New York: John Wiley and Sons, 1984), pp. 159–81. See especially pp. 176–80.

ANNOTATED BIBLIOGRAPHY

DEAL, T. E. and KENNEDY, A. A. *Managing Corporate Cultures*. Reading, Mass.: Addison-Wesley, 1982.

>   For more detail on how corporation culture and strategy shape the design of an organization, this book is a clear and practical guide. The authors examine different types of cultures (tough-guy, bet-your-company, process, and work hard/play hard), corporate heroes and myths, slogans that shape identity (e.g., IBM's "THINK" signs), and rituals that reinforce culture. The second half of the book deals with putting cultures into practice.

FOMBRUN, C. J., TICHY, N. M., and DEVANNA, M. A. *Strategic Human Resource Management*. New York: Wiley, 1984.

>   This is one of the most in-depth books available in its subject area. Major functions of human resources (e.g., rewards, staffing, development) are examined from a strategic point of view. For each function, a company case is presented for illustrative purposes.

GALBRAITH, J. *Organizational Design*. Reading, Mass.: Addison-Wesley, 1977.

>   This is one of the best books available on the general topic of organization structure and design. Galbraith sees design as a process of increasing the congruence

among five elements of the organization: structure, tasks, reward systems, people, and information technology. In addition to being a good integration of relevant theory and research, this text is also rich in case examples that bring the concepts to life.

Murray, V. V. "Organization and Administration of the Human Resources Management Function." In H. Jain (ed.), *Human Resources Management in Canada*. Toronto: Prentice-Hall, 1983.

This is an excellent description of the process and structure of the human resource department. It includes a history of the human resource field, analysis of personnel policies, organizing the human resource department, staffing for human resources, and managing the department in light of day-to-day political realities.

CHAPTER TWENTY-TWO

MANAGING THE HUMAN RESOURCE FUNCTION

From 1979 to 1984, Charles S. Arnold was the Director of Personnel Planning and Professional Employment of Monsanto Company and headed a corporate group of human resource professionals who serve as in-house consultants to line managers. Among the key services they provide are professional recruitment, in-company candidate searches, preparation of career management materials and workshops, internal deployment of surplus employees, outplacement, and development and maintenance of a computerized human resource data base. Arnold stresses the collaboration between the corporate human resource group and line managers. "Organizationally, the human resource planning function is composed of three layers: the corporate group, the operating company planners, and the human resource professionals at individual plants. Since each of these layers, with the exception of the corporate group, reports to line managers, the human resource activities are automatically tied to line management needs."

Arnold states that another key to the success of the group is the close link between business planning by Monsanto's top management and the group's human resource planning. "Line management coordinates the human resource plans with their business plans through a process we call management reviews," Arnold explains. "Every other year, the president conducts an in-depth review of each organization reporting to him, with the head of that organization. They first review the structure of the organization to determine how well it will meet its business needs over the next three to five years. They then review the performance of the incumbents of the top three layers, to decide what, if any, staffing changes will be needed to carry out the business plans. Finally, they review the potential candidates to succeed the incumbents, discuss their career needs, and determine their next most likely job assignment, all within the context of their long-range business needs. The data is kept current through a program of tracking progress against action plans." The human resource professionals serve as consultants during the reviews and then follow up with appropriate activities to meet staffing needs. This process is repeated by the operating company and plant groups so that all managerial and professional employees are reviewed.

Arnold feels the group has been very successful in providing service to the line organization. He comments, "Over a period of eighteen months, for example, the group was able to reduce the salaried work force by over 1800 without resorting to layoff, and with minimum adverse impact on employee morale. Monsanto totally reorganized the corporation in 1982, merging some companies and creating others, without any major disruption to operations. And, we were not forced to go outside the organization to staff any of our critical top management positions in our old line businesses. The exception was the new health care business for which we had no technical or management base.''

Monsanto line managers agree with Arnold's assessment and feel that the human resource professionals have done very well in meeting their needs. They measure the success in many ways, including the performance of new employees, the performance of recommended candidates for promotional jobs, the quality and availability of qualified candidates, organizational effectiveness in working together, the ''sense'' of steadily increasing competence and capability across the organization, and overall employee attitudes, morale, and motiviation. When asked how the Personnel Planning and Professional Employment group might meet their needs more effectively, Monsanto line managers noted that during periods of unusually heavy activity in other human resource areas (e.g., preparing salary increase budgets), the human resource professionals at the operating unit level had less time to spend recruiting new employees or filling job openings. The line managers suggested that the human resource staff be increased to handle the needs better during such peak periods.

There are two keys to the success of the corporate human resource group at Monsanto. First, it establishes a clear link between human resource activities and corporate goals through consultation with line managers about their problems and needs. This link is reinforced by a decentralized departmental structure (Chapter Twenty-One) that has operating company planners and plant human resource professionals reporting directly to line managers. Second, it produces results that line managers value and therefore maintains the group's credibility in the organization.*

*T*hroughout this text we have emphasized the role of human resource professionals in *meeting the needs* of the organization. For example, when new employees are needed in an organization, human resource professionals recruit and screen applicants, and when new knowledge and skills are required on the job, they design and conduct training programs. When new regulations concerning employees are instituted by federal, state, or local governments, human resource professionals see to the organization's compliance with the regulations. In meeting organizational needs, human resource professionals act as internal consultants, providing service and support to the line organization.

We have defined human resource management as the process of achieving an optimal fit between the individual, job, organization, and environment

---

*The authors wish to thank Mr. Charles S. Arnold for his assistance in preparing this material.

to enhance individual satisfaction and performance and organizational effectiveness. Given the importance of individual satisfaction and performance and organizational effectiveness, one might assume that today's organizations are continually striving to adopt sound human resource policies and practices to ensure their own survival and success. Certainly, one might assume that the vast majority of organizations are following the human resource practices advocated in this text. Unfortunately, these assumptions are not correct.

CURRENT HUMAN RESOURCE PRACTICES

In spite of significant advances in human resource management in the last three decades, the human resource policies and practices of many of today's organizations are unsophisticated and inadequate. For example, an extensive survey found in 1969 that only 40 percent of 899 organizations used job analysis,[1] and more recent research suggests little change.[2] This is especially disconcerting in view of the importance of a thorough understanding of the job for so many of the human resource functions covered in this text. Similarly, human resource planning is rare (Chapter Seven), and the ineffective interview is still one of the most common and trusted of all selection tools (Chapter Nine). In a recent comparison of human resource practices recommended in textbooks and those that are common in today's organizations, Jain and Murray concluded that very fundamental human resource functions, such as sophisticated selection procedures, demonstration of training effectiveness, and wage and salary administration, either exist on paper but are not practiced, or have not been adopted widely (Exhibit 22.1).[3] Other functions such as performance appraisal and employee participation have been tried and discarded by many organizations.

Why is there such a gap between recommended and actual human resource practices? Murray and Dimick have proposed two reasons why rational choices are not made in organizations to implement and support human resource practices that would appear to be in the organization's best interests.[4] One reason is the lack of clear evidence of the impact of human resource practices on employee performance. Does it really matter whether job descriptions are out of date? How do selection and training affect employee performance and the bottom line? This imprecise relationship between costs of practices and benefits to the organization makes it difficult for human resource professionals to convince line management to invest time and money in practices recommended in today's textbooks.

The second reason for apparently irrational choices made for human resource practices is the difficulty in determining *which* practices will maximize the chances for the organization's survival and success in today's complex environment. As the organization struggles for survival in an environment of government regulations, changing employees, and the changing work place (see Chapters Three–Five) it is difficult indeed to know which human resource practices to choose. For example, should an organization place more

EXHIBIT 22.1   IMPLEMENTATION OF HUMAN RESOURCE MANAGEMENT PRACTICES

Practice	"Non-Starters" Not widely adopted	"Fads" Often tried but usually discontinued	"Dead Letters" Exist on paper but not in practice
Job Analysis: Job descriptions for all jobs should be provided.	X		X
Selection and Placement: Employers should take full advantage of the whole range of sophisticated selection procedures available to ensure that the best people are hired.	X	X	
Training and Development: Training should be widespread and based on demonstrated needs, closely integrated into the work process, and validated for effectiveness.	X	X	
Performance Appraisal: Appraisals should be extensively used, should have trained raters, be concrete, separate feedback from judgments on salary increases and have top management support.		X	X
Wage and Salary Administration: Inter-job wage differentials should be based primarily in formal job evaluation systems which are fully communicated to employees.	X		X
Employee Participation: Employees should be involved in decisions affecting them to increase motivation.	X	X	X
Employee Relations Research: Organizations should maintain a continuous program of research to ascertain the effectiveness of the human resource function and test the validity of various policies.	X		

SOURCE: Adapted from "Why Human Resources Management Function Fails" by Jain and Murray, *California Management Review,* Summer 1984. Copyright © 1984 by the Regents of the University of California. Reprinted by permission of the Regents.

emphasis on recruiting and selection of college graduates to fill anticipated job openings, or should it train current employees and promote them from within to fill the openings? Should it spend the time and resources needed to comply with all EEOC requirements, or should it take short-cuts and play the odds of not being caught during a period of decreasing enforcement of government regulations? If the technology and jobs in its business are changing so rapidly, should an organization even try to keep written job descriptions up to date? In short, in complex times it is difficult to know which human resource policies and practices are in an organization's best interests.

Since the decision to invest time and money in certain practices is not entirely rational, what factors seem to be important in the decision-making process? Murray and Dimick note two, affordability and power. They conclude that, as funds become available, more time and money are spent on human resource practices. This is especially true of more sophisticated practices, such as validation of selection tools and studies of training effectiveness. These are likely to be considered luxuries except in good times when funds are available.

Power is a more complex determinant of human resource policies and practices. Power can reside outside the organization, in the form of strong pressure from government regulations or unions. These powerful influences are often the impetus for the design and implementation of human resource practices that may not have otherwise been considered affordable or necessary. For example, EEOC guidelines may require the validation of selection tools, or a union may negotiate for additional training or updating of job descriptions.

The other source of power is internal. Senior managers or key decision makers in the organization may favor certain human resource practices and authorize the expenditure of necessary funds. For example, a new vice-president with a preference for employee feedback may provide the impetus for a new performance appraisal system. Similarly, a highly respected human resource professional may convince the organization's senior management team that salaries must be raised to curtail turnover or make the organization competitive in recruiting.

THE NEED TO PROMOTE THE HUMAN RESOURCE FUNCTION

Throughout this text we stressed the responsibility that line managers and human resource professionals share in planning, designing, and carrying out effective human resource policies and practices. Although both parties are involved, the primary responsibility for human resource management rests with human resource professionals, so they must strongly promote policies and practices they feel are vital to the organizations they serve. In short, human resource management is an essential function that must be carefully managed. Human resource professionals need to cultivate and harness sources of power that enable them to influence key decision makers in the organization to commit funds to the human resource function. They cannot wait until good times when more sophisticated policies and practices are considered "affordable." They need to argue that sound human resource management is *vital to the organization's survival*, and that human resource management is especially important during bad times when the organization must make the most efficient use of all its resources—especially its people. The remainder of this chapter deals with how human resource professionals can gain power and influence in their organizations and manage the human resource function effectively.

Another way to establish the credibility of the human resource function and strengthen the role of the human resource professional is to demonstrate that enlightened policies and practices make a difference to the organization. The effectiveness of human resource practices must be clearly identified in terms of outright benefits (e.g., increased productivity following a training course) or cost avoidance (e.g., reduced turnover resulting from a career planning program). This will be discussed further in Chapter Twenty-Three.

HOW HUMAN RESOURCE MANAGEMENT EVOLVES

Success in managing the human resource function is certainly dependent on the organization's receptiveness to that function. Some organizations have a greater need than others for progressive human resource policies and practices. A new, small company, for example, needs only the most rudimentary activities like recruitment and selection of employees, on-the-job training, and administration of payroll and benefits, while older, larger organizations require additional human resource activities like formal training programs, performance appraisal, and career development.

Baird and Meshoulam have described five stages of development of human resource management which are quite useful to our discussion of how the human resource function can be managed.[5] As we outline each stage, we will focus on the person responsible for human resource management, his or her primary goals, and the involvement and reaction of line managers to human resource activities (see Exhibit 22.2). As Baird and Meshoulam point out, the nature of human resource management changes through the five stages. The focus of the first stage is primarily administrative, the middle stages shift toward the design and implementation of programs, and the later stages are concerned with planning and managing human resource activities to solve problems and meet organizational goals.

Stage I: Initiation

At the initial stage of development, characteristic of new and small organizations, human resource management consists of the most fundamental activities necessary to hire and pay employees and to maintain records for employee benefits and government reports. The work is largely administrative and is often done by a clerk or a human resource administrator. Line managers' involvement in policies and practices is minimal, consisting primarily of requests for new employees or salary increases, and they are indifferent to the human resource function except when crises arrive.

EVOLUTION OF HUMAN RESOURCE MANAGEMENT

EXHIBIT 22.2

Stage	Person Responsible	Primary Goals	Line Managers' Involvement	Line Managers' Reaction
I. Initiation	Clerk or human resource administrator	To provide administrative support for hiring and paying employees and maintaining benefits	Minimal	Indifference, except when crises arise
II. Functional Growth	Human resource specialists	To develop and implement programs in recruitment, selection, training, compensation, career development, etc.	Minimal	Confusion about the purpose of the programs and resistance to their implementation
III. Controlled Growth	Human resource specialists with extensive skills	To develop and implement specialized programs within budget constraints To justify expenditures for each program	Minimal; they may provide evaluations of program effectiveness	Confusion about the purpose of the programs and frustration with their sophistication
IV. Functional Integration	Human resource professionals headed by a generalist	To design and implement programs that solve organizational problems	They provide input to program design and assist in implementation	Active support
V. Full Partnership	Human resource professionals headed by a generalist	To design and implement programs that are integrated with organizational goals	They consult with human resource professionals to set goals and strategies	Incorporation of human resource activities into their jobs

SOURCE: Adapted from L. Baird and I. Meshoulam," The HRS Matrix: Managing the Human Resource Function Strategically," *Human Resource Planning*, 1984, 7 (1), pp. 1–21. Reprinted by permission of Human Resource Planning Society.

Stage II: Functional Growth

As organizations grow, human resource specialists are hired to spearhead various functions such as employment, training, compensation and benefits, labor relations, and health and safety. The human resource staff is likely to be centralized as a corporate department (Chapter Twenty-One) that issues formal policies and programs created by specialists concentrating in their own area of expertise. These specialized policies and programs are often poorly integrated and can lead to wasted time and unnecessary paperwork by line managers. For example, managers may be asked by the compensation specialists to complete a questionnaire about job duties of their subordinates for a revision of the organization's job evaluation system (Chapter Eighteen) only six weeks after they complete a similar questionnaire for the training staff's annual training needs analysis. Since human resource specialists seldom consult line managers before developing new policies and programs, managers often respond with confusion and resentment when asked to implement them.

Stage III: Controlled Growth

As the organization continues to grow, specialized human resource programs also grow and the organization begins to assess their effectiveness. Programs that contribute to organizational goals are continued, while others are curtailed. Increasingly expert human resource specialists compete for funding for their programs and may collect evaluations and enlist support from line managers. Such competition can lead to poorly integrated, sophisticated programs that line managers neither understand nor want. Some job evaluation systems described in Chapter Eighteen are examples of complex, technically advanced human resource programs that succeed only in confusing and alienating managers and employees.

Stage IV: Functional Integration

At this stage the entire focus of human resource management changes to diagnosing and solving organizational problems with appropriate human resource programs. The organization's human resource department is likely to be headed by a generalist who integrates all human resource functions and reports directly to the chief executive officer. (Department heads in stages II and III typically report to a vice-president of administration and have considerably less stature and influence.) Human resource professionals confer regularly with line managers to identify problems and then design an integrated package of programs to solve the problems. For example, in the financial controls department of Confederated, Inc. (Chapter One), the causes of employee turnover were identified and new programs in job definition, performance appraisal, training, and job rotation were implemented to reduce turnover. Since line managers are involved in diagnosing the problems and implementing the solutions, they actively support the activities of human resource professionals.

Stage V: Full Partnership

In its most advanced stage of evolution human resource management is integrated with other major functions of the organization (e.g., marketing, finance, production, and sales). Plans for human resource policies and programs are linked with the strategic planning for the entire organization, and the responsibility to implement the policies and programs rests as much with line managers as with human resource professionals. The group Charles Arnold headed at Monsanto operates at this stage through their involvement in top management's business planning and their close collaboration with line managers in human resource activities like recruitment, career development, and placement of current employees. The strategic human resource planning that occurs at this stage to meet the organization's needs for an optimal fit between employees and jobs (see Chapters Two, Seven, and Eleven) requires close collaboration between the organization's chief executive officer and a human resource executive who has earned the respect of line managers throughout the organization.

The difference between stages IV and V is subtle but real; in stage IV the primary goal is to solve problems with integrated human resource policies and programs, while in stage V the goal is to *avoid* problems by planning and implementing integrated human resource policies and programs. Human resource practitioners who operate at stage IV sometimes complain that they spend too much of their time "fighting fires." In the extreme case, they simply move from crisis to crisis, dealing primarily with symptoms rather than with the underlying causes of problems.

Chris Argyris has argued that human resource professionals encourage this *reactive* mode by failing to confront line managers with the futility of continually treating symptoms.[6] For example, suppose an attitude survey shows that employees are very dissatisfied with their organization's performance appraisal system. They complain that their managers evaluate performance unfairly and those who take the time to conduct appraisal interviews provide little or no useful feedback. Suppose also that the appraisal system is used primarily to justify salary increases, consists of trait rating scales, and receives minimal support from top management (see Chapter Fifteen). A human resource professional who accepts top management's suggestion to design a one-day course to train managers in how to do performance appraisals is simply treating the symptom and reinforcing a reactive style of human resource management. Instead, he or she should point out the flaws in the entire appraisal system and argue that a training course will accomplish nothing. If senior managers want to change employee attitudes toward performance appraisal, they must first turn their attention to the appraisal system. Such a confrontation is risky, but it is necessary for human resource professionals to gain credibility in their organizations and reach the stage of full partnership with line managers. And if such a confrontation does *not* take place, management will eventually recognize the flaws in the appraisal system and place the blame for the failure directly on the human resource professional.

Although the stage of human resource management in a particular organization is determined by its size, complexity, and age, stages IV and V are very desirable for any organization. It is especially important for organizations in stages II and III to continue their evolution through the efforts of enlightened managers and progressive human resource professionals.

As we noted earlier, the primary orientation of stages II and III is to develop increasingly sophisticated human resource programs, while the orientation of stages IV and V is to solve or avoid organizational problems with appropriate human resource programs. A key to an organization's evolution to stages IV and V is for human resource professionals to consult actively with line managers *before* developing programs. Before designing training programs, for example, human resource professionals should learn what kind of training line managers feel they need. (See the analysis of training needs in Chapter Twelve). Similarly, a performance appraisal system or a job evaluation system should be viewed as a management tool and should be developed on the basis of line managers' needs and goals.

Another key to an organization's evolution to stages IV and V is for the senior human resource professional to report directly to the chief executive officer and to be an active member of the top management team of the organization (Chapter Twenty-One). This not only strengthens the credibility of the human resource function but also enables the human resource executive to participate in strategic planning sessions and assist in strategic human resource planning (Chapter Two) that will help the organization link human resource programs with organizational goals.

TYPES OF POWER

It is clear that human resource professionals must gain power and influence in their organizations to manage the human resource function more effectively. But they have no direct authority over line managers and executives, with whom they need to collaborate to design and implement policies and programs, or over budget officers, from whom they seek funds. They have no formal power to order anyone in the organization to fund, plan, or implement human resource policies and programs. They must therefore gain other types of power and influence.

Coercive Power

coercive power

One major type of power and influence wielded by human resource professionals is **coercive power,** *the ability of a person to administer punishment to others who do not comply with his or her requests or orders.* As Exhibit 22.3 shows, the person with coercive power usually occupies an important position in the organization and issues orders with the threat of punishment for noncompliance. The person being influenced complies to avoid punishment and may resent being forced to do so.

EXHIBIT 22.3

TYPES OF POWER AVAILABLE TO HUMAN RESOURCE PROFESSIONALS

	Person Exerting Influence		Person Being Influenced		
Type of Power	Basis of Power	How Power Is Used	Characteristic	Need	Effect of Use of Power
Coercive	Control over penalties (reprimands, legal action against the organization)	Gives orders, coupled with threat of punishment	Occupies less powerful position in the organization	Wants to avoid punishment	Complies to avoid punishment but may feel resentment or lose self-esteem
Expert	Expertise, special training and experience	Investigates need for expertise and gives information and advice to others	Lacks expertise	Requires assistance in reaching goals	Understands new options and the consequences of choosing each. Chooses the best option to reach goals
Referent	Perceived as successful and influential	States own opinions and preferences	Perceived as less successful and influential than the other person	Wishes to be similar to, or approved by, the other person	Complies to gain approval from or appear similar to the other person

SOURCE: Adapted from "The Locus and Basis of Influence on Organizational Decisions," by Martin Patchen, *Organizational Behavior and Human Performance*, 1974, *11*, p. 197. Reprinted by permission of Academic Press, Inc. and the author.

Since they lack formal authority, human resource professionals have no absolute claim to coercive power; they must derive it from more powerful sources inside or outside the organization. External sources of coercive power are government legislation, unions, and special interest groups. Internal sources might be senior line managers in the organization who set policies regarding human resource management. In essence, the human resource professional becomes the agent of these sources of power and influences others in the organization through the threat of punishment if they fail to comply.

For example, human resource professionals frequently carry out directives from senior management. When a company president adopts a stance of "promotion from within," human resource professionals acquire the authority to post all job openings and interview current employees before seeking applicants from outside the organization (Chapter Eight), even if this new procedure slows the selection process and annoys line managers. Similarly, a new career development program (Chapter Fourteen) initiated primarily because of the president's wishes might involve extensive discussion of employees' career plans and potential. Human resource professionals who manage such a program would have the authority to set meetings and require the employees' managers to participate in the discussions.

The primary source of human resource professionals' coercive power, however, lies outside the organization. Human resource management grew significantly in stature during the 1960s and 1970s because of increased government regulations and the political activism of union and citizen groups (Chapter Five). The Civil Rights Act of 1964 and subsequent legislation gave human resource professionals unparalleled power to scrutinize organizations' selection processes, validate selection tools, set affirmative action goals, and expand recruiting and training efforts for women and minorities (Chapters Eight and Nine). Similarly, political activity against the "military-industrial complex" and in favor of personal growth and openness put immense pressure on organizations and spawned many programs that emphasized their social responsibility, such as career development, opportunities for the disadvantaged, and pre-retirement counseling. Human resource professionals often initiated and enforced these programs, and some attained the status of "new corporate heroes"[7] with this kind of power and influence.

But coercive power is neither permanent nor especially popular. As major decision makers come and go, human resource professionals gain and lose power and support for their policies and practices. As governments, unions, and societal concerns change, the base of coercive power erodes.

Even more serious is the low popularity of human resource professionals with coercive power. They gain a reputation for their emphasis on control. Line managers may perceive entirely legitimate practices as unnecessary paperwork and delays that interfere with their effectiveness. This perception is particularly likely when the practices are initiated through coercion.

As we noted in Chapter One, human resource professionals perform four functions for the organization—*policy initiation and formulation, advice, service,* and *control.* A degree of control is certainly necessary to ensure that employees are treated uniformly throughout the organization. Imagine the chaos if each manager in an organization were allowed to set salaries for his or her employees. Cries of politics, favoritism, and unfairness would quickly arise. To prevent this chaos, human resource professionals establish a salary system of job grades and pay ranges to ensure that employees are paid fairly and equitably (Chapter Eighteen). A host of similarly uniform policies and practices are established and administered by human resource professionals to govern the selection, training, performance appraisal, and career development of the organization's employees. These controls are just as vital to the organization's success as are the financial, operational, and quality controls that govern the way the organization conducts its business.

But controls are almost always instituted through coercive power. Therefore, human resource professionals who operate primarily on the basis of coercive power soon gain a reputation for control only, and the service, advice, and policies they provide to the organization go unnoticed.

Expert Power

The second major type of power and influence exercised by human resource professionals is **expert power,** *the ability of one person to influence others because of special knowledge or skills.* It is based entirely on the relationship between two parties in which one has a need and the other has the expertise to meet that need (Exhibit 22.3). Unlike coercive power, which is *imposed,* expert power *evolves* from continuing interaction between two parties. The interaction is triggered by a need.

expert power

Human resource professionals have many opportunities to use expert power to perform the other three functions mentioned above. When company presidents turn to them for guidance on how to conform to new legislation on affirmative action, employee pensions, or health and safety, human resource professionals draw upon their knowledge of the legislation and their familiarity with the organization to initiate and formulate appropriate human resource policies. Similarly, line managers request service in the form of new training courses or assistance in placing the right people in the right jobs. For example, Monsanto line managers called upon Charles Arnold to recruit job applicants and transfer employees within the organization. Finally, human resource professionals give advice to line managers who are struggling with problems such as high employee turnover or low morale (see the case of Peter Brown in Chapter One). An excellent strategy for building expert power is to win acceptance for new programs by presenting a proposal for a pilot project and following it up with careful evaluation (Chapter Twenty-Three).

Referent Power

A third type of power and influence available to human resource professionals is **referent power,** *the ability of one person to influence others because they respect and admire him or her* (Exhibit 22.3). It is based on attractive personal characteristics (e.g., charisma) or on the person's association with other powerful people (e.g., a close relationship with the president of the firm). For example, a new vice-president of human resources who is hired by and reports to the CEO or who is transferred to the human resource department after having managed a key operating department for ten years (see Box 2.2 in Chapter Two) probably has referent power. Similarly, the personal and relational power which Don Cornell brought to the human resource department of the bank discussed in Chapter Twenty-One both fall under the category of referent power. People with referent power quickly bring credibility and influence to the human resource function in an organization.

referent power

To establish and exercise expert and referent power, human resource professionals meet the needs of the organization for productive and satisfied employees. In a very real sense, the organization is the client and the human resource professional is the consultant. To act as internal consultants, human resource professionals must demonstrate expertise to line managers and gain their trust. It is in this role that they draw attention to the service, advice, and policies they provide. Box 22.1 contains an interview with Bob Ripston, vice-president of human resource management at Ingersoll-Rand. Bob uses the term "counselor" to refer to his role as an internal consultant. Box 22.2 includes some comments from a line manager of an operating division of Ingersoll-Rand who recently approached Bob for help on work-related and personal problems. The line manager's comments clearly reflect his level of trust in Bob and his respect for Bob's expertise.

HUMAN RESOURCE PROFESSIONALS AS INTERNAL CONSULTANTS

To manage the human resource function most effectively, human resource professionals must use their expert and referent power to serve as internal consultants to line managers throughout the organization. The internal consulting process outlined in Exhibit 22.4, which is also called organization development, is possible in all five stages of development of human resource management, but it is most common in stages IV and V. Many large, progressive organizations include organization development professionals in their human resource departments.

Recognition of Symptoms

The process begins with the recognition of symptoms that suggest a poor fit between the individual, job, and organization. Symptoms can take a wide variety of forms and may appear at the individual, departmental, or organizational level. For example, the attendance of a single employee may drop, or last year's ten new recruits may be rated low on their first annual performance appraisals. Other symptoms may be less tangible, such as a reduction in group morale or an increase in the tension between two departments that work together closely. Any of these symptoms suggests that something is wrong.

Of course, many symptoms are simply ignored or accepted as inevitable, and with some justification. It is clearly impossible for every employee to reach high levels of performance and satisfaction at work. But when the symptoms reach a certain level of severity, they are recognized, either by a line manager or a human resource professional, as an indication of a poor fit between employees, jobs, and the organization. At this point the symptoms suggest a problem that must be addressed and solved.

In many instances supervisors or managers who interact closely with the employees involved will be the first, and sometimes the only, people to rec-

THE ROLE OF HUMAN RESOURCE COUNSELOR

BOX 22.1

Bob Ripston, Vice-President of Human Resource Management at Ingersoll-Rand, spends about one third of his time helping operating managers deal with work-related and personal problems. "It's good for the company to have someone in the organization who functions as a counselor," Ripston explains. "This is particularly important for the top people. As they move up in the ranks, there are fewer and fewer people they can talk to. I become an outlet for both business and personal matters. They need someone they can trust. Recently, a group president called me because his boss told him he had to lay off a certain number of people. He was irate. I knew that he had had a heart attack last year. Basically, I told him to calm down and not have another heart attack. Just talking seemed to help."

Ripston emphasizes the importance of building trust by getting to know people and sometimes sharing his own problems with them to help them open up to him. He also notes that it's essential to suggest viable alternatives and provide information that the person can use.

"Confidentiality is an issue," Ripston says. "I always tell people I will keep their confidence as long as what they're doing is not illegal or unethical. If seven employees come to me about a particular matter and I detect a trend, I will pass the information on without identifying the people. When someone talks with me about his or her career, I know there is a possibility of losing that person. So I might use this information by thinking about what we can do to keep him or her."

Part of Ripston's role is to be a resource person. Depending on the nature of the problem, he refers employees to lawyers, religious people, or psychologists. He sometimes simply sends an employee to a seminar. He also tries to help younger members of his department develop counseling skills by having them watch and participate. He refers some problems to his junior staff members.

Ripston says, "My approach is direct. I readily share my observation about a person with the person. That's how I gain credibility. I am direct but supportive. I always look for positives; everyone has strengths and weaknesses. I have to be aware of the impact of my words on people. I also see myself as a sounding board. Being a good listener is important. I freely give advice and ideas, as well."

Ripston notes that serving as a counselor is sometimes an emotional burden, and knowing about company plans such as layoffs is particularly hard. But he stresses the importance of this part of his job: "The role of counselor in the organization has to be earned. It is informal. Every organization needs such a person. If you don't have credibility in this role, you won't be brought into key problems in the organization. Unless you're approachable, you won't be involved. If I left the company, it would be this role as counselor that would be missed the most, although it is not formally recognized at all."

The authors wish to thank Mr. Robert Ripston for his assistance in preparing this material.

A LINE MANAGER'S USE OF THE COUNSELING FUNCTION

BOX 22.2

A vice-president of Ingersoll-Rand has called upon Bob Ripston for help many times. He views Bob as an excellent resource on both work-related and personal matters.

"We are in a huge company," the vice-president explains. "There is nobody on my level or above to talk to, or to act as a sounding board for my ideas. I turn to Bob to get objective opinions."

The vice-president cites an example of the previous year when business conditions forced the company to lay off many employees. He recalls, "The pressure came down from above to cut back on staff in the form of edicts from headquarters. Most of us had not seen the downtrend coming, and I was very upset. I saw layoffs as a severe threat to my area of the company. I called Bob, and he calmed me down by explaining that the whole company was cutting back. He acted as a filter for me to get the chairman's and my boss's thoughts into perspective.

"Bob's staff has been very helpful to me. They have expertise in areas where my people don't. His people know the laws of the land. He has a group of very skilled people, including a lawyer. From a strategic standpoint they are a great help. During the cutbacks, I was concerned about losing some of our most valuable department managers. We had to cut from 600 down to 120 people in one plant. Bob suggested ways to deal with bad press and the financial community. He helped me broaden my perspective and establish a strategy to deal with the problem. He was particularly helpful recently when I had to deliver a talk to some of my younger employees. My message was 'Hang in there,' but Bob helped me frame the message positively."

When asked about confidentiality in his dealings with Bob Ripston, the vice-president comments, "We just have an understanding. One major aspect of his job is to filter ideas into the chairman's office. Top management needs to know what people are thinking. Bob filters in this information without using names. He keeps up a two-way communication—relaying the chairman's thoughts to group officers and division managers. His function enhances communication. We all need someone in the company we can talk to and go to for help. When we need to get things off our chest, Bob serves as a pressure valve. When we need help with employee problems, Bob provides the necessary expertise to solve the problems."

Speaking about how his relationship with Bob Ripston developed, the vice-president explains, "Our relationship began when I first confided in Bob about a personnel problem. He handled the problem well, and our relationship began to grow. In large organizations, managers rely on people who have been helpful to them. I'm pleased that my division and department managers now also turn to members of Bob's staff to nip problems in the bud. I like to have our problems solved at the lowest level possible, so I am pleased when my people use his people without consulting me."

The authors wish to thank Mr. Robert Ripston for his assistance in preparing this material.

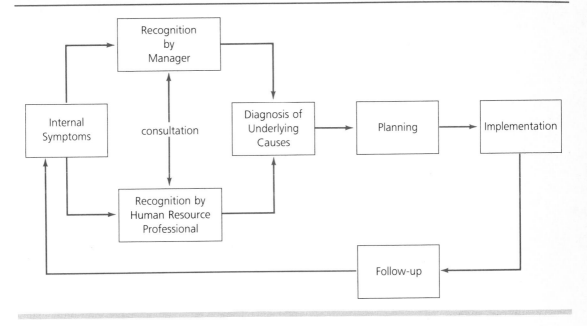

ognize the symptoms as indicative of an underlying problem. They must either alert the organization's human resource professional or deal with the problem alone. For example, the department head may be the only person to notice a drop in department morale or the failure of several employees to reach standard levels of performance in their first three months on the job. Other symptoms, such as increased turnover or a rise in employee discipline cases, are likely to come to the attention of human resource professionals because of their involvement in these matters.

Consultation

After a line manager or a human resource professional has recognized the symptoms, they must collaborate to identify the underlying causes of the symptoms and establish a plan to address the causes. The quality of the collaboration between the two parties is strongly related to the expert and referent power of the human resource professional and the level of trust he or she has earned in the organization. Regardless of which party is the first to recognize the symptoms, there is a degree of risk when one approaches the other.

A human resource professional may detect symptoms and decide to approach the manager of the organizational unit in which they have appeared. Suppose, for example, that department turnover has doubled and formal complaints about the department head have also increased. The human resource professional must approach the department head to discuss potential causes of the turnover very carefully, for the department head may be one of the causes. To initiate this type of discussion in a direct and straightforward manner, human resource professionals must have established a reputation for providing good service to line managers throughout the organization. They must be perceived as experts.

Line managers who have recognized symptoms in their own organizational units may also contact human resource professionals and ask for help. Suppose the president of a small, rapidly growing company detects reduced morale and increased tension within the company's senior management team. How likely is it that the president will confide in the company's senior human resource professional and ask for help to identify the causes of these symptoms? There is a real risk that any manager takes in admitting to people problems in his or her group. Can the human resource professional be trusted with this information? Does he or she have the expertise to deal with the problems effectively? Again, the answers to these questions depend on the perceived competence and trustworthiness of the human resource professional.

Diagnosis of Underlying Causes

To avoid the mistake of treating symptoms rather than causes, line managers and human resource professionals must study the employees, jobs, organization, and environment to identify potential causes of the symptoms. Collaboration is helpful because of the manager's familiarity with his or her employees and their jobs and the human resource professional's neutral status and broader perspective. Human resource professionals also have the skill to interview employees and draw out their opinions and suggestions. For example, careful diagnosis showed that the increases in turnover and complaints about the department head were caused by unchallenging jobs and the manager's reluctance to delegate demanding work to employees. The reduced morale and increased tension within the company's senior management team were traced to unclear company goals, poorly defined job responsibilities of each manager, and salaries that had fallen beneath market values. To make lasting improvements in either situation, the line managers and human resource professionals must change those underlying causes.

Planning

After uncovering causes, line managers and human resource professionals must prepare a comprehensive and well-integrated plan to solve the problem. In organizatons where human resource management has evolved to stage V, such planning occurs periodically and many potential problems can be anticipated and avoided. In organizations in earlier stages of development, special care is needed to identify a number of potential causes of the problem and to develop a comprehensive plan. For example, several causes of the low morale and poor performance among accountants of the financial controls department in Confederated, Inc., were identified (Chapter One), but not all of the causes could be addressed immediately. A two-year plan to increase morale and reduce turnover began with the preparation of new job descriptions, work procedures, and departmental goals. Only after this preliminary work had been completed was it possible to design orientation and training programs, a performance appraisal system, and a job rotation program.

Implementation

The time for action comes only after symptoms have been carefully examined, potential causes have been identified, and a plan for change has been established. The goal is not only to eliminate the original symptoms, but also to prevent their recurrence. As an internal consultant, the human resource professional works closely with line managers and involves them as much as possible in making the planned changes. Under the guidance of the human resource professional, they might update job descriptions, design the content of a training program, or revise recruiting and selection standards.

Follow-Up

Finally, the organizational unit should be monitored over a period of time to ensure that the symptoms are reduced. Measures of learning and performance before and after training (Chapter Twelve) or validation of new selection standards (Chapter Nine) are examples of follow-up to demonstrate the effectiveness of a human resource program or practice. Note in Exhibit 22.4 that this step leads back to the beginning of the internal consulting process. As the effectiveness of various human resource programs and practices is examined, new symptoms may be detected that may also require further study. Consequently, once the internal consulting process has been established in an organization, it tends to repeat itself.

ACCREDITATION OF HUMAN RESOURCE PROFESSIONALS

Throughout this chapter we have stressed the need for human resource professionals to use their expertise and earn the respect and confidence of line managers. In 1975 human resource professionals took a major step toward furthering the acceptance of human resource management as a profession by establishing a voluntary certification program administered by the Personnel Accreditation Institute. Major objectives of the certification program were to specify a common body of knowledge required for successful practice, to enhance public recognition for professional accomplishment, to maintain and improve senior practitioners' competence, and to assist employers by identifying qualified human resource professionals.

The certification program began with extensive research to identify a body of knowledge common to human resource professionals, which formed the basis for accreditation examinations given twice a year in more than fifty American cities. Once accredited, professionals must spend sixty hours every three years updating their knowledge through taking courses, teaching, doing research, or writing articles or books. Currently three different kinds of accreditation are given: Professional in Human Resources Management, Senior Professional in Human Resources Management—specialist, and Senior Professional in Human Resources Management—generalist. Each designation has an examination and experience requirement. The generalist designation is given to those who perform in at least three functional areas, while the specialist is granted to those who concentrate in one area. The six functional areas recognized by the Personnel Accreditation Institute are: employment, placement, and personnel planning; compensation and benefits; training and development; employee and labor relations; health, safety, and security; and personnel research.

To date, the response to this accreditation program has been mixed. By 1983, only 5000 human resource professionals had been accredited and 1000 college students planning to enter the profession had also taken the exams.[8] Of the 380,000 professionals practicing in 1983, therefore, only 1.3 percent have been accredited.[9] A recent survey of members of the American Society for Personnel Administration showed that the Personnel Accreditation Institute has been marginally successful in meeting its original objectives.[10] The accreditation program has successfully specified a common body of knowledge required for successful practice and provided guidance to students and young practitioners, although senior practitioners have shown little interest in the exams. The main weakness of the accreditation program is that senior line managers and executives are largely unaware of the program and therefore do not consider accreditation when selecting human resource professionals.

On balance, accreditation has been a useful step to enhance the stature and credibility of human resource professionals. To strengthen the accreditation program's impact, more human resource professionals must become accredited and a public relations campaign must be initiated to make more line managers and executives aware of accreditation. These developments will add to the expert power of human resource professionals and enable them to manage the human resource function more effectively.

KEY POINTS

- Unsophisticated and inadequate human resource practices are common in many organizations because human resource professionals lack the power and influence to convince senior management to invest sufficient time and money in recommended practices.

- To manage the human resource function effectively, human resource professionals must gain coercive power, which is transient and unpopular, or expert and referent power, which evolves from the respect and confidence of line managers.

■ As human resource management evolves in organizations, it passes through five stages. The focus of the early stages is on developing programs and practices whose value is often unclear to line managers, while in the later stages the focus is on consulting with line managers to help them solve or avoid problems with appropriate programs and practices.

■ To strengthen human resource management in their organizations, human resource professionals need to act as internal consultants who confer with line managers to uncover the underlying causes of organizational problems and design and implement solutions.

■ An accreditation program initiated in 1975 to certify human resource professionals has achieved mixed results. Although it has defined a body of knowledge required for successful practice that guides students and beginning practitioners, the program has not yet gained wide recognition from experienced human resource professionals or line managers.

ISSUES FOR DISCUSSION

1. Suppose that you accepted the job of director of management development and training in a human resource department notorious for its use of coercive power. What steps would you take to initiate training programs that line managers would eagerly attend?

2. Picture yourself in a large organization with a human resource department in stage III of evolution. What kinds of human resource programs would be common in the organization, and how would the typical line manager react to them? As a senior line manager, how would you try to speed the department's evolution to stage IV or V?

3. As the senior human resource professional in a rapidly growing company, you realize that the declining productivity and employee morale and increasing turnover in the production department have been caused primarily by the department head's reluctance to plan, delegate, and communicate with his staff. How would you approach the head of production to try to solve this problem?

4. Summarize the objectives of the certification program of the Personnel Accreditation Institute and the response of human resource practitioners to the program. What must be done to gain the program wider recognition among human resource professionals and line managers?

5. Suppose you were a member of a committee of line managers formed to select a new vice-president of human resources for your company. What would you look for in each applicant's personal style and professional approach? What type of applicant would you favor?

NOTES

1. J. J. Jones, Jr. and T. A. De Cotiis, "Job Analysis: National Survey Findings," *Personnel Journal*, 1969, 48, pp. 805–09.

2. H. Jain and V. V. Murray, "Why the Human Resources Management Function Fails," *California Management Review*, Summer 1984, 26, pp. 95–110.

3. Ibid.

4. V. V. Murray and D. E. Dimick, "Contextual Influences on Personnel Policies and Programs: An Explanatory Model," *Academy of Management Review*, 1978, 3, pp. 750–61.

5. L. Baird and I. Meshoulam, "The HRS Matrix: Managing the Human Resource Function Strategically," *Human Resource Planning*, 1984, 7 (1), pp. 1–21.

6. C. Argyris, "Reinforcing Organizational Defensive Routines: An Unintended Human Resources Activity," unpublished manuscript, Harvard University, Graduate School of Education, 1985.

7. H. E. Meyer, "Personnel Directors Are the New Corporate Heroes," *Fortune*, February 1976, pp. 84–89.

8. E. H. Burack and J. R. Wasdovich, "The Personnel Accreditation Institute (PAI): A Status Report," *Personnel/Human Resources Division News*, Academy of Management, March 1983, 6 (2).

9. G. A. Bayley, J. D. Jackson, and J. G. Johnston, "Accreditation: A Survey to Assess the PAI Program," *Personnel Journal*, July 1984, 63, pp. 58–62.

10. Ibid.

ANNOTATED BIBLIOGRAPHY

BAIRD, L. and MESHOULAM, I. "The HRS Matrix: Managing the Human Resource Function Strategically," *Human Resource Planning*, 1984, 7 (1), pp. 1–21.

Based on a study of twenty corporations, this excellent article stresses the need to manage human resources strategically by linking human resource management to business needs. The authors present five stages of development of human resource management (described in this chapter) and discuss how organizations move through the stages. They also analyze each stage in terms of several factors, including line managers' involvement in implementing human resource programs and human resource professionals' degree of skill, to identifying the gaps between an organization's current and desired level of sophistication in human resource management. This article presents excellent practical guidance for managing the human resource function.

BEER, M. *Organization Change and Development: A Systems View.* Santa Monica, Calif.: Goodyear, 1980.

This book provides sound guidance to the human resource professional who seeks the role of internal consultant. In conceptualizing the organization as a complex system, Chapter Two underscores the need to understand multiple causes of organizational problems, and Chapter Three presents various ways in which organizations can be changed. Also useful are Chapter Six, which introduces several methods of collecting information to diagnose the underlying causes of problems, and Chapter Seven, which deals with planning and managing change.

Personnel Accreditation Institute (P.O. Box 19648, Alexandria, Va. 22320). *Accreditation for Personnel and Human Resource Professionals, undated.*

The booklet describes the three types of accreditation (Basic, Senior Specialist, and Senior Generalist) and the educational and experience requirements for each. It also outlines the procedures and costs for accreditation, describes the comprehensive written examination, and lists testing centers. It provides excellent guidance for students and practitioners interested in becoming accredited.

CHAPTER TWENTY-THREE

EVALUATING THE HUMAN RESOURCE FUNCTION

Consolidated, Inc., has been deeply embroiled in its annual budget process for several weeks, and the senior management team has just convened a meeting to make final decisions. Preparation for this meeting has been especially thorough this year since stiff competition and poor economic conditions have caused Consolidated's revenues to drop 20 percent in the past twelve months, and all departments have been asked to cut expenditures. The vice-presidents of research and development, production, marketing/advertising, sales, and administration have submitted an impressive array of data to document their budget requests for the next fiscal year.

Department managers reporting to the vice-presidents are also in attendance, and the advertising manager has just finished her presentation projecting that more than a 10 percent reduction in the advertising budget will seriously threaten Consolidated's position in the market and further reduce sales volume. She used graphs to demonstrate a close relationship between advertising and sales increases in the past five years as a basis for her projections.

"Susan, everybody in this room is aware of your department's contribution to our growth in market share," comments Consolidated's president, J. B. Moran, "but can't we reduce our television advertising?"

"No, J. B., that's the backbone of our advertising campaign," interjects the vice-president of marketing/advertising.

"Those TV spots attracted three major new customers," adds the vice-president of sales. "I know they're expensive, but I must advise against dropping them."

After little additional discussion, the proposed advertising budget is approved.

Next, Ben Schultz, the manager of human resources, begins his presentation. He and his boss, the vice-president of administration, have struggled to pare down their proposal to the bare essentials, having postponed the revision of the company's performance appraisal system and having eliminated the budget for management development seminars given outside the company. They know the three-week middle-management training program, which they initiated three years ago, is the most expensive item left in their budget and will come under attack. Ben designed the program, consisting of *three one-week training sessions in which industry experts teach various aspects of management like planning, staffing, leadership, motivation, and delegation. He has prepared a chart of training evaluations and testimonials from the seventy-five managers who have completed the program.*

As usual, J. B. Moran leads the charge. "Ben, I know you have worked hard to keep your budget under control, but I'm afraid we're going to have to drop middle-management training next year. It not only costs a great deal to run, but it takes valuable managers off the job for three weeks, and we need everybody working at top capacity to survive this slowdown."

"But our program helps them manage better," Ben counters. "You know how high the training evaluations have been."

The vice-presidents of production and research and development agree that the training has been well received but add that they can't spare any managers right now anyway.

"Look, I've already dropped plans to revise the performance appraisal system, and you all know how unpopular it is," Ben interrupts. "If we drop all external training and the middle-management programs, too, morale within the supervisory ranks will surely drop."

In a half hour of heated discussion, the management team acknowledges that human resource programs are good for employee performance and morale, but concludes that the programs must be curtailed during the critical next year. Ben Schultz's budget is reduced by 50 percent.

L ike Ben Schultz, many human resource professionals have viewed their contribution as "intangible" (e.g., improved job satisfaction and greater opportunity for career development) and have failed to measure the value of human resource activities in *dollars*, the language that business people understand and respect. As a result, very fundamental human resource programs and practices, such as job analysis, evaluation of training effectiveness, and the use of sophisticated selection tools, are non-existent in many organizations (Chapter Twenty-Two). By failing to quantify their contribution to the organization's bottom line, human resource professionals have fueled line managers' perception that they are a "bunch of drones whose apparent missions in life were to create paperwork, recruit secretaries who couldn't type, and send around memos whose impertinence was exceeded only by their irrelevance."[1] Senior executives are quick to proclaim that employees are the organization's most valuable resource, but during economic downswings they are just as quick to cut the budget of the human resource department, whose primary responsibility is to maintain the quality of that most valuable resource.

Because they provide support to the line organization, human resource activities have been traditionally characterized as costs. That is, these activities do not contribute directly to the production of the organization's products

HIERARCHY OF HUMAN RESOURCE ACTIVITIES

EXHIBIT 23.1

High	*Essential Operational Activities*	Tangible
	1. Recruitment and Selection	
	2. On-the-Job Training	
	3. Salary Administration	
	4. Safety Programs	
	5. Employee Records and Benefits	
	6. Labor Relations	
Organization's Perceived Need for the Activity	*Optional Operational Activities*	Perceived Benefits to the Organization
	1. Job Analysis	
	2. Performance Appraisal	
	3. Career Development	
	4. Training Programs	
	5. Communication	
	6. Human Resource Planning	
	Optional Research Activities	
	1. Validation Studies	
	2. Evaluation of Training	
Low	3. Employee Attitude Surveys	Intangible

and services, or its gross revenues, and are therefore expected to cost money, not make money. Of course, human resource professionals provide essential support and service to the organization, and line managers value their assistance in recruitment, selection, training, career development, performance appraisal, compensation, etc. But since their contributions are often indirect and difficult to quantify, they face an uphill battle in their struggle for greater budgets and influence in the organization. A human resource department's status as a cost center makes it a ripe target for cost cutting, and its position is made even weaker if its worth to the organization has not been documented in economic terms.

A HIERARCHY OF HUMAN RESOURCE ACTIVITIES

Let's take a close look at the process of human resource management through the eyes of the chief executive officer of an organization, with particular attention to its costs and benefits. (Since most of you will probably become line managers, you may well share the C.E.O.'s view of human resource management.) The various human resource activities meet a range of needs and provide a range of benefits (Exhibit 23.1).

Essential Operational Activities

A number of human resource activities must be performed for an organization to operate. The need for these activities is high and the benefits they provide are direct and tangible. For example, an organization must have employees who perform at a relatively proficient level. This need can be met through some rudimentary form of selection and on-the-job training to ensure that employees meet performance standards. In small organizations both selection and training are handled by line managers, but in larger organizations it becomes cost effective to delegate recruiting and preliminary screening of applicants to human resource professionals. Similarly, the need to pay employees and offer benefits requires salary administration and record keeping. Finally, human resource professionals must ensure compliance with government regulations concerning equal employment opportunity, employee health and safety, and labor relations.

The need for these human resource activities is real and pressing, and although they represent a substantial cost, they also provide tangible benefits. Recruiting and selection programs produce valuable employees, record keeping for government regulations helps the organization avoid costly penalties and lawsuits, and a good labor relations specialist can save the organization money through skillful negotiation with the union on salaries and benefits and can also help the organization avoid costly strikes. It can be argued, therefore, that the cost of these human resource activities is offset by tangible benefits they provide to the organization.

Optional Operational Activities

At the next level in the hierarchy of Exhibit 23.1 are optional human resource activities like performance appraisal, training programs, and career development. The perceived need for these activities is only moderate in many organizations, and their benefits are not necessarily direct and tangible. Line managers, from the C.E.O. down, may view these activities as luxuries that are useful during good economic times, but can be sacrificed when budgets must be cut. Many of the human resource activities that Jain and Murray found to be uncommon in today's organizations (see Exhibit 22.1 in Chapter Twenty-Two) occur at this level in the hierarchy.[2] The time and effort to keep job descriptions up to date are perceived as providing no tangible benefits in many organizations. Performance appraisal, human resource planning, and communication may be seen as "good for employees," but seldom do human resource professionals document their benefits. Consequently, line managers are likely to view these activities as *optional;* they are useful management tools, but their benefits to the organization are not very tangible.

Optional Research Activities

The activities of this level of the hierarchy in Exhibit 23.1 are the most "ivory tower" in the eyes of line managers and budget committees. The need for research is perceived to be very low primarily because of its intangible benefits. Validation studies of selection tools (Chapter Nine) and the evaluation of actual changes in performance after training (Chapter Twelve) are very rare. Even when legislation of the 1960s and 1970s required validation of selection tools, many organizations did not comply. The dramatic decrease in the use of employment tests during those decades indicates that many organizations, rather than validating their employment tests, simply stopped using them. Unfortunately, little consideration was given to the very real costs of using less valid selection tools like interviews and reference checks. Other types of research, such as employee attitude surveys, are more common but are still not widely used.[3] Until human resource professionals demonstrate the value of research in economic terms, or line managers demand that they do so, these activities will continue to receive low priority.

A COMPREHENSIVE MODEL FOR DOCUMENTING COSTS AND BENEFITS

As we noted in Chapter Twenty-Two, two fundamental reasons have been raised to explain why human resource management is practiced at such a rudimentary level in so many of today's organizations. The first, lack of power, was addressed in Chapter Twenty-Two. The second reason is the lack of evidence that human resource activities affect employee performance and other important organizational outcomes. Cost-benefit analyses have seldom been conducted to document the tangible benefits of costly human resource activities.

The comprehensive model demonstrating the value of various human resource activities in Exhibit 23.2 contains four essential components:

1. An effectiveness model,
2. An economic model,
3. A comparison of costs and benefits,
4. A decision rule for continuation or repetition.[4]

Each component represents a step in an organization's decision to adopt and fund various human resource activities.

For example, suppose the Vice-President of Human Resources wants to evaluate the career planning program described in Box 23.1. First the *effectiveness* of the program must be documented. Were all three phases carried out properly? After two rounds of career planning interviews, had employee morale and performance improved in the department and had employee turnover decreased? A second major concern is *cost*. How much did the consultant charge to design and conduct the two training sessions and what was the cost of the supervisory personnel's time in the first two phases? How much did the program affect employee morale, performance, and turnover and what was the dollar value of its impact? Next, a comparison of the program's *costs* and *benefits* is necessary to determine its net worth to the organization. Finally, some guidelines are necessary to assist key members of the organization to *make the decision* to terminate, continue, or expand the program.

EXHIBIT 23.2 **MODEL FOR COST-BENEFIT ANALYSIS OF HUMAN RESOURCE PROGRAMS**

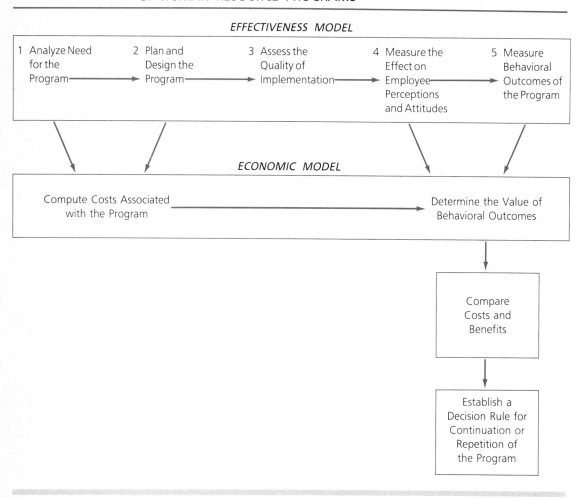

SOURCE: From "Accounting for the Costs and Benefits of Human Resource Development Programs: An Interdisciplinary Approach," by Philip H. Mirvis and Barry A. Macy, *Accounting Organizations and Society,* 1976, *1* (2–3). Reprinted by permission of Pergamon Press.

Wilson Bryant must determine whether the career planning program has been successful enough to be implemented in other departments.

An Effectiveness Model

The five steps in the effectiveness model should be familiar to you by now. Studies of the validity of selection tools or the effectiveness of training programs clearly include some or all of these five steps, as do surveys of em-

BOX 23.1

CAREER PLANNING PROGRAM TO REDUCE EMPLOYEE TURNOVER AND RECRUITMENT COSTS

Jack Nicholson, the Vice-President of Exploration of a major oil company, was concerned because the rate of turnover among the department's geologists and engineers had doubled during the past two years. On the basis of current turnover rates, twenty-five of the department's eighty-five professionals were expected to leave the company within the next twelve months, and only 50 percent were expected to remain with the department for over three years. Such high turnover was affecting the morale and performance of the entire department and was driving up recruitment costs substantially.

In discussions with Wilson Bryant, the Vice-President of Human Resource Management, Jack learned that his departing professionals had expressed great frustration in exit interviews with the lack of feedback about their performance and limited information about career opportunities within the exploration department and the company as a whole. Furthermore, since many of Jack's managers and supervisors routinely turned in performance appraisal forms to the human resource department without employee signatures, Wilson had concluded that they were not conducting appraisal interviews with their employees even once a year. Both vice-presidents were also aware that geologists and engineers were in high demand in the market, but that their company's salaries were competitive.

After conducting confidential interviews with several of the professionals and supervisors in the exploration department and reviewing the department's recruiting costs for the past two years, Wilson Bryant proposed that a career planning program be initiated immediately. It consisted of three phases. In the first phase the supervisory personnel of the exploration department, working with employee training and development specialists from the human resource department, defined the career ladders (a series of jobs to which an employee can be transferred or promoted) available to exploration department professionals. In the second phase a two-day training program on career planning interviewing was designed by a consultant, and all twenty-five department supervisors and managers attended one of the two sessions held. Third, within forty-five days after the training, department supervisors and managers conducted career planning interviews with the professionals reporting to them. These interviews were also scheduled to be repeated in six months.

Initial reactions were very positive. The career ladders were circulated to all departmental geologists and engineers and generated much enthusiastic discussion; morale increased almost immediately. Department supervisors and managers also rated the training sessions very favorably and showed marked improvement during the role-playing interview exercises. Career planning interviews were conducted on schedule with every member of the department, and during the next twelve months turnover of professionals dropped by over two-thirds and the incidence of sick leave and absenteeism decreased by one-half. Plans were made to expand the program to other departments of the company.

ployee attitudes. Indeed, most of the studies that human resource profession-als conduct to demonstrate the value of programs and practices to the organization use the effectiveness model.

1. Analyze need for the program. Throughout this text, we have emphasized the importance of an initial needs analysis to decide which human resource programs are to be designed and implemented in a given organiza-tion. The analysis of needs is also important to an organization's plans to dem-onstrate the effectiveness of a human resource program for two major reasons. First, a program that does not address clearly defined needs is unlikely to be successful, so the more thorough the needs analysis, the greater the program's chances of success. Second, needs analysis provides the basis for a comparison of the state of the organization *before* and *after* a program is instituted (see Chapter Twelve for a discussion of evaluation methods and experimental de-signs). In needs analysis, "before" measures are taken of symptoms and po-tential causes of a poor fit between employees, jobs, and the organization. In the example above, employee morale, performance, and turnover were mea-sured before and after the career planning program was implemented to dem-onstrate its effectiveness. It is useful to include a relatively large number of symptoms to be measured before and after a human resource program is in-troduced in order to improve the chances of detecting changes that can be attributed to the program.

2. Plan and design the program. Next, a human resource program must be planned and designed to meet the needs for a better individual-job-organization fit. It is obvious that the actual choice of a program is crucial to its success. For example, if an organization is attempting to increase employee productivity, it may adopt a more rigorous selection procedure or it may con-duct more extensive training. The choice between these two alternatives will have a major influence on the organization's effectiveness in increasing pro-ductivity. But even at this stage of program selection and design, thought can be given to how the program will be evaluated. A clear plan for evaluating program effectiveness should be set out as the program is being designed. In particular, program planning and design should include clear, concise, com-plete statements of program objectives. Another important consideration is the degree of involvement of human resource professionals as well as line managers and employees that will be necessary to implement the program.[5] For example, a recruiting program to increase the quality of university grad-uates who apply for technical jobs in an organization might have the following goals:

   a. Double the number of ads for the jobs to appear in technical journals and university newspapers.
   b. Send senior managers in the technical areas to twenty universities to serve as guest lecturers in technical courses, visit deans and profes-sors in technical fields, and meet informally with students to discuss career opportunities in technical fields. Schedule one to three months before the formal recruiting season to heighten students' awareness of the organization.

c. Send technical employees and managers to twenty selected universities to conduct screening interviews during the formal recruiting season. Provide interviewing skill training to all technical recruiters before they visit their universities.

These goals are specific and clear, and their attainment depends heavily on the involvement of line managers and employees. The stage is now set for the next step in the effectiveness model.

3. Assess the quality of implementation. No human resource program, no matter how well conceived, can be effective if it is not properly implemented. Therefore, the first truly evaluative step in the effectiveness model in Exhibit 23.2 is the assessment of how the program is implemented. This step is especially important in programs that depend on the support of managers and employees of the line organization. In the recruiting program outlined above, one procedural flaw, such as failure of technical employees and managers to attend the interviewing skill training, could undermine the entire effort. The purpose of this assessment is to monitor the extent to which the program is operating as designed and to keep interested organization members informed of its implementation. The assessment includes:

a. monitoring and documenting procedural events and activities as they occur,
b. collecting and documenting data as specified in the program plans,
c. detecting or predicting defects in program design or implementation, and
d. feeding back to organization members all of the information collected regarding how the program is functioning.[6]

4. Measure the effect on employee perceptions and attitudes Measurement of employee perceptions and attitudes is a very important step in assessing the impact of a human resource program. Many programs are designed to improve employee attitudes as well as performance, and the measurement of perceptual and attitudinal changes provides an interim check on the program's effectiveness. For example, the reactions of line managers to the first two phases of the career planning program are key indicators of the program's potential impact on employee turnover. If line managers rate the career planning training sessions as poor because the trainer was boring and the material was too academic, they are unlikely to conduct effective interviews in the third phase.

Similarly, let's consider a program of job enrichment, designed to increase the variety and challenge of employees' jobs, thereby increasing their job satisfaction, which ultimately leads to reduced absenteeism and turnover. The ultimate indication of success would be a reduction in employee absenteeism and turnover, but what if a comparison of these behaviors taken before and after the job enrichment program showed no change? Measures of employee perceptions and attitudes taken before and after the program could help identify the cause of failure. They could indicate whether the employees actually perceived greater variety and challenge in their supposedly enriched jobs and whether they were more satisfied with their altered jobs. If perceptions and attitudes remained unchanged, then it would not be surprising that the program of job enrichment failed to reduce absenteeism and turnover. Suppose that after the job enrichment program, employee absenteeism and turnover dropped dramatically but employee perceptions of work variety and challenge as well as job satisfaction remained unchanged. These results would strongly suggest that something totally unrelated to job enrichment caused the behavioral changes, and a wise human resource professional would begin looking for other explanations in spite of a strong desire to assign credit to the job enrichment program. For example, if the rate of unemployment rose sharply during the implementation of the program, that might explain the reductions in employee absenteeism and turnover.

5. Measure behavioral outcomes of the program. The ultimate test of the effectiveness of any human resource program is its impact on employee behavior. Measures of productivity, quality of work, absenteeism, turnover, accident rates, grievances, and sick leave must be taken *before* and *after* a program is implemented to measure its effectiveness. Traditional research activities, such as validation of selection tools and evaluation of training effectiveness, include this step of the effectiveness model.

The five steps in the effectiveness model help to document the impact of human resource programs. Each step adds unique information to the assessment process, and all five steps are necessary for a thorough understanding of why programs succeed or fail. These five steps are drawn from the methodology for behavioral science research that has evolved over the last several decades. But as impressive as this methodology is, it is not sufficient to demonstrate the value of human resource management to key decision makers of today's organizations. Behavioral science research methods simply do not enable the human resource professional to communicate in the language of business.

An Economic Model

The language of organizational decision making is financial. Senior managers of organizations want to know the costs of conducting business and the return on those costs. Whether the costs represent investments in property, facilities, and equipment or payment for services, they must be accounted for.

Because the human resource department (whether it consists of one or one hundred employees) is typically viewed as a cost center, its expenditures are categorized as payments for services. Organizations spend a considerable amount of money to attract, select, train, develop, and protect employees, and they budget funds to the human resource department accordingly. But as we pointed out earlier, organizations are apt to cut budgets of cost centers when expenditures must be reduced. This is particularly true for departments that have not documented the *economic* benefits of expenditures for services. Such is the case in a vast majority of human resource departments today.

But the expenditures for human resource activities need not be viewed simply as *costs*. Payment for services can also be viewed as *investments* in people. The cost of a human resource program represents an investment that will increase the value of the organization's human resources. The return on these investments will take the form of benefits to the organization, such as increased employee morale and performance, and decreased absenteeism, turnover, and accident rates. Human resource professionals have traditionally taken the position that the cost of their work is far outweighed by the benefits they provide, and some have used the effectiveness model to demonstrate the positive behavioral outcomes yielded by human resource programs. But they have rarely evaluated programs in economic terms. It is certainly reasonable for an organization's senior managers to ask for documentation of how much is being spent on human resource management and what is being purchased with this money. To compete successfully for influence and funds in today's organizations, human resource professionals must be able to document the costs and benefits of their work. The economic model in Exhibit 23.2 provides them with the means to do so.

Human Resource Accounting ▬ The economic model is based on **human resource accounting,** the *process of measuring the cost and value of people to organizations.*[7] Interest in human resource accounting was spurred in the 1960s by Rensis Likert and others at the University of Michigan.[8] Pioneering work at several companies, notably the R. G. Barry Corporation in 1967, led to the appearance of entries on balance sheets for "net investments in human resources" and "appropriation for human resources."

human resource accounting

Human resource accounting offers two major tools for assessing the economic impact of human resource programs—namely, asset accounting and cost accounting.[9] **Asset accounting** is *the measurement of the value of human resources in terms of the present worth of their expected future services to the organization.* With asset accounting, programs such as training or career development can be viewed as investments in employees that increase their value.

asset accounting

Asset accounting presents major conceptual and operational problems, however. Since asset accounting has been traditionally applied to physical assets *owned* by the organization (e.g., property, facilities, equipment), its use with human resources implies that the organization has purchased its employees or at least their services. Many people find this concept disconcerting. There are also serious operational problems with asset accounting of human resources. It is very difficult to place a dollar value on an individual employee's worth to the organization, and it is equally difficult to assign a dollar value to the increase in worth resulting from an investment such as training or career development.

The second major tool of human resource accounting is much more applicable to the economic approach to cost-benefit analysis of human resource programs. It is **cost accounting,** *the measurement of sacrifices made to obtain some anticipated benefit or service.* This definition applies to many of the

cost accounting

human resource activities covered in this book. For example, recruiting, selection, training, career development, and employee safety measures all entail costs to the organization of acquiring the services of employees.

Cost accounting does not suffer from the conceptual and operational problems that asset accounting does. Since the acquisition of employee services is treated as an expense rather than an investment, the conceptual relationship between the organization and its employees is analogous to *leasing*, rather than ownership. The organization essentially rents its employees' services at a given cost. In operational terms, the cost of acquiring employees is much easier to compute than the worth of their services. The cost of recruiting and training new employees can be estimated with little difficulty.

Now that we are armed with the cost accounting approach to human resource accounting, let's return to the economic model for the cost-benefit analysis of human resource programs shown in Exhibit 23.2.

Compute costs associated with the program. After needs have been analyzed and the program has been planned and designed (steps 1 and 2 in the effectiveness model), the cost of the program can be estimated. For the career planning program in Box 23.1, direct costs include the consultant's time to design and conduct the training sessions, and indirect costs include the time spent by supervisors and managers to define career ladders and attend the training sessions.

Proposals have recently been made to document the costs of human resource activities. Flamholtz has applied the concept of *original human resource cost, the sacrifice actually incurred to acquire and develop employees,* to human resource management.[10] He divides original cost into direct and indirect acquisition costs and direct and indirect learning costs, shown in Exhibit 23.3. A thorough accounting for the human resource activities in this exhibit (e.g., recruiting, selection, hiring, placement, and training) would represent a significant beginning of an effort to compute the costs associated with the activities to provide an organization with productive employees. Fitz-enz argues strongly that human resource professionals need to measure their activities quantitatively to demonstrate their contribution to organizational profits.[11] He points out that most human resource professionals either don't want to or don't know how to measure their activities, and that top management has formed the opinion that human resource management cannot be quantitatively evaluated. He recommends that detailed calculations be made of the time and costs of specific human resource activities. For example, Exhibit 23.4 shows that during one month 217 employee counseling sessions, requiring a total of 141.2 hours, were conducted at a cost of $2824. These records could be used to justify the need for one employee counselor on the human resource department's roster and to report to top management the type of problems that employees are confronting in the organization.

Determine the value of behavioral outcomes. Accounting for the costs of human resource activities is a significant first step in cost-benefit analysis. To complete the analysis, however, the value of the benefits of the activities must also be determined. This step in the economic model coincides

MODEL FOR MEASUREMENT OF ORIGINAL HUMAN RESOURCE COSTS

EXHIBIT 23.3

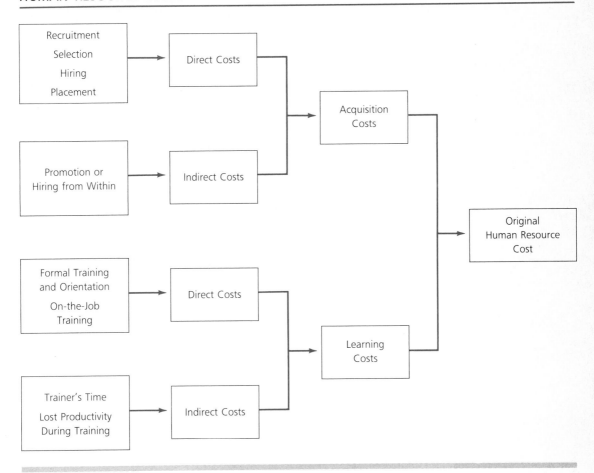

SOURCE: From *Human Resource Accounting* by Eric Flamholtz, Dickenson Publishing Company, Inc. 1974, p. 37. Reprinted by permission of the author.

with step 5 of the effectiveness model of Exhibit 23.2. First, the behavioral outcomes of the human resource activity must be detected, and then their value can be estimated.

Attempts to quantify the benefits of human resource management are not new. One early approach was proposed by Brogden and Taylor through the use of the "dollar criterion."[12] An employee's worth was computed as the dollar value of his or her production minus the dollar cost of the production. The dollar criterion could be applied to cost-benefit analysis of human resource programs by computing the cost of the program (e.g., training) for a group of employees and monitoring the resultant increase in their production.

EXHIBIT 23.4   COMPUTING THE COST OF EMPLOYEE
COUNSELING SESSIONS

Number of Sessions	Major Topic of the Session	Time
48	Problems with Other Employees	26.5 hours
59	Company Policies and Procedures	40.4
13	Transfers	8.8
27	Leaves of Absence	7.9
28	Exit Interviews	14.6
11	Career Counseling	8.5
17	Personal Problems	24.5
14	Problems with Supervisor	10.0
217		141.2
Total Cost @ $20/hour		$2,824.

The value of the increase in production could then be compared with the cost of the training to determine if the expenditure was financially justified. Box 23.2 presents an excellent illustration of how the cost and value of a sophisticated selection process were estimated.

Recently, there have been more complex attempts to estimate the economic value of job performance and thereby to determine the return on investment of human resource programs.[13] These approaches, however, suffer from the same weaknesses of asset accounting discussed in the section on human resource accounting. First, it is very difficult to assign a dollar value to job performance, and this difficulty will grow as the U.S. economy continues its shift from production jobs to service jobs. (The job of claims approver in Box 23.2, with its easily quantified measure of productivity, is an exception.) Second, human resource programs may significantly affect employee attitudes and behavior, but may not result in changes in actual job performance. For example, a program of career development may increase job satisfaction and decrease absenteeism and turnover, but have no measurable impact on job performance. Is it accurate to conclude from the absence of a change in job performance that the human resource program has generated no benefits to the organization?

An Alternative: Cost Avoidance ▬ An alternative to asset accounting to determine the value of human resource programs is derived from the cost model of human resource accounting. Just as the costs of various programs can be computed in the economic model, the costs of specific employee attitudes and behaviors can also be computed. The benefits of human resource

THE DOLLAR VALUE OF A SELECTION PROGRAM

BOX 23.2

To justify the cost of the selection process, human resource professionals must estimate the dollar value of a selection tool and show that the gain in productivity that results from choosing the best job applicants is greater than the cost of the selection process.

Such a study was done at a major U.S. insurance company by the Life Office Management Association, Inc. (LOMA). In conjunction with Personnel Decisions Research Institute, LOMA has developed the Job Effectiveness Prediction System (JEPS). JEPS is a battery of mental ability tests (e.g., numerical ability, reading comprehension) which aids in the selection of applicants for entry-level clerical or professional/technical jobs in the insurance industry.

This study used the following six factors to estimate the dollar value of JEPS for the job of claims approver:

1. Validity—the improvement in prediction when JEPS is added to the selection process,
2. Standard deviation of productivity—the extent to which individual employees differ in productivity,
3. Utility of productivity—the value of each unit of production (i.e., each claim processed) in dollars,
4. Number of applicants—the number of people who apply and take JEPS,
5. Number hired—the number of applicants who are hired,
6. Cost—the cost of administering and scoring JEPS.

To compute the dollar value of JEPS, LOMA researchers meticulously estimated each of the above six factors to enter into the appropriate equation. In the equation for dollar value, factors 4 and 5 were combined to derive factor 7, which is the mean standard score of those applicants who were hired. The average JEPS score depends on the hiring rate, the percentage of applicants actually hired (factor 5) divided by the number of applicants (factor 4). The more selective the organization is, the higher the average JEPS score. The equation for the dollar value of JEPS is:

$$V = (1) \times (2) \times (3) \times (5) \times (7) - (6)$$

Research showed that a reasonable estimate of JEPS's validity was .36, compared with a validity of .14 for conventional selection tools. Therefore, JEPS's improvement in predicting job performance was .36 − .14, or .22 (factor 1). Productivity of individual claims approvers is simply the number of claims processed each day. Company records were used to derive an estimate of 1679.29 claims per year for factor 2. The utility of each claim processed was the total compensation (salary plus benefits) divided by the total number of claims approved. The estimate was $3.30 (factor 3). Since the company hired ten claims approvers during the previous year, ten was used as the estimate of the number of applicants hired. The average score on JEPS (factor 7) was estimated to be 1.428. Finally, the cost of JEPS (factor 6) was estimated to be $1,103.67 per year.

When these estimates are entered into the equation, the value of JEPS equals (.22) × (1679.29) × ($3.30) × (10) × (1.428) − $1,103.67, which equals $16,306. Clearly, JEPS was valuable to the insurance company, and it is currently in use.

The authors wish to thank Dr. Andrew G. Neiner of LOMA for his assistance in preparing this material.

EXHIBIT 23.5   ESTIMATING TURNOVER COSTS

Activity	Nonexempt Cost	Exempt Cost	Total
1. Employment advertising	$ 25,000	$ 30,000	$ 55,000
2. Agency and search fees	5,737	25,000	30,737
3. Internal referrals	10,800	3,979	14,779
4. Applicant expenses	500	9,318	9,818
5. Relocation expenses	3,000	79,132	82,132
6. Employment staff compensation	10,200	25,000	35,200
7. Other employment office expenses	1,150	1,150	2,300
8. Recruiters' expenses	3,000	500	3,500
9. Direct hiring costs (Sum of 1–8)	$ 59,387	$174,079	$ 233,466
10. Number of hires	278	84	362
11. Direct costs per hire (9 ÷ 10)	$ 214	$ 2,072	$ 645*
12. Indirect costs per hire†	3,705	6,180	
13. Total costs per hire (11 + 12)	$ 3,919	$ 8,252	$ 4,840‡
14. Number of replacement hires (turnover)	200	54	254
15. Total turnover costs (13 × 14)	$783,800	$445,608	$1,229,408
16. Target percent reduction	25%	25%	25%
17. Potential savings (15 × 16)	$195,950	$111,402	$ 307,352

*Calculated by dividing total direct hiring costs (line 9) by the total number of hires (line 10).
†Includes the cost of management time and key employees' time spent orienting new employees, cost of training new employees, and cost of reduced productivity until new employees become fully productive.
‡Calculated by dividing the total turnover costs (on line 15) by the total number of replacement hires (on line 14).

SOURCE: Adapted from T. E. Hall, "How to Estimate Employee Turnover Costs," *Personnel,* July-August 1981, *58,* p. 45.

programs can then be assessed in terms of the *avoidance* of the cost of undesirable employee attitudes and behavior.

For example, employee turnover is generally considered to be undesirable in organizations because it costs money to replace lost employees. But how high is an employee's replacement cost and how much should an organization spend on the process of human resource management to *reduce or avoid these costs?* The answer to this question begins with a computation of the cost of employee turnover to the organization. An organization can begin estimating turnover costs by establishing the necessary accounts and accumulating data from the accounting department on costs related to turnover.[14] As Exhibit 23.5 shows, many substantial costs can be traced to employee turnover; the cost of replacing 254 employees is $1,229,408. Human resource activities that contributed to a 25 percent reduction in turnover would therefore produce cost savings of $307,352 for the organization.

There has been additional work to identify and compute the costs of undesirable employee behavior. In developing a procedure to assess quality of work life programs, Macy and Mirvis assigned the behavioral outcomes under study into two main categories:

1. Participation-membership
   a. absenteeism
   b. turnover
   c. strikes
   d. tardiness
2. Performance on the job
   a. production under standard
   b. quality under standard
   c. grievances
   d. accidents
   e. unscheduled downtime and machine repair
   f. material utilization and inventory shrinkage.[15]

All of these outcomes were included because they could be measured and converted to significant costs to the organization, and the costs of the behaviors were estimated and monitored in an organization over three years. Although Macy and Mirvis proposed that this procedure be used to assess the costs and benefits of quality of work life programs, the procedure can also be applied to cost-benefit analysis of other human resource programs.

Using the proposed procedure, Mirvis and Lawler examined the relationship between employee attitudes and the cost of behavioral outcomes in a bank.[16] They measured three employee attitudes (satisfaction with work, feeling of involvement with the organization, and motivation) and three behavioral outcomes (short-term absences or illness, voluntary turnover, and teller balancing shortages). Correlational analysis was used to establish relationships between employee attitudes and behavior, and with cost accounting the *costs* of the behavior to the organization were estimated. Finally, they computed the cost savings that would be realized in the organization if employee attitudes were improved. For example, if satisfaction with work increased by 14 percent, the corresponding reductions in absenteeism, turnover, and shortages for 160 tellers would result in direct savings of over $17,000 in one year. A comparable increase in job involvement would produce savings of over $21,000.

Cost avoidance is a firmly established business principle that appears to be gaining a foothold in human resource management. Cost accounting is a powerful tool that human resource professionals can use to estimate the costs of employee attitudes and behavior. In his excellent book, *Costing Human Resources*, W. F. Cascio presents some eye-opening estimates of the costs of employee turnover, sick leave, and even smoking.[17] For example, employee turnover can lead to separation, replacement, and training costs exceeding $1,000 per employee who leaves the organization, and smoking can cost employers nearly $5,000 per year per smoker in absenteeism, medical care, disease and early mortality, insurance, lost time, property damage and depreciation, maintenance, and involuntary smoking by co-workers. Recognition of these costs, coupled with the programs to reduce them, can be used to significantly increase the influence of human resource professionals in today's organizations.

Comparison of Costs and Benefits

Information from the effectiveness model and the economic model of Exhibit 23.2 can be combined in a cost-benefit analysis of human resource programs. First, the cost of the program can be estimated from the needs analysis and planning for the program. For example, the total cost of the career planning program in Box 23.1, including the time of the consultant, training and development specialists from the human resource department, and supervisors and managers of the exploration department, was $19,400 (Exhibit 23.6). Second, the impact of the program on employee attitudes and behavior can be determined. During the twelve months following the career planning program, turnover of professionals was reduced by over two-thirds and the incidence of sick leave and absenteeism was cut in half. Third, the cost of those employee attitudes and behaviors can be estimated, and costs avoided by the program can be computed. With this information, the costs and benefits of the program can be compared to determine its economic impact on the organization. As Exhibit 23.6 shows, the benefits of the career planning program exceeded its costs by $18,100. A comparable cost-benefit analysis showed that the selection process in Box 23.2 saved the insurance company over $16,000 in one year.

Decision Rule for Continuation or Repetition

The final ingredient in the comprehensive model in Exhibit 23.2 is concerned with the choice of one human resource program over another. A set of guidelines for making this decision is needed to ensure that an organization makes choices that are rational and consistent. An excellent approach has been developed at the Xerox Corporation by Logan Cheek,[18] who made use of program-management techniques to identify four key steps for evaluating and selecting human resource programs:

1. *Define and describe each proposed or ongoing human resource program.* Human resource professionals should list the program's objectives, implementation schedule, and line employees involved and should estimate the knowledge and skills necessary to implement the program, its costs, and its potential benefits.
2. *Identify legal requirements.* Human resource activities required by law (e.g., recruitment of women and minorities, health and safety training,

EXHIBIT 23.6

COST-BENEFIT ANALYSIS OF THE CAREER PLANNING PROGRAM

Activity	Time	Cost
1. Consultant prepares and conducts the training sessions	5 days @ $800	$ 4,000
2. Training and development specialists coordinate the project and conduct the meeting to define career ladders	2 days @ $200	400
3. Twenty-five managers and supervisors of the exploration department attend career ladder meeting and training session	75 days @ $200	15,000
Total Cost of the Program		$19,400

Behavioral Outcomes	Benefits
1. Turnover reduced from the projected level of twenty-five to an actual figure of eight professionals in the twelve months following the program	$34,000 saved in recruitment costs
2. Absenteeism and sick leave dropped by 50 percent during the twelve months following the program	$3,500 saved in overtime to complete work of absent employees
Total Benefits	$37,500
Net Return of the Program	$18,100

and collective bargaining) must be separated from optional programs and given top priority.

3. *Evaluate the feasibility of each program.* This is the most complex and challenging step in Cheek's approach, but fortunately much of the necessary information can be drawn from our comprehensive model in Exhibit 23.2. Cheek suggests that all programs be evaluated in four ways. First, determine the level of sophistication of the program. This evaluation focuses on the technical complexity of the program and the availability of expertise within the human resource department or from outside consultants to successfully undertake the program. These judgments can be made during needs analysis and program planning (steps 1 and 2 of the effectiveness model).

Second, determine the ease of implementation. This evaluation focuses on the receptiveness of the line organization to the human resource program and is dependent on the power and credibility of the organization's human resource professionals as well as line management's perceived need for the program.

Third, determine net economic benefits by estimating the cost of a program and the dollar value of its impact on the organization. For ongoing programs human resource professionals can compute the costs and dollar value of behavioral outcomes, while for proposed programs costs and benefits can only be estimated.

Fourth, determine the economic risks of not acting. Consider how

EXHIBIT 23.7 ESTABLISHING PRIORITIES AMONG HUMAN RESOURCE PROGRAMS

Annotations (left margin):
1. Legally required efforts come first
2. ...then, other programs are ranked by overall feasibility category
3. ...and within feasibility category by net benefits
4. Priorities are indicated here
5. Starting from the lowest priority program, marginal efforts may be trimmed as required by the budget
6. In any case, these programs are eliminated

Legend: |||||||||||| Program and design development   ▬▬ Program implementation

ACTION PROGRAM	Priority	Timing (1972–1977)	Net Annual Dollar Benefit	Cost/Benefit Ratio (1:n)
LEGALLY REQUIRED PROGRAMS				
Labor Relations Strategy	x	1973–1976	($ 619)	n/a
Protect Right to Select Employees	x	1973–1976	($ 86)	n/a
Continue Validation of Selection Tests	x	1973–1976	$35,000	78.17
Redesign Personnel Data System	x	1973	$ 273	1.78
Develop Part-Time Female Employment Approaches	x	1972–1974	$ 227	4.16
VERY DESIRABLE PROGRAMS				
Restructuring Service Force	1	1972–1975	$14,608	9.6
Service College Coop Program	2	1972–1975	$ 4,490	2.74
MODERATELY DESIRABLE PROGRAMS				
Service Job Enrichment	3	1972–1974	$ 9,920	24.3
Assessment Center	4	1973–1975	$ 4,946	15.40
Education & Training Center	5	1972–1974	$ 4,780	3.57
Clerical Selection Program	6	1974–1975	$ 1,799	19.94
Develop College Campus as Primary Employment Source	7	1972–1975	$ 834	2.06
Interfunctional Moves & Fast Track Program	8	1972–1975	$ 679	7.54
Selection Standards for New Sales/Tech. Rep. Types	9	1974–1975	$ 520	11.6
Improve Economics of Field Employment Operations	10	1972–1975	$ 472	1.42
Build Better Technical Recruiting/Selection Capability	11	1972–1975	$ 222	2.48
Monitor Sales & Tech. Rep. Selection Tests	12	1972–1975	$ 211	9.05
MARGINAL BUT DESIRABLE PROGRAMS				
Implement Executive Search Function	13	1972–1975	$ 177	1.67
Refine Career Path Guides	14	1972–1975	$ 110	1.75
Continue National Trend Attitude Surveys	15	1972–1975	$ 107	1.33
Reevaluate Overall Organization Approach	16	1972–1973	$ 93	2.37
NOT WORTHWHILE				
Executive Retreat	x	1972–1975	($ 450)	n/a
Corporate Jet	x	1972–1975	($ 769)	n/a
Savings Plan	x	1972–1973	($ 75)	n/a

SOURCE: Reprinted by permission of the Harvard Business Review. An exhibit from "Cost Effectiveness Comes to the Personnel Function," by Logan M. Cheek (May/June 1973). Copyright © 1973 by the President and Fellows of Harvard College; all rights reserved.

much the organization will lose if a program is discontinued or a proposal is rejected. Estimates of the costs of continued high turnover or poor selection decisions can provide a convincing argument for the value of a human resource program. These estimates can be derived from the economic model in Exhibit 23.2.

4. *Rank all programs, and allocate and deploy resources accordingly.* Finally, Cheek recommends that all programs be ranked in order of priority, as illustrated in Exhibit 23.7. Note that legally required programs receive top priority, in spite of their net annual dollar benefit. The remaining programs are ranked primarily in order of their ease of implementation and economic return to the organizaton. This ranking provides an excellent basis for decisions about the continuation or repetition of specific human resource programs.

Cheek's four steps represent a practical framework for organizing information that can be generated in our comprehensive model for the cost-benefit analysis of human resource programs. The framework contains vital evidence of not only the effectiveness of programs, but also their dollar value.

THE CHALLENGE OF DOCUMENTING COSTS AND BENEFITS

A key concern of American business today is *productivity*. Organizations function in a highly competitive world, and pressure to produce effectively and efficiently is being felt throughout the American economy. All members of an organization—executives, line managers, and operating employees—have a responsibility to critically question the costs and benefits of any activities to which they commit time and money. This critical attitude certainly applies to human resource management. The era in which organizations are willing to spend large sums of money on human resource programs aimed at intangible benefits is ending.

Human resource professionals have the expertise and tools to assist their organizations in the quest for increased productivity and efficiency. Working with line managers to plan, design, and implement human resource policies and practices, they can contribute significantly to organizational goals. But to do so, they must communicate in the language of business. To compete successfully for scarce funds and employee time, they must document the costs and benefits of human resource activities.

Drawing on research methodology from the behavioral sciences, program evaluation techniques, and accounting principles, we have presented practical guidelines to demonstrate the impact of human resource management. Some human resource practitioners follow these guidelines to strengthen their power and influence in the organizations they serve; we urge more to follow suit. We also urge line managers to ask human resource professionals for cost-benefit analyses of human resource activities so the two parties can make more informed choices among the many human resource programs available.

KEY POINTS

▬ Many human resource professionals view their contribution to the organization as intangible and have failed to measure the value of their work in financial terms. As a result, line managers consider some human resource activities as essential, but they perceive others as luxuries to be eliminated when funds are scarce.

▬ To demonstrate the impact of their work, human resource professionals must confer with line managers to design and implement programs that meet well-defined organizational needs, and then measure the programs' effects on employee attitudes, perceptions, and behavior.

▬ Human resource professionals can apply accounting techniques to assess the costs and benefits of human resource programs. In particular, they can use cost accounting to compute the costs of a program and the dollar value of its impact on important organizational outcomes like turnover, absenteeism, and performance.

▬ To make rational recommendations to top management, human resource professionals must assign priorities to proposed and ongoing programs by considering each program's legal requirements, ease of implementation, costs and benefits, and the economic risks of failing to implement the program.

▬ The current climate of high business competition and pressure for productivity has intensified the need for line managers and human resource professionals to document the costs and benefits of human resource programs in their organizations. Without this documentation, the programs will compete poorly for scarce funds and employee time.

ISSUES FOR DISCUSSION

1. Discuss the reasons why human resource professionals have difficulty competing for scarce funds and employee time to mount human resource programs for their organizations.

2. Compare the steps in the effectiveness model for cost-benefit analysis of human resource programs with the Chapter Twelve discussion of the four kinds of evidence to demonstrate training effectiveness. What additional information would you collect about a training program to evaluate it with all five steps of the effectiveness model?

3. What is the difference between cost accounting and asset accounting? Give an example of how each technique can be used to demonstrate the economic benefits of human resource programs.

4. How much can employee turnover and smoking cost an organization, according to T. E. Hall and W. F. Cascio? As a human resource professional, how would you use these costs to strengthen your request for funds to support human resource programs?

5. Summarize Logan Cheek's approach to establishing priorities among human resource programs. How would such an analysis have strengthened Ben Schultz's budget request to the senior management team of Consolidated, Inc.?

NOTES

1. H. E. Meyer, "Personnel Directors Are the New Corporate Heroes," *Fortune*, February 1976, p. 84.

2. H. C. Jain and V. V. Murray, "Why the Human Resources Management Function Fails," *California Management Review*, Summer 1984, 26, pp. 95–110.

3. E. C. Miller, "Consensus: Attitude Surveys: A Diagnostic Tool," *Personnel*, January-February 1978, 55, pp. 4–10.

4. Adapted from a model presented in P. H. Mirvis, and B. A. Macy, "Accounting for the Costs and Benefits of Human Resource Development Programs: An Interdisciplinary Approach," *Accounting, Organizations and Society*, 1976, 1, pp. 179–93.

5. R. A. Snyder, C. S. Raben, and J. L. Farr, "A Model for the Systematic Evaluation of Human Resource Development Programs," *Academy of Management Review*, 1980, 5, pp. 431–44.

6. Ibid. p. 440.

7. E. Flamholtz, *Human Resource Accounting* (Encino, Calif.: Dickenson, 1974).

8. R. Likert, *New Patterns of Management* (New York: McGraw-Hill, 1961).

9. P. H. Mirvis and B. A. Macy, "Accounting for the Costs and Benefits of Human Resource Development Programs: An Inderdisciplinary Approach."

10. Flamholtz, op. cit., p. 33.

11. J. Fitz-enz, *How to Measure Human Resources Management* (New York: McGraw-Hill, 1984); J. Fitz-enz, "Quantifying the Human Resources Function," *Personnel*, March-April 1980, 57, pp. 41–52.

12. H. Brogden and E. Taylor, "The Dollar Criterion—Applying the Cost Accounting Concept to Criterion Construction," *Personnel Psychology*, 1950, 3, pp. 133–54.

13. See W. F. Cascio, *Costing Human Resources: The Financial Impact of Behavior in Organizations* (Belmont, Calif.: Wadsworth, 1982).

14. T. E. Hall, "How to Estimate Employee Turnover Costs," *Personnel*, July–August 1981, 58, pp. 43–52.

15. B. A. Macy and P. H. Mirvis, "A Methodology for Assessment of Quality of Work Life and Organizational Effectiveness in Behavioral-Economic Terms," *Administrative Science Quarterly*, 1976, 21, pp. 212–26.

16. P. H. Mirvis and E. E. Lawler, III, "Measuring the Financial Impact of Employee Attitudes," *Journal of Applied Psychology*, 1977, 62, pp. 1–8.

17. Cascio, op. cit.

18. L. M. Cheek, "Cost Effectiveness Comes to the Personnel Function," *Harvard Business Review*, 1973, 51, pp. 96–105.

ANNOTATED BIBLIOGRAPHY

CASCIO, W. F. *Costing Human Resources: The Financial Impact of Behavior in Organizations.* Belmont, Calif.: Wadsworth, 1982.

In this well-researched and comprehensive book, Cascio shows how accounting methods can be used to estimate the costs and benefits of various human resource activities. With meticulous care he itemizes and computes the many costs of undesirable employee behaviors like turnover, absenteeism, and smoking. He also presents various approaches to placing a dollar value on the results of human resource programs and discusses methods for cost-benefit analysis. Numerous illustrations add clarity and practicality to the book.

FITZ-ENZ, J. *How to Measure Human Resources Management.* New York: McGraw-Hill, 1984.

The author begins by lamenting the common misconception that human resource management is a complex and mysterious art that can be evaluated only in subjective terms, and emphasizes the need to measure its costs and benefits in financial terms. He presents a systematic procedure to identify specific human resource activities to be measured (e.g., orientation and counseling of employees) and compute all the costs needed to support that activity. He then illustrates this procedure for several activities, such as wage and salary administration, career development, and training. The book includes many useful guides for computing costs of human resource activities.

FLAMHOLTZ, E. G., and LACEY, J. M. *Personnel Management, Human Capital Theory, and Human Resource Accounting.* Los Angeles, Calif.: Institute of Industrial Relations Publications, 1981.

The primary objective of this book is to develop a basis for human resource decision making. The authors present a systems model showing how human resource management comprises eight major activities (planning, acquisition, development, allocation, utilization, conservation, evaluation, and reward) aimed at producing valued organizational outcomes, and then use human capital theory and human resource accounting to derive employee value as the basis for human resource decisions and actions. Although they include fewer illustrations than Cascio and Fitz-enz, the authors thoroughly discuss the implications of accounting principles for human resource decision making.

MORRISON ENGINEERS

The following case describes a company with major strategic, managerial, and operational problems.* Morrison Engineers simply isn't being run very well. In addition, there are many indications that human resource policies and practices have not been effectively planned, designed, and implemented; the result is a poor fit between people and jobs. The case consists of a general description of the company, an organization chart, and comments from several of its key employees.

Before you analyze the case, be aware that Morrison Engineers operates in a relatively unpredictable and hostile environment. It faces stiff competition in the oil and gas industry with many engineering and design firms its size as well as major engineering construction firms like Brown and Root, Fluor, and Bechtel. The oil and gas industry is also very complex and dynamic because of shifting consumer demand for petrochemical products and varying world supplies of crude oil. These factors increase the pressure on Morrison Engineers to operate efficiently.

Read the case thoroughly and comprehensively, keeping the following questions in mind:

1. What are the major issues in this case? Look for common symptoms raised by the employees and group them into categories such as strategic, managerial, operational, and human resource management issues.
2. What are the underlying causes of the symptoms? Remember to diagnose the environment, organization, jobs, and individuals in your search for causes. Also, look for causal relationships between issues (e.g., lack of clear organizational goals leads to a lack of focus in marketing the firm).
3. What changes are necessary for Morrison Engineers to survive and prosper, and what priorities would you give to the proposals? Which recommendations must receive top priority and which can wait until a later stage? Make sure your proposals address strategic, managerial, and operational problems, as well as human resource management problems.

When you have read and analyzed the case, you, in your role as senior partner of Human Resource Management, Inc., should provide Randy Mor-

---

*"The Case of Morrison Engineers" by James G. Goodale. Copyright © 1984 by James G. Goodale. Reprinted by permission.

rison with either a written or oral report that answers the preceding questions.

BACKGROUND

Randy Morrison, the General Manager of Morrison Engineers, has invited you, as a senior partner in the management consulting firm of Human Resource Management, Inc., to study his organization. Morrison Engineers has grown rapidly in the past two years, and Randy wants you to help him get the firm running more efficiently so he can back out of the day-to-day management and look for new challenges. In short, Randy wants to be an entrepreneur again, as he was when he started Morrison Engineers.

Morrison Engineers was founded by Randy and his brother-in-law, Chuck Moore, in 1973. Randy had worked as a draftsman and designer for large petrochemical companies before beginning this venture. His brother-in-law was a professional engineer, and together they operated the firm out of Randy's garage.

The partners began by doing farm-out design and drafting work for other engineering design firms, and occasionally got a small project directly from an oil company. Randy and Chuck worked long hours and hired other drafters and engineers as needed. As projects came to a close, Randy and Chuck would try to generate new business to minimize layoffs. During its first three years, Morrison Engineers averaged between ten and twenty employees and existed hand to mouth.

In early 1975 Mike Lane joined the firm. He was a young engineer in his second job since graduating from college. Mike is exceedingly competent, energetic, and ambitious, and he brought a new level of competence and polish to Morrison Engineers. He is personable and works well with clients; in addition, he is an excellent proposal writer, computer programmer, and engineer. A year after he joined the firm, he was made a partner. Randy Morrison held 70 percent of the stock in Morrison Engineers, and Chuck Moore and Mike Lane each held 15 percent. The stock had little real value in 1976, but Randy used it as a gesture of confidence in an employee. As Morrison Engineers' assets have grown over the years, the stock has taken on more value, although it is not liquid.

Today Morrison Engineers has about 100 employees (see chart) and does nearly $6 million of business a year. In the past two years, it has doubled in size, primarily because of a large client for whom it is doing a variety of engineering jobs. The firm still works primarily for major oil companies, doing design and drafting work on renovations of refineries and chemical plants. One mark of its success is that the firm recently designed and built its own office building valued at $900,000.

As an outside consultant, you decide to interview, in addition to Randy, several employees who hold a variety of jobs at Morrison Engineers and represent varying degrees of experience and loyalty. Summaries of all those interviews follow.

Randy Morrison, General Manager

Randy began his interview by reminiscing about starting the firm "on a shoe string" and working eighty hours a week to do good work for his clients. In the early days, Randy did much of the work the firm produced. He and Chuck frequently went without pay when business was slow, and Randy sometimes had to cover payroll checks with his own money. Over the years he built a reputation for delivering the goods and doing quality work. He has always been the kind of manager who gets in there and does the work beside his employees. He has a short time horizon and looks for additional work only when he can't meet the next month's payroll.

As the firm grew to forty or fifty employees, Randy took on the role of people developer. He did the hiring and on-the-job training and served as company "psychiatrist," listening to people's problems and helping with solutions. Occasionally he stepped in when supervisors had to handle an unpleasant task such as firing someone or cracking the whip to get a project back on schedule.

About a year ago Randy took on the job of designing and constructing the building that now houses Morrison Engineers. It was his major project, and during that time Mike Lane played a central role in running the firm. Since the building was completed three months ago, Randy has felt lost. He really doesn't know what his job is. From time to time he serves as project engineer, but he feels he's just a figurehead now. He has delegated most of his work away, and what remains requires only 25 percent of his time. He wants to put the firm in order, help it diversify, and then find challenges, perhaps by starting up a new business.

Randy recognizes the strong division between himself and Mike Lane, and knows that Mike wants more control of the firm. Randy, however, is very concerned about maintaining his equity. He recognizes that Mike has contributed to the firm's success, but feels since he started the firm, he deserves to reap the fruits of his labor.

Mike Lane, Manager of Development

Mike began by expressing resentment that Randy did not consult him before deciding to bring Human Resource Management, Inc., in to study Morrison Engineers. (Although he had attended your first meeting with Randy, the decision to proceed had already been made by Randy.) This beginning demonstrates the division between Randy and Mike—they simply do not communicate. Mike is very frustrated. He feels he has not been sufficiently rewarded for his significant contributions to the firm's growth.

Mike also feels the firm lacks clearly defined, commonly held goals. He wants to build Morrison Engineers into a large engineering design firm but senses resistance from Randy. He thinks the company needs better control in project management and scheduling procedures, and he has spent much of his time designing systems for scheduling and control. He has written all the procedures and designed all the systems currently in use. His job is poorly defined, so he can do many things. As Manager of Development, he meets

MORRISON ENGINEERS ORGANIZATION CHART

EXHIBIT C.1

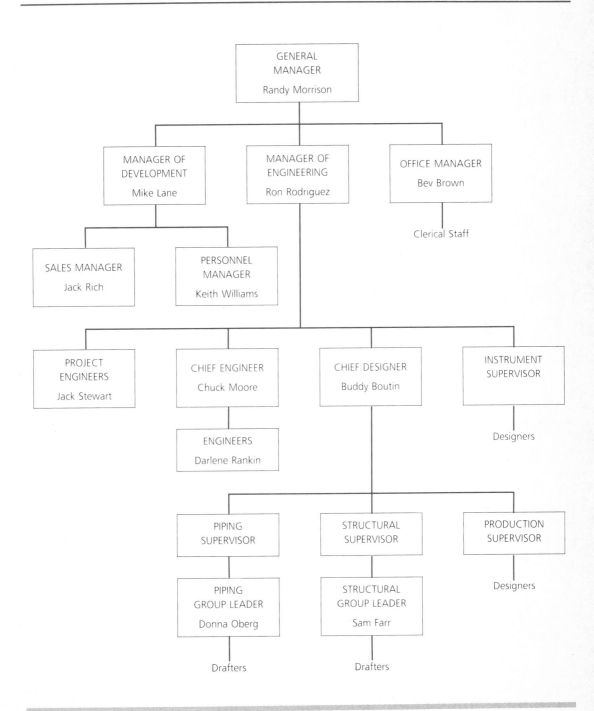

with clients at the initial stages of bidding and selling a project, but he is also one of the firm's best project engineers and manages projects that interest him. In addition, he writes all the firm's computer programs.

Mike's long-term goal is to develop Morrison Engineers into a large firm of 500 employees in six offices located throughout the country. Currently there is one branch office of thirty-five people near the client that constitutes 60 percent of their billings. Mike built that office from scratch and for the first year spent every other week running it. Now the office runs itself.

Now in his mid-thirties, Mike is extremely ambitious. He realizes that he has too little patience with his employees and needs to learn better management skills, but he has shown improvement lately. He considers Randy indecisive, vague, and overly conservative in his strategic planning.

Keith Williams, Personnel Manager

Keith is responsible for personnel management and also helps out with sales (since he receives no sales commissions, however, he puts little effort into sales). He joined Morrison Engineers as a supervisor in the structural department eighteen months ago and recently moved to his present position. He began his career in 1971 as a drafter and has taken sixty hours of civil engineering coursework. He has no formal education in the behavioral sciences.

Keith thinks that employees of Morrison Engineers need to understand their jobs better, that supervisors must delegate more effectively, and that the firm must attract better people. He is currently working on several projects to attract and retain good employees. He is developing job descriptions, job specifications, and salary levels for all positions, setting up a performance appraisal system, and conducting a salary survey. Because he feels he is well liked, he is also trying to assume the role of a counselor whom employees can approach on personal and work-related matters.

Keith enjoys working for Mike Lane and respects him as a boss. He is aware of the rift between Mike and Randy and views Randy primarily as a designer/drafter who has far less ambition than Mike. He sees two different marketing strategies for the firm. Randy's goal is diversification. He wants to branch out into related businesses but does not want the firm to grow. On the other hand, Mike wants to build a large engineering firm. These opposing goals make it difficult for Keith to sell the firm to prospective clients and employees.

Keith also wants to streamline the organization's drafting and engineering procedures. He thinks all supervisors need training and is especially concerned about Chuck Moore's conservative management style. Finally, Keith feels Morrison Engineers has developed some bad habits in dealing with the client representing 60 percent of its billings. Frequent demands from this major client interfere with project planning and management for other clients. In essence, the major client is running the firm as much as Morrison Engineers is.

Jack Rich, Sales Manager

Jack joined the company two years ago. He has bachelor's degrees in chemical engineering and business administration and has been in sales for about twenty years. He formerly worked in purchasing for a large oil company and feels he knows what major oil companies look for in an engineering firm. He also knows many purchasing and engineering people in major oil companies and says this helps him in sales.

Although Jack reports to Mike Lane, he works extensively with both Mike and Randy. Since he directs the firm's sales efforts, he is keenly aware of the lack of coordination between Randy and Mike, especially with regard to their views on growth. When asked about a market plan, he said he doesn't have one—lack of a clear business strategy makes it impossible for him to focus his marketing and sales efforts. He feels Randy and Mike need to agree on Morrison Engineers' business goals, plan a market strategy, capitalize on their strengths, identify a market segment, and get that message across to prospective clients. Jack's current marketing tactic is to meet as many prospective clients as he can in major oil companies. (In his interview, Randy Morrison had earlier questioned whether this "wining and dining" was useful in generating business.)

Jack speaks very highly of Mike Lane, calling him "very dynamic and businesslike." He says Mike gives him direction and feedback, but leaves him alone to do his work. When asked about Randy, he simply says that the general manager is "low key." He adds that Morrison Engineers' planning and scheduling of projects need improvement—"We don't know where we are on a project; we need a better schedule at the outset. Unfortunately, we frequently find out that we're not on schedule too late into the project." He attributes poor project management in part to the firm's major client, but also to poor supervision and delegation throughout the firm.

Bev Brown, Office Manager

Bev joined Morrison Engineers a year ago and has developed office management procedures from scratch. She has a two-year office administration degree and ten years' experience in secretarial work and office management. She manages a number of clerical functions (typing, supply procurement, and scheduling and maintenance of business cars), as well as payroll and invoicing functions. She works extensively with Jack Rich and Keith Williams on their business expenses related to sales.

Bev also has daily contact with Randy Morrison and Mike Lane, and notes that Randy needs to delegate more. Mike is explicit and demanding, but she has trouble understanding what Randy wants. When she joined the firm, she was surprised that neither Randy nor Mike had his own secretary. She serves as secretary to both and distributes their work to her staff.

Mike Lane's computer systems have greatly helped in her work. Payroll, invoicing, manpower inventory, and project scheduling are all on the computer now. When asked about major problems in the firm, she says that nobody really knows how Morrison Engineers should grow. It is unclear whether it should go after big projects from major clients or take farm-out work from other engineering firms. She adds that a real sales program began only this year.

Bev feels very much a part of the firm, but believes the designers and drafters lack loyalty to Morrison Engineers, perhaps because their salaries are below the prevailing market.

Ron Rodriguez, Manager of Engineering

Ron joined Morrison Engineers two years ago, after taking early retirement from a chemical company where he had spent twenty-eight years. His major responsibility is to coordinate all the firm's projects by advising the project engineers. He works extensively with Randy Morrison, Mike Lane, and Bev Brown in planning and coordinating projects. His relationship with Randy is good, although he says Randy needs to delegate more.

When asked about project scheduling and management, Ron raised several concerns. He feels more project management costs should be included in the bids so he does not have to assign so many projects to each project engineer, and the firm needs to spend more time preparing its proposals. Also, the firm lacks clear job descriptions and salary levels for designers and drafters and standard procedures for managing projects. He feels that Morrison Engineers also needs to schedule projects more effectively, and notes that the major client often interferes with his scheduling. Finally, Ron stresses the need for more thorough review of the drawings produced by the drafting departments, and notes that the leaders of the piping and structural groups need training so they can schedule, control, and review their employees' work better.

Ron says Randy and Mike both use a "reactive" style of management and marketing. Morrison Engineers has never had a well-developed, consistent, well-integrated marketing effort. This has resulted in the firm's mixed reputation in the business community. It is respected by existing clients and almost unknown by prospective clients. The conflict between Randy and Mike concerns Ron, but he feels that it will be resolved soon. If Mike leaves Morrison Engineers, Ron believes that the firm will do very poorly.

Buddy Boutin, Chief Designer

Buddy joined Morrison Engineers two years ago, after twenty years of experience in construction and pipe fabrication with a major oil company. His responsibilities include scheduling drafting and design work, ensuring quality control, handling personnel problems, and enforcing company standards and policies. He says he has difficulty finding time to keep in touch with all his people. He works extensively with group leaders in both the structural and piping groups, and says the members of these departments do not communicate enough. He feels project engineers and clients need to meet more often than the weekly project meetings allow.

Buddy also brings up the division between Randy and Mike, saying, "It's hard to figure those two guys out. Mike can sell work for Morrison Engineers, but they go in two different directions." He also raises concerns about project scheduling and management and the lack of clear personnel policies in the firm. Although he's been given stock in the firm and is on the board of directors, he doesn't know what the stock means. He thinks there are incentive and retirement plans, but he doesn't know what they are.

Chuck Moore, Chief Engineer

Chuck is Randy Morrison's brother-in-law and a co-founder of the firm. Until two years ago he held a senior management position, but he felt uncomfortable with the level of responsibility as the firm continued to grow and asked to be moved down to his present position. Chuck supervises a group of engineers who design structures and prepare sketches requested by project engineers. The sketches are then sent to the structural group for detailed drafting. His engineers are not assigned to a specific project, but work on whatever project has priority. Chuck complains about "hot jobs" that take priority over all others and claims that Morrison Engineers needs a better scheduling and priority system. He also feels that the firm has consistently underestimated the time required for engineering on a project to keep its bids competitive. These practices keep his department in a state of crisis.

Darlene Rankin, Engineer

Darlene earned a civil engineering degree five years ago and worked in a testing laboratory until joining Morrison Engineers nine months ago. Her major responsibilities are to take information supplied by project engineers, analyze the project specifications, and make calculations and judgments regarding the foundation of the structure being designed. She receives her work assignments from Chuck Moore, her supervisor.

Darlene is very dissatisfied with Morrison Engineers. She complains that she cannot talk directly with the drafters who will be drafting the work she designs. Instead she must go to Chuck, who goes to the drafting supervisor, who feeds the information to the drafters. This procedure complicates Darlene's already busy schedule. She adds that Chuck supervises all the engineers' work too closely. He's too concerned about reviewing every detail and does not delegate enough to his staff.

Darlene works on two or three projects at a time. The projects are headed by project engineers, who coordinate her work through Chuck Moore. She notes that project engineers are forced to compete for engineering time on their "hot jobs," and no scheduling and priority system exists.

Darlene is considering leaving the firm because she sees little potential for advancement. She's doing highly detailed work with Chuck looking over her shoulder, and she wants to move into supervision. She is also concerned about the competition between Randy and Mike. She has dealt with Randy and feels comfortable with him, but she feels Mike is overly competitive and blames others for problems, rather than working with them to solve those problems.

Jack Stewart, Project Engineer

Jack joined Morrison Engineers three years ago as a project engineer. He majored in engineering technology in junior college and has fifteen years experience in engineering design. He is responsible for planning, scheduling, and anything else to satisfy a client. He views his job as the crucial liaison between the firm and the client. He plans a daily schedule and makes adjustments as clients' needs change. He constantly confers with Ron Rodriguez, Buddy Boutin, and other project engineers to estimate work needs and rate the priority of work the firm is doing for various clients.

Jack's involvement on a project begins at a kick-off meeting with the client, just after Morrison Engineers has secured the contract. He comments that the firm's practice of underestimating labor costs in bids frequently causes him to go over budget. He then estimates the number of people needed for the project and prepares a work schedule. To do this, he must know how to approach his people and keep group leaders in design and drafting informed. The group leaders lack supervisory skills, he feels, and fail to schedule and review their people's work to ensure high quality. This problem is aggravated by the continual turnover among drafters. Jack also says that Buddy Boutin is badly overloaded and is very difficult to find for meetings.

Jack freely admits that the project engineers do not follow their schedules and keep their project status reports current. Ron Rodriguez cannot review the status of projects because this paperwork is not complete. Also, the major client often makes high-priority demands that make the schedules useless. In general, Jack feels Morrison Engineers is not doing a professional job of scheduling and controlling work on the projects he supervises.

Donna Oberg, Piping Group Leader

Donna completed a two-year community college program in industrial arts before beginning her drafting career ten years ago. She joined Morrison Engineers three years ago to head up a group of drafters who prepare drawings and plans for the pipes and tanks of refineries. Her major responsibility is to plan and schedule the drafting work on various projects and ensure the quality of the drawings. In theory, she reports to the piping supervisor, but that position has been vacant for two years so she deals directly with Buddy Boutin and the project engineers. She has no job description, and since Buddy is so busy, she is left on her own to manage her drafters. She says Buddy has a good technical mind but is too busy and channeled in too many directions to be an effective boss. The information she receives from Buddy is sometimes sketchy and leads to poor drawings. Therefore, she interacts primarily with the project engineers to get clear work specifications from them and to juggle their conflicting demands for her people's time.

Donna says she and her drafters need to know why changes must be made so often on their drawings. Drafters are compulsive about their work and resent having to erase and "mess up" a drawing. Instead, they prefer to do the drafting all over again, which runs up costs on a project. Donna notes that there are too few standards on drafting procedures and quality for the piping groups, so drawings often vary, depending on who does the drafting.

Of the several companies she has worked for, Donna considers Morrison Engineers to be the most poorly organized. Everybody seems to be going in different directions. She says the piping and structural groups need to communicate better and coordinate their drawings more carefully. She admits she is not a trained supervisor, and says Morrison Engineers has a habit of promoting good technical employees into supervisory positions without adequate training. She adds that the firm needs better salaries and other incentives to attract more professional managers and to reduce turnover among designers and drafters. Donna is aware of the stock option for employees, but says nobody knows what it means.

Sam Farr, Structural Group Leader

Sam has been a group leader with Morrison Engineers for seven months and has thirteen years of experience in the petroleum industry. His job is to assign work to his three drafters and one checker, review their work, and give them information on a timely basis. He also looks after time sheets and schedules for the entire group and does some design drafting. Sam has a good relationship with his boss and interacts extensively with the project engineers.

Sam comments that the current projects are disorganized. The piping and structural groups do not communicate well and need to have their key people get together at the beginning of a project and lay out a work plan. He adds that lack of clear drafting procedures and standards sometimes leads to poor work. Finally, many of his drafters leave the firm for higher salaries elsewhere.

CASE TWO

COLLECTIVE BARGAINING AND LABOR MANAGEMENT RELATIONS

In this case you will experience some of the dynamics of collective bargaining.* After reviewing the background information, read the role position for your team and prepare for negotiations. You will be given the opportunity to actually negotiate a contract settlement with representatives of another team.

In this case you will be able to observe several things. First, you will see how members of a negotiating team interact and what problems they might face in working together or resolving disagreement among themselves. Second, you will experience the process of developing and executing a strategy in negotiation in order to achieve your objectives. Third, you will see how individual differences in negotiation style can affect final outcomes. Finally, you will experience the difficulties frequently encountered by union and management groups as they try to resolve disputes.

This negotiation will necessarily telescope the planning and negotiating periods into an abnormally short time frame. As a result, it cannot encompass an entire contract package, but must only include a few issues: wages, cost of living increase in wages, differential pay for night shift workers, vacation pay, and hospital/medical benefits package.

PROCEDURE

Your instructor will divide the class into one or more teams of union and management representatives. Observers may also be selected to take notes on each negotiating pair. Specific labor and management negotiating teams should be paired up, so you will know whom you are negotiating against.

Step one. Once your team has been assigned and you have grouped together to begin planning strategy, read the Background section on the Townsford Company, including the Issues for Bargaining, and the Data from

---

* "Collective Bargaining and Labor Management Relations" adapted by Roy J. Lewicki from an exercise developed by Richard J. Campbell and William A. Bigoness from *Experiences in Management and Organizational Behavior* 2nd. ed. by Douglas T. Hall, Donald D. Bowen, Roy J. Lewicki and Francine S. Hall. Reprinted by permission of Richard J. Campbell and William A. Bigoness.

the Independent Community Survey. After you have read and studied this information, read the assigned role position for either the company or union negotiator. Read *only* your own role. Then meet with your team to review this material, and do the following:

1. Make sure you understand each of the issues that will be negotiated. If you have questions, ask the instructor.
2. Select one person to speak for the group. Other members of the team may be asked to be a recorder, or a speaker on a specific issue, or play some other role in the strategy and tactics of the team.
3. Clarify your objectives on each issue. Define the opening demand that you will make on each issue, the point at which you would like to settle on each issue, and the point at which you will "go no further" (resistance point) on each issue.
4. Plan any other strategy or tactics you will use in the negotiation.

Step two.   Meet with the Management or Union team that you have been paired against. Decide who will make the first new set of offers or demands, and then attempt to arrive at a settlement by the end of the time available. Use your time wisely. Remember that you can call a caucus at any point, and/or to control the negotiations in any way that you and your opposing team agree.

Step three.   At the end of the negotiation, record the settlement and cost to the company for each of the following:

_____ Hospital and medical plan,
_____ Wages,
_____ Cost of living sliding scale,
_____ Vacation pay,
_____ Night shift differential,
_____ Total cost of settlement package to company.

Step four.   After the negotiation is over, discuss the following issues:

1. How effectively did your union or management team work together? What kind of problems occurred, if any? How did these affect your negotiation with the other team?
2. Who was selected as negotiator? What criteria were used? Upon hindsight, were these good criteria to use?
3. What other roles were played by other team members? Were these assignments effective?
4. Was your strategy affected by knowing which individuals were on the opposing team? How?
5. How did you determine what you would set as an opening bid, and as a "settlement point?" Upon hindsight, were these good decisions?
6. How was the course of negotiations determined by the style, strategy, and tactics of the negotiators? Which tactics seemed most effective? Least effective? Why?
7. Did you reach a settlement within the time allowed? If not, what factors kept the two groups from agreeing on all five points?

8. How satisfied were you with your settlement after you had completed the negotiations?

9. How satisfied were you with your settlement after you saw how other groups settled? What is the impact of this kind of information on satisfaction with the settlement you achieved?

10. What strategy and tactics are likely to be most effective in this type of situation? Least effective?

11. What can negotiators do to increase the likelihood of achieving a satisfactory solution to a negotiated agreement?

BACKGROUND

The Townsford Company is a small textile company located in a large city in the southeastern United States. Townsford is highly respected for its quality work in the dyeing and finishing of raw woven fabrics. It employs approximately 100 persons. Townsford's employees are among the most skilled to be found in the area.

General business conditions in the country are good, and the financial conditions of Townsford are stable. Townsford is operating at full capacity and has a six-month backlog of orders. Profits are not as high as at previous times, however, since the company has not raised its prices in several years in order to maintain a good competitive position with other sections of the country. The company has been able to maintain a 12 percent shareholders' dividend and has made recent purchases of more modern equipment.

The policies at Townsford are not the most modern but are better than those of most plants the same size. The past president of the company, who retired three months ago, knew most of the workers personally and was well liked. He is largely responsible for the reputation of Townsford as a "good place to work." His successor is viewed with some suspicion by the workers, due mainly to his statements about changing some of the work procedures to achieve greater efficiency.

For the last twenty-five years, a majority of the employees have been members of the union. Relations of the union with the company, for the most part, have been quite good with grievances promptly discussed and settled. The first strike occurred, however, three years ago and lasted fifteen days. The workers lost the fight for a sliding-scale wage based on increases in the cost of living index, but did get the hospital and medical plan, a 10-cent-per-hour wage differential for night shift workers, and several other minor fringe benefits.

Although Townsford's wage scale, $5.94 per hour, compares favorably with that of most other textile firms in the area, it is 3 percent below that of other textile firms that employ workers of equivalent high skill and produce a similar high quality product. Wages in the industry have not increased in proportion to increases in the cost of living or increases in other industries.

Despite occasional small wage increases, over a period of years Townsford's workers have slipped from a relatively high pay scale to a position roughly equivalent to that of low-skilled workers in other industries. This has caused some unrest among the workers, and there is some danger of the workers shifting into these other higher-paying industries. Unemployment is below normal in the area, and it has been difficult to obtain replacements who meet the skill requirements at Townsford.

Townsford gives seven paid holidays and two weeks of paid vacation to all workers with at least one year of service. The company also pays one quarter of each employee's hospital and medical insurance and grants other minor fringe benefits. More detailed information on Townsford and other local firms may be found in Issues for Bargaining.

The three-year contract has now expired. Negotiations broke down in the final week, with both sides adamant in their positions. The only agreement reached was that each side would select a new bargaining agent to represent it, and scheduled a meeting for today (the first day of strike) in an attempt to reach a quick solution and avoid a long strike.

ASSIGNMENT AS UNION NEGOTIATOR

You have been selected by the Union to represent it in its negotiations with the Townsford Company. Negotiations for a new two-year contract broke down last week. The Union is thoroughly irritated with the Company's refusal to grant the workers badly needed wage and benefit increases. Although no compromises were reached in either side's position, it was decided that each side should appoint new negotiating agents in an effort to settle the contract and halt the strike, which began today.

You are to do the best possible job you can to get a good settlement of the contract for labor. Union members were dissatisfied with the last contract three years ago, and there is serious danger of division in the ranks of the Union if a more satisfactory contract is not achieved in these negotiations. It is essential to labor, however, that the contract be settled in this bargaining period. We realize that this involves compromises on both sides, and you are appointed to carry out binding negotiations. Remember, your job is to reach a settlement, one that is good for labor, in this negotiating period.

ASSIGNMENT AS COMPANY NEGOTIATOR

You have been selected by the Townsford Company to represent it in its negotiations with the Union. Negotiations for a new two-year contract broke down last week. The Union demands for general wage and benefit increases

---

EXHIBIT C.2A   ISSUES FOR BARGAINING

Hospital and Medical Plan

Past contract: company paid ¼ cost, employee paid remaining ¾
UNION: demanded company pay full cost
COMPANY: refused to pay more than ¼

	Proportion of company payment				
COMPANY	¼	2/4	¾	4/4	UNION
Total money value per 2 years	$0	$12,000	$24,000	$36,000	

Wages

Past contract: $5.94 per hour
UNION: demanded an increase of 32 cents per hour
COMPANY: refused outright

	Cents increase per hour										
COMPANY	0	4	8	12	16	20	24	28	32	36	UNION
Total money value per 2 years	$0	$16	$32	$48	$64	$80	$96	$112	$128	$144	

(in thousands of dollars)

Sliding pay scale to conform to cost of living

Past contract: pay scale is fixed through the term of the contract
UNION: demanded pay increases in proportion to increases in the cost of living
COMPANY: rejected outright

	NO	YES	
COMPANY			UNION
Total money value per 2 years	$0	$40,000	

Vacation Pay

Past contract: 2 weeks paid vacation for all workers with 1 year service
UNION: wants 3 weeks paid vacation for workers with 10 years of service
COMPANY: rejected

	2 wks for 1 yr service	3 wks for 20 yrs service	3 wks for 15 yrs service	3 wks for 10 yrs service	
COMPANY					UNION
Total money value per 2 years	$0	$500	$2,000	$5,000	

Night Shift Differential

Past contract: $.10 per hour more paid to night shift workers
UNION: demands $.30 per hour more for night shift workers
COMPANY: refused to pay more than the current differential

	Cents per hour differential						
COMPANY	.10	.14	.18	.22	.26	.30	UNION
Total money value per 2 years	$0	$4,000	$8,000	$12,000	$16,000	$20,000	

DATA FROM AN INDEPENDENT COMMUNITY SURVEY

EXHIBIT C.2B

The following table gives information on Townsford, four other local textile plants and averages for nontextile industries in the community. The Moss Plant and the Rose Plant employ highly skilled workers.

	Townsford	Moss	Rose	Baxter	Kraft	Average for other Industries in the Community
Number of Workers	100	300	90	150	300	60
Company Payment for Hosp. & Med. Insurance	¼	¾	¾	4/4	0	½
Hourly Wage Rate	$5.94	$6.00	$6.00	$5.86	$5.88	$6.10
Cost of Living Increases	No	Yes	Yes	No	Yes	40%, yes
Night Shift Differential	$0.10	$0.18	$0.22	$0.16	$0.06	$0.20
Paid Vacation	2 wks for 1 yr	2 wks for 1 yr	2 wks for 1 yr	2 wks for 1 yr	2 wks for 1 yr. 3 wks for 20 yrs	2 wks for 1 yr. 3 wks for 15 yrs

are completely unreasonable. If labor costs are increased, it might necessitate price increases that could seriously hamper the company's competitive standing. Although no compromises were reached in either side's position, it was decided that each side should appoint new negotiators in an effort to settle the contract and halt the strike, which began today.

You are to do the best possible job you can to get a good settlement of the contract for the company. Although the company now has a backlog of orders, it is in danger of losing several major customers if increased labor costs necessitate a significant price increase. It is essential to the company, however, that the contract be settled in this bargaining period. We realize that this involves compromises on both sides, and you are appointed to carry out binding negotiations. Remember, your job is to reach a settlement, one that is good for the company, in this negotiating period.

CASE THREE

THE BARBARA DiBELLA CASE

PART I

Barbara DiBella began work in Spartan Corporation's management trainee program immediately after graduating from college with a major in marketing.* Spartan had recruited her very vigorously as part of its affirmative action efforts to increase the number of women in management positions. While Barbara had had work experience in summer jobs, this was her first full-time position. In the trainee program Barbara would be assigned to the various departments of the corporation for periods of six weeks to six months, so that she could receive an introduction to the complete scope of the organization's activities and also meet the key people. While assigned to each department she would be under the direct supervision of the Department Manager.

Paul Platowski was the corporation's Marketing Manager. He had joined the firm just seven years ago, following completion of an MBA program, and had progressed very rapidly to his current position of power and prominence. He, too, had gone through the management trainee program, following which he had selected marketing for his initial permanent assignment.

As Barbara's training assignment to the Marketing Department approached she became increasingly apprehensive. Her fellow trainees and graduates of previous years' trainee programs told her many stories of Paul's interest in and involvement with young women in the trainee program. Barbara heard of no fewer than three former trainees with whom the grapevine said Paul had been or was intimately involved. Two of the three had excellent positions in the Marketing Department and the third was progressing quickly in one of the Product Groups. The grapevine also indicated that Paul had sought relationships with two other women trainees but had been rejected. One of these women was mired in an undesirable field sales job and the other had left Spartan.

The Manager of the Accounting Department, whom Barbara did not know particularly well but to whom she was assigned just prior to her rotation through Marketing, warned her to be careful of Paul. He said he wouldn't be surprised if top management had stalled the Marketing Manager's rise at its current level until he "cleans up his act."

Barbara was also concerned about her upcoming contact with Paul be-

---

* "Intimacy or Distance? A Case of Male-Female Attraction at Work" by Duncan Spelman and Marcy Crary, *Organizational Behavior Teaching Review*, Spring 1985, 9 (2) pp. 72–85. Reprinted by permission of Organizational Behavior Teaching Society.

cause he seemed to always have his arm around women when he was with them in the halls, at lunch, and at social gatherings.

1. What risks are there to Barbara in getting "involved" with Paul?
2. Are there any risks for Paul in getting "involved" with Barbara?
3. What would you do if you were Barbara?

PART II

On the first day of her assignment in Marketing, Barbara had an early morning meeting with the Department Manager, as was typical when a trainee entered a new department. Paul welcomed her to his office by putting his arm around her and ushering her to a seat on the couch, where he joined her. Paul was extremely warm and animated in their conversation, telling Barbara he was extremely impressed by her credentials. He promised that her stay in Marketing could be an exciting, challenging experience and that a permanent position and unequalled career progress were possible if things worked out. Paul explained her first assignment, which Barbara recognized to be the most exciting she had had by far. After inviting and responding to Barbara's questions and explaining some of the mechanics of the department, Paul wrapped up the meeting by urging her to come to him at any time with questions, problems, or concerns. With that he helped her up from the couch and again put his arm around her as they walked toward the door of his office.

Barbara emerged from the meeting with very mixed emotions. On the one hand she was elated about the assignment she had and the description of how the department operated. On the other hand, she was frightened by the possibility that Paul wanted an intimate relationship with her. She was clear that both personally and professionally she did not want a romantic relationship with her boss. It seemed to her that any short term benefits would be more than outweighed by long term consequences.

Barbara decided she would keep her relationship with Paul strictly business. She would work very hard at her marketing assignments, but would keep the relationship cool and impersonal. She planned to take full advantage of the opportunity that Paul and his department offered for professional development, but be very sure that she was not drawn into the complexities of a personal relationship.

As Barbara considered her future with Paul, she rehearsed in her head a conversation in which she would tell him that she was very interested in an intense professional relationship, but totally uninterested in any kind of intimate relationship. Ultimately, though, she decided against actually having that talk with Paul. She would avoid the chance for things to get personal, but she would not confront the issue directly with Paul.

1. What are the costs and benefits of the strategy Barbara has chosen for managing her relationship with Paul?
2. What other strategies were available to her? What would their costs and benefits have been?

PART III

Over the next couple of months Barbara became more and more comfortable in her relationship with Paul. In fact, as she thought back to her first days in the Marketing Department she almost couldn't remember what she had been so upset about. She was working very hard at her assignments and producing work that Paul acknowledged to be top quality.

There had been a few occasions when her plan for keeping the relationship with her boss businesslike had been tested. For example, he had invited her to accompany him on a two-day trip for the presentation of a marketing plan at one of the key subsidiaries, but the deadline on another project was close enough that she was able to beg off. A couple of times at the beginning Paul had asked her to go to lunch, but again she had been able to use the press of work as an excuse to decline. She had dealt with Paul's touching by simply keeping her physical distance from him, joking about him "keeping his hands off the merchandise," and choosing a chair rather than the couch when meeting with him in his office.

Overall, Barbara was feeling very good about her situation in Marketing and the early threat of a personal relationship with Paul had become a non-issue.

1. How has Barbara's plan worked?
2. Should she have any further concerns?

PART IV

As time passed Barbara noticed that her assignments began to take on a certain sameness. Paul did not seem to be giving her anything new to do. There was nothing wrong with the work she was given—it was interesting and important—but it was not particularly challenging anymore because she had done it several times before. She decided to set up a meeting with Paul to discuss her concerns. Paul had some difficulty finding a time for them to meet but ultimately found fifteen minutes to "squeeze her in." During the meeting he was continually interrupted by phone calls and questions from his secretary. In response to Barbara's concerns Paul said he was sorry to hear she was dissatisfied, but he also indicated that it was really too late to get into anything very new because she had only one month left in the Marketing Department. Barbara decided to raise the issue of a permanent position in Marketing. Paul responded by suggesting that they hold off on any decision about that until she had completed her other assignments and knew what else was available. Rather abruptly Paul stood and thanked Barbara for coming in and walked to the door to discuss something with his secretary.

1. What is happening? How does Paul view the situation?
2. What should Barbara do about it?

PART V

Barbara was quite disappointed with her meeting with Paul, but resigned herself to a final month of the same type of assignments and a delay in discussing a career in marketing.

During her final month Barbara was involved with a project that was supervised by one of "Paul's women" in the Marketing department. Judy had been through the trainee program two years earlier and was now doing extremely well. One evening after Barbara and Judy had been finishing up some work on the project, Judy took a bottle of wine from her desk, poured a glass for Barbara and one for herself, and they began to talk. Three hours and a bottle of wine later Barbara had learned that Judy was not romantically involved with Paul and never had been. In addition, Judy assured her that the other two trainees about whom Barbara had heard rumors of a relationship with Paul were not romantically involved either. Judy acknowledged that Paul felt too free to touch people and that she had talked with him about it to no avail, but added that she had learned to live with it. She described Paul as her mentor and close friend and made an impassioned statement about the centrality of Paul to her career success.

1. How do you explain what happened to Barbara? What mistakes did she make?
2. What should she do now?

EXERCISE ONE

CAREER PLANNING PAPER

The purpose of this exercise is to help you to think explicitly about the resources, priorities, goals, and actions necessary to achieve the most rewarding life and career for you.

Since many of these issues require careful thought, we suggest you *start this paper early* so that some of your ideas have time to "digest."

Your paper will consist of the following separate career planning activities:

I. Self-assessment. What are your major life experiences to date? What are your occupational interests and needs? What are your skills and abilities? What have been the peak experiences (high points) in your career? What sort of life-style and work style would fit best with the sort of person you are? What *patterns* or *themes* do you see in this information?

II. Career opportunity information. What career alternatives are available to you (given your interests and abilities)? How should a person prepare for the positions to which you aspire? What additional education and future assignments do you think would be necessary to qualify you for these career options?

III. Career goals. Discuss your career goals for the next five years (in terms of career, relationships (such as family), and personal development and leisure activities). At this point, what are your career goals for the next twenty years?

IV. Career plan. Discuss the specific steps you can take to help achieve your five-year goals. Identify *barriers* you might need to overcome to achieve these goals. Discuss how you can position yourself in the next few years to be headed in the right direction to achieve your twenty-year goals. Be sure to include *help from other people* that you can solicit to help you achieve these goals.

In view of the importance of the subject, plan on a paper of at least ten pages in length. The paper will be evaluated on:

1. Quantity and quality of information generated. (The "richer" the data base, the stronger your conclusions will be.)
2. Depth of analysis used to reach conclusions.
3. Concreteness and specificity.

Data Inputs

Do the activities listed below to generate input data for your career planning paper.

I. *Self-Assessment*

    A. *Arrange to take the Strong-Campbell Interest Inventory (SCII).* This test can usually be taken in your college counseling and placement office. It can also be ordered directly from NCS Interpretive Scoring Systems, P.O. Box 1416, Minneapolis, MN 55440 (telephone 800-328-6759 or 612-933-3649). Analyze the feedback you get on this test. If possible, arrange to discuss the results with a counselor in your counseling center.

    B. *Conduct a written interview with yourself.* (Do this at a time when you are not feeling rushed, and when you can relax and reflect.)

        1. Write out the story of your life. What are the major events in your life?

        2. List the major *decisions* you made in your life. For each major decision, what other options did you have? What would have happened if you had made a *different* decision?

        3. Describe the major *people* in your life.

        4. Who have your *heroes* been?

        5. List the major *change points* (or turning points or transition points) in your life. How was your life different after each one?

        6. What *disillusionments* have you experienced?

        7. List your *greatest strengths*. What do you do better than most people?

        8. List your *weaknesses*. What parts of you need more development?

        9. What *needs* are *most important* to you? (Security? Money? Self-fulfillment? Achievement? Affiliation or social relationships? Spiritual? Aesthetic? Athletic? Self-esteem? Esteem from others? Power?) Which needs are *least important* to you?

      10. What were the times of your *greatest sadness* in life?

      11. What were the times of your *greatest happiness* in life? What have been the high points in your career?

    C. Share the results of this self-interview and the SCII with someone close to you (a good friend, spouse, fiancee, etc.) Where do their perceptions agree with yours and the test results? Where do their perceptions differ? Can you resolve these differences?

II. *Career Opportunity Information (Information Interview)*

    Interview a person (or people) in the career path to which you aspire (or which you would like to explore further). How did this person get where she or he is now? What previous experiences were needed? How much time should be spent on each assignment? What were the critical points? What skills and abilities were needed? What help from others was needed? What advice does this person offer to people who want to be in his or her position? Examine published information as well (e.g., annual reports, *Wall Street Journal*, *Fortune*, *Business Week* articles).

III. *Career Goals* (next five years)
   A. List five goals related to your work career.
   B. List five goals related to relationships/family/life-style.
   C. List five goals related to personal interests and development.
   D. Go back over these fifteen goals and rank-order them, from 1–15.
   E. Focus on the top three from the combined lists. What kind of goals are these (career, relationships/family/life-style, personal interests)?
   F. Determine how well these career goals fit with your self-assessment information.

IV. *Career Plan*
   This is a logical analysis, working back from your twenty-year and five-year goals to the present. What are the intermediate steps along the way? What steps can *you* take to make things happen? Whom can you ask for help (e.g., bosses, human resource staff, a mentor, friends)? What resources in your employing organization, university, or college are available to you?

PERFORMANCE APPRAISAL INTERVIEW

As noted in Chapter Fifteen, most line managers periodically assess the performance of their employees and discuss the assessments in performance appraisal interviews. In the following exercise the manager of computer services in a consumer products company has assessed the performance of one of her systems analysts six months after he joined the company.* The objective of the interview is *employee development*. Discussion of salary increases or promotional opportunities will occur in the annual salary review six months from now.

The objective of this exercise is to help you practice the techniques and skills required for successful performance appraisal interviewing. You will work in threes, with two students assuming the roles below and the third serving as an observer. Before beginning, review the material on performance appraisal interviewing in Chapter Fifteen.

Preparation

1. Read your role and highlight the key points. Try to identify with the person you are portraying.
2. Since you will use the Problem-solve and Tell approach to conduct the interview, Andrea Thompson should ask Harry to do a self-appraisal and to set some work and developmental goals. In addition, Andrea should evaluate Harry's performance and identify some work and developmental goals for Harry.

Conducting the Interview

1. Remember, Andrea is in charge of the interview. When she and Harry are prepared, she should begin following the format by explaining the purpose of the interview and then asking Harry to summarize his assessment of his own performance. She should continue working through the format until the interview is over.

* "Performance Appraisal Interview" by James G. Goodale © 1984 by James G. Goodale. Reprinted by permission.

2. During the interview, the observer should fill out the feedback forms. In addition, the observer should keep track of the time and signal when twenty-five minutes are up. After thirty minutes, tell the participants to end the interview.

After the Interview

The observer should go immediately through the *Content* and *Conducting* feedback forms with the participants, and then all three students can discuss how effectively the interview was conducted.

Role for Andrea Thompson
Manager of Computer Services

You manage the computer services department of a medium-sized consumer products company with a tradition of responding rapidly to trends in customer demand and aggressively marketing its products. Your company has enjoyed much success because it hires excellent professionals and responds quickly and decisively to opportunities in the marketplace. Your department provides support to all operating departments by writing and updating software and helping users implement and maintain their data processing systems. As manager of computer services, you supervise two systems analysts and six programmers. Harry Jones is one of your systems analysts.

Harry was hired six months ago from a consumer products giant. A placement agency recommended him highly because of his excellent credentials and experience. He has a B.S. and M.S. in computer science and six years of experience with a major firm. During the selection process you were impressed with his education and expertise in programming, and you expected him to quickly establish himself as one of the best members of your staff.

Unfortunately, Harry has not lived up to your expectations. He has been slow to grasp your company's way of doing things and has been slow to produce results. He is consistently behind schedule in developing new software, and the systems he has produced are far too complex and powerful for the user's needs. His logic and documentation are excellent, but again his work is slow.

Harry works hard and freely puts in extra hours, but he seems to get bogged down in details. He also gets into long discussions with programmers about his thesis on the viability of writing programs directly in machine language. These discussions may be interesting, but your group is working for a company, not a university!

Harry is a pleasant young man and has tried hard to fit into the department. He seems to dominate groups, however, and sometimes launches into lectures on technical matters. His strong personality seems to interfere with a joint project with your market research firm. He gets into discussions about data analysis with their field people, and you think he is wasting their time and alienating them.

You have regularly encouraged Harry to work more efficiently, but this will be your first extensive performance appraisal interview with him. You plan to emphasize the importance of achieving work goals in a timely manner, and you want to learn more about how his methods and procedures are slowing him down. In addition, you want him to realize that he cannot be so specialized in a smaller company. He cannot do only work related to his master's thesis.

Role for Harry Jones
Systems Analyst in the Computer Services Department

Six months ago you joined this medium-sized consumer products company because of its excellent reputation. You were impressed with the company's emphasis on quality employees and aggressive marketing. Andrea Thompson, the manager you report to, seemed impressed with your education and experience during your recruiting trip. You have a B.S. and M.S. in computer science and spent six years with a large consumer-products company.

Your current and former employer are very different from one another. There were over twenty systems analysts and 150 programmers in your former computer services group, and you became pretty specialized. Here, there are only two analysts and six programmers, and everybody seems to get involved in every kind of work. Your former company was conservative and bureaucratic, and decision making was quite slow. You became accustomed to designing very detailed, sophisticated computer systems under relatively little time pressure. Here, nobody is a specialist, and time horizons are very short.

You find the fast pace exciting, but it has taken you longer to adjust than you expected. You don't want to sacrifice thoroughness for speed, so you try to work a problem in detail. When you were recruited, Andrea stressed your credentials, so you figure she wants you to take the lead in technical matters. For example, you were able to add some fascinating features to a program for the accounting department a couple of weeks ago, but you missed the project deadline and Andrea seemed really upset.

You also like to compare notes with your colleagues and discuss your areas of expertise. You're the only analyst with a graduate degree, and you want to share your knowledge. Recently you had a chance to talk about part of your thesis on programming in machine language, but nobody seemed very interested. You've also tried to share your expertise with some technical people from the company's market research firm, and a couple of them who just left school seemed really interested, but their boss got on their backs for being behind schedule, and now they are avoiding you.

You're looking forward to meeting with Andrea to discuss your perfor-

EXHIBIT E.1

PERFORMANCE APPRAISAL INTERVIEW FEEDBACK FORM
Content

I. On this sheet, record your comments on the content of the appraisal interview. Also rate how effectively the material was covered on a 5-point scale (1 = least effective; 5 = most effective).

Overall Format	Absent	Present	How Effectively Covered?
Restate Purpose	————	————	—————————
Get Employee Talking	————	————	—————————
Focus on Positives	————	————	—————————
Focus on Negatives	————	————	—————————
Raise Additional Negatives	————	————	—————————
Set Goals	————	————	—————————
Propose Follow-up	————	————	—————————

II. List the major topics covered during the interview and rate how well the boss probed them on the 5-point scale.

Major Topic	How Effectively Probed?
———————————————	—————
———————————————	—————
———————————————	—————
———————————————	—————
———————————————	—————
———————————————	—————
———————————————	—————
———————————————	—————
———————————————	—————
———————————————	—————
———————————————	—————
———————————————	—————
———————————————	—————

mance in the department. You feel your software design has been excellent; you are maintaining your personal standard of sophistication and thoroughness. You are concerned about being behind schedule so much, however, and would really like some suggestions about how to improve. You are very aware that the quantity of your output is low, but the quality is high. You have tried to assume the role of technical consultant in the group, and you'd like to continue to share your advanced training with your co-workers. Perhaps the programmers and you could hold discussions over lunch about new developments and procedures.

PERFORMANCE APPRAISAL INTERVIEW FEEDBACK FORM
Conducting

I. Mark the techniques that were used in the interview you observed and rate how effectively each was used on a 5-point scale (1 = least effective; 5 = most effective).

Technique	Used	How Effectively?
Open-ended Questions	————	————————————————
Specific Probes: How?	————	————————————————
Why?	————	————————————————
How Well?	————	————————————————
Um Huh, Head Nod	————	————————————————
Encouraging Words	————	————————————————
Paraphrasing Ideas	————	————————————————
Reflecting Feelings	————	————————————————
Summarizing Key Themes	————	————————————————
Eye Contact	————	————————————————

II. In addition, please notice the tone of the interview.

   A. Observe how the interview was conducted.

      1. How much did the boss learn how the employee felt about the job in general?

      2. Was the boss accepting of the employee's feelings?

      3. Did the boss criticize the employee? If so, how?

      4. Did the boss praise the employee? If so, how?

      5. Who talked the most?

   B. Observe and evaluate the outcome of the interview.

      1. To what extent did the boss reach a more fair and accurate evaluation of the employee?

      2. How did the boss motivate the employee to improve?

      3. Were relations better or worse after the interview?

EXERCISE THREE

MOTIVATION THROUGH COMPENSATION

For many people, their annual pay raise is the most concrete information they have on how their organization views their performance.* Whether a manager intends it or not, his or her employees will see their pay raises as rewards or punishments for last year's performance. Thus, the raise can be either motivating or demotivating, depending on how the employee views the connection between good performance and financial rewards. Issues of equity, expectancy, psychological needs, and social comparison are also involved in people's reactions to pay decisions.

In this exercise, you should each read the instructions on the Employee Profile Sheet and decide on a percentage pay increase for each employee. After everyone is finished, one student should post and explain the raises he or she has decided on. Then a student who has a different pattern of raises should do the same. Finally, the class as a whole should identify the major differences between the two sets of raises and the reasons behind those differences, and then discuss the following questions:

1. What were the factors that affected your pay raise decisions?
2. What are the reasons for basing pay raises on these factors?
3. What are the behavioral effects of basing pay on these factors?
4. For a pay plan to be effective, to what must employee behavior be linked in employees' minds?
5. What conditions does a good performance appraisal system require?
6. What are some problems associated with using pay as a motivator?

EMPLOYEE PROFILE SHEET

You have to make salary increase recommendations for eight managers that you supervise. They have just completed their first year with the company and are now to be considered for their first annual raise. Keep in mind that you may be setting precedents and that you need to keep salary costs down. However, there are no formal company restrictions on the kind of raises you can give. Decide how large a raise you would like to give each manager, assuming you have a total of $17,000 available in your salary budget to use for pay raises.

* "Motivation Through Compensation" developed by Edward E. Lawler III, adapted by D. T. Hall from *Experiences in Management and Organizational Behavior*, 2nd. ed., by Douglas T. Hall, Donald D. Bowen, Roy J. Lewicki and Francine S. Hall. Reprinted by permission of Edward E. Lawler III.

A. J. Adams. Adams is not, as far as you can tell, a good performer. You have checked your view with others, and they do not feel that Adams is effective either. However, you happen to know Adams has one of the toughest work groups to manage. Adams's subordinates have low skill levels, and the work is dirty and hard. If you lose Adams, you are not sure whom you could find as a replacement. *Salary: $20,000.*

B. K. Berger. Berger is single and seems to live the life of a carefree swinger. In general, you feel that Berger's job performance is not up to par, and some of Berger's "goofs" are well known to the other employees. *Salary: $22,500.*

C. C. Carter. You consider Carter to be one of your best subordinates. However, it is quite apparent that other people don't agree. Carter has married into wealth, and, as far as you know, doesn't need additional money. *Salary: $24,600.*

D. Davis. You happen to know from your personal relationship that Davis badly needs more money because of certain personal problems. As far as you are concerned, Davis also happens to be one of the best of your subordinates. For some reason, your enthusiasm is not shared by your other subordinates, and you have heard them make joking remarks about Davis's performance. *Salary: $22,700.*

E. J. Ellis. Ellis has been very successful so far. You are particularly impressed by this, since it is a hard job. Ellis needs money more than many of the other people and is respected for good performance. *Salary: $23,500.*

F. M. Foster. Foster has turned out to be a very pleasant surprise to you, has done an excellent job, and is seen by peers as one of the best people in your group. This surprises you because Foster is generally frivolous and doesn't seem to care very much about money and promotion. *Salary: $21,800.*

G. K. Gomez. Your opinion is that Gomez just isn't cutting the mustard. Surprisingly enough, however, when you check with others to see how they feel about Gomez, you discover that Gomez is very highly regarded. You also know that Gomez badly needs a raise. Gomez was just recently divorced and is finding it extremely difficult to support a house and a young family of four as a single parent. *Salary: $20,500.*

H. A. Hunt. You know Hunt personally. This employee seems to squander money continually. Hunt has a fairly easy job assignment, and your own view is that Hunt doesn't do it particularly well. You are, therefore, quite surprised to find that several of the other new managers think that Hunt is the best of the new group. *Salary: $21,000.*

Psychological Associates, Inc., 417
Psychological contract of employer-employee, 285
Psychological success and career pattern, 363–64, 370
Public affairs as external communication, 585, 587
Purdue University, 338

Quality circles (QCs), 106, 108–9
Quality-of-work-life (QWL) programs, 77, 105–6, 107, 173, 370

Railway Labor Act, 1926, 159
Ranking vs. evaluation of jobs, 50
Raytheon, 470
RCA (Radio Corporation of America), 403, 404
Reactive style of human resource management, 31, 38
Reality shock, 274–78
Records, employee, 51, 140–43
Recruitment, 209–33, 380–81. *See also* Staffing an organization
by advertising, 222–24, 225
and affirmative action/EEO, 213–14, 231, 232
at colleges, 224, 226–29
costs of 219, 221, 222, 649
defined, 210, 211
employee referrals, 221–22
and employment agencies, 229–31
environmental influences on, 212–14
and job specificatons, 217, 221
methods, 220–32
needs in future, 47, 49
responsibility for, 211–12
and screening applicants, 219–20
and two-career couples, 380–81
from within organization, 217, 220
References and employee selection, 244, 253–54, 255
Relocation assistance, 498
Research-Cottrell, Inc., 116
Research Institute of America, 86
Resumes, 221
Retirement, 466–76
early, and "buy-outs," 468–71
and financial need, 467
financial security in, 471–74
and identity, 466–67
in Japanese firms, 449, 450

phased, 469, 471
planning workshops, 453, 471
as organizational exit, 454
and second career, 370
and self-esteem, 466–67
in U.S. military, 467
Retirement benefits, 467, 495
Retirement styles, 474–76
Retraining, 55, 370
Revenue Act of 1978, 531
Reward and control system, 50, 53
Robots, industrial. *See* Automation
Rockewell, 530
Rockwell, 102
Role and career, 362
Role conflicts of employees, 278–79
Role playing in training, 346
Roman Catholic Church, 316
Ron's Krispy Fried Chicken, 332, 333
Rowe v. General Motors Corporation, 132–33
Rucker Plan of gain-sharing, 505
Russell Reynolds Associates, 209

Salaries. *See also* Compensation
current issues, 533–37
curve and ranges, 514–16
structure, 534
Scanlon Plan of gain-sharing, 505, 506
Schering-Plough, 589
Scientific management theory, 95–98
Search firms, 230–31
Sears Roebuck
career patterns, 369
employee development policy, 315
employee surveys, 155, 284, 578, 579
mentoring at, 373
promotion policy, 308
and union organizing campaigns, 165
voluntary severance at, 469, 471
Selection of employees, 236–68, 356
and affirmative action, 256–60
alternative evaluation approaches, 263–65
assessment phase, 241–45
and body language, 236
and Civil Rights Act of 1964, 238
defined, 236–37
dollar value of program, 657
and equal employment opportunity, 256–60
errors, reasons for, 266–67
fairness of, 248–49
and federal legislation, 242